Algrove Publishing Limited
1090 Morrison Drive
Ottawa, Ontario
Canada K2H 1C2

Canadian Cataloguing in Publication Data

Foster, R. F. (Robert Frederick), 1853-1945
    Hoyle : an encyclopedia of indoor games

(Classic reprint series)
Reprint of Foster's complete Hoyle. 3rd ed. London : F.A. Stokes, 1897.
Includes index.
ISBN 0-921335-53-9

    1. Indoor games. 2. Card games. I. Title. II. Series: Classic reprint series (Ottawa, Ont.)

GV1243.F67 1999   794   C99-901385-8

Printed in Canada
#21000

Publisher's Note

Edmond Hoyle was born in England in 1672. As a teacher of fashionable games in London, he gained sufficient knowledge to publish *A Short Treatise on the Game of Whist, Containing the Laws of the Game* in 1742. It sold for a guinea, a lot of money then, indicating that his reputation as a teacher was very high. The many editions of his book were instrumental in standardizing the playing of whist. Hoyle also wrote authoritative manuals on backgammon, piquet, quadrille, brag and chess. His books established him as the supreme authority on games, causing the phrase "according to Hoyle" to indicate the final authority in any field. Publishers of all sorts of books in the field of rules, both in England and the U.S., appropriated Hoyle's name in their titles, somewhat as is happening today with the name Webster; now that it's in the public domain it is attached to some dictionaries that Noah Webster never contemplated and even some he would have found obnoxious.

Foster was a prolific writer in the Victorian era on the game of whist (a precursor to contract bridge) who expanded his field to codify all of the games popular at the time. His "Hoyle" served the purpose of standardizing the rules for these games so that regional variations would not give rise to conflicts.

As might be expected, the book includes phrases and terms that were commonly used at the time but would be considered objectionable today. As one example, it consistently refers to a cardsharp as a Greek. This expression is not just centuries old (Oxford's first mention of it is 1528) but millennia old.

When the Greeks lifted the siege of Troy, they left behind a giant wooden horse, which the Trojans towed inside the city walls despite the caution of one of their priests who had warned them "Beware of Greeks bearing gifts." History records that there were soldiers secreted in the body of the horse who slipped out at night to open the city gates, allowing the Greeks to capture Troy. It was from this famous Greek deception that the use of the verb "to Greek" came to mean to deceive someone. The phrase is so used in this book.

Leonard G. Lee, Publisher
Ottawa
October 1999

FOSTER'S COMPLETE

HOYLE

*AN ENCYCLOPEDIA OF ALL THE INDOOR GAMES
PLAYED AT THE PRESENT DAY*
With Suggestions for Good Play, a Full Code of Laws
ILLUSTRATIVE HANDS,
AND A BRIEF STATEMENT OF THE DOCTRINE OF CHANCES
AS APPLIED TO GAMES

by

R. F. FOSTER

*Author of "Foster's Whist Manual," "Foster's Whist Tactics,"
"Foster's Duplicate Whist," "Foster's American Leads,"
"Foster on Hearts," "Whist at a Glance,"
"Pocket Guide to Modern Whist,"
and the inventor of the Self-Playing whist cards and the Foster
Whist Markers*

Illustrated with numerous diagrams and engravings

Third Edition.

London and New York
Frederick A. Stokes Company
Publishers

Printed by
Braunworth, Munn & Barber,
Brooklyn, N. Y., U. S. A.

CONTENTS.

PAGE

INTRODUCTION.

THE word " Hoyle " has gradually come to stand as an abbreviation for an Encyclopedia of Indoor Games. The common expression, "played according to Hoyle," usually means, "correctly played;" or, " played according to the standard authorities."

Persons who have never given the subject much attention will be surprised to learn how little authority there is for the rules governing the great majority of our popular games. If we except the table games, such as chess, checkers, billiards, backgammon and ten pins, and such card games as whist and skat, all of which are regulated by well-defined codes of laws, we have very few games left which are not played in different ways in various localities. Even poker, which is undoubtedly the most popular game in the world, is the subject of endless disputes, and decisions which flatly contradict one another are continually given by the editors of the various card columns in the daily press.

The purpose of a Hoyle should be to provide persons with a means of settling all such disputes without referring the matter to a third party, who, perhaps, knows little more than themselves. No one would think of writing to a newspaper to settle a bet as to the correct spelling of the word "billiards"; because it can be found in a dictionary, and any dictionary is recognised as an authority on spelling. But we have seen three different decisions on the spelling of the word, "pinochle," which is not in any dictionary.

There are in the market to-day several Hoyles, each of which claims to be " The Standard Authority." Why are not disputes on games referred to them with the same confidence that a dictionary is referred to in disputes on spelling?

In the opinion of the author it is because they bear within themselves the evidence of their fallibility. There is surely no game so generally known as Whist, nor one with a literature so complete; yet if we turn to the pages on whist in any of the standard Hoyles we find the most absurd mistakes and contradictions. Under the head of "Table of Leads," is given the system now generally known as "American," in which the queen is led from ace, king, queen, and the ace from ace, king, with more than four cards in the suit. Further on we find under the head of "Inferences," the statement that when a queen is led, the leader cannot have either ace or king; and that king is never in a hand from which the ace is led. In another place, under the head of "American Leads," we find the old system, which was used for a hundred years before American Leads were heard of.

It may easily be imagined that a person finding such grave errors in the description of the simplest elements of one of our best-known games, would recall the adage; "false in one, false in all," and would thoroughly distrust the "standard authority" in matters of more difficulty; preferring the decisions of the card editor of some responsible newspaper.

This want of some standard authority, which can command respect as such, is one of the chief causes of the many differences in the methods of playing our popular games. So firmly established have these differences become in various localities, that the author does not believe it possible to compile a work which shall be as universally recognised as an authority on games, as a dictionary is on spelling. But he believes it to be at least possible to select what seems to be the most common usage, or the best rule, and to state it accurately, and bring it up to date.

In minor details, all the Hoyles that the author has examined are sadly deficient. For instance: It is frequently stated that after the cards have been dealt the play shall proceed in such a manner; but nothing is said about who dealt them, or how he came to have that privilege. In many cases it is stated that the players shall cut for the deal; but the rank of the cards in cutting is not given. It is a common remark that no person can learn to play backgammon by reading a description of the game in a Hoyle. This is not so much because the game is difficult of description, as because no method is followed in describing it.

In the following pages the author has followed the very simple plan of actually playing every game described, and setting down, in the order of their occurrence, the various details which need explanation. In a card game, for instance, the first thing is the cards themselves, their number and rank; then comes the apparatus necessary, if any, for counting, etc.; then the number of players who *may take part, their positions at the table and their duties, and how decided; the manner of dealing, penalties for certain irregularities, disposition of the remainder of the pack, if any, and the question of stakes. The method of playing is then described, with notes on possible irregularities, such as revokes, and leads out of turn. Following this in natural order come the manner of taking and arranging the tricks, scoring points, or laying out combinations; the objects of the game, and the manner of scoring and of settling at the end. In important games, these directions are followed by suggestions for good play, and example hands. When the game has a literature of its own, a list of the more important works is given. When the game has a well-known or official code of laws, the code is given in full; but instead of writing out separate rules for every trifling game, the author has framed a general code of laws for all card games, giving the variations under each heading. For instance: In all games the cards are cut by the pone, and are dealt from left to right. It is then necessary to state in what games they are dealt a certain number at a time, and how many are given to each player. It is hoped that this general code will be found useful in providing the most trifling games with a set of rules, framed on the same principles as those which govern the more important ones.

The dictionary of technical terms is as complete as it is possible to make it; the equivalents for many French and German terms being given.

The author has also deemed it advisable to add an occasional paragraph warning the honest card player against the methods of the sharper.

The author trusts his readers will believe that he has made the best of the imperfect and often contradictory authorities which he has consulted, and hopes in future editions to avail himself of the suggestions, criticisms, and descriptions of new games or local usages which his readers may be good enough to send him.

THE WHIST FAMILY.

THE most popular card games of the present day undoubtedly belong to the whist family, which embraces all those played with a full pack of fifty-two cards, ranking from the ace to the deuce, one suit being trumps, and the score being counted by tricks and honours, or by tricks alone.

The oldest and most important of the group is whist itself. The game appears to be of English origin, its immediate parent being "ruff and honours." This was an old English game in which twelve cards only were dealt to each player, the uppermost of the remaining four being turned up for the trump suit. Whoever held the ace of trumps could "ruff" or take in these four cards, discarding in their place any four he chose. As the game developed into whisk, or whist, this ruffing feature disappeared. There was no stock, the four deuces being discarded from the pack instead. Twelve cards were dealt to each player, and the last was turned up for the trump.

About 1680 a variation of the game known as "swabbers" came into vogue. The swabbers were the heart ace, club jack, and the ace and deuce of trumps. The players to whom these cards were dealt were entitled to a certain share of the stakes or payments, independent of the play for tricks and honours. This variety of the game did not long remain in favor, but gave way to make room for one of the most important changes, the restoration of the deuces to the pack, which introduced the feature of the odd trick. This took place early in the last century, and seems to have so much improved the game that attention was soon drawn to its possibilities for scientific treatment.

About this time whist was taken up by a set of gentlemen who met at the Crown Coffee House in Bedford Row, London; chief among whom was Sir Jacob de Bouverie, Viscount Folkestone. After considerable experiment and practice this little whist school laid down the principles of the game as being; "to play from the strong suit; to study the partner's hand; never to force partner unnecessarily, and to attend to the score." It is generally believed that Edmond Hoyle was familiar with the proceedings of this set, and on their experiences based his celebrated "Short Treatise on the Game of Whist," which was entered at Stationers' Hall in London Nov. 17, 1742.

The only works previous to Hoyle touching upon whist were the "Compleat Gamester" of Cotton, which first appeared in 1674, and the "Court Gamester," of Richard Seymour, 1719. One of Hoyle's great points was his calculation of the probabilities at various stages of the rubber. This seems to have been looked upon as most important in guiding persons in their play, for we find that Abraham de Moivre, a famous mathematician, used to frequent the coffee houses, and for a small fee give decisions on questions of the odds at whist.

Bath seems to have been the great rallying-point for the whist-players of the last century; but the passion for the game soon spread all over Europe. In 1767 Benjamin Franklin went to Paris, and it is generally believed that he introduced the American variety of the game known as Boston, which became the rage in Paris some time after the war of independence.

So popular did whist become in Italy that we find the boxes at the opera in Florence provided with card tables in 1790. The music of the opera was considered of value chiefly as, "increasing the joy of good fortune, and soothing the affliction of bad."

A code of laws was drawn up about 1760 by the frequenters of White's and Saunders' in London. These seem to have remained the standard until "Cælebs" published, in 1851, the code in use at the Portland Club. In 1863 John Loraine Baldwin got together a committee at the Arlington, now the Turf Club, and they drew up the code which is still in use all over the world for English whist. In the United States, laws better suited to the American style of play were drawn up by the American Whist League in 1891, and after several revisions were finally adopted, in 1893, as the official code for League clubs.

The literature of whist saw its palmiest days at the beginning of this century. 7,000 copies of Bob Short's " Short Rules for Whist " were sold in less than a year. Mathews', or Matthews', " Advice to the Young Whist-Player," went through eighteen editions between 1804 and 1828. After these writers came Admiral Burney, who published his " Treatise " in 1821 ; Major A. [Charles Barwell Coles,] gave us his " Short Whist " in 1835. Deschapelles published his " Traité du Whiste " in 1839, but it gave little but discussions on the laws. " Whist, its History and Practice " by Amateur, appeared in 1843. General de Vautré's "Génie du Whiste," in 1847. " Cælebs " [Edward Augustus Carlyon] wrote his " Laws and Practice " in 1851. Then in rapid succession came " Cavendish " in 1863, James Clay in 1864, Pole and " Cam " in 1865. Campbell-Walker's "Correct Card " in 1876 ; Drayson's " Art of Practical Whist," with its new theories of trumps, in 1879 ; " Whist, or Bumblepuppy ? " by " Pembridge," [John Petch Hewby,] in 1880 ; G. W. P. [Pettes,] in 1881 ; Proctor's, " How to Play Whist " in 1885 ; and the " Handbook of Whist," by " Major Tenace," 1885. Then began the long list of American authors, Pettes has already been mentioned ; " Foster's Whist Manual " by R. F. Foster, appeared in 1890 ; " Practical Guide to Whist," by Fisher Ames in, 1891 ; Hamilton's " Modern Scientific Whist " in 1894, and in the same year, Coffin s " Gist of Whist ; " and " Foster's Whist Strategy." In 1895, Milton C. Work's " Whist of To-day," and " Foster's Whist Tactics," giving the play in the first match by correspondence ; and in 1896, Val Starnes' " Short-suit Whist."

In periodical literature we find whist taken up in the pages of the " Sporting Magazine " in 1793. The London " Field " has had a card column edited by " Cavendish " for the past thirty years. Proctor's work first appeared in " Knowledge." The " Westminster Papers " devoted a great deal of space to whist games and " jottings " every month for eleven years, beginning in April,

1868. " Whist," a monthly journal devoted exclusively to the game, began publication in Milwaukee in 1891.

Whist is rapidly becoming a " newspaper game." Several of the great American dailies have whist departments in their Sunday issues. The New York Sunday Sun is probably the most important, and the most carefully edited. It devotes two columns every Sunday to the discussion and illustration of moot points in whist tactics, and the analysis of hands played in important matches. In a series of articles begun February 23, 1896, this paper gave to the world the first systematic statement of the theory and practice of the short suit game.

While the parent game has been pursuing this prosperous course, many variations have been introduced. One of the most radical changes in the game itself has been cutting down the points from ten to five, which occurred about 1810. Mathews mentions it in 1813 as having occurred since the publication of his first edition in 1804, and Lord Peterborough, the unlucky gambler for whose benefit the change was introduced, died in 1814. Another great change has taken place in America, where they play for the tricks alone, the honours not being counted at all. Turning the trump from the still pack was first tried by a Welsh baronet, and is mentioned by Southey in his " Letters of Espriella." This custom was revived for a time by the Milwaukee Whist Club, and is still sometimes seen in Europe under the name of " Prussian Whist."

Altogether we can trace nineteen games which are clearly derived from whist. Duplicate, Drive, and Progressive whist are simply changes in the arrangement of the players and in the methods of scoring. Prussian whist introduces the cutting of the trump from the still pack. Dummy and Double-dummy are simply whist with a limited number of players, necessitating the exposure of one or more hands upon the table. The French game of Mort is dummy with a better system of scoring introduced. Favourite Whist simply changes the value of the tricks in scoring, according to the trump suit. Cayenne and Bridge introduce the first changes of importance. In Cayenne, the dealer and his partner have the privilege of changing the trump from the suit turned up; in Bridge they name the trump suit without any turn-up, and play the hands as at dummy. In Boston, and Boston de Fontainbleau, in addition to making the trump suit instead of turning it up, further departures are introduced by naming the number of tricks to be played for, allowing the player to take all or none without any trump suit, and by 'spreading' certain hands, without allowing the adversaries to call the exposed cards. French and Russian Boston are simply varieties of Boston. Solo Whist is an attempt to simplify Boston by reducing the number of proposals and the complications of payments, and eliminating the feature of 'spreads.' Scotch Whist introduces a special object in addition to winning tricks—catching the ten of trumps ; that card and the honours having particular values attached to them. This variety of whist may be played by any number of persons from two to eight; and its peculiarity is that when a small number play, each has several distinct hands, which must be played in regular order, as if held by different players. Humbug Whist is a variety of double-dummy, in which the players may exchange their hands for those dealt to the dummies, and the dealer may sometimes make the trump to suit himself. German Whist is played by two persons, and introduces the element of replenishing the hand after each trick by drawing cards from the remainder of the pack until the stock is exhausted. Chinese Whist is double-dummy for two, three, or four persons, only half of each player's cards being exposed, the others being turned up as the exposed cards are got rid of in the course of play.

As to the respective merits of these various games, the English think there is nothing better than the original whist, counting honours, and playing to the score. The Americans think Duplicate superior to all other forms, especially when two tables are engaged, and four players are opposed by four others for a specified number of deals. We are inclined to agree with Clay that the French game of Mort is "charming and highly scientific." He says English dummy is a "very slow game."

Whether it is because the game has been found 'slow,' or because its more attractive forms are little known, it is certainly true that writers on whist pay little or no attention to dummy. The English authors mention it only in connection with laws and decisions. No American text-book makes any allusion to the game, and there is no reference to it in the American Whist League's code of laws. Nevertheless, it is believed by many that the day is not far distant when dummy will supercede all other varieties of whist among the most expert players; either in the form of the charming Mort, or the fascinating Bridge. Very few persons who have played either of these games sufficiently to appreciate their beauties care to return to the platitudes of straight whist.

WHIST.

CARDS. Whist is played with a full pack of fifty-two cards, ranking A K Q J 10 9 8 7 6 5 4 3 2; the Ace being the highest in play, but ranking below the deuce in cutting. Two packs are generally used, the one being shuffled while the other is dealt.

MARKERS are necessary to keep the score. The most common are red and white circular counters; the white being used for the points in each game, and the red for the games themselves, or for rubber points. It is better to have two sets, of different colours, each set consisting of four circular and three oblong counters, the latter being used for the rubber points, or for games.

PLAYERS. Whist is played by four persons. When there are more than four candidates for play, five or six may form a "table." If more than six offer for play, the selection of the table is made by cutting.

The table being formed, the four persons who shall play the first rubber are determined by cutting, and they again cut for partners, and the choice of seats and cards.

CUTTING. The usual method of cutting for partners, etc., at whist, is to shuffle the cards thoroughly, and "spread" them face downwards on the table; each candidate drawing a card, and turning it face upwards in front of him. The four cutting the lowest cards playing the first game, or rubber.

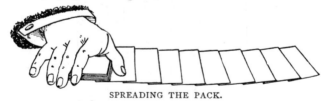

SPREADING THE PACK.

The four having been selected, the cards are again shuffled and spread, and partners are cut for; the two lowest pairing against the two highest; the lowest of the four is the dealer, and has the choice of cards and seats.

TIES. If the first cut does not decide as to which are the two highest or two lowest, or as to which of the two lowest is to be the dealer, those tying must cut again until they decide it.

Two players cutting cards of equal value, cut again for partners, unless the ties are the two highest. If they are the two lowest, they cut again for the deal. For example :—

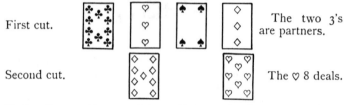

First cut.

Second cut.

The two 3's are partners.

The ♡ 8 deals.

If the ties are the two intermediate cards, they cut again to decide which shall play with the original low. Even should one of the ties cut a card lower than the original lowest, it would not entitle him to the deal, or to the choice of seats and cards. For example :—

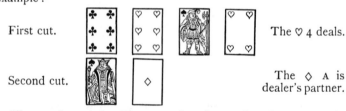

First cut.

Second cut.

The ♡ 4 deals.

The ◇ A is dealer's partner.

Three players cutting cards of equal value, cut again to decide which shall play with the fourth. If the odd card was the highest, the two lowest of the new cut are partners, and the lower of them deals. If the odd card was originally the lowest, it takes the deal, and the two highest of the new cut are partners. For example :—

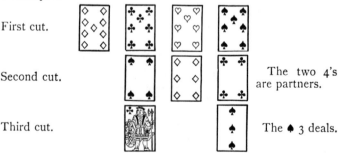

First cut.

Second cut.

Third cut.

The two 4's are partners.

The ♠ 3 deals.

Again :

First cut.  The ♠ 5 deals.

Second cut. The ♡ 2 is dealer's partner.

PLAYERS' POSITIONS. The four players at a whist table are usually distinguished by the letters A, B, Y, Z ; the first two letters of the alphabet being partners against the last two, and their positions at the table being indicated as follows :—

Z is always the dealer ; A the original leader, or first hand ; Y the second hand ; B the third hand ; and Z the fourth hand. After the first trick, some other player may become the leader ; the one on his left being the second hand ; his partner the third hand, and the player on his right the fourth hand.   B is the pone.

DEALING. The cards having been properly shuffled, the dealer presents them to the ***pone*** to be cut.   The American laws require that after separating the pack, the pone shall place the cut part, which he lifts off, nearer the dealer.   Beginning at his left, the dealer distributes the cards one at a time in rotation, until the pack is exhausted.   The last card is turned face up on the table, and the suit to which it belongs is the trump for that hand.

When two packs are used, one is shuffled by the dealer's partner while the other is dealt, and the shuffled pack is placed on the left of the player whose turn it will be to deal next.   Each player deals in turn until the conclusion of the game or rubber.

IRREGULARITIES IN THE DEAL. The following rules regarding the deal should be strictly observed :—

If any card is found faced in the pack, the dealer must deal again.   Should the dealer turn over any card but the trump, while dealing, the adversaries may, if they please, demand a new deal. A player dealing out of turn may be stopped before the trump card is turned ; but after that, the deal must stand, afterwards passing to the left in regular order.   On the completion of the deal, each player should take up and count his cards to see that he has thirteen ; if not, it is a misdeal, and unless the pack is found to be imperfect, the deal passes to the player on the misdealer's left. The dealer loses the deal:—if he neglects to have the pack cut ; if he deals a card incorrectly, and fails to remedy the error before dealing another ; if he counts the cards on the table, or those remaining in the pack ; if he looks at the trump card before the deal is complete ; or if he places the trump card face down, on his own or on any other player's cards.

STAKES. When stakes are played for, it should be distinctly understood at the beginning whether the unit is for a game, for a rubber, for rubber points, or for tricks. The English game is invariably played for so much a rubber point; sometimes with an extra stake upon the rubber itself. In America, it is usual to play for so much a game ; but in some cases the tricks are the unit, deducting the loser's score from seven, or playing the last hand out and then deducting the loser's score. A very popular method is to play for a triple stake : so much a trick, playing each hand out ; so much a game ; and so much a rubber. These three stakes are usually in the proportion of 10, 25, and 50. In clubs it is customary to have a uniform stake for whist, and to fix a limit for all betting on the game beyond the " club stake." Good usage demands that those at the table should have the refusal of any bet made by a player, before it is offered to an outsider.

METHOD OF PLAYING. The player on the dealer's left begins by leading any card he chooses, and the others must all follow suit if they can. Failure to follow suit when able is called **revoking ;** the penalty for which, under the American laws, is the loss of two tricks ; under the English laws, three tricks or points. Any player having none of the suit led may either trump it or throw away a card of another suit, which is called **discarding.** When it is the dealer's turn to play to the first trick, he should take the trump card into his hand. After it has been taken up it must not be named, and any player naming it is subject to a penalty, (see Laws ;) but a player may ask what the trump **suit** is. If all follow suit, the highest card played wins the trick ; trumps win against all other suits, and a higher trump wins a lower. The winner of the trick may lead any card he pleases for the next trick, and so on until all thirteen tricks have been played.

Cards Played in Error, or dropped face upward on the table, or two or more played at once, are called **exposed cards,** and must be left on the table. They can be **called** by the adversaries ; but the fact of their being exposed does not prevent their being played when the opportunity offers. Some persons imagine that the adversaries can prevent an exposed card from being played ; but such is not the case.

Leading out of Turn. Should a player lead out of turn, the adversaries may call a suit from the player in error, or from his partner, when it is next the turn of either of them to lead. American laws require the call to be made by the player on the right of the one from whom the suit is called. The English laws give the adversaries the option of calling the card played in error an exposed card. If all have played to the trick before discovering the error, it cannot be rectified; but if all have not played, those who have followed the false lead must take back their cards, which are not, however, liable to be called.

Revoking Players cannot win the game that hand, no matter what they score; but they may play the hand out, and score all points they make to within one point of game.

Any player may ask the others to *draw cards* in any trick, provided he does so before they are touched for the purpose of gathering them. In answer to this demand, each player should indicate which of the cards on the table he played.

In the English game, any player may look at the last trick turned and quitted; in the American he may not.

Taking Tricks. As the tricks are taken, they should be neatly laid one upon the other in such a manner that any player at the table can count them at a glance. There are several methods of stacking tricks; the first shown being probably the best.

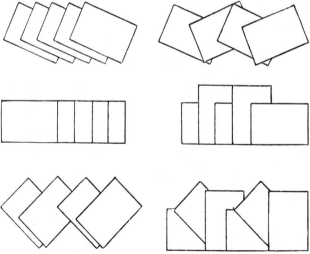

When six have been taken by one side they are usually gathered together to form a **book** ; any subsequently taken being laid apart, as they are the only ones that count. It is customary for the partner of the player winning the first trick on each side to gather the tricks for that deal. In some places it is the custom for the partner of the winner of each trick to gather it, so that at the end of the hand each player has tricks in front of him. Although this method saves time, the practice is not to be recommended, as it hinders the players in counting the tricks already gained by each side.

Immediately upon the completion of the play of a hand, the score should be claimed and marked. Any discussion of the play should be postponed until this has been attended to. The adversaries must detect and claim revokes before the cards are cut for the following deal.

The laws of whist should be carefully studied.

OBJECT OF THE GAME. The object of all whist play is to take tricks, of which there are thirteen in each hand or deal. The first six tricks taken by one side are called a ***book,*** and do not count; but each trick above that number counts one point towards game. The seventh trick is called the ***odd;*** and two or more over the book are called ***two, three,*** etc., ***by cards.*** At the conclusion of each hand, the side that has won any tricks in excess of the book, scores them; the opponents counting nothing. As soon as either side has scored the number of points previously agreed upon as a game, which must be 5, 7, or 10, the cards are again shuffled and spread for the choice of partners, etc., unless it has been agreed to play a rubber.

SCORING. There are several methods of scoring at whist. The English game is 5 points, rubbers being always played. Besides the points scored for tricks, honours are counted; the games have a different value, according to the score of the adversaries; and the side winning the rubber adds two points to its score.

In scoring, the revoke penalty counts first, tricks next, and honours last.

The Revoke. Should the adversaries detect and claim a revoke before the cards are cut for the following deal, they have the option of three penalties: 1st. To take three tricks from the revoking player, adding them to their own. 2nd. To deduct three points from his game score. 3rd. To add three points to their own game score. The penalty cannot be divided. A revoke may be corrected by the player making it before the trick in which it occurs has been turned and quitted. The card played in error must be left face up on the table, and must be played when demanded by the adversaries, unless it can be got rid of previously, in the course of play. In America, the revoke penalty is two tricks.

The Honours are the four highest trumps, A, K, Q, and J; and ***after tricks have been scored,*** partners who held three honours between them are entitled to count two points towards game; four honours counting four points. If each side has two honours, neither can count them. It is not enough to score them; after the last card has been played, they must be claimed by word of mouth. If they are not claimed before the trump is turned for the following deal, they cannot be scored. Partners who, at the beginning of a deal, are at the score of four, cannot count honours; they must get the odd trick to win the game. Should one side be out by tricks, and the other by honours, the tricks win the game, the honours counting nothing.

Rubber Points. At the conclusion of each game, the rubber points are scored, either with the oblong counters, or on the small keys of the whist-marker. If the winners of a game are five points to their adversaries' nothing, they win a *treble,* and count three rubber points. If the adversaries have scored, but have one or two points only, the winners mark two points, for a *double.* If the adversaries have reached three or four, the winners mark one, for a *single.* The rubber points having been marked, all other scores are turned down. The side winning the rubber adds two points to its score for so doing. The value of the rubber is determined by deducting from the score of the winners any rubber points that may have been made by their adversaries. The smallest rubber possible to win is one point; the winners having scored two singles and the rubber, equal to four; from which they have to deduct a triple made by their adversaries. The largest rubber possible is eight points, called a *bumper,* the winners having scored two triples and the rubber, to their adversaries' nothing.

It is sometimes important to observe the order of precedence in scoring. For instance: if, at the beginning of a hand, A–B have three points to Y–Z's nothing, and A–B make two by honours, Y–Z winning three by cards, Y–Z mark first; so that A–B win only a *single,* instead of a *treble.* On the contrary, should A–B make two by cards, Y–Z claiming four by honours, A–B win a treble; as their tricks put them out before it is Y–Z's turn to count.

In America, where rubbers are played without counting honours, it is not usual to reckon rubber points; but simply to add some agreed value to the score of those winning the odd game.

Where single games are played, whether 5, 7, or 10 points, some persons consider the game as finished when the agreed number of points is reached. Others play the last hand out, and count all the tricks made; so that if two partners were at the score of 6 in a 7-point game, and made five by cards, they would win a game of 11 points. When this is done, it is usual to deduct the score of the losers from the total, and to call the remainder the value of the game. In the American Whist League, the rule is to stop at seven points, and to determine the value of the game by deducting the loser's score from seven.

When long sittings occur without change of partners or adversaries, it is a common practice to count the tricks continuously; and on the conclusion of the play, to deduct the lower score from the higher, the winners being credited with the difference.

CUTTING OUT.   If rubbers are played, there is no change of partners, or of rotation in the deal, until one side has won two games, which ends the rubber. If the first two games are won by the same partners, the third is not played. If more than four players belong to the table, those who have just played cut to decide which shall give place to those waiting; those cutting the highest cards going out. If six belong to the table, there will be no further cutting out; as those who are out for one rubber re-enter for the next, taking the places of those who have played two consecutive rubbers. If five belong to the table, the three who remained in for the second rubber must cut to allow the fifth player to re-enter. At the end of the third rubber, the two cut that have not yet been out; and at the end of the fourth rubber, the one who has played every rubber goes out without cutting. After this, it is usual to spread the cards, and to form the table anew. In all the foregoing instances, partners and deal must be cut for, after the cut has decided which are to play.

MARKING.   There are various methods of using the counters. At the beginning of the game they may be placed at the left hand, and transferred to the right as the points accrue. Another method is to stack the four circular counters one upon the other at the beginning of the game, and to count a point by placing one of them beside the others; two points by placing another upon the first; three points by placing a third beyond these two, and four points by placing them all in line.

Nothing. One.   Two.   Three.   Four.

In the seven point game, the score is continued by placing one counter above, and to the right or left of the other three, to indicate five points; and above and between them to indicate six.

Five.   Or this.   Six.

When counters are not used, one of the standard forms of

The Foster Whist Marker.

whist-marker is employed, the most legible and convenient being the "Foster Whist Marker," in which the counting keys are always level with the surface and can be seen equally well from any position at the table.

The four large keys on one side are used to count single points; the single large key on the opposite side being reckoned as five. The three small keys are used for counting rubber points, or games.

In ten point games, the scoring to four points is the same; but beyond four, a single counter placed *below* two or more others, is reckoned as three; and *above* two or more others, as five.

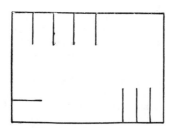

Five. Six. Seven. Eight. Nine.

When proper markers are not obtainable, many persons cut eight slits in a visiting card, and turn up the points.

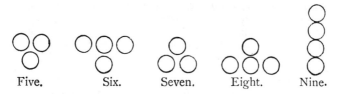

Visiting Card Marker.

Whatever the apparatus employed, it should be such that every player at the table can distinctly see the state of the score without drawing attention to it.

METHODS OF CHEATING. Whist offers very few opportunities to the card-sharper. When honours are counted, he may be able to keep one on the bottom of the pack until the completion of the deal by *making the pass* after the cards have been cut. A *greek* who possessed sufficient skill to do this without detection would be very foolish to waste his talents at the whist table; for, however large the stakes, the percentage in his favour would be very small.

When whist is played with only one pack, a very skillful shuffler may gather the cards without disturbing the tricks, and, by giving them a single *intricate* shuffle, then drawing the middle of the pack from between the ends and giving another single intricate shuffle, he may occasionally succeed in dealing himself and his partner a very strong hand in trumps, no matter how the cards are cut, so that they are not shuffled again. A hand dealt in this manner is framed on the walls of the Columbus, Ohio, Whist Club ; eleven trumps having been dealt to the partner, and the twelfth turned up. In this case the shuffling dexterity was the result of fifteen years' practice, and was employed simply for amusement, the dealer never betting on any game, and making no concealment of his methods.

SUGGESTIONS FOR GOOD PLAY. Although whist is a game of very simple construction, the immense variety of combinations which it affords renders it very complicated in actual practice ; there being probably no game in which there is so much diversity of opinion as to the best play, even with the same cards, and under similar conditions. It has been repeatedly remarked that in all the published hands at whist which have been played in duplicate, or even four times over, with the same cards, no two have been alike.

It would be useless to formulate rules intended to cover every case that might arise, because the conditions are frequently too complicated to allow the average human intellect to select the exact rule which would apply. All that can be done to assist the beginner is to state certain general principles which are well recognised as fundamental at the whist table, and to leave the rest to experience and practice at the whist table.

GENERAL PRINCIPLES. Nothing obstructs the progress of the beginner so much as his attempts to cover all the ground at once. The more ambitious he is, the greater his necessity for keeping in view the maxim ; " One thing at a time : all things in succession." One must master the scales before he can produce the perfect melody.

The novice should first thoroughly understand the object, and the fundamental principle of the game.

The Object is to win tricks. Not to give information, or to count the hands, or to remember every card played ; but simply and only to win tricks.

The Principle is to secure for certain cards a trick-taking value which does not naturally belong to them ; either by getting higher cards out of the way of lower, or by placing the holder of intermediate cards at a disadvantage with regard to the lead.

If any person will take the trouble to deal out four hands, and after turning them face up on the table, count how many tricks each side will probably take with its high cards and trumps, he will find that the total will hardly ever be exactly thirteen tricks.

Let us suppose the following to be one of the hands so dealt ; Z turning up the ♡ 6 for trumps :—

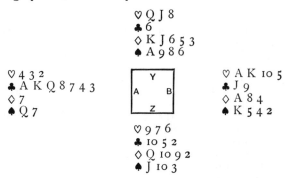

♡ Q J 8
♣ 6
◊ K J 6 5 3
♠ A 9 8 6

♡ 4 3 2
♣ A K Q 8 7 4 3
◊ 7
♠ Q 7

♡ A K 10 5
♣ J 9
◊ A 8 4
♠ K 5 4 2

♡ 9 7 6
♣ 10 5 2
◊ Q 10 9 2
♠ J 10 3

On looking over this hand it would appear that A could only make one trick in Clubs, of which the second round would be trumped. His partner can count on five tricks : the two best and the fourth trumps ; the ◊ A, and the ♠ K ; a total of six tricks. On counting the adversaries' probable tricks, Y should make one of his three trumps, and the ♠ A. Diamonds will not go round twice without being trumped, so we cannot count on his ◊ K. We cannot see any sure tricks for Z. Where are the five other tricks necessary to bring our total up to thirteen ? They must be there, for there are thirteen tricks taken in every hand played.

If we play over the hand, we shall find that A–B may make six, seven, nine, or ten tricks, according to their good management, and the good or bad play of their adversaries. In *Foster's Whist Tactics,* Illustrative Hand No. 13, may be found the various ideas of sixteen of the best players in the American Whist League with regard to the proper management of this hand. They played it in four different ways, and with very different results in the score.

This must show that the accidental distribution of the Aces, Kings, and trumps is not everything in whist, and that there must be ways and means of securing tricks which do not appear on the surface.

There are four ways of taking tricks at whist:

1st. By playing high cards, the suit of which the others must follow. This A does, in the example, on the first round of the Club suit.

2nd. By playing low cards, after the higher ones have been exhausted, and the adverse trumps are out of the way. This Y will do with his Diamonds, or A with his Clubs, according to circumstances.

3rd. By trumping winning cards played by the adversaries. This Y will do if Clubs are led a second time, or A will do if Diamonds are led twice.

4th. By being able to take tricks with cards which are not the best of the suit, the player who holds better cards having already played smaller. This B will do with the ♡ 10 if A leads trumps, and Y does not play either Q or J. If B leads trumps he will lose this advantage.

These four methods of winning tricks suggest four systems of play, which are those in common use by experts at the present day :

1st. Playing high cards to the best advantage, so as to secure the best results from such combinations as may be held. This is the basis of all *systems of leading.*

2nd. Leading from the longest suit, in order that higher cards may be forced out of the way of smaller ones, leaving the smaller ones "established," or good for tricks after the adverse trumps are exhausted. This is called the *long-suit game.*

3rd. Trumping good cards played by the adversaries. This is called *ruffing.* When two partners each trump a different suit, it is called a *cross-ruff,* or *saw.*

4th. Taking advantage of the *tenace* possibilities of the hand by placing the lead with a certain player ; or by avoiding the necessity of leading away from tenace suits. For example : A player holds A Q 10 of a suit, his right hand adversary holding K J 9. These are known as the *major* and *minor* tenaces. Whichever leads makes only one trick ; but if the holder of the major tenace can get the suit led twice, he makes all. This is called the *short-suit game,* or *finesse and tenace.* Its resources may be added to by finessing against certain cards. For example : Holding A Q 3 of a suit led by the partner, to play Q is a finesse against fourth hand having the King.

Each of these systems has its advantages, and almost every hand will offer opportunities for practice in all of them.

The most important thing to impress on the beginner is that whist cannot be played by machinery. Some authorities would have us believe that certain theories alone are sound ; that certain systems of play alone are good ; and that if one will persevere in following certain precepts, in such matters as leading, management of trumps, etc., that the result will be more than average success at the whist table.

Nothing can be further from the truth. As in all other matters largely controlled by chance, there is no system, as a system, which will win at whist. One cannot succeed by slavish adherence to either the long or the short-suit game ; by the invariable giving of information, or the continual playing of false cards. The true elements of success in whist lie in the happy combination of all the resources of long and short suits, of finesse and tenace, of candour and deception, continually adjusted to varying circumstances, so as to result in the adversaries' losing tricks.

HOW TO STUDY WHIST. Any person, anxious to become an expert whist player, may attain to considerable proficiency in a short time, if he will content himself with mastering the following general principles one at a time ; putting each into practice at the whist table before proceeding to the next.

The science of modern whist may be divided into two parts : 1st. *Tactics ;* or the purely conventional rules for leading, second and third hand play, returning partner's suits, etc., all of which may be learnt from books, or gathered from more experienced players. 2nd. *Strategy ;* or the advantageous use of the information given by the conventional plays. This is largely dependent on personal ability to judge the situation correctly, and to select the methods of play best adapted to it.

CONVENTIONAL PLAYS. These may be divided into two parts : those used by the partners who attack, either with their strong suits, or by leading out trumps ; and those employed by their adversaries, who are defending themselves against such suits, or wishing to prevent their trumps being drawn. We shall first consider the conventionalities used in attack.

Leading. The player with the original lead should have a double object in view ; to secure the best results for his own hand, and to indicate to his partner where he is in need of assistance.

The first matter for his consideration will be whether to begin with a trump or with a plain suit. There are two principal uses for trumps. The most attractive to the beginner is that of ruffing the adversaries' winning cards ; and the most important to the expert is leading trumps to prevent this. No matter how strong or well established a plain suit may be, it is of uncertain value as long as the adversaries have any trumps with which to stop it. A suit is established when you can probably take every trick in it. If a player with a good established suit is sufficiently strong to make it probable that he can, with his partner's assistance, exhaust the adverse trumps, he should do so by leading trumps. If they are probably stronger than he, he must *force* them, by leading the established suit which they will be compelled to trump, weakening their hands and gradually reducing their trump strength until it is possible to exhaust what remains by leading. It being to the advantage of the player with a good suit to exhaust the trumps, it must be desirable to his adversaries to keep theirs, if possible, for the purpose of ruffing this good suit.

Trumps are also useful as cards of re-entry, when a player has an established suit, but has not the lead ; their most important use, however, is in defending or stopping established suits.

Rules for Leading Trumps. With five or more trumps, the beginner should always begin by leading them, regardless of the rest of his hand. With three or less, he should never lead them, unless he has very strong cards in *all* the plain suits. With four trumps exactly, he should lead them if he has an established suit and a card of re-entry in another suit. A card of re-entry in plain suits is one which is pretty sure to win a trick, such as an Ace, or a guarded King. The following are examples of hands from which trumps should be led originally by a beginner;—

Hearts are trumps in every case.

♡ J 8 6 4 2 ; ♣ K 3 2 ; ◇ 10 9 2 ; ♠ 7 5.
♡ Q 10 2 ; ♣ A K 5 ; ◇ K Q 10 9 ; ♠ A Q 3.
♡ K J 8 3 ; ♣ A K Q 10 7 3 ; ◇ 3 ; ♠ A 7.

The following are examples of hands from which trumps should not be led :—

♡ A K Q ; ♣ J 8 7 5 3 ; ◇ Q 4 ; ♠ K 4 2.
♡ Q J 10 2 ; ♣ 5 2 ; ◇ A K Q 2 ; ♠ 6 4 3.
♡ A Q 5 4 ; ♣ K Q J 6 3 ; ◇ A 9 2 ; ♠ K.

If at any later stage of the hand, a player finds himself with an established suit and a card of re-entry, he should lead trumps if he has four. For instance : The player with the last example should lead trumps if the first round of Clubs either forced the Ace out of his way, or found it with his partner.

Rules for Leading Plain Suits. It is safest for the beginner to select his longest suit for the original lead ; unless he has a four-card suit which is much stronger. Length and high cards, the two elements of strength, are often very nearly balanced. In the following examples the player should begin with the longest suit :—

♡ A 4 3 ; ♣ J 10 9 8 3 ; ◇ A K Q ; ♠ K 2.
♡ K 10 8 3 ; ♣ 4 2 ; ◇ K Q 10 8 2 ; ♠ A Q.

In the following the four-card suit should be selected :—

♡ J 3 ; ♣ 6 5 4 3 2 ; ◇ J 10 5 3 ; ♠ Q 8.
♡ Q 4 2 ; ♣ 7 ; ◇ 10 6 4 3 2 ; ♠ A K Q 10.

The principle which should guide in the selection of a plain suit for the original lead is, that if there are a number of small cards in one suit, and a few high cards in another, by leading the long suit first, the higher cards in it are forced out of the way, and the high cards in the shorter suit will then bring the holder of the established small cards into the lead again. But if the high cards of the short suit are first led, the long suit of small cards is dead.

Having determined whether to lead the trump or the plain suit, the next point is to select the proper card of the suit to lead. At first the beginner need not trouble himself about making any distinction between trumps and plain suits ; that will come later.

Rules for Leading High Cards. Having a strong suit, but without cards of re-entry or trump strength to support it, the best policy is to make tricks while you can. With such a suit as A K Q 2, no one need be told not to begin with the deuce. Whenever a player holds two or more of the best cards of a suit he should play one of them. If he holds both second and third best, playing one of them will force the best out of his way, leaving him with the commanding card.

The cards which are recognised by whist players as high, are the A K Q J 10, and if we separate the various combinations from which a player should lead each of them, a study of the groups so formed will greatly facilitate our recollection of them.

In the first group are those containing two or more of the best cards. In this and all following notation, the exact size of any card below a Ten is immaterial.

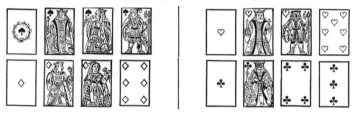

So far as trick-taking is concerned, it is of no importance which of the winning cards is first led; but for the past hundred years it has been the custom for good whist players to lead the ***King*** from all these combinations, in order that the partner may be informed, by its winning, that the leader holds the Ace also.

In the second group are those containing both the second and third best, but not the best.

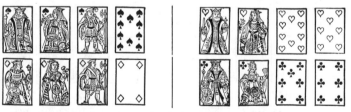

The ***King*** is the proper lead from these combinations. If it wins, the partner should have the Ace; if it loses, partner should know the leader holds at least the Queen.

Both these groups, which contain all the King leads, may be easily remembered by observing that the King is always led if accompanied by the Ace or Queen, or both. Beginners should follow this rule for leading the King, regardless of the number of small cards in the suit, unless they hold the sequence of K Q J, and at least two other cards.

From this combination the **Jack** is the usual lead, in order to invite partner to put on the Ace, if he has it, and get out of the way, thus establishing the suit in the leader's hand. This is the only high-card combination from which the Jack is led.

There is only one combination from which the **Queen** is led. regardless of the number of the small cards.

This may be remembered by observing that there is no higher card in the suit than the one led, and that it contains a sequence of three cards, Q J 10. This lead is an indication to the partner that the leader holds neither Ace nor King.

There is only one combination from which the **Ten** is led, re-gardless of the number of small cards.

The Ten led is an indication to partner that both Ace and Queen are against the leader.

Combinations from which the **Ace** is led contain at least five cards in suit, or both Queen and Jack.

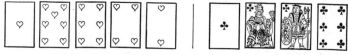

This lead is an indication to partner that the leader has not the King, and that the suit is either long, or contains three honours.

Rules for Leading Low Cards. If the suit selected for the lead contains none of the combinations from which a high card should be led, it is customary with good players to begin with the 4th-best, counting from the top of the suit. This is called the card of uniformity; because it indicates to the partner that there are remaining in the leader's hand exactly three cards higher than the one led. From any of the following combinations the proper lead would be the Four :—

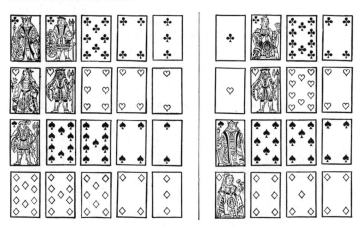

Rules for Leading Short Suits. It will sometimes happen that the only four-card suit in the leader's hand will be trumps, which it is not desirable to lead. In such cases, if there is no high-card combination in any of the short suits, it is usual to lead the highest card, unless it is an Ace or King. Many good players will not lead the Queen from a three-card suit, unless it is accompanied by the Jack. All such leads are called *forced,* and are intended to assist the partner, by playing cards which may strengthen him, although of no use to the leader. The best card should be led from any such combinations as the following :—

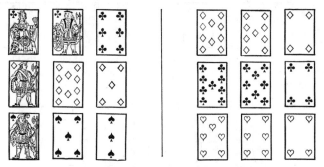

All these rules for leading apply equally to any position at the table when a player opens his own suit for the first time.

Rules for Leading Second Round. On the second round of any suit, the player holding the best card should play it ; or having several equally the best, one of them. If he is Fourth Hand, he may be able to win the trick more cheaply.

If the original leader has several cards, equally the best, such as A Q J remaining after having led the King, he should continue with the lowest card that will win the trick. This should be an indication to his partner that the card led is as good as the best, and that therefore the leader must have the intermediate cards.

Following King, which has been led from these combinations :—

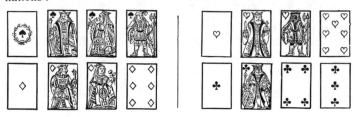

Leading the Jack on the second round would show both Ace and Queen remaining. Leading Queen would show Ace, but not the Jack. Leading Ace would show that the leader had not the Queen.

In combinations which do not contain the best card, the lead may be varied in some cases to show the number remaining in the leader's hand, or to indicate cards not shown by the first lead.

Following King, which has been led from these combinations :—

Leading the Ten on the second round would show both Queen and Jack remaining. Leading the Jack would show the Queen ; but not the ten.

Following the Jack, led from this combination :—

Leading King on the second round would show five cards in the suit originally. Leading the Queen would show more than five.

Following the Queen, led from this combination :—

Leading Jack on the second round shows the suit to have originally contained only four cards ; the Ten would show more than
four.

Following the Ace, led from these combinations :—

Leading the Queen shows the suit was short. Leading the Jack
shows that it contained at least five cards.

When a player holds both the second and third-best of a suit
on the second round, he should always play one of them, whether
he is First, Second, or Third Hand. This protects him, by forcing the command of the suit, if it does not win the trick. Having
led the Ten from K J 10 x, if the Ace or Queen wins the first
trick, the K should be next led. Having led the Four from Q
J 6 4 2, if Ace or King falls to the first trick, the Queen should be
led. If the Jack, Queen, and Ace fall to the first trick, a player
holding both Ten and Nine should lead the Ten.

After leading high cards from some combinations, and winning
the trick, they may no longer contain either the best or the second
and third best. Such are the following :—

The rule in all such cases is to follow with the card of uniformity, the original fourth-best.

If the combinations are those from which the fourth-best had
been led originally, and the leader has neither the best, nor both
second and third best to go on with, he should continue with the

lowest card in his hand, unless he had six or more in suit; in which case he may go on with the remaining fourth-best.

AVOID CHANGING SUITS. A player having once begun with a suit, either for the purpose of establishing it, or of taking tricks in it, should not change it until he is forced to do so. Running off to untried suits is one of the beginner's worst faults. There are five good reasons for changing suits, and unless one of them can be applied, the suit should be continued :

1st. In order to lead trumps to defend it.
2nd. In order to avoid forcing partner.
3rd. In order to avoid forcing both adversaries.
4th. Because it is hopeless, and there is some chance in another.
5th. To prevent a cross ruff, by leading trumps.

Simple Inferences from the fall of the cards usually supply the best guide in the matter of changing suits.

If the Jack is led from K Q J x x, and wins the trick, partner may be credited with the Ace ; and if the original leader has four trumps, and a card of re-entry, he should quit his established suit, and lead trumps to defend it.

If the King and Ace have been led from A K x x, partner dropping the Queen on the second round, the suit should be changed, unless the original leader is strong enough to risk weakening his partner by forcing him to trump the third round. Four trumps are generally considered to be sufficiently strong to justify a force in this position. Some players will force, even with a weak hand, if the two cards played by the partner are small, and he has not availed himself of an artifice known as ***calling for trumps,*** which we shall consider presently.

If the King and Ten have been led from K Q J 10, and on the second round one adversary has dropped the Eight, the other the Nine ; the suit should be changed, as partner must have the Ace, and neither of the adversaries have any more. To lead such a suit again is called ***forcing both adversaries ;*** as it allows one to make a small trump and the other to get rid of a losing card.

If the Four has been led from J 8 6 4, and the adversaries have won the first trick with the Nine or Ten, A K Q must be against the leader and his partner, and the suit should be abandoned as hopeless, unless it is feasible to force the partner.

If at any time there is a strong indication that the adversaries will have a cross-ruff, it is usually best to stop leading plain suits, and attempt to get out the trumps.

THE LEADER'S PARTNER, or the Third Hand, has several conventional plays to remember ; the most important of which are the following :—

When Partner Leads High Cards, the Third Hand has

usually little to do but to play his lowest of the suit. The exceptions are :

If he holds A J alone, on a King led, the Ace should be played.

If he holds A Q alone on a Ten led, the Ace should be played. With A Q x, the Ten should be passed. With Ace and small cards, the Ace should be played on the Ten. With Queen and small cards the Ten should be passed. When Third Hand plays Queen on a Ten led, it should be a certainty that he has no more of the suit.

If he holds A K and only one small card, the King should be played on a Queen led.

If he holds Ace and only one small card, the Ace should be played on the Jack led. If Third Hand has four trumps and a card of re-entry, the Ace should be played on Jack led, regardless of number, in order to lead trumps at once, to defend the suit.

When Partner Leads Low Cards, the Third Hand should do his best to secure the trick. If he has several cards of equal trick-taking value, such as A K Q, or K Q J, he should win the trick as cheaply as possible. The only *finesse* permitted to the Third Hand in his partner's suit, is the play of the Queen, when he holds A Q and others ; the odds being against Fourth Hand having the King.

Foster's Eleven Rule. By deducting from eleven the number of pips on any low card led, the Third Hand may ascertain how far his partner's suit is from being established. For instance : if the card led is the Seven, Second Hand playing the Eight, and Third Hand holding A J 6 3, from which he plays Ace, Fourth Hand playing the Five ; the only card against the leader must be the King or Queen ; he cannot have both, or he would have led one. If the Second Hand has not the missing card, he has no more of the suit. The number of inferences which may be made in this manner by observant players is astonishing. A great many examples and exercises in them are given in ***Foster's Whist Manual.***

Third Hand having None of the Suit, should trump anything but an Ace or a King on the first round. On the second round, if there is only one card against the leader, his partner should pass with four trumps, and allow the suit to be established. For instance : If the leads have been Ace, then Jack, Third Hand holding only one of the suit ; he should pass if the Second Hand does not play King.

Third Hand on Strengthening Cards. Unless Third Hand has both Ace and King of the suit, he should pass any forced or strengthening lead which is not covered by the Second Hand. This obliges the Fourth Hand to open another suit, or to continue at a disadvantage.

Third Hand winning first round has the choice of four lines of play:

1st.   To lead trumps, if he is strong enough.

2nd.   To return the best card of his partner's suit if he has it. This is imperative before opening any other suit but trumps.

3rd.   To lead his own suit, if he can do anything with it.   It is considered better play for the Third Hand to return the original leader's suit than to open a long weak suit of his own, such as one headed by a single honour.

4th.   To return his partner's suit, even with a losing card, in preference to changing.

When the original lead is a trump, it should be returned in every case, either immediately, or as soon as the player can obtain the lead.

The same reasons for changing suits as those given for the original leader will apply to the Third Hand.

RULES FOR RETURNING PARTNER'S SUITS.

When the original leader's suit is returned by his partner, either immediately or upon his regaining the lead, it is usual to show, if possible, how many cards remain in the Third Hand, so that by adding them to his own, the leader may estimate the number held by his adversaries.   This consideration is secondary to the return of the best, or one of the second and third best; but in the absence of such cards, the Third Hand should always return the higher of only two remaining, and the lowest of three or more, regardless of their value.

In addition to the foregoing conventionalities, which are proper to the leader of a suit and his partner, there are two usages which apply equally to any player at the table.   These are discarding and forcing.

Discarding.

When a player cannot follow suit, and does not wish to trump, his safest play is to discard whatever seems of least use to him.   It is not considered good play to unguard a King or to leave an Ace alone; but this may be done if the partner is leading trumps, and there is a good established suit to keep.   Beginners should be careful to preserve cards of re-entry, even if they have to discard from their good suit in order to do so.

When the adversaries have shown strength in trumps, or are leading them, there is little use in keeping a long suit together. It is much better to keep guard on the suits in which they are probably strong, letting your own and your partner's go.

A player having full command of a suit, may show it to his partner by discarding the best card of it.   Discarding the second-best is an indication that the player has not the best; and in general, the discard of any small card shows weakness in that suit.

Forcing. We have already observed that a player who is weak himself should not force his partner. An exception may be made in cases where he has shown weakness, or has had a chance to lead trumps and has not done so. On the contrary, an adversary should not be forced unless he has shown strength, or the player forcing him is weak. The hope of a player with a good suit is to defend it by leading and exhausting the trumps. His adversary tries to keep his trumps in order to stop that suit; at the same time forcing the strong hand, by leading cards which he must trump, hoping that such a force may so weaken him that he will be unable to continue the trump lead.

It is usually very difficult to convince the beginner that the weaker he is himself, the more reason he has for forcing the adversaries to trump his good cards. He is constantly falling into the error of changing from a good suit, which the adversaries cannot stop without trumping, to a weak suit, which allows them to get into the lead without any waste of trump strength. If an adversary refuses to trump a suit, it is imperative to keep on with it until he does; for it is always good play to force an adversary to do what he does not wish to do.

Any person may convince himself of the soundness of this theory of forcing, by giving himself the six highest cards in any suit, three small cards in the others, and four trumps; giving another player the four best trumps, and nine of the highest cards in two suits. If the first player forces the second with his good suit, and continues every time he gets the lead, he must win six tricks; if he does not, the second player makes a slam.

A deliberate force from a partner should always be accepted, if he is a good player.

We may now turn our attention to the conventionalities used by players who are opposed to the establishment of suits in the hands of the leader and his partner. These are divided between the Second and the Fourth Hand, the former being the more important. Generally speaking, they are the tactics of defence.

SECOND HAND PLAY. The player who is second to play on any trick is called the Second Hand. It is his duty to protect himself and his partner, as far as possible, in the adversaries' strong suits. The chief point for the beginner to observe in Second Hand play, is the difference between the circumstances requiring him to play high cards, and those in which he should play low ones.

High Cards Led. When a card higher than a Ten is led on the first round of a suit, the Second Hand has usually nothing to do but to play his lowest card, and make what inference he can as to the probable distribution of the suit. But if he holds the Ace, or cards in sequence with it, such as A K, he should cover any

card higher than a Ten.   If he holds K Q he should cover a J, 10,
or 9 led ; but it is useless for him to cover an honour with a single
honour, unless it is the Ace.

Low Cards Led.   High cards are played by the Second Hand
when he has any combination from which he would have led a
high one if he had opened the suit.   The fact that a player on his
right has already laid a small card of the suit on the table should
not prevent the Second Hand from making the best use of any
combinations he may hold.   The only difference between leading
from such combinations, and playing them Second Hand, is that in
the latter case no attempt is made to indicate to the partner the
exact nature of the combination held.   The general rule is to win
the trick as cheaply as possible, by playing the lowest of the high
cards which form the combination from which a high card would
be led.   Such are the following :—

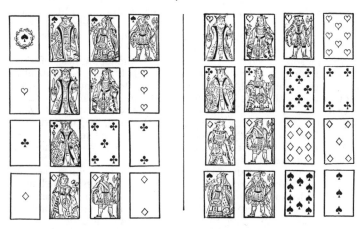

The beginner must be careful with these :—

The combination which makes the first of these a high-card
lead is the A K, and the King must be played Second Hand.   The
Jack has nothing to do with it.   In the second, the Ten does not
form any part of the combination, and the Queen is the card to
play Second Hand.   Some players will not play a high card second
hand with K Q x x unless weak in trumps.

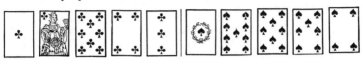

An exception is generally made with these combinations, from which the proper lead is the Ace.

Many will not play Ace Second Hand in any case, and will play the Queen with the first combination only when they are weak in trumps. The reason for this exception is the importance of retaining command of the adverse suit as long as possible.

On the Second Round, the Second Hand should follow the usual rule for playing the best of the suit if he holds it ; or one of the second and third best, if he holds them. He should also be careful to estimate, by the eleven rule, how many cards are out against the leader, which will sometimes guide him to a good finesse. For instance : first player leads Ace, then Eight. If the Second Hand holds K J 9 2, instead of playing the best card to the second round, which would be King, he should finesse the Nine.

With Short Suits. When Second Hand holds such short-suit combinations as :—

and a small card is led, his proper play is one of the high cards, because he cannot save both of them.

On Strengthening Cards Led. This is a difficult point for the beginner, and his best plan is to follow the rules already given for covering cards higher than the Ten. One of the most common errors is to cover a Jack led with a Queen, when holding A Q and others. The Ace should be put on invariably. To play the Queen in such a position is called *finessing against yourself.*

Singly Guarded Honours. Many players put on the King Second Hand, if they hold only one small card with it, and a small card is led. This will win the trick as often as it will lose it ; but it betrays the hand to the adversary, and enables him to finesse deeply if the suit is returned. It may be done in order to get the lead, and in trumps the practice is very common, and generally right. With Queen and only one small card, it can be demonstrated that it is useless to play the Queen Second Hand, except as an experiment, or to get the lead in desperate cases.

With any combination weaker than J 10 x, it is useless to attempt to win the trick Second Hand, and only makes it difficult for the partner to place the cards correctly.

The Fourchette. When the Second Hand has cards immediately above and below the one led, he should cover. The beginner may have some difficulty in recognising the fact that he holds fourchette if the suit has been round once or twice, and the intermediate cards have been played. Such cards as a Queen and a Seven may be fourchette over a Nine, if Jack, Ten and Eight have been played.

Second Hand Having None of the suit led, on either first or second round, must decide whether or not to trump it. If the card led is the best of the suit, he should certainly do so ; but if it is not, and there is any uncertainty as to who will win the trick, it is usual for the Second Hand to pass when he has four trumps. With five trumps, there should be some good reason for keeping the trumps together, as a player with so many can usually afford to trump. If he does not trump, his play comes under the rules for discarding.

FOURTH-HAND PLAY. The Fourth Hand is the last player in any trick. He is the partner of the Second Hand, but has not so many opportunities for the exercise of judgment, his duties being simply to win tricks if he can, and as cheaply as possible. If he cannot win the trick, he should play his lowest card.

A bad habit of Fourth-Hand players is holding up the tenace A J when a King or Queen is led originally. This is called the **Bath Coup,** and the suit must go round three times for it to succeed in making two tricks. The holder of the tenace should equally make two tricks by playing the Ace at once, provided he does not lead the suit back.

The Turn-up Trump. When trumps are led by the adversaries, it is a common practice to play the turn-up as soon as possible, unless it is a valuable card. On the contrary, it is usual to keep it as long as possible when the partner leads trumps.

Changing Suits. If the Second or Fourth Hand wins the first or second round of the adversaries' suit, it is seldom right to return it, as that would probably be playing their game. The player should open his own suit, as if he were the original leader. If he is strong enough to lead trumps under ordinary circumstances, he may be deterred from so doing if the adversaries have declared a strong suit against him. The same consideration may prevent his leading trumps in the hope of making a suit of his own, as the adversaries might reap the benefit by bringing in their suit instead. On the contrary, when the Second or Fourth Hand holds command of the adverse suit, they may often risk a trump lead which would otherwise be injudicious. Having once started a suit, it should not be changed, except for one of the reasons already given for the guidance of the First Hand.

When the Adversaries Lead Trumps, and the Second Hand has a chance either to establish a suit against them or to force his partner, he should stop the trump lead if he can. If his partner has led trumps, the Second Hand should generally play his winning cards on his right hand opponent's plain-suit leads, to stop them; and continue the trumps.

These are about all the conventionalities necessary for the beginner. After at least a year's practice with them, he will either discover that he has no aptitude for the game, or will be ready to go into further details. A beginner who attempts to handle the weapons of the expert simply plays with edged tools, which will probably cut no one but himself and his partner.

THE SIGNAL GAME. Having become thoroughly familiar with the elementary conventionalities of the game, so that they can be used without the slightest hesitation at the whist table, the player may proceed to acquaint himself with the details of what is commonly known as the Signal Game, which comprises all the various methods of signalling up hands between partners, according to certain arbitrary and pre-arranged systems of play. Many players object to these methods as unfair; but they are now too deeply rooted to yield to protest; and the best thing for a player to do is to familiarise himself with his adversaries' weapons.

The Trump Signal. A player anxious to have trumps led, but who has no immediate prospect of the lead, may call on his partner to lead trumps at the first opportunity, by playing any two cards of a suit led, the higher before the lower. Let us suppose him to hold five good trumps, with the Six and Two of a suit of which his partner leads King, then Jack. By playing first the Six, and then the Two, he calls upon his partner to quit the suit, and lead a trump.

Among some players, the lead of a strengthening card when an honour is turned, is a call for trumps to be led through that honour at the first opportunity, but it is not good play.

Passing a certain winning card is regarded by most players as an imperative call for trumps.

The discard of any card higher than a Seven is known as a single-card-call. Even if it was not so intended, it is assumed that a trump lead cannot injure a player with nothing smaller than a Nine in his hand.

Answering Trump Signals. In response to partner's call, a player should lead the best trump if he holds it; one of the second and third best if he holds them; the highest of three or less; the lowest of four; and the fourth-best of more than four. Holding any of the regular high-card combinations in trumps, he should lead them in the regular way in answer to a call.

After a Force. If the player is forced before he can answer the call, he may indicate the number of trumps originally held by playing them in this manner :—

With 3 or less; trumping with the lowest; leading the highest.

With 4 exactly; trumping with the 3rd-best; leading the highest.

With 5 or more; trumping with the 3rd-best; leading the 4th-best.

These methods of taking the force must not be carried to extremes. For instance: A player holding K J 10 2, would hardly be justified in trumping with the 10 to show number. Some experts, holding the best trump with at least four others, will not lead it; preferring to show number first, by leading the fourth-best. Others, holding four, lead the lowest after trumping with the third-best.

The Echo in Trumps. When the partner leads high trumps, the Third Hand should echo with four or more, by signalling in the trump suit. The universal form of the echo is to play first the third-best, then the fourth-best. When a player has called, and his partner leads, it is unnecessary for the caller to echo. Players seldom echo on adverse trump leads, even with five trumps.

The Four-Signal. There are several ways of showing four or more trumps without asking partner to lead them. Among some players the original lead of a strengthening card is an evidence of four trumps, and is called an ***Albany Lead.*** A player holding three cards of any plain suit, such as the 3, 4, 5, may show the number of his trumps by playing these small cards as follows :—

No of trumps.	1st trick.	2nd trick.	3rd trick.
3 or less	3	4	5
4 exactly	4	5	3
5 "	4	3	5
6 "	5	3	4
7 or more	5	4	3

The second of these is the four-signal; the last three are trump signals. They are used only in following suit.

The four-signal is sometimes used in the trump suit as a ***Sub-echo,*** to show three trumps exactly.

Apart from signalling, trump strength may often be inferred, especially from player's passing doubtful tricks, forcing their partners, etc.

Trump Suit Leads. When trumps are not led for the purpose of exhausting them immediately, but simply as the longest suit, the fourth-best may be led from the following :—

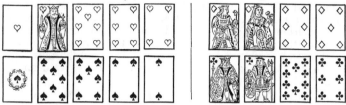

If the Ten accompanies the King and Queen, in the third combination, it is best to adhere to the usual lead of the King.

In leading trumps from combinations containing a winning sequence, such as the following :—

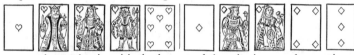

many players begin with the lowest of the winning cards, continuing with the next above it.

Speculative Trump Leads. The whist player will often find himself with a single good suit, a card of re-entry, and few trumps. Certain conditions of the score may prompt him to make a speculative trump lead from such a hand. If his trumps are high, such as A K x, he may safely begin by leading them; but if they are weak, and he is depending largely on his partner's possible strength, he should show his suit first by leading it once.

Overtrumping is generally regarded as bad policy when a player has a good suit, and sufficient trump strength to justify him in hoping to do something with it. The refusal to overtrump, unless the trump played is a high one, should be regarded by the partner as a call.

It is sometimes necessary to overtrump partner in order to get the lead. For instance : A player holds the two best trumps, and all winning cards of a plain suit, while the player on his right has a losing trump. In such a position the player with the two best trumps should trump any winning card his partner leads, or over trump him if he trumps, so as to prevent the adversary from making that losing trump.

Undertrumping, or the Grand Coup, is playing a low trump on a trick that partner has already trumped with a higher, in order to avoid the lead. For instance : A player holds major tenace in trumps with a small one, and knows that the minor tenace is on his right. Four cards remain in each hand. The player on the left leads ; Second Hand trumps ; Third Hand follows suit. If the Fourth Hand keeps his three trumps, he must win the next trick, and lose the advantage of his tenace,

A player will sometimes have the best card in two suits, and a small trump, and will know that the two best trumps and an unknown card are on his right. If the missing suit is led, and the player on the right trumps, his unknown card must be one of the two other suits, and the player with the command of them should keep both, and throw away his small trump. The discards on the next trick may enable him to determine the suit of the losing card on his right.

The Last Trump. If two players have an equal number of trumps, each of them having an established suit, it will be the object of both to remain with the last trump, which must bring in the suit. The tactics of each will be to win the third round of trumps ; and then, if the best trump is against him, to force it out with the established suit, coming into the lead again with the last trump. So often is it important to win the third round of trumps that few good players will win the second round, unless they can win the third also. With an established suit, a card of re-entry, and four trumps King high, a player should lead trumps ; but if his partner wins the first round and returns a small trump, the King should not be put on, no matter what Second Hand plays, unless the card next below the King is fourchette. Some of the most brilliant endings in whist are skirmishes for the possession of the last trump ; the player who is at a disadvantage often persistently refuses the fatal force, hoping the leader will be compelled to change his suit, or will lose the lead.

Drawing the Losing Trump. It is usually best to draw losing trumps from the adversaries, unless a player can foresee that he may want the best to stop a strong adverse suit.

A Thirteenth Card, played by the partner, is usually considered an invitation to put on the best trump. The Second Hand should not trump a thirteenth card unless he is weak in trumps.

AMERICAN LEADS. Advanced players, who have had so much practice that they can infer the probable position of the cards without devoting their entire attention to it, have adopted a new system of leading from the four combinations following, in order to show the number of small cards in the suit :—

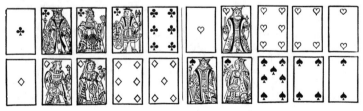

From these the King is never led if there are more than four cards in the suit. Having more than four, the lowest of the sequence of high cards is led. From the first this would be the Jack ; from the second the Queen ; from the third the Ace, (because the King is barred ;) and from the fourth the Queen. The Ten is not ranked among the high cards in American Leads.

On the second round, with the first two combinations, the difference between a suit of five or one of six cards may be indicated by following with the Ace if five were held originally ; the King, if more than five. Seven cards may be shown with the first combination, by leading the Queen on the second round.

The chief difference these leads make in the play of the Third Hand is that he should not trump any court card led, even if weak in trumps. The misunderstanding as to the meaning of the first lead, especially if it is a Queen, often occasions confusion and loss ; but this is claimed to be offset by the value of the information given. Some lead 10 from Q J 10 ; 4th-best from K J 10.

To the adversaries these leads are often of value, as they are frequently enabled to place the cards very accurately from the information given by the lead itself, regardless of the fall of the cards from the other hands. For instance : Second Hand holds A J of a suit in which King is led ; Third Hand plays the Four ; Fourth Hand plays the Nine. The leader remains with Q 3 2 ; Third Hand still has 8 7 6 5 ; and if he has also the 10, Fourth Hand has no more. Again : The leader shows a suit of six ; Second Hand holding two only. If the suit is led a third time it is a doubtful trick, and with four trumps the Second Hand should pass. If the leader shows the exact number of the suit originally led, and then changes to a four-card suit, the adversaries know at least nine of his cards.

So obvious is this that it is an almost invariable rule for a player, on quitting his suit, to conceal the length of the second suit led by leading the highest card of a short suit.

If it were allowable to exercise some judgment in using these leads, they might not be open to so many objections ; but they are worse than useless unless the partner can depend on their being uniformly adopted.

The Minneapolis Lead. This is another variation in the leads, which is confined to one combination ; that of Ace and any four other cards, not including the King. With strength in trumps the fourth-best is led instead of the Ace, the theory being that the Ace is more likely to be valuable on the second or third round of such a suit than on the first, and that the trump strength justifies the finesse of the original lead. With weak trumps the Ace is led. Some players extend this principle to the Second Hand, and play Ace on a small card led, when holding A x x x with weak trumps. This is open to the objection that it gives up command of the adverse suit too early in the hand ; but it saves many a trick.

The Plain-suit Echo. This is another device for giving information as to number. When the original leader begins with a high card, the Third Hand should play his third-best if he holds four or more; and on the second round his second-best, always retaining his fourth-best and any below it. The value of this echo is much disputed, and the adversaries can usually render it ineffective by holding up small cards; a practice very much in vogue with advanced players.

Low's Signal. This is the latest system of indicating to the leader the number of cards in his suit held by the Third Hand. With four or more of the suit, the third-best is played to the lead of a high card, or when no attempt is made to win the trick. In returning the suit, the second-best is led if three or more remain, and on the third round, or in a discard, the highest is played, always retaining the fourth-best and those below it. For instance: With the 8 7 5 2 of a suit which partner leads, the 5 is played to the first round. If the suit is returned, the 7 is played; and next time the 8. Holding only three originally, the lowest is played to the first round, and the higher of two returned, in the usual way. The chief value of this signal is that the return of the lowest of a suit shows absolutely no more, instead of leaving the original leader in doubt as to whether it is the only one, or the lowest of three remaining. It is also a great exposer of false cards.

Discard Signalling is another method of indicating plain suits. When a player is known to have no trumps, and therefore cannot be calling for them, he may use the trump signal in any plain suit which he wishes led to him. As a general rule, a player should not use this signal unless he has a certain trick in the suit in which he signals. Some players use what is called the reverse discard; a signal in one suit meaning weakness in it, and an invitation to lead another. This avoids the necessity for using the good suit for signalling purposes.

Unblocking. When the original leader shows a suit of five cards, and the Third Hand has four exactly, the latter should keep his lowest card, not for the purpose of echoing, but in order to retain a small card which will not block the holder of the longer suit. If the Third Hand has three cards of the suit led, and among them a card which may block his partner, he should give it up on the second round. For instance: Holding K 4 3, and partner showing a five-card suit by leading Ace then Jack, Third Hand should give up the King on the second round. Again: Holding Q 9 3, partner leading Ace then Eight; Second Hand playing King second round, Third Hand should give up the Queen. Again: Holding K Q, partner leading the 8 originally, won by Fourth Hand with Ace; the King should be discarded or otherwise got rid of at the first opportunity.

Short-suit Leads. Many players will not lead a long weak suit unless they have sufficient strength to justify them in hoping to establish, defend, and bring it in, with **reasonable** support from the partner. With a long suit, headed by a single honour, weak trumps, and no cards of re-entry, they prefer selecting a strengthening card for the original lead, hoping it may be of some assistance to partner by affording a successful finesse. It is claimed that it is better for a person, especially with a strong hand, to play with the knowledge that his partner is weak, than under the impression that he may be strong. Such an opening lead should warn the Third Hand to finesse deeply, to hold any tenaces he may have, and to let nothing pass him which might be too much for his weak partner to attend to. This is a very difficult game to play well, and is seldom resorted to except by the most expert.

Deschapelles Coups. It often happens that after the adverse trumps are exhausted, a player will find himself with the lead, but unable to give his partner a card of his established suit. In such cases the best course is to sacrifice the King or Queen of any suit of which he has not the Ace, in the hope that it may force the best of the suit, and leave partner with a card of re-entry. For instance : The leader has established the Club suit ; his partner has exhausted the trumps, Hearts ; and having no Clubs, leads the King of Spades from K x x x. If the holder of the Club suit has Spade Queen, and the King forces the Ace, the Club suit will be brought in. If he has not the Queen, the Clubs are probably hopeless. The *coup* risks a trick to gain several.

Players should be careful not to fall into this trap in the end-game ; and it is generally right to hold up the Ace if the circumstances are at all suspicious.

Tenace Positions. Many expert players will not lead away from a suit in which they hold tenace. Having two suits, one containing a tenace, and the other without it, they will select the latter, although it may be much weaker. It is noteworthy that players who disregard the value of holding a tenace in the opening lead, are well aware of its importance toward the end of the hand. When one player holds tenace over another, the end game often becomes a struggle to place the lead ; and players frequently refuse to win tricks in order to avoid leading away from tenaces, or to compel another player to lead up to them.

Underplay is often resorted to by the Fourth Hand in suits in which the Third Hand has shown weakness. For instance : A small card is led ; Third Hand playing the Ten, and Fourth Hand holding A Q J x. It is a common artifice to win with the Queen, and return the small card. When the original leader is underplayed in his own suit, he should invariably put up his best card.

Finessing. The expert may finesse much more freely than the beginner. Having led from such a suit as K J x x and partner having won with Ace and returned a small card, the Jack may be finessed with strong trumps. If the adversaries lead trumps, and the Ace wins the first round, a player holding the King second hand on the return, may finesse by holding it up, trusting his partner for the trick.

In all cases that mark the best of the suit against a player, and on his left, he may finesse against the third-best being there also. For instance: A player leads from K 10 x x x. Third Hand plays Queen and returns a small card   The Ten should be finessed, regardless of trump strength, as the Ace must be on the left, and the finesse is against the Jack being there also. Many varieties of this finesse occur.

Placing the Lead. This is usually a feature of the end-game. A player may have an established suit, his adversary being the only person with any small cards of it. If the lead can be placed in the hand of this adversary, he must eventually lead the losing cards.

A player begins with a weak suit of four cards, on the first round of which it is evident that his partner has no more, the adversaries having all the high cards. The suit is not played again, and for the last six tricks the original leader finds himself with three cards of it, and the Q x x of another suit. If the adversaries play King and Ace of the latter suit, the Queen should be given up, trusting partner for the Jack, for the Queen will force the holder of the three losing cards into the lead. It is sometimes necessary to throw away an Ace in order to avoid the lead at critical stages of the end-game.

False Cards. It requires more than ordinary skill to judge when a false card will do less harm to the partner than to the adversaries. There are some occasions for false-card play about which there is little question. Having a sequence in the adverse suit, the Second or Fourth Hand may win with the highest card, especially if the intention is to lead trumps. Holding K Q only, Second Hand may play the King, especially in trumps. Holding A K x, the Fourth Hand should play Ace on a Queen led by an American leader. With such a suit as K J 10 x, after trumps have been exhausted, the Ten is not a safe lead ; Jack or fourth-best is better. Holding up the small cards of adverse suits is a common stratagem ; and it is legitimate to use any system of false-carding in trumps if it will prevent the adversaries who have led them from counting them accurately.

Playing to the Score. The play must often be varied on account of the state of the score, either to save or win the game in the hand. If the adversaries appear to be very strong, and likely to go out on the deal, all conventionalities should be disregarded until the game is saved; finesses should be refused, and winning cards played Second Hand on the first round. If the adversaries are exhausting the trumps, it will often be judicious for a player to make what winning cards he has, regardless of all rules for leading, especially if they are sufficient to save the game.

It often happens that the same cards must be played in different ways according to the state of the score, and the number of tricks in front of the player. A simple example will best explain this. Hearts are trumps; you hold two small ones, two better being out against you, but whether in one hand or not you cannot tell. You have also two winning Spades, one smaller being still out. The game is seven-point whist. The importance of playing to the score will be evident if you consider your play in each of the following instances, your score being given first :

> Score 6 to 6 ; you have 5 tricks in front of you.
> Score 6 to 6 ; you have 4 tricks in front of you.
> Score 6 to 5 ; you have 4 tricks in front of you.
> Score 5 to 4 ; you have 5 tricks in front of you.

INFERENCES. The great strength of the expert lies in his ability to draw correct inferences from the fall of the cards, and to adapt his play to the circumstances.

Inferences from the various systems of leads and returns are too obvious to require further notice; but attention may be called to some that are often overlooked, even by advanced players :

If a suit led is won by Third Hand with King or Ace ; and the original leader wins the second round with King or Ace, the adversaries must have the Queen.

If the Third Hand plays Ace first round, he has neither King nor Queen. If he plays Queen on a Ten led, he has no more. If he plays Ace on a King led, he has the Jack alone, or no more.

If the Second Hand plays King first round on a small card led, he has Ace also, or no more. If he plays Ace under the same conditions, he has no more. [See Minneapolis Lead.]

If a suit is led, and neither Third nor Fourth Hand has a card in it above a Nine, the original leader must have A Q 10, and the second player K J. When neither Third nor Fourth Hand holds a card above the Ten, the major and minor tenaces are divided between the leader and the Second Hand. If it can be inferred that the leader held five cards in the suit originally, he holds the minor tenace.

When a player, not an American leader, begins with a Jack and wins the trick, the adversaries may conclude that his partner had two small cards with the Ace, and had not four trumps and another winning card.

When a good player changes his suit, he knows that it will not go round again, or that the command is against him. This is often a valuable hint to the adversaries. When he quits his original suit and leads trumps, without his partner having called, the adversaries may conclude that the suit has been established.

When a player puts Ace on his partner's Jack led, and does not lead trumps, the adversaries may count on him for only one small card of the suit led.

When an adversary finesses freely, he may be credited with some strength in trumps.

When a player changes his suit, the adversaries should note carefully the fall of the cards in the new suit. As already observed, the leader almost invariably opens the new suit with the best he has. Suppose a player to lead two winning cards in one suit, and then the Eight of another, which the Second Hand wins with the Ten; The four honours in the second suit must be between the Second and Fourth Hands.

Having won the first or second round of the adverse suit, and having no good suit of his own, the Second or Fourth Hand may be able to infer a good suit with his partner, by the play. For instance: A player opens Clubs, showing five, his partner wins second round, and opens the Diamond suit with the Jack, on which Second Hand plays Ace, his partner dropping the 9. Having now the lead, and no good suit, it is evident that the play should be continued on the assumption that partner is all Spades and trumps.

———

THE HOWELL GAME. Many of those who adopt the short-suit game as a regular system of play use the original or opening lead to indicate the general character of the hand, rather than any details of the individual suit. In the long-suit game the original leader is always assuming that his partner may have something or other, and playing on that supposition. The short-suit player indicates the system of play best adapted to his own hand, without the slightest regard to the possibilities of his partner. It is the duty of the partner to indicate his hand in turn, and to shape the policy of the play on the combined indications of the two. This system was elaborated by E. C. Howell.

By his original lead the short-suit player can indicate which of the five following lines of play will best suit his individual hand:—

First. The trump attack; showing that he is anxious to exhaust the trumps. The details of his holding in plain suits is immaterial; he wants the trumps out of his way first. This is indicated by an original lead of a trump of any size.

Second. The high-card game; showing that he is anxious to make what tricks he can with his high cards, while in the lead.

This is shown by the original lead of an ace or king in any plain suit, and is sometimes called "running."

Third. The tenace game; showing that he holds cards that offer chances for successful finesse in his own hand, or that may strengthen the third hand. This is indicated by the lead of any supporting card, such as a Q, J, 10, or 9. Third Hand should pass all such cards, unless he holds both ace and king. If he holds ace and queen, he should either put the ace on the J, 10, or 9, or pass altogether, according to his trump strength, and the general character of his hand. If the last play on the next trick would probably be advantageous, he should pass.

Fourth. The ruffing game; showing that he has not five trumps, and that he thinks the best use he can make of what he has is to trump the second or third round of the suit he leads. This is indicated by the lead of a 6, 7, or 8, which are too weak to be supporting cards, and too strong to be the lowest of a long unestablished suit. Such are never led with more than two cards in the suit, and are preferably singletons.

Fifth. The invitation to lead trumps; showing that the leader's hand is more than usually strong, and that the fear of partner's weakness is the only thing that prevents an original trump lead. This is indicated by the lead of a 2, 3, 4, or 5; which should be the lowest of a long unestablished suit; or at least a suit that may be safely led back by partner. Such a suit must be well supported by cards of re-entry and some trump strength. If the trumps are very weak, all the plain suits should be well protected. A small card of a short suit may often be selected to show a desire for partner to lead trumps if he is strong in them, provided there is no objection to the short suit being returned. For instance : Hearts trumps; and you hold ♡ K 2 ; ♣ K Q 4 ; ◊ A Q ; ♠ A Q J 10 9 6. The best original lead is the club 4. If partner has four or five good trumps, you make a great game ; if not, you are warned to play more cautiously.

None of these openings compel the partner to follow them up. He develops his own hand according to its possibilities, tempered by the indications given by the original leader. For instance : if the leader invites a ruff, by an original opening of a 6, 7, or 8, he probably does not hold five trumps ; or if he does, his plain suits must all be absolutely worthless.

In the leads there is no attempt to indicate the number of cards held in the suit. The king is led only from A K, or K Q J and others; never from K Q or K Q 10 and others; the latter should never be opened at all, unless the lowest card is led to indicate a desire for trumps. Ace is not led from suits of less than six cards, and then only when "running," because it is unlikely that there is anything more in the suit than the ace. Queen is never led except as a supporting card, and frequently with one other in the suit, or as a singleton. The Jack or Ten is led from the top of weak suits, or as an intermediate card from suits headed by Q or K. From long, unestablished, but well-supported suits, the lowest card is led ; never the fourth-best.

In leading trumps from strength, all the number showing leads are used, and the echo is used with three or more ; sub-echoing in a plain suit with four or more.

All false cards are tabooed ; nothing is so dangerous in a game where partner may be unexpectedly strong. The system of leads must be adhered to with the greatest strictness, or the whole game becomes a nightmare. The most dangerous lead is the small card, which should never be used unless the leader is quite willing to have trumps led, either by his partner or by the adversaries. Trumps must never be counted as cards of re-entry, unless there are five or more. There should be as many cards of re-entry in the leader's hand as there will be leads necessary to establish and bring in his long suit. If he leads from Q J 10 x x, two cards of re-entry will be required in plain suits ; one to lead a second time ; another to bring the suit in.

The fundamental principle of the game is that high cards which are not in sequence are more valuable when led up to than when led away from. For instance : A king guarded is a certainty for a trick, bar trumping, if the holder of it is Fourth Hand. It is two to one that it wins a trick if it held Second or Third Hand. But it is two to one against it if it is led. An ace led will probably win a trick ; but only small cards will fall to it. If the suit is led by some other player, the ace may kill a king or a queen ; not only winning a trick, but capturing a card that would otherwise have been good for another trick. For this reason the short-suit player will not lead from suits of five cards containing the ace but not the king ; not even from A Q J. If there are six cards in the suit, there is little hope for a tenace to make, or for the suit to go round more than once. The ace may be led from all such, and the lead should indicate to partner a suit of at least six cards.

Suits containing major, minor, or potential tenaces are not led originally. The major tenace is A Q ; the minor, K J ; and the potentials, A J, and K 10. Suits which develop into tenace suits during the play should not be led. For instance : A J fall on the first round of a suit in which you hold K 10. Your cards are now tenace over the Q, and should not be led.

The original lead often requires careful consideration, and, in order to avoid deceiving partner, a player is often driven to select intermediate cards, such as a 10 from A 10 9 ; a 9 from K 9 7 ; or a J from Q J x x x. As an example of the difference between the long and the short-suit systems of leading, here are two hands, from both of which the long-suit player would lead the club 6 ;

hands of totally different strength and construction, and yet led from in precisely the same way. The heart Q turned.

♡	9	6	4				♡	K	4	2	
♣	10	9	8	6	3	2	♣	K	J	9	6
◇	8	7					◇	K	Q	2	
♠	A	6					♠	A	Q	10	

From the first hand the short-suit player might either invite a ruff by leading the diamond 8, or support his partner by leading the club 10. The latter would not be so good as the first, because the partner might read the leader for a finessing hand. From the second hand the short-suit player would lead the diamond 2, indicating general strength, and a desire that his partner should lead trumps if he wins the first trick, and is strong enough to venture a trump lead. Some would begin with the trump suit; but the conservative player would not take such an unnecessary risk while he had the alternative of making the trump lead dependent on his partner's trump strength.

By some short-suit players, the lead of a 5, 4, 3 or 2 is considered a positive call for trumps if an honour is turned ; not otherwise.

IN CONCLUSION. These are the principal refinements used by experts in whist conventionalities. They are worse than useless to the beginner, as they only confuse him, and withdraw his attention from matters which he could probably understand and make good use of. Many believe they equally handicap the expert.

The first-class whist-player is usually developed gradually. If he possess the faculty of paying close attention to the game while he is playing, nothing should prevent his rapid progress. At first he may care little or nothing for " book " whist, but after some experience with book players, he is rather in danger of running to the other extreme, and putting more book into his game than it will carry. Having passed that stage, his next step is usually to invent some system of his own, and to experiment with every hand he plays. By degrees he finds that all special systems of play have some serious defects, which overbalance their advantages ; and this discovery gradually brings him back to first principles. If he gets so far safely, his game for all future time will probably be sound, common-sense whist, without any American leads, plain-suit echoes, or four-signals, and free from any attempts to take fourteen tricks with thirteen cards.

When a whist player reaches that point, he is probably as near the first class as the natural limitations of his mental abilities will ever permit him to go.

THE LAWS will be found at the end of the Whist Family of Games.

ILLUSTRATIVE WHIST HANDS.

A and B are partners against Y and Z. A is always the original leader, and Z is the dealer. The underlined card wins the trick, and the card under it is the next one led.

No. 1. Long Suits; ♡ 5 turned. — No. 3. Short Suits; ♡ Q turned.

A	Y	B	Z	TRICK	A	Y	B	Z
♣K	♣5	♣7	♣3	1	Q♢	K♢	**A♢**	2♢
♡10	♡J	**♡Q**	♡5	2	2♠	**A♠**	J♠	5♠
♣Q	♣J	♣2	♣10	3	4♢	10♢	3♢	**J♢**
♡7	♡3	**♡9**	♡8	4	♡2	♡5	♡3	**♡Q**
J♠	9♠	2♠	5♠	5	♡6	**♡A**	♡4	♡J
♣A	♡4	♡6	5♢	6	♣8	♣2	♣3	**♣K**
4♠	**♡K**	A♠	6♠	7	**♡7**	8♢	5♢	7♢
J♢	7♢	2♢	**K♢**	8	**♡K**	4♠	6♢	♡9
♡2	3♢	4♢	A♢	9	**K♠**	7♠	6♠	8♠
♣9	6♢	3♠	8♢	10	**Q♠**	♣4	♣5	10♠
♣8	9♢	7♠	8♠	11	9♠	♣Q	♣6	**♡10**
♣6	10♢	K♠	10♠	12	♡8	9♢	♣7	**♣J**
♣4	Q♢	**♡A**	Q♠	13	**3♠**	♣A	♣10	♣9

No. 2. Howell Game; ♡ 8 turned, — No. 4. Play to Score; ♡ J turned.

A	Y	B	Z	TRICK	A	Y	B	Z
6♢	J♢	**A♢**	9♢	1	K♠	4♠	3♠	**A♠**
♡3	3♢	2♢	10♢	2	♡3	♡9	**♡Q**	♡2
♣9	♣K	**♣A**	♣3	3	2♠	7♠	5♠	**♡4**
♡6	4♢	5♢	♣4	4	♣2	**♣K**	♣6	♣3
♣Q	♣8	♣2	♣7	5	♡5	♡7	♡8	**♡J**
♣6	♡4	**♡9**	♣10	6	♡10	♣5	♡K	**♡A**
♡10	7♢	8♢	♣J	7	♣8	**♣J**	3♢	♣4
♣5	♡K	**♡A**	7♠	8	5♢	J♢	**A♢**	2♢
4♠	Q♢	**♡Q**	♡5	9	10♠	9♠	8♠	**♡6**
2♠	5♠	**♡J**	♡7	10	♣Q	♣7	4♢	**♣A**
A♠	6♠	Q♠	K♠	11	Q♠	J♠	6♠	**♣10**
J♠	9♠	3♠	10♠	12	10♢	7♢	6♢	**♣9**
8♠	K♢	♡2	**♡8**	13	Q♢	8♢	9♢	**K♢**

No. 1. This is a fine example of the **Long-suit Game.** The leader begins with one of the high cards of his long suit. Missing the 2, he knows some one is signalling for trumps, and as it is very unlikely that the adversaries would signal while he was in the lead, he assumes it is his partner, and leads his best trump. His partner does not return the trump, because he holds major tenace over the king, which must be in Y's hand. At trick 5 B still holds major tenace in trumps, and leads a small card of his long suit to try to get A into the lead again. If A leads trumps again, his only possible card of re-entry for his club suit is gone. At trick 7, if B draws Y's king, he kills A's card of re-entry at the same time.

No. 2. This is an excellent example of the **Howell Game.** A's clubs are weak, and he has a potential tenace in spades, so he invites a force in diamonds. His partner, having nothing in plain suits, immediately returns the diamond. A now leads an intermediate club, and B forces him again. At trick 6, A avoids changing suits. If the long spade suit is opened, and Z returns the diamond 10, A-B will make four tricks less on this hand.

No. 3. This example of the **Short-suit Game** is from Val Starnes' Short-Suit Whist. This is sometimes called the Gambit opening. The leader, having no reason to lead trumps, even with five, and not having three honours in his long suit, prefers the gambit opening of the singly guarded queen. Y holds what is called a potential or imperfect fourchette, and covers, in order to make A-B play two honours to get one trick. B also makes a gambit opening by returning a supporting spade. Three tricks are gained by the two leads of the supporting cards, and five would have been made but for Y's covering on the first trick.

No. 4. This is an example of **Playing to the Score.** The game is English Whist, 5 points, counting honours. The first lead of trumps shows Z that honours are divided, and that he must make 11 tricks to win the game. At trick 3, he must trump; to discard clubs would be inconsistent with refusing to trump in order to bring them in. At trick 4, if Y cannot win a trick in clubs and give Z a finesse in trumps, Z cannot win the game. At trick 7, both black queens are against Z, and he must take the best chance to win if the diamond ace is also against him. The adversaries cannot place the club ace, and so Z underplays in clubs as his only chance for the game.

PRUSSIAN WHIST. This is the ordinary 5, 7 or 10 point whist, with or without honours, except that instead of turning up the last card for trump, the player to the left of the dealer cuts a trump from the still pack, which is shuffled and presented to him by the dealer's partner.

FAVOURITE WHIST. This is the regular 5, 7 or 10 point whist, with or without honours, except that whichever suit is cut for the trump on the first deal of the rubber is called ***the favourite.*** Whenever the suit turns up for trump, after the first deal, tricks and honours count double towards game. There must be a new favourite at the beginning of each rubber, unless the same suit happens to be cut again.

A variation is to attach a progressive value to the four suits; tricks being worth 1 point when Spades are trumps; when Clubs 2; when Diamonds 3; and when Hearts 4. Honours do not count, and the game is 10 points, made by tricks alone. The hands are played out; the winners score all tricks taken, and the winners of the rubber add 10 points for bonus. The value of the rubber is the difference between the scores of the winners and that of the losers. For instance: If the rubber is in A-B's favour with the score shown in the margin A-B win a rubber of 8 points.

1st game ;	10 to	6
2nd game ;	4 to	16
3rd game ;	14 to	8
Rubber ;	10	
Totals	38 to	30

This is a good game for superstitious people, who believe that certain trump suits are favourable to them.

TEXT-BOOKS.

The following list of works on ***whist***, alphabetically arranged, contains the principal standard text-books on the game. Those marked * are especially for the beginner. Those marked x are chiefly devoted to the Short-suit game.

Art of Practical Whist, by Major Gen. Drayson.
* Foster's Whist Manual, by R. F. Foster.
* Foster's Whist Tactics, by R. F. Foster.
* Foster's Self-Playing Cards, by R. F. Foster.
x Foster's Duplicate Whist, by R. F. Foster.
Foster's American Leads, by R. F. Foster.
* Foster's Whist at a Glance, by R. F. Foster.
* Gist of Whist, by C. E. Coffin.
x Howell's Whist Openings, by E. C. Howell.
Laws and Principles of Whist, by "Cavendish."
Modern Scientific Whist, by C. D. P. Hamilton.
Philosophy of Whist, by Dr. W. Pole.
* Practical Guide to Whist, by Fisher Ames.
x Short-Suit Whist, by Val. W. Starnes.
* Short Whist, by James Clay.
* Theory of Whist, by Dr. W. Pole.
* Whist, or Bumblepuppy, by "Pembridge."
Whist Developments, by "Cavendish."
* Whist of To-day, by Milton C. Work.
* *Whist à Trois*, by Ch. Lahure. [Dummy.]
x Whist, and its Masters, by R. F. Foster.
* Whist, A monthly journal ; pub. Milwaukee, Wis., U. S. A.

DUPLICATE WHIST,

OR REJOUÉ.

Duplicate, or more properly speaking, overplayed whist or Rejoué, is not a distinct game, but is simply the name given to that manner of playing whist in which a number of hands are played over again with the same cards, but by different persons.

CARDS. The cards have the same rank as at whist; they are dealt in the same manner, and the same rules apply to all irregularities in the deal, except that a misdealer must deal again. The objects of the game are the same, and so are all the suggestions for good play. The only differences that require attention are the positions of the players, the manner of counting the tricks, and the methods of keeping and comparing the scores.

THEORY. It may briefly be stated that rejoué proceeds upon the principle that if two partners have made a certain number of tricks with certain cards, under certain conditions with respect to the lead, distribution of the other cards in the adversaries' hands, etc., the only way to decide whether or not two other players could have done better, or cannot do so well, is to let them try it, by giving them the same cards, under exactly similar conditions.

This comparison may be carried out in various ways; but in every instance it depends entirely upon the number and arrangement of the players engaged. The most common forms are: club against club; team against team; pair against pair; or man against man. The reason for the arrangement of the players will be better understood if we first describe the method of playing rejoué.

METHOD OF PLAYING. There is no cutting for partners, and choice of seats and cards as at whist, because the players take their places and deal according to a prearranged schedule.

The player to the left of the dealer begins by placing the card he leads face up on the table, and in front of him. The second player follows by placing his card in front of him in the same manner; and so the third, and so the fourth. The four cards are then turned face down, and the dealer takes up the trump. The partners winning the trick place their cards lengthwise, pointing towards each other; the adversaries place theirs across. At the end of the hand, the number of tricks taken by each side can be seen by glancing at any player's cards. If there is any discrepancy, a comparison of the turned cards will show in which trick it occurs, and the cards can be readily faced and examined.

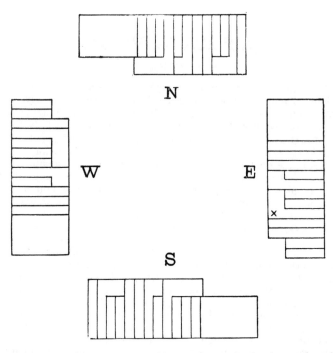

N & S 6 ; E & W 7. East has made a mistake in turning the fifth trick.

COUNTERS. In some places 13 counters are placed on the table, the winner of each trick taking down one.   This system often leads to disputes, as there can be no check upon it, and there is nothing to show in which trick the error occurred.

COUNTING TRICKS. At the end of each hand, the players sitting North and South score the **total** number of tricks they have taken; instead of the number in excess of a book.   Their adversaries, sitting East and West, do the same.   Each player then slightly shuffles his 13 cards; so as to conceal the order in which they were played, and the four separate hands of 13 cards each are then left on the table, face down ; the trump being turned at the dealer's place.

TRAYS. When any apparatus is used for holding the cards, such as trays, boxes, or envelopes, each player puts his 13 cards in the compartment provided for them.   The four hands can then be conveniently carried or handed to any other table to be overplayed.

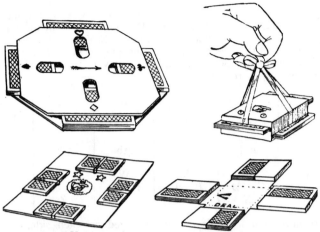

VARIOUS APPARATUS FOR REJOUÉ.

SCORING. There should be two score cards at each table, ruled for seven columns, and having at least 24 lines for 24 hands. This will be found to answer for any form of competition. The various methods of putting down and comparing the scores can best be described in connection with the variety of competition to which they belong. It is the general practice to note the trump card on the score sheets.

POSITION OF THE PLAYERS. The four players at each table are distinguished by the letters N S E W ; North and South being partners against East and West. West should always be the dealer in the first hand, North having the original lead. In all published illustrative hands, North is the leader, unless otherwise specified.

The deal passes in rotation to the left, and the number of hands played should always be some multiple of four, so that each player may have the original lead an equal number of times. 24 hands at each table is the usual number, and is the rule at all League tournaments. The partners and adversaries should be changed after each eight hands. Three changes in 24 hands will bring each member of a set of four into partnership with every other member for an equal number of hands.

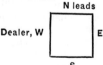

N leads

Dealer, W   E

S

If two teams of four on a side, A B C D, and W X Y Z, play

against each other, the arrangement in a League tournament would be as follows :—that A B C D should represent the players of the visiting club, or challengers, and W X Y Z the home club, or holders ; and that the positions of the players should be changed after every four hands. It is usual to play 24 hands in the after-oonn, and 24 more at night.

A	A	A	A	A	A
W X	Y Z	W Y	X Z	X Y	W Z
B	B	C	C	D	D
1st.	2nd.	3rd.	4th.	5th.	6th.
Y	W	X	W	W	X
C D	C D	B D	B D	B C	B C
Z	X	Z	Y	Z	Y

If more than four players are engaged on each side, this ar-rangement must be repeated with every additional four ; the tables being always in sets of two each, but in such cases, and in fact in anything but League matches, it is usual to play only the 1st, 3rd and 5th sets.

CLUB AGAINST CLUB. The smaller club should put into the field as many multiples of four as it can ; the larger club presenting an equal number to play against them. The op-posing sides are then so arranged that half the members of each club sit North and South, the other half East and West. If we distinguish the clubs by the marks O and X, and suppose 16 to be engaged on each side, they would be arranged at 8 tables, thus :—

O	O	O	O
X 1 X	X 3 X	X 5 X	X 7 X
O	O	O	O
1st set	2nd set	3rd set	4th set
X	X	X	X
O 2 O	O 4 O	O 6 O	O 8 O
X	X	X	X

If apparatus is used, the players may sit still for four hands, put-ting the trays aside, and then exchanging them for the four trays played at the other table in their set. If not, the cards are left on the table, as already described, and the fours change places ; those at table No 1 going to table No. 2, while those at No. 2 go to No. 1, the other sets changing in the same manner. This brings them into this position :—

X O 1 O X	X O 3 O X	X O 5 O X	X O 7 O X
O X 2 X O	O X 4 X O	O X 6 X O	O X 8 X O

The two O's that have just played the N & S hands at table No. 1, proceed to play at table No. 2, the N & S hands which have just been played by two X's; while the two O's that played the E & W hands at table No. 2, overplay at table No. 1, the E & W hands just held by the two X's.

It is now evident that the four O's have held between them all the 52 cards dealt at each table; for the first pair have held all the N & S hands dealt at both tables, and the second pair have held all the E & W hands. The same is true of the four X players; and if there is any difference in the number of tricks taken by the opposing fours, it is supposed to be due to a difference in skill, other matters having been equalised as far as the limitations of the game will permit.

The overplay finished, the cards are gathered, shuffled, cut, and dealt afresh, East now having the original lead. It must be remembered that the deal can never be lost, and that no matter what happens, the player whose proper turn it is to deal must do so.

NUMBERING HANDS. The hands simultaneously played are scored under the same number, but distinguished by the number of the table at which they are first dealt. Each pair of partners in a team play two No. 1 hands, in one of which they are N & S; in the other E & W.

SCORING. The result of the hand is entered upon the score sheets, which the opposing players at each table should then compare, and turn them face down, leaving them on the table when they change places. In case of disagreement in the scores, the League rule is to take the E & W score as the correct one, and to change the N & S to agree with it.

Let us suppose the N & S partners of the O team to make 7 tricks at table No. 1; the E & W partners of the X team making 6. Each pair enters on its own score-card the number it makes. The E & W partners of the O team now come to table No. 1, and play the 26 cards which the other members of their team did not hold. They are not permitted to look at the score-card until the hand has been overplayed. Then they enter the result, which should be 6 tricks. If the total of the tricks taken by the same team on the N & S and the E & W hands is not 13, it must be a loss or a gain. At the end of the 24 hands, the result of the

MANHATTAN WHIST CLUB

Table No. 7.....May. 6. 1895

St Team

1 D. Jones 3 M. Boyce
2 E. Wilson 4 H. Jones.

E-W	Gain	Trump	HAND	N-S	Check	
6		DK	1	7	✓	
9	1	47	2	5	✓	3+4
4	2	H7	3	11	✓	
5		S4	4	7	✓	
3		S9	5	10	✓	2+4
7		D3	6	5	✓	
9	1	C5	7	3	✓	
9		H8	8	5	✓	1+4
4	1	DK	9	8	✓	
3		S4	10	9	✓	
8	+5	S3	11	6	✓	
10		C2	12	2	✓	
			13			
			14			
			&c			

MANHATTAN WHIST CLUB

Table No. 7.....May. 6. 1895

O Team

1 Chinery 3 Bullock
2 Lewis 4 Izard

B-W	Gain	Trump	HAND	N-S	Check	
6		DK	1	7	✓	
8		47	2	4	✓	1+2
2	1	H7	3	8	✓	
6		S4	4	10	✓	
3	1 1	S9	5	6	✓	1+3
8		D3	6	4	✓	
10	1 1	C5	7	4	✓	
8		H8	8	9	✓	1+4
5	1	DK	9	10	✓	
4		S4	10	5	✓	
7	+6	S3	11	3	✓	
1		C2	12			
			13			
			14			
			&c			

MANHATTAN WHIST CLUB

Table No. 1...... May 6. 1895

Y Team

1 D. Jones   3 M. Boyce
2 E. Wilson   4 H. Jones

E-W	Gain	Trump	HAND	N-S	Check	
4		CJ	1	8	✓	3+4
8		S3	2	5	✓	
3		CA	3	8	✓	
7		H8	4	6	✓	2+4
11	1	D4	5	3	✓	
6	2	D7	6	3	✓	
6	1	C6	7	9	✓	1+4
2	1	S4	8	8	✓	
11	3	C7	9	12	✓	
5	1	S4	10	5	✓	
		D3	11	4	✓	
		DQ	12	9	✓	
			13		✓	
5	+9		14		✓	
			&c			

MANHATTAN WHIST CLUB

Table No. 2...... May 6. 1895

O Team

1 Olivery   3 Bullock
2 Lewis   4 Izard

E-W	Gain	Trump	HAND	N-S	Check	
5	1	CJ	1	9	✓	1+2
8	2	S3	2	5	✓	
5	3	CA	3	10	✓	1+3
7		H8	4	6	✓	
10		D4	5	6	✓	1+4
10		D7	6	2	✓	
4		C6	7	7	✓	
5		S4	8	7	✓	
1		C7	9	11	✓	
8		S4	10	2	✓	
9		D3	11	4	✓	
4	+6	DQ	12	8	✓	
			13			
			14			
			&c			

match can be immediately ascertained by laying side by side the score cards of the East and West hands played at the same table. The North and South scores are not compared, because the laws say they may be incorrect, but the East and West must be, officially, right.

We give on the two preceding pages an illustration of the full score of a match. The check marks in the 6th column show that the N & S players compared the score with the E & W before turning down their cards. The figures in the 2nd column are the gains on the various hands. The figures in the 7th column show which of the four players whose names appear at the top of the score-card were partners for that series of hands. The result shows that the O team had a majority of one trick at table No. 1, while the X team had a majority of three tricks at table No. 2, leaving them the winners of the match by two tricks.

If sixteen players were engaged, it would be necessary to institute a similar comparison between each set of tables, and there would be sixteen score-cards to compare, two at a time, instead of four.

TEAM AGAINST TEAM. The methods just described for a match of club against club are identical with those which are used in a contest between two teams of four ; the only difference being that of proportion. In the latter case there will be only one set, of two tables, and only four score-cards to compare.

The change of partners should be exhaustive in team matches ; which will require six sets.

TEAMS AGAINST TEAMS. When several quartette teams compete with one another, Howell's system of arrangement will be found the best. There are two methods ; for odd and for even numbers of teams.

Odd Numbers of Teams. This is the simplest form of contest. Let us suppose five teams to offer for play, which we shall distinguish by the letters, *a, b, c, d, e,* arranging each at its own table thus :—

N	a	b	c	d	e
W + E	a 1 a	b 2 b	c 3 c	d 4 d	e 5 e
S	a	b	c	d	e

The names of the N & S and the E & W members of each team should first be entered on the score-cards ; then all the N & S players move to the next table East ; those at table 5 going to table 1 ; and each table dealing and playing four hands, afterwards putting them away in trays.

	e	a	b	c	d
	a 1 a	b 2 b	c 3 c	d 4 d	e 5 e
	e	a	b	c	d
Hands :—1 to 4	5 to 8	9 to 12	13 to 16	17 to 20

The peculiarity of this system is in the movement of the trays; those at the middle table always going to the extreme West of the line, the others moving up as many tables at a time as may be necessary to follow them. In this instance the trays at table 3 go to 1, all others moving up two tables. At the same time the N & S players all move one table further East, bringing about this position :—

2nd set.	d	e	a	b	c
	a 1 a	b 2 b	c 3 c	d 4 d	e 5 e
	d	e	a	b	c
Hands :—9 to 12	13 to 16	17 to 20	1 to 4	5 to 8

This movement of the trays and players is continued for two more sets, which completes the round :—

3rd set.	c	d	e	a	b
	a 1 a	b 2 b	c 3 c	d 4 d	e 5 e
	c	d	e	a	b
Hands :—17 to 20	1 to 4	5 to 8	9 to 12	13 to 16

4th set.	b	c	d	e	a
	a 1 a	b 2 b	c 3 c	d 4 d	e 5 e
	b	c	d	e	a
Hands :—5 to 8	9 to 12	13 to 16	17 to 20	1 to 4

If we now take any two of the teams engaged, *a* and *d* for instance, we shall find that the E & W *a* and the N & S *d* pairs of those teams have played hands 9 to 12 at table 1, in the 2nd set; and that N & S *a* and E & W *d* pairs have overplayed the same hands at table 4, in the 3rd set; so that we have really been carrying out a number of matches simultaneously, between five teams of four players each.

If there are 5, 7, 9 or 11 tables in play, the movement of the trays must be 2, 3, 4 or 5 tables at a time; but the movement of the players remains the same; one table at a time, in the direction opposite to the trays.

Even Numbers of Teams. There is a choice between two systems of arranging these. The first is Mr. W. H. Barney's improvement on Howell's system.   The other is Mitchell's, which is better suited to social gatherings, at which persons naturally wish to play all the time.   The former is the more accurate for match play.

Barney's System.   Although the number of teams is even, the number of tables must still be odd, the one on the East end of the line being a dummy, provided with four trays, but no players. When the first movement of the players takes place, those moving to the dummy table will find themselves without adversaries ; so will those left at table 1.   These unoccupied players may shuffle and deal the hands that will be required for the trays they find on these tables.   At each of the other tables four hands are dealt and played.   The trays then move to the West, those at the middle table going to table 1, the others following on precisely the same system as just described for an odd number of teams.   The N & S players move East one table, which will leave table 2 without adversaries.   The next movement will put table 3 out of play, dummy being always idle, and so on until the round is finished.   At the end, the result will be exactly as if an odd number of teams had competed, and a comparison of the score-cards will show that the same series of matches have taken place.

SCORING.   In both the foregoing systems, each pair should have its own score-card, and should mark in the 7th column the name of the team it plays against for each series of four hands. The winner is the team that wins the most matches ; not the one that gains the most tricks.   In case of ties, the number of tricks won must decide.   If the number of tricks taken by each side is a tie in any match, the score is marked zero, and each team counts half a match won.   We give an illustration of the final score in a match between five teams.   The *c* and *d* teams are tied for a second place in the number of matches ; but the *c* team takes third place, because it has lost one more trick than the *d* team.   The *b* and *c* teams score a half match ; so do the *c* and *e* teams.

Teams	a	b	c	d	e	Matches	Tricks
a	\	+5	−1	+1	+4	3	+9
b	−5	\	0	−1	+2	1½	−4
c	+1	0	\	-2	0	2	−1
d	−1	+1	+2	\	−2	2	0
e	−4	−2	0	+2	\	1½	−4

Mitchell's System. If the number of teams offering for play is such that half of it is an odd number; such as 6, 10, 14, or 18, the tables can be divided into an odd number of sets, containing two each. In each set one team sits still during the entire play; one of the pairs sitting N & S at one table, the other pair E & W at the other table. Their adversaries move from set to set. If we designate the players sitting still as *X Y Z,* and those moving as *a b c,* we have this initial position for six tables :—

1st set	2nd set	3rd set
X	Y	Z
a 1 a	b 3 b	c 5 c
X	Y	Z
Hands :—1 to 4	5 to 8	9 to 12
a	b	c
X 2 X	Y 4 Y	Z 6 Z
a	b	c

The tables in each set exchange trays with each other ; No. 1 exchanging with No. 2 ; 3 with 4, etc.; the players not moving until this overplay is finished. The trays are then passed to the set next further West, and the moving players go to the set further East.

X	Y	Z
c 1 c	a 3 a	b 5 b
X	Y	Z
Hands :—5 to 8	9 to 12	1 to 4
c	a	b
X 2 X	Y 4 Y	Z 6 Z
c	a	b

Another change will exhaust the combinations for six teams, and each will have overplayed the entire series of hands. This system is deficient in one respect ; the teams sitting still never play against one another, but simply overplay the same hands. For this reason the winner must be the team gaining the greatest number of tricks on the total number of hands played.

When this system is used for pairs, instead of fours, there must be two winners, one pair N & S, and one E & W.

PAIR AGAINST PAIR. This is the most interesting form of competition, especially for domestic parties, as the arrangement of the players will allow of great latitude in the number engaged, table after table being added as long as players offer to fill them.

Two Pairs. When only four players are engaged at a single table, the game is called Memory Duplicate ; which is forbidden in all first-class clubs. The players retain their seats until they have played an agreed number of hands, which are laid aside one by one in trays. No trump is turned in Memory Duplicate ; one suit being declared trumps for the entire sitting.

Instead of the players changing positions for the overplay, the trays are reversed. If the indicators pointed N & S on the original deals, they must lie E & W for the overplay.

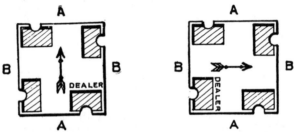

ORIGINAL POSITION OF TRAYS.   POSITION FOR OVERPLAY.

Scoring. The E & W hands only are scored, the card being laid aside after the original play is completed, and a new card used for the overplay. The difference in the totals of these two sets of score-cards will show which pair gained the most tricks.

Four Pairs. These should be arranged at two tables, changing adversaries after every 8 hands. The third set will exhaust the combinations, and it will then be found that each pair has played and overplayed an equal number of hands against every other pair.

	1st set	2nd set	3rd set
	b	c	d
	a a	a a	a a
	b	c	d
Hands :—	1 to 8	9 to 16	17 to 24
	d	b	c
	c c	d d	b b
	d	b	c

Four hands are dealt at each table in each set, and then exchanged. The trump card is turned for every original deal.

Scoring. Each pair carries its own score-card with it from table to table, until the 24 hands have been played. The 7th column is used to designate the pair played against. The pairs at the second table should begin scoring with hands Nos. 5, 13 and 21 respectively; as they will presently receive from the first table the series beginning 1, 9 and 17 respectively. Eight hands complete a match, and the result must be tabulated in the same manner as for teams of four, ties being decided by the majority of tricks won. We give an example.

Pairs	a	b	c	d	Matches	Tricks
a	\	+3	−2	+5	2	+6
b	−3	\	+4	−1	1	0
c	+2	−4	\	−2	1	−4
d	−5	+1	+2	\	2	−2

The **a** pair wins the tie with **d,** being 6 tricks plus.

Six Pairs. This is a very awkward number to handle, and should be avoided if possible. The whole could be played at three tables simultaneously; but such a course would necessitate their changing places ten times, following a very complicated schedule in so doing. The simplest way to handle six pairs is to arrange them at three tables, two of which are constantly in play, the third only half the time. This is the first position :—

<pre>
        b   d   f
      a 1 a   c 2 c   e 3 e
        b   d   f
</pre>

Tables 1 and 2 deal and play two hands each, and then exchange trays with each each other. At table 3, two hands are dealt and played, both being left in the trays.

The players at tables 1 and 2 then change adversaries; dealing, playing and exchanging two fresh hands. The players at the third table remain idle, or look on.

<pre>
        c   d | f
      a 1 a   b 2 b | e 3 e
        c   d | f
</pre>

Hands 5 and 6 played and exchanged. | None.

The *b* and *c* pairs now give way to *e* and *f :*—

e	d	b
a ɪ a	f 2 f	c 3 c
e	d	b
Hands 7 and 8 played and exchanged.		3 and 4.

While tables ɪ and 2 are playing two fresh hands, the trays containing hands Nos. 3 and 4 which were left at table 3 are overplayed by the *b* and *c* pairs, which makes a match between them and the *e* and *f* pairs.

Again the pairs at the first two tables change adversaries ; dealing, playing and exchanging two more hands ; the third table remaining idle.

f	d	b
a ɪ a	e 2 e	c 3 c
f	d	b
Hands 9 and 10 played and exchanged.		None.

The pairs *a* and *d* now give way to *b* and *c,* and the *b c e f* pairs play two hands and exchange them ; then change adversaries for two more hands ; *a* and *d* remaining idle all the time. All the pairs have now been matched but *a* and *d,* and they take seats E & W at two tables, the N & S positions being filled up by any of the other players in the match.

any	any
a ɪ a	d 2 d
any	any

No notice is taken of the scores made by the N & S hands in the last set ; as it is simply a match between the *a* and *d* pairs.

Scoring. Each pair against each is considered a match, and the winner of the most matches wins ; tricks deciding ties.

More than Six Pairs. When we come to handle large numbers, the changes of position become too complicated, and the simplest plan is to arrange them at as many tables as they will fill, and deal as many hands at each as will make an evening's play. If seven tables are filled, four hands at each would make a good number.

In the Chicago Whist Club, famous for matches of this kind, the minimum is 24 hands. If there are less than 24 and more than 12 tables, only one hand is dealt at each table except the last. At the last table a sufficient number of hands are dealt, played, and passed down to the first table in trays, to make the number up to 24; those coming up to the last from the other tables being allowed to accumulate. For instance: If 15 tables are filled, 10 hands will be dealt, played, and passed on at the last table before any of the 14 dealt at the other tables are overplayed. Then the hands 14, 13, 12 etc., are taken up and played at the last table, while the 10 hands dealt there are going the rounds of the other tables.

It is the practice in this club to divide the known strong players as equally as possible between the N & S, and the E & W positions.

The players may either sit still, and pass the hands from one table to the other until they have made the circuit; or the N & S players may move in one direction, and the trays in another, as already described for fours. The only difference will be in the scoring; as there can be no comparison between the players sitting N & S, and those sitting E & W, unless the average of the hands is computed. The players having the greatest number of tricks above the average of the N & S or the E & W hands, whichever series they played, are declared the winners. We give an illustration of the score of 10 pairs, who dealt 6 hands at each of the five tables; making the match 30 hands.

N & S			E & W		
a	201	—6	f	189	+6
b	204	—3	g	186	+3
c	211	+4	h	179	—4
d	207	=	j	183	=
e	212	+5	k	178	—5
5	1035		5	915	
Aver. 207, N & S.			Aver. 183, E & W.		

The *e* and *f* pairs make the best scores N & S and E & W respectively; the *f* pair, having won the greatest number of tricks above the average of the hands, would be the winners.

This system, sometimes called **Compass Whist,** is the one generally used in clubs that have regular evenings set apart for duplicate whist, as it is of no importance how many players present themselves. In the Chicago Whist Club it is not uncommon for 30 or 40 tables to fill up on Compass Whist nights.

INDIVIDUALS. When four play memory duplicate, one of the four, usually S, retains his seat and keeps the score, the others changing places right and left alternately, each playing with S as a partner for 8 hands. These changes successively bring about the three following positions :—

```
        c                    b                    a
    a       b            a       c            c       b
        S                    S                    S
Hands :—1 to 4           5 to 8               9 to 12
```

For the overplay, the trays are reversed, the hands originally dealt N & S being placed E & W; but the players continue to change right and left alternately. This brings the same partners together, but on different sides of the table.

```
        c                    b                    a
    b       a            c       a            c       b
        S                    S                    S
Hands :—1 to 4           5 to 8               9 to 12
```

Scoring. The names of the four players should be written at the head of each score-card, and as there is no trump turned in memory duplicate, the third and seventh columns can both be used for the numbers of the players that are partners, and the sixth column for the N & S gains.

When the match is finished, a tabulation of the tricks lost or won by each player will readily show which is the winner. In the illustration which we give, No. 3 finishes plus 6; No. 4 plus 2; No. 1 minus 4; and No. 2 minus 4.

MANHATTAN WHIST CLUB

Table No.......... *31 May.* 1896.

1 *Chimery*   3 *Bullock*
2 *Lewis*   4 *Izard*

E-W	Gain	Part's	HAND	N-S	Gain	Part's
8			1	10	2	
4		1&2	2	5	1	3&4
6	1	−4	3	5		+4
3			4	5	2	
7			5	8	1	
6	2	1&3	6	4		2&4
3		+1	7	4	1	−1
10	1		8	9		
5			9	6	1	
9		1&4	10	10	1	2&3
10	2	−1	11	8		+1
2			12	3	1	

	Summary	1 to 4	5 to 8	9 to 12	Total
No	1	−4	+1	−1	−4
	2	−4	−1	+1	−4
	3	+4	+1	+1	+6
	4	+4	−1	−1	+2

It must be remembered that the hands which are here scored N & S, in the 5th column, were E & W when originally dealt ; so that the 1st and 5th columns are really the same hands. The score-card should be folded down the middle during the overplay, so that the original scores cannot be seen. It is even better to use a new card.

Eight Individuals. This form of contest is seldom used, because players dislike the continual changing of position, and the delay in arriving at the results of the score. It would require seven sets to exhaust the combinations ; and at each table two hands should be dealt, played, and exchanged with the other table in the set, before the players change positions. This would require 28 hands to complete the match.

Safford's System for arranging the players is to have indicator cards on the tables :—

The players take their seats in any order for the first set ; after which they go to the next higher number ; 8 keeping his seat, and 7 going to 1.

Scoring. Each individual must keep his own score, adding up the total tricks taken in each set of four hands. These totals must then be compared with those of the player occupying the same position, N, S, E, or W, at the other table in the set; and it will save time in the end if these are tabulated at once, on a sheet prepared for the purpose. For instance : Let this be the arrangement of eight players in the first set :—

$$\begin{array}{ccc} \text{b} & & \text{f} \\ \text{a\ 1\ c} & \text{Hands 1 to 4.} & \text{e 2 g} \\ \text{d} & & \text{h} \end{array}$$

If *a* and *c* take 34 tricks E & W ; *e* and *g* taking only 30 with the same cards, either *a* and *c* must have gained them, or *e* and *g* must have lost them. It is a waste of time to put down both losses and gains, and all that is necessary is to call the top score zero, and charge all players with the loss of as many tricks as their total is short of the top score. In this case we charge *e* and *g* with a loss of 4 each. It must be obvious that *f* and *h* have also made 4 more tricks than *b* and *d ;* and that the latter must be charged with a loss of 4 on the same hands that *e* and *g* lose on.

We give as an illustration a sheet balanced in this way, showing the losses of the various players. The totals at the end of the match show that *c* is the winner, losing less tricks than any other player.

Players	a	b	c	d	e	f	g	h
Set 1	–	4	–	4	4	–	4	–
2	–	2	–	2	–	2	–	2
3	5	5	–	–	–	–	5	5
4	1	–	–	1	1	–	–	1
5	–	–	3	3	–	–	3	3
6	–	–	–	–	3	3	3	3
7	4	–	–	4	–	4	4	–
Totals	10	11	3	14	8	9	19	14

Large Numbers of Individuals. Several ingenious methods have been devised for handling large numbers of players, especially in domestic parties; Safford and Mitchell having both distinguished themselves in this line. The simplest form has been suggested by Mitchell, and is especially adapted for social gatherings of ladies and gentlemen.

As many tables as possible are filled; all the ladies sitting N & E; the gentlemen S and W.

The number of hands dealt at each table must be adjusted to the number of tables filled, and the time to be devoted to play. The trays containing the hands are passed to the West, and all the gentlemen move one table to the East, the ladies sitting still. In all the changes each gentleman keeps to his original point of the compass, South or West. When he arrives at the table he started from, the round is finished. If an odd number of tables are engaged in play, the changes may take place in regular order to the end. If even, a dummy must be put in; but as that is objectionable in a social gathering, it is better to adopt one of the two systems following. unless half the number of tables is an odd number, when the method already described may be used.

1st Method.   Some table in the series, which must not be either the first or the last, deals no original hands, but overplays all the hands coming from the other tables to the East of it.   The four players sit still, taking no part in the progression ; thus obliging those whose turn it would be to play at their table to pass on to the next.

2nd Method.   Each gentleman should carefully note the number of the hand originally dealt at the table from which he starts.   He progresses until he meets this hand again.   The first to observe this should give notice to the company by a bell tap, as all the gentlemen must meet their original hands at the same time. Instead of stopping at the table at which this tray is encountered, all the gentlemen move on to the next, leaving the trays as they are.   This skip enables each to finish the round without playing any of the hands twice.

Scoring.   There must be four winners ; the ladies with the best scores for the N & E hands respectively, and the gentlemen with the best S & W scores.   If a choice is necessary, the lady and the gentleman taking the greatest number of tricks above the average should be selected as the winners.

MARRIED COUPLES.   Safford has an ingenious schedule for eight married couples, so arranged in two sets that no husband and wife are ever in the same set at the same time.   When seven sets have been played, every lady will have overplayed four hands against every other lady and gentleman, including four held by her husband.   The same will be true of every man.   Indicators are placed on the tables to show players their successive positions. The numbers represent the husbands, and the letters the wives, the couples being a-1, b-2, etc.   The couple a-1 always sit still ; the ladies go to the next higher letter of the alphabet, and the men to the next higher number ; *h* going to *b,* as *a* sits still ; and 8 to 2.

N	N	N	N
6	3	f	c
W a 1 2 E	W d 2 8 E	W 1 3 b E	W 4 4 h E
g	e	6	5
S	S	S	S

One hand is dealt at each table, and overplayed at each of the others.   A different point of the compass should deal at each table, in order to equalise the lead.

Scoring.   The score of each four hands should be added up by each individual player, and the results tabulated at the end of every four hands, in the manner described for eight individuals. The winner is the player who loses the fewest tricks.   This is the only known system for deciding whether or not a man can play whist better than his wife.

PROGRESSIVE DUPLICATE WHIST is the generic name by which those systems of duplicate are known in which the purpose is to have as many as possible of the players meet one another during the progress of the match. Most of the systems we have been describing belong to this class.

There are at present only two works on Duplicate Whist; but a number of articles on the subject may be found in " *Whist.*"

Duplicate Whist; by John T. Mitchell, 1896.

Foster's Duplicate Whist; 1894.

Whist; Jan., 1892; Jan., 1894; Aug., 1894; Oct., 1894; Jan., 1895; Mar., 1895; May, 1895; July, 1895; Oct., 1895.

DRIVE WHIST.

There are several methods of playing Drive Whist; the most popular being to fill as many tables as possible with the players that present themselves, regardless of any order further than that partners should sit opposite each other. The players may select their own partners, or they may be determined by lot, according to the decision of the hostess.

Straight whist is played; the cards being shuffled and cut afresh for every hand. Each deal is a game in itself.

Drawing for Partners. If there is an equal number of ladies and gentlemen, and the number is less than fifty-two, a sufficient number of red and black cards should be sorted out, and the ladies asked to draw from the red, the men from the black; those getting the same denominations being partners. For instance: 16 couples present themselves for play. The thirteen Hearts and the A 2 3 of Diamonds should be put into one hat for the ladies; the thirteen Clubs, and the A 2 3 of Spades being put into another for the men. Those drawing the same denomination of Hearts and Clubs, or of Spades and Diamonds, are partners.

Before play begins, the number of hands which it is proposed to play should be announced, or a time set for adjournment.

Driving. There is no rank attached to the tables, but they should be arranged in such a manner that players may know which table to go to next. The partners seat themselves wherever they please, and at the tap of the bell at the head table the deal is cut for, and play begins. The winners of the majority of the thirteen tricks at each table go to the next table. Here they may either continue to play as partners, or may divide, whichever has been the style of play decided upon by the hostess. When the partnerships have been drawn for, it is usual to preserve them for the evening.

The losing gentleman at each table has the deal for the next hand.

Scoring. Every hand must be played out for all it is worth, both winners and losers scoring all the tricks they take. If the same partners play together throughout the evening, one score-card will do for the couple. If they divide, each individual must have his or her own score-card. The winners are those who have taken the greatest number of tricks in the agreed number of hands, or during the time limit. When partners divide as they drive on, there should be two prizes, one for ladies, and one for gentlemen.

DUMMY.

There are three forms of Dummy: The English game, for three players; the French game, for three or four; and the game now generally known as Bridge, or Bridge Whist. Dummy is not recognized in any form by the American Whist League, and there are no American Laws governing it. We shall describe each variety of the game in its turn; beginning with the English.

Cards. ENGLISH DUMMY, is played with a full pack of fifty-two cards, ranking as at whist both for cutting and playing. Two packs are generally used.

Markers are necessary, and are of the same patterns as those used in whist.

Players. According to the English usage, Dummy is played by three persons, and the table is complete with that number.

They cut for partners and for the deal; the player cutting the lowest card takes dummy for the first rubber; the one cutting the next lowest takes dummy for the second rubber; and the one cutting the highest takes it for the last rubber. It is considered obligatory to play three rubbers, in order that each may have whatever advantage or disadvantage may be supposed to attach to the dummy. The three rubbers so played are called a Tournée. It is sometimes agreed that one player shall take dummy continuously, on condition that he concedes to his adversaries one point in each rubber. When this is done, the largest rubber that the dummy's partner can win is one of seven; and he may win nothing; whereas his adversaries may win a rubber of nine, and must win at least two. This concession of a point is not made, as many imagine, because it is an advantage to have the (dummy) partner's hand exposed; but because it is an advantage to have the player's hand concealed. He knows the collective contents of the adversaries' hands; each of them knows only the contents of dummy's hand and his own.

Cutting.   The player cutting the lowest card has the choice of seats and cards; but he must deal the first hand for his dummy; not for himself. The methods of spreading, cutting, deciding ties, etc., described in connection with whist, are those employed in dummy.

Position of the Players.   The players are distinguished, as at whist, by the two first and last letters of the alphabet, and their positions at the table are indicated in the same manner. There is no mark to distinguish the dummy hand; a defect which is remedied in the French system.

Dealing.   At the beginning of a rubber, dummy's partner presents the pack to his ***left-hand*** adversary to be cut, and deals from right to left, beginning with the player on his right, and turning up the last card for dummy's trump. When two packs are used, there is no rule as to which player shall collect and shuffle the still pack. On this point the French rules are very explicit.

The general rules with regard to irregularities in the deal are the same as at whist.

The cards having been dealt, it is usual for dummy's partner to take up and sort the dummy first. There are several ways of laying out dummy's hand; the most common being to run the suits down in rows, with the turn-up across and to the right of the other trumps, if any.

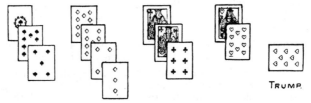

METHOD OF SPREADING DUMMY'S CARDS.

Stakes.   The remarks made on this subject in connection with whist apply equally to dummy. Dummy's partner must pay to, or receive from each adversary the amount agreed.

Method of Playing.   The general method of playing is identical with that of whist, with the following exceptions :—

When it is dummy's turn to play, his partner selects the card.

The Revoke. For this dummy is not liable to any penalty, as his adversaries can see his cards. Even should the revoke be occasioned by dummy's cards being disarranged, or one of them covered up, the adversaries should be as able to detect the error as the partner. Should dummy's hand revoke, it cannot be remedied after the trick in which it occurs has been turned and quitted ; and the game must proceed as if no revoke had occurred. All the penalties for a revoke may be enforced against dummy's partner, should he renounce in error, and not correct it in time. There being no American laws for dummy, the English penalty of three tricks or three points may be enforced, and the revoking player cannot win the game that hand.

Cards Played in Error. Dummy's partner is not liable to any penalty for cards dropped face upwards on the table, or two or more played at once, because it is obvious that Dummy cannot gain any advantage from such exposed cards.

Leading out of Turn. Should either dummy or his partner lead out of turn, the adversaries may call a suit from the one that should have led. It should be noticed that if it was not the turn of either to lead, there is no penalty ; for neither can have gained any advantage from knowing what suit the other wished to lead, or from the exposed card. Should all have played to the erroneous lead, the error cannot be corrected, and no penalty remains.

The methods of ***Taking Tricks ; Scoring ; Claiming and Counting Honours ; Marking Rubber Points,*** etc., are the same as in whist, and the counters are used in the same manner.

Cutting Out. As already observed, there is no change of partners, or of the rotation of the deal, until the completion of a rubber ; but at the beginning of each rubber, dummy must deal the first hand. Should one side win the first two games in any rubber, the third is not played. At the end of the tournée, should any player wish to retire, and another offer to take his place, the cards must be shuffled and cut as at the beginning ; a player's position in one tournée giving him no rights in the next. There is nothing in the English game to recognize that there may be more than three candidates for dummy ; as it is supposed that if four were present, they would prefer playing whist.

Suggestions for Good Play. As these are equally proper to any form of dummy, we shall postpone their consideration until we have described the other varieties of the game ; French dummy, and Bridge ; giving them all at the end of the chapter on " Bridge."

DOUBLE DUMMY.

CARDS. Double Dummy is played with a full pack of fifty-two cards, ranking as at whist both for cutting and playing. Two packs are generally used.

MARKERS are necessary, and are of the same description as those used in whist.

PLAYERS. According to the English usage, double dummy is played by two persons, and the table is complete with that number.

CUTTING. The players cut for the deal ; the player cutting the lowest card deals for his dummy first, and has the choice of sitting to the right or left of his opponent. It is usual to select the seat on the right of the living player, because it is possible that one may forget whether or not certain cards have been played, and under such circumstances it is better to lead up to an exposed hand than to one whose contents you are not sure of.

The methods of spreading, cutting, deciding ties, etc., are the same as those employed at whist.

POSITION OF THE PLAYERS. It is not usually considered necessary to distinguish the players further than to indicate which hand had the original lead. For this purpose the whist notation is used, A being the leader, and Z the dealer.

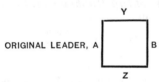

DEALING. When two packs are used, the still pack should be shuffled by the non-dealer, and placed on the left of the player or dummy whose turn it will be to deal next.

The general rules with regard to irregularities in the deal are the same as in whist.

The cards being dealt, it is usual to sort the dummy hands first, running the suits down in rows, with the turn-up trump across, and to the right of the others.

STAKES. The remarks already made on this subject in connection with whist and dummy, apply equally to double dummy, except that there is no double payment ; but each player wins from or loses to his living adversary the unit agreed upon.

METHOD OF PLAYING. This so closely resembles dummy as to need no further description. Neither dummy can revoke, and there are no such things as exposed cards, or cards played in error. It is very common for one player to claim that he will win a certain number of tricks, and for his adversary to admit it, and allow him to score them, without playing the hand out.

LEADING OUT OF TURN. Should either of the dummies or the players lead out of turn, the adversary may call a suit from the one that ought to have led ; but if it was the turn of neither, there is no penalty. If all four have played to the trick, the error cannot be corrected, and no penalty remains.

The methods of ***Taking Tricks ; Scoring ; Claiming and Counting Honours ; Marking Rubber Points,*** etc., are the same as in whist, and the counters are used in the same manner.

RUBBERS. If the first two games are won by the same player and his dummy, the third is not played. Tournées are not played, and the completion of the rubber breaks up the table.

CUTTING IN. The table being complete with two, at the end of a rubber a new table must be formed.

SUGGESTIONS FOR GOOD PLAY. The player should first carefully examine the exposed hands, and by comparing them with his own, suit by suit, should fix in his mind the cards held by his living adversary. This takes time, and in many places it is the custom to expose the four hands upon the table. Players who have better memories than their opponents object to this, for the same reason that they prefer sitting on the right of the living player. It is not at all uncommon for a player to forget that certain cards have been played, to his very serious loss.

The hands once fixed in the mind, some time should be given to a careful consideration of the best course to pursue ; after which the play should proceed pretty rapidly until the last few tricks, when another problem may present itself.

There is nothing in the game beyond the skilful use of the tenace position, discarding, and establishing cross-ruffs. Analysis is the mental power chiefly engaged. There are no such things as inferences, false cards, finesse, underplay, speculative trump leads, or judgment of human nature. The practice of the game is totally different from any other form of whist, and much more closely resembles chess.

The laws of Dummy will be found at the end of the English Whist Laws.

HUMBUG WHIST.

This is a variation of double dummy, in which two players sit opposite each other. The deal and seats are cut for in the usual manner; four hands of thirteen cards each are dealt, and the last card is turned for trump.

Each player examines the hand dealt to him, without touching those to his right or left. If he is content with his hand, he announces it; if not, he may exchange it for the one on his right. In case of exchange, the discarded hand is placed on the table face down; and the other taken up and played. If a player retains the hand originally dealt him, he must not look at the others. If the dealer exchanges, he loses the turn-up card, but the trump suit remains the same. Each player deals for himself in turn, there being no deal for the dead hands. Whist laws govern the deal and its errors.

METHOD OF PLAYING. The dealer's adversary has the first lead; the other must follow suit if he can, and the highest card of the suit led wins the trick. Trumps win all other suits.

SCORING. Each trick above six counts one point towards game. Of the four honours, A K Q J of trumps, if each player holds two, neither can count. But if one player has only one honour, or none, the other counts 2 points for two honours, if he holds them; 3 points for three; and 4 points for four. The honours count towards game as in whist. The penalty for a revoke is three tricks, and it takes precedence of other scores; tricks count next, honours last. Five points is game.

SUGGESTIONS FOR GOOD PLAY. It is considered best for a player not finding four reasonably sure tricks in his hand to exchange; for there is a certain advantage to be gained by knowing thirteen cards which cannot be in the adversary's hand. Before changing, the player should fix in his memory the exact cards of each suit in the hand which he is about to discard. By combining his knowledge of them with his own cards, he may often be able to direct his play to advantage. Beyond this there is little skill in the game.

A variation is sometimes made by the dealer announcing a trump suit after he has examined his hand, instead of turning up the last card. His adversary then has the right either to play his hand, or to exchange it for the one on his right; but the dealer must play the hand dealt to him.

MORT.

WHIST À TROIS; OR FRENCH DUMMY.

MORT means simply the dead hand; and is the equivalent of the English word Dummy; the partner being known as **Vivant,** or the living hand. In these words the English usually sound the **t,** as they do in such words as **piquet,** and **valet.**

CARDS. Mort is played with a full pack of fifty-two cards, ranking as at whist for cutting and playing. Two packs are generally used.

MARKERS are necessary to count the game points only. Four circular counters for each side, preferably of different colours, are employed, or the ordinary whist markers may be used. At the end of each game, the score of the points won or lost by each player must be transferred to a score-sheet, kept for that purpose.

PLAYERS. Mort is played by three persons; but the table is usually composed of four. If there are more than four candidates, the methods described in connection with whist are adopted for deciding which four shall play the first tournée.

The table being formed, the cards are again shuffled and spread to cut for partners and deal.

TIES are decided in the same manner as at whist.

CUTTING. If there are three players, the one cutting the lowest card takes dummy for the first game; he also has the choice of seats and cards, and may deal the first hand for himself or for Mort, as he pleases; but having once made his choice, he must abide by it. The player cutting the intermediate card takes dummy for the second game; and the player cutting the highest card takes it for the third game; each in turn having the choice of seats and cards. These three games finish the rubber or tournée, each having once had the advantage or disadvantage of playing with Mort. It is obligatory to finish the tournée, no player being allowed to withdraw and substitute another without the consent of the other players. In Mort it is very unusual for one person to take dummy continuously.

If there are four players, the one cutting the highest card of the four sits out, and takes no part in the first game. It is customary for him to take Mort's seat, and to make himself useful in sorting dummy's cards for him. He plays in the three following games, taking Mort in the fourth, or last. Four games complete the tournée for four players.

POSITION OF THE PLAYERS. The players or hands are distinguished by the letters, M, V, L, and R; which stand respectively for Mort, Vivant, Left, and Right. The Mort is the dead hand, which is turned face up on the table. The Vivant is his partner, who sits opposite him, and plays his cards for him. The Left and Right are the adversaries who sit on the left and right of **Mort.**

Special attention must be called to the use of the term **adversaries** in any description of Mort. It is used exclusively to designate the two partners opposed to the Mort and Vivant. In all other cases where opposition is implied, the term **opponents** must be used.

When necessary to distinguish the dealer from the first, second, or third hand, it is usual to add the letters employed for that purpose in whist; placing them inside the diagram of the table, thus:—

This diagram shows that Vivant dealt, and that the adversary on the Right of Mort had the original lead.

With Three Players. Vivant having selected his seat and cards, the adversaries may select their seats. It is usual for the strongest adversary to sit Right.

With Four Players, we can best describe the arrangement by numbering them 1, 2, 3, and 4, respectively, the lowest number, 1, having cut the lowest card, and the others having the right to play Vivant in their numerical order. The initial arrangement would be as follows:—

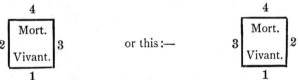

For the three succeeding games the arrangement would be:—

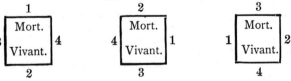

It will be seen that each player, immediately after being Vivant, sits out, or takes Mort's place, for the next game.

DEALING. It is usual for Vivant to deal the first hand for himself, as the disadvantage of exposing fourteen cards is more than compensated for in compelling the adversary to open the game by leading up to an unknown hand. If Vivant deals the first hand for Mort, he must present the pack to the player on dummy's right to be cut, and deal the cards from right to left, turning up the trump at Mort's place. If he deals for himself, he presents the pack to the pone to be cut, and proceeds as in whist.

When two packs are used, the French laws require that if the deal is for Mort, the Right shall gather and shuffle the still pack; and that if Vivant deals for himself, the pone shall gather and shuffle. I have found this to be awkward, because the player who is gathering and shuffling the cards of one pack is called upon to cut the other. For this reason I recommend that whichever adversary is the pone for the deal in hands should allow his partner to gather and shuffle the still pack. When either adversary deals, his partner will, of course, gather and shuffle the still pack.

The general rules with regard to irregularities in the deal are the same as at whist, with the following exceptions:—

A misdeal does not lose the deal unless the opponents so elect; they may prefer a new deal by the same dealer. The reason for this is that the deal is a disadvantage, especially for Mort.

If Vivant or Mort offers the pack to one adversary to cut, and then deals as if the other had cut, it is a misdeal; and it is not admissible to shift the packets in order to remedy matters.

It might be imagined that a card exposed in dealing, if dealt to Mort, would make no difference, as all his cards will presently be exposed. But the laws give the opponents of the dealer the option of either allowing the deal to stand, or having a new deal, or calling it a misdeal.

According to the French laws, if there is any discussion in progress with regard to the previous hand or play, the dealer may lay aside the trump card, face down, until the discussion is finished. If this law prevailed in America, I think the trump would very seldom be turned immediately.

STAKES. In Mort the stake is a unit, so much a point. It may assist players in regulating the value of the stake to remember that six is the smallest number of points that can be won or lost on a single game, and that thirty-seven is probably the highest, although fifty, or even a hundred is not impossible. The average is about twelve. The same customs as at whist prevail with regard to outside betting.

The Vivant must pay or receive double, as he has to settle with each adversary. If four play, the one sitting out has nothing to do with the stakes; but he may make outside wagers on the result of the game.

THE METHOD OF PLAYING is practically the same as at whist, with the following exceptions :—

When it is the turn of Mort to play, Vivant selects the card for him.

The Revoke. The rules governing this are the same as those already given for English Dummy. Mort is not liable to penalty under any circumstances. If any other player revokes, his opponents may take three points from the score of his side ; or add three points to their score ; or take three of his tricks. The penalty cannot be divided ; but if two or more revokes are made by the same side, the penalty for each may be enforced in a different manner. For instance : If the score is 3 to 2 in favor of the adversaries, Vivant may take three points from their score for one revoke, and add three to his own score for the other. It is not permissible to reduce the revoking player's ***tricks*** to nothing. At least one must be left in order to prevent slams being made through revoke penalties.

Cards Played in Error. Vivant is not liable to any penalty for dropping his cards face up on the table ; but if he or Mort plays two cards at once to a trick, the adversaries may select which they will allow to be played. The adversaries are subject to the same penalties as in whist for all cards played in error.

Leading Out of Turn. If Vivant or Mort lead out of turn, the adversaries may let the lead stand, or demand it be taken back. If it was the turn of neither, no penalty can be enforced, and if all have played to the trick, the error cannot be corrected.

Taking Tricks. The methods of taking tricks, and placing them so that they can be easily counted, have been fully described in connection with whist.

OBJECT OF THE GAME. As in whist, the object is to take tricks ; the highest card played of the suit led wins, and trumps win against all other suits. The first six tricks taken by one side, and forming a ***book***, do not count ; but all above that number count toward game. At the end of each hand, the side that has taken any tricks in excess of the book scores them, their opponents counting nothing. As soon as either side reaches five points, they win the game, but the concluding hand must be played out, and the winners are entitled to score all the points over five that they can make on that hand. For instance : The score is 4 to 3 in favor of Vivant and Mort. They win the first seven tricks, which makes them game ; but they do not cease playing. If they succeed in gaining eleven tricks out of the thirteen, they win a game of 9 points, instead of 5.

As already observed, Vivant loses or gains double the value of the points in each hand. In the three-handed game this must be so ; but in my opinion it would be a great improvement in the four-handed game to allow the player sitting out to share the fortunes of the Vivant, as in Bridge, and in many German games of cards, notably Scat.

SLAMS. The two great differences between French and English Dummy are that honours are not counted in Mort, and that a special value is attached to slams. A slam is made when one side takes the thirteen tricks. These must be actually won, and cannot be partly made up of tricks taken in penalty for revokes. Players cannot score a slam in a hand in which they have revoked.

A slam counts 20 points to the side making it; but these 20 points have nothing to do with the game score. For instance: The score is 4 all. Vivant and Mort make a slam. This does not win the game; but the 20 points are debited and credited on the score-sheet; the deal passes to the left, and the game proceeds with the score still 4 all, as if nothing had happened.

SCORING. The number of points won on each game are put down on the score-sheet, each side being credited with the number of points appearing on their markers when the game is finished. To the winners' score is added: 3 points, for a triple game, if their opponents have not scored; 2 points, for a double game, if their opponents are not half way; or 1 point, for a simple game, if their opponents are 3 or 4. In addition to this, the winners add 4 points, for bonus or consolation, in every instance. From the total thus found must be deducted whatever points have been scored by the losers, whether game points, slams, or both. For instance: Vivant and Mort win a game with the score 8 to 2 in their favor, which is a double. This is put down on the score sheets thus:—

$8 + 2$ for the double, $+ 4$ consolation, $= 14$, minus 2 scored by the opponents; making 12 the net value of the game. Vivant therefore wins 24 points, and each of the adversaries, R and L, lose 12. Again:—

R and L win a simple with a score of 5 to 4, V and M having made a slam. $5 + 1$ for the simple, $+ 4$ for consolation, $= 10$, minus 4 points scored, and 20 for the slam $= 24$; showing that R and L lose 14 points each, although they won the game. Again:—

V and M win a triple, with a score of 8 to 0; R and L having revoked. $8, + 3, + 4, + 3$ for the revoke $= 18$, from which there is nothing to deduct.

The greatest number of points that can be made on a game, exclusive of slams and revokes, is 17; and the least number is 6.

MARKING. The methods of using the counters in scoring the game points have already been described in connection with whist.

CUTTING OUT. If there are more than four candidates for play at the conclusion of a tournée, the selection of the new table must be made as if no tournée had been played; all having equal rights to cut in.

CHEATING. Mort offers even less opportunity to the greek than whist, as the deal is a disadvantage, and nothing is gained by turning up an honour, beyond its possession.

SUGGESTIONS FOR GOOD PLAY will be postponed until we have described the third variety of dummy, viz : Bridge.

BRIDGE,

OR BRIDGE WHIST.

CARDS. Bridge is played with a full pack of fifty-two cards, which rank as at whist, for both cutting and playing. Two packs are generally used.

MARKERS suitable for scoring the various points made at Bridge have not yet been invented. Some persons use the bezique marker; but it is not a success. The score is usually kept on a sheet of paper, and it should be put down by each side, for purposes of verification.

PLAYERS. Bridge is played by four persons, and the table is complete with that number. When there are more than four candidates for play, the selection of the four is made by cutting. These cut again for partners, and the choice of seats and cards, as at whist. The player cutting the lowest card takes the deal.

CUTTING. The methods of cutting are the same as those described in connection with whist, and ties are decided in the same manner.

POSITION OF THE PLAYERS. The disposition of the four players at the bridge table is the same as at whist, and they are indicated by the same letters; A and B are partners against Y and Z ; Z always represents the dealer ; and Y the dummy, A having the original lead.

DEALING. The cards are shuffled, cut, and dealt in the same manner as at whist ; but no trump is turned. When two packs are used, the dealer's partner shuffles one while the other is dealt, and the deal passes in regular rotation to the left until the rubber is finished.

The general rules with regard to irregularities in the deal are the same as at whist ; except that a misdeal does not pass the deal. The misdealer must deal again, and with the same pack.

The cards being dealt, each player sorts his hand to see that he has the correct number, thirteen ; and the player or players keeping the score should announce it at the beginning of each hand.

STAKES. In bridge, the stake is a unit, so much a point. The number of points won or lost on the rubber may be only two or three, or they may run into the hundreds. The average will vary according to the style of play ; some persons habitually bidding up hands to much beyond their value. In settling at the end of the rubber, it is usual for each losing player to pay his right-hand adversary.

MAKING THE TRUMP. This is the chief peculiarity in bridge. The trump is not turned up, but the suit is named by the dealer or his partner, after they have examined their cards. In order properly to understand the considerations which guide them in making the trump, one should first be familiar with the values attached to the tricks when certain suits are trumps. As in whist, the first six tricks taken by one side do not count ; but each trick above that number counts toward game according to the following table :—

> When Spades are trumps, each trick counts 2 points.
> " Clubs " " " " " 4 "
> " Diamonds " " " " " 6 "
> " Hearts " " " " " 8 "
> " there is no trump " " " 12 "

Better to understand the importance of this variation in value, it should be noticed that the game is 30 points ; so that if two partners won 3 by cards with no trump, or 4 by cards with hearts for trumps, they would win the game in one deal. On the other hand, if either of the black suits were trumps, they could not lose the game, even if a slam were made against them.

It will thus be evident that two considerations influence the player whose privilege it is to make the trump : First, to win as much as possible, if he has the cards to do it. Second, to save himself, if he is weak ; or the game, if it is in danger. As a general proposition, it may be said that his decision will be indicated by the colour of the trump he names. If it is red, he is strong, and plays to win ; if it is black, he is taking to the woods. A further element may enter into his calculations, the state of the score. If he feels sure of the few points necessary to win the game or the rubber with a black trump, there is no necessity to risk making it red. This is a part of the subject which we shall go into further when we come to the suggestions for good play.

The dealer has the first say in making the trump. If he does not feel himself strong enough to make it red, although his hand may be black enough to promise a good score in clubs or spades, he should transfer to his partner the privilege of making the trump by simply saying: " You make it, partner." Guided by this indication, his partner must fix on some suit for the trump, and must announce it. If he does not do so, the hand must be played without a trump suit, and each trick above the book will be worth 12 points to the partners winning it. In America it is imperative that the dealer or his partner announce a trump suit or "grand."

Either the dealer or his partner may elect to play without a trump, if he has sufficient strength in all the suits to do so. In such a case he announces " grand." The difference between announcing grand, and letting the trump go by default will appear presently.

If a player declares the trump out of turn, his adversaries may consult as to the propriety of demanding a new deal.

SETTLING THE VALUE OF THE TRICKS. The
trump suit having been announced, the first hand or leader, A, before he plays a card, has the privilege of doubling the value of the tricks if he thinks the opponents cannot win the odd trick with the trump named. To do this, he simply says: " I double." If he does not feel justified in doubling, he transfers the opportunity to his partner, by asking him: "Shall I play?" That is to say, " shall we play without doubling?" If his partner will not double, he answers: "Yes." Either A or B having doubled, it becomes the privilege of the player who made the trump to double him again; making the value of the trick four times greater than that given in the table. If he does not do so, he says: "I pass"; and his partner then has the privilege. If either the dealer or his partner doubles, the adversary who first doubled may repeat it; or if he passes, his partner may double. This doubling may be continued indefinitely, until both sides declare to pass. A player with the six highest trumps and an entire suit has been known to double sixteen times; his adversary having seven trumps and command of two suits.

The final value of the tricks should be noted before play begins, in order to avoid later disputes as to how often it was doubled.

If neither the dealer nor his partner will name a trump suit, the hand must be played without a trump; but in such a case the adversaries have no right to double, no announcement having been made. If a grand is announced, they may double.

If any player double out of turn, his adversaries may consult as to whether or not they will allow the double to stand.

METHOD OF PLAYING. The trump suit and the value of the tricks settled, the player on the dealer's left begins by leading any card he pleases. After he has played, the second player, Y, lays his hand face up on the table, and takes no further part in the play beyond availing himself of the privilege of asking his partner if he has none of a suit to which he renounces. From the moment that Y's cards are exposed the game becomes Dummy, the dealer, Z, playing Y's cards for him.

The Revoke. The rules governing this have already been given fully in connection with Dummy and Mort. Y cannot revoke under any circumstances; but the penalty for any other player is the loss of three tricks; or the value of three tricks in points; or the addition of a like amount to his opponent's score. As in Mort, a slam cannot be made by taking tricks for the revoke penalty. At least one trick must be left to the revoking players. The side making a revoke cannot win the game that hand, no matter what they score; but they may play the hand out, and count all they make to within two points of game, or 28. Players cannot score a slam in a hand in which they have revoked.

Cards Played in Error. The dealer is not liable to any penalty for dropping his cards face up on the table after Y's cards have been exposed. A and B are liable to the same penalties as in Whist for all cards played in error.

Leading Out of Turn. If Y or Z leads out of turn, the adversaries cannot call a suit from the one that should have led. If it was the turn of neither to lead, there is no penalty, and if all have played to the trick, the error cannot be corrected.

Players may be asked to draw their cards, and the last trick turned and quitted may be looked at.

Taking Tricks. The method of gathering and stacking the tricks is the same as in Whist, and has been fully described in connection with that game.

OBJECT OF THE GAME. As in all members of the whist family, the object in Bridge is to win tricks, the highest card played of the suit led winning, and trumps, if any, winning against all other suits. At the end of each hand the side that has won any tricks in excess of the book, scores them, after multiplying their number by the unit of value settled upon by the doubling, if any took place. As soon as either side reaches or passes 30, they win the game; but the hand must be played out, as in Mort, and all tricks taken must be counted. The total is written on the score-sheet; the score of the losers standing to their credit until the final accounting at the end of the rubber.

RUBBERS. Three games, of 30 points each, constitute a rubber; but if the first two are won by the same players, the third is not played. The side winning the majority of the games adds 100 (rubber) points to its score.

SCORING. Apart from the game score, which is made entirely by tricks and revoke penalties, there are several additional scores which are entered to the credit of the players; but which have no influence in winning or losing the game, and are not in any way affected by the doubling process, the latter applying only to the value of the tricks. These additional points are kept together under the general heading, "Honour Score."

Chicane. Any player finding himself without a trump in his thirteen cards, may announce it, after the hand is played, and add to his honour score 4, 8, 12, or 16 points, according to the trump suit; the 4 being for spades, and the others for clubs, diamonds, and hearts respectively. If he announces chicane before the hand is played, he is penalized the same number of points, instead of winning them; his hand is exposed, and his opponents may call his cards. In America, if one side claims chicane and the other honours, chicane is simply deducted from the honour score.

Honours are the five highest cards in the trump suit, A K Q J 10; and in grand, or when there is no trump, they are the four Aces. The partners holding three, four, or five honours between them, or four honours in one hand, or four in one hand and the fifth in the partner's, or all five in one hand, are entitled to claim and score them, according to the following table. It will be seen that their value varies according to the trump suit; and it must be remembered that this value cannot be increased by doubling.

TABLE OF HONOUR VALUES.

If the trump suit is :—

	♠	♣	◇	♡
3 honours count..........	4	8	12	16
4 honours count..........	8	16	24	32
5 honours count..........	10	20	30	40
4 in one hand count.......	16	32	48	64
4 in one hand, 5th in partner's } count...	18	36	54	72
5 in one hand count......	20	40	60	80

When there is no trump :—

3 Aces, between partners, count   30.
4 Aces, between partners, count   40.
4 Aces in one hand count   100.

Slams. Little Slam is made by taking twelve of the thirteen tricks; it counts 20 points. Grand Slam is made by taking the thirteen tricks, and it counts 40. Either score must be exclusive of revoke penalties.

All scores made by chicane, honours, or slams, must be kept separate from the game score, which consists of nothing but tricks.

A–B	Y–Z
Honours	
	40
	64
30	20
16	24
Tricks	
24	18
	48
36	
	32
106	246
	100
	346
	106
Y-Z win 240	

It is customary to have *scoring blanks* ruled especially for Bridge, so that the trick score may be kept below the double line, and the honour score above it. Lines drawn under the trick score show the termination of each game. In the illustration here given Z dealt the first hand, and made diamonds trumps, winning three by cards and four by honours. In the next deal, A–B made hearts trumps, and won three by cards and three by honours. Then Y–Z made a little slam, with hearts trumps; for which they scored 48 for tricks, 20 for little slam, and 64 for four honours in one hand. A line was then drawn under that game. In the next hand, A–B played without a trump, and made three by cards and three aces, winning the game. In the third and last game, Y–Z made hearts trumps, and made four by cards and five honours, winning the game and the rubber. The total tricks and honours for each side were then added up, 100 points being added to Y–Z's score for winning the rubber, and A–B's score being deducted from the total, leaving Y–Z the winners of a rubber worth 240 points.

SETTLING THE SCORE. When the rubber is finished, each side adds up the various scores it has made by tricks, slams, chicanes, honours, and rubber points, (if it won the rubber). The two totals are then compared, and the value of the rubber is the difference between them. It is quite possible for one side to win the rubber, and yet lose 100 points or more; so largely does the element of luck enter into the various counts for holding honours.

CUTTING OUT. At the conclusion of the rubber, if there are more than four candidates for play, the selection of the new table is made by cutting; those who have just played having an equal chance with the new-comers. The reason for this is that a Bridge table is complete with four, and that a rubber is usually too long, with its preliminaries of making the trump, and its finalities of settling the score, for players to wait their turn. A rubber at Short Whist is often over in two hands; but a carefully played rubber at Bridge sometimes occupies an hour.

CHEATING. When the cards are shuffled by the adversary, and no player can tell what the trump suit will be, there is little opportunity for the greek to exercise his skill. As already observed, none of the whist family of games offers any inducements to the philosopher.

SUGGESTIONS FOR GOOD PLAY.   The points which the beginner may profitably study in Bridge, not common to other forms of Dummy, are chiefly in making the trump, and in doubling.

Making the Trump.   The bridge-player's first consideration should be the state of the score, which will show how many points he needs to win the game.   Let us suppose this number to be 12, he having already scored 18.   These 12 points can be made by winning six by cards with spades for trumps ; three by cards with clubs ; or two by cards with diamonds or hearts.   But if the hand can be played without a trump, the odd trick wins the game.

It is hardly necessary to say that a player would be very foolish to engage himself to win six by cards if the odd trick would equally answer his purpose ; nor would he undertake to win three by cards with clubs for trumps, if he had as good a chance of making two by cards with diamonds or hearts.   In other words, the player should not make the trump which promises the greatest number of tricks, but should select that which will yield the largest number of points.

It is for this reason that every good player first considers the advisability of announcing "grand" ; and if he thinks that injudicious, hearts or diamonds, leaving the black suits as a last resort.

It is the custom invariably to announce grand with three Aces.

In estimating the probabilities of trick-taking, it is usual to count the partner for three tricks on the average.   Conservative players do not depend on him for more than two.   Generally speaking, the maker of the trump should have four pretty certain tricks in his own hand ; but if the score of the adversaries is such that they would go out if they won the odd trick, there should be five reasonably sure tricks in the trump-maker's hand.

The dealer should seldom announce a black trump unless he has a certainty of the game in his own hand, without any assistance from his partner.   If he cannot safely make it grand or red, he should pass, and allow his partner the chance.   With such a hand as seven clubs, including four honours, and absolutely worthless cards otherwise, the dealer should make it clubs, except when the adversaries have won the first game, and are about 20 points in the second.   This makes it not unlikely that they will win the rubber on the next hand with their deal.   Under such circumstances the dealer must invariably leave it to his partner, in the hope that he can save the rubber by making it a grand.   The dealer must never announce spades unless he can certainly win the game in his own hand.

The dealer's partner should be aware that there cannot be any reasonable hope of four tricks in red in the leader's hand, or a red trump would have been announced ; and unless he has at least five probable tricks in his own hand he should not make it red. With three Aces he should announce grand. If he is obliged to make it black, and has three or four probable tricks, he should announce whichever suit he is best in. Attention should be paid to the score ; for in many instances the suit must be selected so that the adversaries cannot win the game with the odd trick, even if they double.

An example will make this clear. Y holds these cards : ♡ A 4 2 ; ♣ K 3 2 ; ◇ 7 5 4 2 ; ♠ K 8 7. The score is 24 to 12 in his favour, and the dealer tells him to make the trump. His partner's hand being presumably black, he can count on both his black Kings to win, which, with the ♡ A, should make three tricks. If he announces spades, and the adversaries double, he cannot lose the game, even if they make four by cards. On the other hand, he can win the game with two by cards ; but that is a very unlikely result if he is doubled. If he announces clubs, and the adversaries double, they must make three by cards to win ; while he can win with only the odd trick, which is not improbable if his partner is strong in either black suit. But the thing to be considered is that if the adversaries double on clubs, and go out on this hand, it is not impossible that they will win the rubber on their deal. Therefore, at this state of the score, if it is the first game of the rubber, Y's safest plan is to make it spades. But if it were the second game of the rubber, the adversaries having won the first, it would be the duty of Y to make it a grand ; and if the adversaries were 20 points or more on the second game, such a course would be imperative. This is an excellent example of the care and judgment required in making the trump at Bridge, and of paying close attention to the score. Under some circumstances a player will make it spades for safety ; while with exactly the same cards, but under other conditions of the score, he must play without a trump.

Doubling. The dealer or his partner having announced the trump, the adversary should carefully consider the score before doubling or playing. Most players consider themselves justified in doubling when they have six reasonably certain tricks in their own hands, trusting partner for one only. Great caution should be used in doubling a grand, the position of the lead being carefully studied ; because the odd trick usually settles the game in a doubled grand. While a player with the lead, and seven certain tricks in one suit, should double a grand, his partner would be very foolish to do so, unless he had, in addition to his long suit, the heart ace ; for it is a conventionality of the game for A to lead hearts if B doubles a grand.

The original maker of the trump should be very strong to justify him in re-doubling the adversary. If he had four probable tricks originally, he may count the adversary who doubles for five, and of the four doubtful tricks remaining, the odds are against partner having the three which would be necessary to win the odd trick. With seven reasonably certain tricks, including five trumps, the original maker of the trump should re-double, unless he can win the game with the odd trick without quadrupling its value.

The Original Lead. Another point in which Bridge differs from other forms of Dummy, is that the first card must be played before Y's hand is exposed. The experience of the best players has been, that the original lead should be governed by the same principles as at Whist; opening the best suit, and giving as much information as possible to the partner as to the general characteristics of the hand. The most common exception is that it is seldom right to lead trumps.

The following suggestions apply equally to any of the three games, Dummy, Mort, or Bridge. It will simplify matters if we divide them into several parts; first giving those for the player who has dummy for his partner. The terms Mort and Dummy may be considered as synonymous.

DUMMY'S PARTNER, or Vivant. The chief difference between the play of the dummy and partner, and that of their adversaries, is that there is no occasion for the former to play on the probability of partner's holding certain cards, because a glance will show whether he holds them or not. There is no hoping that he may have certain cards of re-entry, or strength in trumps, or that he will be able to stop an adverse suit, or anything of that sort, for the facts are exposed from the first. Instead of adapting his play to the slowly ascertained conditions of partner's hand, Vivant should have it mapped out and determined upon before he plays a card. He may see two courses open to him; to draw the trumps and make a long suit, or to secure such discards as will give him a good cross-ruff. A rapid estimate of the probable results of each line of play, a glance at the score, and his mind should be made up. Several examples of this foresight will be found in the example hands.

Another point of difference is, that Vivant should play false cards whenever possible. He has not a partner who, if he plays the King, might jump to the conclusion that he is signalling; or can trump a suit, or has not the Queen. The more thoroughly the adversaries are confused, the greater the advantage to Vivant, especially in the end game.

Selecting a Suit for the original lead. If there is any choice, that suit should be selected which contains the longest sequence, or the sequence with the fewest breaks. It should be noticed that the sequence need not be in one hand; for it is almost as valuable if divided, and it is especially advantageous to have the higher cards concealed in Vivant's hand. Its continuity is the chief point. For instance : Vivant and Mort hold between them one suit of K J 9 7 5 4 3, and another of Q J 10 9 8 7 5. The latter should be selected, because two leads must establish it.

In establishing a long suit it is very important to note the fall of the missing cards in the sequences. In the first of the two combinations just given, Vivant should be as careful to watch for the fall of the 8 and 6 as for the A Q and 10.

Leading. It is quite unnecessary to follow any system of leads, further than to distinguish between the combinations from which high or low cards are led. But it is important to remember that although a high-card combination may be divided, it should be played as if in one hand. For instance : Vivant holds Q J x x x of a suit ; Dummy having A x x. By leading Q or J, Dummy is enabled to finesse, as if he held A Q J. Vivant holds K J x x x ; Dummy having Q x x. The play is to force the Ace, as if the combination of K Q J x x were in one hand.

Many opportunities arise for leading the Ace first from a short suit, in order to secure a ruff on the second or third round.

Second Hand Play. If any card is led by the adversaries which the fourth hand cannot win, the second hand should cover it if possible ; for unless he does so, his weakness will be exposed, and the suit will be continued. This is especially true of cases in which the second hand holds single honours, such as Jack and others, or Queen and others. Even the King should be played second hand in such cases, unless it is so well guarded that the Ace must fall before the King can be forced out.

If the fourth hand can win the card led, it is seldom necessary to cover second hand. For instance : If the Jack of trumps is led, Vivant holding Q 9 7 4, and Dummy having A 6 3 2 ; there is no need to play the Queen. If the King is in third hand, such play would establish the Ten. If the King is with the leader, it or the Ten must make. If Dummy were second hand with the same cards, Jack being led, he should not play the Ace, for third hand must play the King to shut out the Queen.

With A Q 9, partner having K and others, it is best to play A on J led.

If Vivant has Ace and several others of a suit led, Dummy having only two small cards, a force may be certainly secured by passing the first round. If Dummy has the Ace, and passes second hand, Vivant failing to win the trick, the adversaries will of course see that the play is made in order to force Vivant on the third round.

If Dummy is weak in trumps, and has only one card of a suit in which Vivant has Ace and others, the Ace should be played, and Dummy forced, unless there is a better game.

It is a disadvantage to play in second hand from suits in which each has a guarded honour.   If Vivant has Q x x, and Dummy has J x, they must make a trick in that suit if they play a small card second hand, and avoid leading the suit.   The same is true of the adversaries; but they must play on the chance that the partner has the honour, whereas Vivant knows it.

DUMMY'S ADVERSARIES.   To play well against Dummy, a person should thoroughly understand the variations in his play required by his position with regard to Dummy and to the lead.   He may be first, second, or third hand, and in each he may be on the Right or Left of Dummy; added to which he may be fourth player, which will make seven varieties of position requiring consideration.

There are three great principles in playing against Dummy:—

1st.   Lead through the strong suits, and up to the weak.

2nd.   Do not lead through a fourchette.

3rd.   Do not lead up to a tenace.

These rules must not be blindly followed in every instance. They are simply general principles, and some of the prettiest *coups* arise from the exceptional cases.

It way be well to repeat that Right, and Left, are the terms distinguishing the player sitting on the Right, or Left, of Dummy; so that "first hand left," refers to the first player in any trick, who sits on Dummy's Left.   We shall consider this position first, because it is the easiest to play.

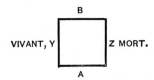

FIRST HAND LEFT.   As already observed, this position does not occur in the original lead at Bridge, but Left may become first hand any time after the first trick.

The general principle of leading up to weakness suggests that we should know what weakness is.   Dummy may be considered weak in suits of which he holds three or four small cards, none higher than an 8; Ace and one or two small cards; or King and one or two small cards.   In leading up to such suits, your object should be to give your partner a finesse, if possible; and in calculating the probabilities of success it must be remembered that there are only two unknown hands, so that it is an equal chance that he holds either of two unknown cards.   It is 3 to 1 against his holding both, or against his holding neither.   Of three unknown cards, it is 7 to 1 against his holding all three, or none of them; or about an equal chance that he holds two of the three; or one only.

If Dummy holds any of the weak suits just given, you holding nothing higher than the Ten, you should lead it. Suppose you have 10 9 6 ; Dummy having A 3 2. The K Q J may be distributed in eight different ways, in any of which your partner will pass your Ten if second hand does not cover. In four cases, second hand would cover with the King, and in one with the Queen and Jack. In the remaining three your partner's hand would be benefited.

If Dummy has King and one or two small cards, it is not so disadvantageous to lead up to the King as would at first appear ; because it is forced out of his hand on the first round, unless Vivant plays Ace ; and it is usually good policy to force out Dummy's cards of re-entry early in the hand.

In leading from high-card combinations, the usual whist leads should be followed ; but exceptions must be made on the second round when certain cards are in Dummy's hand. For instance : With A K J and others, it is usual to stop after the first round, and wait for the finesse of the Jack. This is obviously useless if the Queen is not in Dummy's hand. So with K Q 10, unless Dummy has the Jack ; or K Q 9, unless Dummy has the 10. The lead from A Q J should be avoided if Dummy has the King.

With A Q 10 and others, J in Dummy's hand, begin with the Queen.

With A J 9 and others, 10 in Dummy's hand, lead the Jack.

With A J 10, Dummy having K Q x, play the Jack, and do not lead the suit again.

In trumps, with K Q and others, if Dummy has the J singly guarded, begin with the King as usual, but follow it with the Queen instead of the smallest ; for Vivant may have passed in the hope of making a Bath coup with both Ace and Jack. In plain suits this is a dangerous lead, because Vivant having Ace, and wishing to force Dummy, would hold his Ace as a matter of course.

With short suits, such as K x, Q x ; or even with King or Queen alone, the honour is a good lead if Dummy has no court cards in the suit. The Queen is rather a better lead than the King, the only danger being that second hand holds fourchette.

With Q J x, or J 10 x, one of the high cards should be played, as in Whist. With Q 10 x, Dummy having Ace or King, the Queen should be led.

With K 10 x, Dummy having Jack, the suit should not be led.

With such combinations as K x x x, Dummy having Q x, the suit should not be led.

When you have a suit which is both long and strong, such as A K x x x, and Dummy has no honour in the suit, it is a common artifice to underplay, by beginning with the smallest, if playing against a grand, and you have a card of re-entry. This should not be done unless you have the general strength to justify such a finesse.

If you open a long suit, Dummy having only small cards, and your partner wins with Q. J, or 10, and does not return it ; he has evidently a finesse in the suit, and wants it led again.

Leading Trumps. Many players fall into the error of leading from weak trumps up to weakness in trumps. This should not be done without a very strong hand in plain suits. It must be borne in mind that the dealer and his partner have made the trump to suit their hands, and their adversaries should be very cautious about leading trumps for them. When the dealer has named the trumps, and dummy is weak in them, a player with an established suit and weak trumps might show his suit to his partner and then lead trumps through the dealer. Under other circumstances, a player in this position should not lead trumps up to dummy except in answer to a call, or when his partner has doubled the dealer.

The usual whist methods of signalling, echoing, etc., may be used to advantage in any form of Dummy.

End Games. In the end game there are several variations which are made possible by the fact that the cards on your right are exposed.

With A J x, Dummy having Q x x, the small card should be led.

With Q x, and an odd card, Dummy having K x x of the first suit ; it is better to play the odd card , but if for any reason this should not be done, lead the Q. hoping to find A 10 with your partner.

The state of the score must be a constant guide in all end games. For instance : You hold Q 10 x, Dummy having J 9 x. If you want only one trick, play the Queen ; but if you want two, play the small card.

FIRST HAND RIGHT. This is the first player in any trick sitting on Dummy's Right.

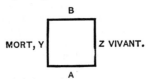

With the original lead in this position, the bridge-player must follow the general principles that prevail in Whist ; for Y's cards are not exposed until after A has played. But after the first trick in Bridge, and at any time in Dummy or Mort, he should remember the importance of leading through Dummy's strong suits.

It must be remembered that the first lead must necessarily be made in the dark, but the selection of the suit will often depend on the trump, and whether it was named by the dealer or by his partner.

If the dealer has made it red, and A has the A K of a plain suit, he should play the King, so as to retain the lead until Dummy's hand is exposed.

If the dealer has made it a grand, A must play a low card from his best protected suit, never leading an Ace, even from A Q and others. But if he has A K and others he may play the King to retain the lead until the exposure of Dummy's hand.

If the dealer passes it to his partner, he is weak in red. If Y makes it hearts, A should lead a supporting diamond, unless he has great strength in another suit. If Y has made it diamonds, A should lead a supporting heart. But in either case, if A has in his hand such cards as A K, even of a black suit, he should play the King, and wait to see Dummy's hand. If Y has made it black, A must be guided by his own cards, but should give a red suit the preference for his opening lead.

If Y makes it a grand, it is unadvisable to lead the black suits, unless very strong in them, and as a general rule, A should lead hearts. If A's partner has doubled a grand, it is imperative for A to lead a heart. In playing against a grand, not doubled, if A has a sure card of re-entry, in addition to a suit headed by A K, he should lead a small card from the A K suit.

Suits which it is good policy to lead through are A x x x, K x x x, or any broken sequences of high cards.

Suits in which Dummy is long, or holds any of the regular high-card combinations, should be avoided ; winning or high sequences being especially dangerous. To lead such suits through Dummy's strength is an invitation to partner to force you in the suit led.

It is not necessary for you to be strong in a suit which you lead through Dummy ; and if you are both weak, is often advantageous ; especially if it avoids leading one of his strong suits.

With A Q 10 x ; Dummy having J x x x ; play the 10. If partner has the King you make every trick in the suit.

With A Q 10 x ; Dummy having K x x ; play the Q. If Dummy passes, you make two tricks ; if he covers, you have tenace over the Jack.

With A 10 9 x ; Dummy having J x x x ; play the 10. If partner has the K, your A 9 is tenace over the Q.

With A J 10 x ; Dummy having Q x x x ; if the suit must be led, play the Jack ; but such positions should be avoided, except in the end game, or when you play for every trick.

With A J 10 x ; Dummy having no honour in the suit ; if you must lead the suit, play the 10.

In trumps, with K Q x x ; Dummy having A J x x ; play the Queen. If Dummy wins with A, play a small card for the second round, and he may refuse to put on the J. A good Vivant player, not having the 10, would make Dummy cover; but nothing is lost if he does, and it marks the 10 with your partner.

With King and others of a suit in which Dummy has not the Ace; avoid leading the suit until the Ace has fallen.

With King alone, play it if Dummy has the Ace; keep it if he has not.

Trumps. If a player in this position is strong in trumps, he should keep quiet about it, and let the maker of the trumps develop the suit. False-carding is perfectly legitimate in trumps, and will deceive the dealer more than your partner.

End Games. There are cases in which it is necessary to play as if partner was known to possess a certain card, for unless he has it the game is lost. For instance: You want one trick, and have Q 10 x x, Dummy having K x x, of an unplayed suit. The Queen is the best play; for if partner has any honour you must get a trick; otherwise it is impossible.

You have K x in one suit, a losing card in another, and the thirteenth trump. You want all four tricks to save the game. Play the King, and then the small card; for if your partner has not the Ace and another winning card you must lose the game.

You have a losing trump, and Q x x of a suit in which Dummy has K 10 x. If you want one trick, play the losing trump, counting on partner for an honour in the plain suit. If you must have two tricks, lead the Queen, trusting your partner to hold Ace.

SECOND HAND LEFT. This is the second player in any trick, sitting on Dummy's Left.

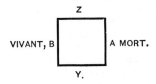

As a general principle, it may be assumed that any high card led by Dummy forms part of a combination, the unseen part of which is in Vivant's hand. If Dummy leads a Queen from Q x x; you holding A J x, it is almost a certainty that Vivant holds the King. If you have A K x, Vivant must have J 10 and several others. If you have K x x, Vivant probably holds Ace, or a long suit headed by J 10.

When Dummy leads strengthening cards, they must be to give Vivant a finesse. If he leads a small card from small cards, some high-card combination must be in Vivant's hand. In such cases it is useless for you to finesse. If you have any sequence superior to the card led, cover with the lowest. There should be no false-carding in this, because your partner is the only one that can be deceived.

With A K and others, play the King, whatever Dummy leads.

With A Q and others, Dummy having nothing higher than the 9, play the Ace.

With K Q 10, play the Queen on a small card led, unless Dummy has the Jack.

With A J 10 x, play Ace if Dummy has no honour in the suit. But if Dummy leads the 9, cover with the 10 ; if it loses, you lie tenace over the dealer.

With A J x, play the Jack on a 9 led. This prevents the finesse of the 9, and retains command of the suit. If Dummy has both K and Q, play your Ace. It is usless to play the Bath coup, for Vivant knows your cards, and your partner only is deceived.

With K x x, if Dummy has not the Ace, do not play the King, no matter what is led.

With Q x x, unless Dummy has both A and K, do not play the Queen. If your partner has the Jack guarded, one of you must make a trick. If Dummy has A J, and leads J, put on the Queen ; it may make the 9 or 10 good in your partner's hand.

With A x x, Dummy leading Jack, play the Ace.

With any fourchette, cover the card led.

If Dummy remains with one or two small cards of a suit that has been led, and you have the best, play it on the second round. Dummy's play is evidently for the ruff, and if Vivant has not the second-best, your partner has.

If you have King, and only one or two small cards, Dummy leading Queen from Q 10 x x, play your King. You cannot save yourself ; but you may make the 9 good in partner's hand. If you have three or more small cards, do not play the King, for either partner or Vivant must be short in the suit. So if Dummy leads Jack from J 10 and others, play the King with a short suit. If partner has Queen you establish it ; if not, you cannot make a trick in the suit.

With short suits it is usually best to cover an honour with an honour ; but with several small cards, such as K x x x, Dummy leading a singleton Queen, you should pass.

With K 10 x, Dummy having J and others, play honour on honour ; small card on small card, whichever Dummy leads.

It is often important for the second hand to cover with what is called an ***imperfect fourchette.*** A true fourchette is the card immediately above and below the one led ; such as K J over the Q, or Q 10 over the J. An imperfect fourchette is the card above the one led, and another next but one below it ; such as K 10 over a Q led, or Q 9 over a J led. Covering forces the opponents to play two honours to win one trick, and will often make an intermediate card good in your partner's hand.

SECOND HAND RIGHT. This is the second player in
any trick, sitting on Dummy's Right.

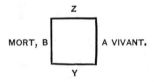

This position is one of the easiest to play, as a glance at
Dummy's cards will show what is best to be done. If a small
card is led, you having King, put it on if Dummy has not the Ace ;
unless you want partner to get the lead. If Dummy has only two
cards of the suit, neither of them the Ace, always play your
King.

When Vivant leads a suit, it is often important to count how
many he and your partner can possibly hold. For instance : You
have four, K x x x ; Dummy has four, A J 10 x, and Vivant leads
the Queen. It is useless to play your King ; for either the Queen
is a singleton, and Vivant cannot continue the suit, which will compel Dummy to lead it to you eventually ; or, the third round will
be trumped, perhaps by your partner. If you have only two small
cards with the King, put it on the Queen. You cannot save it,
but you may establish your partner's 9.

In the last three tricks, if you find yourself with a doubtful card,
and the best and a small card of a suit which Vivant leads
through you, win the trick and lead the doubtful card, for if Vivant
held the best of that suit he would have led it first, to be sure of a
trick.

THIRD HAND LEFT. This is the third player in any
trick, sitting on Dummy's Left.

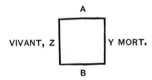

The third hand will require constant practice in putting himself
in his partner's place, asking himself what the object is in leading
certain cards through Dummy's hand. The inferences from the
conventional leads should be sufficiently familiar to need no further
explanation ; but even good players occasionally overlook indications that partner holds certain cards. For instance : A leads a
small card ; Y, Dummy, holds Q x x, and plays Q. You play the

King and win the trick. This marks not only the Ace, but the *Jack* in partner's hand ; because on the principle already stated, Vivant would not play a twice guarded Queen from Dummy's hand, if he had the Jack guarded himself.

False cards should be avoided by the third hand as much as possible. Vivant will give your partner enough to puzzle over without your adding to the confusion. There are some exceptions in trumps. For instance : You have K Q x ; Dummy has A J x x, and your partner leads. Unless Dummy plays Ace, you should put on the King, and change the suit.

If you hold Ace and others in a plain suit, partner leading Jack, pass it if Dummy has no honour. If it is not led from K Q J x x, it must be a doubleton, and by winning the second round you can give the invited force. With any other honours than the Ace, pass a partner's Jack led.

If partner leads you a suit of which he knows, or should know, you have not the best, he must have a good finesse in the suit which he does not lead, and you should take the first opportunity to lead that suit to him.

The usual whist principles prevail in returning partner's suits, except when some modification may be suggested by the condition of Dummy's hand. For instance : With K x x ; Dummy having A Q J x ; if you win, third hand, on Dummy's finesse, you may be sure your partner's lead was a singleton. If Dummy is weak in the two other plain suits, your partner may have a good finesse in one or both of them.

When your partner wins the first round of an adverse suit, and immediately returns it, he is inviting a force. If Vivant or Mort make this move, you should at once get out as many rounds of trumps as possible, if they made it black for safety.

THIRD HAND RIGHT. This is the third player in any trick, sitting on Dummy's Right.

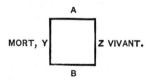

The general principles of inference are the same as in the preceding case, and cards may often be inferred in the same manner from the evident intention of partner. For instance : You hold K x x ; partner leads J, Vivant covering with Queen. A glance at Dummy's cards shows him to have 10 x x ; so your partner may be credited with A 9. You have x x ; your partner leading Q, covered by Vivant with K, and Dummy having J x x. You may credit your partner with A 10. You have x x ; your partner leads Q, and Vivant wins with Ace ; Dummy holding 10 x x. Your partner must have J 9 and others, and Vivant has the King.

There are several cases in which you should not allow Dummy to win the trick. If you have only one card of a suit in which your partner leads Ace then Queen, and Dummy has the King twice guarded, trump at once, if weak, to prevent Dummy from getting into the lead. Your partner leads Queen ; you holding A 10 x, and Dummy having K x x. Let the King make on the first round.

If your partner leads a small card up to strength in Dummy's hand, he is either inviting a force, or trying to establish a long suit. Under such circumstances, if you have the Ace, play it, and lead a second round of the suit immediately, which will settle the question.

If you have Q J 10 of a suit in which partner leads King, play the Jack, so that he will count you for Q or no more, and will not go on with the Ace.

IN GENERAL. Both the adversaries of Dummy should adopt the usual whist tactics for unblocking, etc., especially in grand, and in some cases Dummy's exposed cards will make the matter more simple. For instance : You hold A Q alone, of a suit which partner leads. If you are Left, and Dummy has not the King, play Ace and return the Queen.

Plain suit echoes are of no value in Dummy, owing to the false cards played by Vivant.

The lead of a thirteenth card is usually an invitation to put on the best trump, as in Whist.

FOURTH HAND, RIGHT OR LEFT. There is only one difference from the usual whist methods in playing fourth hand, and that is in indicating sequences by winning with the best and returning the lowest to show the intermediate cards. For instance: Fourth player, holding K Q J x, wins with King and returns the Jack. Or with A K Q, wins with Ace and returns the Queen. The reason for this is that Vivant gains nothing by the information, for he knows from the first what cards are out against him ; but the information may be valuable to your partner, the second hand. If it is not the intention to return the suit at once, the lowest of the sequence should be played.

PLAYING TO THE SCORE. This is the most important element in any form of Dummy, and there is no surer indication of a careless or weak player than his inattention to the score.

One cannot be too early impressed with the importance of saving the game before trying to win it ; although great risks may be taken to win a game that cannot be lost that hand.

Never risk a sure odd trick in the hope of making two ; unless the two will win the game, and the odd trick will not lose it. Never risk a trick that will save the game in the hope of winning more.

An illustration has already been given, in connection with whist, showing that the same combination of cards must often be played in various ways, according to the number of tricks required to save or win the game.

DISCARDING. For the adversaries of Dummy the general principles of discarding are the same as at Whist. It is usual to keep a card of the suit which the partner discards, especially if either Vivant or Mort is leading trumps. When a grand is played, discard from your weak suit, unless it unguards an honour, or unless you show your strength by signalling in the discards.

Dummy and his partner should be able to reduce their discarding to an exact science. Such simple cases as getting rid of cards in one hand that block a good suit in the other are too obvious to require notice ; but there are many cases in which it is necessary to plan in advance for one or more discards, as in the celebrated Vienna Coup. Some excellent examples of foresight in discarding will be found in the illustrative hands.

PLACING THE LEAD. The end game offers many fine opportunities for the display of skill in this branch of whist tactics. The problem is usually some variation of the tenace position, and in its solution Vivant and Mort have the advantage of knowing exactly the cards against them, if not their location.

MAKING SLAMS. Owing to the possibility of planning the general scheme of the hand in advance, slams are more common at Dummy than at Whist, and in the great majority of cases they are made by Mort and Vivant. Hands should be carefully examined before playing a card, to be sure that a possible slam is not overlooked. There are many simple slam hands at Dummy which would not yield more than four or five by cards at Whist.

There are at present no *text books* on the subject of Bridge, the small handbooks on the game by " Boax " and " Hoffman " being chiefly confined to the laws, and the rules of play. Dummy in all its forms seems to have been sadly neglected by the writers on card games ; the only book that goes into the tactics peculiar to this form of Whist being Charles Lahure's "*Whist à Trois.*" This work being a text-book for Mort, gives the student no hint of the variations necessary in a game like Bridge, in which the trump is made by the dealer and his partner, and not turned up.

ILLUSTRATIVE BRIDGE HANDS.

The dealer, Z, names hearts in both instances, and A leads. The underlined card wins the trick, and the card under it is the next one led.

A	Y	B	Z		A	Y	B	Z	
♣ A	**♡ 2**	♣ 10	♣ 2	I	**♣ K**	♣ 5	♣ 3	2 ◇	I
6 ◇	**Q ◇**	2 ◇	7 ◇	2	**♣ Q**	♣ 6	♣ 4	3 ◇	2
8 ◇	3 ◇	9 ◇	**J ◇**	3	**♣ A**	♣ 10	♣ 7	4 ◇	3
♣ 3	**♡ 3**	♣ J	♣ 4	4	9 ♠	**K ♠**	5 ♠	2 ♠	4
♡ 6	♡ 5	♡ 9	**♡ 10**	5	♡ 2	**♡ Q**	♡ 6	♡ 3	5
2 ♠	**A ♠**	10 ♠	3 ♠	6	♡ 4	♡ 8	♡ 9	**♡ 10**	6
♡ 7	♡ 4	♡ J	**♡ Q**	7	♡ 5	♡ 7	♡ K	**♡ A**	7
10 ◇	4 ◇	♡ K	**♡ A**	8	7 ♠	10 ♠	6 ♠	4 ♠	8
♣ 5	5 ◇	♣ Q	**♣ K**	9	♣ 2	**♣ J**	♣ 8	K ◇	9
♣ 6	4 ♠	J ♠	**♣ 9**	10	6 ◇	3 ♠	8 ♠	**J ♠**	10
♣ 7	5 ♠	Q ♠	**♣ 8**	11	9 ◇	7 ◇	5 ◇	**A ♠**	11
7 ♠	6 ♠	K ◇	**A ◇**	12	10 ◇	8 ◇	♣ 9	**Q ♠**	12
8 ♠	9 ♠	K ♠	**♡ 8**	13	J ◇	Q ◇	A ◇	**♡ J**	13

In the first example the dealer is almost strong enough to announce a grand. After dummy's hand is exposed, the dealer's object is to establish the club suit by allowing dummy to trump the high cards. After the successful finesse of the diamond Jack, a little slam is possible. If the trump 10 wins, a grand slam is possible. At trick 9, as A led ace originally, he can be counted for three more clubs, no diamonds and two spades; so B must have one club, which must be the Queen.

The dealer and his partner score 56 and game for tricks; 16 for honours, and 40 for grand slam.

In the second example, as soon as dummy's hand is exposed the dealer sees that the entire club suit is against him, and that if he trumps and leads trumps, the King will win, and he will be forced again. A's best lead on quitting his own suit is undoubtedly through dummy's strength, as the dealer's discards would indicate that he was safe in diamonds. The method of getting a discard of the diamond King should be carefully studied, as such cases are common.

Dealer and partner score 32 and game for tricks, and 32 for honours.

For the Laws of Bridge, see Whist Family Laws.

CAYENNE,

OR CAYENNE WHIST.

CARDS. Cayenne is played with two full packs of fifty-two cards, which rank as at Whist, both for cutting and playing.

MARKERS are necessary, and must be suitable for counting to ten points. A sheet of paper is used for scoring the results of the games.

PLAYERS. Cayenne is played by four persons. When there are more than four candidates for play the selection of the table must be made as at Whist. Partners and deal are then cut for.

CUTTING. One of the packs having been spread on the table, face down, each of the four players draws a card; the two lowest pairing against the two highest. The lowest of the four is the dealer, and has the choice of seats and cards. Ties are decided in the same manner as at Whist.

POSITION OF THE PLAYERS. The partners sit opposite each other, and the players are distinguished, as at Whist, by the letters A-B and Y-Z. Z is the dealer, and A has the original lead.

DEALING. One pack of cards is shuffled and cut as at Whist. The dealer then gives four cards to each player, beginning on his left; then four more, and finally five, no trump being turned. In many places six cards are first dealt to each player, and then seven; but the 4-4-5 system is better, and is the rule in the very similar game of Boston.

The general rules with regard to irregularities in the deal are the same as at Whist; except that a misdeal does not lose the deal. The misdealer must deal again, and with the same pack.

CAYENNE. After the cards are all dealt, the player to the left of the dealer cuts the still pack, which is shuffled and presented to him by the dealer's partner, and the top card of the portion left on the table is turned up for Cayenne. This card is not a trump, but is simply to determine the rank of the suits.

STAKES. In Cayenne the stake is a unit, so much a point. The largest number of points possible to win on a rubber is 24, and the smallest, 1. The result of the rubber may be a tie, which we consider a defect in any game. In settling at the end of the rubber it is usual for the losers to pay their right-hand adversaries.

MAKING THE TRUMP. The trump suit must be named by the dealer or his partner, after they have examined their cards. The dealer has the first say, and he may either select cayenne or any of the other suits; or he may announce *grand,* playing for the tricks without any trump suit; or he may call *nullo,*

playing to take as few tricks as possible, without a trump suit. If
the dealer makes the choice, his partner must abide by it; but if he
has not a hand to justify him in deciding, he should leave the
selection to his partner, who must decide one way or the other.

The considerations which should guide players in their choice
are the scoring possibilities of their hands, in tricks and in honours.
As in Whist, the first six tricks taken by one side do not count;
but each trick above that number counts one, two, etc., *by cards.*
There are five honours in the trump suit in Cayenne ; A K Q J 10;
and the partners holding the majority of them count 1 for each
honour that they hold in excess of their opponents, and 1 in addition, for *honours.* For instance : If A–B have three honours
dealt them, they must have one more than their adversaries, and 1
for honours; entitling them to score 2. If they have four, they
have 3 in excess, and 1 for honours, a total of 4. If they have
five, they count 6 by honours.

At the end of the hand the points made by cards and by honours
are multiplied by the value of the trump suit. This value varies
according to the suit which is cayenne, which is always first preference. If cayenne is also the trump suit the points made by
cards and honours are multiplied by 4. If the trump suit is the
same colour as cayenne, the multiplier is 3. If it is a different
colour the multiplier is 2 or 1, according to the suit. The rank of
the suits as multipliers will be readily understood from the following table :—

If Cayenne is	♡	◇	♣	♠	If trumps, multiply by 4.
Second color is	◇	♡	♠	♣	If trumps, multiply by 3.
Third color is	♣	♣	♡	♡	If trumps, multiply by 2.
Fourth color is	♠	♠	◇	◇	If trumps, multiply by 1.

Better to understand the importance of considering this variation
in value when making the trump, it should be noticed that
although the game is 10 points, several games may be won in a
single hand, as everything made is counted, and any points over
10 go to the credit of the second game. If more than 20 points
are made, the excess goes on the third game, and so on. Another
important point is the great value attached to honours, and the
maker of the trump should never forget that he can better afford
to risk his adversaries winning 2 by cards with a trump in which
he has three honours, than he can to risk a trump in which they
may have three honours, and he can probably win only the odd
trick.

A further element may enter into his calculations, the state of
the score. Tricks count before honours, and if he feels certain of
making, by cards, the few points necessary to win the rubber, he
may entirely disregard the honours.

With such a hand it would be better to play without a trump, and to announce a **grand**, in which there are neither trumps nor honours, and every trick over the book is multiplied by 8. Two by cards at grand is worth more than two by cards and two by honours with any trump but cayenne.

There is still another resource, to announce **nullo**, in which there is no trump, and the object of the players is to take as few tricks as possible. In nullo, every trick over the book counts for the adversaries, and is multiplied by 8. A peculiarity of nullo is that the Ace of each suit ranks below the deuce, unless the player holding it wishes to declare it higher than the King. In the latter case he must announce it when he plays it, and before his left-hand adversary plays to the trick.

If the dealer transfers the right of making the trump to his partner, he must use the phrase, "You make it, partner." If a player makes the trump out of turn, his adversaries may consult as to the propriety of demanding a new deal.

METHOD OF PLAYING. The trump suit, grand, or nullo having been announced, the player on the dealer's left begins by leading any card he pleases, and the others must all follow suit if they can. The penalty for a revoke is the loss of three tricks; or the value of three tricks in points; or the addition of a like amount to the adversaries' score. The side making a revoke cannot win the game that hand, no matter what they score; but they may play the hand out, and count all they make to within one point of game, or 9. Revoking players cannot count points for slams.

The rules for cards played in error, leading out of turn, and all such irregularities, are the same as in Whist. The last trick turned and quitted may be seen.

The methods of gathering and stacking the tricks is the same as at Whist.

OBJECTS OF THE GAME. The chief object in Cayenne, either with a trump or in a grand, is to take tricks; in a nullo it is not to take them. In any case the highest card played of the suit led wins the trick, and trumps, if any, win against all other suits. At the end of each hand the side that wins any tricks in excess of the book scores them, after multiplying their number by the unit of value settled upon by the announcement. If a nullo is played the adversaries score them. Honours are then claimed; but the game cannot be won by honours alone, as at Whist; those holding honours must stop at the score of 9, unless they also win the odd trick. As soon as either side reaches or passes 10 points, they win a game; but the hand must be played out, and all tricks taken must be counted. If one side goes out by cards, the other cannot score honours. Thirteen tricks taken by one side is called a **slam,** and it counts 6 points. Twelve tricks is a *little slam,* and it counts 4. Either of these must be made exclusive of revoke penalties.

RUBBERS. The rubber is won by the side that first wins four games of ten points each; and the winning side adds 8 points to its score.

SCORING. The game score should be kept on a whist marker, using the four large keys on one side for single points, and the single large key on the opposite side for five points. The three small keys are used to show how many games of the rubber have been won by that side.

TWO GAMES WON, AND 2 POINTS SCORED ON THE THIRD.

The method of using counters for scoring 10-point games has already been described in connection with Whist.

In addition to either markers or counters, there must be a sheet of paper to keep the final results of the games.

In scoring, the revoke penalty counts first, tricks next, and honours last.

The side first reaching 10 points wins a *quadruple,* or game of 4, if their adversaries have not scored; a *triple,* or game of 3, if their adversaries have not reached 4; a *double,* or game of 2, if the adversaries have not reached 7; and a *single,* or game of 1, if their adversaries are 8 or 9 up. These game points are put down on the score-sheet, and all the points on the *adversaries'* marker are then turned down. If the winners make any points in excess of 10, such points are left to their credit on the marker, and count toward the next game. For instance: The score is A–B, 6; and Y–Z, 8; shown on the markers thus :—

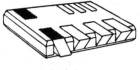

A-B 6 POINTS.

Y-Z 8 POINTS.

Let us suppose that Z announces cayenne, and makes 2 by cards; A–B claiming two by honours. Y–Z multiply by 4, mak-

ing them 8, and bringing their total score on the marker to 16;
that is, a game, and 6 points to their credit on the second game.
This must now be put down on the score-sheet. A-B's honours
not counting, as Y-Z went out by cards, the game is a double;
A-B not having reached 7 points. The score and markers now
stand :—

A-B | o | | | | | | |
Score: | | | | | | | | |
Y-Z | 2 | | | | | | |

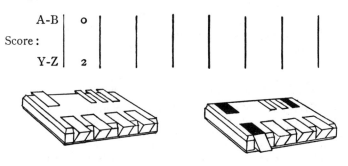

A-B's, NOTHING.   Y-Z's, 1 GAME, 6 POINTS.

Let us suppose A-B to announce grand on their deal, and to
make four by cards, which, multiplied by 8, gives them 32 points;
that is, three games, and 2 points to their credit on the marker.
The first of these games is a double, Y-Z having 6 points up.
The two others are quadruples, put down on the score-sheet
thus :—

A-B | o | 2 | 4 | 4 | | | |
Score: | | | | | | | | |
Y-Z | 2 | o | o | o | | | |

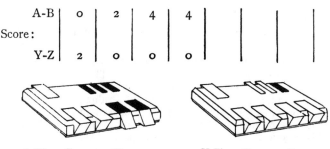

A-B's, 3 GAMES, 2 POINTS.   Y-Z's, 1 GAME, 0 POINTS.

In the next hand let us suppose clubs to be cayenne. Y deals,
and plays in colour, spades. Y-Z win 6 by cards, and 4 by
honours; 10 points multiplied by 3, = 30. For this they score
three games, the first being a triple, and the others quadruples.
These three games win the rubber, for which they add 8 points,

and 4 points for the little slam. This is all put down on the score-sheet :—

A-B	o	2	4	4	c	o	o	—=10
Score :								
Y-Z	2	o	o	o	3	4	4	8 4=25

Both scores being added up, the value of the rubber won by Y-Z is found to be 15, after deducting the 10 points made by A-B.

CUTTING IN. If there are more than four persons belonging to the table, those waiting cut in, as at Whist.

METHODS OF CHEATING. In all games in which the cards are dealt in bulk, four or six at a time, there is more or less temptation for the greek to gather desirable cards in the pack, leaving them undisturbed in the shuffle. If he can pick up two tricks of the previous deal with eight good cards of the same suit in them, by placing any two tricks of other cards between them, and dealing six at a time, he can tell exactly how many of the eight located cards are in his partner's hand. For this reason a player who does not thoroughly shuffle the cards should be carefully watched ; and an immediate protest should be made against any disarrangement of the tricks as they are taken in during the play, such as placing the last trick taken under the first. If the player doing this is to be the next dealer, any one observing the movement should insist upon his right to shuffle the cards thoroughly ; if not to leave the game.

We are strongly opposed to dealing the cards in bulk at Cayenne, and see no reason why the methods that prevail in the very similar game of Bridge should not be adopted.

SUGGESTIONS FOR GOOD PLAY. There is little to add to the rules already given for Whist. The principles that should guide in the making of the trump have been given in connection with the more important game of Bridge ; and the suggestions for playing nullo will be fully discussed in the games in which it is a prominent characteristic : Solo Whist, and Boston. Grand is practically Whist after the trumps are exhausted.

For the Laws of Cayenne, see Whist Family Laws.

SOLO WHIST,

OR WHIST DE GAND.

CARDS. Solo Whist is played with a full pack of fifty-two cards, which rank as at Whist, both for cutting and playing. Two packs are generally used, the one being shuffled while the other is dealt.

MARKERS are not used in Solo Whist, every hand being a complete game in itself, which is immediately settled for in counters representing money. At the beginning of the game each player should be provided with an equal number of these counters. They are usually white and red, the red being worth five times as much as the white. Twenty white and sixteen red is the usual allotment to each player when the game begins. Some one player should be the banker, to sell and redeem all counters.

PLAYERS. Solo Whist is played by four persons. If there are five candidates for play, they all sit at the same table, each taking his turn to sit out for one hand while the four others play. The dealer is usually selected to sit out. If there are only three players, one suit must be deleted from the pack, or the 2, 3, and 4 of each suit must be thrown out.

CUTTING. The table being formed, the players draw from an outspread for the deal, and choice of seats and cards. The player drawing the lowest card deals the first hand, and it is usual for him to dictate to the other players what seats they shall occupy with relation to himself. Ties are decided in the same manner as at Whist.

POSITION OF THE PLAYERS. The four players at Solo Whist are usually distinguished by the letters A B Y Z.

Z is the dealer, and A is known as the **eldest hand.** The position of the players does not imply any partnership ; for, as we shall see presently, any player may have any one of the others for a partner, without any change taking place in their positions at the table.

The players having once taken their seats are not allowed to change them without the consent of all the others at the table.

DEALING. The cards having been properly shuffled, are presented to the pone to be cut. Beginning on his left, the dealer distributes the cards three at a time, until only four remain. These he deals one at a time, turning up the last for the trump. When two packs are used, the player sitting opposite the dealer shuffles the still pack while the other is dealt. The deal passes in regular rotation to the left.

When three play with a pack of forty cards, the last card is turned up for trumps, but it does not belong to the dealer, and is not used in play.

The general rules with regard to irregularities in the deal are the same as at Whist; except that a misdeal does not pass the deal. The misdealer must deal again, and with the same pack.

The cards dealt, each player sorts and counts his hand to see that he has the correct number of cards, thirteen. If not, he should immediately claim a misdeal; for a player having more or less than his right proportion of cards cannot win anything on that hand, but will have to stand his proportion of all losses incurred by him or his side.

OBJECTS OF THE GAME. There are seven distinct objects in the Solo Whist, and before play begins each player has an opportunity of declaring to which of these objects he proposes to attain. They are:—

1st. To win 8 of the 13 tricks, with the assistance of a partner. This is called a *Proposal;* the partner's share is an *Acceptance.*

2nd. To win 5 of the 13 tricks, against the three other players combined. This is called a *Solo.*

3rd. To take no tricks, there being no trump suit, and the three other players being opposed. This is called *Misere,* or Nullo.

4th. To win 9 of the 13 tricks against the three other players combined; the single player to name the trump suit. This is called *Abundance.*

5th. To win 9 of the 13 tricks against the three other players comhined, with the trump suit that is turned up. This is called *Abundance in Trumps.*

6th. To take no tricks, there being no trump suit, and the three other players being opposed; the single player's cards being exposed face up on the table after the first trick is complete. This is called Misère sur table, or *A Spread.*

7th. To win all 13 tricks against the three other players combined; the single player to name the trump suit, and to have the original lead whether eldest hand or not. This is called Abundance Déclarée, or *A Slam.*

While the object of the proposing player is to win or lose the declared number of tricks, that of his adversaries is to prevent him from doing so, if possible. There are no honours, and the only factor in the count is the number of tricks actually taken. The highest card played of the suit led wins the trick, and trumps, if any, win against all other suits.

METHOD OF DECLARING. The eldest hand has the first say, and after examining his cards he may make any of the several propositions just enumerated. The smallest proposal he can make is to take 8 tricks with the assistance of a partner. To do this he should have four reasonably sure tricks in his own hand. Some players say he should be strong in trumps ; while others claim that the eldest hand should propose only on general strength. The former is the better plan. No other player should propose on trumps alone. This announcement is made by saying : *" I propose."* If a player thinks he can take five tricks against the combined efforts of the three other players, he announces : *" Solo."* If he feels equal to a misère, he calls : *" Misère ; "* and so on, according to the strength of his hand. If he does not feel justified in making a call, he says : *" I pass ; "* and the next player on his left has the opportunity ; and so on, until some player has proposed to do something, or all have passed.

If any player has proposed for a partner, any of the others, in their proper turn, may accept him by simply saying : *" I accept."* By so doing, a player intimates that he has four probable tricks also, but in the plain suits, and that he is willing to try for eight tricks with the proposer for a partner. All the other calls are made by a single player with the intention of playing against the three others. Any player except the eldest hand having once said, " I pass," cannot afterwards make or accept any proposal. The eldest hand, after passing once, can accept a proposal, but he cannot make one.

It is the custom in some places, when no one will make a proposal of any sort, to turn down the trump, and play the hands without any trump suit, each man for himself ; the winner of the last trick losing to each of the others the value of a solo. This is called a *Grand.*

RANK OF THE PROPOSALS. The various calls outrank one another in the order in which we have given them. If one player says, " I propose," and another calls " Solo," the solo call shuts out the proposal, even though it has been accepted by a second player. The call of a misère would in turn shut out a solo ; abundance would take precedence of misère ; and abundance in trumps would be a better call than simple abundance. The slam of course outranks all other bids. This making of a better proposition than one already made is known as *" Overcalling."*

A player who has made a call of any kind, or has accepted a proposal, may amend his proposition to a better one, only in case he is overcalled ; or a player who can not get a partner to accept him may amend his call to solo. For instance : A player may have a hand which he feels sure is good for 8 tricks, perhaps 9. To be safe, he calls solo, and hopes to make three or four over-tricks. If he is outbid by some player overcalling him with a misère, he may be tempted to amend his call to abundance.

No call is good until every player who has not already passed does so, by saying distinctly, " I pass."

STAKES. The losses and gains of the players are in propor-tion to the difficulties of the tasks they set themselves.

The most popular method of settling is to pay or take red counters for the various calls, and white counters for the tricks under or over the exact number proposed. If the callers succeed in their undertakings, their adversaries pay them ; if they fail, they pay their adversaries. A red counter is worth five white ones.

Proposal and Acceptance wins or loses........1 red counter.
Solo wins or loses...........................2 red counters.
Misère, or Nullo, wins or loses..............3 red counters.
Abundance, of any kind, wins or loses........4 red counters,
Open Misère, or Spread, wins or loses........6 red counters.
Declared Abundance, or Slam, wins or loses .8 red counters.
Each Over or Under-trick wins or loses......1 white counter.

In Proposal and Acceptance, each of the partners pays one of his adversaries. In all cases in which a single player is opposed to the three others, he wins or loses the amount shown in the foregoing table with each of them individually ; so that a single player calling a solo would win or lose 6 red counters. If he lost it, making only four tricks, he would also have to pay to each of his three adversaries a white counter. If he won it, making seven tricks, each of them would have to pay him two red and two white counters.

Misères, Spreads, and Slams pay no odd tricks. The moment a Misère player takes a trick, or a Slam player loses one, the hands are abandoned, and the stakes paid.

The usual value attached to the counters in America is 25 cents for the red, and 5 cents for the white. In England the proportion is sixpence and a penny.

POOL SOLO. When players wish to enhance the gam-bling attractions of the game, a pool is introduced. For this pur-pose a receptacle is placed upon the table, in which each player puts a red counter at the beginning of the game. Any person playing alone against the three others, wins this pool if he is suc-cessful ; if he fails, he must double the amount it contains, be-sides paying each of his adversaries in the regular way. In some places it is the custom for each player to contribute a red counter when he deals. The proposals and acceptances do not touch the pool.

METHOD OF PLAYING. If a proposal is accepted, and no one overcalls it, the proposer and acceptor are partners ; but make no change in their positions at the table. The eldest hand, sitting to the left of the dealer, begins by leading any card he pleases, and the play proceeds exactly as at Whist, the tricks being so stacked that they may be readily counted at any time.

If a single player has called solo, misère, or abundance, the eldest hand still has the original lead, and there is no change in the positions of the players. The position of the lead is often a serious consideration with a player calling a solo or a misère.

In all calls except misères and slams, the hands must be played out, in order to give each side an opportunity to make all the overtricks they can. The moment a misère player takes a trick, or a slam player loses one, the hands are thrown up, and the stakes paid.

When a spread is called, the trump is taken up, and the eldest hand leads. As soon as all have played to the first trick, the caller spreads his remaining twelve cards face upward on the table, so that each of his adversaries may see them ; but they have no control of the order in which they shall be played. The adversaries play their hands in the usual manner, with no further guidance than that possible by inference from the play and the exposed hand. The caller plays according to his best judgment.

When a slam is called, the player proposing it has the original lead ; but that does not alter the position of the deal for the next hand.

REVOKES. A revoke is a serious matter in Solo Whist. The penalty for it is the loss of three tricks, and the revoking players must pay the *red* counters involved in the call whether they win or lose ; but they may play the hand out to save overtricks. For instance : A proposer and acceptor make 11 tricks ; their adversaries having claimed a revoke. After deducting the revoke penalty, 3 tricks, the callers still have 8 tricks left, enough to make good the call. They each lose a red counter ; but no white ones, having saved their over-tricks. Had they taken only 8 tricks altogether, the penalty for the revoke would have left them only 5, and they would each have had to pay one red and three whites. If either adversary of the callers revokes, the individual player in fault must pay for all the consequences of the error. If the player in fault can show that the callers would have won in spite of the revoke, his partners must pay their share ; but the revoking player must settle for the three tricks lost by the revoke. For instance : Z calls solo ; A revokes ; Z makes 6 tricks, which it can be shown he must have done in spite of the revoke. A, Y, and B each pay Z 1 red and 1 white counter, and then A pays Z 9 white counters in addition for the tricks taken as revoke penalty.

If the single player revokes, either on solo or abundance, he loses the red counters involved, and must pay whatever white counters are due after three of his tricks have been added to those of the adversaries as penalty for the revoke. For instance: A calls solo, and revokes, but wins 6 tricks in all. He pays two red counters to each adversary. They then take three of his tricks, leaving him three only, and demand two white counters each, for the two under-tricks. If a player revokes who has called a misère or a slam, he immediately loses the stakes. If a revoke is made by any adversary of a player who has called misère or slam, the player in fault must individually pay all the stakes.

CARDS PLAYED IN ERROR. In the simple proposal and acceptance, the rules with regard to cards played in error, or led out of turn, are the same as at Whist. In the case of a single player against three adversaries, the caller is not liable to any penalty for cards played in error, or led out of turn ; but his adversaries are subject to the usual whist penalties for all such irregularities, such as having the cards laid on the table as exposed, or a suit called, or the highest or lowest of a suit led demanded from an adversary who has followed suit out of turn.

For the better protection of the single player, who is much more liable to be injured by irregularities than partners would be, he is allowed to prevent the use of an exposed trump for ruffing, and to demand or *to prevent* the play of any exposed card in plain suits. If a suit is led of which an adversary has an exposed card on the table, the single player may call upon him to play his highest or lowest of that suit.

If any adversary of a misère player leads out of turn, or exposes a card, or plays before his proper turn in any trick, the caller may immediately claim the stakes, and the individual player in fault must pay for himself, and for his partners.

METHODS OF CHEATING. While the practice of dealing three cards at a time gives a little more opportunity to the greek than would occur if they were dealt as at Whist, there is little to be feared if two packs are used, unless two greeks are in partnership. When such partners sit next each other, there is more or less danger, if only one pack is used, that one may shuffle so that the other may cut understandingly ; or that a good shuffler may run up six cards for a dealer that is not embarrassed by the cards being cut. A shrewd greek can often help a silent partner who is playing under the disguise of a single caller, especially in misère. Persons who play in the many public cafés of Europe should be especially careful to avoid this style of partnership, where it is very common.

SUGGESTIONS FOR GOOD PLAY. Apart from the general principles common to all forms of Whist, such as the play of high or low cards, trumps or plain suits, etc., there are several points peculiar to Solo Whist which require attention.

Proposing. It is better to propose on two or three sure tricks, with strong probabilities of several more, than on a certainty of four only. For instance: The two highest trumps, and two suits containing Aces, with no other trick probable, is not such a good hand for a proposal as one containing four average trumps, with one plain suit of K Q J x x, and another of K Q x x. It is not improbable that the latter may be good for seven or eight tricks. Nothing but experience will teach a player what combinations of cards are " probably " good for tricks; but K x x, or Q J 10 x, or K Q, may be counted on.

There should be some intelligible system of proposing, so that the players may understand each other. The eldest hand should not propose except on strong trumps, and this should be a warning to other players not to accept him on trump strength alone.

Four trumps with two or three honours may be called strong; or five trumps, even without an honour. Five trumps with two or more honours is great strength.

Any player other than the eldest hand should propose on general strength, and the player accepting him should do so on trump strength. Some such distinction should be clearly understood, in order that there may be no such contretemps as two players proposing and accepting on trumps alone, and finding themselves without a trick in the plain suits after the trumps are drawn.

If the eldest hand is strong in trumps, but has not four sure tricks, he should pass, which will give him an excellent opportunity to accept a player proposing on general strength in the plain suits. If the proposal should be accepted before it comes to his turn, the eldest hand should be in a good position to defeat it.

If any player, other than the eldest hand, has sufficient trump strength to justify a proposal, he will usually find that he can risk a solo; or by passing, defeat any proposal and acceptance that may be made.

Accepting. A proposal by the eldest hand should not be accepted by a player with only one strong suit. The probability of tricks in several suits is better than a certainty in one suit; but if one strong suit is accompanied by a card of re-entry, or by four trumps, it should prove very strong, particularly in partnership with the eldest hand.

When the partners will sit next each other, proposals may be accepted on slightly weaker hands than would be considered safe otherwise.

Playing Proposals and Acceptances. If the eldest hand has proposed, and his partner sits next him on the left, the commanding trumps should be first led, in order to secure as many rounds as possible. If the eldest hand has no high-card combination in trumps, it is sometimes better to lead a small card from a weak suit, hoping to put the partner in. If successful, the partner will first show his suit, and then lead trumps through the adversaries. If the acceptor sits on the right of the proposing eldest hand, trumps should be led immediately, and the highest of them first, no matter what they are. The Q or J at the head of five trumps may be of great use to a partner with an honour. When the eldest hand has proposed, and his partner sits opposite him, trumps should be led at once, and all combinations played as at Whist.

The foregoing principles equally apply when the eldest hand has accepted a proposal, if the player can be depended on to have proposed on general strength.

When partners sit opposite each other, the general principles of leading, establishing, defending, and bringing in suits, are the same as at Whist, and the usual trump signals and echoes are made use of. The game is practically Whist, with the additional knowledge that both proposer and acceptor have strong hands.

When partners sit next each other, there are many opportunities for leading strengthening cards through the adversaries, especially in the partner's known or inferred strong suit.

Finesse. If neither proposer nor acceptor is the eldest hand, they should make no finesses; but get into the lead as soon as possible, and exhaust the trumps. The greatest danger of defeat for a proposal and acceptance is that the adversaries, with the original lead, may establish a cross-ruff, or get six tricks with their winning cards before the calling players get a lead.

It is a common artifice for the proposer and acceptor, after they have exhausted the adversaries' trumps, each to show a strong suit by leading it once, and then to lead the highest card of a weaker suit; thus offering each other chances for successful finesse.

If a partner sitting on the right leads a suit, there should be no finesse; and, in general, finessing should be avoided until the declaration is assured. It may then be used to secure probable over-tricks.

Adversaries' Play. The players opposed to the call are always designated as the adversaries.

Players opposed to a proposer and acceptor should make no finesses that they are not certain will win more tricks if successful than they will lose if they fail. If the adversaries sit together, and are the last to play on any trick, the third hand should not trust anything to his partner that he can attend to himself, unless he is very anxious to be the last player on the next trick.

When the adversaries sit opposite each other, their play will differ very little from that in Whist, except that they will make no efforts to establish long suits, and will not lead small cards from combinations containing an Ace. Every trick possible should be made sure of at once, before the calling players get any chance to discard. Weak suits should be protected, as they are in Whist when opposed to strong hands.

If an adversary has the first lead, it is usually best for him to make what winning cards he has at once, unless he is pretty sure that the proposal will be defeated.

It is very seldom right for the adversaries to lead trumps. Some exceptions will naturally present themselves, such as an eldest hand leading to his partner's turned-up King. In the middle or end game, it may be advantageous to bring down the caller's trumps together, or to draw two for one.

If an adversary finds himself with a pretty strong hand, he should utterly disregard his partner, and play as false as he can; for if the callers have eight probable tricks between them, it is impossible for the fourth player to have anything, unless there has been some mistake in the call.

In General. There are one or two exceptions to the methods of playing sequences at Whist, dependent on the position of the players holding them. For instance : If first or second hand holds any sequence of high cards, he should play the highest if his partner sits next him on the left, and the adversaries are to play after him; otherwise the partner might think the higher cards of the sequence were against the leader. If a caller should hold K Q x second hand, and play the Q as at Whist, his partner following him, and holding Ace, would have to play it, thinking the King might be beyond.

SOLO. In speaking of the players in a solo, misère, or abundance, it is usual to distinguish those opposed to the single player by calling them respectively, Left, Right, and Opposite.

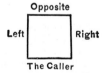

This arrangement does not affect the use of the letters A Y B Z, and the terms first, second, third, and fourth hand ; indicating the position of the deal, and of the lead.

Calling. Those solos are easiest which are declared by the eldest hand, or by the dealer; the hardest being those called by second hand. The safest solos are those called on trump strength ;

but average trumps and winning cards in the plain suits are more advantageous if the caller is not eldest hand. To call a solo on plain suits alone, with only one or two trumps, is extremely dangerous; and a solo called on a single suit must have at least five or six good trumps in order to succeed.

PLAYING. When a call has been made entirely upon trump strength, it is much better to make tricks by ruffing, than by leading trumps. There is little use for a solo player to hold a tenace in trumps, hoping it will be led to him. If he has good suits, he should make sure of two rounds of trumps by leading the Ace.

When the solo player is depending on the plain suits for tricks, and has one long suit, he should make what winning cards he has in the other plain suits in preference to leading trumps, for his only danger is that his long suit will be led often enough to give his adversaries discards in the other suits.

If a proposal was made before the solo was called, it is better for the solo player to sit on the left of the player that proposed.

The caller should never play single honours second hand, unless he has only one small card of the suit, or the honour is the Ace.

With A Q x, second or third hand, the Q must be finessed if the caller has counted on both A and Q for tricks. If he can probably win without the finesse, he should play Ace. If he has tricks enough to win without either A or Q, he should play neither of them.

A solo player should be very sure of his call before finessing for over-tricks.

Adversaries' Play. The player to the left of the caller should not lead trumps; but if the solo player has had a lead, and has not led trumps himself, the player on his right should take the first opportunity to lead them through him.

The player to the left of the caller should not lead from suits headed only by the King; nor from those containing major or minor tenaces. The best leads are from suits headed by Q J or 10, even if short.

With such high-card combinations as can be used to force the command in one round, such as K Q, or K Q J, the regular whist leads should be used. With suits headed by winning sequences, held by the player on the left, it is often right to lead them once, in order to show them, and then to lead a weaker suit to get rid of the lead. It is sometimes better to play winning sequences as long as it seems probable that the caller can follow suit.

Many persons use the Albany lead to indicate a wish for trumps to be led through the caller. In response to such a signal the best trump should be led, whatever it is.

When the adversary who leads in any trick is not on the left of the solo player, the caller will, of course, not be the last player, as at least one adversary must play after him. In such cases it is best to lead the longest suits.

MISÈRE. The great difficulty in Misère is not in playing it ; but in judging what hands justify such an undertaking.

Calling. As a general proposition it may be stated that misère should not be called with a long suit not containing the deuce. But the longer the suit the less the danger there is for a player who is determined to risk it ; because the deuce is more likely to be found alone in some adversary's hand. Short suits may be risked, even with no card smaller than a 5 or 6, and it is of course a great advantage to have a suit altogether missing.

Leading. The lead is a disadvantage to the caller, because he must begin with a small card, and the adversaries can play their highest. The only satisfaction to the caller is that he can usually locate the high cards of the suit under such circumstances. For instance : Suppose he originally leads a 4 ; second hand playing the 9; third hand the Ace ; and fourth hand the 10. The third hand is marked with whatever cards of the sequence K Q J are not in the caller's hand.

Many players fall into the error of leading the highest card of a losing sequence, such as a 6 from 6 5 4 3. This accomplishes nothing, and only discloses to the adversaries the fact that the caller is safe in that suit. The three is the better lead.

Following Suit. The caller should usually play a card as little inferior as he can to the highest already on the trick. When he has cards of equal value, such as the 5 and 2, the 3 and 4 being already on the table, he should play the lower card of the four-chette ; for although it may be said that the fourth player must take the trick, there is no certainty that he will follow suit.

When second hand, if there is a choice between two cards, such as the 6 and 2, an intermediate card having been led, it is often a nice point to decide whether or not to risk covering, and keeping the deuce. If the deuce is played, it must be remembered that the adversaries will follow with their highest cards, leaving two cards out against the caller, both smaller than the 6.

Discarding. The misère player should never discard from his long suits. The high cards of short suits, and single intermediate cards, such as 5's and 6's, should be got rid of at every opportunity.

Adversaries of the Misère. In playing against a misère the chief difficulty is to prevent the caller from discarding, and to place the lead with the player who can probably do him the most harm.

It is an axiom with solo-whist players that every misère can be defeated, if the weak spot in it can be found ; because if the misère was absolutely safe, it would be played as a spread, which would pay the caller twice as much. This is not true, however, for it often happens that the cards are so distributed in the other hands that the call cannot be defeated, however risky it may have been.

The weak point in a misère is usually a short suit with one high card in it ; or a suit of intermediate length, without the deuce.

As it is probable that the caller is short in suits in which the adversaries are long, and long in those in which they are short, he is less likely to get a discard if they lead their shortest suits first. If the misère player has overcalled a proposal or a solo, he is likely to be short in the trump suit, or at least safe in it. It is not good play to lead a single Ace ; but a King may be very effective ; for if no one plays the Ace on it, that card may be absolutely marked in the caller's hand. In such a case the adversary with the greatest number of that suit should keep it for the attack. If this player can get into the lead, he is not only sure of preventing the caller from discarding, but of allowing the other adversaries to discard to advantage.

With an honour and one small card, a player on the left should lead the small card first ; if on the right, the honour should be led first. A long suit containing the deuce should be avoided as long as possible.

The caller's cards may sometimes be inferred if there has been a previous call on the hand. For instance : A misère may be a forced call ; that is, the player first called a proposal, and not being accepted, was forced to amend his call, choosing misère in preference to solo. This would indicate a long weak suit of trumps. If the dealer calls misère, the turn-up trump should be carefully noted.

It is useless to persevere in suits in which the caller is evidently safe. If he plays a very low card to a trick in which there is already a high card, that suit should be stopped.

Discarding. An adversary should get rid of some one suit, if possible ; for when that suit is afterwards led he will have free choice of his discards in the other suits. Short suits should be discarded in preference to high cards in long suits, unless the cards in the short suit are very low. Discards give great information to the adversaries if the rule is followed to discard the highest of a suit ; because all cards higher than those discarded must be between the two other adversaries and the caller, and each adversary is thus furnished with a guide. It is useless to discard a suit of which the caller is void ; and it is best to keep discarding from one suit until it is exhausted, or only the deuce remains. The trump signal is frequently used in discarding to indicate that the signaller wishes to get into the lead.

Returning Suits. Whether or not to return a partner's lead may often be decided by inferences from the fall of the cards. It is frequently an easy matter to locate the cards in the various suits, if it is borne in mind that adversaries who play after the caller get rid of their highest cards. For instance: Right leads the 9; caller plays the 5; left the 10; and the last player finds he holds K Q J 6 of the suit. He should know that the caller has nothing between the 5 and the 9, and must have the Ace; so his cards were probably A 5 4 3 2. While it is manifestly impossible to catch him on that suit, it may still be led three times, in order to give the partners discards, as both of them must be short. If this estimate of the caller's cards is wrong in anything, it is not with regard to the Ace, so there is not the slightest danger in continuing the suit.

As a general rule, the suit first led by an adversary should be returned, unless the player winning the trick has a singleton in another suit, when he should lead that.

The suit led by the caller, if he was eldest hand, should not be returned.

Some judgment of character must be used in playing on a caller's own lead. An adventurous player will sometimes call a misère on a hand which contains a singleton 5 or 6, and will lead it at once; trusting that second hand will imagine it to be safe, and cover it. Players should be aware of this trap, and never cover a misère player's own lead if they can help it, unless the card led is below a 4.

ABUNDANCE. Very few persons will risk calling an abundance which they are not pretty certain of; but a player may be forced to the call on a doubtful hand, especially if he is overcalled on his original proposal to play a solo. The lead is a great advantage, because trumps can be exhausted immediately, and the suits protected. If the caller has not the lead he must calculate in advance for trumping in, and if his plain suits are not quite established, he will require more trumps than would otherwise be necessary. The greatest danger to an abundance player who has not the original lead, is that his best suit will be led through him, and trumped, either on the first or second round. The caller is often trapped into unnecessarily high trumping when suits are led through him a second or third time.

The Adversaries have little chance to defeat an abundance unless they can over-trump the caller, or ruff his good cards before he can exhaust the trumps. It is best for the Right to lead his longest suit, and for the Left to lead his shortest. A guarded King suit should not be led under any circumstances; nor a short suit Ace high. If an adversary has a single trump of medium size, such as a J or 10, it is often good play to trump a partner's winning cards, so as to be sure of preventing the caller from making a small trump. If an adversary has trumped or over-trumped, it is very important to lead that suit to him again as soon as possible.

The rules for discarding that are given in connection with Whist should be carefully observed ; especially in the matter of showing command of suits.

SPREADS. These should not be called except with hands in which every suit contains the deuce, and all the cards are low enough to insure the player that nothing short of extraordinary circumstances will defeat him. Open sequences, or Dutch straights, as they are sometimes called, in which the cards are all odd or all even, such as 2 4 6 8 10, are quite as safe as ordinary sequences, provided the deuce is among the cards.

The player calling a spread must remember that it will be impossible for him to get any discards after the first trick without the consent of the adversaries ; for they will not lead a suit of which they see he is void. In order to reduce the caller's chances of a discard on the opening lead, before his cards are exposed, the adversaries should select their shortest suits, unless they have a bottom sequence to the deuce.

THE SLAM. This feature of Solo Whist is even rarer than the *grand coup* at Whist. It is not very marvellous for an abundance player to make twelve or thirteen tricks; but to announce thirteen tricks before a card is played is something phenomenal. All the adversaries can do against such a call is to show each other, by their discards, in which of the suits they have a possible trick. It is very annoying to have a player succeed in making a slam just because two of his adversaries keep the same suit.

SOLO WHIST FOR THREE PLAYERS.

The best arrangement for this form of the game is to play with a pack of forty cards, deleting the 2 3 and 4 of each suit. The last card is turned up to determine the trump, but it is not used in play.

There is no proposal and acceptance ; solo being the lowest call. If all three players pass, the trump card is turned down, and each player in turn has the option of calling a six-trick abundance, naming his own trump suit. In some places it is the custom to allow the players to overcall each other, after the trump is turned down, each increasing the number of tricks he proposes to take. For instance : Z deals ; all pass, and Z turns down the trump. A calls six tricks ; Y passes ; B calls seven ; and Z eight. If neither A nor Y will bid nine, Z names the trump suit, and A leads. A misère overcalls eight tricks

TEXT BOOKS.

Solo Whist, by R. F. Green.
How to Play Solo Whist, by Wilks & Pardon.

For the Laws of Solo Whist, see Whist Family Laws.

ILLUSTRATIVE SOLO WHIST HANDS.

The dealer, Z, turns up the heart 3 in both hands, and A leads. The underlined card wins the trick, and the card under it is the next one led.

A Solo.				TRICK	A Misère.			
A	Y	B	Z		A	Y	B	Z
10◊	8◊	Q◊	**K◊**	1	**K♠**	7♠	J♠	10♠
3◊	9◊	**A◊**	2◊	2	**Q♠**	5♠	9♠	8♠
♡6	♡2	**♡A**	♡3	3	Q◊	5◊	**A◊**	J◊
♣8	♡4	♡Q	**♡K**	4	9◊	4◊	**K◊**	10◊
♣9	**♣A**	♣4	♣7	5	♡6	3♠	**6♠**	8◊
A♠	9♠	K♠	4♠	6	♡7	2♠	**4♠**	♣A
♣K	♣2	♣6	♣5	7	♣10	♣8	♣7	**♣K**
7♠	2♠	**Q♠**	6♠	8	♣9	♣6	7◊	**♣Q**
5◊	♣3	♣Q	**♡8**	9	♣5	♣4	6◊	**♣J**
6◊	3♠	**♡5**	J◊	10	♡8	♣2	♡K	**♣3**
7◊	♡10	♡9	**♡J**	11	**♡A**	♡2	♡Q	♡3
8♠	5♠	**♡7**	4◊	12	2◊	**3◊**	♡9	♡4
J♠	♣J	♣10	10♠	13	♡J	**A♠**	♡10	♡5

Solo player wins.   *Misère player loses.*

In the first example, A and Y pass, and B calls Solo. A follows the modern practice of leading the top of his long weak suit, as a card of warning and support for his partners. Z knows Y must have 9 or Ace of diamonds, or no more, and he avoids the error of opening another suit, especially a weak one. B continues with the trump Queen, hoping to drop King and Jack together. At trick 5, Z cannot give up the command of trumps, and as A's lead and discard indicate that he wants spades led up to him, Z's best chance is that Y has some clubs. Y leads to A. At trick 9, Z knows B cannot have 10 and 9 of trumps, or he would have led one of them to prevent the J and 8 both making, so Y must have one of those trumps. At trick 11, if B leads the club, he loses his call. He must again take the chance of bringing the trumps down together.

In the second example A proposes, or calls Solo, and Y over-calls him with Misère. The great point in playing against Misère is to continue leading suits in which he is known to be long, so as to give your partners discards. This B does with the two long spades, the caller being marked with the ace and others on the second trick. Then Z allows B to discard his high diamonds on the clubs.

SCOTCH WHIST,

OR CATCH THE TEN.

CARDS. Scotch Whist is played with a pack of 36 cards, which rank in plain suits, A K Q J 10 9 8 7 6; the Ace being highest both in play and in cutting. In the trump suit the Jack is the best card, the order being, J A K Q 10 9 8 7 6.

MARKERS. There are no suitable counters for Scotch Whist, and the score is usually kept on a sheet of paper.

PLAYERS. Any number from two to eight may play. When there are five or seven players, the spade 6 must be removed from the pack. In some places this is not done; the thirty-fifth card being turned up for the trump, the thirty-sixth shown to the table, and then laid aside.

CUTTING. Whatever the number of persons offering for play, the table is formed by cutting from the outspread pack for partners, seats, and deal.

When two play, the one cutting the lowest card has the choice of seats and cards, (if there are two packs).

When three play, the lowest deals, and chooses his seat and cards. The next lowest has the next choice of seats.

When four play, partners are cut for; the two lowest pairing against the two highest; the lowest of the four is the dealer, and has the choice of seats and cards.

When five play, each for himself, the lowest cut deals, and has the first choice of seats and cards. The next lowest has the next choice of seats, and so on.

When six play, they cut for partners, the two lowest pairing together; the two highest together; and the two intermediates together. The player cutting the lowest card of the six has the choice of seats and cards, and deals the first hand. If the six play, three on a side, the three lowest play against the three highest; the lowest cut of the six taking the deal, and choice of seats and cards.

When seven play, each for himself, the lowest deals, and has the choice of seats and cards; the others choosing their seats in the order of their cuts.

When eight play, they may form two sets of four each, or four sets of two each. In either case the partnerships are decided by cutting, and the lowest cut of the eight has the deal, with choice of seats and cards.

TIES are decided in the manner already described in connection with Whist.

POSITION OF THE PLAYERS. Two players sit opposite each other. Three, five or seven sit according to their choice. Four sit as at Whist, the partners facing each other. Six, playing in two partnerships, sit alternately, so that no two partners shall be next each other. Six, playing in three partnerships of two each, sit so that two adversaries shall be between each pair of partners. Eight, playing in two sets of four each, or as four pairs of partners, arrange themselves alternately. If we distinguish the partners by the letters A, B, C, D, the diagram will show the arrangement of the tables.

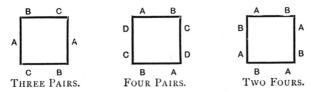

| THREE PAIRS. | FOUR PAIRS. | TWO FOURS. |

The player to the left of the dealer is the original leader.

DEALING. The method of dealing varies with the number of players engaged. When only one pack is used, any player may shuffle, the dealer last. The pack must be presented to the pone to be cut, and the entire pack is then dealt out, one card at a time.

When two play, the dealer gives each six cards, one at a time. These two hands are kept separate, and two more are dealt in the same manner, and then a third two, the last card being turned up for the trump. When the deal is complete, there will be six hands on the table, three belonging to each player.

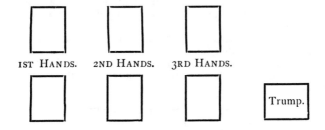

ist HANDS.   2ND HANDS.   3RD HANDS.

Trump.

When three play, the cards are dealt in much the same manner; two separate hands of six cards being given to each player.

When four, five, six, seven, or eight play, the cards are dealt in rotation from left to right until the pack is exhausted, the last card being turned up for the trump. When five or seven play, either the spade 6 must be thrown out of the pack, or the thirty-sixth card must be shown, after the dealer has turned the thirty-fifth for the trump. When eight play, all four sixes are deleted.

The deal passes to the left, each player dealing in turn until the game is finished.

The general rules with regard to irregularities in the deal are the same as at Whist.

STAKES. When stakes are played for, they are for so much a game. Rubbers are not played. It is usual to form a pool, each player depositing the stake agreed upon, and the winner taking all. In partnership games, each losing player pays the successful adversary who sits to his right. If three pairs were engaged, and A-A won, C and B would each pay the A sitting next him. Before play begins, it should be understood who pays for revokes ; the side or the player.

METHOD OF PLAYING. The player on the dealer's left begins by leading any card he chooses, and the others must all follow suit if they can. Failure to follow suit when able is a revoke, the penalty for which, if detected and claimed by the adversaries, is the immediate loss of the game. When there are more than two players or two sets of partners, the revoking player or side must pay the two or more adversaries as if each had won the game. In some places the individual is made to pay, not the side. This should be understood before play begins. If seven are playing, and one is detected in a revoke, his loss is equal to six games. Any player having none of the suit led may either trump or discard. The dealer should take up the trump card when it is his turn to play to his first trick ; after which it must not be named, although a player may be informed what the trump suit is. If all follow suit, the highest card played of the suit led wins the trick, trumps win all other suits. The winner of the trick may lead any card he chooses for the next ; and so on, until all the cards have been played.

It is not necessary to keep the tricks separate, as at Whist ; but one player should gather for his side.

When two or three play, the hands must be played in the order in which they were dealt. For instance : If these are the hands :—

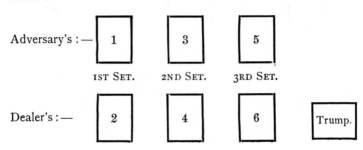

Adversary's :— 1   3   5

1ST SET.   2ND SET.   3RD SET.

Dealer's :— 2   4   6   Trump.

The players first take up hands Nos. 1 and 2 ; a card is led from No. 1, the dealer follows suit from No. 2, or trumps, or discards, and the play continues until these two hands are exhausted. The second set are then taken up and played in the same manner ; the player who won the last trick in one set having the first lead in the next. Finally, the third set are played in tne same manner ; all the cards taken by each side being gathered into one pile by the player who has won them. The trump card must remain on the table until the dealer takes up the last hand. When three play, the set of hands first dealt must be first played, and then the second set taken up.

The rules for cards played in error, leading out of turn, etc., are the same as at Whist.

OBJECTS OF THE GAME. The side first scoring 41 points wins the game ; and the chief object is to secure tricks containing cards to which a certain value is attached. These all belong to the trump suit, and are the following :—

The Jack of trumps counts...... 11
The Ace of trumps counts...... 4
The King of trumps counts...... 3
The Queen of trumps counts.... 2
The Ten of trumps counts...... 10

The other trumps, and the plain suit-cards, have no counting value.

The Jack of trumps, being the best, must be taken in by the player to whom it is dealt ; but any court card in trumps will win the Ten, so that one of the principal objects in Scotch Whist is to *catch the ten.*

At the end of each hand the players count the number of cards they have taken in tricks, and they are entitled to score one point for each above the number originally dealt to them. For instance : If four play, nine cards were originally dealt to each, so each pair of partners held eighteen. If at the end of the hand they have taken in eight tricks, or thirty-two cards, they score 14 points toward game, in addition to any score they may have made by winning honours in trumps, or catching the Ten. If five play, beginning with seven cards each, and at the end of the hand one player has taken in fifteen, and another ten ; they score 8 and 3 respectively, for cards.

SCORING. At the end of each hand, each player or side should claim all honours won, and cards taken in. One player should keep the score, and announce it distinctly, in order that it may be known how many points each player or side requires to win the game.

In the case of ties, the Ten counts out first ; then cards ; then A K Q of trumps in their order, and the Jack last A revoke, if detected and claimed before the cards are cut for the next deal, immediately ends the game.

METHODS OF CHEATING. When only one pack is used, the greek can often succeed in dealing himself the Jack of trumps, and usually loses no time in marking the Ten, so that he can at least distinguish the player to whom it is dealt. A player should be carefully watched who keeps his eyes on the pack while shuffling, or who rivets his attention on the backs of the cards as he deals. Two packs should be used in all round games of cards.

SUGGESTIONS FOR GOOD PLAY. The chief counting elements that are affected by the play being the trump Ten and the cards, it is usual to devote particular attention to winning them. With J A of trumps, or A K, it is best to lead two rounds immediately; but with a tenace, such as J K, or A Q it is better to place the lead on your left if possible. The high cards in the plain suits are capable of being very skilfully managed in this matter of placing the lead. It sometimes happens that a player with the Ten may be fourth hand on a suit of which he has none; or he may catch the Ten with a small honour if it is used in trumping in. The partnership games offer many fine opportunities for playing the Ten into the partner's hand, especially when it is probable that he has the best trump, or a better trump than the player on the left.

In calculating the probabilities of saving the Ten by trumping in, it must be remembered that the greater the number of players, the less chance there is that a suit will go round more than once, because there are only nine cards of each suit in play.

Many players, in their anxiety to catch the Ten, overlook the possibilities of their hands in making cards, the count for which often runs into high figures.

Close attention should be paid to the score. For instance: A wants 4 points to win; B wants 10; and C wants 16. If A can see his way to win the game by cards or small honours, he should take the first opportunity of giving C the Ten; or allowing him to make it in preference to B. As the Ten counts first, cards and honours next, B may be shut out, even if he has the Jack.

LAWS. There are no special laws for Scotch Whist. The whist laws are usually enforced for all such irregularities as exposed cards, leading out of turn, etc. The most important matter is the revoke, and it should be clearly understood before play begins whether the revoke penalty is to be paid by the individual in fault, or by the side to which he belongs. Some players think there should be some regulation for penalties in such cases as that of a player taking up the wrong hand, when two or more are dealt to each player; but as no advantage can be gained by the exchange. it is hard to see what right the adversary would have to impose a penalty.

ILLUSTRATIVE SCOTCH WHIST HAND.

We give a simple example hand, as an illustration of the manner of playing with four persons; two being partners against the other two.

Z deals and turns heart 8.

	A	Y	B	Z
1	Q ◊	K ◊	8 ◊	9 ◊
2	♣ A	♣ K	♣ J	♣ 8
3	♣ 7	♣ 9	♣ 6	6 ♠
4	8 ♠	J ♠	K ♠	A ♠
5	J ◊	9 ♠	A ◊	Q ♠
6	7 ◊	10 ♠	♣ Q	7 ♠
7	♡ A	10 ◊	6 ◊	♡ Q
8	♡ 9	♡ 6	♡ K	♡ 7
9	♣ 10	♡ 10	♡ J	♡ 8

A-B win 30 *by honours.*

Y-Z win 2 *by cards.*

Trick 1. *Y* plays King second hand, hoping it will be taken by the Ace, so that he may become third or fourth player, and perhaps save his Ten. *B,* with the major tenace in trumps, plays to avoid the lead as long as possible.

Trick 2. *Y* gets rid of another winning card; *B* keeping a small card to avoid the lead.

Trick 3. *A* returns the Club, reading *B* for the Q or no more. *B* still avoids the lead, and *Z* is marked as not having the trump Ten, or he would have saved it.

Trick 4. *Z* plays to win what cards he can.

Trick 5. *B* throws ◊A to avoid the lead, knowing *Y* has the trump Ten; for *A* would have made it on the second round of Spades. *A* also marks it with *Y,* as *B* does not save it.

Trick 6. *B* is not sure whether *Y* has a Diamond or a Club left, and discards the winning card.

Trick 7. *Z* plays Queen to shut out the Ten, if with *A.* *A* knows each player has two trumps left, and that as the turn-up is still with *Z, B* must have J or K; for if he held only 7 and 6 he would have trumped in to make cards.

Trick 8. *A* leads trumps. If *Y* does not play the Ten, and *B* has not the Jack, *B* must make four cards and the King by passing. If *B* has the Jack, he must catch the Ten, no matter how *Y* and *Z* play.

FRENCH WHIST is the name given to a variety of Scotch Whist in which the Ten of Diamonds counts ten to those winning it, whether it is a trump or not.

BOSTON.

CARDS. Boston is played with two packs of fifty-two cards each, Which rank as at Whist, both for cutting and playing.

MARKERS are not used in Boston, every hand being immediately settled for in counters. These are usually of three colours ; white, red, and blue ; representing cents, dimes, and dollars respectively. At the beginning of the game each player should be provided with an equal number, the general proportion being 20 white, 18 red, and 8 blue for each. Some one player should be selected to act as the banker, selling and redeeming all counters.

STAKES. The stakes in Boston depend upon the value of the counters. One cent for a white counter is considered a pretty stiff game ; because it is quite possible for a single player to win or lose a thousand white counters on one hand, and the payments very seldom fall short of fifty.

THE POOL. In addition to the counters won and lost on each hand, it is usual for the players to make up a pool at the beginning of the game by each of them depositing one red counter in a small tray provided for the purpose. This pool may be increased from time to time by penalties ; such as one red counter for a misdeal ; four for a revoke, or for not having the proper number of cards, etc. The whole amount in the pool may be won or lost by the players, according to their success or failure in certain undertakings, which will presently be described. When empty, the pool is replenished by contributions from each player, as at first.

The pool proper is usually limited to 25 red counters. When it exceeds that amount, the 25 are set aside, and the surplus used to start a fresh pool. Any player winning a pool is entitled to 25 red counters at the most. It will often happen that several such pools will accumulate, and each must be played for in its turn. At the end of the game any counters remaining in the pool or pools must be divided among the players.

PLAYERS. Boston is played by four persons. If more than four candidates offer for play, five or six may form a table ; if there are more than six, the selection of the table must be made by cutting, as at Whist.

CUTTING. The four persons who shall play the first game are determined by cutting, and they again cut for the deal, with the choice of seats and cards. The player drawing the lowest card deals, and chooses his seat ; the next lower card sits on his left, and so on, until all are seated. Twelve deals is a game, at the end of which the players cut to decide which shall go out, as at Whist.

It is usual to count the deals by opening the blade of a pocket-knife, which is placed on the table by the player on the dealer's right. When it comes to his turn to deal, he partly opens one blade. When he deals again he opens it entirely, and the third time he closes it ; that being the third round, and the last deal of the game.

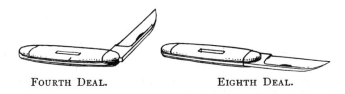

FOURTH DEAL. EIGHTH DEAL.

POSITION OF THE PLAYERS. The four players at Boston are distinguished by the letters A Y B Z.

Z is the dealer, and A is known as the *eldest hand.* There are no partnerships in Boston, except that of three players combined against the fourth, who is always spoken of as *the caller.* The players having once taken their seats are not allowed to change them without the consent of all the others at the table.

DEALING. At the beginning of the game the two packs are thoroughly shuffled ; after which they must not again be shuffled during the progress of the game. If a hand is dealt and not played, each player must sort his cards into suits and sequences before they are gathered and dealt again.

At the beginning of each deal, one pack is presented to the players to be cut ; each having the privilege of cutting once, the dealer last. Beginning on his left, the dealer gives four cards to each player, then four more, and finally five ; no trump being turned.

The general rules with regard to irregularities in the deal are the same as at Whist, except that a misdeal does not lose the deal. The misdealer must deal again with the same pack, after the players have sorted their cards into suits. It is a misdeal if the dealer fails to present the pack to the other players to cut, or neglects to cut it himself.   Should the dealer expose any of his own cards in dealing, that does not invalidate the deal.   The deal passes in regular rotation to the left, each pack being used alternately.

MAKING THE TRUMP.   The deal being complete, the player opposite the dealer cuts the still pack, and the player on his right turns up the top card for the trump.   The suit to which this card belongs is called *First Preference,* and the suit of the same colour is called *Second Preference,* or *Colour.*   The two remaining suits are known as *Plain Suits* for that deal.

The cards having been dealt, and the trump turned, each player carefully sorts and counts his cards, to see that he has the correct number, thirteen.   A player having more or less than his right proportion should at once claim a misdeal; for if he plays with a defective hand he cannot win anything that deal, but must stand his proportion of all losses incurred, besides paying a forfeit of four red counters to the pool.

OBJECTS OF THE GAME.   In Boston, each player has an opportunity to announce that he is willing to undertake to win a certain number of tricks, if allowed the privilege of naming the trump suit; or to lose a certain number, there being no trumps. In either case, he proposes to play single-handed against the three other players.   The player proposing the undertaking which is most difficult of accomplishment is said to *overcall* the others, and must be allowed to try.   If he is successful, he wins the pool, and is paid a certain number of counters by each of his adversaries.   If he fails, he must double the amount in the pool, and pay to each of the other players a certain number of counters.

ANNOUNCEMENTS.   The bids rank in the following order, beginning with the lowest.   The full-faced type shows the words used by the players in calling their bids :—

To win five tricks ;   *Boston.*

To win *Six Tricks.*

To win *Seven Tricks.*

To lose twelve tricks, after having discarded a card which is not to be shown ;   *Little Misère.*

To win *Eight Tricks.*

To win *Nine Tricks.*

To lose every trick ;   *Grand Misère.*

To win *Ten Tricks.*

To win *Eleven Tricks.*

To lose twelve tricks, after having discarded a card which is not to be shown ; the single player's remaining twelve cards being exposed face up on the table, but not liable to be called ;   *Little Spread.*

To win *Twelve Tricks.*

To lose every trick ; the single player's cards exposed on the table, but not liable to be called ; *Grand Spread.*

To win Thirteen Tricks ; *Grand Slam.*

The object of the proposing player, if successful in his bid, is to win or lose the proposed number of tricks ; while that of his three adversaries is to combine to prevent him from so doing. There are no honours, and the only factor in the count is the number of tricks taken. The highest card played of the suit led wins the trick ; and trumps, if any, win against all other suits.

METHOD OF BIDDING. The eldest hand has the first say, and after examining his cards, and estimating the number of tricks he can probably take, making the trump to suit his hand, he bids accordingly. It is not necessary for him to state which suit he wishes to make the trump ; but only the number of tricks he proposes to win. If he has no proposal to make, he says distinctly ; *" I pass,"* and the other players in turn have an opportunity to bid. If any player makes a bid, such as six tricks, and any other player thinks he can make the same number of tricks with a trump of the same colour as the turn-up, that is, Second Preference, he overcalls the first bidder by saying *" I keep ; "* or he may repeat the number bid, saying *" Six here."* This is simply bidding to win the number of tricks *in colour.* The original caller may hold his bid, or a third player may overbid both, by saying ; *" I keep over you,"* or *" Six here."* This means that he will undertake to win the number of tricks already bid, with the *turn-up* suit for trumps. In order to overcall such a bid as this, any other player would have to announce a greater number of tricks. For instance ; Z deals, and turns a heart. A calls six tricks, intending to name hearts trumps ; but not saying so. B passes ; Y says " I Keep." This announces to the table that Y will play with a red trump, and A knows he is bidding on diamonds. Z passes, and A says ; " I keep over you." B then bids seven tricks, and if A will not risk seven tricks in hearts, B will be the successful bidder. If A should bid seven tricks by keeping over B, the latter must know that it is useless for him to bid again unless he can make more tricks in diamonds than A can in hearts ; for A's bid, being in first preference, will always outrank B's for the same number of tricks.

A player once having passed cannot come into the bidding again, except to call one of the misères. In the example just given, either Y or Z, after having twice passed, might have outbid the seven tricks by calling a little misère. Such a bid can, of course, be entertained only when it outranks any bid already made.

A player is not compelled to bid the full value of his hand ; but it is to his interest to go as near to it as he can with safety ; because, as we shall see presently, the more he bids the more he is paid. For instance : If he can make ten tricks, but bids seven only, he will be paid for the three over-tricks, if he makes them; but the payment for seven bid and ten taken, is only 22 counters; while the payment for ten bid and ten taken is 42. As he receives from each adversary, a player who underbid his hand in this manner would lose 60 counters by his timidity.

It sometimes happens that no one will make a proposal of any sort. It is very unusual to pass the deal. The trump is generally turned down, and a *Grand* is played, without any trump suit. This is sometimes called a *Misère Partout*, or "all-round poverty"; and the object of each player is to take as few tricks as possible.

METHOD OF PLAYING. No matter who is the successful bidder, the eldest hand always leads for the first trick, and the others must follow suit if they can, the play proceeding exactly as at Whist. The tricks should be carefully stacked, so that they can be readily counted by any player without calling attention to them. The laws provide a severe penalty for drawing attention to the score in this manner. Suppose a player has called eight tricks. An adversary hesitates in his play, and another reaches over and counts the tricks in front of the caller, finding he has seven. This is tantamount to saying to the player who hesitates: "If you don't win that trick, the call succeeds." In such a case, the single player may at once demand the play of the highest or lowest of the suit; or that the adversaries trump or refrain from trumping the trick.

In all calls except misères and slams, the hands should be played out, in order to allow the players to make what over-tricks they can; but the moment a misère player takes a trick, or a slam player loses one, the hands are thrown up, and the stakes paid. It is usual to show the cards to the board, in order to satisfy each player that no revoke has occurred.

When Little Misère is called, each player discards one card, which must not be shown, and the hand is then played out with the remaining twelve cards.

When Spreads are called, the caller's cards must be placed face upwards on the table before a card is played. If it is a Little Spread, the discard of each player must remain unknown. The adversaries have no control of the manner of playing the exposed cards, which cannot be called, and may be played in any manner suited to the judgment of the single player, provided he follows suit when able.

REVOKES. If a player opposed to the caller revokes, but discovers his mistake in time to save himself, he may be called upon by the single player for his highest or lowest of the suit led; or the card played in error may be claimed as an exposed card. If the highest or lowest of the suit is called, the card played in error is taken up.

If the caller revokes, and discovers his mistake in time, he is not liable to any penalty, unless an adversary has played to the next trick. In that case the revoking card must be left on the table, and is liable to be called. When the single player revokes, he loses the call in any case, and at least one trick besides, He must also double the pool, and add to it a revoke forfeit of four red counters. For instance : A bids eight tricks, and his adversaries detect and claim a revoke. As he is supposed to have lost his bid, and one trick more, he may be said to have bid eight, and taken only seven ; losing 23 white counters to each of his adversaries, doubling the pool, and then paying a forfeit of four red counters. In some places the forfeit is omitted, and in others it takes the place of doubling the pool. It is not usual to play the hand out after a revoke is claimed and proved.

If an adversary of the single player revokes, he and his partners must each pay the caller just as if he had been successful, and must also pay him for three over-tricks as forfeit, provided his bid was not more than nine tricks ; for the bid and the over-tricks together must not exceed thirteen tricks. In addition to this, the individual player in fault must pay four red counters as forfeit to the pool. In some places he is made to double the pool ; but this is manifestly unfair, as he could not win the amount in the pool in any case, and therefore should not lose it.

In a Misère Partout, the revoking player pays five red counters to each adversary, and deposits a forfeit of four red counters in the pool. The hands are immediately thrown up if the revoke is claimed and proved.

CARDS PLAYED IN ERROR. The single player is not liable to any penalty for cards played in error, or led out of turn, except those taken back to save a revoke ; but his adversaries are liable to the usual whist penalties for all such irregularities. The single player can forbid the use of an exposed trump for ruffing, and can demand or prevent the play of an exposed card in plain suits, provided he does not ask the adversary to revoke. If a suit is led of which an adversary has an exposed card on the table, the single player may call upon him to play his highest or lowest of that suit.

If a player has announced Little Misère, and one of the adversaries leads before the others have discarded, the caller may immediately claim the pool and stakes. If any adversary of a misère player leads out of turn, or exposes a card, or plays before his proper turn in any trick, the bidder may at once claim the pool and stakes. In all such cases it is usual for the individual in fault to pay a forfeit of four red counters toward the next pool.

In Misère Partout, there is no penalty for cards played in error, or led out of turn.

PAYMENTS. If the caller succeeds in winning the proposed number of tricks, he is paid by each of his adversaries according to the value of his bid, and the number of over-tricks he wins, if any. The various payments are shown in this table :—

Number of tricks bid by player.	Number actually taken by him.								
	5	6	7	8	9	10	11	12	13
Five....................	12	12	13	13	14	14	14	15	15
Six.....................		15	16	16	17	18	19	20	20
Seven..................			18	20	21	22	23	24	26
Eight...................				23	24	26	28	29	31
Nine					32	34	36	39	41
Ten....................						42	45	48	52
Eleven.................							63	68	72
Twelve.................								106	114
Thirteen...............									166

The American system is not to pay the successful bidder for any over-tricks. This is to make him bid up his hand, and to save time ; as hands need not be played out when the bidder has made or can show the number of tricks bid.

Tricks bid	5	6	7	8	9	10	11	12	13
Amount.	10	15	20	25	35	45	65	105	170

If the caller fails in his undertaking, he must pay each adversary according to the number of tricks by which he failed to reach his bid. For instance : A player bidding eight, and taking only seven, is said to be "*put in for*" one trick, and he would have to pay each adversary 23 white counters. These payments are shown in this table :—

Tricks bid by the player.	Number of tricks by which the player falls short of his declaration.												
	1	2	3	4	5	6	7	8	9	10	11	12	13
Five.....	11	21	31	41	50								
Six......	15	24	35	45	55	66							
Seven...	19	29	40	50	60	72	82						
Eight....	23	34	46	56	67	78	89	110					
Nine.....	33	44	57	68	82	92	103	115	127				
Ten	44	56	70	82	94	107	119	132	145	157			
Eleven...	67	80	95	109	123	138	151	165	180	194	208		
Twelve ..	113	130	148	165	182	200	217	234	252	270	286	304	
Thirteen..	177	198	222	241	262	284	305	326	348	369	390	412	433

We give the same table reduced to the American decimal system, in which form it is commonly found in the clubs. It may be remarked in passing that the table is very illogical and inconsistent, the payments bearing no relation to the probabilities of the events. Some of them provide for impossibilities, unless the player has miscalled the trump suit, and is held to it, but we have no authority to change them.

Tricks bid.	Number of tricks bidder is "put in for."												
	1	2	3	4	5	6	7	8	9	10	11	12	13
Five.....	10	20	30	40	50								
Six......	15	25	35	45	55	65							
Seven....	20	30	40	50	60	70	80						
Eight....	25	35	45	55	70	85	100	115					
Nine.....	35	45	55	65	80	95	110	125	140				
Ten	45	55	70	80	95	110	125	140	155	170			
Eleven...	70	80	95	110	125	140	155	170	185	200	220		
Twelve ..	120	130	145	160	180	200	220	240	260	280	300	320	
Thirteen..	180	200	220	240	260	280	300	320	340	360	390	420	450

If a misère is bid, the caller wins from, or loses to each adversary according to the following table, there being no over-tricks:—

Little Misère,	20 white counters.
Grand Misère,	40 white counters.
Little Spread,	80 white counters.
Grand Spread,	160 white counters.

It may be observed that each of these is twice the amount of the next lower.

When misère partout is played, the person winning the largest number of tricks is the only loser, and he must pay each of the other players the difference between the number of his tricks and theirs in red counters. The number of red counters lost will always be found to be three times the number of tricks taken, minus the number of tricks not taken. For instance : A wins 4 tricks, three times which is 12 ; from which he deducts 9, the number he did not take, and finds his loss to be 3 red counters. Again ; A wins 7 tricks ; three times which is 21 ; minus 6 tricks not taken, a net loss of 15. No matter in what proportion the other tricks may be divided between the three other players, this total payment will always be found correct. For instance : A wins 6 tricks ; Y 2 ; B 5 ; and Z none. A loses 6 × 3 = 18 — 7 = 11, of which he gives 4 to Y ; 1 to B ; and 6 to Z.

If two players tie for the greatest number of tricks taken, they calculate their losses in the same manner ; but each pays only half the total. For instance : A and Y each take 5 tricks ; B taking 1, and Z 2. The 7 red counters lost by A and Y being divided, shows a loss of 35 white counters for each of them. If three players take four tricks apiece, they each pay the fourth man a red counter.

WINNING THE POOL. Besides the white counters won and lost by the players individually, the successful caller takes the pool, provided he has made a bid of seven tricks or better, which is called a ***pool bid.*** Any lower bid does not entitle him to the pool, unless the other players compel him to play the hand out. In order to save the pool, it is usual for the adversaries, before playing to the second trick, to say : *" I pay."* If all agree to pay, the bidder must accept the amount of his bid without any over-tricks, and the pool is not touched. If a player has made a pool bid, and the adversaries, before playing to the second trick, agree to pay, they cannot prevent the caller from taking the pool ; but they save possible over-tricks. The agreement of the adversaries to pay must be unanimous.

Misère Partout does not touch the pool.

If the hand is played out, and the caller fails, he must double the pool, whether he has made a pool bid or not. If there is more than one pool, he must double the first one, which will of course contain the limit. This will simply have the effect of forming an additional pool to be played for.

When there are several pools on the table, a successful caller takes any of those that contain the limit. When there is only one pool on the table, he must be satisfied with its contents, however small.

At the end of the game, after the twelfth hand has been settled for, it is usual to divide the pool or pools equally among the players. But sometimes a grand is played without trumps, making a thirteenth hand, and the pool is given to the player winning the last trick.

METHODS OF CHEATING. There being no shuffling at Boston, and each player having the right to cut the pack, the greek must be very skilful who can secure himself any advantage by having the last cut, unless he has the courage to use wedges. But Boston is usually played for such high stakes that it naturally attracts those possessing a high degree of skill, and the system adopted is usually that of counting down. The greek will watch for a hand in which there is little changing of suits, and will note the manner of taking up the cards. The next hand does not interest him, as he is busy studying the location of the cards in the still pack. When this comes into play on the next deal, he will follow every cut, and finally cut for himself so that the desired distribution of the suits shall come about. Even if he fails to secure an invincible hand for bidding on himself, he knows so nearly the contents of the other hands that he can bid them up, and afterwards play against them to great advantage.

It is unnecessary to say that if a greek can mark the cards, the game becomes a walkover, even if he can recollect only the hand on his left.

SUGGESTIONS FOR GOOD PLAY. Boston so closely resembles Solo Whist in such matters as bidding, and playing single-handed against three others, that the reader may be referred to that game for the outlines of the principles that should guide him in estimating the probable value of his hand, playing for tricks or for misères, and combining forces with his partners for the purpose of defeating the single player.

For laws, see Whist Family Laws.

BOSTON DE FONTAINBLEAU.

This game is sometimes, but incorrectly, called French Boston. The latter will be described in its proper place.

CARDS. Boston de Fontainbleau is played with a full pack of fifty-two cards. Two packs are generally used. The cards rank as at Whist, both for cutting and playing.

MARKERS are not used, counters taking their place. These are usually of the colours and values, and are distributed among the players as already described in Boston.

STAKES. As a guide in settling upon the unit value, it may be noted that the largest amount possible to win or lose on a single hand is 2,400 white counters; the smallest amount being 30. The average is about 300.

THE POOL. In addition to the counters won or lost on each hand, a pool is formed by each dealer in his turn placing five counters in a small tray provided for the purpose. This pool may be increased by penalties, etc., and the whole amount may be won under certain conditions, as at Boston. There is no limit to the amount of a single pool.

PLAYERS. The number of players, methods of *Cutting, Dealing,* etc., are the same as those already described in connection with Boston, except that no trump is turned for first preference, the suits always having a determined rank; diamonds being first, hearts next, then clubs, and last spades. No-trump, or "grand," outranks diamonds.

Twelve deals is a game; after which the players cut out if there are more than four belonging to the table, or if other candidates are waiting to play.

PENALTIES, for playing with more or less than the proper number of cards, etc., are the same as at Boston.

OBJECTS OF THE GAME. These are identical with Boston, but instead of doubling the pool, the player who is unsuccessful in his undertaking pays into the pool the same amount that he loses to each of the other players.

ANNOUNCEMENTS. The bids rank in the order following; beginning with the lowest. The full-faced type show the words used by the players in calling their bids. It will be noticed that the order is not the same as in Boston, and that an additional bid is introduced, called Piccolissimo.

To win 5 tricks, ***Boston.***

To win ***Six Tricks.***

To lose 12 tricks, after having discarded a card which is not to be shown ; ***Little Misère.***

To win ***Seven Tricks.***

To win one trick, neither more nor less, after having discarded a card which is not to be shown, there being no trump suit ; ***Piccolissimo.***

To win ***Eight Tricks.***

To lose every trick, no trump suit, ***Grand Misère.***

To win ***Nine Tricks.***

To lose 12 tricks, after having discarded a card which is not to be shown ; the single player's remaining twelve cards being exposed face up on the table, but not liable to be called ; ***Little Spread.***

To win ***Ten Tricks.***

To lose every trick, no trump suit, the single player's cards being exposed on the table, but not liable to be called ; ***Grand Spread.***

To win ***Eleven Tricks.***

To win ***Twelve Tricks.***

To win 13 tricks ; ***Slam.***

To win 13 tricks, the single player's cards exposed face up on the table, but not liable to be called ; ***Spread Slam.***

The object of the bidder, if successful in securing the privilege of playing, is to win or lose the proposed number of tricks, against the combined efforts of his adversaries. Having once made a bid, he must play it unless he is over-called.

METHOD OF BIDDING. The eldest hand has the first say, and after examining his hand, and deciding on the bid most appropriate to it, if any, he makes his announcement. If his proposal is to win a certain number of tricks with a certain suit for trumps, he must name the suit, saying, " Eight Spades," or " Seven Diamonds," as the case may be. If he proposes to play without any trump suit, he announces, " Seven Grand," or whatever the number may be. Such a bid overcalls one of the same number in diamonds. If the eldest hand has no proposal to make, he says, " I pass," and the others in turn have an opportunity to bid. The bids outrank one another according to their order in the foregoing table, and the rank of the suits in which they are made. The players bid against one another, until all but one declare to pass, he then becomes the single player against the three others.

A player having once passed cannot come into the bidding again, even to call a misère. In this respect the game differs from Boston. A player is not compelled to bid the full value of his hand, but it is to his interest to do so, and he should make the full announcement the first time he bids ; because if he has had a good hand for ten tricks, and begins with a bid of seven, he cannot increase his proposal unless some player bids over him.

PARTNERS. Before playing, the successful bidder may call for a partner if he chooses to do so. The player accepting him undertakes that the two together shall win three tricks more than the number bid. For instance : A has successfully bid seven in diamonds, and asks for a partner. If Y accepts him, they make no change in their positions at the table, but play into each other's hands, just as at Solo Whist, B and Z being partners against them. A and Y together must win ten tricks, with diamonds for trumps.

If no one makes a proposal of any sort, ***Misère Partout*** is played ; there being no trump suit. The player or players taking the least number of tricks win or divide the pool. There are no other losses or gains in Misère Partout.

HONOURS. In any call in which there is a trump suit, the A K Q and J of trumps are honours, and may be counted by the successful bidder if he carries out his proposal, If the single player, or a caller and his partner have all four honours dealt them, they score as for four over-tricks ; if three, as for two over-tricks. Honours do not count for the adversaries under any circumstances.

In bidding on a hand, it must be remembered that although honours will count as over-tricks in payments, they cannot be bid on. If a player has nine tricks and two by honours in his hand, he cannot bid eleven. If he bids nine and fails to make so many, he cannot count the honours at all. It is growing less and less the custom to count honours in America.

A player making a bid can be compelled to play it ; but it is usual to allow him to pay instead of playing, if he proposes to do so, either because he has overbid his hand or for any other reason.

METHOD OF PLAYING. No matter who is the successful bidder, the eldest hand always leads for the first trick, and the others must follow suit if they can, the play proceeding exactly as in Whist. Tricks should be carefully stacked, there being the same penalties as in Boston for calling attention to the score. The methods of playing misères and spreads have already been described in connection with Boston. When piccolissimo is played, the moment the single player takes more than one trick the hands are thrown up, and the stakes paid.

REVOKES. The rules governing these and cards played in error, are the same as at Boston. In piccolissimo, the penalties are the same as in misère.

PAYMENTS. If the caller succeeds in winning the proposed number of tricks, he is paid by each of his adversaries according to the value of his bid, as shown in Table No. 1. Overtricks, if any, and honours, if played, are always paid at the uniform rate of five white counters each. If the caller fails, he must pay each adversary the amount he would have won if successful, with the addition of five white counters for every trick that he falls short of his proposal. For instance : He bids nine hearts, and wins six tricks only. He must pay each adversary 115 white counters.

TABLE No. 1.

	No trump.	The trump being			Extra tricks.
		♣ ♠	♡	◇	
Boston, five tricks......	....	10	20	30	5
Six tricks..............	....	30	40	50	5
Little misère........	75				
Seven tricks............	....	50	60	70	5
Piccolissimo........	100				
Eight tricks...........	....	70	80	90	5
Grand misère......	150				
Nine tricks.............	....	90	100	110	5
Little spread.......	200				
Ten tricks.	....	110	120	130	5
Grand spread......	250				
Eleven tricks..........	....	130	140	150	5
Twelve tricks.........	....	150	160	170	5
Slam, thirteen tricks....	....	400	450	500	
Spread slam...........	....	600	700	800	

TABLE No. 2.

In America, the last two items are usually reduced, and are given as follows:—

		♠ ♣	♡	◊	
Slam, thirteen tricks....	....	250	300	350	
Spread slam..........	....	350	400	450	

Why a player should be paid more for spreads than for eleven or twelve tricks while the trick bid outranks the spreads, is difficult to understand; but we have no authority to change the tables.

Misère Partout wins nothing but the pool.

If partners play, it is usual for the losers to pay the adversaries on their right; or, if partners sit together, to pay the adversary sitting next.

THE POOL. Besides the white counters won and lost by the players individually, the successful player takes the pool. Successful partners divide it equally, regardless of the number of tricks bid or taken by each. If the partners fail, they must contribute to the pool an amount equal to that which they pay to one adversary. For instance: A calls seven diamonds, and asks for a partner. Y accepts him, and the pair win only nine tricks. Each pays 135 counters to the adversary sitting next him, and then they make up 135 more between them for the pool.

Asking for a partner is not a popular variation of the game, and is seldom resorted to unless the successful bid is very low, or has been made on a black suit.

If the adversaries of the caller declare to pay, before playing to the second trick, they can save nothing but possible overtricks The pool goes with every successful play.

If the single player is unsuccessful, he does not double the pool, as in Boston, but pays into it the same amount that he loses to each adversary, overtricks and all; so that he really loses four times the amount shown in the table.

At the end of the game, or on the twelfth hand, if the caller does not succeed, he pays the pool as usual, and his adversaries then divide it amongst themselves.

The **Suggestions for Good Play,** etc., are given in connection with Solo Whist and need no further amplification for Boston de Fontainbleau.

The **Laws** vary so little from those used in the regular game of Boston that it is not necessary to give an additional code, either for Fontainbleau or for French Boston, which follows.

FRENCH BOSTON.

CARDS. French Boston is played with a full pack of fifty-two cards, which rank as at Whist, both for cutting and playing ; except that the diamond Jack is always the best trump unless diamonds are turned up, in which case the heart Jack becomes the best trump, and the diamond Jack ranks next below the diamond Queen.

COUNTERS are used as in Boston, their value being a matter of agreement before play begins.

THE POOL is made up by the dealer's contributing ten counters for the first eight rounds, and twenty for the last two. It is increased from time to time by penalties, and is won or lost by the players, just as in Boston. There is no limit to the pool. If any player objects to dividing it at the end of the game, it must be played for until some player wins it.

PLAYERS. The number of players, their arrangement at the table, etc., is precisely the same as at Boston.

CUTTING. Instead of cutting for the first deal, any one of the players takes a pack of cards, and gives thirteen to each player in succession, face up. The player to whom he gives the diamond Jack deals the first hand, and has the choice of seats and cards. The others sit as they please.

DEALING. The cards are shuffled before every deal. The player on the left of the dealer cuts, and cards are given first to the player on the dealer's right, dealing from right to left. The cards may be dealt one at a time, or three at a time, or four at a time, always dealing the last round singly, and turning up the last card. A misdeal loses the deal. Other irregularities are governed by the same laws as in Boston.

The deal passes to the right, and the next dealer is indicated by the position of the tray containing the pool, which the dealer always passes to the player on his right, after putting in his ten or twenty counters.

Forty deals is a game ; the first thirty-two of which are called "simples," and the last eight "doubles." In the doubles, all stakes and contributions to the pool are doubled. If anything remains in the pool at the end, it is divided equally, unless a player demands that it shall be played for until won. Such extra deals are simples.

RANK OF THE SUITS. The suit turned on the first deal is called "belle" for that game. The suit turned on each succeeding deal is called "petite." If belle turns up again, there is no petite for that deal. The suits are not first and second preference, as in Boston, but are used only to determine the value of the payments, and to settle which suits partners must name for trumps. The rank of the suits is permanent, as in Boston de Fontainbleau, but the order is, hearts, diamonds, clubs, and spades ; hearts being highest. In France, the suits rank in this order in Boston de Fontainbleau, but in America diamonds outrank hearts.

OBJECTS OF THE GAME. Each player in turn has an opportunity to announce that he is willing to undertake to win a certain number of tricks, if allowed the privilege of naming the trump suit ; or to lose a certain number, there being no trump suit. If he proposes to play alone, he may select any suit for trumps ; but if he takes a partner the trump suit must be belle or petite. The announcements outrank each other in certain order, and the player making the highest must be allowed to play. If he succeeds in his undertaking, he wins the pool, and is also paid a certain number of counters by each of his adversaries. If he fails, he must double the pool, and pay each of his adversaries. The table of payments will be given later.

ANNOUNCEMENTS. The proposals rank in the order following, beginning with the lowest. The French terms are given in ***italics :*** —

Five tricks ; or eight with a partner, in petite. ***Simple in petite.***

Five tricks ; or eight with a partner, in belle. ***Simple in belle.***
Six tricks solo, in any suit. ***Petite independence.***
Little misère. ***Petite misere.***
Eight tricks solo in any suit. ***Grand independence.***
Grand misère. ***Grand misère, or misère sans ecart.***
Misère with four aces. ***Misère des quatre as.***
Nine tricks in any suit. ***Neuf.***
Nine tricks in petite. ***Neuf en petite.***
Nine tricks in belle. ***Neuf en belle.***
Little spread. ***Petite misère sur table.***
Grand spread. ***Grand misère sur table.***

METHOD OF BIDDING. The player to the right of the dealer has the first say. If he proposes to take a partner as in Solo Whist, he says, " Je demande," at the same time placing one of his cards face downward on the table. This card must not be shown or named, but must be of the suit which he proposes to make the trump. He is not allowed to announce the suit, so that any player accepting him as a partner does so in ignorance as to whether he will play in belle or in petite. If the demand is accepted, the proposer and his partner make no change in their positions at the table, but must make eight tricks, just as in Solo Whist.

If a player cannot propose, he says : " Je passe," and each of the others in turn from right to left have the opportunity to make a proposal. When any player proposes, any player in turn after him may accept, although such a one may have already passed. If the fourth player proposes, the three others having passed, and no one will accept him, he is bound to play solo against three such weak adversaries, and must make five tricks, either in belle or in petite. He is not allowed to play in a plain suit if he has made a simple " demand."

The only solo bids allowed are those for six, eight, or nine tricks, which outrank one another. A player cannot bid seven to overcall six ; he must go to eight ; and a player cannot *bid* five tricks without a partner, although, as we have just seen, he may be forced to *play* in that manner.

When six, eight, or nine tricks are bid, the suits outrank one another for equal numbers of tricks ; but as the suit called need not be the bidder's true intention, nor the same as the card laid on the table, the proposer must be careful that his play will be as good as his bid. For instance : He intends nine tricks in spades, but proposes eight in diamonds. He cannot bid nine in diamonds, for that would be a better bid than he intends to play ; but the ruse may succeed in inducing a player not to bid against him, hoping diamonds is the true suit. It is a common artifice to bid the true suit, because few will believe it to be such.

If clubs are belle, and diamonds petite, and a player who " demands " is over-called by a demand in belle, or a call of six tricks, the first caller cannot advance his bid to six tricks except in the suit which he has already laid on the table ; but he may accept the player over-calling him, instead of bidding against him. After a player has once accepted or passed, he cannot bid misère.

If no one makes a proposition of any kind, the hands are thrown up ; the next dealer contributes to the pool, and a fresh hand is dealt.

METHOD OF PLAYING. As in Boston, the eldest hand has the first lead, and the others must follow suit if they can, except in the misère des quatre as. When this is played, the bidder may renounce at pleasure for the first ten tricks.

GATHERING TRICKS. When a partnership is formed, each gathers the tricks he takes. If the partnership loses, the one who has not his complement of tricks must pay the adversaries and double the pool. If the demander has not five, and the acceptor has three, the demander pays. If the proposer has five, and the acceptor has not three, the acceptor pays ; but they both win if they have eight tricks between them, no matter in what proportion. If neither has taken his proper share, they must both pay. When they are successful, they divide the pool.

SLAMS. If a player has demanded, and not been accepted, and has been forced to play alone for five tricks, but wins eight, it is called a slam. But as he did not wish to play alone, his only payment, besides the pool, is 24 counters from each player if he played in petite ; 48 if in belle ; double those amounts if the deal was one of the last eight in the game.

If two partners make a slam, thirteen tricks, they take the pool, and receive from each adversary 24 counters if they played in petite ; 48 if in belle ; double if in one of the last eight hands in the game.

EXPOSED CARDS. The laws governing these are almost identical with those in Boston, with the additional rule that a player allowing a card to fall upon the table face up before play begins, can be forced to play independence in that suit.

REVOKES. The individual player who is detected in a revoke must double the pool, and pay both adversaries.

PAYMENTS. Payments are made according to the table. The player holding diamond Jack receives two counters from each of the other players in a simple ; four in a double; except in misères, in which the card has no value.

Misères are paid for according to the trump turned in the deal in which they are played. If a heart is turned, and little misère is played, the payment is 64 counters to or from each player. If a spade was turned, the payment would be 16 only.

Three honours between partners count as three ; four as four. Being all in one hand does not increase their value.

The Bid.	♠	♣	◇	♡
Five tricks alone, or partners' 8.	4	8	12	16
Three honours.........	3	6	9	12
Four honours..........	4	8	12	16
Each extra trick........	1	2	3	4
Six tricks, or petite independence.	6	12	18	24
Three honours..........	4	8	12	16
Four honours..........	6	12	18	24
Each extra trick........	2	4	6	8
Eight tricks, or grand independence.	8	16	24	32
Three honours..........	6	12	18	24
Four honours..........	8	16	24	32
Each extra trick........	4	8	12	16
Petite misère..........	16	32	48	64
Grand misère..........	32	64	96	128
Misère de quatre as.....	32	64	96	128
Misère sur table.......	64	128	192	256
Slam à deux (partners)...	50	100	150	200
Slam seul (alone).......	100	200	300	400
Slam sur table..........	200	400	600	800

RUSSIAN BOSTON.

This is a variation of Boston de Fontainbleau. A player holding carte blanche declares it before playing, and receives ten counters from each of the other players. Carte blanche is the same thing as chicane in Bridge, no trump in the hand. But in Bridge the player is penalized for announcing it until after the hand is played.

The order of the suits is the same as in American Boston de Fontainbleau: diamonds, hearts, clubs, and spades.

When a player bids six, seven, or eight tricks, he is supposed to be still willing to take a partner, unless he specifies solo. When a partner accepts him, the combination must make four tricks more than the original proposal.

Four honours are paid for as four over-tricks; three honours as two over-tricks.

Piccolissimo is played, and comes between the bids of seven and eight tricks.

GERMAN WHIST.

CARDS. German Whist is played with a full pack of fifty-two cards, which rank as at Whist, both for cutting and playing.

PLAYERS. Two persons play. They cut for the first deal, and the choice of seats.

DEALING. The dealer presents the pack to his adversary to be cut, and then gives thirteen cards to each player, one at a time, turning up the twenty-seventh card for the trump, and laying it on the talon, or remainder of the pack.

PLAYING. The non-dealer begins by leading any card he pleases, and his adversary must follow suit if he can. The winner of the first trick takes the trump card into his hand, and his adversary takes the card immediately under it, but without showing or naming it. Each player thus restores the number of cards in his hand to thirteen. The card which is now on the top of the talon is turned up, and the winner of the next trick must take it, his adversary taking the one under it, as before, and turning up the next. In this manner it will be seen that the winner of each trick must always get a card which is known to his adversary, while the loser of the trick gets one which remains unknown.

When the talon is exhausted, the thirteen cards in each hand should be known to both players if they have been observant, and the end game becomes a problem in double dummy.

STAKES. The game is usually played for so much a point, the player having won the majority of the tricks receiving the difference between the number of his tricks and those of his adversary. Each game is complete in one hand.

In many respects the game resembles single-handed Hearts, except that in Hearts none of the cards drawn are shown.

CHINESE WHIST.

CARDS. Chinese Whist is played with a full pack of fifty-two cards, which rank as at Whist, both for cutting and playing.

MARKERS. Ordinary whist markers are used for scoring the points.

PLAYERS. Two, three or four persons can play Chinese Whist. When three play, the spade deuce is thrown out of the pack. Partners and deal are cut for from an outspread pack, as at Whist.

POSITION OF THE PLAYERS. When four play, the partners sit opposite each other. When three play, the one cutting the lowest card chooses his seat, and dictates the positions of the two other players.

DEALING. When four play, the pack is shuffled and cut as at Whist. The dealer then gives six cards to each player, one at a time, beginning on his left. These six cards are then spread face down on the table in front of the players to whom they have been dealt, but without being looked at. Six more are then dealt to each, one at a time, and these are turned face up, and sorted into suits. They are then laid face up on the top of the six cards which are lying on the table face down, so as to cover them. The last four cards are then dealt, one to each player, These last are retained in the hand, and must not be shown or named ; they are usually called the *" down cards."*

MAKING THE TRUMP. After examining the cards exposed on the table, and the down card in his own hand, the dealer has the privilege of naming any suit he pleases for trumps. No consultation with partner is allowed.

METHOD OF PLAYING. The player to the left of the dealer begins by leading any one of his exposed cards, and the others must follow suit if they can ; either with one of their exposed cards, or with their down cards. A player having none of the suit led may either discard or trump. The highest card played of the suit led wins the trick, and trumps win all other suits. The side winning the trick takes it in and arranges it just as at Whist. Before leading for the next trick all cards which have been uncovered are turned face up. If any person has played his down card he will have no card to turn up, none having been uncovered. The cards cannot under any circumstances be shifted from their original positions. If a player has five cards face up, covering five cards face down, he cannot shift one of the exposed cards to the empty sixth place, and uncover another card. All covering cards must be got rid of in the course of play.

PENALTIES for revokes, cards led out of turn, etc., are the same as at Whist.

OBJECTS OF THE GAME. As in Whist, the object is to win tricks, all above six counting one point toward game. Five, seven, or ten points may be made the game, at the option of the players, but ten is the usual number. Honours are not counted except by agreement.

STAKES. It is usual to play for so much a point or a game. If points are played, the loser's score must be deducted from the winner's, and the difference is the value of the game won.

WHEN THREE PLAY, eight cards are dealt to each person, and arranged face down ; then eight more, arranged face up, and then one to each for down cards. There are no partnerships ; each plays for himself against the others.

WHEN TWO PLAY, twelve cards are dealt to each player, and arranged face down ; then twelve more, arranged face up, and then two down cards to each. It is usual to deal all the cards two at a time.

SUGGESTIONS FOR GOOD PLAY. Chinese Whist very closely resembles Dummy, and the chief element of success is the skilful use of tenace. Memory also plays an important part, it being especially necessary to remember what cards are still unplayed in each suit. While the down cards are held a player cannot be sure of taking a trick by leading a card higher than any his adversary has exposed, because one of the down cards may be better. If a player is short of trumps, but has as many and better than those of his adversary, it is often good play to lead and draw the weaker trumps before the adversary turns up higher ones to protect them. For instance : One player may have 10 8, and his adversary the 9 alone. If the 10 is led the 9 will probably be caught, unless one of the adverse down cards is better. If the 10 is not led the adversary may turn up an honour, and will then have major tenace over the 10 and 8.

The end game always offers some interesting problems for solution by the expert in tenace position, and in placing the lead.

WHIST FAMILY LAWS.

While the code of laws drawn up by the American Whist League, and finally approved and adopted at the Third Congress, [in Chicago, June 20th to 24th, 1893,] refers exclusively to the parent game of Whist, its general provisions equally apply to all members of the whist family of games. The author believes it will save much repetition and confusion to interlineate the exceptions which are necessary in order to cover the special features of such important variations as Boston, Bridge, Cayenne, and Solo Whist. Where no exceptions are made, the law applies equally to these games and to Whist. The unnumbered paragraphs show the inserted laws.

It is a common practice for the framers of laws to insert rules which are simply descriptive of the manner of play. The author believes in adhering to the proper definition of a law, which is a rule carrying with it some penalty for its infraction, or defining the rights of individual players. Such a statement as that the dummy player in Bridge may not overlook his adversary's hand is not a law, because there is no penalty if he does so.

The author is not responsible for the peculiar grammar employed in both the American and English Laws.

THE GAME.

1. A game consists of seven points, each trick above six counting one. The value of the game is determined by deducting the losers' score from seven.

In ***Boston,*** the game is finished in twelve deals.

In ***Bridge,*** a game consists of thirty points, each trick above six counting towards game according to the table of values. Honours, Chicane, and Slams do not count towards game. Every hand must be played out, and all points made in excess of the thirty required to win the game are counted. A rubber is the best of three games; but if the first two are won by the same players, the third is not played. The value of the rubber is determined by adding 100 points to the winner's score for tricks and honours, and then deducting the scores of the losers.

In ***Cayenne,*** a game consists of ten points, each trick above six counting towards game according to the table of values. Honours and Slams also count towards game. Every hand must be played out, and all points made in excess of the ten required to win the game are counted on the next game; so that it is possible to win two or three games in one hand. In Nullo, every trick over the book is counted by the adversaries. Players cannot count out by honours alone;

they must win the odd trick or stop at the score of nine. If one side goes out by cards, the other cannot score honours. The rubber is won by the side that first wins four games of ten points each. The value of the rubber is determined by adding 8 points to the winners' score for tricks, honours, and slams, and then deducting the score of the losers.

In *Solo Whist,* the game is complete in one deal, and the value of it is determined by the player's success or failure in his undertaking, and must be settled for at the end of the hand, according to the table of payments.

FORMING THE TABLE.

2. Those first in the room have the preference. If, by reason of two or more arriving at the same time, more than four assemble, the preference among the last comers is determined by cutting, a lower cut giving the preference over all cutting higher. A complete table consists of six; the four having the preference play. Partners are determined by cutting; the highest two play against the lowest two; the lowest deals and has the choice of seats and cards.

In *Boston* and in *Solo Whist,* a table is complete with four players. In cutting for positions at the table, the lowest has the choice of seats and cards, and the two highest sit opposite each other.

3. If two players cut intermediate cards of equal value, they cut again; the lower of the new cut plays with the original lowest.

4. If three players cut cards of equal value, they cut again. If the fourth has cut the highest card, the two lowest of the new cut are partners, and the lowest deals. If the fourth has cut the lowest card, he deals, and the two highest of the new cut are partners.

5. At the end of a game, if there are more than four belonging to the table, a sufficient number of the players retire to admit those awaiting their turn to play. In determining which players remain in, those who have played a less number of consecutive games have the preference over all who have played a greater number; between two or more who have played an equal number, the preference is determined by cutting, a lower cut giving the preference over all cutting higher.

In *Boston, Cayenne,* and *Solo Whist,* at the end of a game a new table must be formed, those already in having no preference over fresh candidates.

6. To entitle one to enter a table, he must declare his intention to do so before any one of the players has cut for the purpose of commencing a new game or of cutting out.

In *Boston, Cayenne,* and *Solo Whist,* this rule does not apply.

CUTTING.

7. In cutting, the ace is the lowest card. All must cut from the same pack. If a player exposes more than one card, he must cut again. Drawing cards from the outspread pack may be resorted to in place of cutting.

SHUFFLING.

8. Before every deal, the cards must be shuffled. When two packs are used, the dealer's partner must collect and shuffle the cards for the ensuing deal and place them at his right hand. In all cases the dealer may shuffle last.

In **Boston** and in **Cayenne,** two packs must be used; and in Boston there must be no shuffling of either pack after the first deal.

9. A pack must not be shuffled during the play of a hand, nor so as to expose the face of any card.

CUTTING TO THE DEALER.

10. The dealer must present the pack to his right hand adversary to be cut; the adversary must take a portion from the top of the pack and place it toward the dealer; at least four cards must be left in each packet; the dealer must reunite the packets by placing the one not removed in cutting upon the other.

11. If, in cutting or reuniting the separate packets, a card is exposed, the pack must be reshuffled by the dealer, and cut again; if there is any confusion of the cards, or doubt as to the place where the pack was separated, there must be a new cut.

In **Boston,** the pack must be cut again; but not shuffled.

12. If the dealer reshuffles the pack after it has been properly cut, he loses his deal.

In **Boston, Bridge, Cayenne,** and **Solo Whist,** the misdealer must deal again.

DEALING.

13. When the pack has been properly cut and reunited, the dealer must distribute the cards, one at a time, to each player in regular rotation, beginning at his left. The last, which is the trump card, must be turned up before the dealer. At the end of the hand, or when the deal is lost, the deal passes to the player next to the dealer on his left, and so on to each in turn.

In **Bridge,** no trump is turned.

In **Solo Whist,** the cards are distributed three at a time until only four remain in the pack. These are dealt one at a time, and the last turned up for trump.

In **Boston** and in **Cayenne,** the cards are dealt four at a time for two rounds, and then five at a time. No trump is turned. After the cards have been dealt the player opposite the dealer presents the still pack to be cut by the player on the dealer's left, and the top card of the portion left on the table is turned up.

In **Boston, Bridge, Cayenne,** or **Solo Whist,** the deal is never lost. The same dealer deals again with the same pack.

14.   There must be a new deal by the same dealer :—
    I.   If any card except the last is faced in the pack.
    II.   If, during the deal or during the play of the hand, the pack is proved incorrect or imperfect ; but any prior score made with that pack shall stand.

In **Bridge,** if any player declares out of his turn, either adversary may, without consultation, claim a fresh deal.

15.   If, during the deal, a card is exposed, the side not in fault may demand a new deal, provided neither of that side has touched a card. If a new deal does not take place, the exposed card is not liable to be called.

In **Bridge,** if either the dealer or his partner exposes a card before the trump suit has been declared, the adversaries may claim a new deal. If any player exposes a card before the eldest hand has led to the first trick, the partner of the player in fault forfeits his right to double or re-double. If the leader's partner exposes a card, the dealer may either require that suit not to be led, or may claim the card as liable to be called.

16.   Any one dealing out of turn, or with his adversaries' pack, may be stopped before the trump card is turned, after which, the deal is valid, and the packs, if changed, so remain.

In **Boston, Bridge,** and **Cayenne,** the dealer must be stopped before the last card is dealt.

MISDEALING.

17.   It is a misdeal :—
    I.   If the dealer omits to have the pack cut, and his adversaries discover the error before the trump card is turned, and before looking at any of their cards.
    II.   If he deals a card incorrectly, and fails to correct the error before dealing another.
    III.   If he counts the cards on the table or in the remainder of the pack.
    IV.   If, having a perfect pack, he does not deal to each player the proper number of cards, and the error is discovered before all have played to the first trick.

v.   If he looks at the trump card before the deal is completed.

vi.   If he places the trump card face downward upon his own or any other player's cards.

A misdeal loses the deal, unless, during the deal, either of the adversaries touches a card or in any other manner interrupts the dealer.

In *Boston, Bridge, Cayenne,* and *Solo Whist,* the misdealer deals again with the same cards. In Boston he forfeits a red counter to the pool for his error.

THE TRUMP CARD.

18.   The dealer must leave the trump card face upward on the table until it is his turn to play to the first trick; if it is left on the table until after the second trick has been turned and quitted, it is liable to be called. After it has been lawfully taken up, it must not be named, and any player naming it is liable to have his highest or his lowest trump called by either adversary. A player may, however, ask what the trump suit is.

This law does not apply to Boston, Bridge, or Cayenne.

In *Boston* and in *Cayenne,* no trump is turned, but a card is cut from the still pack to determine the rank of the suits. See Law 13.

In *Bridge* and in *Cayenne,* the trump suit must be named by the dealer or his partner after they have examined their cards. The dealer has the first say, and he may select any of the four suits, or he may announce " grand," playing for the tricks without any trump suit. In Cayenne, he may announce " nullo," playing to take as few tricks as possible, there being no trump suit. If the dealer makes his choice, his partner must abide by it; but if the dealer has not a hand to justify him in deciding, he may leave the choice to his partner, who must decide. A declaration once made cannot be changed.

In *Bridge,* after the trump is declared, or a grand announced, the adversary on the left of the dealer has the right to double the standard value of the tricks. If he does not double, he must ask his partner's permission to play, by saying: " May I play, partner?" The partner must then double, or direct the leader to play. Should either the leader or his partner double, the player who made the declaration has the right to re-double, or if he declines, his partner may double. Should the dealer or his partner re-double, their adversaries may re-double again, the one who first doubled having the first option. This may be continued until all decline to double further. The value of honours, chicane, slams, etc., is not affected by the doubling; only the trick score is increased.

IRREGULARITIES IN THE HANDS.

19. If, at any time after all have played to the first trick, the pack being perfect, a player is found to have either more or less than his correct number of cards and his adversaries have their right number, the latter, upon the discovery of such surplus or deficiency, may consult and shall have the choice:—

  I.   To have a new deal; or

  II. To have the hand played out, in which case the surplus or missing card or cards are not taken into account.

If either of the adversaries also has more or less than his correct number, there must be a new deal.

If any player has a surplus card by reason of an omission to play to a trick, his adversaries can exercise the foregoing privilege only after he has played to the trick following the one in which such omission occurred.

In ***Boston,*** if at any time it is discovered that a player opposed to the bidder has ***less*** than his proper number of cards, whether through the fault of the dealer, or through having played more than one card to a trick, he and his partners must each pay the bidder for his bid and all over-tricks. If the bidder has ***less*** than his proper number of cards, he is put in for one trick at least, and his adversaries may demand the hand to be played out to put him in for over-tricks. In Misère Partout, any player having ***less*** than his proper number of cards forfeits five red counters to each of the other players, and the hands are abandoned. If any player has ***more*** than the proper number of cards, it is a misdeal, and the misdealer deals again, after forfeiting one red counter to the pool.

In ***Solo Whist,*** the deal stands good. Should the player with the incorrect number of cards be the caller or his partner, the hand must be played out. Should the caller make good his proposition, he neither receives nor pays on that hand. If he fails, he must pay. Should the player with the defective hand be the adversary of the caller, he and his partners must pay the stakes on that hand, which may then be abandoned. Should two players have an incorrect number of cards, one of them being the caller, there must be a new deal.

CARDS LIABLE TO BE CALLED.

20. The following cards are liable to be called by either adversary:—

  I.   Every card faced upon the table otherwise than in the regular course of play, but not including a card led out of turn.

II.   Every card thrown with the one led or played to the current trick. The player must indicate the one led or played.

III.   Every card so held by a player that his partner sees any portion of its face.

IV.   All the cards in a hand lowered or shown by a player so that his partner sees more than one card of it.

V.   Every card named by the player holding it.

In *Boston, Bridge,* and *Solo Whist* there are no penalties for cards exposed by the single player, because he has no partner to take advantage of the information. In Bridge, cards exposed before play begins are covered by law 15.

21.   All cards liable to be called must be placed and left face upwards on the table. A player must lead or play them when called, provided he can do so without revoking. The call may be repeated at each trick until the card is played. A player cannot be prevented from leading or playing a card liable to be called ; if he can get rid of it in the course of play, no penalty remains.

In *Boston* and in *Solo Whist,* if the exposed card is a trump, the owner may be called upon by his adversary not to use it for ruffing. If the suit of the exposed card is led, whether trump or not, the adversary may demand that the card be played or not played ; or that the highest or lowest of the suit be played. If the owner of the exposed card has no other of the suit, the penalty is paid.

Penalties must be exacted by players in their proper turn, or the right to exact them is lost. For instance : In Solo Whist, A is the proposer, B the acceptor, and B has an exposed card in front of him. When Y plays he should say whether or not he wishes to call the exposed card. If he says nothing, B must await Z's decision.

22.   If a player leads a card better than any his adversaries hold of the suit, and then leads one or more other cards without waiting for his partner to play, the latter may be called upon by either adversary to take the first trick, and the other cards thus improperly played are liable to be called ; it makes no difference whether he plays them one after the other, or throws them all on the table together, after the first card is played, the others are liable to be called.

23.   A player having a card liable to be called must not play another until the adversaries have stated whether or not they wish to call the card liable to the penalty. If he plays another card without awaiting the decision of the adversaries, such other card also is liable to be called.

LEADING OUT OF TURN.

24. If any player leads out of turn, a suit may be called from him or his partner, the first time it is the turn of either of them to lead. The penalty can be enforced only by the adversary on the right of the player from whom a suit can be lawfully called,

If a player, so called on to lead a suit, has none of it, or if all have played to the false lead, no penalty can be enforced. If all have not played to the trick, the cards erroneously played to such false lead are not liable to be called and must be taken back.

In **Bridge,** if either the dealer or his partner leads out of turn there is no penalty.

In **Boston,** if the adversary of the bidder leads out of turn, and the bidder has not played to the trick, the latter may call a suit from the player whose proper turn it is to lead: or, if it is the bidder's own lead, he may call a suit when next the adversaries obtain the lead ; or he may claim the card played in error as an exposed card. If the bidder has played to the trick the error cannot be rectified. Should the bidder lead out of turn, and the player on his left follow the erroneous lead, the error cannot be corrected.

In Misères, a lead out of turn by the bidder's adversary immediately loses the game, but there is no penalty for leading out of turn in Misère Partout.

PLAYING OUT OF TURN.

25. If the third hand plays before the second, the fourth hand also may play before the second.

26. If the third hand has not played, and the fourth hand plays before the second, the latter may be called upon by the third hand to play his highest or lowest card of the suit led or, if he has none, to trump or not to trump the trick.

In **Bridge,** this law does not apply to the dealer and his partner.

In **Boston,** and in **Solo Whist,** should an adversary of the single player play out of turn, the bidder may call upon the adversary who has not played to play his highest or lowest of the suit led, or to win or not to win the trick. If the adversary of a Misère player leads or plays out of turn, the bidder may immediately claim the stakes. In Solo Whist, the individual player in fault must pay for himself and for his partners.

ABANDONED HANDS.

27. If all four players throw their cards on the table, face upwards, no further play of that hand is permitted. The result of the hand, as then claimed or admitted, is established, provided that, if a revoke is discovered, the revoke penalty attaches.

In *Solo Whist,* should the bidder abandon his hand, he and his partner, if any, must pay the stakes and settle for all over-tricks as if they had lost all the remaining tricks. If a player, not the bidder, abandons his hand, his partner or partners may demand the hand to be played out with the abandoned hand exposed, and liable to be called by the adversary. If they defeat the call they win nothing, but the player who abandoned his hand must pay the caller just as if he had been successful. If the partner or partners of the exposed hand lose, they must pay their share of the losses.

REVOKING,

28. A revoke is a renounce in error, not corrected in time. A player renounces in error, when, holding one or more cards of the suit led, he plays a card of a different suit.

A renounce in error may be corrected by the player making it, before the trick in which it occurs has been turned and quitted, unless either he or his partner, whether in his right turn or otherwise, has led or played to the following trick, or unless his partner has asked whether or not he has any of the suit renounced.

In *Boston, Bridge, Cayenne,* and *Solo Whist,* a player may ask his partner if he has none of the suit led ; but in Whist such a question establishes the revoke.

29. If a player corrects his mistake in time to save a revoke, the card improperly played by him is liable to be called ; any player or players, who have played after him, may withdraw their cards and substitute others ; the cards so withdrawn are not liable to be called.

In *Bridge,* the dealer is not liable to any penalty if he corrects his mistake before the trick is turned and quitted.

In *Boston,* if the bidder revokes and corrects himself in time, there is no penalty unless an adversary has played after him, in which case the bidder's card may be claimed as exposed. The player who followed him may then amend his play. If a player opposed to the bidder discovers and corrects a revoke made by himself or any of his partners, the bidder may either claim the card played in error as exposed, or may call on the revoking player for his highest or lowest of the suit led.

30. The penalty for revoking is the transfer of two tricks from the revoking side to their adversaries ; it can be enforced for as many revokes as occur during the hand. The revoking side cannot win the game in that hand; if both sides revoke, neither can win the game in that hand.

In *Bridge, Cayenne,* and *Solo Whist,* as a penalty for a revoke, the adversaries of the revoking player may take from him three tricks ; or may deduct the value of three tricks from his score ; or may add the value of three tricks to their own score. The revoking players cannot score slams or game that hand. All slams must be made independently of the revoke penalty.

In *Boston,* the penalty for a revoke on the part of the bidder is that he is put in for one trick, and must pay four red counters into the next pool. Should an adversary of the bidder revoke, he must pay four red counters into the next pool, and he and his partners must pay the bidder as if he had been successful. On the discovery of a revoke in Boston the hands are usually abandoned ; but the cards should be shown to the table, in order that each player may be satisfied that no other revoke has been made. A player revoking in Misère Partout pays five red counters to each of his adversaries and the hands are then abandoned.

31. The revoking player and his partner may require the hand in which the revoke has been made, to be played out, and score all points made by them up to the score of six.

In *Boston,* the hands are abandoned after the revoke is claimed and proved.

In *Bridge,* the hand must be played out, and all points made may be scored, but the revoking players must stop at 28, or within two points of game.

In *Cayenne,* the revoking players must stop at nine.

In *Solo Whist,* the revoking players must pay all the red counters involved in the call, whether they win or lose, but they may play the hand out to save over-tricks. If the caller or his partner revokes they must jointly pay the losses involved ; but if an adversary of the caller revokes, he must individually pay the entire loss unless he can show that the callers would have won in spite of the revoke. Should he be able to do this, his partners must stand their share of the losses, but the revoking player must individually pay for the three tricks taken as the revoke penalty. If the single player revokes, either on solo or abundance, he loses the red counters involved in any case, but may play the hand out to save over-tricks. If the single player in a misère or a slam revokes, the hand is abandoned and he must pay the stakes. If an adversary of a misère or a slam revokes, he must individually pay the whole stakes.

32. At the end of a hand, the claimants of a revoke may search all the tricks. If the cards have been mixed, the claim may be urged and proved, if possible ; but no proof is necessary and the revoke is established, if, after it has been claimed, the accused player or his partner mixes the cards before they have been examined to the satisfaction of the adversaries.

33. The revoke can be claimed at any time before the cards have been presented and cut for the following deal, but not thereafter.

MISCELLANEOUS.

34. Any one, during the play of a trick and before the cards have been touched for the purpose of gathering them together, may demand that the players draw their cards.

35. If any one, prior to his partner playing, calls attention in any manner to the trick or to the score, the adversary last to play to the trick may require the offender's partner to play his highest or lowest of the suit led or, if he has none, to trump or not to trump the trick.

36. If any player says "I can win the rest," "The rest are ours," "We have the game," or words to that effect, his partner's cards must be laid upon the table and are liable to be called.

In *Bridge*, this law does not apply to the dealer.

37. When a trick has been turned and quitted, it must not again be seen until after the hand has been played. A violation of this law subjects the offender's side to the same penalty as in case of a lead out of turn.

In *Boston, Bridge, Cayenne,* and *Solo Whist,* it is still the custom to permit looking at the last trick, except in Misères. The penalty in a misère game is the same as for a lead out of turn.

38. If a player is lawfully called upon to play the highest or lowest of a suit, or to trump or not to trump a trick, or to lead a suit, and unnecessarily fails to comply, he is liable to the same penalty as if he had revoked.

39. In all cases where a penalty has been incurred, the offender must await the decision of the adversaries. If either of them, with or without his partner's consent, demands a penalty to which they are entitled, such decision is final. If the wrong adversary demands a penalty, or a wrong penalty is demanded, none can be enforced.

The following rules belong to the established code of Whist Etiquette. They are formulated with a view to discourage and repress certain improprieties of conduct, therein pointed out, which are not reached by the laws. The courtesy which marks the intercourse of gentlemen will regulate other more obvious cases.

1. No conversation should be indulged in during the play, except such as is allowed by the laws of the game.

2. No player should in any manner whatsoever give any intimation as to the state of his hand or of the game, or of approval or disapproval of a play.

3. No player should lead until the preceding trick is turned and quitted.

4. No player should, after having led a winning card, draw a card from his hand for another lead until his partner has played to the current trick.

5. No player should play a card in any manner so as to call particular attention to it, nor should he demand that the cards be placed in order to attract the attention of his partner.

6. No player should purposely incur a penalty because he is willing to pay it, nor should he make a second revoke in order to conceal one previously made.

7. No player should take advantage of information imparted by his partner through a breach of etiquette.

8. No player should object to referring a disputed question of fact to a bystander who professes himself uninterested in the result of the game, and able to decide the question.

9. Bystanders should not in any manner call attention to, or give any intimation concerning the play or the state of the game, during the play of a hand. They should not look over the hand of a player without his permission ; nor should they walk round the table to look at the different hands.

DUMMY.

In **Bridge,** the dealer's partner may ask him if he has a card of the suit in which he renounces ; but if he calls the dealer's attention to any penalty which might be enforced against the adversaries, the dealer forfeits the right to exact such penalty. A card drawn from Dummy's hand is not played until actually quitted. Dummy is not liable to any penalties for revokes or leads out of turn ; if a trick in which he has revoked is turned and quitted, the trick stands good. Should Dummy in any way suggest to the dealer the play of a card from Dummy's hand, the adversaries may prevent its being played.

ERRONEOUS SCORES.

Any error in the trick score may be corrected before the last card has been dealt in the following deal ; or if the error occurs in the last hand of a game or rubber, it may be corrected before the score is agreed to. Errors in other scores may be corrected at any time before the final score of the game or rubber is agreed to.

BIDDING.

In **Boston,** or **Solo Whist,** any player making a bid must stand by it, and either play or pay. Should he make a bid in error and correct himself, he must stand by the first bid unless he is overcalled, when he may either amend his bid or pass.

LAWS OF DUPLICATE WHIST

AS ADOPTED BY THE

FOURTH AMERICAN WHIST CONGRESS, 1894.

Duplicate Whist is governed by the laws of Whist, except in so far as they are modified by the following Special Laws:

THE GAME AND THE SCORE.

(*a*) A game or match consists of any agreed number of deals, each of which is played once only by each player.

The contesting teams must be of the same number, but may each consist of any agreed number of pairs, one-half of which, or as near thereto as possible, sit north and south, the other half east and west.

Every trick taken is scored, and the match is determined by a comparison of the aggregate scores won by the competing teams. In case the teams consist of an odd number of pairs, each team, in making up such aggregate, adds, as though won by it, the average score of all the pairs seated in the positions opposite to its odd pair.

Each side keeps its own score, and it is the duty of the north and south players at each table to compare the scores there made and see that they correspond. In case they fail to perform this duty, the east and west scores are taken as correct, and the north and south scores made to correspond thereto.

In a match between two teams, the team which wins a majority of all the tricks, scores the match as won by that number of tricks which it has taken in excess of one-half the total.

In a match between more than two teams, each team wins or loses, as the case may be, by the number of tricks which its aggregate score exceeds or falls short of the average score of all of the competing teams.

In taking averages, fractions are disregarded, and the nearest whole number taken, one-half counting as a whole, unless it is necessary to take the fraction into account to avoid a tie, in which case the match is scored as won by "the fraction of a trick."

FORMING THE TABLE.

(*b*) Tables may be formed by cutting or by agreement.

In two-table duplicate, if the tables are formed by cutting, the four having the preference play at one table, and the next four at the other. The highest two at one table are partners with the lowest two at the other. The highest two at each table sit north and south; the lowest two east and west.

DEALING AND MISDEALING.

(*c*) The deal is never lost; in case of a misdeal, or of the exposure of a card during the deal, the cards must be redealt by the same player.

THE TRUMP CARD.

(*d*) The trump card must be recorded before the play begins, on a slip provided for that purpose. When the deal has been played, the slip on which the trump card has been recorded must be placed by the dealer on the top of his cards, but the trump card must not be again turned until the hands are taken up for the purpose of overplaying them, at which time it must be turned and left face upwards on the table until it is the dealer's turn to play to the first trick. The slip on which the trump card is recorded must be turned face downwards as soon as the trump card is taken up by the dealer.

IRREGULARITIES IN THE HANDS.

(*e*) If a player is found to have either more or less than his correct number of cards, the course to be pursued is determined by the time at which the irregularity is discovered.

I. Where the irregularity is discovered before or during the original play of a hand :—

There must be a new deal.

II. Where the irregularity is discovered when the hand is taken up for overplay, and before such overplay has begun :—

The hand in which the irregularity is so discovered must be sent back to the table from which it was last received and the error be there rectified.

III. Where the irregularity is not discovered until after the overplay has begun : —

In two-table duplicate there must be a new deal ; but, in a game in which the same hands are played at more than two tables, the hands must be rectified as above, and then passed to the next table without overplay at the table at which the error was discovered ; in which case, if a player had a deficiency and his adversary the corresponding surplus, each team takes the average score for that deal ; if, however, his partner had the corresponding surplus, his team is given the lowest score made at any table for that deal.

PLAYING THE CARDS.

(*f*) Each player, when it is his turn to play, must place his card face upwards, before him, and towards the center of the table, and allow it to remain upon the table in this position until all have played to the trick, when he must turn it over and place it face downwards, and nearer to himself, placing each successive card, as he turns it, on top of the last card previously turned by him. After he has played his card, and also after he has turned it, he must quit it by removing his hand.

A trick is turned and quitted when all four players have turned and quitted their respective cards.

The cards must be left in the order in which they were played, until the scores for the deal are recorded.

CLAIMING A REVOKE.

(*g*) A revoke may be claimed at any time before the last trick of the deal in which it occurs has been turned and quitted and the scores of that deal recorded, but not thereafter.

SINGLE-TABLE OR MNEMONIC DUPLICATE.

The Laws of Duplicate Whist govern, where applicable, except as follows :

Each player plays each deal twice, the second time playing a hand previously played by an adversary.

Instead of turning the trump, a single suit may be declared trumps for the game.

On the overplay, the cards may be gathered into tricks instead of playing them as required by Law (*f*).

In case of the discovery of an irregularity in the hands there must always be a new deal.

ENGLISH WHIST LAWS.

THE RUBBER.

1. The rubber is the best of three games. If the first two games are won by the same players, the third game is not played.

SCORING.

2. A game consists of five points. Each trick, above six, counts one point.

3. Honours, *i. e.*, Ace, King, Queen, and Knave of trumps, are thus reckoned :

If a player and his partner, either separately or conjointly, hold—

    I.   The four honours, they score four points.

    II.   Any three honours, they score two points.

    III.   Only two honours, they do not score.

4. Those players who, at the commencement of a deal, are at the score of four, cannot score honours.

5. The penalty for a revoke (*see* Law 72) takes precedence of all other scores. Tricks score next. Honours last.

6. Honours, unless claimed before the trump card of the following deal is turned up, cannot be scored.

7. To score honours is not sufficient; they must be called at the end of the hand; if so called, they may be scored at any time during the game.

8. The winners gain—

    I.   A treble, or game of three points, when their adversaries have not scored.

    II.   A double, or game of two points, when their adversaries have scored less than three.

    III.   A single, or game of one point, when their adversaries have scored three or four.

9. The winners of the rubber gain two points (commonly called the rubber points), in addition to the value of their games.

10. Should the rubber have consisted of three games, the value of the losers' game is deducted from the gross number of points gained by their opponents.

11. If an erroneous score be proved, such mistake can be corrected prior to the conclusion of the game in which it occurred, and such game is not concluded until the trump card of the following deal has been turned up.

12. If an erroneous score, affecting the amount of the rubber, be proved, such mistake can be rectified at any time during the rubber.

CUTTING.

13. The Ace is the lowest card.

14. In all cases, every one must cut from the same pack.

15. Should a player expose more than one card, he must cut again.

FORMATION OF TABLE.

16. If there are more than four candidates, the players are selected by cutting; those first in the room having the preference. The four who cut the lowest cards play first, and cut again to decide on partners; the two lowest play against the two highest; the lowest is the dealer, who has choice of cards and seats, and, having once made his selection, must abide by it.

17. When there are more than six candidates, those who cut the two next lowest cards belong to the table, which is complete with six players; on the retirement of one of those six players, the candidate who cut the next lowest card has a prior right to any aftercomer to enter the table.

CUTTING CARDS OF EQUAL VALUE.

18. Two players cutting cards of equal value, unless such cards are the two highest, cut again; should they be the two lowest, a fresh cut is necessary to decide which of those two deals.

19. Three players cutting cards of equal value cut again; should the fourth (or remaining) card be the highest, the two lowest of the new cut are partners, the lower of those two the dealer; should the fourth card be the lowest, the two highest are partners, the original lowest the dealer.

CUTTING OUT.

20. At the end of a rubber, should admission be claimed by any one, or by two candidates, he who has, or they who have, played a greater number of consecutive rubbers than the others is, or are, out; but when all have played the same number, they must cut to decide upon the outgoers; the highest are out.

ENTRY AND RE-ENTRY.

21. A candidate wishing to enter a table must declare such intention prior to any of the players having cut a card, either for the purpose of commencing a fresh rubber or of cutting out.

22. In the formation of fresh tables, those candidates who have neither belonged to nor played at any other table have the prior right of entry; the others decide their right of admission by cutting.

23. Any one quitting a table prior to the conclusion of a rubber may, with consent of the other three players, appoint a substitute in his absence during that rubber.

24. A player cutting into one table, whilst belonging to another, loses his right of re-entry into that latter, and takes his chance of cutting in, as if he were a fresh candidate.

25. If any one break up a table, the remaining players have the prior right to him of entry into any other, and should there not be sufficient vacancies at such other table to admit all those candidates, they settle their precedence by cutting.

SHUFFLING.

26. The pack must neither be shuffled below the table nor so that the face of any card be seen.

27. The pack must not be shuffled during the play of the hand.

28. A pack, having been played with, must neither be shuffled by dealing it into packets, nor across the table.

29. Each player has a right to shuffle, once only, except as provided by Rule 32, prior to a deal, after a false cut [*see* Law 34], or when a new deal [*see* Law 37] has occurred.

30. The dealer's partner must collect the cards for the ensuing deal, and has the first right to shuffle that pack.

31. Each player after shuffling must place the cards properly collected, and face downwards, to the left of the player about to deal.

32. The dealer has always the right to shuffle last; but should a card or cards be seen during his shuffling, or whilst giving the pack to be cut, he may be compelled to re-shuffle.

THE DEAL.

33. Each player deals in his turn; the right of dealing goes to the left.

34. The player on the dealer's right cuts the pack, and, in dividing it, must not leave fewer than four cards in either packet; if in cutting, or in replacing one of the two packets on the other, a card be exposed, or if there be any confusion of the cards, or a doubt as to the exact place in which the pack was divided, there must be a fresh cut.

35. When a player, whose duty it is to cut, has once separated the pack, he cannot alter his intention; he can neither re-shuffle nor re-cut the cards.

36. When the pack is cut, should the dealer shuffle the cards, he loses his deal.

A NEW DEAL.

37. There must be a new deal—
   I.   If during a deal, or during the play of a hand, the pack be proved incorrect or imperfect.
   II.   If any card, excepting the last, be faced in the pack.

38. If, whilst dealing, a card be exposed by the dealer or his partner, should neither of the adversaries have touched the cards, the latter can claim a new deal; a card exposed by either adversary gives that claim to the dealer, provided that his partner has not touched a card; if a new deal does not take place, the exposed card cannot be called.

39. If, during dealing, a player touch any of his cards, the adversaries may do the same, without losing their privilege of claiming a new deal, should chance give them such option.

40. If, in dealing, one of the last cards be exposed, and the dealer turn up the trump before there is reasonable time for his adversaries to decide as to a fresh deal, they do not thereby lose their privilege.

41. If a player, whilst dealing, look at the trump card, his adversaries have a right to see it, and may exact a new deal.

42. If a player take into the hand dealt to him a card belonging to the other pack, the adversaries, on discovery of the error, may decide whether they will have a fresh deal or not.

A MISDEAL.

43. A misdeal loses the deal.

44. It is a misdeal—

   I. Unless the cards are dealt into four packets, one at a time in regular rotation, beginning with the player to the dealer's left.

   II. Should the dealer place the last (*i. e.*, the trump) card, face downwards, on his own, or any other pack.

   III. Should the trump card not come in its regular order to the dealer; but he does not lose his deal if the pack be proved imperfect.

   IV. Should a player have fourteen cards, and either of the other three less than thirteen.

   V. Should the dealer, under an impression that he has made a mistake, either count the cards on the table or the remainder of the pack.

   IV. Should the dealer deal two cards at once, or two cards to the same hand, and then deal a third; but if, prior to dealing that third card, the dealer can, by altering the position of one card only, rectify such error, he may do so. except as provided by the second paragraph of this Law.

   VII. Should the dealer omit to have the pack cut to him, and the adversaries discover the error, prior to the trump card being turned up, and before looking at their cards, but not after having done so.

45. A misdeal does not lose the deal if, during the dealing, either of the adversaries touch the cards prior to the dealer's partner having done so ; but should the latter have first interfered with the cards, notwithstanding either or both of the adversaries have subsequently done the same, the deal is lost.

46. Should three players have their right number of cards—the fourth have less than thirteen. and not discover such deficiency until he has played any of his cards, the deal stands good ; should he have played, he is as answerable for any revoke he may have made as if the missing card, or cards, had been in his hand ; he may search the other pack for it, or them.

47. If a pack, during or after a rubber, be proved incorrect or imperfect, such proof does not alter any past score, game, or rubber ; that hand in which the imperfection was detected is null and void ; the dealer deals again.

48. Any one dealing out of turn, or with the adversary's cards, may be stopped before the trump card is turned up, after which the game must proceed as if no mistake had been made.

49. A player can neither shuffle, cut, nor deal for his partner, without the permission of his opponents.

50. If the adversaries interrupt a dealer whilst dealing, either by questioning the score or asserting that it is not his deal, and fail to establish such claim, should a misdeal occur, he may deal again.

51. Should a player take his partner's deal and misdeal, the latter is liable to the usual penalty, and the adversary next in rotation to the player who ought to have dealt then deals.

THE TRUMP CARD.

52. The dealer, when it is his turn to play to the first trick, should take the trump card into his hand ; if left on the table after the first trick be turned and quitted, it is liable to be called ; his partner may at any time remind him of the liability.

53. After the dealer has taken the trump card into his hand, it cannot be asked for ; a player naming it at any time during the play of that hand is liable to have his highest or lowest trump called.

54. If the dealer take the trump card into his hand before it is his turn to play, he may be desired to lay it on the table ; should he show a wrong card, this card may be called, as also a second, a third, etc., until the trump card be produced.

55. If the dealer declare himself unable to recollect the trump card, his highest or lowest trump may be called at any time during that hand, and unless it cause him to revoke, must be played ; the call may be repeated, but not changed, *i. e.*, from highest to lowest, or *vice versa*, until such card is played.

CARDS LIABLE TO BE CALLED.

56. All exposed cards are liable to be called, and must be left on the table ; but a card is not an exposed card when dropped on the floor, or elsewhere below the table. The following are exposed cards :—

    I.   Two or more cards played at once.

    II.   Any card dropped with its face upward, or in any way exposed on or above the table, even though snatched up so quickly that no one can name it.

57. If any one play to an imperfect trick the best card on the table, or lead one which is a winning card as against his adversaries, and then lead again, or play several such winning cards, one after the other, without waiting for his partner to play, the latter may be called on to win, if he can, the first or any other of those tricks, and the other cards thus improperly played are exposed cards.

58. If a player, or players, under the impression that the game is lost—or won—or for other reasons—throw his or their cards on the table face upward, such cards are exposed, and liable to be called, each player's by the adversary ; but should one player alone retain his hand, he cannot be forced to abandon it.

59. If all four players throw their cards on the table face upward, the hands are abandoned ; and no one can again take up his cards. Should this general exhibition show that the game

might have been saved, or won, neither claim can be entertained, unless a revoke be established. The revoking players are then liable to the following penalties : they cannot under any circumstances win the game by the result of that hand, and the adversaries may add three to their score, or deduct three from that of the revoking players.

60. A card detached from the rest of the hand so as to be named is liable to be called ; but should the adversary name a wrong card, he is liable to have a suit called when he or his partner have the lead.

61. If a player who has rendered himself liable to have the highest or lowest of a suit called, fail to play as desired, or if when called on to lead one suit he lead another, having in his hand one or more cards of that suit demanded, he incurs the penalty of a revoke.

62. If any player lead out of turn, his adversaries may either call the card erroneously led, or may call a suit from him or his partner when it is next the turn of either of them to lead.

63. If any player lead out of turn, and the three others have followed him, the trick is complete, and the error cannot be rectified ; but if only the second, or the second and third, have played to the false lead, their cards, on discovery of the mistake, are taken back ; there is no penalty against any one, excepting the original offender, whose card may be called, or he, or his partner, when either of them has next the lead, may be compelled to play any suit demanded by the adversaries.

64. In no case can a player be compelled to play a card which would oblige him to revoke.

65. The call of a card may be repeated until such card has been played.

66. If a player called on to lead a suit have none of it, the penalty is paid.

CARDS PLAYED IN ERROR, OR NOT PLAYED TO A TRICK.

67. If the third hand play before the second, the fourth hand may play before his partner.

68. Should the third hand not have played, and the fourth play before his partner, the latter may be called on to win, or not to win the trick.

69. If any one omit playing to a former trick, and such error be not discovered until he has played to the next, the adversaries may claim a new deal ; should they decide that the deal stand good, the surplus card at the end of the hand is considered to have been played to the imperfect trick, but does not constitute a revoke therein.

70. If any one play two cards to the same trick, or mix his trump, or other card, with a trick to which it does not properly

belong, and the mistake be not discovered until the hand is played out, he is answerable for all consequent revokes he may have made. If, during the play of the hand, the error be detected, the tricks may be counted face downward, in order to ascertain whether there be among them a card too many ; should this be the case, they may be searched, and the card restored ; the player is, however, liable for all revokes which he may have meanwhile made.

THE REVOKE.

71.   Is when a player, holding one or more cards of the suit led, plays a card of a different suit.

72.   The penalty for a revoke—

I.   Is at the option of the adversaries, who at the end of the hand may either take three tricks from the revoking player or deduct three points from his score, or add three to their own score ;

II.   Can be claimed for as many revokes as occur during the hand ;

III.   Is applicable only to the score of the game in which it occurs ;

IV.   Cannot be divided, *i. e.*, a player cannot add one or two to his own score and deduct one or two from the revoking player ;

V.   Takes precedence of every other score—*e. g.*, the claimants two, their opponents nothing ; the former add three to their score, and thereby win a treble game, even should the latter have made thirteen tricks, and held four honours.

73.   A revoke is established if the trick in which it occur be turned and quitted, *i. e.*, the hand removed from that trick after it has been turned face downward on the table, or if either the revoking player or his partner, whether in his right turn or otherwise, lead or play to the following trick.

74.   A player may ask his partner whether he has not a card of the suit which he has renounced ; should the question be asked before the trick is turned and quitted, subsequent turning and quitting does not establish the revoke, and the error may be corrected, unless the question be answered in the negative, or unless the revoking player or his partner have led or played to the following trick.

75.   At the end of the hand, the claimants of a revoke may search all the tricks.

76.   If a player discover his mistake in time to save a revoke, the adversaries, whenever they think fit, may call the card thus played in error, or may require him to play his highest or lowest card to that trick in which he has renounced ; any player or

players who have played after him may withdraw their cards and substitute others: the cards withdrawn are not liable to be called.

77.   If a revoke be claimed, and the accused player or his partner mix the cards before they have been sufficiently examined by the adversaries, the revoke is established.   The mixing of the cards only renders the proof of a revoke difficult; but does not prevent the claim and possible establishment of the penalty.

78.   A revoke cannot be claimed after the cards have been cut for the following deal.

79.   The revoking player and his partner may, under all circumstances, require the hand in which the revoke has been detected to be played out.

80.   If a revoke occur, be claimed and proved, bets on the odd trick or on amount of score, must be decided by the actual state of the latter, after the penalty is paid.

81.   Should the players on both sides subject themselves to the penalty of one or more revokes, neither can win the game; each is punished at the discretion of his adversary.

82.   In whatever way the penalty be enforced, under no circumstances can a player win the game by the result of the hand during which he has revoked; he cannot score more than four.   (*See* Law 61.)

CALLING FOR NEW CARDS.

83.   Any player (on paying for them) before, but not after, the pack be cut for the deal, may call for fresh cards.   He must call for two new packs, of which the dealer takes his choice.

GENERAL RULES.

84.   Where a player and his partner have an option of exacting from their adversaries one of two penalties, they should agree who is to make the election, but must not consult with one another which of the two penalties it is advisable to exact; if they do so consult, they lose their right ; and if either of them, with or without consent of his partner, demand a penalty to which he is entitled, such decision is final.

[This rule does not apply in exacting the penalties for a revoke ; partners have then a right to consult.]

85.   Any one during the play of a trick, or after the four cards are played, and before, but not after, they are touched for the purpose of gathering them together, may demand that the cards be placed before their respective players.

86.   If any one, prior to his partner playing, should call attention to the trick—either by saying that it is his, or by naming his card, or, without being required so to do, by drawing it toward him—the adversaries may require that opponent's partner to play the highest or lowest of the suit then led, or to win or lose the trick.

87.   In all cases where a penalty has been incurred, the offender is bound to give reasonable time for the decision of his adversaries.

88.   If a bystander make any remark which calls the attention of a player or players to an oversight affecting the score, he is liable to be called on, by the players only, to pay the stakes and all bets on that game or rubber.

89.   A bystander, by agreement among the players, may decide any question.

90.   A card or cards torn or marked must be either replaced by agreement, or new cards called at the expense of the table.

91.   Any player may demand to see the last trick turned, and no more.   Under no circumstances can more than eight cards be seen during the play of the hand, *viz.:* the four cards on the table which have not been turned and quitted, and the last trick turned.

ETIQUETTE OF WHIST.

The following rules belong to the established Etiquette of Whist. They are not called laws, as it is difficult—in some cases impossible—to apply any penalty to their infraction, and the only remedy is to cease to play with players who habitually disregard them :

Two packs of cards are invariably used at Clubs ; if possible, this should be adhered to.

Any one, having the lead and several winning cards to play, should not draw a second card out of his hand until his partner has played to the first trick, such act being a distinct intimation that the former has played a winning card.

No intimation whatever, by word or gesture, should be given by a player as to the state of his hand, or of the game.

A player who desires the cards to be placed, or who demands to see the last trick, should do it for his own information only, and not in order to invite the attention of his partner.

No player should object to refer to a bystander who professes himself uninterested in the game, and able to decide any disputed question of facts ; as to who played any particular card—whether honours were claimed though not scored, or *vice versâ*—etc., etc.

It is unfair to revoke purposely ; having made a revoke, a player is not justified in making a second in order to conceal the first.

Until the players have made such bets as they wish, bets should not be made with bystanders.

Bystanders should make no remark, neither should they by word or gesture give any intimation of the state of the game until concluded and scored, nor should they walk round the table to look at the different hands.

No one should look over the hand of a player against whom he is betting,

DUMMY.

Is played by three players.

One hand, called Dummy's, lies exposed on the table.

The laws are the same as those of Whist, with the following exceptions :

I. Dummy deals at the commencement of each rubber.

II. Dummy is not liable to the penalty for a revoke, as his adversaries see his cards ; should he revoke, and the error not be discovered until the trick is turned and quitted, it stands good.

III. Dummy being blind and deaf, his partner is not liable to any penalty for an error whence he can gain no advantage. Thus, he may expose some or all of his cards—or may declare that he has the game, or trick, etc., without incurring any penalty ; if, however, he lead from Dummy's hand when he should lead from his own, or *vice versâ*, a suit may be called from the hand which ought to have led.

DOUBLE DUMMY.

Is played by two players, each having a Dummy or exposed hand for his partner. The laws of the game do not differ from Dummy Whist, except in the following special Law : There is no misdeal, as the deal is a disadvantage.

THE POKER FAMILY.

Properly speaking, Poker is not the founder, but simply the most famous representative of a very ancient and always very popular family of games, all of which can be traced to one source, the old French game of Gilet, which was undoubtedly of Italian origin, perhaps a variety of Primero. Gilet we find changed to Brelan in the time of Charles IX., and although Brelan is no longer played, the word is still used in all French games to signify triplets, and "brelan-carré" is the common French term for four of a kind in *le poker Americain*. From Brelan we trace the French games of Bouillotte, and Ambigu, and the English game of Brag; which are undoubtedly the forerunners of American Poker, the only difference being in the number of cards dealt to each player.

The peculiar and distinguishing characteristic of Poker we find well described by Seymour, in his chapter on "Brag," in the "Court Gamester," 1719: "The endeavour to impose on the judgment of the rest who play, and particularly on the person who chiefly offers to oppose you, by boasting or bragging of the cards in your hand. Those who by fashioning their looks and gestures, can give a proper air to their actions, as will so deceive an unskilful antagonist, that sometimes a pair of fives, trays or deuces, in such a hand, with the advantage of his composed countenance, and subtle manner of over-awing the other, shall out-brag a much greater hand, and win the stakes, with great applause and laughter on his side from the whole company."

Quite a number of card games retain the feature of pairs, triplets, sequences, and flushes, but omit the element of brag or bluff, and can therefore hardly be considered full-blooded members of the poker family. Whiskey Poker, for instance, has really little or nothing in common with the true spirit of poker, and is simply the very ancient game of Commerce, played with five cards instead of three. The descriptions of this game in the earliest Hoyles betray its French origin ; particularly in the use of the piquet pack ; the French custom of cutting to the left and dealing to the right ; and the use of the words "brelan," and "tricon." In later descriptions of the "new form" of Commerce, about 1835, we find 52 cards are used, and dealt from left to right, and the names of the combinations are changed to "pairs-royal," "sequences," and "flushes."

There appears to be little or nothing modern in the game of Poker but the increased number of cards dealt to each player, which makes it possible for one to hold double combinations, such as two pairs, triplets with a pair, etc. The old games were all played with three cards only, and the "brelan-carré," or four of a kind, could be made only by combining the three cards held by the player with the card which was sometimes turned up on the talon, or remainder of the pack. The blind, the straddle, the raise, the bluff, table stakes, and freeze-out, are all to be found in Bouillotte, which flourished in the time of the French Revolution, and the "draw" from the remainder of the pack existed in the old French game of Ambigu.

It is a curious fact that in none of the many text-books on Poker is there any satisfactory explanation of how or where the game, in its present form, originated. Poker is not mentioned in the American Hoyles of forty years ago, nor in the standard English work, Bohn's "Handbook of Games," as late as 1879. Many persons must be still living who could give some account of when the change from three cards to five took place, and the circumstances that brought it about. If Poker continues to increase in popularity as it has done, such historical data will be very valuable some day.

There is no authoritative code of laws for the game of Poker, simply because the best clubs do not admit the game to their card rooms, and consequently decry the necessity for adopting any laws for its government. In the absence of any official code, the daily press is called upon for hundreds of decisions every week. The author has gathered and compared a great number of these newspaper rulings, and has drawn from them and other sources to form a brief code of poker laws, which will be found amply sufficient to cover all irregularities for which any penalty can be enforced, or which interfere with the rights of any individual player.

DRAW POKER.

CARDS. Poker is played with a full pack of fifty-two cards, ranking: A K Q J 10 9 8 7 6 5 4 3 2 ; the ace being the highest or

 lowest in play, according to the wish of the holder, but ranking below the deuce in cutting. In some localities a special pack of sixty cards is used, the eight extra cards being elevens and twelves in each suit, which rank above the ten, and below the Jack. It is very unusual to play

Poker with two packs.

COUNTERS, or CHIPS. Although not absolutely necessary, counters are much more convenient than money. The most
common are red, white, and blue circular chips, which should
" stack up " accurately, so that equal numbers may be measured
without counting them. The red are usually worth five whites,
and the blue worth five reds, or twenty-five whites. At the beginning of the game one player should act as banker, and be responsible for all counters at the table. It is usual for each player to
purchase, at the beginning of the game, the equivalent of 100
white counters in white, red, and blue.

PLAYERS. Poker may be played by any number of persons
from two to seven. When there are more than seven candidates
for play, two tables should be formed, unless the majority vote
against it. In some localities it is the custom for the dealer to take
no cards when there are eight players, which is thought to make a
better game than two tables of only four players each. When the
sixty-card pack is used, eight players may take cards.

CUTTING. The players who shall form the table, and their
positions at the beginning of the game, must be decided by throwing round a card to each candidate, face up, or by drawing cards
from an outspread pack. If there are more than eight candidates,
the four cutting the highest cards should play together at one table,
and the others at another table. If there are an even number of
candidates, the tables divide evenly, but if the number is odd, the
smaller table is formed by those cutting the highest cards.

The table formed, the pack must be shuffled and spread, and
positions drawn for. The player cutting the lowest card has the
choice of seats, and must deal the first hand. The player cutting
the next lowest has the next choice, and so on, until all are seated.

TIES. If the first cut does not decide, those tying must cut
again. Should two or more players cut cards of equal value, the
new cut will decide nothing but the tie; for even should one of
those cutting to decide a tie draw a card lower than one previously
cut by another player, the original low cannot be deprived of his
right. For instance : there are six players.

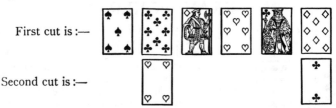

First cut is :—

Second cut is :—

The 5 and 7 have the first and second choice of seats; the 2
and 4 the third and fourth choice.

PLAYERS' POSITIONS. There are only three distinctive positions at the poker table : the ***dealer ;*** the ***pone;*** and the ***age.*** The pone is the player on the dealer's right, and the age is the one on his left.

STAKES. Before play begins, or a card is dealt, the value of the counters must be decided, and a ***limit*** must be agreed upon. There are four limitations in Draw Poker, and they govern or fix the maximum of the four principal stakes : the blind ; the straddle ; the ante ; and the bet or raise.

The ***blind*** is the amount put up by the age before he sees anything, and should be limited to one white counter, as the blind is the smallest stake in the game. In some places it is permissible for the age to make the blind any amount he pleases within half the betting limit ; but such a practice is a direct violation of the principles of the game, which require that the amount of the blind shall bear a fixed proportion to the limit of the betting.

The ***straddle*** is a double blind, sometimes put up by the player to the left of the age, and like the blind, without seeing anything. This allows the player on the left of the straddler to double again, or put up four times the amount of the original blind. This straddling process is usually limited to one-fourth of the betting limit ; that is, if the betting limit is fifty counters, the doubling of the blind must cease when a player puts up sixteen, for another double would carry it to thirty-two, which would be more than half the limit for a bet or raise.

The ***ante*** is the amount put up by each player after he has seen his cards, but before he draws to improve his hand. The terms "ante" and "blind" are often confused. The blind is a compulsory stake, and must be put up before the player has seen anything. He does not even know whether or not he will be dealt a foul hand, or whether it will be a misdeal. He has not even seen the cards cut. The ante, on the other hand, is a voluntary bet, and is a sort of entrance fee, which is paid before the hand is complete, but after the first part of it has been seen. The ante is always twice the amount of the blind, whatever that may be. If the blind has been increased by the process of straddling, the ante must be twice the amount of the last straddle, but must not exceed the betting limit. This is why the straddles are limited.

The largest ***bet,*** or ***raise,*** which a player is allowed to make is generally known as ***the limit.*** This limit is not the greatest amount that may be bet on one hand, but is the maximum amount by which one player may increase his bet over that of another player. For instance : If no one has bet, A may bet the limit on his hand ; B may then put up a similar amount, which is called ***seeing*** him, and may then ***raise*** him any further sum within the limit fixed for betting. If B raises the limit, it is obvious that he has placed in the pool twice the amount of the betting limit ; but his *raise* over A's bet is within the betting limit. If another player should raise B again, he would be putting up three times the limit ; A's bet, B's raise, and his own raise.

In the absence of any definite arrangement, it is usual to make the betting limit fifty times the amount of the blind. That is, if the value of the blind, or one white counter, is five cents, the limit of a bet or raise will be two dollars and a half, or two blue counters. This fixes the ante at two white counters, or ten cents, in the absence of straddles, and limits the straddling to the fourth player from the age, or sixteen white counters. This proportion makes a very fair game, and gives a player some opportunity to vary his betting according to his estimate of the value of his hand. Where the blind is five cents, the ante ten, and the limit twenty-five, the game ceases to be Poker, and becomes a species of *show-down.* It is universally admitted by good judges that a player can lose more money at twenty-five cent show-down than he will at two-and-a-half Poker.

There are several other variations in the manner of arranging the stakes and the betting limits, but they will be better understood after the game itself has been described.

DEALING. The age having put up the amount of the blind, and the cards having been shuffled by any player who chooses to avail himself of the privilege, the dealer last, they are presented to the pone to be cut. The pone may either cut them, or signify that he does not wish to do so by tapping the pack with his knuckles. Should the pone decline to cut, no other player can insist on his so doing, nor do it for him. Beginning on his left, the dealer distributes the cards face down one at a time in rotation until each player has received five cards. The deal passes to the left, and each player deals in turn.

IRREGULARITIES IN THE DEAL. The following rules regarding the deal should be strictly observed :—

If any card is found faced in the pack the dealer must deal again. Should the dealer, or the wind, turn over any card, the player to whom it is dealt must take it ; but the same player cannot be compelled to take two exposed cards. Should such a combination occur, there must be a fresh deal by the same dealer. If the player exposes his cards himself, he has no remedy.

Should any player receive more or less than his correct number of cards, and discover the error before he looks at any card in his hand, or lifts it from the table, he may demand a fresh deal if no bet has been made ; or he may ask the dealer to give him another from the pack if he has too few ; or to draw a card if he has too many. Cards so drawn must not be exposed, but should be placed on the bottom of the pack.

If the number of the hands dealt does not agree with the number of players, there must be a new deal.

If two or more cards are dealt at a time, the dealer may take back the card or cards improperly dealt if he discovers the error before dealing to the next player ; otherwise there must be a new deal.

A misdeal does not lose the deal. The misdealer must deal again.

Should a player take up his hand, or look at any card in it, he is not entitled to any remedy. If he has less than his proper number of cards, he must play them or pass out ; but if he has more than the proper number, his hand is foul, and must be abandoned, the player forfeiting any interest he may have in that deal, and any stake he may have put up on that hand. In some places the rule is to call a short hand foul ; but there should be no objection to playing against a man with only four cards, which cannot be increased to five, even by the draw.

STRADDLING. During the deal, or at any time before he looks at any card in his hand, the player to the left of the age may *straddle the blind* by putting up double the amount put up by the age. The only privilege this secures to the straddler is that of having the last *say* as to whether or nor he will make good his ante and draw cards. Should he refuse to straddle, no other player can do so ; but if he straddles, the player on his left can straddle him again by doubling the amount he puts up, which will be four times the amount of the blind. This will open the privilege to the next player on the left again, and so on until the limit of straddling is reached ; but if one player refuses to straddle, no other following him can do so. Good players seldom or never straddle, as the only effect of it is to increase the amount of the ante.

METHOD OF PLAYING. The cards dealt, the players take up and examine their hands. The careful poker player always " spreads " his cards before taking them up, to be sure that he has neither more nor less than five, and he lifts them in

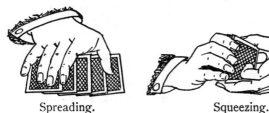

Spreading. Squeezing.

such a way that the palm and fingers of his right hand conceal the face of the first card, while the thumb of the left hand separates the others just sufficiently to allow him to read the index or " squeezer " marks on the edges.

The object of this examination is to ascertain the value of the hand dealt to him, and to see whether or not it is worth while trying to improve it by discarding certain cards and drawing others in their place. The player should not only be thoroughly familiar with the relative value of the various combinations which may be held at Poker, but should have some idea of the chances for and against better combinations being held by other players, and should also know the odds against improving any given combination by drawing to it.

The value of this technical knowledge will be obvious when it is remembered that a player may have a hand dealt to him which he knows is comparatively worthless as it is, and the chances for improving which are only one in twelve, but which he must bet on at odds of one in three, or abandon it. Such a proceeding would evidently be a losing game, for if the experiment were tried twelve times the player would win once only, and would lose eleven times. This would be paying eleven dollars to win three; yet poker players are continually doing this.

RANK OF THE HANDS. The various combinations at Poker outrank one another in the following order, beginning with the lowest. Cards with a star over them add nothing to the value of the hand, and may be discarded. The figures on the right are the odds against such a hand being dealt to any individual player.

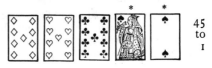

Five cards of various suits; not in sequence, and without a pair.	Even
One Pair. Two cards of one kind and three useless cards.	13 to 10
Two Pairs. Two of one kind; two of another kind; and one useless card.	20 to 1
Threes. Three of one kind, and two useless cards.	45 to 1

Straight. All five cards in sequence, but of various suits.

Flush. All five cards of one suit, but not in sequence.

Full Hand. Three of one kind, and two of another kind; no useless cards.

Fours. Four cards of one kind, and one useless card.

Straight Flush. Five cards of the same suit, in sequence with one another.

Royal Flush. A straight flush which is ace high.

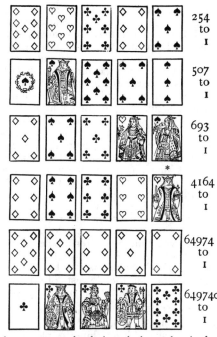

254 to 1

507 to 1

693 to 1

4164 to 1

64974 to 1

649740 to 1

When hands are of the same rank, their relative value is determined by the denomination of the cards they contain. For instance : A hand without a pair, sequence, or flush is called by its highest card ; "ace high," or " Jack high," as the case may be. As between two such hands, the one containing the highest card would be the better, but either would be outclassed by a hand with a pair in it, however small. A hand with a pair of nines in it would outrank one with a pair of sevens, even though the cards accompanying the nines were only a deuce, three and four, while those with the sevens were an ace, King and Queen. But should the pairs be alike in both hands; such as tens, the highest card outside the pair would decide the rank of the hands, and if those were also alike, the next card, or perhaps the fifth would have to be considered. Should the three odd cards in each hand be identical, the hands would be a tie, and would divide any pool to which each had a claim. Two flushes would decide their rank in the same manner. If both were ace and Jack high, the third card in one being a nine, and in the other an eight, the nine would win. In full hands the rank of the triplets decides the value of the hand. Three Queens and a pair of deuces will beat three Jacks and a pair of aces.   In straights, the highest card of the sequence wins; not necessarily the highest card in the hand, for a player may have a sequence of A 2 3 4 5, which is only five high, and would be beaten by a sequence of 2 3 4 5 6. The ace must either begin or end a sequence, for a player is not allowed to call such a combination as Q K A 2 3 a straight.

It was evidently the intention of those who invented Poker that the hands most difficult to obtain should be the best, and should outrank hands that occurred more frequently.   A glance at the table of odds will show that this principle has been carried out as far as the various denominations of hands go; but when we come to the members of the groups the principle is violated.   In hands not containing a pair, for instance, ace high will best Jack high. but it is much more common to hold ace high than Jack high. The exact proportion is 503 to 127.   A hand of five cards only seven high but not containing a pair, is rarer than a flush; the proportion being 408 to 510.   When we come to two pairs, we find the same inversion of probability and value.   A player will hold " aces up," that is, a pair of aces and another pair inferior to aces, eleven times as often as he will hold " threes up."   In the opinion of the author, in all hands that do not contain a pair, "seven high " should be the best instead of the lowest, and ace high should be the lowest.   In hands containing two pairs, " threes up " should be the highest, and " aces up " the lowest.

MISTIGRIS.   In Europe it is not uncommon to leave the joker, or blank card, in the pack.   The player to whom this card is dealt may call it anything he pleases.   If he has a pair of aces, and the joker, he may call them three aces.   If he has four clubs, and the joker, he may call it a flush; or he may make the joker fill out a straight.   If he has four of a kind, and the joker, he can beat a royal flush by calling his hand five of a kind.   In case of ties, the hand with the mistigris wins; that is to say, an ace and the joker will beat two aces.   The mistigris is comparatively unknown in America, and is a relic of the old English game of Brag.

PROBABILITIES.   In estimating the value of his hand as compared to that of any other player, before the draw, the theory of probabilities is of little or no use, and the calculations will vary with the number of players engaged.   For instance: If five are playing, some one should have two pairs every fourth deal, because in four deals twenty hands will be given out.   If seven are playing, it is probable that five of them will hold a pair of some kind before the draw.   Unfortunately, these calculations are not of the slightest practical use to a poker player, because although three of a kind may not be dealt to a player more than once in forty-five times on the average, it is quite a common occurrence for two players to have threes dealt to each of them at the same time. The considerations which must guide the player in judging the comparative value of his hand, both before and after the draw, must be left until we come to the suggestions for good play.

THE ANTE. The player to the left of the age is the one who must make the first announcement of his opinion of his hand, unless he has straddled, in which case the player on the left of the last straddler has the first **"say."** If he considers his hand good enough to draw to, let us say a pair of Kings, he must place in the pool, or toward the centre of the table, double the amount of the blind, or of the last straddle, if any. This is called the ante, because it is made before playing the hand, whereas the blind is made before seeing it. The player is not restricted to double the amount of the blind or straddle; he may bet as much more as he pleases within the limit fixed at the beginning of the game. For instance: If there has been only one straddle he must put up four white counters or pass out of the game for that deal. But if he puts up the four, he may put up as many more as he pleases within the limit, which is two blues, or fifty whites. This is called *raising the ante.* If he does not care to pay twice the amount of the blind or straddle for the privilege of drawing cards to improve his hand, he must throw his cards face downward on the table in front of the player whose turn it will be to deal next. Reasonable time must be allowed for a player to make his decision; but having made it, he must abide by it; a hand once thrown down cannot be taken up again, and counters once placed in the pool, and the hand removed from them, cannot be taken out again, even though placed in the pool by mistake.

The player who has the first say having made his decision, the player next him on the left must then decide. He must put into the pool an amount equal to that deposited by the first player, or abandon his hand. Suppose there has been no straddle, and that all conclude to *stay,* as it is called. They each in turn put up two white counters until it comes to the age. The one white counter he has already put up as a blind belongs to the pool, but by adding one to it he can make his ante good, and draw cards, always provided no player has raised the ante. If any player has put more counters into the pool than the amount of the ante, all the other players must put up a like amount, or throw down their hands. Suppose five play, and A has the age. B antes two counters, and C puts up seven, the ante and a raise of five. If D and E come in, they must put up seven counters also; and the age, A, must put up six to make his ante good. It now comes to B, who must either lose the two he has already put up, or add five more to them. Let us suppose that D puts up the seven, and that E, the dealer, puts up twelve. This will force the age to put up eleven; B to put up ten; and C to put up five more, This will make each player's ante an equal amount, twelve counters, and they will then be ready to draw cards. No one can now raise the ante any further, because it is no one's turn to " say."

It will thus be seen that every player in his turn can do one of three things, which are sometimes called the *a b c* of Poker : He can *Abdicate ;* by throwing down his hand, and abandoning whatever money he has already placed in the pool. He can *Better ;* by putting up more money than any player before him, which is sometimes called " going better." Or, he can *Call,* by making his amount in the pool equal to the highest bet already made.

Should any player increase the ante to such an extent that none of the others care to call him, they must of course throw down their hands, and as there is no one to play against him, the one who made the last increase in the ante takes down all the counters in the pool. This is called *taking the pot,* and the cards are gathered, shuffled, and dealt again, the deal passing to the player who was the age.

DRAWING CARDS. All those who have made the ante good have the privilege of discarding, face downward, as many cards as they please, in the place of which they may draw others. The age has the first draw, and can take any number of cards from one to five, or he may *stand pat,* refusing to draw any. A player cannot receive from the dealer more or less cards than he discards ; so that if a person is allowed to play with a short hand, of four cards only, he will still have only four cards after the draw. If his hand was foul, it will remain so after the draw In drawing, a player may keep or discard what cards he pleases. There is no rule to prevent his throwing away a pair of aces and keeping three clubs if he is so inclined ; but the general practice is for the player to retain whatever pairs or triplets he may have, and to draw to them. Four cards of a straight or a flush may be drawn to in the same way, and some make a practice of drawing to one or two high cards, such as an ace and a king, when they have no other chance. Some hands offer opportunities to vary the draw. For instance : A player has dealt to him a small pair ; but finds he has also four cards of a straight. He can discard three cards and draw to the pair ; or one card, and draw to the 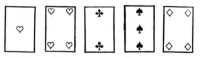 straight ; or two cards, keeping his ace in the hope of making two good pairs, aces up. The details of the best methods of drawing to various combinations will be discussed when we come to suggestions for good play.

In drawing cards, each player in turn who has made good his ante, beginning with the age, must ask the dealer for the number of cards he wants. The demand must be made so that every player can hear, because after the cards have been delivered by the dealer no one has the right to be informed how many cards any player drew. When the dealer comes to his own hand, he must distinctly announce the number of cards he takes. He must also inform any player asking him how many cards he took, provided the question is put before the player asking it has made a bet, and it is put by a player who has made good his ante and drawn cards.

In dealing the cards for the draw, the pack is not cut again, the cards being dealt from the top, beginning where the deal before the draw left off. As each player asks for his cards he must discard those he wants replaced, and he must receive the entire number he asks for before the next player is helped. In some places it is the custom for all those who have made good the ante to discard before any cards are given out. This is not good poker, as it prevents the dealer from seeing that the number discarded is equal to the number asked for. Should any card be found faced in the pack, it must be placed on the table among the discards. Should any card be exposed by the dealer in giving out the cards, or be blown over by the wind before the player has touched it, such card must not be taken by the player under any circumstances, but must be placed with the discards on the table. A player whose card is exposed in this manner does not receive a card to take its place until all the other players have been helped. [The object of this rule is to prevent a dealer from altering the run of the cards in the draw.]

Should a player ask for an incorrect number of cards and they be given him, he must take them if the next player has been helped. If too many, he must discard before seeing them. If too few, he must play them. If he has taken them up and has too many, his hand is foul, and shuts him out of that pool. If the dealer gives himself more cards than he needs he is compelled to take them. For instance: He draws three cards to a pair; but on taking up his hand he finds he had triplets, and really wanted only two cards. He cannot change his draw, and must take the three cards he has dealt off. There is a penalty for not following the strict rule of the game, which is for each player, including the dealer, to discard before he draws.

Should the dealer give any player more cards than he asked for, and the player discover the error before taking them up or looking at any of them, the dealer must withdraw the surplus card, and place it on the top of the pack. Should the dealer give a player fewer cards than he asks for, he must supply the deficiency when his attention is called to it, without waiting to supply the other players. If a player has more than five cards after the draw, his hand is foul, and he must abandon it, together with all he may have already staked in the pool. Should he have too few cards, he may play them if he pleases; but he must announce to the table that he plays with four cards only, and he cannot claim to have either a straight or a flush with a short hand.

The last card of the pack must not be dealt. When only two cards remain, the discards and abandoned hands must be gathered, shuffled, and presented to the pone to be cut, and the deal then completed.

BETTING UP THE HANDS. All those who made good the ante having been supplied with cards, the next player who holds cards on the left of the age must make the first bet. Should the age have declined to make good his ante, or have passed out before the draw, that does not transfer the privilege of having the last say to any other player; because the peculiar privilege of the age,—having the last say,—is given in consideration of the blind, which he is *compelled* to pay, and no other player can have that privilege, because no other player is obliged to play. Even if a player has straddled the blind, he must still make the first bet after the draw, because he straddled of his own free will, and knew at the time that the only advantage the straddle would give him was the last say as to whether or not he would make good his ante and draw cards.

If the player next to the age has passed out before the draw, the next player to the left who still holds cards must make the first bet. The player whose turn it is to bet must either do so, or throw his hand face downward in front of the player whose turn it will be to deal next. If he bets, he can put up any amount from one white counter to the limit, two blues. It then becomes the turn of the player next on his left who still holds cards to abdicate, better, or call. If he calls, he does so by placing in the pool an amount equal to that staked by the last player, and it then becomes the turn of the next player on the left to say what he will do. But if he goes better, he adds to the amount staked by the player on his right any further sum he sees fit, within the limit of two blues. Each player in turn has the same privilege, the age having the last say.

Suppose five play, and that A has the age. B has straddled, and all but the dealer have made good the ante and drawn cards. There are sixteen white counters in the pool, B's straddle having made the ante four instead of two. Suppose B bets a red counter, and C then throws down his hand. D *sees* B, by putting up a red counter; and he then ***raises*** him, by putting up two blues, increasing his bet as much as the limit will allow him. The age must now abandon his hand or put up one red and two blues to call D, without knowing what B proposes to do. Let us suppose he sees D, and raises another two blues. B must now retire, or put up four blues to call A, without knowing what D will do. He can raise the bet another two blues, or one blue, or a red, or a white even, if he is so minded. If he declines to raise, he cannot prevent D from so doing, because D still has the privilege of replying to A's raise, and as long as a player has any *say* about anything, whether it is to abdicate, better, or call, he can do any one of the three. It is only when there is no bet made, or when his own bet is either not called or not raised, that a player has nothing to say. Let us suppose B puts up the four blues to call A. It is now D's turn. If he puts up two blues, each will have an equal amount in the pool, and as no one will have anything more to say, the betting must stop, and the hands must be shown. But if D raises A again, by putting up four blues instead of two, he gives A another say, and perhaps A will raise D in turn. Although B may have had quite enough of this, he must either put up four more blues, the two raised by D and the further raise by A, or he must abandon his hand. If B throws down his cards he loses all claim to what he has already staked in the pool, four blues and a red, besides his straddle and ante. Let us suppose he drops out, and that D just calls A, by putting up two blues only, making the amount he has in the pool exactly equal to A's, eight blues and a red, besides the antes. This prevents A from going any further, because it is not his turn to say anything. He is not asked to meet any one's raise, nor to make any bet himself, but simply to show his hand, in order to see whether or not it is better than D's.

SHOWING HANDS. It is the general usage that the hand *called* must be shown first. In this case A's hand is called, for D was the one who called a halt on A in the betting, and stopped him from going any further. The strict laws of the game require that both hands must be shown, and if there are more than two in the final call, all must be shown to the table. The excuse generally made for not showing the losing hand is that the man with the worse hand paid to see the better hand ; but it must not be forgotten that the man with the better hand has paid exactly the same amount, and is equally entitled to see the worse hand. There is an excellent rule in some clubs that a player refusing to show his hand in a call shall refund the amount of the antes to all the other players, or pay all the antes in the next jack pot. The rule of showing both hands is a safeguard against collusion between two players, one of whom might have a fairly good hand, and the other nothing ; but by mutually raising each other back and forth they could force any other player out of the pool. The good hand could then be called and shown, the confederate simply saying, " That is good," and throwing down his hand. Professionals call this system of cheating, " raising out."

When the hands are called and shown, the best poker hand wins, their rank being determined by the table of values already given. In the example just given suppose that A, on being called by D, had shown three fours, and that D had three deuces. A would take the entire pool, including all the antes, and the four blues and one red staked by B after the draw. It might be that B would now discover that he had *laid down* the best hand, having held three sixes. This discovery would be of no benefit to him, for he abandoned his hand when he declined to meet the raises of A and D.

If the hands are exactly a tie, the pool must be divided among those who are in at the call. For instance: Two players show aces up, and each finds his opponent's second pair to be eights. The odd card must decide the pool; and if that card is also a tie the pool must be divided.

If no bet is made after the draw, each player in turn throwing down his cards, the antes are won by the last player who holds his hand. This is usually the age, because he has the last say. If the age has not made good his ante, it will be the dealer, and so on to the right. There is no necessity for the fortunate player to show his hand; the mere fact that he is the only one holding any cards is prima facie evidence that his hand is the best. On the same principle, the player who has made a bet or raise which no other player will see, wins the pool without showing his hand, as he must be the only one with cards in his hand; for when a player refuses to see a bet he must abandon his hand, and with it all pretensions to the pool. If he wishes to call, but has not money enough, he must borrow it. He cannot demand a show of hands for what counters he has, except in table stakes.

During the betting, players are at liberty to make any remarks they see fit, and to tell as many cheerful lies about their hands as they please. A player may even miscall his hand when he shows it; the cards speak for themselves, just as the counters do, and what a player says does not affect either in the slightest. If a player says: " I raise you two blues," the statement amounts to nothing until the blues have been placed in the pool, and the owner's hand removed from them. There is no penalty if a player, during the betting, tells his adversaries exactly what he holds; nor is he likely to lose anything by it, for no one will believe him.

JACK POTS. The addition of jack pots has probably done more to injure Poker than the trump signal has injured Whist In the early days, when poker parties were small, four players being a common number, it was frequently the case that no one had a pair strong enough to draw to, and such a deal was regarded as simply a waste of time. To remedy this, it was proposed that whenever no player came in, each should be obliged to ante an equal amount for the next deal, and just to demonstrate that there were some good hands left in the pack no one was allowed to draw cards until some one had *Jacks or better* to draw to.

The result of this practice was to make jack pots larger than the other pools, because every one was compelled to ante, and this seems to have prompted those who were always wanting to increase the stakes to devise excuses for increasing the number of jack pots. This has been carried so far that the whole system has become a nuisance, and has destroyed one of the finest points in the game of Poker,—the liberty of personal judgment as to every counter put into the pool, except the blind. The following excuses for making jack pots are now in common use :

After a Misdeal some parties make it a jack ; but the practice should be condemned, because it puts it in the power of any individual player to make it a jack when he deals.

The Buck is some article, such as a penknife, which is placed in the pool at the beginning of the game, and is taken down with the rest of the pool by whichever player wins it. When it comes to his deal, it is a jack pot, and the buck is placed in the pool with the dealer's ante, to be won, taken down, and make another jack in the same way.

The usual custom is to fix the amount of the ante in jack pots, a red, or five whites, being the common stake. In some places it is at the option of the holder of the buck to make the ante any amount he pleases within the betting limit. Whichever system is adopted, every player at the table must deposit a like amount in the pool. Players are sometimes permitted to *pass a jack ;* that is, not to ante nor to take any part in the game until the jack is decided. If this is to be allowed, it should be so understood at the beginning of the game.

The High Hand jack pot is played whenever a hand of an agreed value, such as a flush or a full, is shown to the board ; that is, called. In some places four of a kind calls for *a round of jacks,* every player in turn making it a jack on his deal.

Only Two In. It is a common custom in large parties, say six or seven players, to make it a jack when no one but the dealer will ante. Instead of allowing the blind to make his ante good, and draw cards against the dealer, each player contributes two white counters, the age adding one to his blind, and the cards are redealt for a jack pot. Another variety of this custom is when the blind is opposed by only one ante, to allow the age to make this player take down his two counters, and to pay two counters for him, to make it a jack. For instance : Five play, and A has the age. B and C pass, and D antes two counters. The dealer, E, says : " I pass for a jack." A then puts up three counters, one of which is added to his blind, the other two paying D's ante in the ensuing jack. D takes down his two counters, and the cards are redealt. This cannot be done if more than one player has anted, nor if the ante has been raised or the blind straddled. In the example just given, had D raised the ante to five counters and E passed, the age would have had to put up four more white counters and draw cards, or allow D to win his blind.

Progressive Jacks. In some localities it is the custom to make the pair necessary to open a jack pot progress in value; Jacks or better to open the first round; Queens the next; then Kings; then Aces; and then back to Kings, Queens, and Jacks again. This is very confusing, and is not popular.

Fattening Jacks. When the original ante is two counters only, and no one holds Jacks or better on the first deal, each player must contribute another white counter to "fatten," and the cards are dealt again. This continues until the pot is opened; that is, until some player holds a hand as good or better than a pair of Jacks. The fattening process is followed when the dealer can make the original ante what he pleases; but if the ante for jacks is a fixed sum, such as a red counter, it is not usual to fatten the pot at all. This saves all disputes as to ***who is shy,*** one of the greatest nuisances in Poker.

Opening Jacks. As there is no age or straddle in any form of jack pot, the player to the left of the dealer has the first say, and must examine his hand to see if he has Jacks or better; that is to say, either an actual pair of Jacks, or some hand that would beat a pair of Jacks if called upon to do so, such as two pairs, a straight, or triplets. In some localities it is allowed to open jacks with a ***bobtail;*** that is, four cards of a flush or straight. If the player on the dealer's left has not openers, or does not care to open the pot if he has, he says: " I pass; " but he does not abandon his hand. The next player on his left must then declare. In some places players are allowed to throw down their cards when they pass; but in first-class games a penalty of five white counters must be paid into the pool by any player abandoning his hand before the second round of declarations, as it gives an undue advantage to players with medium hands to know that they have only a limited number of possible opponents. For instance: If six play, and the first three not only pass, but throw down and abandon their cards, a player with a pair of Jacks will know that he has only two possible adversaries to draw against him, which will so increase his chances that it may materially alter his betting.

If no one acknowledges to holding Jacks or better, the pot is fattened, and the cards are re-shuffled and dealt. The best practice is for the same dealer to deal again until some one gets Jacks or better. This is called ***dealing off the jack.*** If any player has forfeited his right in one deal, such as by having a foul hand, that does not prevent him coming into the pot again on the next deal with rights equal to the other players.

If any player holds Jacks or better, he can open the pot, or " the jack," for any amount he pleases within the betting limit.

The expression " open " is used because after one player has declared that he holds Jacks or better, all restrictions are removed, and the pool is then open to any player to come in and play for it, regardless of what he may hold. Each player in turn, beginning on the left of the opener, must declare whether or not he will *stay.* If he stays, he must put up an amount equal to that bet by the opener, and has the privilege of raising him if he sees fit. If he passes, he throws his cards face downward on the table in front of the player whose turn it will be to deal next. Should the opener be raised, and not care to see that raise, he must show his hand to the table before abandoning it, in order to demonstrate that he had openers. Some players show only the cards necessary to open, but the strict rules require the whole hand to be shown before the draw. When once the jack is opened, the betting before the draw proceeds exactly as in the ordinary pool. Any player on the right of the opener, who passed on the first round, may come in after the pot is opened. For instance : E deals. A and B pass, but hold their hands. C opens, and D throws down his hand. E sees the opener's bet, and it then becomes the turn of A and B, who have passed once, to say whether or not they will play, now that the pot is opened.

When all those who have declared to stay have deposited an equal amount in the pool, they draw cards to improve their hands, just as in the ordinary pool, the player on the dealer's left being helped first. In some places the opener is allowed to *split his openers* in order to try for a better hand. For instance · He has opened with a pair of Jacks, but has four of one suit in his hand. Four other players have stayed, perhaps the bet has been raised, and he knows that his Jacks will probably be worthless, even if he gets a third. So he breaks the pair, and draws for a flush. This is not good poker, and should not be permitted under any circumstances. The opener should be compelled to keep his openers. Some contend that the opener should be allowed to lay aside the card of the split pair, so as to show that he had openers originally ; but that is no proof that the other card of the pair was in his hand before the draw.

False Openers. Should a player open a jack without the hand to justify it, and discover his error before he draws, the best usage demands that his hand is foul, and that he forfeits to the pool whatever amount he may have opened for, and any raises that he may have stood. There are then three ways to play : *First.* Those who have come in under the impression that the pot had been legitimately opened but who have not openers themselves, can withdraw their money, and allow any one to open it who has openers. This is very unfair to those on the left of the false opener who have abandoned their hands. *Second.* Those who have come into the pot after the false opening are allowed to

stay in, and play for it, no matter what their hands are. **Third.**
On discovery of the false opening, each player is allowed to take
down whatever amount he may have paid into the pool, including
his original ante and all fatteners, and the false opener must then
make the entire amount good.   The cards are then dealt afresh.
This is a very harsh punishment for a very trifling and common
error.   The second method is the most popular, and probably the
fairest.

If the false opener does not discover his mistake until he has
drawn cards, his action is at least suspicious, and he should be
compelled to put up the total amount in the pool, as in case three.
In some localities such a player is barred from playing the next
two jacks, but compelled to ante his share in each.

Betting Jacks.   When a jack pot has been properly opened,
and all have declared whether or not they will stay, and have
drawn cards, the players proceed to bet on their hands.   As there
is no age in jack pots, the rule is for the opener to make the first
bet ; or, if he has been raised out before the draw, the player next
on his left who still holds cards.   The opener may decline to bet
if he pleases ; but if he does so, he must show his openers, and
then abandon his hand.   If no bet is made, the last player holding cards takes the pool without showing his hand.   If a bet is
made, each player in turn on the left must abdicate, better, or call,
just as in the ordinary pool.   At the conclusion of the betting, if
there is a call, the best poker hand wins, of course.   If there is no
call, the player making the last bet or raise takes the pool without
showing his hand, unless he is the opener, when the whole hand
need not be shown, as it is no one's business what the opener got
in the draw, no one having paid to see it.   All he need show is
openers.   But should the opener be one of those in the final call,
he must show his whole hand.   Should it then be discovered that
he has not openers, the usual penalty is for each player to take
down all he has contributed to the pool in the way of antes,
fatteners, or bets, and the false opener is then compelled to pay
the entire amount of the pool to the holder of the best hand
against him.

The Kitty is now an almost universal adjunct to the pool.   In
clubs, it pays for the cards, and for an occasional round of refreshments ; in small poker parties it defrays the expense of the
weekly supper.   When the amount is excessive, or accumulates
too rapidly, it is often used to give the players a " free ride " by
paying all their antes in a " kitty jack pot."

The kitty is usually kept by the banker, who takes a white
counter out of every pool in which triplets or better are shown to
the board, and a red counter out of every jack pot.   These
counters must be kept apart from the other chips, and must be

accounted for at the end of the game by paying the kitty so much in cash, just as if it was one of the players.

Gambling houses and poker rooms are supposed to derive their entire revenue from this source, and those of the lowest class invent endless excuses for taking out for the kitty. In many houses there is a sliding scale for various hands ; one counter being taken for two pairs; two counters for triplets ; three for straights or flushes ; and a red for fours, jack pots, and misdeals. It is not uncommon for the proprietors of such games to find thirty or forty dollars in the kitty after a night's play with five-cent chips.

TABLE STAKES. This is one of several variations in arranging the stakes and the betting limit. In some localities it is the custom to allow each player to purchase as many counters as he pleases ; in others it is the rule to compel each to buy an equal number at the start, usually two hundred times the amount of the blind. In table stakes the betting limit is always the amount that the player has in front of him ; but no player is allowed either to increase or diminish that amount while he has any cards in front of him. Before the cards are dealt for any pool he may announce that he wishes to buy counters, or that he has some to sell to any other player wishing to purchase ; but for either transaction the consent of all the other players must be obtained. No player is allowed under any circumstances to borrow from another, nor to be " shy " in any pot ; that is, to say, " I owe so many." If he has any counters in front of him, his betting is limited to what he has ; if he has none, he is out of the game, for that hand at least. As a player cannot increase the amount he has in front of him during the play of a hand, it is best to keep on the table at all times as much as one is likely to want to bet on any one hand.

It is the usual custom, and an excellent one, to fix upon a definite hour for closing a game of table stakes, and to allow no player to retire from the game before that hour unless he is *decavé,* (has lost all his capital). Should he insist on retiring, whatever counters he has must be divided among the other players, and if there are any odd ones after the division, they must be put into the current pool.

In table stakes, any player may **call a sight** for what money or counters he has in front of him, even should another player have bet a much larger amount. For instance : A has bet three dollars, and B has only two dollars in front of him, but wishes to call A. B calls for a sight by putting his two dollars in the pool, and A must then withdraw his third dollar from the pool, but leave it on the table to be called or raised by any other player. Should C wish to call A, or even to raise him, A and C may continue the betting independently of B's part of the pool. Should C have even less money than B, say one dollar, he may still further reduce the original pool, leaving the two dollars aside for settlement between

A and B, and A's third dollar still aside from that again for the decision of any other player.

Let us suppose that A and C continue the betting until one calls. When the hands are shown, if either A's or C's is better than B's, B loses his interest; but if B's hand is better than either A's hand or C's hand, he takes the part of the pool for which he called a sight, while A and C decide the remainder between them. For instance: A calls C, and C shows three tens. Neither A nor B can beat it, and C takes everything. But if B had three Jacks, and A only three fives, B would take the part of the pool for which he called a sight, and C would take the remainder.

Should C have raised and bluffed A out, or have bet so much that A finally refused to call, A would have no interest in either pool, and C would take all the money outside the pool for which B called a sight. Should it then transpire, on the show of hands between B and C, that A had laid down a better hand than either of them, that would not entitle A to claim the sight pool from B, because in laying down his hand he has practically acknowledged that C's hand is better, and has retired from the game. If B's hand is better than C's, B takes the sight pool.

FREEZE OUT.

This might be called a variety of table stakes. At the start, each player is supplied with an equal number of counters; but no one is allowed to replenish his stock, or to withdraw or loan any part of it. As soon as any player has lost his capital he is decavé, or **frozen out,** and must permanently retire from the game. The other players continue until only one remains, who must of course win everything on the table. This is not a popular form of Poker, because it is sometimes a long time before a player who is frozen out can get into a game again.

FLAT POKER.

In this variety of the game, before the cards are dealt, the age puts up, for a blind, any amount he pleases within the limit. Those who are willing to bet a similar amount on the possibilities of their hands put up a similar amount. Those who decline are not given any cards. There are no straddles, raises, or antes. Immediately after the deal each player who is in the pool draws cards, the age first. There are then two ways to play: The hands are shown and the best wins; or, beginning with the age, each player may say if he will back his hand against the field; *i. e.,* all the others in the pool. If he will, he must put up as much as their combined stakes. He cannot be raised; but if any one player or combination of players call him, and one of them can beat his hand, the field divide the pool. For instance: Age makes it a blue, and three others stay with him. After the draw C puts up three blues against the field. D and A call it, and all show hands. If any of the three, A, B or D can beat C they divide the pool, B getting his third, although he did not contribute to the call. This game is a pure gamble ; except that a bold player may occasionally bluff the field off.

METHODS OF CHEATING. Poker and its congeners have received more attention from the greeks than any other family of card games. In fact it is generally believed that the term greek, as applied to a card sharper, had its origin in the Adam of the poker family, which was a gambling game introduced by the Greeks in Italy.

So numerous and so varied are the methods of cheating at Poker that it is an axiom among gamblers that if a pigeon will not stand one thing he will another. The best informed make it a rule never to play Poker with strangers, because they realize that it is impossible for any but a professional gambler to know half the tricks employed by the poker sharp. It is a notorious fact that even the shrewdest gamblers are continually being taken in by others more expert than themselves. What chance then has the honest card player ?

There are black sheep in all flocks, and it may be well to give a few hints to those who are in the habit of playing in mixed companies.

Never play with a man who looks attentively at the faces of the cards as he gathers them for his deal ; or who stands the pack on edge, with the faces of the cards towards him, and evens up the bunch by picking out certain cards, apparently because they are sticking up. Any pack can be straightened by pushing the cards down with the hand. The man who lifts them up is more than probably a cheat.

Never play with a man who looks intently at the pack and shuffles the cards slowly. If he is not locating the cards for the ensuing deal he is wasting time, and should be hurried a little.

Never play with a person who leaves the cut portion of the pack on the table, and deals off the other part. In small parties this is a very common way of working what is known as ***the top stock.*** If such a dealer is carefully watched it will usually be found that he seizes the first opportunity to place the part cut off on the top of the part dealt from. The top stock is then ready for the draw, and the judicious player should at once cash his chips and retire from the game.

Never play with a man who continually holds his cards very close to his body, or who completely conceals his hand before the draw, or who takes great care to put his discard among previous discards, so that the exact number of cards put out cannot be counted. He is probably working a vest or sleeve hold-out. Some clumsy or audacious sharpers will go so far as to hold out cards in their lap, or stick them in a "bug" under the table. One of the most successful poker sharps ever known, "Eat-um-up Jake" Blackburn, who had a hand like a ham, could hold out five cards in his palm while he carried on all the operations of shuffling, dealing, and playing his hand. Such men require great dexterity and nerve to get rid of their "deadwood," or surplus cards, without detection. ***Holding out*** is regarded by the professional as a most dangerous experiment, but it is very common.

Never play with a man who keeps his eyes rivetted on the cards as he deals, and who deals comparatively slowly. He is probably using marked cards, or has marked the important ones himself during the play. Poker sharps who mark cards by scratching them with a sharp point concealed in a ring are obliged to hold the cards at a certain angle to the light in order to see the scratches. Those who dig points in the cards with the thumb nail depend on touch instead of sight. If you find such points on the cards, either dig other points on other cards, or retire from the game.

Against the hold-out or marked cards there is no protection, because the dealer does not care how much the cards in the pack are shuffled or cut ; but every method of running up hands, or stocking cards, can be made ineffective if the pone will not only cut the cards, but carefully re-unite the packets. If the two parts are straightened after the cut, it will be impossible for the dealer to shift the cut, and bring the cards back to their original position. The dealer will sometimes bend the top or bottom card so as to form a ***bridge,*** which will enable him to find the place where the cards were cut. This can only be overcome by shuffling the cards instead of cutting them, which every player has the right to do. If you insist on shuffling, the greek will do the same in his turn, and will run up hands to be dealt to himself. It is perfectly useless to endeavour to protect yourself against a poker sharp ; the only remedy is to leave the game.

Many persons have a strong prejudice against playing with a man who shuffles his chips. The mere fact of his being an expert at chip shuffling has nothing to do with the game of poker, the accomplishment usually being the result of long experience at the faro table. The reason for the prejudice is that a chip shuffler is usually cold blooded, courageous, and seldom a loser at any game that requires nerve.

SUGGESTIONS FOR GOOD PLAY. Volumes might be written for the guidance of the poker player without improving his game a particle, unless he possesses at least one of four qualifications : Control over his features and actions ; judgment of human nature ; courage ; and patience. The man whose face or manner betrays the nature of his hand, or the effect of an opponent's bet or raise, will find everyone to beat his weak hands, and no one to call his strong ones. Unless he is a fair judge of human nature he will never be able to estimate the strength or peculiarities of the players to whom he is opposed, and will fail to distinguish a bluff from an ambuscade. Without courage he cannot reap the full benefit of his good hands ; and without patience he cannot save his money in the time of adversity.

Of one thing every player may rest assured, and that is that Poker cannot be played by mathematical formulas. Beyond the most elementary calculations of the chances in favour of certain events the theory of probabilities is of no assistance. It is not necessary to call in a mathematician to prove that a player who habitually discards a pair of aces to draw to three cards of a suit will lose by the operation in the long run. Nor will any amount of calculation convince some players that they are wasting their money to stay in a jack pot in order to draw to a pair of tens, although such is the fact.

The various positions occupied by the player at the poker table may be briefly examined, and some general suggestions offered for his guidance in each of them. In the first place he should look out for his counters. It is always best for each player to place the amount of his ante or his bet immediately in front of him, so that there need be no dispute as to who is up, or who is shy. Above all it should be insisted that any player who has once put counters in the pool, and taken his hand from them, should not again take them down.

The Age is the most valuable position at the table, but it is seldom fully taken advantage of. The age should never look at his hand until it is his turn to make good his blind. He may pick up his cards, but he should use his eyes in following the manner and facial expression of the other players as they sort their cards. One of the greatest errors made by the age is in thinking that he must save his blind. The player who draws to nothing because he can do so cheaply, will usually have nothing to draw at the end of the game. The age can usually afford to draw to four-card flushes, and to straights open at both ends, but should not do so when there are less than three who have paid to draw cards, or when the ante has been raised.

If the age holds Kings or better before the draw, he should invariably raise the ante unless there are five players in the pool besides himself, or unless some other player has already raised. If he holds two pairs, he should do all his betting before the draw. If any other player has raised, or his own raise is re-raised, the age must use his judgment of the player and the circumstances. It is useless for the age to disguise his hand by such manœuvres as holding up an odd card to a pair, unless he raises the blind at the same time. If he draws one or two cards only, and has not raised the blind, every one will credit him for a small pair and an ace, or for a bobtail, and will inevitably call any bluff he may make. The age is the poorest position at the table for a bluff, but it is decidedly the best in which to win large pots with moderate hands.

The Dealer has the next best position to the age, and in large parties there is very little difference in the way in which the two positions should be played.

The ***first bettor*** has the worst position at the table and he should seldom come in on less than Queens. He should seldom raise the ante, even with two pairs, as he will only drive others out. In this position very little can be made out of good hands, because every one expects to find them there; but it offers many excellent opportunities for successful bluffing. A player in this position should never straddle. Many players endeavour to force their luck in this way, but it is a losing game, and the best players seldom or never straddle. Having to make the first bet after the draw, it is usualfor the player in this position, if he has an average hand, to ***chip along***, by simply betting a single counter, and waiting for developments. With a strong hand, it is best to bet its full value at once, on the chance that the bet may be taken for a bluff, and called.

Other Positions. As the positions go round the table from the first bettor to the age, they become more desirable, and little need be said of them beyond the consideration of the average strength necessary for a player to ***go in*** on.

GOING IN. There is a great difference of opinion as to the minimum value of a hand which should justify a player in drawing cards if he can do so for the usual ante. In close games many players make it a rule not to go in on less than tens, while in more liberal circles the players will draw to any pair. In determining which course to follow, the individual must be guided by his observation and judgment. Suppose five play, and A observes that B and C constantly draw to small pairs, while D and E never come in on less than tens. If A has the age, B, D, and E having anted, A may be sure that there are at least two good hands against him, and will guide himself accordingly. But if B and C are the only players in, A may safely draw to a small pair. It can be mathematically demonstrated that what is called an ***average go-in hand*** should be at least a pair of tens; but a player who waits for tens in a liberal game, in which others are drawing to ace high, will ante himself away if there are many jack pots, and will get no calls when he gets a hand.

BETTING. Good players are guided by the general character of the game in which they take part. Some parties play a very liberal game, and the players bet high on medium hands, and give every one a good fight. It is best to have liberal or lucky players on your right; because if they sit behind you, they will continually raise you, and you will be forced either to overbid your hand on the same liberal scale that they adopt, or lose what you have already put up. If a liberal player sits on your right you will often be able to make large winnings on moderate hands. In a close game, when the players bet in a niggardly manner, the liberal player is at a great disadvantage; for he can win little or nothing on his good hands, but will lose large amounts when he runs up the betting on a good hand which is opposed to one that is better. When a liberal player finds a close player following him freely, he may be sure there is a very strong hand against him.

VARIETY. Above all things a player should avoid regularity in his play, because observant adversaries will soon learn his methods. The best players usually play two pairs pat, without drawing, about half the time. This gives them the reputation of betting on pat hands which are not genuine, and when they get one that is real, they will often succeed in getting a good bet, or even a raise, from those holding triplets or two large pairs, who have noticed them play two pairs pat. In the same way it is advisable to hold up an odd card occasionally, without raising the ante; so that when you do hold triplets, and draw two cards, you will not frighten every one at the table. The chances of improving a pair by drawing three cards, are one in three; and by drawing two cards only, one in four. The difference is worth the moral effect of the variation in the play.

PROBABILITIES. The endless poker statistics that have been published are of little or no value to the practical player, and there are only a few figures that are worth remembering. It is a general law in all games of chance that you should never do a thing which you would not be willing to repeat under the same circumstances a hundred times. The best example of the application of this law is in drawing to bobtails. If you have a four-card flush to draw to, the odds against getting it are about four to one; and unless you can obtain the privilege of drawing to it by paying not more than one-fifth of the amount in the pool, you will lose by it in the long run. The best players never draw to four-card flushes except when they have the age, and the ante has not been raised.

There are some players who pretend to be so guided by probabilities that they never go into a pool unless the chances in favour of their having a good hand after the draw are at least equal to the odds they have to bet by going into the pool. This is all nonsense; for no player knows when he goes into a pool how much it will cost him to get out, and the value of his individual hand is an unknown quantity at the best, because it cannot be compared to the others. One thing only is certain, and that is that in the long run the player who goes in with the strongest hand will still have the strongest hand after the draw. This is an important thing to remember in jack pots, in which the value of at least one hand is known. If you draw to a pair smaller than

Jacks, you do so with the full knowledge that the pair itself is not strong enough to win. Now what are the odds against your winning the pool? Suppose you hold tens, and draw three cards. Your chance of improving your hand is a little better than one in five. The opener of the jack pot has exactly the same chance, and if both of you draw cards a hundred times under those circumstances, he will beat you in the long run, to say nothing of the other players who may come in and beat both of you. It is therefore evident that in backing tens against openers, it is four to one against your beating the openers to begin with, and if you do beat them the odds are still against your winning the pot. If there were five players, and the jack pots were all equal in amount, you would have to win one pot out of five to make your investment pay. Can you make this average when your original pair will not beat openers?

There are three principles with regard to the draw that should never be lost sight of:

(1) An average go-in hand is a hand which will win its proportion of the pools, according to the number playing, taking all improvements and opposition into account. This can be demonstrated to be a pair of tens.

(2) The draw is much more valuable to a weak hand than to a strong one, and weak hands will improve in much greater proportion than strong ones will. For instance: The chances for a player to improve by drawing to a pair of Queens are one in five. He may make two pairs, or triplets, or a full hand, or four of a a kind. The chances of improvement for a player drawing to two pairs, say Eights up, are only one in thirteen. This consideration leads players to adopt two lines of play: To bet all they intend to on two pairs before the draw, in order to prevent weaker hands drawing cards and improving; or, to discard the smaller pair in order to increase their chances of improvement.

(3) The smaller the number of players, the greater the value of the hands; and the larger the number of players, the greater the chance that any given hand will be beaten. When only two play, you can safely bet the limit on a pair of Eights; but in a party of eight players they are hardly worth drawing to. For this reason average hands should force the weaker out, and reduce the number of players *before the draw.*

For the benefit of those interested in such matters *the probable improvement by the draw* may be briefly given.

It is 3½ to 1 against improving *a pair* by drawing three cards; the chances against making triplets or two pairs being 8 to 1; against a full hand, 61 to 1; and against four of a kind, 364 to 1. It is 4 to 1 against improving a pair by drawing two cards; the chances against triplets being 12 to 1, and 8 to 1 against two pairs.

It is 12 to 1 against making a full hand by drawing to *two pairs.*

It is 8 to 1 against improving *triplets* by drawing two cards; 11 to 1 against a full hand, and 23 to 1 against four of a kind. It is 12 to 1 against improving if one card is drawn; 16 to 1 against the full, and 47 to 1 against four of a kind.

It is 12 to 1 against making a straight out of a sequence of four cards which is open in the middle, or at one end only. It is 5 to 1 against making a straight out of a sequence of four which is open at both ends.

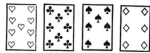

In-between Straight. | Open-end Straight.

It is 4½ to 1 against filling a four-card flush. It is 23 to 1 against filling a three-card flush. It is 95 to 1 against filling a two-card flush.

It is 3 to 1 against improving a four-card straight flush which is open at both ends. The chances against getting the straight or the flush have been given; the odds against getting the straight flush are 24 to 1. The chance for getting a pair exists; but the pair would probably be worthless.

It is 4 to 1 against improving a four-card straight flush open in the middle, or at one end only; the odds against getting the straight flush being 46 to 1.

There are several minor or speculative draws which may be of interest. Drawing to an ace and a King, it is 3 to 1 against making a pair of either. It is 4 to 1 against making a pair of aces by drawing four cards to an ace; and 12 to 1 against making aces up, or better. It is 24 to 1 against making a straight by drawing to three cards of it, open at both ends. It is 12 to 1 against making either a straight or a flush by drawing to three cards of a straight flush, open at both ends.

HOW TO WIN AT POKER. There have been many alleged infallible receipts for winning at Poker. Proctor thought that refusing to go in on less than triplets would prove a certainty; but in the same paragraph he acknowledges that the adversaries would soon learn the peculiarity, and avoid betting against the player. Triplets before the draw occur about once in every 45 hands. If five were playing, a person following Proctor's advice would have to blind 9 times, and ante in at least 12 jack pots in every 45 hands, to say nothing of fattening. This means an outlay of at least 75 counters. When the triplets come, will he get back 75 counters on them? He will probably win the blind, and one or two antes; but the moment he makes his own ante good, every player who cannot beat triplets, knowing his system, will lay down his hand.

An extensive observation of the methods of the best players has led the author to the conclusion that the great secret of success in Poker, apart from natural aptitude for the game, and being a good actor, is to *avoid calling.* If you think you have the best hand, raise. If you think you have not the best, lay it down. Although you may sometimes lay down a better hand than the one that takes the pool, the system will prove of immense advantage to you in two ways: In the first place, you will find it a great educator of the judgment; and in the second place, it will take almost any opponent's nerve. Once an adversary has learned your method, it is not a question of his betting a red chip on his hand; but of his willingness to stand a raise of two blues, which he will regard as inevitable if you come in against him at all. The fear of this raise will prompt many a player to lay down a moderately good hand without a bet; so that you have all the advantage of having made a strong bluff without having put up a chip. The system will also drive all but the most courageous to calling your hand on every occasion, being afraid of a further and inevitable raise; and it is an old saying that a good caller is a sure loser.

The theory of calling is to get an opportunity to compare your hand with your adversary's. Now, if you think that after the comparison yours will prove the better hand, why not increase the value of the pool? If, on the contrary, you fear that his hand will beat yours, why throw good money after bad? If you don't think at all about it, and have no means of forming an opinion as to the respective merits of your hands, you are not a poker player, and have no business in the game.

BLUFFING. There is nothing connected with Poker on which persons have such confused ideas as on the subject of bluffing. The popular impression seems to be that a stiff upper lip, and a cheerful expression of countenance, accompanied by a bet of five dollars, will make most people lay down three aces; and that this result will be brought about by the five-dollar bet, without any regard to the player's position at the table, the number of cards he drew, his manner of seeing or raising the ante, or the play of his adversaries before the draw. The truth of the matter is that for a bluff to be either sound in principle or successful in practice, the player must carefully select his opportunity. The bluff must be planned from the start, and consistently played from the ante to the end. To use a common expression: "The play must be right for it, or the bluff will be wrong."

There are many cases in which a bluff of fifty cents would be much stronger than one of five dollars; the difference depending on the player's position at the table, his treatment of the ante, and the number of cards he had drawn. As an example of the play being right for a bluff, take the following case : Five play in a jack pot. A and B have passed when C opens it for the limit. D and E pass out, but A and B both stay. and each draws one card. C takes two cards, and as it is his first bet he puts up the limit on his three aces. A drops out, but B raises C the limit in return. Now, if C is a good player he will lay down his three aces, even if he faintly suspects B is bluffing, because B's play is sound in any case. He either could not, or pretended he could not open the jack ; but he could afford to pay the limit to draw one card against openers, and he could afford to raise the limit against an opener's evidently honest two-card draw. As a matter of fact the whole play was a bluff; for B not only had nothing, but had nothing to draw to originally.

Another variety of the bluff, which is the author's own invention, will often prove successful with strangers, but it can seldom be repeated in the same company. Suppose six play in a jack pot. A passes, and B opens it by quietly putting up his counters. C and D pass, and E, pretending not to know that B has opened it, announces that he will open it for the limit, although he has not a pair in his hand. He is of course immediately informed that it has been opened, upon which he unhesitatingly raises it for the limit. Whatever the others do, E stands pat, and looks cheerful. The author has never known this bluff to be called.

Holding a strong hand, a player may often coax another to raise him, by offering to divide the pool.

The successful bluffer should never show his hand. Even if he starts the game by bluffing for advertising purposes, hoping to get called on good hands later, he should not show anything or tell anything that the others do not pay to see or know. Bluffing is usually more successful when a player is in a lucky vein than when he has been unfortunate.

POKER LAWS.

1. Formation of Table. A poker table is complete with seven players. If eight play the dealer must take no cards, or a sixty-card pack must be used. If there are more than seven candidates for play, two tables must be formed unless the majority decide against it.

2. Cutting. The players who shall form the table, and their positions at the beginning of the game may be decided by drawing from an outspread pack, or by throwing round a card to each candidate, face up. If there are eight or more candidates, the tables shall divide evenly if the number is even, those cutting the highest cards playing together. If the number is odd, the smaller table shall be formed by those cutting the highest cards. In cutting, the ace is low. Any player exposing more than one card must cut again.

3. The table formed, the players draw from the outspread pack for positions. The lowest cut has the first choice, and deals the first hand. The player cutting the next lowest has the next choice, and so on until all are seated.

4. *Ties.* If players cut cards of equal value they must cut again ; but the new cut decides nothing but the tie.

5. *Stakes.* Any player may be the banker, and keep the kitty, if any. In Draw, Straight, or Stud Poker, each player may purchase as many counters as he pleases. In Freeze-out, Table Stakes, Whiskey Poker, and Progressive Poker, each player must begin with an equal amount.

6. *Betting Limits.* Before play begins limits must be agreed upon for the amount of the blind, the straddle, the ante in jack pots, and for betting or raising.

7. *Shuffling.* Before the first deal the pack must be counted to see that it contains the proper number of cards. Should the first dealer neglect this he forfeits five counters to the pool. Before each deal the cards must be shuffled. Any player may shuffle, the dealer last.

8. *Cutting to the Dealer.* The dealer must present the pack to the pone, [the player on his right,] to be cut. The pone may either cut, or signify that he does not wish to do so, by tapping the pack with his knuckles. Should the pone decline to cut, no other player can insist on his doing so, nor do it for him. If he cuts, he must leave at least four cards in each packet, and the dealer or the pone must re-unite the packets by placing the one not removed in cutting upon the other.

9. If in cutting, or in re-uniting the packets, a card is exposed, the pack must be re-shuffled and cut.

10. If the dealer re-shuffles the pack after it has been properly cut, he forfeits five counters to the current pool.

11. *Dealing Before the Draw.* After the age, [the player on the dealer's left,] has put up the amount of the blind, the dealer distributes the cards face down, one at a time, in rotation, until each player has received five cards.

12. The deal passes to the left, except in jack pots, when it may be agreed that the same dealer shall deal until the pot is opened.

13. *Misdealing.* A misdeal does not lose the deal ; the same dealer must deal again. It is a misdeal : If the dealer fails to present the pack to the pone ; or if any card is found faced in the pack ; or if the pack is found imperfect ; or if the dealer gives six or more cards to more than one player ; or if he deals more or fewer hands than there are players ; or if he omits a player in dealing ; or if he deals a card incorrectly, and fails to correct the error before dealing another.

14. *Irregularities in the Hands.* Should the dealer, or the wind, turn over any card, the player to whom it is dealt must take it ; but the same player cannot be compelled to take two exposed cards. Should such a combination occur there must be a new deal. If the player exposes cards himself, he has no remedy,

15. Should any player receive more or less than his proper number of cards, and discover the error before he looks at any card in his hand, or lifts it from the table, he may demand a new deal if no bet has been made ; or he may ask the dealer to give him another card from the pack if he has too few, or to draw a card if he has too many. Cards so drawn must not be exposed, but should be placed on the top of the pack. If a bet has been made, there must be a new deal. Should the player take up his hand, or look at any card in it, he has no remedy.

16. Should a player take up a hand containing more than five cards, or look at any card in it, such a hand is foul, and he must abandon it, forfeiting any interest he may have in that pool. Should his hand contain less than five cards, he must play them, or pass out. If he decides to play the short hand he must announce it before putting up his ante or drawing cards, or the hand is foul.

17. *Straddling.* During the deal, or at any time before he looks at any card in his hand, the player to the left of the age may straddle the blind by putting up double the amount put up by the age. Should he straddle, the player on his left may double the amount again, provided he has not seen any of his cards ; and so on, until the limit of the straddling is reached. This limit must not exceed one-fourth of the betting limit. Should any player in his turn refuse to straddle, no other player on his left can straddle.

18. *The Ante.* After the cards are dealt, each player in turn, beginning with the one to the left of the age, or to the left of the last straddler, if any, must either abandon his hand or put into the pool twice the amount of the blind, or of the last straddle. When it comes to the turn of the age, and the straddlers, if any, they must either abandon their hands, or make the amount they have in the pool equal to twice the amount of the blind, or of the last straddle, if any.

19. *Raising the Ante.* Each player, when it is his turn to come in, may add to the amount of the ante any sum within the betting limit. This will compel any player coming in after him to equal the total of the ante and the raise, or to abandon his hand ;

and it will also give such following player the privilege of raising again by any further amount within the betting limit. Should any player decline to equal the amount put up by any previous player, he must abandon his hand, together with all his interest in that pool. Any player who has been raised in this manner may raise again in his turn ; and not until each player holding cards has anted an equal amount will the game proceed.

20. Winning the Antes. Should any player have put up an amount which no other player will equal, he takes whatever counters are then in the pool, without showing his hand, and the deal passes to the next player on the dealer's left. Should only one player come in, and the age decline to make good his ante, the player who has come in wins the blind, unless jack pots are played. Should any player have straddled the blind, or raised the ante, there can be no jack pot.

21. Making Jacks. If no player will come in, it is a Natural Jack, and all the hands must be abandoned, each player putting up for the ensuing deal the amount agreed upon. If no one has straddled the blind, or raised the ante, and only one player has come in, the age may do one of four things : He may forfeit his blind ; or he may make the ante good ; or he may raise it ; or he may demand that the single player who has come in shall take down his ante, the age putting up twice the amount agreed upon for jack pots ; once for himself, and once for the player who came in. All the other players must then put up for the ensuing deal. This is an Only-Two-In Jack.

22. Drawing Cards. When two or more players have come in for an equal amount, the others having abandoned their hands, each of them in turn, beginning with the one on the dealer's left, may discard any or all of the cards originally dealt him, and draw others in their place. The number discarded and drawn, if any, must be distinctly announced by each player, including the dealer ; and the fresh cards must be given face down from the top of the pack, without any further shuffling or cutting. Each player must receive the entire number he asks for before the next player is helped. No player shall receive from the dealer more or fewer than he discards ; so that if he is playing with a short hand, such as four cards only, he will still have four cards after the draw ; and if his hand was originally foul, it will so remain.

23. Exposed Cards. In dealing for the draw, should any card be found faced in the pack, or should any card be exposed by the dealer in giving out the cards, or be blown over by the wind before the player has touched it, such cards must be placed on the table with the discards. The player whose card has been exposed does not receive another in its place until all the other players, including the dealer, have been helped.

24. Incorrect Draws. Should any player ask for an incorrect number of cards, he must take them ; unless he discovers the error before the next player has been helped. If too many have been asked for, he must discard before seeing them. If too few, he must play with the short hand, or not at all. No player is allowed to take back into his hand any card that has once been discarded. If he has taken up the cards, or has seen any of them, and has too many, his hand is foul, and must be abandoned. If the dealer gives himself more cards than he needs, he must take them ; but if less, he can supply the deficiency, provided he has not looked at any of the drawn cards.

25. Incorrect Dealing. Should the dealer give any player more or fewer cards than he asks for, and the player discover the error before taking them up or seeing any of them, the dealer must withdraw the surplus card, and place it on the top of the pack. Should the dealer give a player fewer cards than he asks for, he must supply the deficiency when his attention is called to it, without waiting to supply the other players. Should the dealer give cards to any player out of his proper turn, he may correct the error if none of the cards have been seen ; not otherwise.

26. The Last Card of the pack must not be dealt. When only two cards remain, and more than one is asked for, they must be placed on the table with the discards and abandoned hands, and the whole shuffled together, and presented to the pone to be cut.

27. After the cards have been delivered by the dealer, no player has the right to be informed how many cards any player drew ; and any person, bystander or player, volunteering the information, except the player himself, may be called upon to pay to the player against whom he informs an amount equal to that then in the pool. Any player who has made good the ante and drawn cards may, before making a bet, ask how many cards the dealer drew, and the dealer must inform him.

28. Betting After the Draw. The first player who holds cards on the left of the age must make the first bet, whether he has straddled or not. If he declines to bet he must abandon his hand. The fact that the age is not playing makes no difference, as his privilege cannot be transferred to any other player. Bets may vary in amount from one counter to the betting limit. If no player will bet, the age takes the pool without showing his hand ; or, if he has passed out before the draw, the last player on his right who holds cards wins the pool.

29. Raising the Bets. Should any player make a bet, each player in turn on his left must either bet an equal amount or abandon his hand. Should any player bet an equal amount, he has the privilege of increasing the bet to any further sum within the betting limit. The players on his left must then either meet the total amount of the original bet and the raise, or abandon their hands. Any player meeting the amount already bet has the privilege of increasing it to any further amount within the limit, and so on, until no further raises take place. Any player whose bet has been raised must abandon his hand or meet the raise, with the privilege of raising again in return. Should one player make a bet or raise which no other player will see, he takes the pool without showing his hand, and the cards are shuffled and cut for the next deal.

30. Calling the Bets. As long as one player raises another's bets, he gives that player the privilege of raising him again; but if a player who has made a bet is not raised, the others simply betting an equal amount, the first bettor is called, and all betting must cease. The players must then show their hands to the table, in order to decide which wins the pool.

31. Bets must be actually made by placing the counters in the pool, and no bet is made until the player's hand has been withdrawn from the counters. Any counters once placed in the pool, and the owner's hand withdrawn, cannot be taken down again, except by the winner of the pool.

32. Betting Out of Turn. Should any player bet out of his turn, he cannot take down his counters again if he has removed his hand from them. Should the player whose proper turn it was raise the bet, the player who bet out of turn must either meet the raise or abandon his hand, and all interest in that pool.

33. Mouth Bets. Any player stating that he bets a certain amount, but failing to put up the actual counters in the pool, cannot be called upon to make the amount good after the hands are shown, or the pool is won. If the players opposed to him choose to accept a mouth bet against the counters they have already put up, they have no remedy, as no value is attached to what a player says; his cards and his counters speak for themselves. Any player wishing to raise a mouth bet has the privilege of raising by mouth, instead of by counters; but he cannot be called upon to make the amount good after the hands are shown, or the pool has been won.

34. Showing Hands. When a call is made, all the hands must be shown to the table, and the best poker hand wins the pool. Any player declining to show his hand, even though he admits that it is not good, must pay an amount equal to the ante to each of the players at the table; or, if jack pots are played, he must put up for all of them in the next jack pot. When the hands are called, there is no penalty for mis-calling a hand; the cards, like the counters, speak for themselves.

35. Rank of the Hands. The best poker hand is a **Royal Flush;** A K Q J 10 of the same suit, which beats a

Straight Flush; any sequence of five cards of the same suit.

Four of a Kind; such as four 10's and an odd card.

Full Hand; three of a kind and a pair, such as three 8's and a pair of Q's, which beats a

Flush; five cards of the same suit, but not in sequence.

Straight; five cards in sequence, but of various suits. In straights, the Ace cannot be used to form such combinations as Q K A 2 3; but it may be used as the bottom of 5 4 3 2, or the top of 10 J Q K. Straights beat

Three of a Kind; such as three K's and two odd cards.

Two Pairs; such as two 9's and two 7's, with an odd card.

A Pair; such as two Aces and three odd cards.

If no pair is shown, the **Highest Card** wins.

A short hand, such as four cards, cannot be claimed as either a straight or a flush.

36. Ties. In case of ties, the highest of the odd cards decides it. Ultimate ties must divide the pool. When combinations of equal rank are shown, the one containing the highest cards wins, the rank of the cards being, A K Q J 10 9 8 7 6 5 4 3 2; so that two pairs, K's and 4's, will beat two pairs, Q's and J's. Three 5's and a pair of 2's, will beat three 4's and a pair of aces.

JACK POT LAWS.

37. The Antes. There is neither age nor straddle in jack pots. Every one at the table must ante an equal amount. Any player may decline to ante, by saying: "I pass this jack;" and the dealer will give him no cards.

38. Opening. After the cards are dealt, each player in turn, beginning on the dealer's left, may open the pot for any amount he pleases within the betting limit, provided he holds a pair of Jacks, or some hand better than a pair of Jacks. If he does not hold openers, or does not wish to open the pot with them, he must say: "I pass;" but must not abandon his hand, under penalty of paying five counters to the pool.

39. False Openers. Should a player open a jack without the hand to justify it, and discover his error before he draws, his hand is foul, and he forfeits whatever amount he may have already placed in the pool. Those who have come into the pool after the false opening, stay in and play for the pot, regardless of the value of the hands dealt them.

40. Fattening. If no player will open, the cards are re-shuffled, cut, and dealt, usually by the same dealer, and each player adds one counter to the pool.

41. Coming In. If any player opens the pot for a certain amount, each player in turn, on his left, can come in by putting up a similar amount, regardless of the value of his hand. Any player on the right of the opener who passed on the first round may now come in. Any player declining to put up the amount for which the pot is opened must abandon his hand, and all his interest in the pool.

42. Raising the Opener. Any player coming into the pool has the privilege of raising the original opener any amount within the betting limit, and he may in turn be raised again, just as in the ordinary pools. Should the opener decline to meet such a raise, he must show his entire hand before abandoning it. If he declines to do so, he must pay the antes for all the other players for another jack. It is not enough to show openers before the draw, the whole hand must be shown.

43. Drawing Cards. Each player in turn who has come in, beginning on the left of the dealer, may discard and draw, to improve his hand. The opener is not allowed to split his openers. No matter how much he may have been raised, he must retain Jacks or better ; but if he had two pairs originally, such as J's and 4's, he may discard the 4's. If his two pairs were 10's and 8's, he must keep them both, because neither pair alone constitute openers.

44. False Hands. If a false opener does not discover his mistake until after he has drawn cards, his hand is foul, and must be abandoned. As a penalty he must put up an amount equal to that then in the pool, each of the other players taking down whatever amount he may have put in, including his original ante and all fatteners.

45. Betting the Hands. The opener makes the first bet ; or, if he has withdrawn, the player next on his left. Should the opener decline to bet after the draw, he must show his openers before abandoning his hand. He need not show the cards he has drawn. If no bet is made, the last player holding cards takes the pool without showing his hand. If a bet is made, the game proceeds as in the ordinary pools. Should the opener retire during the betting, he must show his openers ; if he is in the final call he must show his entire hand, whether it is the best or not. If he or any other player declines to show his hand when a call is made, he must ante for all the other players for another jack.

46. Shy Bets. If any player is shy in a jack pot, whether from failure to put up his ante, to fatten, or to substantiate his mouth bets with counters, nothing can be collected from him after a call has been made, or the pot has been won.

STRAIGHT POKER.

Straight Poker or *Bluff* is played with a full pack of fifty-two cards, and any number of players from one to eight. The arrangements for counters, seats, and deal are exactly the same as in Draw Poker, but the method of anteing and betting up the hands is slightly different. There is no draw to improve the hand, and no such combination as a straight flush is recognized, four of a kind being the highest hand possible.

The ante and betting limit must be decided before play begins. The first dealer is provided with a *buck,* which should be a pen-knife, or some similar article. Before dealing, he puts up the amount of the ante for all the players, and then *passes the buck* to the player on his left, who must ante for all the players in the next pool. There is no variation of the amount of the ante under any circumstances, and the buck is passed round the table in this manner irrespective of the deal, which is taken by the player winning the pool. The laws for the deal and its irregularities are the same as in Draw Poker, except that it does not pass to the left.

The cards dealt, each in turn, beginning with the player to the left of the dealer, may either bet or pass. Should all pass, the holder of the buck antes, making a double pool, and passes the buck. The deal then passes to the left. Should any player make a bet, each in turn, beginning with the one on his left, must call it, raise it, or abandon his hand. Players who have passed the first time, must now decide. The rules for seeing, raising, calling, and showing hands are precisely the same as at Draw Poker.

Owing to the absence of the draw, there is no clue to the strength of an opponent's hand, except his manner, and the amount of his bet. The hands shown are much weaker than the average of those at Draw Poker, being about equal to hands that a player in that game would come in on. Triplets are very strong at Straight Poker, and two pairs will win three out of four pools in a five-handed game. The great element of success is bluff.

STUD POKER.

The arrangements for the cards, seats, antes, buck, etc., are precisely as at Straight Poker ; but in dealing, only the first card is dealt face down, the remaining four being turned up by the dealer as he gives them out. Each player in turn then looks at his *down*

card, and the betting proceeds as in Straight Poker, each player having the privilege of passing once before a bet is made.

The game is sometimes varied by stopping the deal at two cards, each player having received one face down, and another face up. Betting is then in order, and if any bet is made, each player in turn must meet it, raise it, or pass out of that pool. If no one will call, the player making the last bet takes the pool, and the next deal. If a bet is made and called, those in the call do not show their down cards, but are each given another card, face up, and the same betting process is gone through. As long as two or more players remain in the pool they are given more cards until they have five. Then the final betting is done, and if a call is made, the down cards are shown, and the best poker hand wins the pool. Straight flushes do not count.

WHISKEY POKER.

The arrangements for the cards, seats, etc., are the same as in Draw Poker. Each player is provided with an equal number of white counters, which may have a value attached to them, or which may simply represent markers. If the counters represent money, each player should have at least twenty ; if they are only markers, five is the usual number.

If the game is played for money, each player puts one counter in the pool before the cards are dealt. There is no raising or betting of any kind.

An extra hand, called ***the widow,*** is dealt face down at Whiskey Poker. The dealer gives each player and the widow five cards, one at a time, beginning on his left, and dealing to the widow just before he deals to himself. Each player in turn, beginning with the age, then examines his hand, and has the option of exchanging it for the widow ; keeping it for the purpose of drawing to it ; or risking his chances of winning the pool with it as it is.

If he wishes to exchange, he must place his five cards face upward on the table, and take up the widow, but without showing it to any other player. The hand he abandons then becomes the widow. If he prefers to draw to his hand, he says : **"*I pass,*"** which transfers to the next player the option of taking the widow. If he wishes to stand on the merits of the hand dealt to him, without drawing to it, he **knocks** on the table, which also passes the option of taking the widow to the next player on his left.

If any player takes the widow, the next player on his left can do any one of three things : He may discard from his own hand any card he pleases, taking one from the widow in its stead ; the card which he discards being placed on the table face upward, and becoming part of the widow ; or he may exchange his entire hand for the widow ; or he may stand on the hand dealt him, and knock. Whether he draws one card, exchanges his entire hand, or knocks, the next player on his left has the option of drawing, exchanging, or knocking ; and so on, until some player does knock.

Should no player take the widow until it comes to the dealer's turn, he must either take it, or turn it face upward on the table. Even if the dealer knocks, he must turn up the widow, and allow each player an opportunity to draw from it, or to exchange his entire hand for it.

When a player knocks, he signifies that no matter what the players following him may do, when it comes to his turn again the hands must be shown. A player cannot draw and knock at the same time ; but a player can refuse to draw or exchange after another player has knocked, not before. In some localities it is the rule to turn the widow face up at once if any player knocks before it is taken ; allowing all those after the knock an opportunity to draw or exchange ; but this is not the usual custom.

Suppose five play. E deals, and A passes ; B takes the widow ; C and D draw from B's abandoned hand, and E knocks ; without drawing, of course. A, who passed the first time, now has an opportunity to draw or exchange. So have each of the others in turn, up to D ; but after D draws or exchanges, the hands must be shown, because the next player, E, has knocked.

When the hands are shown, there are two ways to settle : If the counters have a money value, the best poker hand wins the pool, and the deal passes to the left. If the counters have no money value, there is no pool ; but the player who has the worst hand shown puts one of his counters in the middle of the table. This continues until some player has lost all five of his counters, and he is then called upon to pay for the whiskey, or whatever refreshments may be at stake upon the game. Hence the name : Whiskey Poker.

PROGRESSIVE POKER.

There are several ways to play Progressive Poker, but the description of one will suffice. The simplest method of arranging the players is to take two packs of cards, one red and one blue, and to select two aces from each for the four positions at the head table ; three deuces, treys, etc., for the six positions at each of the other tables until the last or booby table is reached, at which there must be only four players at starting. If there are not enough players to make exactly six at each of the intermediate tables, the numbers may be varied from four to seven, cards being selected to agree with the number required; but the head and booby tables must start with four only. The cards thus selected are then thoroughly shuffled, and presented face downward to the ladies to draw from. Each lady takes a red-backed card, the gentlemen drawing the blue cards only. The number of pips on the card drawn will indicate to each person the table at which they are to sit. Should the number of men and women not be equal, some of the men must represent women or *vice versâ.*

Each player is provided at starting with a certain number of counters, usually fifty. The head table is supplied with a box of counters differing in colour from any of those used by the players, and also with a bell. The choice of seats, deal, etc., is decided at each table exactly as at Draw Poker.

One deal is made at each table, ordinary Draw Poker is played, and when the pool is decided at the head table the bell is struck. This is the signal for the winner of the pool at each of the other tables to move up to the table next above. At the head table, the chips are counted, and the player with the smallest number in his possession goes down to the booby table, unless he was one of the players in the call. Should the player with the smallest number of chips be the winner of the pool, or one of those who called the winner, he retains his seat, and the player with the smallest number of counters who was not in the call goes to the booby table. This arrangement effectually prevents players at the head table from waiting for big hands. In case of ties, the players cut to decide which shall go down, the lowest cut remaining. The winner of each pool at the head table is given one of the special chips provided for that purpose, and which are usually yellow, the others being red, white, and blue,

Any player losing all his counters at any table must get a fresh stake of fifty more from the banker, and must then exchange seats with the player at the booby table who has the most counters.

Three or four prizes are usually provided for: One for the player who has won the greatest number of yellow chips at the head table, and one each for the lady and gentleman winning the greatest number of counters during the evening's play. Those who have been provided with an extra stake must be charged with it when settling up. In case of ties for the number of yellow chips, the player with the largest number of ordinary counters wins. The booby prize, if any, is usually given to the player with the smallest number of ordinary chips, or the fewest number of yellow ones.

BRAG.

There are two varieties of this old English game; single, and three-stake Brag. Both are played with a full pack of fifty-two cards; the positions of the players, arrangements for counters, decision of the betting limit, etc., being the same as in Draw Poker. Three to twelve players may form a table.

There is a special value attached to three cards which are known as **braggers.** These again have a rank of their own; the best being the *ace of diamonds;* then the *Jack of clubs,* and then the *nine of diamonds.* All other cards rank as in Poker. A player to whom any one of these braggers is dealt may call it anything he pleases. If he has a pair of nines and a bragger, or a nine and two braggers, he may call them three nines, and bet on them as such. In this respect braggers resemble mistigris, already described in connection with Draw Poker; but in Brag a natural pair or triplet outranks one made with the aid of a bragger. Three eights will beat an eight and two braggers.

The dealer must put up an ante before the cards are cut. This ante may be any amount he pleases within the betting limit. No player can straddle or raise this ante until the cards are dealt. Beginning on his left the dealer distributes the cards face down, and one at a time, until each player has received three. Beginning with the age, [eldest hand,] each player in turn must put up an amount equal to the dealer's ante, or abandon his hand. He may, if he chooses, raise the ante any further amount within the betting limit. All those following him must meet the total sum put up by any individual player, increase it, or pass out. In this respect Brag is precisely similar to the betting after the draw at Poker.

If no one will see the dealer's ante, he must be paid one white counter by each of the other players, and the deal passes to the left. Should any player bet an amount which no other player will meet, he takes the pool without showing his hand. Should a call be made, all the hands must be shown, and the best brag hand wins.

Pairs and triplets are the only combinations of any value, and of course three aces is the best hand; two aces and the club Jack being the next best. If none of the hands shown contains either a natural pair or a bragger, the highest card wins, the ace ranking above the King. In case of equal natural pairs, the highest card outside the pair wins. Should the pairs tied both be made with a bragger, the highest bragger wins. Two odd cards, seven high, with the club Jack, would beat two cards seven high with the diamond nine.

Three Stake Brag. In this variation each player puts up three equal amounts to form three equal pools. These amounts must be invariable, and should be agreed upon before play begins. The dealer then gives two cards to each player, one at a time, face down ; and then a third card to each, face up. The highest card turned up in this manner wins one of the pools, the ace being the highest and the deuce the lowest. The diamond ace, being a bragger, outranks any other ace ; the club Jack any other Jack ; and the diamond nine any other nine. Ties are decided in favour of the eldest hand, or the player nearest him on the left.

The players then take up the other two cards, without showing them, and proceed to brag on their hands as in single stake Brag. The winner takes the second pool ; but those who pass out do not abandon their hands until the third pool is decided. If no bet is made for the second pool, it is won by the dealer.

All hands are shown to decide the last pool. Each player counts up the pip value of his three cards, reckoning the aces for eleven, and court-cards as ten each. The player coming nearest to thirty-one takes the third pool. Ties are decided in favour of the eldest hand, as before.

In some places a further variation is introduced by allowing the players to draw cards for the third pool, in order to increase the pip value of their hands. Beginning with the eldest hand, each player in turn pays into the pool a counter for each card he draws. These cards are given by the dealer face up, and one player must be given all he needs before passing to the next. Should a player pass thirty-one, he is out of the pool. Some judgment is necessary in drawing in this manner, for all the hands are exposed, and each player knows exactly what he has to beat.

In *American Brag*, there are eight braggers ; the Jacks and nines of each suit, and they are all of equal rank when used as braggers. Pairs or triplets formed with the aid of braggers outrank naturals, so that three Jacks is an invincible hand, beating three aces. Two braggers and an ace outrank two aces and a bragger ; but the absurd part of the arrangement is that three Jacks and three nines are a tie.

The method of playing differs from English Brag. If the players simply equal the dealer's ante, nothing unusual occurs, and all the hands are shown at once. But if any player raises, and another sees this raise, these two immediately exchange hands, without showing them to the other players, and the one who held the worse hand retires from that pool, returning the better hand to its original holder, who then awaits a call or raise from the next player in order, the entire amount staked still remaining in the pool. This lose-and-drop-out system is continued until only one player remains to dispute the pool with the dealer. If they come to a call, both hands are shown to the table. If the bragger is not called, he takes the pool without showing his hand.

COMMERCE.

This old English game is evidently the forerunner of Whiskey Poker. It is played with a full pack of fifty-two cards, and the arrangements for the seats, counters, etc., are the same as at Draw Poker. Three to twelve players may form a table. There are two methods of playing Commerce ; with and without a widow. We shall take the older form first.

Without a Widow. The counters have a money value, and each player deposits one in the pool. The dealer then distributes the cards one at a time, face down, until each has three. The players then examine their cards, and each in turn, beginning with the eldest hand, may exchange one card. If he trades *for ready money,* he gives his card and one white counter to the dealer, and receives another card, face down, from the top of the pack. The discard is left on the table, and the counter is the dealer's perquisite. If he trades *for barter,* he passes his discard to the player on his left, who must give one of his own in exchange before looking at the one he is to receive. If the player will not exchange, he must *knock* on the table, to signify that he will stand by the cards he has. If he exchanges, he takes up the offered card, and then has the privilege of trading for ready money or for barter himself. The trading goes on in this way round and round, until some player knocks, when all trading is immediately stopped, and the hands are shown. The best hand wins the pool, the rank of the various combinations being as follows, beginning with the highest :—

Triplets. Three aces being the highest, and three deuces the lowest. Pairs have no value.

Sequence Flushes ; the ace being allowed to rank as the top or the bottom ; Q K A, or A 2 3.

The Point ; the greatest number of pips on two or three cards of the same suit in one hand, counting the ace for eleven, and the other court-cards for ten each. A single card of a suit does not count for the point. In case of ties, a point made with three cards will beat one made with two cards. If the number of cards is also a tie, the dealer, or the player nearest him on his left wins.

If no triplet is shown, the best straight flush wins. If there is no straight flush, the best point wins. The deal passes to the left, and a misdeal loses the deal, as the deal is an advantage, owing to the trade for ready money.

If the dealer does not win the pool, he must pay one white counter to the player who does. If the dealer holds a combination of the same rank as the one that wins the pool, he must pay one white counter to every other player at the table. For instance ·

No triplet is shown, and a straight flush, Jack high, wins the pool. The dealer has a straight flush, 9 high, and must pay one counter to every player at the table. If the dealer had no sequence flush, he would pay the winner of the pool only.

With a Widow. This is almost three-card Whiskey Poker. Each player is provided with three counters only, which are of no value, and three cards are dealt to each player and to the widow, face down, and one at a time. The widow is turned face up immediately, and the dealer has the first say. Before he looks at the cards he has dealt to himself, he may exchange his whole hand for the widow, otherwise the eldest hand has the first draw. No other player may exchange his whole hand, but each in turn may draw one card until some player knocks. The moment any player knocks, all drawing must cease, and the hands are shown at once. Triplets, straight flushes, and points determine the value of the hands, as already described, and the best hand takes the pool. The dealer makes no extra payments, as he has no perquisites. The first player to lose his three counters pays for the whiskey; and if two or more are frozen out at the same time, the one with the worst hand pays. The game is sometimes varied by playing freeze-out, a value being attached to the three counters, and players who are decavé retiring from the game until all the counters have been won by a single player.

Two other combinations are sometimes introduced in either form of Commerce: A flush, three cards of one suit, ranking next below the straight flush; and a single pair outranking the point.

Another variety of Commerce is variously known as **My Ship Sails; or My Bird Sings.** The counters have a money value, and three are given to each player. Three cards are dealt, face down, and one at a time. There is no widow. The eldest hand may then exchange one card with the player on his left, who must give his card before seeing the one he is to receive. The exchange goes round to the left. The moment any player finds himself with a flush, three cards of the same suit, regardless of their value, whether dealt to him, or made by exchange, he says: "My Ship Sails;" and all exchange is stopped, and the hands are shown. Should there be more than one flush, the pips win, counting ace for 11, and other court-cards for 10 each. If no player has secured a flush after two rounds of exchanges, the hands are shown, and the highest number of pips in the two-card flushes wins the pool. The elder hand wins ties.

BOUILLOTTE,

OR BRELAN.

This is an old and famous French gambling game, often referred to in stories of fast life in European society. It was the rage during and long after the French Revolution, but has lately had to share public attention with Baccara, and even with Le Poker Américain. It has many points in common with three-stake Brag, and is evidently descended from the same stock. By many persons Bouillotte is considered superior to Poker, because it offers the player many opportunities to speculate on winning by the aid of cards that are not in his own hand.

Cards. Bouillotte is played with a piquet pack, reduced to twenty cards, only the A K Q 9 8 of each suit being retained. The ace is the highest card in play and in cutting. If five persons play, the Jack of each suit is added ; if only three play, the Queens are discarded, reducing the pack to sixteen cards. Two packs are generally used alternately.

Counters or chips are used, as in Poker, instead of money. Any player may be the banker.

Players. Three, four, or five persons may play ; but four is the proper number, and all descriptions of the game suppose it to be four-handed.

Cutting. To decide the positions of the players, a sequence of cards is sorted out, equal in number with the number of players. These cards are then shuffled, face downward, and each player draws one. The highest of the sequence has the choice of positions, and so on down until all are seated. The player who draws the King deals the first hand.

Stakes. Each player purchases an equal number of counters from the banker, usually 100. This original ***cave*** cannot be added to or deducted from. As long as a single counter of it remains the player must call for a sight, just as in freeze-out or table stakes ; and not until he is ***decavé,*** [has lost everything,] can he purchase another stake, the amount of which is usually at his own option.

Blind and Straddle. Before the distribution of the cards, the dealer puts up a blind, usually five counters, which the player on his right has the privilege of straddling. If he straddles, he may be straddled again, and so on. In Bouillotte the straddle practically buys from the dealer the privileges of the age. If it goes round until the dealer buys it back himself, the straddling must then be stopped.

Dealing. As in all French games, the cards are cut by the player on the dealer's left, and are dealt from right to left. Three cards are given to each player, one at a time, face down, and the thirteenth is then turned face up on the pack. This card is called the ***retourne.***

Misdeals. If any card is exposed during the deal, either in the pack or in giving it to a player, it is a misdeal; but the distribution of the cards is continued until each player has received three cards, the exposed card being given out in its regular order. If any player can show triplets, he receives one white counter from each of the other players, and the hands are then abandoned. If more than one triplet is shown, the inferior does not pay the higher. If no triplet is shown, the cards are redealt. A misdeal does not lose the deal.

The deal passes to the right; but should the player whose turn it is to deal have lost everything on the previous deal, and have just purchased another stake, the deal passes to the player beyond him. If a player withdraws from the table when it is his turn to deal, the deal passes any new-comer who may take his place.

Betting. The cards dealt, each player in turn, beginning with the one to the right of the dealer, or to the right of the last straddler, if any, can do one of three things: Equal the amount of the ante; increase it as much as he pleases within the limits of his cave; or pass, retaining his cards but betting nothing. If any player ***opens*** the game by making a bet, the player on his right may equal or raise it; but he cannot pass after the game is opened, unless he withdraws from the pool. Any player may call for a sight for the amount in front of him, but that does not prevent the others from continuing the betting. If no one will open, the deal is void, and each player puts five counters in the pool for the next deal. If a player opens, and no one will equal or raise him, he wins the antes and straddles, if any. If any player makes a raise which no one will meet, he takes whatever is in the pool, unless a player has called for a sight for a small part of it.

Calling and Showing. If only two players bet against each other, either may call the other, and demand a show of hands at any time; but if three or four are betting, the privilege of calling falls upon each in turn from right to left. For instance: A, B, C, and D play. D blinds five counters, and deals. A passes, and B opens for five reds. C passes out, while D and A both meet the bet of five reds, but neither will raise it. This does not call B, who has the privilege of raising the bet if he pleases. Suppose he raises, and D and A both meet it. On this second round, C having passed out, it is D's turn to say whether or not he will raise. On the next round it will be A's turn, and after that it will be B's second turn, and so on. Should any player meet the bet but refuse to raise, although it is his turn, he still cannot call. If he does not avail himself of his privilege of raising, he must **pass the word** to the player on his right; that is, transfer the privilege to him. If he declines, it is a call; if he raises, it goes on until every player has refused to avail himself of the privilege. If a player chooses to raise without waiting for his turn, of course he can do so. One of the fine points in the game is knowing when to raise the bet yourself, and when to pass the word.

Rank of the Hands. If a call is made, the hands are shown, and the best Bouillotte hand wins. There are only two classes of hands recognized in Bouillotte, the brelan, and the point; but there are three kinds of brelans, which rank in the following order:

A Brelan Carré is four of a kind; three in the player's hand, and the fourth turned up on the pack. If any player holds a brelan, [three of a kind,] of a higher denomination than the brelan carré, the player may turn up the card under the retourne, and if this makes his hand a brelan carré also, he wins the pool. In addition to winning the pool, the holder of a brelan carré receives from each player four white counters.

A Simple Brelan is three of a kind in the player's hand, three aces being the highest, and three eights the lowest. In addition to winning the pool, the holder of a simple brelan receives one counter from each of the other players at the table. If two are shown, neither pays the other. Should the brelan be formed by uniting the retourne with two cards in the player's hand, it is a **brelan favori,** and the holder of it receives an extra counter from every player at the table, whether he wins the pool or not. For instance: The retourne is an eight; a brelan of Queens is shown, and wins the pool. Another player holds a pair of eights, and claims brelan favori. He does not pay the winning brelan, but receives one counter from its holder, and also from each of the other players. If the brelan favori wins the pool, it is paid two counters by each player. If two simple brelans are shown, the higher wins the pool; but both must be paid by each of the other two players, who did not hold brelans.

The Point. If no brelan is shown, the hands of all the players are shown, including those who passed out during the betting. This will expose thirteen cards, including the retourne. The pips in each suit are then counted, the ace reckoning for 11, court cards for 10 each, and the 9 and 8 at their face value. Whichever suit has the greatest number of pips is called **the suit that wins,** and the player who holds the highest card of it takes the pool; provided, of course, that he was one of those who backed his hand until the last call. If the player who holds the best card of the winning suit has dropped out during the betting, his cards count for the player who has the highest card of the suit among those who backed their hands. For instance: D deals and turns the heart 8. A and B have passed out, but C has made a bet which D has called. Neither has a brelan, so all four players show their cards, and it is found that they lie thus:—

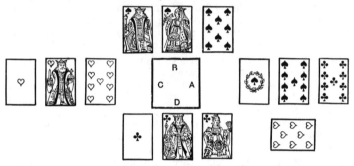

Spades are the winning suit: but neither C nor D has a spade, and as neither A nor B is in the call, the spade suit cannot win anything. As between clubs and hearts, D's point is 40, and C's 38; so D wins the pool. C of course had a great advantage in betting, as he knew four hearts were out, his own and the retourne; and all he feared was a brelan. A would have won the pool if he had backed his hand, because he would have had the highest card of the winning suit.

Calling for a Sight. Suppose four players have the following caves in front of them: A, 35; B, 60; C, 120; and D, 185. D blinds five, deals, and turns the heart 9. A puts up all his 35 counters. B passes out. C raises 50, putting up 85; and D bets everything, 180 more than his blind. A demands a sight for his 35, and C puts up the remainder of his 120, and calls a sight for them. Then D withdraws his superfluous 65, and it is a call. No one has a brelan, so all the hands are shown, and the cards lie thus:—

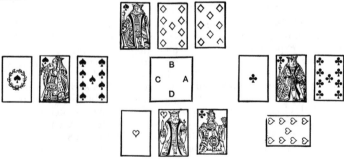

The point is exactly even for clubs and spades, 40 in each. In case of ties, the dealer, or the player nearest him on the right wins. In this case A wins on account of his position, so clubs is the winning suit, and A has the best card of it. But he can win from C and D only the amount for which he called a sight, *i. e.* 35 counters. He therefore takes down 105 as his share of the pool, leaving 170 to be decided between C and D. Now, although C has a better point than D, it is one of the principles of the game that the suit that wins cannot lose at the same time ; and as D has a card of the winning suit, while C has not, D wins the remainder of the pool. If neither C nor D had a card of the winning suit, C would win from D on account of his better point.

If we transposed the club ace and spade ace, spades would be the winning suit, because the elder hand, A, had the best card of it ; but C would take the remainder of the pool, because he held a spade, while D did not.

As it is, C is decavé, and must purchase another stake, or retire from the game. If C had lost this pool with a brelan in his hand, he would not be decavé ; because after losing the pool, and all he had staked therein, B, who had passed out, would have to pay him for the brelan, and with this one white counter he would have to call for a sight in the next pool he entered.

Methods of Cheating. As in all games in which winning depends entirely on the cards held, and not on the manner of playing them, Bouillotte offers many opportunities to the greek. The small number of cards in the pack, and the consequent ease with which they may be handled, enable even the clumsiest card sharpers to run up brelan carrés, make false shuffles, and shift cuts. There is one trick, called the poussette, which consists in surreptitiously placing more counters on the table when the player finds he has a hand worth backing. Marked cards, and packs trimmed to taper one way, biseautés, are among the most common weapons of the French tricheurs. As in Poker, it is best to avoid playing with strangers.

Suggestions for Good Play. Beyond the usual qualifications necessary to succeed with any member of the poker family, Bouillotte requires some study of the probable value of the point, which value will vary with the number of players engaged in the coup. For instance : The first player to say, having only 21 in his hand, should ante ; but if two other players had already anted, 31, or even 40 would be a doubtful hand. If a bet had been made and met by another player, such a point should generally be laid down.

With good cards it is always better for the eldest hand to pass, especially with a brelan, for he will then have an opportunity to judge of the value of the hands against him, and he can raise the bet to his advantage. Good players will not bet on an ace alone, unless the suit is turned up; nor on a point of 21 with a weak card of the turn-up suit. If three play in a pool the point should be very strong to follow beyond the first raise; and if four players are engaged, it is almost a certainty that brelans will be shown.

When a player with a brelan has frightened off his opponents with a big bet, it is usual to *stifle* the brelan, as it is considered more to the player's advantage to leave his adversaries under the impression that he may have been bluffing than to show the hand for the sake of the one white counter to which it entitles him. With three cards of one suit to the King, it is usual to bet high, in order to drive out anything but a brelan. Any player holding ace and another of the suit will of course abandon his hand, as his point is worth only 21 at the most, and the player with three to the King will get the benefit of his cards when the point is counted.

AMBIGU.

Cards. Ambigu is played with a pack of forty cards, the K Q J of each suit being deleted. The cards rank in the order of their numerical value, the 10 being the highest, and the ace the lowest. Two packs may be used alternately.

Players. Any number from two to six may form the table, and the arrangements for seats, first deal, etc., should be decided as at Bouillotte.

Stakes. Each player begins with an equal number of counters, the value of which must be determined beforehand. A betting limit should be agreed upon, and one player should be the banker for the evening.

Blind. Before the cards are dealt, each player deposits one counter in the pool; there is no straddle.

Dealing. The cards are cut to the left, and dealt to the right, and two cards are given to each player, one at a time, face down.

Method of Playing. Each player in turn, beginning on the dealer's right, examines his hand, and if satisfied with it he says: "Enough." If not satisfied, he may discard one or both of his cards, and receive others from the top of the pack. In either case he places two white counters in the pool for his ante. All having decided to stand or to draw, the remainder of the pack, exclusive of the discards, is reshuffled and cut ; each player is then given two more cards, one at a time, and face down. Each in turn examines his four cards, and if satisfied he says : " I play ; " if not, he says : " I pass." If all pass, the dealer has the choice of two things : He may gather the cards and deal again, each player putting another counter into the pool, or he may put up two white counters himself, and compel the players to retain the cards dealt them, the dealer keeping his also.

Any person announcing to play may put up as many counters as he pleases within the betting limit. If no person will stay with him, he takes back his raise, leaving the antes, and is paid two counters by the last player who refuses. If two or more declare to play they can either meet the amount offered by the first player, or raise him. If any player declines to meet a raise, he must abandon his hand. If no one will call the last raise, the player making it takes the pool, and then shows his hand, and demands payment from each of the other players for whatever combination he holds. If two or more players call, by making their bets equal, they again draw cards, having the privilege of discarding any number from one to four, or of standing pat. After the draw each in turn can pass or play. If all pass, the hands are abandoned, and the pool remains; each player adding one counter for the next deal. This is to force players to bet on their hands. If a bet is made, the calling and raising proceeds as in Draw Poker.

When there are not enough cards to supply the players, the discards must be gathered, shuffled, and cut. Any player with too many or too few cards must abandon his hand as foul. Any player showing his cards must abandon his hand, and forfeit four counters to the pool.

The general laws of Poker governing all irregularities may be applied to Ambigu; but it must be remembered that the French are very much averse to penalties of all kinds, and if an error can be rectified without doing an injustice to any player, it is usual to set things right in the simplest manner possible.

Value of the Hands. There are seven combinations of value in Ambigu, which rank in the following order, beginning with the lowest :—

The Point. The total number of pips on two or more cards of the same suit. A single card does not count for the point. Three cards of one suit are a better point than two cards, even if there are more pips on the two cards. If no higher combination than a point is shown, the player with the winning point receives ***one counter*** from each of the other players at the table, besides winning the pool, and everything in it. In case of ties, the player having two cards in sequence wins. For instance : an 8 and a 7 will beat a 10 and a 5. If this does not decide it, the elder hand wins.

The Prime. Four cards of different suits, sometimes called a Dutch flush, is a better hand than the point. If a prime is the best combination shown, the holder wins the pool, and receives **two counters** from each of the other players. If the pips in the prime aggregate more than thirty, it is called **Grand Prime,** and the holder receives **three counters** from each of the other players, instead of two. If two or more primes are shown, the one with the highest number of pips wins. If this is still a tie, the elder hand wins.

A Sequence is a bobtail straight flush; that is, three of the four cards are in sequence, such as the 2, 3 and 4 of spades, with an odd card, such as a 9. This is a better combination than a prime, and the holder receives **three counters** from each player. In case of ties, the highest sequence wins. If the sequence flush is one of four cards, it is a doublet.

A Tricon, or three of a kind, is better than a straight, and entitles the holder to **four counters** from each of the other players. Pairs have no value.

A Flush is four cards of the same suit, not necessarily in sequence, and is better than a tricon. The holder is paid **five counters** by each of the other players, in addition to winning the pool.

Doublets. Any hand containing a double combination will beat any single combination. For instance : A player holds three of a kind, and the fourth card in his hand is of a different suit from any of his triplet. His hand is a double combination, prime and tricon, and will beat a flush. A sequence of four cards of the same suit is a double combination, and will beat anything but a fredon. When doublets are shown, the holder is paid for both combinations, **six** for tricon and prime, or **eight** for sequence and flush, as the case may be.

A Fredon, or four of a kind, is the best possible hand, and the holder is paid **ten or eleven counters** by each of the other players, according to the pip value of his cards. He is paid eight counters for fredon, and two for the prime, if it is smaller than 8's ; but he claims grand prime if he has four 9's, or four 10's, and gets eleven counters.

In case of **ties** which cannot be decided by the pip values, the elder hand wins.

Even if a player has lost his entire stake in the pool, he must pay the various combinations shown, and it is usual to reserve about ten counters for this purpose.

Betting the Hands. After the last cards have been drawn, the players proceed to bet upon their hands precisely as at Poker. If a player makes a bet or raise which no one will call, he takes the pool, and then shows his hand and demands payment for the combination he holds. It is very unusual for a player to stifle a hand at Ambigu, as he would at Bouillotte. If a call is made, the players in the call show and compare their cards, and the best hand wins the pool. Only the player who wins the pool can demand payment for combinations held.

TEXT-BOOKS ON POKER.

Draw Poker, by John W. Keller.
Round Games, by Baxter–Wray.
Complete Poker Player, by John Blackbridge.
Proctor on Draw Poker.
Schenck's Rules for Draw Poker.
The Poker Book, by Richard Guerndale.
The Gentlemen's Handbook of Poker, by J. W. Florence.
Poker Rules in Rhyme, by Geo. W. Allen.

THE EUCHRE FAMILY.

This family embraces four of the best known and most popular games in the world, each of which has been considered the national game in its own country : Écarté in France ; Napoleon in England ; Spoil Five in Ireland ; and Euchre in America.

It has always been the custom to trace the origin of Euchre to a variety of Triomphe, or French Ruff, probably introduced to America by the French of Louisiana ; and to claim Ecarté as its cousin, and the French survivor of the parent game. In the opinion of the author, both the game and its name go to show that Euchre is of mixed stock, and probably originated in an attempt to play the ancient Irish game of Spoil Five with a piquet pack. "Euchre" is not a French word, but the meaning of it is identical with "Spoil Five" ; both names signifying that the object of the game is to prevent the maker of the trump from getting three tricks. In the one game he is "spoiled ;" in the other he is "euchred." In the old game of Triomphe, in Écarté, and in the black suits in Spoil Five, the order of the court cards in plain suits is the same, the ace ranking below the Jack, But in Euchre the Jack ranks above the ace when the suit is trumps, exactly as it does in Spoil Five. In the latter game the five is the best trump ; but as there is no five in a piquet pack, that trump was probably disregarded, leaving the Jack the best. Taking up, or "robbing" the turn-up trump, is another trait common to both Spoil Five and Euchre.

Spoil Five and Triomphe are mentioned in the earliest works on card games. Triomphe can be traced to 1520, when it was popular in Spain ; and the origin of Maw, the parent of Spoil Five, is lost in the mists of Irish antiquity. It was the fashionablega me during the reign of James I.

The old Spanish game of Triomphe, now obsolete, seems to have undergone several changes after its introduction to France. At first it was played either by two persons, or by two pairs of partners. If one side had bad cards, they could offer to abandon the hand, and allow the adversaries to count a point without playing. If the adversaries refused, they were obliged to win all five tricks or lose two points. It was compulsory to win the trick if possible, and to trump, overtrump, or undertrump if the player had none of the suit led. This peculiarity survives in the games of Rams and Loo, which also belong to the euchre family.

After a time we find a variation introduced in which any number from two to six could play, each for himself, and the player first winning two tricks out of the five marked the point. Later still we find the ace ranking above the King, thus becoming the best trump. If the ace was turned up, the dealer had the privilege of robbing it, or the holder of the ace of trumps could rob the turn-up, discarding any card he pleased, just as in Spoil Five. But in Triomphe the dealer turned up another card, and if that was of the trump suit the holder of the ace could rob that also, and so on until he turned a card of a different suit. This did not alter the trump, but merely stopped the robbing process. Whether or not Triomphe borrowed this feature from Spoil Five or Maw, it is now impossible to say.

Whatever its origin, Euchre has always been the most respectable member of the family, and the game of all others that has best served the card-playing interest in social life. Spoil Five probably comes next in point of respectability; but Écarté has often fallen into evil hands, and the very name is in some places regarded as synonymous for gambling. The same is true of Napoleon, but in less degree. Euchre, unlike the other members of the family, is not essentially a gambling game, but belongs rather to the intellectual group of card games; a position which we hope it may long maintain.

EUCHRE.

CARDS. Euchre is played with what is commonly known as the piquet pack, 32 cards, all below the 7 being deleted. In plain suits the cards rank as at Whist; but in the trump suit the Jack is the best, and it is called the ***Right Bower.*** The Jack of the same colour as the trump suit, red or black, is the second-best trump, and it is called the ***Left Bower ;*** so that if clubs were trumps the rank of the nine cards in the trump suit would be as follows :—

The rank of the cards in the other suits would be :—

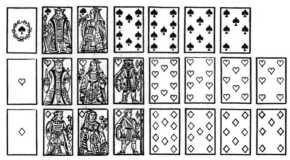

When the **Joker,** or blank card is used, it is always the best trump, ranking above the right bower. In cutting, the ace is low, the other cards ranking as in plain suits. A player cutting the Joker must cut again.

COUNTERS or whist markers may be used for keeping the score, but it is much more common to use the small cards from the deleted portion of the pack. The game is five points, and the best method of scoring is to use the 4 and 3 of any suit. When the 3 is face up, but covered by the 4 face down, it counts **one.** When the 4 is face up, covered by the 3 face down, it counts **two.** When the 4 is face down, covered by the 3 face up, it counts **three.** When the 3 is face down, covered by the 4 face up, it counts **four.**

ONE. TWO. THREE. FOUR.

The number of pips exposed on the card which is face up is immaterial ; the relative position of the two cards will always determine the score.

Rubber or game scores must be kept on a whist marker, or on a sheet of paper.

PLAYERS. Euchre may be played by any number of persons from two to seven ; but in the seven-handed game the full pack of fifty-three cards is used. Whatever the number of players, they cut for positions at the table, for partners, and for the deal.

CUTTING. The cards are usually spread, face down, and each candidate for play draws a card.

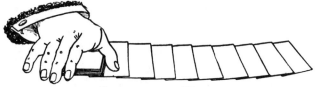

SPREADING THE HAND.

When ***two*** or ***three*** play, the lowest cut has the choice of seats, and takes the first deal. When ***four*** play, they cut for partners ; the two highest pairing against the two lowest. The lowest has the choice of seats, and deals the first hand. When ***five*** or ***seven*** play, they have the choice of seats in their order, the lowest first, and the lowest cut deals. When ***six*** play, the three lowest are partners against the three highest, the lowest cut having the choice of seats, and the first deal.

TIES. Players cutting cards of equal value cut again ; but the new cut decides nothing but the tie.

PLAYER'S POSITIONS. The ***eldest hand,*** or age, sits on the left of the dealer, and the ***pone*** sits on the dealer's right. There are no distinctive names for the other positions.

When ***two*** play, they sit opposite each other. When ***three*** play, each for himself, the game is known as ***Cut Throat,*** and the position of the players is immaterial. When ***four*** play, the partners sit opposite each other. When ***five*** or ***seven*** play, the maker of the trump in each deal selects his partners, and they play against the others without any change in their positions at the table. When ***six*** play, three are partners against the other three, and the opposing players sit alternately round the table.

STAKES. If there is any stake upon the game, its amount must be settled before play begins. When ***rubbers*** are played, it is usual to make the stake so much a rubber point. If the winners of the game are five points to their adversaries' nothing, they win a ***treble,*** and count three rubber points. If the losers have scored one or two points only, the winners mark two points for a ***double.*** If the losers have reached three or four, the winners mark one for a ***single.*** The side winning the rubber adds two points to its score for so doing ; so that the largest rubber possible is one of eight points ;—two triples to nothing, and two added for the rubber. The smallest possible is one point ;—two singles and the rubber, against a triple. If the first two games are won by the same partners, the third is not played.

DEALING. Any player has the right to shuffle the cards, the dealer last. The pack must be presented to the pone to be cut, and he must leave at least four cards in each packet. Beginning on his left, the dealer distributes the cards either two at a time and then three, or three and then two to each player in rotation, until all have five cards. Whichever number, two or three, the dealer begins with, he must continue giving the same number to every player, including himself, for the first round. After the cards are dealt, the next card is turned face up on the remainder of the pack, except in five and seven-handed Euchre, in which no trump is turned. Each player deals in turn to the left, until the conclusion of the game or rubber.

Irregularities in the Deal. If any card is found faced in the pack, the dealer must deal again. Should the dealer expose any card but the trump while dealing, the adversaries may demand a new deal by the same dealer. Should any adversary of the dealer expose a card, the dealer may elect to deal again. A player dealing out of turn may be stopped before the trump card is turned; but after that the deal must stand, afterward passing to the left in regular order. On the completion of the deal, if any player has more or less than five cards, it is a misdeal, and the deal passes to the player on the misdealer's left.

The dealer loses his deal if he neglects to have the pack cut; if he deals a card incorrectly, and fails to remedy the error before dealing another; if he counts the cards on the table, or those remaining in the pack; or if he deals two cards to one player and three to another in the same round.

If the pack is found to be imperfect, the deal in which the error is discovered is void; but all previous scores stand good.

MAKING THE TRUMP. Although a card is turned up at the end of the deal, the suit to which it belongs is not necessarily the trump for that hand. Each player in turn, beginning on the dealer's left, whether he be an adversary or a partner of the dealer's, may insist on the turn-up suit remaining the trump; or he may declare that he is indifferent as to which suit is the trump, the one turned up or some other. But should one player in his proper turn decide in favour of the turn-up, no player after him can alter the decision. When it comes to the dealer's turn, if no other player has decided to retain the suit turned up, he must either let the trump remain as it is, or insist on its being changed.

As the individual or side that settles which suit shall be the trump is said to *make the trump,* it will be necessary to describe the method of scoring in order to understand the principles that guide the players in deciding on the trump suit.

SCORING. Euchre is played for tricks. If the side that makes the trump takes three or four tricks out of the five possible, it scores one point. If the side wins all five tricks, it scores two points for a ***march.*** If the player that makes the trump fails to win three tricks, he is ***euchred,*** and his adversaries score two points for the euchre. ***When four play,*** if the player who makes the trump declares to play ***alone,*** that is, without any assistance from his partner, who must lay down his cards, the maker of the trump scores four points if he succeeds in winning all five tricks, and one point if he wins three or four tricks. But if he fails to win three tricks, he is euchred, and the adversaries score two points. ***When three play,*** a lone hand counts three if the player wins all five tricks. ***When two play,*** five tricks is simply a march, and counts two points. ***When five or seven play,*** there are special scores for lone hands. When all five tricks are taken by one side, but not by an individual playing a lone hand, it is simply a march, and counts two points, no matter how many are playing. When two or three are playing, a march must of course be a lone hand, as there are no partnerships. As we shall see later, there are some varieties of Euchre in which a lone hand may play against a lone hand, but this is not permitted in the ordinary game.

No one but the individual player who makes the trump can play alone.

Except in five and seven-handed Euchre, the player or side first reaching five points wins the game. If three are playing, and two of them reach five points simultaneously by euchreing the third, they both win a game. If they are playing for stakes, they divide the pool.

TAKING UP THE TRUMP. After the trump is turned up, each player in turn examines his cards, and if he does not care whether the trump suit remains unchanged or not, he says: ***"I pass."*** If all pass, the dealer must decide. The dealer has the advantage of being allowed to take the trump card into his own hand, discarding one of his worthless cards in its place. If he thinks he can make three tricks with the turn-up suit for trumps, and his partner's probable assistance, or can win five tricks by playing alone, he discards any card he pleases, placing it under the remainder of the pack, face down, and without showing or naming it. If the dealer decides to play alone, it is usual for him to pass his discard across the table to his partner, face down, so that there may be no misunderstanding his intention.

The dealer may take up the trump card at any time during the play of the hand; but it is usual to leave it on the pack until it is played to a trick. No one but the dealer can take the trump into his hand.

TURNING DOWN THE TRUMP. If the dealer fears that he and his partner cannot make three tricks with the turn-up suit for trumps, or would prefer to have the suit changed, he can pass. If he passes, he takes the trump card from the top of the pack, and places it face upward, and partly under the pack, in such a manner that it can be distinctly seen.

TAKEN UP.

TURNED DOWN.

CHANGING THE TRUMP. It then becomes the turn of the other players, each in succession to the left of the dealer, to name some other suit for the trump, or to pass a second time. If the suit of the same colour as the turn-up is named for the new trump, it is usual to say: *" I make it next."* If a suit of a different colour is named, it is called ***crossing the suit,*** and some players, if a red suit is turned, will say: " I *cross* to clubs."

Any player naming a new suit may announce to play alone at the same time. The side that makes the new trump must make at least three tricks, or it will be euchred, and the adversaries will count two points. If a player names the suit that has just been turned down, he loses his right to make the trump; and if he corrects himself, and names another suit, he debars not only himself but his partner from making the trump. One player having named a new trump suit in his proper turn, his decision is binding on all the others; but should a player name a suit out of his proper turn, both he and his partner are debarred from making that suit the trump. If no one will name a new trump, the deal is void, and passes to the next player on the dealer's left.

ORDERING UP THE TRUMP. Instead of passing the turn-up trump on the first round, any player who thinks it would be to his advantage to have the turn-up remain the trump, may order the dealer to take it up. In doing so he says: *"I order it,"* if he is an adversary; or: *" I assist,"* if he is the dealer's partner. In either case the player making the trump may announce a lone hand at the same time. His side must make at least three tricks, whether he plays alone or not, or it is a euchre, and the adversaries will count two points. In case an adversary of the dealer plays alone, he must distinctly announce it when he orders up the trump. The usual expression is: *" I order it alone."* His partner then lays his cards face downward on the table and takes no further part in the play of that hand. If he exposes any card of the abandoned hand, the adversaries can call upon him to take up the hand and play it, leaving the exposed card on the table as liable to be called. This of course prevents the lone hand.

If the dealer's partner wishes to play alone, instead of assisting, he says: *" I play this alone,"* and the dealer lays down his cards, leaving the trump on the pack.

PLAYING ALONE. No player but the one that takes up, orders up, or makes the trump can play a lone hand. If the dealer takes up the trump card of his own accord, he can play alone. If any player orders up or assists, that player can play alone. Any player making a new trump after the first has been turned down, can play alone. If one player orders up the trump, neither his partner nor his adversary can play alone; and if the dealer's partner assists, that prevents the dealer from playing a lone hand. In many clubs the mistake is made of allowing the dealer to play alone on his partner's assist; or letting the pone play alone after the dealer has been assisted; or letting the partner of the player who makes the new trump play alone. This is not good Euchre, because it gives an unfair advantage to one side, as we shall see when we come to the suggestions for good play, especially in connection with ordering up at what is called the " bridge ;" that is, when the score is 4 to 1, or 4 to 0.

METHOD OF PLAYING. The trump settled, the eldest hand, or the player next him on the left, if the partner of the eldest hand is playing alone, begins by leading any card he pleases, and the others must follow suit if they can. Failure to follow suit when able is a *revoke,* if the error is not discovered and corrected before the trick in which it occurs is turned and quitted. If the player discovers his mistake in time, the card played in error must be left on the table, and is liable to be called. When a revoke is discovered and claimed by the adversaries, it is usual to abandon the hand, and the adversaries of the revoking player can either deduct two points from his score, or add two to their own score, for every revoke made during the hand. The penalty cannot be divided. If both sides revoke, the deal is void, and the same dealer must deal again.

Any player having none of the suit led may either trump, or throw away a card of another suit. The highest card played, if of the suit led, wins the trick, trumps winning against all other suits, and a higher trump winning a lower. The winner of the trick may lead any card he pleases for the next trick, and so on, until all five tricks have been played. If the dealer takes the trump into his hand, any player naming it is liable to have his highest or lowest trump called; but a player may ask and must be informed what the trump suit is.

Cards Played in Error. All cards led out of turn, played in error, or two or more played to a trick, or dropped face upward on the table, are called ***exposed cards,*** and must be left face up on the table. These must be played when called by the adversaries, unless compliance with the demand would make the player revoke ; but the fact of their being exposed does not prevent their being got rid of in the course of play if the opportunity offers. Some persons imagine that the adversaries can prevent an exposed card from being played ; but such is not the case in Euchre. A person playing a lone hand is not liable to any penalty for exposing his cards, nor for leading out of turn, for he has no partner to derive any benefit from the information conveyed.

Leading Out of Turn. Should any person, not playing alone, lead out of turn, the adversaries may call a suit from the player in error, or from his partner, when it is next the turn of either of them to lead. The demand must be made by the person who will be the last player on the trick in which the suit is called. If all have played to the lead before discovering the error, it cannot be rectified ; but if all have not played, those who have followed the false lead must take back their cards, which are not liable to be called.

Any player may ask the others to ***draw cards*** in any trick, provided he does so before the cards are touched for the purpose of gathering them. In answer to this demand, each player should indicate which card of those on the table he played. No one is allowed to see any trick that has been turned and quitted.

Taking Tricks. As the tricks are taken they should be neatly laid one upon the other in such a manner that any player at the table can count them. All tricks belonging to one side should be kept together. At the end of each hand the score should be claimed and marked. Revokes must be detected and claimed before the cards are cut for the following deal.

CUTTING OUT. When the play is confined to four players, rubbers are usually played, and the table is complete with six persons, two looking on, and awaiting their turn. At the end of a rubber, if there are more than four players belonging to the table, those who have just played cut to decide which shall give place to those waiting, the players cutting the highest cards going out. If six belong to the table, there will be no further cutting out, as those who are out for one rubber re-enter for the next, taking the places of those who have played two consecutive rubbers. If five belong to the table, the three who remained in for the second rubber must cut to allow the fifth player to re-enter. At the end of the third rubber, the two cut that have not yet been out ; and at the end of the fourth rubber the one who has played every rubber goes out without cutting. Partners and deal are cut for at the beginning of each new rubber.

METHODS OF CHEATING. All the Euchre family of games, especially Écarté and Napoleon, offer numerous opportunities to the greek. So well is this known in Europe that it is considered extremely foolish for any person to play Écarté in mixed companies. The small number of cards in the pack, and the custom of dealing two and three at a time, gives the dealer an opportunity to bunch four valuable cards, of which he can give himself three, and turn up the fourth. False shuffles, shifted cuts, and marked cards are formidable weapons. The telegraph between partners, and the variation in tone or words in passing are frequently used by card-sharpers. One of the commonest devices in America is the use of what are known as "jack strippers" These are two Jacks, usually both of the same colour, which can be withdrawn from any portion of the pack by the fingers of an expert, and placed on the top. When the sharp deals, he places cards enough on these to supply the other players on the first round, so that the strippers will come to him. When only two are playing, he strips them out and leaves them on the top when he cuts the cards, so that they shall be dealt to him. Never play Euchre or Écarté with a man who cuts the pack with both hands.

Any person who is tempted to bet on any game in the Euchre family should remember the advice of the worldly-wise Parisian to his son: "Until you have four eyes in your head, risk not your gold at Écarté."

SUGGESTIONS FOR GOOD PLAY. The chief points for the beginner to understand are: When to order up; when to assist; when to take up; when to play alone; and what to make the trump if it is turned down. His decision in each case will be governed largely by his position at the table, and by the score. The following suggestions are for four players, two being partners against the other two, and playing without the Joker; that being the most common form of the game. The general principles underlying these suggestions for the four-handed game will be found equally valuable in any form of Euchre.

ORDERING UP. Although probabilities are of little practical value in Euchre, it may be well to remember that there are nine cards in the trump suit; but as only two-thirds of the pack is dealt out, the average number of trumps among four players will be six. Of these, the dealer always has the advantage of being sure of one more than his share, and it is safe to reckon upon the dealer to hold at least two trumps. He may also be counted for a missing suit, for he will discard any losing card of an odd suit when he takes up the trump.

The Eldest Hand should not order up the trump unless he has such cards that he is reasonably certain of three tricks without any assistance from his partner, and cannot be sure of two tricks if the trump is turned down. When he holds one or two bowers, especially if he has cards of the next suit; that is, the suit of the same colour as the turn-up, he should always pass; because if the dealer takes it up he will probably be euchred, and if he turns it down, the eldest hand will have the first say, and can make it next. It is seldom right to order up a bower, because the dealer will rarely turn down such a card.

There are exceptional cases in which the eldest hand may order up with little or nothing. One of the most common is when the adversaries of the dealer are at the **bridge;** that is, when their score is 4, and the dealer's side has only 1 or 2 marked. It is obvious that if the dealer or his partner plays alone, he will win the game; but if the trump is ordered up the most he can score is 2 points for a euchre, and the player who orders up will then have a chance to go out on his own deal. For this reason it has come to be regarded as imperative for the eldest hand to order up at the bridge, unless he holds the right bower, or the left bower guarded, or the ace twice guarded, any one of which combinations is certain to win a trick against a lone hand if the eldest hand does not lead trumps himself. Another case is when the score is 4 to 4, and the eldest hand has average trump strength, good side cards, but nothing in the next suit. It is better to order it up, and risk the game on such a hand than to take the chance of the dealer's turning it down.

The Pone, who is the partner of the eldest hand, orders up at the bridge on exactly opposite principles. The fact that the eldest hand did not order up shows that the dealer cannot make a lone hand. This should indicate to the pone that his partner has a certain trick in trumps, and if the pone holds any good trumps himself, he can often guess what his partner's trumps are. For instance: The ace is turned, and the pone holds the left bower guarded. The eldest hand must have the right bower, or four trumps to the King. If the eldest hand has passed at the bridge, and the pone has strong trumps himself, especially the ace or left bower and two small trumps, he should order up the trump; not to save the game, but to be sure of winning it by preventing the dealer from turning it down. If the pone does not order up at the bridge, the eldest hand may infer that he is weak in trumps.

When it is not a bridge, the pone should be guided by the same principles as those given for the eldest hand, because he may be sure that his partner will make it next if it is turned down, unless he has a certainty of three tricks by crossing.

If a player calls his partner's attention to the fact that they are at the bridge, both lose their right to order up.

ASSISTING. The dealer's partner usually assists on plain-suit cards, such as two aces, rather than on trumps. The score and the turn-up trump will often be a guide as to whether or not to assist. For instance: If the score is 1 all, or to 2 to 1, and a bower is turned, it is rarely right to assist, because it prevents the dealer from playing alone. If the partner has good suit cards, they may be useful to make a march; if he has strong trumps, especially if sure of three tricks, he should play alone, instead of assisting. If the score is 3 in the dealer's favour, he does not need a lone hand to win the game, and with two reasonably certain tricks in his own hand the dealer's partner should assist, as they may win the game by a march.

If the dealer's side is at the bridge, the score being 4 to 1 or 4 to 0 in their favour, and the eldest hand passes, the dealer's partner must be on the alert to prevent the pone from playing a lone hand. He should assist unless a bower is turned, or he has it himself, or holds such cards that, combined with the turn-up, he is sure of a trick. For instance: The dealer's partner has the King and two other trumps, and the ace is turned. It is impossible for the pone to make a lone hand, even if he has both bowers, and the ace is bare; for he cannot catch the King, even if his partner leads the trump through it. But if a small trump was turned, the pone might easily make a lone hand with both bowers and the ace.

TAKING UP. The average expectation of the dealer is something over two trumps, including the turn-up. With more than two trumps, or with two strong trumps, and a reasonably certain trick in a plain suit, the dealer should take up the trump. Three trumps of any size and an ace in plain suits is a strong take-up hand. It is better to take up the trump with only one plain suit in the hand, and small trumps, than with two strong trumps and two weak plain suits. The score will often decide the dealer in taking up the trump. For instance: At 4 all, it is useless to turn anything down unless you have a certain euchre in the next suit, and nothing in the turn-up. Even then, the adversaries are almost certain to cross the suit and go out. With the score 3 all, the dealer should be very careful about taking up on a weak hand, because a euchre loses the game. If he is weak, but has a chance in the next suit, or a bower in the cross suits, he should turn it down. It is a common stratagem to turn it down for a euchre when the dealer is better in the next suit, and has only 2 to go.

PLAYING ALONE. The dealer has the best chance to get a lone hand; but the eldest hand is more likely to succeed with one, on account of the advantage of the lead. It is an invariable rule for any player to go alone when he has three certain tricks, unless he is 3 up, and can win the game with a march. A lone hand should be played with both bowers and the ace, no matter how worthless the other cards; or with five trumps to the ace without either bower; or two high trumps and three aces in plain suits; or three good trumps and two aces. The theory of this is that while the march might possibly be made with partner's assistance, if partner has the cards necessary to make a march, the adversaries have little or nothing, and there is a very good chance to make a lone hand if three tricks of it are certain. Both bowers and the ace, with only the seven and eight of a plain suit have made many a lone hand. If the lone player is not caught on the plain suit at the first trick, the adversaries may discard it to keep higher cards in the other suit; or they may have none of it from the first. There is always a chance, and it should be taken.

The dealer's partner, and the pone, should be very careful in playing lone hands, and should never risk them except with three certain tricks, no matter what suit is led first. The pone's partner will of course lead trumps, if he has any, when the pone announces to play alone.

MAKING THE TRUMP. When the trump is turned down the general rule is for the eldest hand to make it next. The exceptions are when he has nothing in the next suit, but has at least two certain tricks in the cross suit, and a probable trick in a plain suit. It is safer to make it next with a weak hand than to cross it on moderate strength, for the presumption is that neither the dealer nor his partner had a bower in the turn-down suit, and therefore have none in the next suit. Such being the case, it is very likely that one or both may be strong in the cross suits, and it is not considered good policy to cross the suit unless so strong in it as to be reasonably certain of three tricks. Some players invariably make it next, regardless of their hands, unless they can play alone in the cross suit. Such a habit exposes them to the common artifice of the dealer's turning it down for a euchre. A dealer holding a bower and three cards of the next suit, will often turn it down, and trust to the eldest hand making it next, which will give the dealer four trumps instead of two. The eldest hand should be on his guard against this when the dealer's side has 3 scored.

The dealer's partner, on the other hand, should cross the suit almost as invariably as the eldest hand should make it next; for if his partner cannot take up the trump, and the eldest hand cannot make it next, their hands must be weak, and if it is passed to the pone, he will probably turn out to have a lone hand. The best chance is to cross the suit, unless the player has three certain tricks in his own hand by making it next, such as five trumps to the ace, or four trumps and a plain-suit ace. With such cards he should play alone.

The pone should never make the trump unless he has three certain tricks, and is willing to play a lone hand. If the dealer turns it down, and both the eldest hand and the dealer's partner pass a second time, there must be a nigger in the woodpile somewhere.

LEADING. The general principle of leading is to make
tricks while you can. It is useless to save up tenaces in plain
suits, because there are only five tricks to play, two of which are
certain to fall to the trumps, and it is very improbable that any
player will lead up to you a small card of a plain suit that will go
round twice. It is seldom right to lead small cards of a plain suit.
There is a better chance to make a trick with the King by leading it than by keeping it guarded. In the trump suit, tenaces are
very strong, and should be preserved, especially if the tenace is
over the turn-up trump. There is a familiar example of the importance of tenace when only two play, in which one person holds
the major tenace in trumps, hearts, and must win three tricks, no
matter which player leads. The cards in one hand are :—

and those in the other hand are ;—

If the player with the major tenace has to lead first, all he has to
do is to force his adversary with the plain suit, spades. Whatever
the adversary leads, the player with the major tenace simply wins
it, and forces again. If the player with the four trumps has the
first lead, it does not matter what card he plays ; the player with
the major tenace wins it, and forces with the plain suit. As long
as the major tenace in trumps is not led away from, it must win
three tricks in trumps.

Leading Trumps. With strong cards in plain suits, the
eldest hand may often lead trumps to advantage if the dealer's
partner has assisted, especially if the turn-up trump is small. It
is seldom right to lead trumps if the dealer has taken up the trump
of his own accord ; but an exception is usually made when the
eldest hand holds three trumps, and two aces in plain suits. The
best chance for a euchre is to exhaust the trumps, so as to make
the aces good for tricks. If the pone has ordered up the trump,
the eldest hand should lead trumps to him immediately ; but the
pone should not lead trumps to his partner if the eldest hand has
ordered up at the bridge. If a bower is turned, the dealer's partner should lead a small trump at the first opportunity.

In playing against a lone hand the best cards in plain suits
should always be led, trumps never. In playing alone, it is best
to lead winning trumps as long as they last, so as to force discards, which will often leave intermediate cards in plain suits good
for tricks.

Second Hand. Play the best card you have second hand, and cover everything led if you can. With King and another or Queen and another, it is usually best to put up the honour second hand, on a small card led.

Trumping. It is seldom right to trump partner's winning cards, unless he has ordered up the trump, and you think you can lead through the dealer to advantage. In playing against a lone hand, it is sometimes good play to trump your partner's ace with an unguarded left bower or ace of trumps, as it may prevent the dealer from getting into the lead with a small trump, and may save a King or Queen of trumps in your partner's hand. If you don't trump, the dealer will probably get in and swing the right bower, and your trump will be lost.

If your partner has ordered, made, or taken up the trump, and you have only one trump, even a bower, trump with it at the first opportunity. Trump everything second hand, unless it takes the right bower for a doubtful trick, or breaks into the major tenace in trumps.

Discarding. It is best to throw away singletons, unless they are aces. If you have two cards of equal value, but of different colours, one of which must be discarded, it is usual to keep the one of the same colour as the turn-up when playing against the dealer. Discard suits that the adversaries are trumping. If your partner discards a suit in which you have a high card, keep that suit, and discard another. If you have both ace and King of a plain suit, discard the ace, to show partner that you can win a trick in the suit. It is very often important to discard correctly when playing against a lone hand, especially if the lone player leads trumps for the fourth trick. It is a common practice for modern players to signal in the discard if they have a certain trick in a suit. This is done by discarding two cards in another suit, the higher before the lower. For instance : You have two aces, spades and diamonds. The dealer plays alone on hearts, and trumps your spade ace the first time. If you have two clubs, such as King and ten, discard the King first, and then the ten, and your partner will know you can stop the diamond suit. This should advise him to keep his clubs.

CUT-THROAT EUCHRE.

The chief element in the three-handed game is playing to the score. The player with the strong hand must always be kind to the under dog, and partnerships are always formed against the man with the high score. Suppose *A, B,* and *C* are playing, and

that *A* has 3 points to his adversaries' nothing on *B's* deal. It is
to the interest of *A* to euchre *B;* but it is to the interest of *C* to
let *B* make his point, because if *B* is euchred, *A* wins the game.
B having made his point, *C* deals, and it is then to the interest of
B to let *C* make his point. Suppose *C* makes a march, 3 points,
which puts him on a level with *A.* On *A's* deal it is *C's* game to
euchre him, but *B* must let *A* make his point ; so that instead of
being opposed by both *B* and *C,* as he was a moment ago, *A*
finds a friend in *B,* and the two who were helping each other to
beat *A,* are now cutting each other's throats. On *B's* deal, *A*
does not want to euchre him, for although that would win the
game for both *A* and *C, A,* who now has 4 points up, does not
wish to divide the pool with *C* while he has such a good chance
to win it all himself. Suppose *B* makes his point. *A* will do all
he can to euchre *C,* but *B* will oppose the scheme, because his
only chance for the game is that *A* will not be able to take up the
trump on his own deal, and that *B* will make a march.

SET-BACK EUCHRE.

This is simply a reversal of the ordinary method of scoring, the
players starting with a certain number of points, usually ten, and
deducting what they make on each deal. The peculiarity which
gives the game its name is that if a player is euchred he is **set
back** two points, his adversaries counting nothing. The revoke
penalty is settled in the same way. The game is usually counted
with chips, each player starting with ten, and placing in the centre
of the table those that he is entitled to score.

AUCTION EUCHRE.

This form of the game is sometimes erroneously called **French
Euchre.** The French know nothing about Euchre in any form.
Auction Euchre is exactly the same as the ordinary four or six-
handed game, except that the trump is not turned up, the players
bidding in turn for the privilege of naming the trump suit. The
bidder names the number of tricks he proposes to take. There is
no second bid, and the player who has made the highest bid names
the trump suit. No matter who is the successful bidder, the eldest
hand leads for the first trick. The number of points won or lost
on the deal are the number of points bid, even if the bidder ac-

complishes more. If a player has bid 3, and he and his partner take 4 or 5 tricks, they count 3 only. If they are euchred, failing to make the number of tricks bid, the adversaries count the number of points bid. Fifteen points is usually the game.

This is probably the root of the much better games of five and seven-handed Euchre, which will be described further on.

PROGRESSIVE EUCHRE.

This form of Euchre is particularly well suited to social gatherings. Its peculiarity consists in the arrangement and progression of a large number of players originally divided into sets of four, and playing, at separate tables, the ordinary four-handed game.

Apparatus. A sufficient number of tables to accommodate the assembled players are arranged in order, and numbered consecutively; No. 1 being called ***the head table,*** and the lowest of the series ***the booby table.*** Each player is provided with a blank card, to which the various coloured stars may be attached as they accrue in the course of play. These stars are usually of three colours; red, green, and gold. The head table is provided with a bell, and each table is supplied with one pack of cards only. It is usual to sort out the thirty-two cards used in play, and the four small cards for markers, before the arrival of the guests.

Drawing for Positions. Two packs of differently coloured cards are used, and from the two black suits in each a sequence of cards is sorted out, equal in length to the number of tables in play. For instance: If there are sixteen ladies and sixteen gentlemen, or thirty-two players in all, they will fill eight tables, and all the clubs and spades from the ace to the eight inclusive should be sorted out. These are then thoroughly shuffled and presented, face down, to the players to draw from. The ladies take only the red-back cards, and the gentlemen only the blue. The number of pips on the card drawn indicates the number of the table at which the player is to sit, and those drawing cards of the same suit are partners for the first game.

Playing. All being seated, the deal is cut for at each table, and play begins. There is no cutting for partners, that being settled in the original drawing. Five points is a game, and after that number is reached by either side at the head table, the bell is struck. Lone hands are usually barred at the head table, so as to give the other tables time to make a certain number of points, and so to avoid ties. Upon the tap of the bell all play immediately ceases, even if in the middle of a deal. If the players at any but the head table have reached five points before the bell rings, they play on, counting all points made until the bell taps,

Progressing. The partners winning the game at the head table each receive a gold star, and retain their seats for the next game. The losing players at the head table go down to the booby table. All the winning players at the other tables receive red stars, and go to the table next in order above, those at table No. 2, going to No. 1. Those losing and remaining at the booby table each receive a green star.

Changing Partners. At all but the head table the partners that progress to the next table divide, the lady who has just lost at each table retains her seat, and takes for her partner the gentleman who has just arrived from the table below. At the head table the newly arrived pair remain as partners ; but at the booby table the players who have just arrived from the head table divide. All being seated, they cut for the deal, and play is resumed until the next bell tap.

Ties. In case of ties in points at any table when the bell taps, those having won the most tricks on the next hand are declared the winners. If that is also a tie, the ladies cut to decide it, the lowest cut going up. In cutting, the ace is low, and the Jack ranks below the Queen.

Prizes. Six prizes are usually provided for large companies. The lady and gentleman having the largest number of gold stars taking the first prizes ; the largest number of red stars winning the second prizes ; and the largest number of green stars the booby prizes. One player cannot win two prizes. In case of ties for the gold stars, the accompanying red stars decide it ; if that is also a tie, the player with the fewest number of green stars wins ; and if that is still a tie, the players must cut for it.

The hostess decides the hour at which play shall cease, and is the referee in all disputes.

RAILROAD EUCHRE.

Railroad Euchre is the name given to any form of the four-handed game in which every expedient is used to make points rapidly.

Cards. A pack of twenty-five cards is used, all below the 9 being deleted, and the Joker added. The Joker is always the best trump.

Players. There are four players, two being partners against the other two. Partners, deal, and seats are cut for as in the ordinary game.

Dealing. The cards are distributed as in the ordinary game ; but it is usual to agree beforehand upon a suit which shall be the trump if the Joker is turned up.

Playing Alone. The chief peculiarity in Railroad Euchre is in playing alone. Any player announcing to play alone, whether the dealer or not, has the privilege of passing a card, face down, to his partner. In exchange for this, but without seeing it, the partner gives the best card in his hand to the lone player, passing it to him face down. If he has not a trump to give him, he can pass him an ace, or even a King. Even if this card is no better than the one discarded, the lone player cannot refuse it. If the dealer plays alone, he has two discards ; the first in exchange for his partner's best card, and then another, in exchange for the trump card, after seeing what his partner can give him. In this second discard he may get rid of the card passed to him by his partner. If the dealer's partner plays alone, the dealer may pass him the turn-up trump, or any better card he may have in his hand.

Any person having announced to play alone, either of his adversaries may play alone against him ; discarding and taking partner's best card in the same manner. Should the lone player who makes the trump be euchred by the lone player opposing him, the euchre counts four points. It is considered imperative for a player holding the Joker, or the right bower guarded, to play alone against the lone hand, taking his partner's best ; for as it is evident that the lone hand cannot succeed, there is a better chance to euchre it with all the strength in one hand than divided.

If any player, in his proper turn, announces to play alone, and asks for his partner's best, the partner cannot refuse ; neither can he propose to play alone instead.

Scoring. With the exception of the four points for euchreing a lone hand, the scoring is exactly the same as in the ordinary four-handed game ; but there are one or two variations which are sometimes agreed upon beforehand in order to make points still more rapidly.

Laps. If a player makes more points than are necessary to win the game, the additional points are counted on the next game, so that there is always an inducement to play lone hands, even with 4 points up.

Slams. If one side reaches five points before the other has scored, it is a slam, and counts ***two games.***

When laps and slams are played, it is sometimes agreed that if a person plays alone without taking his partner's best card, or the dealer plays alone without taking up the trump or asking for his partner's best, and such a player succeeds in winning all five tricks with a pat hand, it counts *five* points.   If he fails to win all five tricks, the adversaries count *one.*   If he is euchred, they count *three;* but they are not permitted to play alone against him.

Jambone.   Any person playing a lone hand may announce Jambone, and expose his cards face up on the table.   The adversaries then have the right to call any card they please, either for the lead, or in following suit; but they cannot make the player revoke, nor can they consult, or in any way expose their hands.   If a lead is required, it must be called by the person on the jambone player's left.   If a card is called on a trick, it must be called by the person on the jambone player's right.   If in spite of these difficulties the jambone player succeeds in winning five tricks, he scores *eight* points.   If he wins three or four only, he counts *one* point.   If he is euchred he loses *two.*   It is not allowable to play alone against a jambone.

Jamboree.   This is the combination of the five highest trumps in one hand, and need only be announced and shown to entitle the holder to score *sixteen* points.   If held by the dealer, it may be made with the assistance of the turn-up trump; and any player may make it with the assistance of his partner's best; but it does not count unless the holder of it has made the trump.   If a player with a pat Jamboree is ordered up, all he can score is a euchre.

As in other forms of Euchre, no one but the maker of the trump can play alone, or announce Jambone or Jamboree.   Lone hands are very common in Railroad Euchre, and ordering up to prevent lone hands is commoner still.

SEVEN-HANDED EUCHRE.

Cards.   Seven-handed Euchre is played with a full pack of fifty-three cards, including the Joker.   The cards in plain suits rank as at Whist; but the Joker is always the best trump, the right and left bowers being the second and third-best respectively.

Counters.   One white and four red counters are necessary. The white counter is passed to the left from player to player in turn, to indicate the position of the next deal.   The red counters are placed in front of the maker of the trump and his partners, to distinguish them from their opponents.   Markers are not used, the score being kept on a sheet of paper.   The score is usually kept by a person who is not playing, in order that none of those in the game may know how the various scores stand. Should an outsider not be available for scoring, there are two methods : One is for one player to keep the score for the whole table, who must inform any player of the state of the score if asked to do so. The other is to have a dish of counters on the table, each player being given the number he wins from time to time. These should be placed in some covered receptacle, so that they cannot be counted by their owner, and no other player will know how many he has. As it is very seldom that a successful bid is less than five, and never less than four, counters marked as being worth 4, 5, 6 and 7 each will answer every purpose, and will pay every bid made.

Cutting. The players draw cards from an outspread pack for the choice of seats, those cutting the lowest cards having the first choice. The lowest cut of all deals the first hand, passing the white counter to the player on his left, whose turn it will be to deal next. Ties are decided in the usual way.

Dealing. The cards are dealt from left to right, two being given to each player for the first round, then three, and then two again, until each player has received seven cards. The four remaining in the pack are then placed in the centre of the table, face down, and form the *widow.* No trump is turned.

The rules governing all irregularities in the deal are the same as in ordinary Euchre.

Making the Trump. The cards dealt, each player in turn, beginning with the eldest hand, bids a certain number of points, at the same time naming the suit which he wishes to make the trump. There is no second bid, and the suit named by the highest bidder must be the trump for that deal. The successful bidder takes the widow, selecting from it what cards he pleases, and discarding others in their stead, so as to restore the number of his cards to seven. He then places a red counter in front of him, and chooses his partners, passing a red counter to each of them. These counters must be placed in front of the players to distinguish them as belonging to the bidder's side ; but the players make no changes in their respective positions at the table. Each player should bid on the possibilities of his hand, however small, so as to guide the others in their selection of partners.

Partners. If the bidder has proposed to take not more than *five* tricks out of the seven possible, he chooses two partners, and these three play against the remaining four. If he has bid to make *six* or *seven* tricks he chooses three partners, and these four play against the remaining three. Partners cannot refuse to play.

Playing Alone. Should a player think he can take all seven tricks without any partners, he may bid *ten,* which would outrank a bid of seven ; but such a bid must be made before seeing the widow. If a player thinks he can win all seven tricks without either widow or partners, he may bid **twenty**, which is the highest bid possible. When twenty is bid the cards in the widow must remain untouched.

Playing. The successful bidder has the lead for the first trick. The general rules for following suit, etc., are the same as in ordinary Euchre. The bidder takes in all the tricks won by himself and his partners, and one of the adversaries should gather for that side. If a player on either side **revokes**, the adversaries score the number bid, and the hand is abandoned.

Scoring. If the bidder is successful in his undertaking, he and his partners, if any, are credited by the scorer with the number of points bid, but no more. Should a player bid five, and his side take seven, it would count them only five points. If the player making the trump fails to reach his bid, he is euchred, and the adversaries are credited with the number of points lost.

Prizes. It is usual to give two prizes for each table in play; one for the highest number of points won during the evening, and one for the smallest number ; the latter being usually called the "booby" prize.

Suggestions for Good Play. It is very risky to bid seven without the Joker, the odds being 11 to 1 against finding it in the widow. A bid of ten should not be made without both Joker and Right Bower, and all the other cards winners and trumps. To bid twenty, a player should have a practically invincible hand, with at least five winning leads of trumps.

The first bidders are always at a disadvantage, because they know nothing of the contents of the other hands ; but after one or two players have made a bid, those following them can judge pretty well how the cards lie. For instance : The seven players are *A B C D E F G.* *A* deals, and *B* bids 2 in hearts. *C* and *D* pass. *E* bids 3 in clubs; and *F* says 4 in hearts. It is evident that *F* is bidding on *B's* offer in hearts, and intends to choose him for a partner. *G* finds in his hand four good spades and the Joker, but neither Bower. He may safely bid 5 or 6, taking *E* for a partner if successful, as *E* very probably has one or both the black Bowers. If he bids 5 only, the dealer, *A,* would have an excellent chance to bid 6 in hearts, and to take *B* and *F* for two of his partners, and *G* for the third, trusting to find him with the Joker, or at least protection in one or both black suits.

If the successful bidder has had no previous bids to guide him in his choice of partners, he should take those who have the lowest scores, if the scores are known ; because it is to his advantage to avoid advancing those who are perhaps already ahead. When the scores are not known, there is nothing but luck to guide one, unless a person has a very good memory, and knows which players are probably behind.

Leading. If the successful bidder wants 6 or 7 tricks, and holds the Joker, he should lead it at once. If he has not the Joker, he should begin with a low trump, and give his partners a chance to play the Joker on the first round. If the leader cannot exhaust the trumps with one or two rounds, it will sometimes be to his advantage to lead any losing card he may have in the plain suits, in order to let his partners win the trick if they can. In playing alone, it is absolutely necessary to exhaust the trumps before opening a plain suit.

Partners should avail themselves of the methods common to four-handed Euchre to support one another in trumps and plain suits. The discard should invariably be from weakness if the player is the bidder's partner; and from strength, if opposed to him.

EUCHRE FOR FIVE PLAYERS. This is practically the same as the seven-handed game, but the pack is reduced to 28 cards, all below the Eight in each suit being deleted. The Joker is not used. Five cards are dealt to each player, by two and three at a time, and the three remaining form the widow. The player bidding ***three*** tricks takes one partner only. The player bidding ***four*** or ***five*** tricks, takes two partners. A player who intends to take the widow, but no partners, can bid ***eight*** and one who intends to take neither widow nor partners can bid ***fifteen.*** In this form of Euchre the scores are generally known, and 100 points is game.

In some clubs it is the practice for the successful bidder to select one of his partners by asking for the holder of a certain card. For instance: B has the lead, and has bid five in hearts, holding the three best trumps, the club ace, and a losing spade. Instead of selecting his partners at random, he asks for the spade ace, and the player holding that card must say, "Here"; upon which the bidder will pass him a counter, marking him as one of his partners.

EUCHRE LAWS.

1. SCORING. A game consists of five points. If the players making the trump win all five tricks, they count ***two*** points towards game; if they win three or four tricks, they count ***one*** point; if they fail to win three tricks, their adversaries count ***two*** points.

2. If the player making the trump plays ***alone,*** and makes five tricks, he counts as many points as there are players in the game: Two, if two play; three if three play; four if four play, etc. If he wins three or four tricks only, he counts one; if he fails to win three tricks, his adversaries count two.

3. *The Rubber* is the best of three games. If the first two are won by the same players, the third game is not played. The winners gain a **triple,** or three points, if their adversaries have not scored; a **double,** or two points, if their adversaries are less than three scored; a **single,** or one point, if their adversaries have scored three or four. The winners of the rubber add two points to the value of their games, and deduct the points made by the losers, if any; the remainder being the value of the rubber.

4. *FORMING THE TABLE*. A Euchre table is complete with six players. If more than four assemble, they cut for the preference, the four lowest playing the first rubber. Partners and deal are then cut for, the two lowest pairing against the two highest. The lowest deals, and has the choice of seats and cards.

5. *Ties*. Players cutting cards of equal value cut again, but the new cut decides nothing but the tie.

6. *Cutting Out*. At the end of a rubber the players cut to decide which shall give way to those awaiting their turn to play. After the second rubber, those who have played the greatest number of consecutive games give way; ties being decided by cutting.

7. *Cutting*. In cutting, the ace is low, the other cards ranking, K Q J 10 9 8 7, the King being the highest. A player exposing more than one card, or cutting the Joker, must cut again.

8. *SHUFFLING*. Every player has a right to shuffle the cards, the dealer last.

9. *DEALING*. The dealer must present the pack to the pone to be cut. At least four cards must be left in each packet. If a card is exposed in cutting, the pack must be re-shuffled, and cut again. If the dealer re-shuffles the pack after it has been properly cut, he loses his deal.

10. Beginning on his left, the dealer must give to each player in rotation **two** cards on the first round, and **three** on the second; or three to each on the first round, and two on the second. Five cards having been given to each player in this manner, the next card is turned up for the trump. The deal passes to the left.

11. There must be a new deal by the same dealer if any card but the trump is found faced in the pack, or if the pack is proved incorrect or imperfect; but any previous scores made with the imperfect pack stand good.

12. The adversaries may demand a new deal if any card but the trump is exposed during the deal, provided they have not touched a card. If an adversary exposes a card, the dealer may elect to deal again.   If a new deal is not demanded, cards exposed in dealing cannot be called.

13.   The adversaries may stop a player dealing out of turn, or with the wrong pack, provided they do so before the trump card is turned, after which the deal stands good.

14.   *MISDEALING.*   A misdeal loses the deal.   It is a misdeal: If the cards have not been properly cut; if the dealer gives two cards to one player and three to another in the same round; if he gives too many or too few cards to any player; if he counts the cards on the table, or those remaining in the pack; or if he deals a card incorrectly, and fails to correct the error before dealing another.   If the dealer is interrupted in any manner by an adversary, he does not lose his deal.

15.   *THE TRUMP CARD.*   After the trump card is turned, each player in turn, beginning with the eldest hand, has the privilege of passing, assisting, or ordering up the trump. Should a player pass, and afterward correct himself by ordering up or assisting, both he and his partner may be prevented by the adversaries from exercising their privilege.   If a player calls his partner's attention to the fact that they are at the bridge, both lose their right to order up the trump.

16.   The dealer may leave the trump card on the pack until it is got rid of in the course of play.   If the trump card has been taken up or played, any player may ask, and must be informed by the dealer, what the trump suit is; but any player naming the trump card may be called upon by an adversary to play his highest or lowest trump.

17.   If the dealer takes up, or is ordered up, he must ***discard*** a card from his own hand, placing it under the remainder of the pack.   Having quitted such discard, it cannot be taken back.   If the dealer has not discarded until he has played to the first trick, he and his partner cannot score any points for that hand.

18.   If the eldest hand leads before the dealer has quitted his discard, the dealer may amend his discard, but the eldest hand cannot take back the card led.

19.   If the dealer takes up the trump to play alone, he must pass his discard across the table to his partner.   If he fails to do so, the adversaries may insist that his partner play with him, preventing the lone hand.

20.   *MAKING THE TRUMP.*   If the dealer does not take up the trump, he must place it under the remainder of the pack, face upward, so that it can be distinctly seen.   Each player in turn, beginning on the dealer's left, then has the privilege of naming a new trump suit.

21. If any player names the suit already turned down, he loses his right to name a suit ; and if he corrects himself, and names another, neither he nor his partner is allowed to make that suit the trump. If a player names a new trump suit out of his proper turn, both he and his partner are forbidden to make that suit the trump.

22. If no one will name a new trump, the deal is void, and passes to the next player on the dealer's left.

23. IRREGULARITIES IN THE HANDS. If any player is found not to have his correct number of cards, it is a misdeal ; but if he has played to the first trick the deal stands good, and he cannot score anything that hand.

24. EXPOSED CARDS. The following are exposed cards, and must be left face up on the table, and are liable to be called by the adversaries :

    I.   Every card faced upon the table otherwise than in the regular course of play.

    II.   Two or more cards played to a trick. The adversaries may elect which shall be played.

    III.   Any card named by the player holding it.

25. If an adversary of a person playing alone exposes a card, the lone player may abandon the hand, and score the points. Should the partner of the lone player expose a card, the adversaries may prevent the lone hand by compelling the player in error to play with his partner, leaving the exposed card on the table.

26. CALLING EXPOSED CARDS. The adversary on the right of an exposed card must call it before he plays himself. If it will be the turn of the player holding the exposed card to lead for the next trick, the card, if wanted, must be called before the current trick is turned and quitted. Should a player having an exposed card and the lead, play from his hand before the previous trick is turned and quitted, the card so led may also be claimed as exposed.

27. LEADING AND PLAYING OUT OF TURN. If a player leads when it was his partner's turn, a suit may be called from his partner. The demand must be made by the last player to the trick in which the suit is called. If it was the turn of neither to lead, the card played in error is exposed. If all have played to the false lead, the error cannot be rectified. If all have not followed, the cards erroneously played must be taken back, but are not liable to be called.

28. If an adversary of a lone player leads out of turn, the lone player may abandon the hand, and score the points.

29. If the third hand plays before the second, the fourth hand may play before his partner, either of his own volition, or at the direction of the second hand, who may say : " Play, partner." If the fourth hand plays before the second, the third hand may call upon the second hand to play his highest or lowest of the suit led, or to trump or not to trump the trick.

30. REVOKING. A revoke is a renounce in error, not corrected in time ; or non-compliance with a performable penalty. If a revoke is claimed and proved, the hand in which it occurs is immediately abandoned. The adversaries of the revoking player then have the option of adding two points to their own score, or deducting two points from his score. If both sides revoke, the deal is void. If one person is playing alone, the penalty for a revoke is as many points as would have been scored if the lone hand had succeeded.

31. A revoke may be corrected by the player making it before the trick in which it occurs has been turned and quitted, unless the revoking player or his partner, whether in his right turn or otherwise, has led or played to the following trick.

32. If a player corrects his mistake in time to save a revoke, the card played in error is exposed ; but any cards subsequently played by others may be taken back without penalty.

33. PLAYING ALONE. No one but the individual maker of the trump can play alone.

34. The dealer must announce his intention to play alone by passing his discard over to his partner. Any other player intending to play alone must use the expression " alone " in connection with his ordering up or making the trump ; as, " I order it, alone ; " or " I make it hearts, alone."

35. The partner of a player who has announced to play alone must lay his cards on the table, face down. Should he expose any of his cards, the adversaries may prevent the lone hand, and compel him to play with his partner, the exposed card being left on the table and liable to be called.

36. The lone player is not liable to any penalty for exposed cards, nor for a lead out of turn.

37. Should either adversary lead or play out of turn, the lone player may abandon the hand, and score the points.

38. MISCELLANEOUS. No player is allowed to see any trick that has once been turned and quitted, under penalty of having a suit called from him or his partner.

39. Any player may ask the others to indicate the cards played by them to the current trick.

40. A player calling attention in any manner to the trick or to the score, may be called upon to play his highest or lowest of the suit led ; or to trump or not to trump the trick during the play of which the remark was made.

ÉCARTÉ.

Écarté is usually described as a very simple game, but unfortunately the rules governing it are very complicated, and as no authoritative code of law exists, disputes about trifling irregularities are very common. In the following directions the author has selected what appears to be the best French usage. The code of laws adopted by some of the English clubs is unfortunately very defective, and in many respects quite out of touch with the true spirit of the French game. The English are very fond of penalties; the French try to establish the status quo.

CARDS. Écarté is played with a pack of thirty-two cards, which rank, K Q J A 10 9 8 7. When two packs are used, the adversary shuffles one while the other is dealt.

MARKERS. In France, the game is always marked with the ordinary round chips or counters, never with a marker. As five points is the game, four of these counters are necessary for each player.

PLAYERS. Écarté is played by two persons, who sit opposite each other. One is known as the dealer, and the other as the pone, the adversary, the elder hand, the non-dealer, the leader, or the player.

THE GALLERY. In clubs that make a feature of Écarté, and in which there is a great deal of betting on the outside by the spectators, it is not usual to allow more than one game between the same players, the loser giving place to one of those who have been backing him, and who is called a ***rentrant.*** This is known as playing the *cul-levé.* Any person in the gallery is allowed to draw attention to errors in the score, and may advise the player he is backing, or even play out the game for him, if he resigns. The player need not take the advice given him, which must be offered without discussion, and by pointing only, not naming the suit or cards. If a player will not allow the gallery to back him, taking all bets himself, no one may overlook his hand nor advise him without his permission, and he need not retire if he loses the game.

CUTTING. The player cutting the highest écarté card deals the first hand, and has the choice of seats and cards. If a person exposes more than one card in cutting, the lowest is taken to be his cut. If he does not cut, or will not show his cut, he loses the first deal.

STAKES. Écarté is played for so much a game. If the gallery is betting, all money offered must be placed on the table, and if the bets are not taken by the players, they may be covered by the opposing gallery.

DEALING. It is usual for the dealer to invite his adversary to shuffle the cards, but if two packs are used this is not necessary. The dealer must shuffle the pack and present it to his adversary to be cut. At least two cards must be left in each packet, and the upper part of the pack must be placed nearer the dealer. Five cards are given to each player, and the eleventh is turned up for the trump. The cards are distributed two and three at a time, or three and then two, and in whichever manner the dealer begins he must continue during the game. If he intends to change his manner of dealing in the following game, he must so advise his adversary when presenting the cards to be cut.

MISDEALING. A player dealing out of turn, or with the wrong cards, may be stopped before the trump is turned. But if the trump has been turned, and neither player has discarded or played to the first trick, the pack must be set aside, with the cards as dealt, and the trump turned, to be used for the ensuing deal. The other pack is then taken up and dealt by the player whose proper turn it was to deal. If a discard has been made, or a trick played to, the deal stands good, and the packs, if changed, must so remain.

There must be a new deal if any card but the eleventh is found faced in the pack. If the dealer exposes any of his own cards, the deal stands good. If he exposes any of his adversary's cards, the non-dealer may claim a fresh deal, provided he has not seen any of his cards.

It is a misdeal if the dealer gives too many or too few cards to his adversary or to himself. If the hands have not been seen, and the pone discovers that he has received more than five cards, he has the choice to discard the superfluous cards at hazard, or to claim a misdeal, which loses the deal. If the pone has received less than the proper number, he may supply the deficiency from the remainder of the pack, without changing the trump card, or he may claim a misdeal. If the dealer has given himself too many or too few cards, the pone may claim a misdeal, or he may draw the superfluous cards from the dealer's hand, face downward, or allow him to supply the deficiency from the remainder of the pack, without changing the trump.

If the cards have been seen, the pone, having an incorrect number, may supply or discard to correct the error, or he may claim a misdeal. If he discards, he must show the cards to the dealer. If the dealer has an incorrect number, the pone may draw from his hand, face downward, looking at the cards he has drawn, (as the dealer has seen them,) or allow him to supply the deficiency, or claim a misdeal.

When any irregularity is remedied in this manner, the trump card remains unchanged.

If the dealer turns up more than one card for the trump, his adversary has a right to select which card shall be the trump, or he may claim a new deal by the same dealer, provided he has not seen his hand. If he has seen his hand, he must either claim a misdeal, or the eleventh card must be the trump, the other exposed card being set aside.

If the pack is found to be imperfect, all scores previously made with it stand good.

TURNING THE KING. If the King is turned up, the dealer marks one point for it immediately. If a wrong number of cards has been dealt, and a King is turned, it cannot be scored, because it was not the eleventh card.

PROPOSING AND REFUSING. The cards dealt, the pone examines his hand, and if he thinks it strong enough to win three or more tricks, he stands; that is, plays without proposing, and says to the dealer: *" I play."* If he thinks he can improve his chances by drawing cards, allowing the dealer the same privilege of course, he says: *" I propose;"* or simply: *" Cards."* In reply the dealer may either accept the proposal by asking: *" How many ?"* or he may refuse, by saying: *" Play."* If he gives cards, he may also take cards himself, after having helped his adversary. If he refuses, he must win at least three tricks or lose two points; and if the pone plays without proposing, he must make three tricks, or lose two points. The hands on which a player should stand, and those on which the dealer should refuse are known as *jeux de règle,* and will be found in the suggestions for good play.

A proposal, acceptance, or refusal once made cannot be changed or taken back, and the number of cards asked for cannot be corrected.

DISCARDING. If the pone proposes, and the dealer asks : " How many ? " the elder hand discards any number of cards from one to five, placing them on his right. These discards, once quitted, must not again be looked at. A player looking at his own or his adversary's discards can be called upon to play with his cards exposed face upward on the table, but not liable to be called. The number of cards discarded must be distinctly announced, and the trump is then laid aside, and the cards given from the top of the pack, without further shuffling. It is considered imperative that the player who has proposed should take at least one card, even if he proposed with five trumps in his hand. The pone helped, the dealer then announces how many cards he takes, placing his discards on his left. The dealer, if asked, must inform his adversary how many cards he took, provided the question is put before he plays a card.

After receiving his cards, the pone may either stand or propose again, and the dealer may either give or refuse, but such subsequent stands or refusals do not carry with them any penalty for failure to make three tricks. Should these repeated discards exhaust the pack, so that there are not enough cards left to supply the number asked for, the players must take back a sufficient number from their discards. If the dealer has accepted a proposal, and finds there are no cards left for himself, that is his own fault ; he should have counted the pack before accepting. The trump card cannot be taken into the hand under any circumstances.

MISDEALING AFTER DISCARDING. If the dealer gives the pone more or less cards than he asks for, he loses the point and the right to mark the King, unless it was turned up.

If the dealer gives himself more cards than he wants, he loses the point and the right to mark the King, unless he turned it up. If he gives himself less cards than he wants, he may make the deficiency good without penalty; but if he does not discover the error until he has played a card, all tricks for which he has no card to play must be considered as won by his adversary.

If the pone asks for more cards than he wants, the dealer can play the hand or not, as he pleases. If he plays, he may draw the superfluous card or cards given to the pone, and look at them if the pone has seen them. If the dealer decides not to play, he marks the point. In either case the pone cannot mark the King, even if he holds it.

If the pone asks for less cards than he wants, he must play the hand as it is, and can mark the King if he holds it ; but all tricks for which he has no card to play must be considered as won by his adversary.

If a player plays without discarding, or discards for the purpose of exchanging, without advising his adversary of the fact that he has too many or too few cards, he loses two points, and the right of marking the King, even if turned up.

If either player, after discarding and drawing, plays with more than five cards, he loses the point and the privilege of marking the King.

Should the dealer forget himself in dealing for the discard, and turn up another trump, he cannot refuse his adversary another discard, if he demands it, and the exposed card must be put aside with the discards.

If any cards are found faced in the pack when dealing for the discard, the deal stands good if they will fall to the dealer. But if the exposed card will go to the pone, he has the option of taking it, or claiming a fresh deal by the same dealer.

During all the discards the trump card remains the same.

MARKING THE KING. The discards settled, the first and most important thing before play begins is to mark the King. If the King is turned up, the dealer marks one point for it immediately. If the pone holds it, he must **announce** and mark it before he plays a card. If he leads the King for the first trick, he must still announce it by saying distinctly : " I mark the King ; " and unless this announcement is made before the King touches the table, it cannot be marked. So important is this rule that in some European Casinos it is found printed on the card tables. Having properly announced the King, it may be actually marked with the counters at any time before the trump is turned for the following game.

If the dealer holds the King he must announce it before his adversary leads for the first trick. It is in order that there may be no surprises in this respect that the elder hand is required to say distinctly : " I play," before he leads a card. The dealer must then reply : " I mark the King," if he has it ; if not, he should say : " Play." A player is not compelled to announce or mark the King if he does not choose to do so.

If a player announces and marks the King when he does not hold it, his adversary can take down the point erroneously marked, and mark one himself, for penalty. This does not prevent him from marking an additional point for the King if he holds it himself. For instance : The pone announces King, and marks it, at the same time leading a card. Not having notified the dealer that he was about to play, the dealer cannot be deprived of his right to mark the King himself, if he holds it. The dealer marks the King, marks another point for penalty, and takes down the pone's point, erroneously marked. If the player announcing the King without holding it, discovers his error before a card is played, he simply amends the score and apologizes, and there is no penalty. If any cards have been played after an erroneous announcement of the King, such cards can be taken back by the adversary of the player in error, and the hand played over again.

METHOD OF PLAYING. The elder hand begins by leading any card he pleases, at the same time announcing the suit ; " hearts ; " " spades ; " or whatever it may be. This announcement must be continued at every trick. If a player announces one suit and leads another, his adversary may demand that he take back the card played, and lead the suit announced. If he has none of the announced suit, the adversary may call a suit. If the adversary is satisfied with the card led, but improperly announced, he may demand that it remain as played.

RENOUNCING. When a card is led the adversary must not only follow suit, but must win the trick if he can. If he can neither follow suit nor trump, he may discard any card he pleases. Should a player not follow suit, or should he decline to win the trick, when able to do so, it is a renounce, and if he makes the odd trick he counts nothing ; if he makes all five tricks, he counts one point only, instead of two. Should he trump the trick when he can follow suit, he is subject to the same penalty. There is no such thing as a *revoke* in Écarté. When it is discovered that a player has not followed suit when able, or has lost a trick that he could have won, the cards are taken back, and the hand played over again, with the foregoing penalty for the renounce.

The highest card played, if of the suit led, wins the trick, and trumps win all other suits.

Leading Out of Turn. Should a player lead out of turn, he may take back the card without penalty. If the adversary has played to the erroneous lead, the trick stands good.

Gathering Tricks. The tricks must be turned down as taken in, and any player looking at a trick once turned and quitted may be called upon to play with the remainder of his hand exposed, but not liable to be called.

Abandoned Hands. If, after taking one or more tricks, a player throws his cards upon the table, he loses the point; if he has not taken a trick, he loses two points. But if the cards are thrown down claiming the point or the game, and the claim is good, there is no penalty. If the cards are abandoned with the admission that the adversary wins the point or the game, and the adversary cannot win more than is admitted, there is no penalty.

SCORING. A game consists of five points, which are made by tricks, by penalties, and by marking the King. A player winning three tricks out of the five possible, counts one point toward game; winning all five tricks, which is called ***the vole,*** counts two points. The player holding or turning up the King of trumps may mark one point for it, but he is not compelled to do so.

If the pone plays without proposing, and makes three or four tricks, he counts one point; if he makes the vole he counts two points; but if he fails to make three tricks the dealer counts two.

If the dealer refuses the first proposal, he must make three tricks to count one point; if he makes the vole he counts two points; but if he fails to win three tricks the player who was refused counts two points.

If the dealer accepts the first proposal, and gives cards, subsequent proposals and refusals do not affect the score; the winner of the odd trick scoring one point, and the winner of the vole two points.

In no case can a player make more than two points in one hand by tricks. If the dealer refuses the first proposal, and the pone makes the vole, it counts two points only. If the pone should play without proposing, and the dealer should mark the King and win the vole, it would count him only three points altogether.

The player first reaching five points wins the game. If a player has four scored, and turns the King, that wins the game, provided the King was the eleventh card.   Rubbers are seldom played.

CHEATING.   The methods of cheating at Écarté would fill a volume.   There are many tricks which, while not exactly fraudulent, are certainly questionable.   For instance : A player asks the gallery whether or not he should stand, and finally concludes to propose, fully intending all the time to draw five cards.   Another will handle his counters as if about to mark the King ; will then affect to hesitate, and finally re-adjust them, and ask for cards, probably taking four or five, having absolutely nothing in his hand. The pone will ask the dealer how many points he has marked, knowing perfectly well that the number is three.   On being so informed, he concludes to ask for cards, as if he were not quite strong enough to risk the game by standing ; when as a matter of fact he wants five cards, and is afraid of the vole being made against him.

There are many simple little tricks practiced by the would-be sharper, such as watching how many cards a player habitually cuts, and then getting the four Kings close together in such a position in the pack that one of them is almost certain to be turned.   Telegraphic signals between persons on opposite sides of the gallery who are nevertheless in partnership, are often translated into advice to the player, to his great benefit.   Besides these, all the machinery of marked cards, reflectors, shifted cuts, wedges, strippers, and false shuffles are at the command of the philosopher, who can always handle a small pack of cards with greater freedom, and to whom the fashion of dealing in twos and threes is always welcome. The honest card-player has not one chance in a thousand against the professional at Écarté.

SUGGESTIONS FOR GOOD PLAY.   The French claim that any person may become an expert at a game like Piquet, simply by dint of long practice ; but that the master of Écarté must be a born card-player, as no game requires in such degree the exercise of individual intelligence and finesse.   While this may be true, there are many points about the game which may be learned by the novice, and which will greatly improve his play.

There are two things which the beginner should master before sitting down to the table for actual play : the hands on which it is right to stand, or play without proposing , and those with which it is right to refuse, or play without giving cards.   These are called stand hands, or *jeux de règle,* and the player should be able to recognize them on sight.

In the following paragraphs the words *dealer* and *player* will be used to distinguish the adversaries at Écarté.

The principle underlying the jeux de règle is the probable distribution of the cards in the trump suit, and the fact that the odds are always against the dealer's holding two or more. There are thirty-two cards in the Écarté pack, of which eight are trumps, and one of these is always turned up. The turn-up and the player's hand give us six cards which are known, and leave twenty-six unknown. Of these unknown cards the dealer holds five, and he may get these five in 65,780 different ways. The theory of the jeux de règle is that there are only a certain number of those ways which will give him two or more trumps. If the player holds one trump, the odds against the dealer's holding two or more are 44,574 to 21,206; or a little more than 2 to 1. If the player holds two trumps, the odds against the dealer's holding two or more are 50,274 to 15,506; or more than 3 to 1. It is therefore evident that any hand which is certain to win three tricks if the dealer has not two trumps, has odds of two to one in its favour, and all such hands are called jeux de règle. The natural inference from this is that such hands should always be played without proposing, unless they contain the King of trumps.

The exception in case of holding the King is made because there is no danger of the dealer's getting the King, no matter how many cards he draws, and if the player's cards are not strong enough to make it probable that he can win the vole, it is better for him to ask for cards, in hope of improving his chances. If he is refused, he stands an excellent chance to make two points by winning the odd trick.

While it is the rule for the player to stand when the odds are two to one in his favour for making the odd trick, and to ask for cards when the odds are less, there are exceptions. The chances of improving by taking in cards must not be forgotten, and it must be remembered that the player who proposes runs no risk of penalty. He has also the advantage of scoring two for the vole if he can get cards enough to win every trick, whereas the dealer gets no more for the vole than for the odd trick if the player does not propose. Some beginners have a bad habit of asking for cards if they are pretty certain of the point. Unless they hold the King this is not wise, for the player cannot discard more than one or two cards, but the dealer may take five, and then stands a fair chance of getting the King, which would not only count a point for him, but would effectually stop the vole for which the player was drawing cards.

The most obvious example of a jeux de règle is one trump, a winning sequence of three cards in one suit, and a small card in another. For instance: Hearts trumps—

         44,724 to 21,056.

If the dealer does not hold two trumps, it is impossible to prevent the player from winning the point with these cards ; because he need only lead his winning sequence until it is trumped, and then trump himself in again. With this hand the player will win 44,724 times out of 65,780.

There are about twenty hands which are generally known as jeux de règle, and every écarté player should be familiar with them. In the following examples the weakest hands are given, and the trumps are always the smallest possible. If the player has more strength in plain suits than is shown in these examples, or higher trumps, there is so much more reason for him to stand. But if he has not the strength indicated in plain suits, he should propose, even if his trumps are higher, because it must be remembered that strong trumps do not compensate for weakness in plain suits. The reason for this is that from stand hands trumps should never be led unless there are three of them ; they are to be kept for ruffing, and when you have to ruff it does not matter whether you use a seven or a Queen. The King of trumps is of course led ; but a player does not stand on a hand containing the King.

The first suit given is always the trump, and the next suit is always the one that should be led, beginning with the best card of it if there is more than one. The figures on the right show the number of hands in which the player or the dealer will win out of the 65,780 possible distributions of the twenty-six unknown cards. These calculations are taken, by permission of Mr. Charles Mossop, from the eighth volume of the " *Westminster Papers,*" in which all the variations and their results are given in full.

						PLAYER WINS.	DEALER WINS.
2	♣	♣	♡	♡	♡	47,768	18,012
3	♡	♡	♔	♠	♢	46,039	19,741
4	♠	♠	♢	♣	♔	43,764	22,016
5	♢	♢	♣	♣	♕	45,374	20,406

			PLAYER WINS.	DEALER WINS.
6			44,169	21,611
7			43,478	22,302
8			44,243	21,537
9			44,766	21,014
10			44,459	21,321
11			44,034	21,746
12			43,434	22,346
13			44,766	21,014
14			46,779	19,001
15			45,929	19,851

The player should always stand on a hand containing three trumps, not including the King, and should lead the trump :—

16    42,014 to 23,766

An example of a hand containing only one trump has already been given, and some hands are jeux de règle which contain no trumps. The strongest of these is the King of each plain suit, and any queen. Lead the K Q suit :—

17    48,042 to 17,738

The odds in favour of this hand are greater than in any other jeux de règle. Another which is recommended by Bohn is this, the odds in favour of which have not been calculated ; the player to begin with the guarded King :—

18

Another is any four court cards, not all Jacks ; unless one is the trump Jack guarded. From the example the Queen should be led :—

19

There are two hands which are usually played with only one trump, from both of which the best card of the long suit is led :—

20

21

THE LEADER. There are a great many more opportunities to make the vole than most players are aware of ; especially with jeux de règle. Where the vole is improbable or impossible, tenace is very important, and all tenace positions should be made the most of. In No. 5, for instance, if the clubs were the Queen and ace, it would be better to begin with the heart King, instead of leading away from the minor tenace in clubs. Observe the lead in No. 4. Many tenace positions cannot be taken advantage of because the player must win the trick if he can. For instance : Several discards have been made, and each player suspects the other holds three trumps, with three tricks to play. The Queen is led, and the adversary holds K A 7. If he could pass this trick, he must lie tenace ; but as he has to win it with the King, he gives tenace to his adversary, who evidently has J and another.

When the dealer is four, the player may stand on much weaker hands.

It is usually best to lead from guarded suits, in preference to single cards. Lead the best of a suit if you have it. If the third trick is the first you win, and you have a trump and another card, lead the trump ; but if you have won two tricks, lead the plain suit.

THE DEALER. When the player asks for cards, the dealer knows that his adversary probably does not hold a jeux de règle. The dealer must not be too sure of this, however, for proposals are sometimes made on very strong hands in order to try for the vole, or to make two points on the refusal. The dealer should assume that he is opposed by the best play until he finds the contrary to be the case, and it is safest to play on the assumption that a player who proposes has not a jeux de règle.

For all practical purposes it may be said that the dealer can refuse to give cards with hands a trifle less strong than those on which the player would stand. The general rule is for the dealer to give cards unless he is guarded in three suits ; or has a trump, and is safe in two suits ; or has two trumps, and is safe in one suit. If the dealer has only one suit guarded, and one trump, he must take into account the risk of being forced, and having to lead away from his guarded suit.

There are eight recognized hands on which the dealer should refuse. The full details of the calculations can be found in the ninth volume of the " *Westminster Papers*." As in the case of the player, the weakest trumps have been taken for the examples, and the weakest holdings in plain suits. If the dealer has better plain suits, or stronger trumps, he has of course so much more in his favour if he refuses. The first column of figures gives the number of times in 65,780 that there will be no proposal, so that the dealer has no choice but to play. The other columns give the number of times the dealer or the player will win if the player proposes and the dealer refuses.

The first suit given in each instance is the trump.

					No Proposal.	Dealer Wins.	Player Wins.
22	♣	♣	♣	♦	♠	6,034	36,974	22,772
23	♡	♡	❀	♠	♠	9,826	38,469	17,485
24	♠	♠	Q	♡	♣	8,736	41,699	15,345
25	♦	♦	K	♣	♡	9,256	40,524	16,000
26	♣	♣	♦	♦	K	10,336	37,484	17,960
27	♡	♡	♣	♣	J	9,776	37,439	18,565
28	♠	♠	♡	♡	♣	9,776	36,909	19,095
29	♦	♦	♣	♦	♦	9,776	36,733	19,271

In giving cards, some judgment of human nature is necessary. Some players habitually propose on strong hands, and it is best to give to such pretty freely.

DISCARDING. The general principle of discarding is to keep trumps and Kings, and let everything else go. If you hold the trump King you may discard freely in order to strengthen your hand for a possible vole. If you have proposed once, and hold the King, and feel pretty sure of the point, you may propose again on the chance of getting strength enough to make the vole.

When only two cards can be discarded, it is a safe rule to stand on the hand ; either to play without proposing, or to refuse cards ; unless you hold the King.

There are no authoritative laws for Écarté, and the various French and English codes do not agree. The code adopted by the English clubs is not in accord with the best usage, and fails to provide for many contingencies. All that is essential in the laws will be found embodied in the foregoing description of the game.

TEXT BOOKS. The best works on the subject of Écarté are usually to be found in conjunction with other games. The student will find the following useful :—

The Westminster Papers, Vols. IV to XI, inclusive.
Bohn's Handbook of Games ; any edition.
Écarté and Euchre, by Berkeley, 1890.
Cavendish on Écarté, 1886.
Jeux de Cartes, (Fr.), by Jean Boussac.
Règles de Tous les Jeux, (Fr.), M. Dreyfous, Edit.
Académie des Jeux, (Fr.), by Van Tenac.
Académie des Jeux, (Fr.), by Richard.
Short Whist, by Major A. (Écarté Laws in appendix.)

POOL ÉCARTÉ.

Pool Écarté is played by three persons, each of whom contributes an agreed sum, which is called a ***stake,*** to form a pool. They then cut to decide which shall play the first game, the lowest écarté card going out. The players then cut for the first deal, choice of seats and cards, etc., exactly as in the ordinary game.

The winner of the first game retains his seat; the loser pays into the pool another stake, equal to the first, and retires in favour of the third player, who is called the ***rentrant.*** The rentrant takes the loser's seat and cards, and cuts with the successful player for the first deal. The loser of the second game adds another stake to the pool, and retires in favour of the waiting player.

The pool is won by any player winning two games in succession. If the winner of the first game won the second also, he would take the pool, which would then contain five stakes; the three originally deposited, and the two added by the losers of the two games. A new pool would then be formed by each of the three depositing another stake, and all cutting to decide which should sit out for the first game.

In some places only the two players actually engaged contribute to the pool, the loser retiring without paying anything further, and the rentrant contributing his stake when he takes the loser's place.

The outsider is not allowed to advise either player during the first game, nor to call attention to the score ; but on the second game he is allowed to advise the player who has taken his seat and cards. This is on the principle that he has no right to choose sides on the first game ; but that after that he has an interest in preventing his former adversary from winning the second game, so as to preserve the pool until he can play for it again himself.

NAPOLEON,

OR NAP.

This is one of the simplest, and at the same time most popular of the euchre family. Few games have become so widely known in such a short time, or have had such a vogue among all classes of society. So far as the mere winning and losing goes, the result depends largely upon luck, and skill is of small importance. Except in a long series of games the average player has little to fear from the most expert.

CARDS. Napoleon is played with a full pack of fifty-two cards, which rank A K Q J 10 9 8 7 6 5 4 3 2 ; the ace being highest in play ; but ranking below the deuce in cutting.

COUNTERS. As each deal is a complete game in itself it must be settled for in counters, to which some value is usually attached. One player is selected for the banker, and before play begins each of the others purchases from him a certain number of counters, usually fifty. When any player's supply is exhausted, he can purchase more, either from the banker or from another player.

In many places counters are not used, and the value of the game is designated by the coins that take their place. In "penny nap," English coppers are used in settling ; sixpences in "sixpenny nap," and so on. In America, nickel and quarter nap are the usual forms.

PLAYERS. Any number from two to six can play ; but four is the best game. If five or six play it is usual for the dealer to give himself no cards.

CUTTING. The players draw from an outspread pack to

form the table, and for choice of seats. A lower cut gives preference over all higher; the lowest cut has the first choice of seats,
and deals the first hand. Ties cut again, but the new cut decides nothing but the tie.

In some places the players take their seats at random, and a
card is then dealt to each face upward; the lowest card or the
first Jack taking the deal.

DEALING. Any player has a right to shuffle the cards, the
dealer last. They are then presented to the pone to be cut, and
at least four cards must be left in each packet. Beginning at his
left, the dealer gives each player in rotation two cards on the first
round, and three on the next; or three on the first and two on
the next. No trump is turned. In some places the cards are distributed one at a time until each player has five; but the plan is
not popular, as the hands run better and the bidding is livelier
when the cards are dealt in twos and threes. The deal passes
to the left, each player dealing in turn.

MISDEALING. A misdeal does not lose the deal in Napoleon, because the deal is a disadvantage. For this reason, if
any player begins to deal out of turn, he must finish, and the deal
stands good. If any card is found faced in the pack, or is exposed
by the dealer ; or if too many or too few cards are given to any
player ; or if the dealer does not give the same number of cards to
each player in the same round ; or if he fails to have the pack cut,
it is a misdeal, and the misdealer must deal again with the same
pack.

BIDDING. Beginning on the dealer's left, each player in
turn bids for the privilege of naming the trump suit, stating the
number of tricks he proposes to win, playing single-handed against
the three other players, and leading a trump for the first trick. In
bidding, the trump suit is not named, only the number of tricks.
If a player proposes to win all five tricks he bids ***nap,*** which is
the highest bid possible, and precludes any further bidding, except in some of the variations which will be described later on.
If a player will not make a bid, he says **"*I pass.*"** A bid having
been made, any following player must either increase or pass.
If all pass until it comes to the dealer, he is bound to bid at least
one trick, and either play or pay. The hands are never abandoned
except in case of a misdeal.

In some places a ***misère*** bid is allowed, which outranks a bid
of three tricks, and is beaten by one of four. There is no trump
suit in misère, but the bidder, if successful, must lead for the first
trick.

Any bid once made can neither be amended nor recalled, and
there is no second bid.

METHOD OF PLAYING. The player bidding the highest number of tricks has the first lead, and the first card he plays must be one of the trump suit. The players must follow suit if able, but need not win the trick unless they choose to do so. The highest card played of the suit led wins the trick, and trumps win all other suits. The winner of the trick leads again for the next trick, and so on, until all five tricks have been played. After the first trick any suit may be led.

The bidder gathers all tricks he wins, stacking them so that they may be readily counted by any player at the table. One of the other side should gather all tricks won by the adversaries of the bidder. A trick once turned and quitted cannot again be seen. In some places they have a very bad habit of gathering tricks with the cards face up, turning down one card only. This always results in numerous misdeals, on account of cards being continually found faced in the pack.

The hands are usually abandoned when the bidder succeeds in his undertaking, or shows cards which are good for his bid against any play. If it is impossible for him to succeed, as when he bids four and the adversaries have won two tricks, the hands are thrown up, because nothing is paid for under or over-tricks. Players should show the remainder of their hands to the board, as evidence that no revoke has been made.

IRREGULARITIES IN HANDS. If a player, before he makes a bid or passes, discovers that he holds too many or too few cards, he must immediately claim a misdeal. If he has either made a bid or passed, the deal stands good, and the hand must be played out. If the bidder has his right number of cards and succeeds, he must be paid. If he fails, he neither wins nor loses; because he is playing against a foul hand. If the bidder has more than his right number of cards he must pay if he loses; but wins nothing if he succeeds. If he has less than his right number of cards, he is simply supposed to have lost the trick for which he has no card to play.

PLAYING OUT OF TURN. If any adversary of the bidder leads or plays out of turn, he forfeits three counters to the bidder, independently of the result of the hand, and receives nothing if the bid is defeated. If the bidder leads out of turn, the card must be taken back, unless all have followed the erroneous lead, in which case the trick is good. There is no penalty if he plays out of turn.

REVOKES. When a revoke is detected and claimed, the hands are immediately abandoned, and the individual player in fault must pay all the counters depending on the result. If he is the bidder, he pays each adversary; if he is opposed to the bidder, he pays for himself and for each of his partners. In England it is the rule to take back the cards and play the hand over again, as at Écarté, the revoking player paying all the stakes according to the result. This is often very unfair to the bidder, and leads to endless disputes as to who held certain cards which have been gathered into tricks. Sometimes the difference between a seven and an eight in a certain player's hand will change the entire result.

PAYMENTS. If the bidder succeeds in winning the specified number of tricks, each adversary pays him a counter for every trick bid. If he bid three tricks, they pay him three counters each; four counters each for four tricks bid; and the value of three tricks for a misère. If he fails to win the specified number of tricks, he pays each adversary; three counters if he bid three tricks, or a misère; four if he bid four. Any player bidding nap, and succeeding in winning all five tricks, receives ten counters from each adversary; but if he fails, he pays only five to each.

When penny nap is played, the settlement being in coin, it is usual to make naps win a shilling or lose sixpence, in order to avoid handling so much copper.

SUGGESTIONS FOR GOOD PLAY. In calculating his chances for success in winning a certain number of tricks, the player will often have to take into consideration the probability of certain cards being out against him. This will vary according to the number of players engaged. For instance: If four are playing, and the bidder holds K Q of a plain suit, the odds against the ace of that suit being out against him are about 2 to 1. As it would be impossible for any person to remember all the jeux de règle for three tricks at Napoleon, each must learn from experience the trick-taking value of certain hands. Trump strength is, of course, the great factor, and the bidder should count on finding at least two trumps in one hand against him. Nap should never be bid on a hand which is not pretty sure of winning two rounds of trumps, with all other cards but one winners. One trick may always be risked in a nap hand, such as A Q of trumps, or a King, or even a Queen or Jack in a plain suit; the odds against the adversaries having a better card being slightly increased by the odds against their knowing enough to keep it for the last trick.

If the bid is for three tricks only, tenaces, or guarded minor honours in plain suits should be preserved. After the first trick it will sometimes be advantageous for the player to get rid of any losing card he may have in plain suits. It is seldom right to continue the trumps if the bidder held only two originally, unless he has winning cards in two plain suits, in which case it may be better to lead even a losing trump to prevent a possibility of adverse trumps making separately.

In playing against the bidder, leave no trick to your partners that you can win yourself, unless a small card is led, and you have the ace. In opening fresh suits do not lead guarded honours, but prefer aces or singletons. If the caller needs only one more trick, it is usually best to lead a trump. If you have three trumps, including the major tenace, pass the first trick if a small trump is led ; or if you remain with the tenace after the first trick, be careful to avoid the lead.

Discards should indicate weakness, unless you can show command of such a suit as A K, or K Q, by discarding the best of it. This will direct your partners to let that suit go, and keep the others. It is usually better to keep a guarded King than a single ace. The player on the right of the bidder should get into the lead if possible, especially if he holds one or two winning cards. These will either give his partners discards, or allow them to over-trump the bidder.

In playing misères, it is better to begin with a singleton, or the lowest of a safe suit. An ace or King two or three times guarded is very safe for a misère, as it is very improbable that any player will be able to lead the suit more than twice ; and if the bidder's missing suit is led, the high card can be got rid of at once.

In playing against a misère, discards are important, and the first should be from the shortest suit, and always the highest card of it. A suit in which the bidder is long should be continued, in order to give partners discards. More money is lost at Napoleon by playing imperfect misères than in any other way.

Variations. The foregoing description applies to the regular four-handed game ; but there are several variations in common use.

Better bids than " nap " are sometimes allowed, on the understanding that the bidder will pay double or treble stakes if he fails, but will receive only the usual amount if successful. For instance : One player bids *Nap,* and another holds what he considers a certainty for five tricks. In order not to lose such an opportunity the latter bids *Wellington,* which binds him to pay ten counters to each player if he fails. Another may outbid this again by bidding *Blucher,* which binds him to pay twenty to each if he loses, but to receive only ten if he wins. In England, the bidder, if successful, receives double or treble stakes for a Wellington or a Blucher, which is simply another way of allowing any person with a nap hand to increase the stakes at pleasure, for a player with a certain five tricks would of course bid a Blucher at once, trebling his gains and shutting off all competition at the same time. This variation is not to be recommended, and benefits no one but the gambler.

Pools. Napoleon is sometimes played with a pool, each player contributing a certain amount, usually two counters, on the first deal. Each dealer in turn adds two more ; revokes pay five, and leads out of turn three. The player who first succeeds in winning five tricks on a nap bid takes the pool, and a fresh one is formed.

If a player bids nap and fails, he is usually called upon to double the amount then in the pool, besides paying his adversaries.

Purchase Nap ; sometimes called **Écarté Nap,** is a variation of the pool game. After the cards are dealt, and before any bids are made, each player in turn, beginning on the dealer's left, may discard as many cards as he pleases, the dealer giving him others in their place. For each card so exchanged, the player pays one counter to the pool. Only one round of exchanges is allowed, and bids are then in order. A player having once refused to buy, or having named the number of cards he wishes to exchange, cannot amend his decision. Any player winning five tricks on a nap bid takes the entire pool. This is a very good game, and increases both the bids and the play against them.

Widows. Another variation is to deal five cards in the centre of the table, face downward, the dealer giving the cards to the widow just before helping himself in each round. Any player in his proper turn to bid may take the widow, and from the total of ten cards so obtained select five on which he must bid nap, discarding the others face downward.

Peep Nap. In this variety of the pool game one card only is dealt to the widow, usually on the first round. Each player in turn, before bidding or passing, has the privilege of taking a private peep at this down card, on paying one counter to the pool. The card is left on the table until the highest bidder is known, and he then takes it into his hand, whether he has paid to peep at it or not. He must then discard to reduce his hand to five cards. If a player bids nap it usually pays those following him to have a peep at the down card in case the bidder should retain it in his hand.

SPOIL FIVE.

Spoil Five is one of the oldest of card games, and is generally conceded to be the national game of Ireland. It is derived from the still older game of Maw, which was the favourite recreation of James the First. The connecting link seems to have been a game called Five Fingers, which is described in the "*Compleat Gamester*," first published in 1674. The Five Fingers was the five of trumps, and also the best, the ace of hearts coming next. In Spoil Five, the Jack of trumps comes between these two.

CARDS. Spoil Five is played with a full pack of fifty-two cards. The rank of the cards varies according to the colour of the suit, and the trump suit undergoes still further changes, the heart ace being always the third best trump. In the plain suits, the

K Q J retain their usual order, the King being the best. The rank of the spot cards, including the aces of diamonds, clubs, and spades, is generally expressed by the phrase: **Highest in red ; lowest in black.** That is to say, if several cards of a suit, not including a King, Queen or Jack, are played to a trick, the highest card will win if the suit is red ; and the lowest if the suit is black. This will give us the following order for the plain suits, beginning with the highest card in each :—

	No change.			Highest in red.								
♡	K	Q	J	10	9	8	7	6	5	4	3	2
◇	K	Q	J	10	9	8	7	6	5	4	3	2 A

				Lowest in black.								
♣	K	Q	J	A	2	3	4	5	6	7	8	9 10
♠	K	Q	J	A	2	3	4	5	6	7	8	9 10

In the trump suit the same order of cards is retained, except that four cards are always the best trumps. These are the Five, Jack, and ace of the suit itself, and the ace of hearts, the latter being always the third best. This gives us the rank of the cards as follows, when the suit is trump :—

	No change,					Highest in red.								
♡ 5 J			♡ A K Q	10	9	8	7	6	5	4	3	2
◇ 5 J	♡ A		◇ A K Q	10	9	8	7	6	5	4	3	2

			Lowest in black.								
♣ 5 J	♡ A	♣ A K Q	2	3	4	5	6	7	8	9	10
♠ 5 J	♡ A	♠ A K Q	2	3	4	5	6	7	8	9	10

COUNTERS. Spoil Five is played with a pool, for which counters are necessary. One player should act as banker, and the others should purchase from him, each beginning with 20 counters. Coins may take the place of counters, shillings being the usual points.

PLAYERS. Any number from 2 to 10 may play ; but 5 or 6 is the usual game.

CUTTING. This is unknown at Spoil Five. The players take their seats at random, and one of them deals a card face up to each in succession. The first Jack takes the first deal. Some note should be made of the player who gets the first deal, as the rules require that when the game is brought to an end the last deal shall be made by the player on the right of the first dealer.

THE POOL. Before play begins each player deposits one

counter in the pool, and to this amount each successive dealer adds a counter until the pool is won, when all contribute equally to form a new one. In some places it is the practice for each successive dealer to put up for all the players, whether the pool is won or not. This simply makes larger pools.

DEALING. Any player has the right to shuffle the pack, the dealer last. The cards are then presented to the pone to be cut, and as many cards as there are players must be left in each packet. Beginning on his left, the dealer gives five cards to each player ; two on the first round and three on the next, or three and then two. After all are helped, the next card is turned up on the remainder of the pack, and the suit to which it belongs is the trump for that deal.

MISDEALING. If there is any irregularity in the deal which is not the dealer's fault, such as any card except the trump found faced in the pack, or the pack found imperfect, the same person deals again. But if the dealer neglects to have the pack cut, or deals too many or too few cards to any player, or exposes a card in dealing, or does not give the same number of cards to each player on the same round, or counts the cards on the table or those remaining in the pack, it is a misdeal, and the deal passes to the next player on the misdealer's left. In some places the misdealer is allowed to deal again if he forfeits two counters to the pool.

ROBBING THE TRUMP CARD. If the trump card is an ace, the dealer may discard any card he pleases in exchange for it. He may take up the ace when he plays to the first trick, or may leave it on the pack until got rid of in the course of play. When an ace is turned, the eldest hand, before leading, should call upon the dealer to discard if he has not already done so. If the dealer does not want the trump, he answers : " I play these."

If the trump card is not an ace, any player at the table holding the ace of trumps is bound to announce the fact when it comes to his turn to play to the first trick. The usual plan is for him to pass a card to the dealer face downward, and in return the dealer will give him the turn-up trump. If the holder of the ace does not want the turn-up, he must tell the dealer to turn the trump down, which shows that he could rob, but does not wish to. If the holder of the ace of trumps plays without announcing it, he not only loses his right to rob, but his ace of trumps becomes of less value than any other trump for that deal, and even if it is the ace of hearts he loses the privileges attached to that card.

METHOD OF PLAYING. The eldest hand begins by leading any card he pleases. It is not necessary to follow suit except in trumps ; but if a player does not follow suit when he is able to do so, he must trump the trick, or it is a revoke. If he cannot follow suit, he may trump or discard at his pleasure. The highest card played of the suit led wins the trick, and trumps win all other suits. The winner of the first trick leads any card he pleases for the next, and so on, until all five tricks have been played. Each player gathers his own tricks, as there are no partnerships.

RENEGING. The three highest trumps have special privileges in the matter of not following suit. Any player holding the Five or Jack of the trump suit ; or the ace of hearts, but having no smaller trump with them, may refuse to follow suit if any inferior trump is led ; but if he has also a smaller trump, he must play one or the other. If a superior trump is led, the player must follow suit in any case. For instance : If the Five of trumps is led, no one can refuse to follow suit, no matter what trumps he holds ; but if the Jack is led, and any player holds the Five alone, he need not play it to the inferior trump lead. If the heart ace is led, and one player holds the Jack alone, and another the Five alone, neither of these cards need be played, because the trump led is inferior to both of them. If a superior trump is played in following suit, such as the Five played on an Eight led, the holder of the lone Jack of trumps or ace of hearts, need not play it, because the lead was inferior. This privilege of reneging is confined to the three highest trumps.

OBJECTS OF THE GAME. In Spoil Five there are three things to play for. If any one person can win three tricks he takes the pool. If he can win all five tricks he not only gets the pool, but receives an extra counter from each of the other players. If he has no chance to win three tricks, he must bend all his energies to scattering the tricks among the other players, so that no one of them shall be able to get the three tricks necessary to win the pool. When this is done, the game is said to be *spoiled,* and as that is the object of the majority in every deal it gives the game its name. In the older forms of the game the winner of three tricks counted five points, and if he could be prevented from getting three tricks his five points were spoiled.

JINK GAME. When a player has won three tricks, he should immediately abandon his hand and claim the pool, for if he continues playing he must *jink it,* and get all five tricks or lose what he has already won, the game being spoiled just as if no one had won three tricks. It is sometimes a matter for nice judgment whether or not to go on, and, for the sake of an extra counter from each player, to risk a pool already won. The best trump is often held up for three rounds to coax a player to go on in this manner.

IRREGULARITIES IN THE HANDS. If, during the play of a hand, it is discovered that any one holds too many or too few cards, that hand is foul, and must be abandoned, the holder forfeiting all right to the pool for that deal. Those who have their right number of cards finish the play without the foul hand, but any tricks already won by the holder of the foul hand remain his property.

IRREGULARITIES IN PLAY. If any player robs when he does not hold the ace; leads or plays out of turn; reneges to the lead of a higher trump; renounces in the trump suit; revokes in a plain suit; or exposes a card after any player has won two tricks, he loses all his right and interest in the current pool, which he cannot win, either on that or any subsequent deal, but to which he must continue to contribute when it comes to his turn to deal. After the pool has been won, and a fresh one formed, the penalty is removed.

SUGGESTIONS FOR GOOD PLAY. Observation, quickness, and good judgment of character are the essentials for success at Spoil Five, the last being probably the most important. The peculiar order of the cards; the privilege of renouncing when holding a card of the suit led; and the right of passing inferior trump leads, are very confusing to the beginner; but with practice the routine and strategy of the game soon become familiar.

The player should first make up his mind whether he is going to try to win the pool or to spoil it. Particular attention should be paid to the player who robs, because he must have at least the ace and the turn-up in trumps, and is more likely to need spoiling than any other player. When a player wins a trick, some judgment will be necessary to decide whether he is trying for the pool himself, or simply spoiling it for some one else. When he wins two tricks, every other player at the table must combine against him.

With only one small or medium trump, it is better to use it at the first opportunity. Unless the player has some hopes of winning the pool himself, he should trump all doubtful cards; that is, cards that may win the trick if not trumped. With two good trumps, it is better to wait for developments; even if you cannot win the last three tricks yourself, you may effectually spoil any other player. Do anything you can to prevent the possibility of a third trick being won by a player who has already won two.

FORTY-FIVE, OR FIVE AND TEN.

These names are given to Spoil Five when it is played by two persons only, or by four or six divided into two equal partnerships. There is no pool, as one side or the other must win three tricks every deal. The side winning the odd trick counts five points towards game, or ten points if it wins all five tricks. Forty-five points is game. In another variation, each trick counts five points, and the winners' score is deducted from the losers', so that if one side wins four tricks it counts fifteen towards game. When this manner of counting is adopted, the players count out; that is, if each side is 35 up, the first to win two tricks counts out.

Minor variations are sometimes introduced; such as robbing with the King, if the ace is not in play; counting five for the dealer's side if the ace or King is turned up, etc.

There are no *Text Books* on Spoil Five; but descriptions and laws of the game are to be found in the " Westminster Papers," Vol II., and in " Round Games," by Berkeley.

RAMS,

OR RAMMES.

This game seems to be the connecting link between the more strongly marked members of the Euchre family and Division Loo.

CARDS. Rams is played with the euchre pack, thirty-two cards, which rank as at Écarté, K Q J A 10 9 8 7. It has lately become the fashion, however, to adopt the rank of the cards in the piquet pack, A K Q J 10 9 8 7.

PLAYERS. Any number from three to six may play; but when six play the dealer takes no cards. The general arrangements for the players, first deal, counters, etc., are exactly the same as at Spoil Five.

THE POOL. Each successive dealer puts up five counters, to form or to augment the pool.

DEALING. The cards having been properly shuffled and cut, five are given to each player; two the first round and three the next, or three the first round and two the next. An extra hand, known as the *widow,* is dealt face downward in the centre of the table. The dealer gives cards to the widow just before dealing to himself in each round. When all are helped, the next card is turned up for the trump. Irregularities in the deal are governed by the same rules as in Spoil Five.

DECLARING TO PLAY. Each player in turn, beginning with the eldest hand, may either play or pass. If he passes, he lays his cards face downward in front of him, and takes no further part in that deal unless a general rams is announced. If he plays, he engages himself to take at least one trick, or forfeit five counters to the pool. He may play with the hand originally dealt him, or he may risk getting a better by taking the widow in exchange. If he exchanges, his original hand is dead, and must not be seen by any player. If any player takes the widow, those following him must play the hand dealt them or pass out. In some clubs the eldest hand is obliged to play, either with his own hand or with the widow.

If all pass except the pone, he must play against the dealer, either with the cards dealt him, or with the widow. If he declines to play, he must pay the dealer five counters, and the pool remains. The dealer must play if he is opposed by only one player; but if two others have announced to play, the dealer may play or pass as he pleases. If he plays, he may discard and take up the trump card. No other player may rob the trump.

METHOD OF PLAYING. The eldest hand of those who have declared to play begins by leading any card he pleases. Each player in turn must head the trick; that is, play a higher card if he can. If he has two higher, he may play either. If he has none of the suit led, he must trump if he can, even if the trick is already trumped by another player. For instance: Hearts are trumps, and A leads a club. B follows suit, but neither C nor D has a club. Suppose C trumps with the King, and that the only trump D has is the Queen, he must play it on the trick, losing it to C's King. When a player can neither follow suit nor trump, he may discard any card he pleases. The winner of the trick leads for the next trick, and so on until all five tricks have been played.

PENALTIES. There is only one penalty in Rams; to win nothing on the deal, and to forfeit five counters to the next pool. This is inflicted for playing with more or less than five cards; for exposing any card; for leading or playing out of turn; for renouncing; and for refusing to head or trump a trick when able to do so.

DIVIDING THE POOL. Pools may be simple or double. The usual custom is to compel every one to play when the pool is a simple, containing nothing but the five counters put up by the dealer. When there are more than five counters in the pool they must be some multiple of five, and the pool is called a double. In double pools the players may play or pass as they please. No matter how many counters are already in the pool, the dealer must add five.

Each player gathers in the tricks he wins, and at the end of the hand he is entitled to take one-fifth of the contents of the pool for every trick he has won. If he has played his hand, and failed to get a trick, he is ramsed, and forfeits five counters to form the next pool, in addition to those which will be put up by the next dealer. If two or more players fail to win a trick, they must each pay five counters, and if the player whose turn it will be to deal next is ramsed, he will have to put up ten ; five for his deal, and five for the rams.

GENERAL RAMS. If any player thinks he can win all five tricks, with the advantage of the first lead, he may announce a general rams, when it comes to his turn to pass or play. This announcement may be made either before or after taking the widow. When a general rams is announced, all at the table must play, and those who have passed and laid down their hands, must take them up again. If the widow has not been taken, any player who has not already refused it may take it. The player who announced general rams has the first lead. If he succeeds in getting all five tricks, he not only gets the pool but receives five counters in addition from each player. If he fails, he must double the amount then in the pool, and pay five counters to each of his adversaries. Any player taking a trick that spoils a general rams gets nothing from the pool, and it is usual to abandon the hands the moment the announcing player loses a trick.

ROUNCE.

This is an American corruption of Rams. It is played with the full pack of fifty-two cards, which rank as at Whist, and any number of players from three to nine. Six cards are dealt to the widow, one of which must be discarded by the player taking it. All pools are alike, there being no difference between simples and doubles, and there is no such announcement as general rounce. There is no obligation to head the trick, nor to trump or under-trump ; but the winner of the first trick must lead a trump if he has one.

BIERSPIEL.

This is a popular form of Rams among German students. Three crosses are chalked on the table in front of each player, representing five points each. When a trick is won, a beer-soaked finger wipes out the centre of a cross, and reduces its value to four. Successive cancellings of the remaining arms of the cross as tricks are taken gradually reduce it to nothing, and the player who is last to wipe out his third cross pays for the beer. No player is allowed to look at his cards until the trump is turned, and the dealer gives the word of command: "Auf." The seven of diamonds is always the second-best card of the trump suit, ranking next below the ace. If it is turned up, the dealer turns up the next card for a trump, and when it comes to his turn, he can take both cards into his hand, discarding others in their place. If the dealer passes, the eldest hand may take up the trump. If only two declare to play, a trump must be led for the first trick; if three play, trumps must be led twice; if four play, three times. If the leader has no trump, he must lead his smallest card, face downward, which calls for a trump from such of the other players as have one. All penalties are made by adding fresh crosses to the delinquent's score.

LOO,

OR DIVISION LOO.

This was at one time the most popular of all round games at cards; but its cousin Napoleon seems to have usurped its place in England, while Poker has eclipsed it in America. There are several varieties of the game, but the most common form is Three-card Limited Loo, which will be first described.

CARDS. Loo is played with a full pack of fifty-two cards, which rank, A K Q J 10 9 8 7 6 5 4 3 2; the ace being the highest.

COUNTERS. Loo being a pool game, counters are necessary. They should be of two colours, white and red, one red being worth three whites. The object of this is to provide for an equal division of the pool at all times. One person should act as banker, to sell and redeem all counters. Each player should begin with 18 red and 6 white, which is equal to 20 reds.

PLAYERS. Any number of persons from three to seventeen may play, but eight is the usual limit, and five or six makes the best game. The players take their seats at random.

CUTTING. A card is dealt round to each player, face up, and the first Jack takes the first deal.

THE POOL. Each successive dealer places three red counters in the pool. The pool is added to from time to time by penalties for infractions of the rules, and by forfeitures from players who have failed in their undertakings. Such payments are always made in red counters, the number being always three or six. When the pool is divided, it sometimes happens that a player is not allowed to withdraw his share. In such cases the red counters representing it should be changed for their value in white ones, so that the forfeited share may be divided in three parts.

The difference between **Limited Loo,** and **Unlimited Loo,** is in the amounts paid into the pool. In Limited Loo the penalty is always three or six red counters. In Unlimited Loo, it is the same for irregularities, and for infraction of the rules; but any player failing in his undertaking must put up for the next pool an amount equal to that in the current pool. When two or more fail on successive deals the pool increases with surprising rapidity. A player at twenty-five cent Loo has been known to lose $320 in three consecutive deals.

DEALING. The pack having been properly shuffled and cut, the dealer gives three cards to each player, one at a time in rotation, beginning on his left. The first deal, and every deal in which the pool contains only the three red counters put up by the dealer, is known as a **simple,** and no trump card is turned up until one or two tricks have been played to. If there are more than three red counters in the pool, it is known as a **double,** and an extra hand must be dealt for the **widow,** and after all have been helped, the next card in the pack is turned up for a trump. The dealer gives cards to the widow just before helping himself in each round.

Irregularities in the Deal. If the pack is found to be imperfect, or any card except the trump is found faced in the pack, the same dealer must deal again without penalty. If the dealer neglects to have the pack cut; re-shuffles it after it has been properly cut; deals a card incorrectly and fails to correct the error before dealing another; exposes a card in dealing; gives any player too many or too few cards; or deals a wrong number of hands, it is a misdeal, and he loses his deal, and forfeits three red counters to the current pool. The new dealer adds his three counters as usual, and the pool becomes a double.

METHOD OF PLAYING. A description of the method of playing will be better understood if it is divided into two parts, as it varies in simple and in double pools.

In Simple Pools, no trump is turned, and no widow dealt. Should the dealer inadvertently turn a trump, he forfeits three red counters to the current pool, but it remains a simple. If he deals a card for a widow, and fails to correct himself before dealing another card, it is a misdeal.

The eldest hand leads any card he pleases, and the others must not only follow suit, but must head the trick if they can. This does not necessarily mean that they shall play the best card they hold of the suit led, but that they shall play a better one than any already played. The cards are left in front of the players. If all follow suit the winner of the trick leads any card he pleases for the next trick. If all follow suit to that again, the winner leads for the next, and if all follow suit again, that ends it, and the winners of the several tricks divide the pool. All those who have not won a trick are **looed,** and must contribute three red counters each for the next pool, which, added to the three to be deposited by the next dealer, will make the ensuing pool a double. But if in any trick any player is unable to follow suit, as soon as the trick is complete the dealer turns up the top card on the remainder of the pack, and the suit to which it belongs is the trump. If any trump has been played, the highest trump wins the trick. In any case, the winner of the trick must lead a trump for the next trick if he has one. When all three tricks have been played, the winner of each is entitled to one-third of the contents of the pool. Those who have not won a trick are looed, and must contribute three red counters each for the next pool.

In Double Pools, an extra hand is dealt for the widow, and a trump is turned. No player is allowed to look at his cards until it comes to his turn to declare. The dealer, beginning on his left, asks each in turn to announce his intentions. The player may **stand** with the cards dealt him ; or may **take the widow** in exchange ; or may **pass.** If he passes or takes the widow, he gives his original hand to the dealer, who places it on the bottom of the pack. If he takes the widow or stands, he must win at least one trick, or he is looed, and will forfeit three red counters to the next pool.

If all pass but the player who has taken the widow, he wins the pool without playing, and the next deal must be a simple. If only one player stands, and he has not taken the widow, the dealer, if he will not play for himself, must take the widow and play to defend the pool. If he fails to take a trick, he is not looed ; but the payment for any tricks he wins must be left in the pool, and the red counters for them should be changed for white ones, so that the amount may be easily divided at the end of the next pool.

Flushes. If any player in a double pool holds three trumps, whether dealt him or found in the widow, he must announce it as soon as all have declared whether or not they will play. The usual custom is to wait until the dealer declares, and then to ask him : " How many play ? " The dealer replies : " Two in ; " " Three in : " or : " Widow and one ; " as the case may be. The player with the flush then shows it, and claims the pool without playing, each of those who are " in " being looed three red counters. If two players hold a flush in trumps, the elder hand wins, whether his trumps are better or not ; but the younger hand, holding another flush, is not looed.

Leading. In all double pools, the eldest hand of those playing must lead a trump if he has one. If he has the ace of trumps he must lead that ; or if he has the King and the ace is turned up. The old rule was that a player must lead the higher of two trumps, but this is obsolete. The winner of a trick must lead a trump if he has one. Each player in turn must head the trick if he can ; if he has none of the suit led he must trump or over-trump if he can ; but he need not under-trump a trick already trumped.

Irregularities and Penalties. There is only one penalty in Loo, to win nothing from the current pool, and to pay either three or six reds to the next pool. If the offender has won any tricks, the payment for them must be left in the pool in white counters, to be divided among the winners of the next pool.

The offences are divided, some being paid for to the current pool, such as those for errors in the deal, while others are not paid until the current pool has been divided. If any player looks at his hand before his turn to declare, or the dealer does so before asking the others whether or not they will play, or if any player announces his intention out of his proper turn ; the offender in each case forfeits three red counters to the current pool, and cannot win anything that deal, but he may play his hand in order to keep counters in the pool. If he plays and is looed, he must pay.

Revokes. If a player, when able to do so, fails to follow suit, or to head the trick, or to lead trumps, or to lead the ace of trumps, (or King when ace is turned,) or to trump a suit of which he is void, the hands are abandoned on discovery of the error, and the pool is divided as equally as possible among those who declared to play, with the exception of the offender. Any odd white counters must be left for the next pool. The player in fault is then held guilty of a revoke, and must pay a forfeit of six red counters to the next pool. The reason for the division of the pool is that there is no satisfactory way to determine how the play would have resulted had the revoke not occurred. It is impossible to take back the cards and replay them, because no one would have a right to judge how much a person's play was altered by his knowledge of the cards in the other hands.

If a player, having already won a trick, renders himself liable to any penalty, as for exposing a card, leading or following suit out of turn, or abandoning his hand, he is looed for three red counters, payable to the next pool, and the payment for the tricks he has won must be left in the pool in white counters.

IRISH LOO.

In this variation, no widow is dealt, and there is no distinction between simple and double pools. A trump is always turned up, and the dealer asks each in turn, beginning on his left, whether or not he will play, taking up the cards of those who decline to stand. He then announces his own decision, and proceeds to ask those who have declared to play whether or not they wish to exchange any of the cards originally dealt them. The usual question is simply: "How many?" and the player names the number of cards he wishes to exchange, if any; at the same time discarding others in their places. The number first asked for cannot be amended or recalled. The trump is laid aside, and the cards called for are dealt from the remainder of the pack, without further shuffling. In all other respects, the game is Three-card Loo.

FIVE-CARD LOO.

This is Irish Loo with some additional variations. Each red counter should be worth five white ones, and the players will require about fifty red counters each at starting. The dealer puts up five red counters. Any player holding a flush of five cards in any suit may immediately claim the pool, and every person at the table, whether playing or not, is supposed to be looed, and pays five red counters to the next pool. If two players hold flushes, the elder hand wins, even if the younger hand holds a flush in trumps.

Another variation is to make the club Jack, which is known as **Pam,** always the best trump. Combined with four cards of any suit, this card will make a flush. If any player leads the trump ace, the holder of Pam must pass the trick if he can do so without revoking. The old usage was for the holder of the trump ace to notify any player holding Pam to pass, if he wished him to do so; but that is quite superfluous, as no player wants to lose his ace of trumps, and it goes without saying that he wants Pam to pass it.

Interesting articles on Loo will be found in "Bell's Life," the "Field," the "Sportsman," and the "Westminster Papers;" Vol. II. of the latter especially.

ALL FOURS FAMILY.

All Fours is to be found amongst the oldest games of cards, and is the parent of a large family of variations, all of which are of American birth. The youngest member of the family, Cinch, seems to have a bright future before it, and bids fair to become one of our most popular games. The chief defect in Cinch has been the method of scoring, which left too much to luck. In the following pages the author has attempted to remedy this.

The name, "All Fours," seems to have been varied at times to "All Four," and was derived from four of the five points which counted towards game; the fifth point, for "gift" having been apparently quite overlooked. The game was originally ten points up, and the cards were dealt one at a time. According to the descriptions in some of the older Hoyles, the honours and Tens of the plain suits did not count towards game; but this is evidently an error, for we find in the same editions the advice to trump or win the adversary's best cards in plain suits. This would obviously be a mere waste of trumps if these plain-suit cards did not count for anything.

All Fours seems to have been popular with all classes of society at one time or another. Cotton's "Compleat Gamester" gives it among the principal games in his day, 1674. Daines Barrington, writing a hundred years later, speaks of All Fours in connection with Whist. "Whist," he says, "seems never to have been played on principles until about fifty years ago; before that time [1735] it was confined chiefly to the servants' hall, with All Fours and Put." Another writer tells us that Ombre was the favourite game of the ladies, and Piquet of the gentlemen *par excellence;* clergymen and country squires preferring Whist, "while the lower orders shuffled away at All Fours, Put, Cribbage, and Lanterloo." In 1754 a pamphlet was published containing: "Serious Reflections on the dangerous tendency of the common practice of Card-playing; especially the game of All Four." For many years All Fours was looked upon as the American gambler's game *par excellence*, and it is still the great standby of our coloured brother; who would sooner swallow a Jack than have it caught.

ALL FOURS,

SEVEN-UP, OR OLD SLEDGE.

CARDS. Seven-up is played with the full pack of fifty-two cards, which rank A K Q J 10 9 8 7 6 5 4 3 2; the ace being the highest, both in cutting and in play.

COUNTERS. Each player or side should be provided with seven counters. As the points accrue, these counters are got rid of by placing them in a pool in the centre of the table. By this method a glance will show how many each side or player has " to go," that is, how many will put him out.

PLAYERS. Two, three or four persons may play. When three play, the game resembles Cut-throat Euchre, each for himself. When four play, two are partners against the other two, and the partners sit opposite each other. The player on the dealer's left, or his adversary if only two play, is always spoken of as the eldest or elder hand. The one on the dealer's right is the pone.

CUTTING. If there are four players, they cut for partners, deal, and choice of seats. The two lowest are partners against the two highest; the highest cut has the choice of seats, and deals the first hand. When two or three play, they cut for seats and deal. In cutting, the ace is high. Ties cut again; but the new cut decides nothing but the tie.

STAKES. If there is any stake, it is for so much a game. Rubbers are never played.

DEALING. Each player has the right to shuffle the pack, the dealer last, and the cards are then presented to the pone to be cut. At least four cards must be left in each packet. Beginning on his left, the dealer gives six cards to each player, three on the first round, and three more on the second round, turning up the next card for the trump, and leaving it on the remainder of the pack. If this card is a Jack, the dealer counts one point for it immediately; but if any player is found to have an incorrect number of cards, and announces it before he plays to the first trick, the Jack cannot be counted, as it could not have been the proper trump.

In ***Pitch, or Blind All Fours,*** no trump is turned. The first card led or "pitched" by the eldest hand is the trump suit for that deal.

MISDEALING. If any card is found faced in the pack, or the pack is proved to be imperfect, the same dealer deals again. If he deals without having the cards cut, or gives too many or too few cards to any player, it is a misdeal, and the deal passes to the next player on the misdealer's left. If the dealer exposes a card, the adversaries may elect to have the deal stand, or to have a new deal by the same dealer. In *Pitch*, a misdeal does not lose the deal, because the deal is no advantage.

BEGGING. The deal completed, and the trump turned, the eldest hand looks at his cards, the other players leaving theirs untouched. If the eldest hand is not satisfied, he says : *I beg ;* and the dealer, after examining his own hand, has the option of giving him a point or *running the cards.* If he decides to give the point, he says : *Take it,* and the eldest hand immediately scores one for the *gift.* If the dealer will not give, he lays the trump card aside, and deals three more cards to each player, including himself ; turning up another trump. Should this be a Jack of another suit, the dealer scores a point for it at once. Should it be of the same suit as that first turned up, the Jack cannot be scored, as the dealer has declined to have that suit for the trump. When the same suit is turned up a second time, the card is laid aside ; three more cards are given to each player, another trump is turned, and so on until a different suit comes up for the trump. If the pack is exhausted before another suit turns up, the cards must be *bunched,* and the same dealer deals again.

The dealer's partner and the pone are not permitted to look at their cards until the eldest hand and the dealer have decided whether to stand or run the cards. Among strict players, if a person looks at his hand before the proper time, the adversaries score a point. The object of this rule is to prevent the possibility of any expression of satisfaction or disapproval of the turn-up trump.

No second beg is allowed, but when only two play, if either player is dissatisfied with the new trump he may propose to *bunch the cards.* If the proposition is agreed to, the cards are re-shuffled and dealt again by the same dealer. If three play, the dealer must give a point to both adversaries if he refuses to run the cards, although only one begs.

DISCARDING. When the cards have been run, the usual practice is to discard all superfluous cards, each player reducing his hand to six, with which he plays. In some clubs it is the rule to keep all the cards if only nine are in each hand, but to discard down to six if two or more rounds were dealt after turning the first trump.

OBJECTS OF THE GAME. The object in Seven-up is to secure certain points which count towards game. As its name implies, the game is won when a player has put up seven of his counters, each of which represents a point. There are six different ways of making these points, and it is possible for one player

to make all six of them in one deal ; but he cannot by any possibility make seven. The following count one point each :

1st. Turning up the *Jack* of trumps.
2nd. Being *given* a point by the dealer.
3rd. Holding the *Highest* trump.
4th. Holding the *Lowest* trump.
5th. Winning a trick with the *Jack* of trumps in it.
6th. Making the majority of the pips that count for what is
called *Game.*

Turning the Jack is entirely a matter of chance, and should
not occur more than once in thirteen deals. If a Jack is turned
every few deals, you may be sure that unfair methods are being
used. Nothing is more common among advantage players than
turning up Jacks every few deals.

Begging is resorted to by a player who holds no trumps, or
such indifferent ones that it is very unlikely they will be either
High or Low. If he has anything better, such as very high or
low cards in other suits, such a hand is called, " a good hand to
run to," and the player begs, hoping the new trump will better fit
his hand. If he has nothing better in other suits than in the turn-
up, it will still be slightly in his favour to beg, unless he has trumps
enough to give him some hopes of making the point for Game. It
is a fatal error to beg on good cards, and gamblers have a saying
that he who begs a point to-day, will beg a stake to-morrow.

High and *Low* count to the player to whom those cards are
dealt, and there is no chance to alter the fortunes of the deal except by begging and running the cards. These two points may
both be made by the same card, if it is the only trump in play ;
because High is counted for the best trump out during the deal,
and Low for the lowest, no matter what the cards are.

Catching the Jack, or saving it, is one of the principal objects of the game, and as a rule a player holding the Jack should
lose no opportunity to save such a valuable counting card. On
the other hand, a player holding higher trumps will often have to
use good judgment as to whether to lead them to catch the Jack,
if it happens to be out ; or to keep quiet until the last few tricks,
when if the Jack is not out, such trumps may be useful to win
cards that count for Game.

The Game is generally known as *the gambler's point,* because it is the only point that must be played for in every hand,
and its management requires more skill than all the others put together. The cards that count for Game are the four honours and
the Ten of each suit. Every ace counts 4 ; every King 3 ; every
Queen 2 ; every Jack 1 ; and every Ten 10. After the last card has
been played, each player turns over the tricks he has won, and
counts up the pip value of the court cards and Tens that he has

won. Whoever has the highest number counts the point for Game. For instance : Two are playing. The elder hand has taken in an ace, two Kings and a Jack, which are collectively worth 11. The dealer has taken in a Queen and a Ten, which are worth 12 ; so the dealer marks the point for Game. If both players have the same number, or if there is no Game out, which rarely happens, the non-dealer scores Game. If three play, and Game is a tie between the two non-dealers, neither scores. The non-dealer is given the benefit of counting a tie for Game as an offset to the dealer's advantage in turning Jacks. When no trump is turned, as in Pitch, no one can count Game if it is a tie.

METHOD OF PLAYING. The eldest hand begins by leading any card he pleases. If a trump is led, each player must follow suit if able. When a plain suit is led he need not follow suit if he prefers to trump ; but if he does not trump, he must follow suit if he can. If he has none of the suit led he may either trump or discard. This rule is commonly expressed by saying that a player may *follow suit or trump.* The highest card played of the suit led wins the trick, and trumps win all other suits. The winner of the trick takes it in, and leads for the next one, and so on until all the cards have been played. The tricks themselves have no value except for the court cards and Tens they contain.

As High, Jack, and Game are always counted by the player holding those points at the end of the play, there can be no question about them ; but serious disputes sometimes arise as to who played Low. The best method of avoiding this is for each player, as the game proceeds, to announce and claim the lowest trump which has so far appeared, and instead of giving it to the current trick, to leave it turned face up in front of him if it is of no counting value. For instance : Four are playing, and a round of trumps comes out, the six being the lowest. The player holding it announces : " Six for Low," and keeps the card face up in front of him until some smaller trump appears. It often happens that a player holds a 7 or 8, and having no idea that it will be Low, takes no notice of it. At the end of the hand it is found that both the 7 and 8 are out, the 7 being Low, and the holders of those two cards get into an argument as to which card each of them held.

SCORING. The last card played, the various points for High, Low, Jack, (if in play), and the Game are claimed, and the player or side holding them puts a counter in the pool for each. The side first getting rid of its seven counters wins the game. If both sides make points enough to win the game on the same deal, High goes out first, then Low, then Jack, and then Game. As already noticed, one card may be both High and Low ; the Jack may be High, Low, Jack ; and it is even possible, if there is no other trump or counting card in play, for the Jack to be High, Low, Jack, and the Game.

In the variety known as **All Fives,** the score is kept on a crib-bage board, and part of it is pegged as the hand progresses. A player winning a trick containing any of the following cards in the trump suit pegs them immediately :—For the trump ace, 4 points ; for the King 3 ; for the Queen 2 ; for the Jack 1 ; for the Ten 10, and for the Five 5. After the hand is over, all these cards are counted over again in reckoning the point for Game, the Five of trumps counting 5. Sixty-one points is game.

IRREGULARITIES IN PLAY. The most serious error in Seven-up is the *revoke.* If a player does not follow suit when able, it is a revoke unless he trumps the trick. A player holding two small trumps and the Ten of a plain suit, may trump both the ace and King of that suit instead of giving up his Ten. But if on the third round the Queen is led, and he cannot trump it, he must play his Ten if he has no other card of the suit.

The only points affected by the revoke are Jack and Game. **If the Jack is not in play,** there is only one point that can be affected by the revoke, the score for Game ; and the revoke penalty is one point, which the adversary may add to his own score, or deduct from the score of the revoking player. The adversary may also score the point for Game if he makes it ; but it cannot be scored by the revoking player ; who may mark only High or Low if he holds either or both of those points.

If the Jack is in play, two points may be affected by a revoke. The player in fault cannot score either Jack or Game, and the penalty for the revoke is two points ; in addition to which the adversary of the revoking player may score either or both Jack and Game if he makes them.

The revoking player cannot win the game that hand, no matter what he scores, but must stop at six. A revoke is established as soon as the trick in which it occurs has been turned and quitted, or a card has been led or played to the next trick.

Exposed Cards. When four play, all exposed cards must be left on the table, and are liable to be called by the adversaries if they cannot be previously got rid of in the course of play. All cards led or played out of turn are exposed, and liable to be called. If two or more cards are played to a trick, the adversaries may select which shall remain ; the other is exposed.

METHODS OF CHEATING. Few games lend themselves more readily to the operations of the greek than Seven-up. Turning Jacks from the bottom of the pack ; setting up the half-stock for the beg ; dealing oneself more than six cards, and dropping on the tricks already won those counting for Game ; getting the A J 10 and 2 of a suit together during the play of a hand, and then shifting the cut to get them on the next deal, turning up the Jack ; marked cards ; strippers ; wedges ; reflectors ;

these and many other tricks are in common use. Those who are not expert enough to deal seconds or shift cuts will sometimes resort to such trifling advantages as abstracting one of the Tens from the pack, so that they may know a suit from which a small card can always be led without any danger of the adversary's making the Ten. One very common swindle in Seven-up is known as *the high hand,* which consists in giving the intended victim the A K J 10 9 2 of trumps, and then inducing him to bet that he will make four points. No matter how skilful the player may be, he will find it impossible to save both Jack and Game.

CALIFORNIA JACK.

This is a variety of Seven-up for two players, in which the number of cards in the hand is constantly restored to six by drawing from the remainder of the pack.

The trump suit is cut for before the cards are shuffled and dealt. The usual method is to cut for seats and deal, and the highest cut determines the trump suit at the same time, After each player has been given six cards, three at a time, the remainder of the pack is turned face up on the table, and the winner of each trick takes the top card, his adversary taking the next one. When the stock is exhausted, the last six cards are played as in the ordinary game of Seven-up.

Seven points is game, the points being the same as in Seven-up ; but everything, including Low, counts to the player winning it.

Shasta Sam is California Jack with the remainder of the pack turned face down, and is a much better game on that account.

AUCTION PITCH,

SELL OUT, OR COMMERCIAL PITCH.

This very popular round game derives its name from the fact that the first card led or " pitched " is the trump suit, and that the privilege of pitching it belongs to the eldest hand, who may sell it out to the highest bidder.

The number of *cards* and their rank is the same as at Seven-up ; A K Q J 10 9 8 7 6 5 4 3 2, the ace being the highest in cutting and in play.

Players. Any number from four to seven may play, each for himself ; five is considered the best game. The players cut for choice of seats, the highest cut taking the first choice and the deal.

Counters. Each player should be provided with seven white counters to mark the game. If stakes are played for, red counters are used to make up the pool, one player acting as the banker to sell and redeem all red counters.

Dealing. Six cards are dealt to each player, three at a time, but no trump is turned. All the rules for irregularities in the deal are the same as in Seven-up, but a misdeal does not lose the deal under any circumstances.

Objects of the Game. As in Seven-up, the object of each player is to get rid of his seven counters, one of which he is entitled to put in the pool for each of the following points : For holding the *highest* trump in play ; for holding (having dealt to him) the *lowest* trump in play ; for winning a trick with the *Jack* of trumps in it ; for making the greatest number of the pips that count for the *game* point. The details of these points have already been explained in connection with Seven-up. If the count for Game is a tie, no one scores it.

Bidding. The eldest hand sells. If he pitches without waiting for a bid he must make four points, or he will be set back that number. Each player in turn, beginning on the left of the eldest hand, bids for the privilege of pitching the trump, naming the number of points he thinks he can make. If he will not bid, he must say distinctly : ***"I pass."*** After a bid has been made, any following player must bid higher or pass. There are no second bids. The highest number any player can bid is four, which will require him to make High, Low, Jack, and the Game against the combined efforts of all the other players. The eldest hand must either accept the number bid, or pitch the trump himself, and make as many points as the highest bidder offered him. If the eldest hand accepts, he pushes into the pool as many counters as he is bid, and the successful bidder pitches the trump. If no bid is made, the eldest hand must pitch the trump himself.

There is no penalty for bidding out of turn. If a player chooses to expose to a preceding player what he is prepared to bid, that is usually to his own disadvantage.

Playing. The successful bidder has the first lead, and whatever card he plays, whether by mistake or not, is the trump suit for that deal. After that, the winner of the trick may lead any suit he pleases. A player must follow suit in trumps if he is able to do so ; but in a plain suit he may trump if he chooses, although holding a card of the suit led. If he does not trump, he must follow suit if he can. If he has none of the suit led, he may trump or discard as he pleases. The highest card played of the suit led wins the trick, and trumps win all other suits.

Scoring. At the end of the hand the various players claim the points made, and score them by placing white counters in the pool. If the bidder makes any points in excess of the number bid, he scores them. The first player to get rid of his seven white counters wins the pool, and takes down all the red counters it contains. The white counters are then re-distributed, and the players cut for the first deal of the new game.

If two players can count out on the same deal, and one of them is the bidder, he wins the pool if he has made good his bid. If neither of the ties is the bidder, the points count out in their regular order, High first, then Low, then Jack, and finally Game. For instance : Seven are playing. A sells to B, who bids two. B and C have each two to go. B pitches a trump of which C has both High and Low; but if B makes Jack and Game he wins the pool, because he bid only two points, and made them. This is generally expressed by the rule : *bidder goes out first.*

A bidder is not allowed to give the seller enough points to put him out, and should he do so by mistake, he forfeits his right to bid at all for that deal. If the seller has only two to go, and a player is able to bid three or four, he loses nothing by bidding one only, for no one can overbid him, and he is entitled to count all he makes. The only risk he runs is that the .bidder can afford to refuse one, and will go out on his own pitch. To remedy this it is the custom in some clubs to allow a player to bid the full value of his hand. If the seller accepts, he scores to within one of game ; but if he refuses, he must make as many as bid, even if he does not actually want them. It is one of the fine points of the game for the seller to refuse when the number of points offered would put the bidder out if he was successful.

Setting Back. If the player who pitches the trump fails to make the number of points bid, he is set back, and scores nothing for any points he may have made. A player who is set back, either for overbidding his hand, or for refusing to sell and failing to make the number of points offered him, must withdraw from the pool as many white counters as were bid, and add them to his own. For instance : It is A's sell. A and B each have two to go. B bids three, which A refuses, pitching the trump himself. A makes only two points, B scoring one, and a third player D, another. B and D score one each, but A scores nothing for the two points he made, and must take three white counters from the pool, which will make him five to go. Had the bid which A refused been two only, he would have won the game, as he made two points. In many clubs it is the custom for a player who is set back to add a red counter to the pool.

Irregularities in Play. If any adversary of the player who pitches the trump leads or plays out of turn, he may be called upon by the bidder to play his highest or lowest of the suit led ; or to trump or not to trump the trick. If any player but the pitcher has followed the erroneous lead, the cards must be taken back ; but if the pitcher has followed, the error cannot be rectified.

In case of a *revoke,* the hand is played out as if the revoke had not occurred, and each player except the person in error counts whatever points he makes. If the pitcher of the trump fails to make the number of points bid, he cannot be set back, but must be allowed to score any points he makes. The revoking player is then set back the number of points bid, and forfeits a red counter to the pool. If no bid was made, he is set back two points.

PEDRO.

Pedro, Pedro Sancho, Dom Pedro, and Snoozer, are all varieties of Auction Pitch, in which certain counting cards are added, and secondary bids are allowed.

Everything counts to the player winning it, instead of to the one to whom it is dealt. The game point is scored by the player who wins the trick containing the Ten of trumps. If that card is not in play there is no Game.

In *Pedro Sancho,* the Five and Nine of trumps count their pip value in scoring, so that 18 points can be bid and made on one deal ; one each for High, Low, Jack, and Game, and fourteen more for the Nine and Five of trumps. These two trumps have no special rank. The Ten will win the Nine, and the Six will take the Five. In some places all the cards in the pack are dealt out, which makes a much better game in any form of Pedro.

The eldest hand sells, as at Auction Pitch. If a player's first bid is raised he may raise again in his proper turn.

Fifty points is game, and the players are usually provided with two varieties of counters for scoring ; one worth five points, and the other worth one. The rank of the points in scoring is ; High, Low, Jack, Ten (Game), Five, and Nine. The revoke penalty is to be set back the number of points bid, or ten points if there is no bid, and the player in fault cannot score anything that hand. In all other respects the rules are the same as in Auction Pitch.

In *Dom Pedro, or Snoozer,* the Joker is added to the pack, and the Three, Five, and Nine of trumps count their pip value in scoring. The Joker, or Snoozer, counts fifteen, so that thirty-six points can be bid and made on one deal. The Joker is the lowest trump, so that the deuce of trumps will win it, but it will win any trick in plain suits. Fifty or a hundred points is the game. In counting out, the order of precedence is: High, Low, Jack, Ten (Game), Three, Five, Nine, Snoozer.

CINCH,

DOUBLE PEDRO, OR HIGH FIVE.

This is now regarded as the most important variety of All Fours, and bids fair to supplant the parent game altogether. Properly speaking, Cinch is one of the pedro variations of Auction Pitch, the difference being that no one sells, and that there is added the always popular American feature of a draw to improve the hand.

The derivation and meaning of the name, Cinch, seems to be very much misunderstood. Many persons assume it is simply a name for the Left Pedro, but such is not the case. Cinch is a Mexican word for a strong saddle-girth, and when used as a verb it refers to the manner of adjusting the girth on a bucking broncho so that no amount of kicking will get him free. The word is used in this sense to describe one of the principal tactics of the card game, which is to " cinch " certain tricks, so that the adversary cannot possibly get either of the Pedroes free.

CARDS. Cinch is played with a full pack of fifty-two cards which rank A K Q J 10 9 8 7 6 5 4 3 2. When the suit is trumps the 5 retains its natural position, and is known as the ***Right Pedro ;*** but the 5 of the same colour as the trump suit, which is known as the ***Left Pedro,*** ranks between the 5 and 4 of the trump suit. The ace is highest in cutting and in play. Whist-players, who have taken up Cinch as a side issue, are in the habit of making the ace lowest in cutting; but such a practice is out of harmony with all other members of the Seven-up family of games.

COUNTERS. The score is usually kept on a sheet of paper; but it is more convenient to provide each side with 8 red and 11 white counters, representing 51 points; the whites being worth 1, and the reds 5 each. A good pull-up cribbage board is still better.

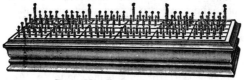

PULL-UP GAME COUNTER.

PLAYERS. Any number from two to six can play; but the regular game is for four persons, two of whom are partners against the other two. The player on the dealer's left is the **eldest hand;** on the dealer's right is the **pone.**

CUTTING. The players draw from an outspread pack for partners, seats, and deal. The two lowest play against the two highest; the highest cut has the choice of seats and cards, and deals the first hand. Partners sit opposite each other.

DEALING. Each player has the right to shuffle the pack, the dealer last. The cards are then presented to the pone to be cut, and at least four cards must be left in each packet. Beginning on his left, the dealer gives nine cards to each player, three at a time in three separate rounds. No trump is turned, and the remainder of the pack is left on the table face downward.

MISDEALING. If any card is found faced in the pack, the cards must be re-shuffled and dealt again. If the dealer exposes a card in dealing, or turns up a trump by mistake, the adversaries may elect to have a new deal by the same dealer, or to let the deal stand. If the dealer gives too many or too few cards to any player, or fails to give the same number of cards in each round, it is a misdeal, and the deal passes to the next player on the left. Any player dealing out of turn, or with the wrong cards, may be stopped before the last three cards are dealt; but after that the deal stands good. If a misdeal is not discovered until after a bid has been made, the deal stands good if three players have their right number of cards. The deal passes in regular rotation to the left.

OBJECTS OF THE GAME. The game is fifty-one points, and the side first pegging that number, or getting rid of its fifty-one counters is the winner. Fourteen points are made on every deal, as follows :—

1	For **High,** the ace of trumps.
1	For **Low,** the deuce of trumps.
1	For the **Jack** of trumps.
1	For the Ten of trumps, or **Game.**
5	For the Five of trumps, or **Right Pedro.**
5	For the Five of the same colour, or **Left Pedro.**
14	points altogether; all in the trump suit.

All these points, including Low, count to the player winning them, and not to the players to whom they are dealt. This saves endless disputes.

BIDDING. Beginning with the eldest hand, each player in turn, after examining his nine cards, can make **one bid** for the privilege of naming the trump suit. The peculiarity of this bidding is that nobody sells, the bids being made **to the board,** as it is called.   The bidder announces the number of points he thinks he can make (with his partner's assistance) but does not name the trump suit.   If a player will not bid, he says : *" I pass."*   After a bid has been made in its proper turn, any following player must bid higher or pass.   No one is allowed to bid more than fourteen. There are no second bids, and a bid once made cannot be amended or withdrawn.   The player who has made the highest bid is called upon to name the trump suit.

Irregular Bids.   If any player bids before the eldest hand has bid or passed, both the player in error and his partner lose their right to make any bid that deal ; but the side not in error must bid against each other for the privilege of naming the trump suit.   If the eldest hand has decided, and the pone bids without waiting for the dealer's partner, the pone loses his bid, and the dealer may bid before his partner, without penalty.   If the dealer bids before his partner has decided, both he and his partner lose their right to bid that deal ; but the pone is still at liberty to over-bid the eldest hand for the privilege of naming the trump.   If the dealer's partner has bid, and the dealer bids without waiting for the pone, the dealer loses his right to bid for that deal.

If a player whose partner has not yet bid names the trump suit, his partner loses the right to bid.   If no bid is made, the dealer may name any suit he pleases, without bidding.   If any player exposes a card beforte he trump suit is named, the adversaries may elect to have a new deal by the same dealer.

DISCARDING AND DRAWING.   The trump suit named, each player discards and leaves *face upward* on the table as many cards as he pleases.   He must discard three, to re-duce his hand to six cards.   If he discards more than three he must draw from the remainder of the pack to restore the number of his cards to six ; so that after the discard and draw each player at the table will have exactly six cards, although nine were originally dealt him.

The dealer, beginning on his left, gives to each player in turn as many cards from the top of the pack as may be necessary to re-store the number in his hand to six.   When it comes to the dealer's turn, instead of taking cards from the top of the pack, he may search the remainder of the pack, and take from it any cards that he pleases.   This is called *robbing the deck.*   Should he find in his own hand and the remainder of the pack more than six trumps, he must discard those he does not want, showing them face up on the table with the other discards.

Should any player discard a trump, his partner has the right to call his attention to it, and if the player has not been helped to cards, or has not lifted the cards drawn, the trump erroneously discarded may be taken back ; otherwise it must remain among the discards until the hand has been played, when, if it is of any counting value, it must be added to the score of the side making the trump.

Although there is no law to that effect, it is considered imperative for each player except the dealer to discard everything but trumps. This is partly because no other cards are of the slightest use, and partly because one of the points of the game is that the number of trumps held by each player before the draw should be indicated by his discard.

METHOD OF PLAYING. The player who has named the trump suit begins by leading any card he pleases. If a trump is led, every one must follow suit if able to do so, and it must be remembered that the Left Pedro is one of the trump suit. When a plain suit is led, any player may trump if he chooses, although holding one of the suit led; but if he does not trump, he must follow suit if he can. If he has none of the suit led he may trump or discard at pleasure. The highest card played of the suit led wins the trick, and trumps win all other suits. The Five of trumps, or any higher, will win the Left Pedro; but the Left Pedro will win the Four of trumps, or any lower. The winner of the trick gathers it in, turning it face down, and leads for the next trick, and so on, until all six tricks have been played. The tricks themselves have no value, and need not be kept separate. The last trick turned and quitted may be seen, but no other.

Irregularities in Playing. If, during the play of a hand, any person is found to have too many cards, his hand is foul, and neither he nor his partner can score any points for that deal, but they may play the hand out to prevent the adversaries from scoring everything. If he has too few cards there is no penalty.

If a player leads out of turn, and the three others follow him, the trick stands good. If all have not followed the false lead, their cards must be taken back, but only the leader's card is liable to be called. If it was the turn of the partner of the player in error to lead, the adversary on his right may call upon him to lead or not to lead a trump; but he cannot specify the plain suit. If it was the turn of either adversary of the player in error to lead, the card led in error is simply exposed.

If the third hand plays before the second, the fourth may play before the second also. If the fourth hand plays before his partner, third hand not having played, the trick may be claimed by the adversaries, regardless of who wins it; but the player who actually wins it leads for the next trick.

If a player has a card of the suit led, and neither follows suit nor plays a trump, it is a *revoke;* and, if detected and claimed by the adversaries, neither the player in error nor his partner can score any points that hand; but the hand may be played out to prevent the adversaries from scoring everything If an adversary of the bidder revokes, the bidder's side scores all points it makes, regardless of the number bid. For instance : A has bid nine ; and Y revokes. A-B make eight only, which they score, Y-Z scoring nothing. When a player renounces, his partner should ask him if he is void of the suit.

If any player abandons his hand, the cards in it may be exposed and called by the adversaries. The practice of throwing down the hand as soon as one renounces to trumps, cannot be too strongly condemned.

All *exposed cards,* such as cards dropped on the table ; two or more played at once ; cards led out of turn ; or cards named by the player holding them, must be left face up on the table, and are liable to be called by the adversaries, unless they can be previously got rid of in the course of play. If the exposed card is a trump, the adversaries may prevent its being played, but the holder of it is not liable for a revoke in such cases.

SCORING. When the last card has been played, each side turns over all the tricks won, and counts the points they contain ; High, Low, Jack, Game, Right and Left Pedro. Everything, including Low, counts to the side winning it. The number of points won or lost is determined by deducting the lower score from the higher, the difference being the number of points won on that deal. If it is a tie, neither side scores. If either side has incurred a penalty which prevents them from scoring any points they may have won, the adversaries have nothing to deduct, and score all they make.

If the side that named the trump fails to make as many points as it bid, it scores nothing, and the number of points bid are scored by the adversaries, in addition to any points that the adversaries may have made in play. For instance : A-B are partners against Y-Z. B has bid to make 8, and named hearts for trumps. A-B make 10, which is 2 more than they bid, Y-Z getting the other 4 ; which leaves A-B 6. These are scored by placing one red and one white counter in the pool. But suppose A-B got only 5 points, Y-Z getting 9. A-B would score nothing, as they did not make good their bid ; while Y-Z would score the 9 points actually won, and the 8 points bid in addition, or 17 altogether.

The old way of scoring was to *set back* the side that failed to make the number bid ; but that system of counting entirely destroyed the interest in the game when one side got much behind ; because it could not recover in time to prevent the other side from *sweating out,* as it is called. Suppose A-B have been set back 18 points on two failures, Y-Z having made 16 points on those two deals, and 23 on their own bids. The score will stand : A-B 64 to go ; Y-Z, 12 to go. Even if we suppose that A-B make 11 on each of the next four deals, they will still have 20 to go, while

Y-Z will be out. Again : A-B want 15, Y-Z want 2. Even if A-B can bid 12 and make it, Y-Z will sweat out.

With the system of scoring here recommended, this sweating out is impossible, and it is not uncommon for a side that wants one to go, to be beaten by an adversary that wants forty-nine.

The side first pegging out on a cribbage-board, or getting rid of its fifty-one counters, wins the game. When the game is counted on a pull-up cribbage marker, it is usual to start with ten up, and peg out to the game-hole, or 61.

VARIATIONS. There are quite a number of minor differences in the manner of playing Cinch. Sometimes, instead of discarding and drawing, after the successful bidder has been ascertained, but before he names the trump, four more cards are given to each player, including the dealer. Having seen thirteen cards, the bidder names the trump suit, and the hands are then reduced to six cards each. This method gives no clue to the number of trumps originally held, and deprives the dealer of one of the greatest advantages of his position, robbing the deck.

Another method is to discard and draw after the trump is named, but to make the dealer take his cards from the top of the pack to complete his hand, without seeing what he is to get. This often leaves counting cards in the remainder of the pack, which must remain face down, and be kept separate from the discards. Such points count for neither side ; but any points found among the discards may be counted by the side making the trump, as in the ordinary game. Owing to the uncertainty as to the number of points actually in play, the result is controlled more largely by luck than skill.

In some places the *first lead* from the successful bidder must be a *trump.* This makes the game too much like Auction Pitch, and spoils some of the finer points in leading.

Low is sometimes counted for the person to whom it is dealt. Such a rule causes endless confusion and disputes.

The old method of *scoring* has already been mentioned. Another variation is that if the bidder's side do not make at least 8 points they cannot score anything, no matter what they bid. If both sides score 7, neither having bid more than 7, neither scores. If one side bids 6, and makes 8, it scores 8 ; but the adversaries score the 6 they make. If the side bidding 6 had made 6 only, it would score nothing, while their adversaries would mark the 8 they made. The only good result of the 6 bid in this case is to prevent the adversaries from scoring for a failure ; for if 7 had been bid, and only 6 made, the adversaries would have scored the 7 bid in addition to the 8 they made, or 15 in all. This system, while better than the old way, because it never sets players back, still allows one side to sweat out ; because if the bidder does not make 14, the adversaries must count something every deal.

Five or six players, each for himself, may play what is called *Auction Cinch,* or *Razzle-dazzle.* Only six cards are dealt to each player, three on the first round and three on the second. Then the privilege of naming the trump suit is bid for as usual. After the trump is named, superfluous cards are thrown out, and others drawn in their place, restoring the hands to six cards each. The successful bidder then calls upon the holder of any given card to be his partner. The person holding the card named cannot refuse, and says : " I play with you." The partnership thus formed plays against the combined forces of the other players, but without changing seats. The maker of the trump leads first, any card he pleases. For instance : A B C D E are playing. C bids 8 and names clubs. After the draw he finds he holds A J 10 5 2 of trumps. He calls for the club King as his partner, and leads his Pedro at once for the King to take it in. He is then certain to catch the other Pedro, or to save three of the four points for High, Low, Jack, and the Game. Those who have played Seven-handed Euchre will at once recognize the similarity of the two games. Both are excellent round games for the family circle.

Progressive Cinch is played by dealing one round at each table ; that is, four deals, each player having the deal once only. The ordinary game of Cinch is played, and the pair having the fewest points to go at the end of the four deals progress to the next higher table. Ties cut to decide, high going up. On arriving at the next table, the partners divide, and another game of four deals is played, the winning pair again progressing. The general arrangements for the original positions of the players, and the prizes to be given, are the same as in Progressive Euchre, and have been fully described in connection with that game.

SUGGESTIONS FOR GOOD PLAY. There is a great diversity of opinion on bidding. Some persons always bid six on an ace, if they hold neither of the Pedroes. This is based on the sound principle that the odds are five to four in favour of your partner having one of the Pedroes, which he will immediately give up if you lead the ace. The odds are five to two that your partner will hold one or more of any three named counting cards which you do not hold. If you have no Pedro, count on him for one, and if you have King and Queen, you can risk his having a guard to it, and bid as if you were sure of getting his Pedro home. If you have none of the points for High, Low, Jack, or Game, or only one of them, count on him for one at least, and bid accordingly.

It is very difficult to give exact rules for bidding, the state of the score having much to do with it ; but as a general rule it is much better to bid on *catching cards* than on the points themselves. For instance : A K Q of trumps should certainly be good for eight points ; some players habitually bid twelve on them, reckoning to catch both Pedroes and one of the minor points. This is risky unless there are one or two small trumps with the A K Q. On the other hand, two Pedroes, with Jack and Low, are not worth bidding more than five on ; because it is very unlikely that you will save more than one of the Pedroes, if that. The very fact that you bid five diminishes your chances, for you betray the fact that your only hope is to save a well-guarded Pedro. Long experience with players who bid their hands correctly will give a player a very good idea of what the bidder has in his hand. To the partner this is a great point, for it enables him to judge when to give up points himself, and when to play for his partner to throw them to him.

The number of cards asked for by each player should be very carefully noted ; for it will frequently happen that the entire trump suit can be located by this means. It is useless to keep anything but trumps, for tricks, as such, have no value, and every card you draw increases your chances of getting another trump.

The most important point in the game is to **cinch** every trick in which an adversary plays after you ; that is, to play some trump higher than a Pedro, if the Pedroes have not been played, and you do not hold them yourself. Examples of cinching will be found in the Illustrative Hands. If your partner leads a certain winning trump, such as the ace, or the King if the ace is gone, give him the best counting card you have ; but if you have two, one of them being Low, give up the lower card first ; you may catch something with the Jack or Ten. If your partner leads any trump higher than the Five, play your smallest trump unless second hand covers, in which case you must cinch the trick, to prevent the fourth hand from giving up a Pedro on his partner's trick.

If you are forced to win your partner's first lead of trumps, return the best trump you have, unless it is the Jack or Ten, in which case you must be guided by the number of points you are playing for, and your chances of making them if you lose the card you lead.

If your partner begins by leading a plain suit, you must cinch the trick if you can ; if second hand follows suit, any trump better than the Five will do. If second hand puts on a trump, you must cinch higher.

If the player on your right renounces to trumps, get into the lead if possible, and play your best cards in plain suits. This may give your partner a tenace position over the player on your left.

If partner begins with a high card in trumps, not the ace, credit him with the sequence below it, and put in your Pedro at the first opportunity. For instance : Partner leads King, won by the ace second hand. Whatever this player leads, put in your Pedro, if you have one, your partner must have Queen of trumps.

Playing to the score is very important. Do not attempt to get ınore than the number bid until that is assured. On the other hand, if it is certain that the adversary cannot make good his bid, do not let him get as close to it as possible, but play boldly to win all you can, for every point he makes is simply lost.

Here are a few example hands, which will give a very good idea of some of the fine points in the game.

No.1				TRICK	No.2			
No. 1. A bids 8 on hearts.					**No. 2.** A bids 8 on hearts.			
The draw : A 2 ; Y 2 ; B 4 ; Z 5.					The draw : A 2 ; Y 3 ; B 4 ; Z 4.			
A	Y	B	Z		A	Y	B	Z
♣ Q	♣ 3	♥ 8	♣ 5	I	♥ 3	♥ 7	♥ 10	♥ 8
♥ 2	♥ 6	♥ Q	♥ 4	2	♥ Q	♥ 2	♥ 4	♥ 9
♥ 10	♥ J	♣ J	♥ 9	3	♥ 6	♥ J	A ◊	♣ 4
♥ K	5 ◊	2 ♠	4 ♠	4	♣ 2	7 ♠	K ◊	6 ♠
♥ A	♥ 7	6 ♠	♣ 9	5	♥ K	♥ A	♣ 3	♣ 6
♥ 3	♥ 5	10 ♠	K ◊	6	♥ 5	5 ◊	2 ◊	♣ 10

No. 1. Y's draw shows that he holds at least four trumps, so A must trust his partner to cinch the first trick and return the trump. [See our suggestions for good play.] At trick 3, Z cinches, to make A play a high trump. It is evident to A that neither B nor Z holds either Jack or Seven of trumps; so both those cards must be with Y. As B has no more trumps the adversaries must have both Pedroes, and Y must have one, as he holds four trumps. If they are divided, A can catch both by cinching this trick with the King and leading the Ace; but if Y has both Pedroes, such a course would lose Jack, Game, and one Pedro. If A cinches this trick with the Ten, allowing Y to win with the Jack, A must catch both Pedroes, no matter how they lie, provided Y leads the trump Seven, for A will refuse to win it.

Y sees his danger, and by leading a Pedro to A, forces him either to pass it, or to get into the lead and free the other Pedro.

A–B score nothing : Y–Z score 7 for Jack, Game, Pedro ; and 8 in addition, for points bid but not made by A–B ; 15 altogether.

No. 2. At trick 2, Y sees that he cannot save Low, and the lead would be a great disadvantage, because either A has all the remaining trumps, or Y's partner has an unguarded Pedro. At trick 3, A knows that if Y has Ace, and Z Pedro, A can still make his bid by catching Jack, and saving his own Pedro. If the Pedro is not with Z the small trump is still the best lead, for it puts the lead on A's left. B gets rid of cards which might get him into the lead to his partner's disadvantage. Unfortunately, Z is unable to take the lead away from Y at trick 4. As Y is still in the lead, there is no necessity for A to save his Pedro, for Y cannot possibly catch it, and A must catch Y's, no matter how Y plays.

A–B score 10 points; Low, Game, and both Pedroes, 12, from which they deduct the 2 points made by Y–Z.

	No. 3. A bids 12 on hearts. The draw : A 3; Y 5; B 3; Z 2.			TRICK	**No. 4.** A bids 8 on hearts. The draw : A 2; Y 4; B 4; Z 4.			
A	Y	B	Z		A	Y	B	Z
♡ A	♡ 3	5 ◇	♡ 6	1	♡ A	♡ 6	♡ J	♡ 3
♡ K	♡ 4	♡ 8	♡ 10	2	♡ 8	♡ 7	♡ 4	♡ 9
♡ 2	♡ 7	♡ 9	♡ J	3	♡ Q	♡ 2	4 ◇	♡ K
♣ Q	♣ K	♣ 3	♣ J	4	Q ♠	♣ 2	♣ A	♣ 9
8 ♠	♣ A	♣ 10	2 ◇	5	5 ◇	♡ 5	♣ J	♣ 7
♡ Q	Q ♠	K ◇	♡ 5	6	♡ 10	4 ♠	J ◇	2 ◇

No. 3. At the second trick, A knows that his partner still holds another trump, because he drew only three cards. This trump must be the 9. Z holds two more trumps, and they must be the Jack and Right Pedro, because Z would not throw away Game if he had anything smaller. The 7 must be with Y, and if A now leads trump Queen, he will leave the Pedro good over his Deuce, leaving him only 8 points, whereas he has bid 12. If A leads the Deuce, his partner's nine will cinch the trick, and Z can make only the Jack.

A–B score 10. The 12 actually taken make good the bid; but the 2 points won by the adversaries must be deducted, leaving 10 to be scored by A–B.

No. 4. At the third trick, a hasty or careless player would have been only too glad of the opportunity to get in his Pedro. But Y reasons that there are only two trumps unaccounted for, the Ten and Left Pedro. If B has one, it must fall to this trick. He cannot have both, for A drew only two cards. If A has both, Y must catch his Pedro, no matter how A plays; and as long as Y does not get into the lead himself, he cannot lose his own Pedro. At trick 5, A naturally places the Pedro with Z, as Y did not save it on the King, and it is perfectly natural for A to trump with his Pedro, intending to lead the Ten to catch Z's.

A–B score nothing, not having made good their bid. **Y–Z** score Right and Left Pedro, and Low, 11 points; adding the 8 points bid but not made by A–B, 19 altogether.

CINCH LAWS.

Formation of Table. A cinch table is complete with six players. If more than four assemble, they cut for preference, the four highest playing the first game. Partners and deal are then cut for, the two lowest pairing against the two highest. Partners sit opposite each other. The highest deals, and has the choice of seats and cards. The Ace is high, both in cutting and in play. A player exposing more than one card must cut again.

Ties. If the first cut does not decide, the players cutting equal cards cut again ; but the new cut decides nothing but the tie.

Cutting Out. At the end of the game, the players cut to decide which shall give way to those awaiting their turn to play, the lowest cuts going out. After the second game, those who have played the greatest number of consecutive games give way, ties being decided by cutting.

Dealing. Every player has the right to shuffle the cards, the dealer last. The dealer must present the pack to the pone to be cut. At least four cards must be left in each packet. If a card is exposed in cutting, the pack must be re-shuffled, and cut again. If the dealer re-shuffles the pack after it has been properly cut, he loses his deal.

Beginning on his left, the dealer must give to each player in rotation three cards at a time for three rounds. No trump is turned. The deal passes to the left.

There must be a new deal by the same dealer if any card is found faced in the pack ; or if the pack is proved incorrect or imperfect ; but any previous cutting or scores made with the imperfect pack stand good.

The adversaries may demand a new deal if any card is exposed during the deal, provided they have not touched a card. If an adversary exposes a card, the dealer may elect to deal again. If a new deal is not demanded, cards exposed in dealing cannot be called.

The adversaries may stop a player dealing out of turn, or with the wrong pack, provided they do so before the last three cards are dealt, after which the deal stands good.

Misdealing. A misdeal loses the deal. It is a misdeal : If the cards have not been properly cut ; if the dealer does not give the same number of cards to each player on the same round ; if he gives too many or too few cards to any player ; if he counts the cards on the table, or those remaining in the pack ; or if he deals a card incorrectly, and fails to correct the error before dealing another. If the dealer is interrupted in any way by an adversary, he does not lose his deal.

Bidding. After receiving his nine cards, each player in turn, beginning on the dealer's left, announces the number of points he will undertake to win if he is allowed to name the trump suit. No player is allowed to bid more than fourteen. If he will not bid, he must say : " I pass." A bid having been regularly made, any following player must bid higher or pass. There are no second bids. A bid once made can neither be amended nor withdrawn.

Irregular Bids. If any player bids before the eldest hand has bid or passed, both the player in error and his partner lose their right to bid ; but the side not in error must bid to decide which of them shall name the trump. If the eldest hand has decided, and the pone bids without waiting for the dealer's partner, the pone loses his bid, and the dealer may bid before his partner. If the dealer bids without waiting for his partner, both lose their bids ; but the pone may overbid the eldest hand.

If the dealer's partner has bid, and the dealer bids without waiting for the pone, the dealer loses his bid.

If a player whose partner has not yet bid names the trump suit, his partner loses his bid.

If a player bids with more than nine cards in his hand, his bid is lost, and the adversaries must draw the superfluous cards from his hand, face down, placing them about the middle of the undealt portion of the pack.

If no bid is made, the dealer may name any trump he pleases, without bidding.

If any player exposes any of his cards before the trump suit is named, the adversaries may elect to have a new deal by the same dealer.

Discarding. The trump named, each player must put out at least three of his cards, and may discard as many more as he pleases. All such discards must be placed on the table face up. Should a player discard a trump, his partner may call his attention to it, and it may be taken back, provided the player has not been helped to cards, or has not lifted the cards drawn.

Drawing. The players having discarded, the dealer, beginning on his left, must give to each in turn from the top of the pack, face down, as many cards as may be necessary to restore the number in each hand to six.

Robbing the Deck. When it comes to the dealer's turn to draw cards, instead of taking them from the top of the pack, face down, he may search the remainder of the pack, and take from it any cards he pleases to restore the number in his hand to six. Should he find in his own hand and in the remainder of the pack, more than six trumps, he must discard those he does not want, face upward on the table.

Irregular Drawing. Should a player ask for too many or too few cards, and not discover his error until the next player has been helped, if he has too few he may make his hand good from the discards, but must not take a trump therefrom. If he has too many, the adversaries must be allowed to draw the superfluous ones at random, face down, placing them on the top of the pack.

Playing. The maker of the trump must lead for the first trick, any card he pleases. If a trump is led, all must follow suit if able. If a plain suit is led, a player may trump, even when holding a card of the suit led; but if he does not trump he must follow suit if he can, or he is liable to the penalty for a revoke.

The last trick turned and quitted may be seen, but no other.

Irregularities in the Hands. If any player is found to have an incorrect number of cards, it is a misdeal if no bid has been made. If a bid has been made, the deal stands good if three players have their right number of cards. If the first trick has been played to by a person holding too many cards, neither he nor his partner can score anything that hand; but they may play the hand out to save what points they can. If a player has too few cards, there is no penalty, but he should draw from the discard to make up the deficiency, plain-suit cards only being available.

Exposed Cards. The following are exposed cards, which must be left face up on the table, and are liable to be called by either adversary: 1. Every card faced upon the table otherwise than in the regular course of play. 2. Two or more cards played to a trick; the adversaries may elect which shall be played. 3. Any card named by the player holding it.

The adversary on the right of an exposed card must call it before he plays himself. If it will be the turn of the player holding the exposed card to lead for the next trick, the card, if wanted, must be called before the current trick is turned and quitted. Should a player having the lead, and an exposed card in front of him, play before the previous trick is turned and quitted, the card so led may also be claimed as exposed.

If a trump is exposed after the trump suit has been named, the adversaries may prevent the playing of such a card; but the holder of it is not liable to any penalty for a revoke under such circumstances.

Leading Out of Turn. If a player leads when it was his partner's turn, the partner may be called upon by his right-hand adversary to lead or not to lead a trump; but a specified plain suit cannot be called. If it was the turn of neither of the side in error to lead, the card played in error is simply exposed. If all have played to the false lead, the error cannot be rectified. If all have not followed, the cards played to the false lead may be taken back, and are not liable to be called.

Playing Out of Turn. If the third hand plays before the second, the fourth may play before the second also ; either of his own volition, or by the direction of the second hand, who may say : "Play, partner." If the fourth hand plays before the second, the third hand not having played, the trick may be claimed by the adversaries, no matter who actually wins it ; but the actual winner of it must lead for the next trick.

If any player abandons his hand, the cards in it may be claimed as exposed, and called by the adversaries.

The Revoke. A revoke is a renounce in error, not corrected in time, or non-compliance with a performable penalty. It is a revoke if a player has one of the suit led, and neither follows suit nor trumps.

A person prohibited from playing an exposed trump is not liable to any penalty if it causes him to revoke.

A revoke is established when the trick in which it occurs has been turned and quitted ; or when either the revoking player or his partner, whether in his right turn or otherwise, has led or played to the following trick.

If a revoke is claimed and proved, the revoking side cannot score any points that deal ; but they may play the hand out to prevent the adversaries from making points.

If an adversary of the bidder revokes, the bidder's side scores whatever points it makes that deal, regardless of the number bid.

A player may ask his partner whether or not he has a card of the suit in which he renounces and does not trump, and the player may correct his error if the question is asked before the trick is turned and quitted. But if he answers in the negative, there is no remedy.

Drawing Cards. Any player may ask the others to indicate the cards played by them to the current trick ; but he must confine himself to the expression : "Draw cards."

Irregular Remarks. A player calling attention in any manner to the trick or to the score, may be called upon to play his highest or lowest of the suit led ; or to trump or not to trump the trick during the play of which the remark is made.

Scoring. A game consists of fifty-one points ; fourteen of which must be made on every deal, as follows :—

1 for ***High,*** or the Ace of trumps.

1 for ***Low,*** or the Deuce of trumps.

1 for the ***Jack*** of trumps.

1 for ***Game,*** or the Ten of trumps.

5 for ***Right Pedro,*** or the Five of trumps.

5 for ***Left Pedro,*** or Five of the same colour as the trump suit. All points count to the side winning them.

Any trumps found among the discards at the end of the hand count for the side that made the trump.

At the end of the hand, the number of points won by each side is added up, and the lower deducted from the higher, the difference being scored by the winners of the majority. If the result is a tie, neither scores. For instance : If A-B make 11, Y-Z must make the remaining 3, which deducted from 11 leaves 8 points for A-B to score.

If the side naming the trump suit fails to make as many points as they bid, they score nothing for that deal, and the number bid is scored by the adversaries, in addition to any other points that the adversaries may have made in play. The number bid and the number actually won, must be compared before deducting the points made by the adversaries.

The side first making fifty-one points wins the game.

Text Books. There are two very good text-books on the game.

The Laws and Principles of Cinch, by G. W. Hall, 1891.

The Laws and Etiquette of Cinch, issued by the Chicago Cinch Club, 1890.

HEARTS.

Hearts is supposed by some persons to be an entirely new game ; but its leading principle, losing instead of winning tricks, is to be found in many other card games, some of which are quite old. Slobberhannes, Enflé, Schwellen, Polignac, and The Four Jacks, all belong to the same family, but most of them have given way to the more popular game of Hearts.

There are several varieties of Hearts, but the principal arrangements are the same in all, and the chief differences are in the manner of settling at the end of the hand.

CARDS. Hearts is played with a full pack of fifty-two cards, which rank A K Q J 10 9 8 7 6 5 4 3 2 : the ace is the highest in play, but in cutting it ranks below the deuce. There is no trump suit.

When three persons play, the deuce of spades is thrown out of the pack ; when five play, both the black deuces are laid aside, and when six play, all four deuces are discarded. It is usual to play with two packs, one being shuffled while the other is dealt.

COUNTERS. Every deal is a game in itself, and must be settled for in counters immediately. It is usual for each player to begin with fifty counters, which are purchased from some person who is agreed upon to act as banker. When only two play, the game may be scored on a pull-up cribbage board, and settled for at the end.

PLAYERS. Any number from two to six persons may play, but four is the usual number, each playing for himself against all the others. The players on the dealer's right and left are known as the ***pone*** and the ***eldest hand,*** respectively.

STAKES. The value of the counters must be agreed upon before play begins, and the method of settling should also be understood, Sweepstake Hearts and Howell's Settling being entirely different games, and requiring totally different methods of play.

CUTTING. If seven players assemble, it is usual to make up a table in which the dealer takes no cards. If there are more than seven candidates for play, two tables must be formed.

Players draw from an outspread pack for the choice of seats and cards, the lowest cut having the first choice, and the others following in their order. The player cutting the lowest card takes the first deal, which afterward passes in regular rotation to the left.

In cutting, the ace is low. Any player exposing more than one card must cut again.

TIES. If the first cut does not decide, those tying must cut again, but the new cut decides nothing but the tie.

DEALING. Any player has the right to shuffle the pack, the dealer last. The cards are then presented to the pone to be cut, who must leave at least four in each packet. The cards are dealt from left to right, one at a time to each player in rotation until the pack is exhausted. No trump is turned. In Two-handed Hearts, the dealer stops when each player has received thirteen cards. The deal passes to the left.

Misdealing. It is a misdeal if the dealer omits to have the pack cut, and the error is discovered before the last card is dealt ; if he deals a card incorrectly, and does not remedy the error before dealing another ; or if he counts the cards on the table, or those remaining in the pack ; or if it is discovered before all have played to the first trick that any player has too many or too few cards. A misdeal loses the deal unless one of the other players has touched the cards, or has in any way interrupted the dealer.

If any card is exposed by the dealer, the player to whom it is dealt may demand a new deal, provided he has not touched any of his cards. Any one dealing out of turn, or with the wrong cards, may be stopped before the last card is dealt. After that the deal stands good, and the packs, if changed, must so remain.

IRREGULAR HANDS. If, after the first trick has been played to, any two players are found to have more or less than their correct number of cards, the pack being perfect, the one having less must draw, face downward, from the hand of the one having more ; and each must pay five counters into the pool.

OBJECTS OF THE GAME. As a general proposition, the object of each player is to avoid getting any hearts in the tricks he takes in. In some varieties of the game his object must be to take no hearts ; in others it will be to take less than his adversaries ; while in others it will be to take less than four. After a person has taken in one or more hearts, his object will be to *load* the others ; that is, to see that they get some hearts also ; or it may be to see that a given player takes at least one heart ; or that no one but himself takes any. The manner in which a person must vary his play in accordance with these different objects will be discussed when we come to the suggestions for good play. In the meantime, it is necessary to bear in mind only the general principle that the object of the game is to avoid winning any tricks that contain hearts.

METHOD OF PLAYING. The cards dealt, the player to the left of the dealer begins by leading any card he pleases, and the others must follow suit if they can. The highest card played, if of the suit led, wins the trick. There is no trump suit. If a player has none of the suit led, he may discard anything he pleases. The winner of the trick takes it in and leads for the next trick, and so on until all the cards have been played. The tricks themselves have no value as such, and need not be kept separate.

Irregularities in Play. If any player omits to play to a trick, and plays to a following one, he is not allowed to correct his error, but is compelled to take the thirteenth or last trick, with whatever hearts it may contain. If a player is found, during or at the end of a hand, to be a card short, all others at the table having their right number, and all having played to the first trick, the player with the short hand is compelled to take the last trick, with whatever hearts it may contain.

Exposed Cards. Should a person lead or play two cards to one trick, he is allowed to indicate the one intended; but he must leave the other face upward on the table. All exposed cards are liable to be called by any player at the table, and should one player call such a card, his decision is binding on the others. A player with an exposed card in front of him must play it when called upon, provided he can do so without revoking; but he cannot be prevented from getting rid of the exposed card in the course of play, if the opportunity offers.

Leading Out of Turn. Should a player lead out of turn, he may be called upon to lead or not to lead a heart when it is next his turn to lead. This penalty can be enforced only by the player on his right. If all have played to the false lead the error cannot be rectified; but if all have not played, their cards must be taken back, and are not liable to be called.

If any person plays out of turn in any trick, the player on his left, not having played, may demand that the card be taken back, and after the proper player has played the player in error may be called upon to play his highest or lowest of the suit led, or not to discard a heart. If the person on the left of the player in error was the leader in the trick, either he or the player whose proper turn it was to play may demand the penalty.

Revoking. Any player failing to follow suit, when able to do so, may amend his error if he discovers his mistake before the trick in which it occurs has been turned and quitted. The card played in error then becomes an exposed card. Those who have played after him have the privilege of withdrawing their cards and substituting others, without penalty. Should the revoking player not discover his error in time, the hand must be played out, and if the revoke is detected and claimed the player in error must pay all the losses on that hand. Should the revoking player win the pool himself, he must pay the thirteen counters to the pool, and leave them for a *Jack.* Should he divide the pool with another player, he must pay his co-winner six counters, and put up the other seven for a Jack.

If two or more players revoke in the same hand, each must pay the entire losses in that hand as if he were alone in error ; so that if two should revoke and a third win the pool, the latter would receive twenty-six counters instead of thirteen. In Auction Hearts, the revoking player must also refund the amount put up by the bidder. A revoke must be claimed and proved before the pool is divided. Non-compliance with a performable penalty is the same as a revoke.

SETTLING. After the last card has been played, each player turns over his tricks, counts the number of hearts he has taken in, and announces it. Players should be careful not to gather or mix the cards until all thirteen hearts have been accounted for. Each player then pays into the pool for the number of hearts he has taken in, according to the system of settlement agreed upon before play began. The pool is then taken down by the player or players winning it, and the deal passes to the left. The game is at an end any time the players wish to stop, after a hand has been settled for ; but it is usual to agree upon some definite hour.

There are two ways of settling at the end of the hand, each of which has its good points.

SWEEPSTAKE HEARTS. After the hand has been played, each player announces the number of hearts he has taken in, and pays into the pool one counter for each. All thirteen hearts having been paid for, any player having taken no hearts wins the entire pool ; two having taken none, divide it. If all the players have taken hearts, or if one player has taken all thirteen, the pool remains, and forms a *Jack.* This can be won only by a single player in some subsequent deal taking no hearts, all the others having taken at least one. These jack pools are of course increased thirteen counters every deal until some player wins the whole amount. Some clubs make it a Jack after two players have divided a pool, using the odd counter as a starter. It will be found that natural Jacks occur quite frequently enough without resorting to this expedient.

HOWELL'S SETTLING. The great objection to the method of settling at Sweepstake Hearts is that it makes the game almost entirely one of chance. No matter how good a player one may be, good luck alone will bring success. In a four-handed game it is possible for one player to take in only 58 hearts in 60 deals, and still to be 46 counters behind ; while another player may take in 500 hearts in 60 deals and be 46 counters ahead. It may be claimed that the player who has 46 counters ahead at the end was the better player, because he won ; but most persons will agree that a player who takes in only 58 hearts in 60 deals is a much better player than one who has taken in 500 hearts in the same time.

It was to remedy this defect, and to give skill its proper percentage of value, that Mr. E. C. Howell of Boston proposed the manner of contributing to and dividing the pools which is now known as Howell's Settling.

Each player begins with an equal number of counters, usually 100. At the end of the hand, after the hearts have been counted and announced, each player pays into the pool, for every heart he holds, as many counters as there are players besides himself. For instance : A, B, C and D play. A takes three hearts ; B and C five each, and D none. There being three players besides himself, A puts up three times three, or 9 counters. B and C put up 15 each, and D none ; so that there are 39 in the pool. Each player then takes out of the pool 1 counter for every heart he did *not* hold when the hearts were announced. D, having taken no hearts, gets 13 counters. A, having taken three hearts only, is entitled to 10 counters for the 10 hearts he did not hold, while B and C get 8 each. This exhausts the pool. There are no Jacks in this way of settling.

Matters may be facilitated by having counters of different colours, the white being the unit, and the red representing the number which it will be necessary to pay for one heart. Practice will make the players so familiar with the amount of the various profits or losses that they simply pay or take what is due to them.

The first time this is played it looks like a pretty severe game for a player who takes in a large number of hearts on one deal; but it will be found that he rapidly recovers. During a sitting of any length the player who takes in the smallest number of hearts must be the winner. In the case mentioned in connection with Sweepstake Hearts, in which one player lost 46 counters while another won 46, in 60 deals, the result at Howell's Settling would have been that the player who took in only 58 hearts would be 548 counters ahead instead of losing 46 ; while the one who took in 500 hearts would lose 1220 counters, instead of winning 46.

METHODS OF CHEATING. Under the rule for dealing the cards one at a time, the greek must be very skilful to secure any advantage at Hearts. But when it is the practice to deal the cards three at a time, and four on the last round, it is an easy matter to get four small hearts together on the bottom of the pack. Any person who is observed to hold three or four small hearts every time he deals, should be carefully watched, and it will usually be found that he gathers the small hearts from the hands of the other players while the pool is being divided. Marked cards are of little use to the greek at hearts, because so much depends on what a player holds, and so little on his play.

VARIETIES OF HEARTS.

Before proceeding to suggestions for good play, it will be better to describe some of the variations of the game in common use, because what would be good play in one variation would not be in another.

TWO-HANDED HEARTS. The two players having cut for the deal, thirteen cards are given to each, one at a time, and the remainder of the pack is left on the table, face down. The dealer's adversary, usually called the pone, begins by leading any card he pleases, and the dealer must follow suit if he can, as in the ordinary game. The winner of the trick takes it in, but before leading for the next trick he draws one card from the top of the pack lying on the table, restoring the number of his cards to thirteen. His adversary then draws the next card, and the cards are played and drawn in this manner until the pack is exhausted. The thirteen cards remaining in the hands of the two adversaries are then played, and after the last trick has been won, each turns over his cards and counts the number of hearts he has taken in. The object of the game is to take fewer hearts than your opponent, and the method of settling is either for the greater number to pay the lesser the difference ; or, for the first six hearts taken by the loser to count nothing, but all above six to be paid for. The most popular way is to peg up the difference on a cribbage board, and to settle at the end of the sitting.

THREE-HANDED HEARTS. The deuce of spades is discarded, and seventeen cards are dealt to each player, one at a time, after which the game proceeds in the usual way. There are several methods of settling. Howell's method is undoubtedly the best, but Sweepstakes is very common. An excellent way is for the player who takes the largest number of hearts to pay the two others as many counters as he has hearts in excess of theirs. If two have an equal number, both pay the low man. There are no Jacks.

AUCTION HEARTS. This is usually played by four persons, although five or six may form a table. After the cards have been dealt in the usual way, the player to the left of the dealer examines his cards, and determines which suit he would prefer to play to get clear of. It may be that if the game were to get rid of clubs instead of hearts, his hand would be a very good one , whereas if the suit were to remain hearts it would be a very bad hand. As the pool will contain thirteen counters to a certainty, he can afford to pay something for the better chance he will have to win it if he is allowed to make clubs the suit to be avoided, instead of hearts. He bids whatever amount he is willing to pay for the privilege of changing the suit, without naming the suit he prefers. The next player then has a bid, and so on in turn, the dealer bidding last. There are no second bids.

The player making the highest bid pays into the pool the amount he has bid. He then names the suit to be avoided, and leads for the first trick, regardless of his position with respect to the deal. The dealer's position is a great advantage, on account of its having the last bid.

After the hand is played, those who have taken in any cards of the suit announced to be avoided, pay one counter to the pool for each of them. If any one player gets clear, each of the others having at least one of the tabooed suit, he takes the entire pool. If two get clear, they divide the pool, leaving any odd counter to form the basis of a Jack, as at Sweepstakes. If one player takes all thirteen, it is a Jack; but instead of the next choice being sold to the highest bidder, the one who named the suit on the hand that made the pool a Jack has the choice of suits again for the next deal, and he must select some suit without paying anything further for it, until some player wins what he paid for the choice in the first place. That is, the pool must be won before the choice can be sold again.

The general principle of the game is for the players to combine against the successful bidder, and to spare no effort to prevent him from winning the pool.

SPOT HEARTS. In this variation, when the hearts are announced at the end of the hand, the spots on them are the units of value, the Jack being worth 11, the Queen 12, the King 13, and the Ace 14. This adds nothing to the interest or skill of the game; but rather tends to create confusion and delay, owing to the numerous disputes as to the correctness of the count.

The total to be accounted for in each deal is 104. In settling, the player with the smallest number collects from each of the others the amount they have in excess of his. If two or more players have an equal number, or none at all, they divide the amount collected from each of the others. For instance: Four play, A has 8 points, B 24, C 18, and D 54. As 8 points is the lowest, B pays A 16, C pays him 10, and D pays him 46. If A and B had 8 each, C 32, and D 56, C would pay 24, and D 48; and A-B would divide the amount between them.

The chief variation in play arises from the fact that one who must win a heart trick cannot always afford to play his highest heart as in the ordinary game.

JOKER HEARTS. In this variation, the heart deuce is discarded, and the Joker takes its place. The Joker occupies a position between the Jack and the Ten in value, with the added peculiarity that it cannot be discarded on a plain suit; for if it is, it wins the trick unless there is a higher heart in the same trick. If a player has the Joker dealt to him, his only chance to get rid of it is to play it on a trick in which hearts are led, or to discard it on a plain suit on which some other player has already discarded a higher heart than the Ten. Under such circumstances, the holder of the Joker is allowed to discard it, even if he has one of the suit led, and the Joker being in the trick compels the player who discarded the higher heart to take it in.

In settling, the Joker is worth five counters. If the player to whom it was dealt takes it in, he pays these five counters to the pool. If another player gets the Joker, he must pay the five counters to the player who got rid of it. The remainder of the pool is then divided in the usual way. This is a most exasperating game.

PROGRESSIVE HEARTS. The general arrangements for the players and their positions are exactly the same as those already described in connection with Progressive Euchre. The players at each table cut for the deal, and play begins with the tap of the bell at the head table. Only one deal is played at each table.

There are no counters. At the end of the hand the ladies compare their cards, and the one having the fewer hearts goes to the next higher table. The gentlemen then compare their cards in the same way, so that one lady and one gentleman go up from each table at the end of every hand. They take the seats vacated by those leaving the table they go to. All ties are determined by cutting, those cutting the lower cards going up. In cutting, the ace is low.

Each player is provided with a score card, to which the gold, red and green stars are attached as in Euchre. The gold stars are given to those at the head table who have the fewest hearts. Those moving from other tables receive red stars; and those taking in the most hearts at the booby table receive green stars. Prizes are given to the ladies and gentlemen having the greatest number of each variety of star; but the same player cannot win two prizes. If there is a tie in one class, the number of other stars must decide; equal numbers of gold being decided by the majority of red on the same card; red ties, by the greater number of gold; and green ties by the fewest number of gold stars.

HEARTSETTE. Heartsette differs from hearts only in the addition of a widow. When four play, the spade deuce is deleted; twelve cards are given to each player, and the three remaining form the widow, which is left face downward in the centre of the table. When any other number play, the full pack is used. If there are three players, three cards are left for the widow: two cards are left when five play, and four when six play. The player winning the first trick takes in the widow, with any hearts it may contain. He is entitled to look at these cards, but must not show or name them to any other player. The game then proceeds in the usual way. Payments are made to the pool for all hearts taken in, and the pool is then won, divided, or remains to form a Jack, just as at Sweepstake Hearts. The chief difference in the game is that the other players do not know whether the winner of the first trick is loaded or not, and he is the only player who knows how many or what hearts are still to be played.

SUGGESTIONS FOR GOOD PLAY.

A good player, after sorting his hand, carefully estimates its possibilities. The hand may be such that it is evidently impossible to avoid taking some hearts. The player must then decide whether he will play to give each of the others hearts, or will take them all himself. If he succeeds in either object he has a chance to win back his money in the ensuing Jack. In deciding on his chances to get clear without taking a single heart, the player must first consider the advisability of beginning with a heart, or with a plain suit. If hearts, he should know the probability of the heart he leads not winning the trick; if a plain suit, he should know the probability of the suit going round one or more times without hearts being discarded on it, especially if he intends to lead high cards. These chances must then be balanced one against the other and the more favourable selected.

LEADING HEARTS ORIGINALLY. When your hearts are so small as to be absolutely safe, such as the 7 5 3 2, it might be supposed that the best play would be to lead them at once, in order to get a large number of hearts out of your way. But with such cards it is usually much better play, unless you have a very dangerous hand in plain suits, to reserve these small hearts until you have a more definite idea, from the fall of the cards, to whom you are giving them. Such cards are particularly useful for getting rid of the lead at dangerous stages in the end-game.

When the plain-suit cards are high or dangerous, but the hearts are reasonably safe, it is usually better to lead the hearts, and to continue leading them every time you get in. By following these tactics it is quite possible for you to take almost every trick in the plain suits, and yet to win the pool by rapidly exhausting the hearts.

If you lead the ♡ 4, the only chance for it to win is that one player has no hearts, and that the 2 and 3 are divided. The odds against this combination of circumstances will vary with the number of hearts you hold with the 4, but may be generally stated on the average as about 50 to 1. It is usually considered a safer lead than a high card of a plain suit, even if you have only three of the suit.

If your only heart is the 5, and you propose to lead it, the chances that the 2, 3, and 4 are not each in separate hands are about 19 in 25, or 19 to 6 against it, which is about 3 to 1. If you lead the 5, the odds against your winning the trick decrease as the number of hearts you hold with the 5 increases. If you have four hearts, the 5 being the lowest, the odds against its winning the trick, if you lead it, are about 29 to 11. If you have eight hearts, the 5 being the lowest, it is about an even chance. If your only heart is the 6, it is about an even chance that it will win the trick; but the odds against you increase rapidly with the number of additional hearts that you hold. If you propose to lead the 7, the chances that it will win the trick are 2 to 1 under the most favourable circumstances, which are when it is your only heart. These odds against you increase rapidly with the number of additional hearts that you hold.

LEADING PLAIN SUITS ORIGINALLY. It will often happen that you will have to decide between the lead of a comparatively dangerous heart and a risky plain suit. Your knowledge of probabilities should enable you to select the safer course. The odds against getting a heart on the first round of a plain suit depend upon how many cards of the suit you hold. If you lead an Ace, or any card which is sure to win the trick, the odds against your getting a heart on it are as the following :—

If you have	4	cards of the suit,	22 to 1.
"	5	"	15 to 1.
"	6	"	7 to 1.
"	7	"	4 to 1.
"	8	"	2 to 1.

These odds may be slightly increased by taking into account the fact that players who cannot follow suit do not always discard hearts, having perhaps more dangerous cards to get rid of.

The odds against a suit going round a second time may be influenced by the cards played to the first round; but it sometimes happens that you have to calculate in advance for two rounds of a suit, regardless of the cards that may be played by others. This is especially the case when you fear that the suit will be led to you, and you have such cards as must win two rounds. If you have 4 cards of the suit the odds *against* your getting a heart in two rounds are 2 to 1. The odds *in favour* of your getting a heart in two rounds are :—

If you have	5	cards of the suit,	4 to 3.
"	6	"	2 to 1.
"	7	"	6 to 1.

As an example of the value of a thorough knowledge of these odds to a careful player, suppose he had to win two rounds of a plain suit, of which he held six cards ; or to lead the ♡ 7, having three higher. The suit would be the better play, because it takes in only one heart, while the lead of the heart might take in four.

The following table shows the exact number of times in 1,000 deals that a heart would probably be discarded on a plain suit led, according to the number of cards in the suit held by the leader, and the number of times the suit was led :

Cards held by the leader.	1, 2, 3, 4	5	6	7	8
Times hearts will be discarded :—					
On first round...........	44	63	122	200	315
On second round	358	430	659	857	1000
On third round..........	842	1000	1000	1000	1000

This shows that 158 times in 1,000, when the leader has 1, 2, 3, or 4 cards of the suit, it will go round three times, because 158 is the balance necessary to bring our last figure, 842, up to 1,000. Reducing this to a small fraction, the odds are about 5⅛ to 1 that a suit will not go round three times without affording to some player the chance of discarding hearts on it. This calculation shows the hopeless nature of all hands that contain at least three cards of each suit, unless the smallest card in every suit is below a 6 ; for if any one of the suits is led three times, it is even betting that you will have to win the third round, and 5⅛ to 1 that you get a heart on it if you do.

PLAIN-SUIT LEADS. The favourite lead with most heart players is a singleton ; or, failing that, a two-card suit. This is a mistake, unless the singleton is a high card ; for if the adversaries are sharp players they will at once suspect the nature of the lead, and carefully avoid the suit. But if you wait until some other player opens the suit, it will very probably be led twice in succession. The best original plain-suit lead is one in which you are moderately long, but have small cards enough to be safe, and from which you can lead intermediate cards which probably will not win the first trick.

A very little experience at Hearts will convince any one that it is best, in plain suits, to play out the high cards first. This agrees with the theory of probabilities ; for while the odds are 22 to 1 against your getting a heart on the first round of a plain suit of which you have 4 cards, the odds are only 2 to 1 against it on the second round, and on the third they are 5⅛ to 1 in favour of it. Accordingly, on the first round most players put up their highest card of the suit led, no matter what their position with regard to the leader ; but in so doing, they often run needless risks. The

object in Sweepstake Hearts is to take none, and the most successful players will be found to be those who play consistently with
the greatest odds in their favour for taking none.

Suppose that you hold such a suit as A 10 9 7 4 2. This is a safe
suit ; because it is very improbable that you can be compelled to
take a trick in it. The best lead from such a suit is the 10 or 9.
If the suit is led by any other player, the same card should be
played, unless you are fourth hand, and have no objection to the
lead. This avoids the risk, however slight, of getting a heart on
the first round, which would be entailed by playing the ace. In
Sweepstake Hearts it is a great mistake to play the high cards of a
suit in which you are safe ; for no matter how small the risk, it is
an unnecessary one. In the case we are considering, when you
have six cards of the suit, the odds are 7 to 1 against your getting
a heart if you play the ace first round. That is to say, you will
probably lose one pool out of every eight if you play it. Take the
greatest odds in your favour, when you have only four cards of a
suit ; they are 22 to 1 against your getting a heart the first round,
so that you would lose by it only once in 23 times. But this is a
heavy percentage against you if you are playing with those who
do not run such risks, for you give up every chance you might
otherwise have in 5 pools out of every 110.

When you have a dangerous hand in hearts, but one absolutely
safe long suit, it is often good play to begin with your safe suit,
retaining any high cards you may have in other suits in order to
get the lead as often as possible for the purpose of continuing
your safe suit, which will usually result in one or more of the
other players getting loaded.

When you have at least three of each plain suit it is obvious
that you cannot hope for any discards, and that you must take into
account the probability of having to win the third round of one or
more suits, with the accompanying possibility of getting hearts at
the same time. If you have the lead, this probability must be
taken into account before any of the other players show their
hands, and as it may be set down as about 5½ to 1 that you will
get a heart, any better chance that the hand affords should be
taken advantage of.

It will often occur that a player's attention must be so concen-
trated on getting clear himself that he has no opportunity to
scheme for " loading " the others. But if it unfortunately happens
that he is compelled to take in one or more hearts, he should at
once turn his attention to taking them all, or to loading the
other players, with a view to making a Jack of the pool. Should
he succeed in either object, he has another chance for his money.

It is usually bad policy to return the suit opened by the original
leader. He has picked that out as his safest suit, and although he
may be the only one safe in it, by continuing it you are reducing

your chances to two players, when you might share them with all three.

FOLLOWING SUIT.   When a player is not the original leader, his policy becomes defensive ; for, as the first player is plotting to give hearts to every one but himself, each of the others must be a prospective victim, and should do his best to avoid the traps prepared by the one who plans the opening of the hand.

When you are second or third player, the first time a suit is led, it is usually best to play your highest card, unless you are safe in the suit, or have so many that there is danger of getting a heart, even on the first round.   As fourth player, you should always play your highest card, unless there is already a heart in the trick, or some decided disadvantage in the lead.   The risks you run in playing high cards while following suit must be judged by the same probabilities that we examined in considering the original lead. The fact that one or more players have already followed suit, and perhaps the cards they have played, may enable you to arrive at a still closer estimate of your chances.   It is generally conceded that the odds against a player who holds up on the first round are about 1 to 11.   That is to say, in 12 pools, he will sacrifice his chances of one simply by holding up.

After one or two tricks have been played, the conditions may be such that it becomes necessary to hold up, in order to win the second round.   This is especially the case after you have been loaded, and are anxious to keep a certain player out of the lead. For an example see Illustrative Hand No. 4, in which **Y** holds up the ◇ King to keep A from getting in and leading another round of hearts.   In the same hand Z tries hard to make the pool a Jack by holding up the ♣ Q.   Had not A been entirely safe in diamonds the stratagem would have succeeded.

In following suit it is important to keep count of the cards played, in order to avoid the unwitting lead of a suit of which the other players have none.   The suits that need close watching are those in which you have nothing smaller than a six or eight, You should be careful to note which player appears to have the smaller cards, after the suit has been led once or twice, and be on the watch to take the lead away from him in other suits if you can, or he may load you by leading the small cards of your dangerous suit, in which he is safe.   When this danger is apparent, it is best to retain, until the second round, such high cards as Kings and Queens of the suits led.   Even if you have four of the suit, you run only a 2 to 1 risk in winning the second round instead of the first, as against a certainty that you will be out of the pool at once if the dangerous player gets the lead.   For an example of this, see B's play in Illustrative Hand No. 2.

Where you have a certain safe card, and others of another suit not absolutely safe, it is better to keep the safe card, in order to be sure of getting rid of the lead if you are put in on your dangerous suit.

In following suit, the most annoying hand that one can hold is one containing at least three cards of each suit, none of them below a 6. There is no hope of a discard, unless two players make a fight in some one suit, which they lead four or five times in order to load each other, regardless of the escape of the other players. This very seldom occurs, and never among good players. With such a hand escape is almost impossible, and it is usually best to make the losses as small as possible. Many good players. with such a hand, will deliberately take in hearts on the plain suits, hoping to escape with only one or two in each trick, instead of having to carry the whole load by getting into the lead at the end. It should never be forgotten that when you must inevitably take some hearts it is cheaper to take them in on plain suits than to win heart tricks.

CONTROL OF THE LEAD. One of the strongest points in good heart play is the proper control of the lead at certain times. A player whose hand contains no commanding cards, and who is unable to do anything but follow suit on the first two or three rounds, will often find himself compelled to win one of the later rounds with a small card, taking in one or two hearts with it ; and this misfortune usually overtakes him because a certain player gets into the lead at a critical period of the hand. If he sees the impending danger, and has K, Q or J of a suit led, he will not give up his high card, even if the ace is played to the trick ; but will retain it in order to prevent the possibility of the dangerous player getting into the lead on the second round of the suit. In doing this, he of course decreases the odds against his getting hearts, by deliberately winning the second round. But 2 to 1 in his favour is a much better chance than the certainty, almost, that he will be loaded if a particular player is allowed the opportunity to lead a certain suit again. See B's play in Illustrative Hand No 2, and Y's in No 4.

A player may have no desire to prevent any particular adversary from getting the lead ; but may be anxious simply to carry out a certain line of play. In order to do this it may be essential that he should have some direction of the course of the hand. This is impossible if his play is confined to following suit helplessly, whatever is led. He must be able to assume the lead himself in order so to change the course of the play as to better suit his game.

Let us suppose that he has a dangerous hand in plain suits, but is safe in hearts, and decides that his best chance is to lead hearts at every opportunity ; or that he has a certain safe suit which it is manifestly to his advantage to have led as often as possible. The other players, being the ones who are to suffer from this line of play, will of course prevent it if possible ; and in order to carry out the plan in spite of their opposition, it will be necessary for the individual player to gain the lead a certain number of times, and so force his game upon them.

Again, a player may know that he can load a certain adversary if he can get in and lead a certain suit or card ; or he may know that by giving one player the lead, that player can load another. In such cases commanding cards must be held or retained, in order to give the player a certain control of the lead.

When a player is attempting to take all thirteen hearts, the control of the lead, especially in the end game, is very important ; because the design of each of the other players will be to get the lead into some other hand, in the hope that they may load the player having it, and so at least divide the pool.

THE DISCARD. One of the most important elements in heart play is the discard. The beginner is too apt to discard hearts at every opportunity ; but a little experience will teach him that even a 3 in a plain suit may be a better card to part with.

The most important thing in discarding is to reduce the odds against your winning the pool. Let us suppose that you have the A K Q of a plain suit. It is 5½ to 1 that you get a heart if this suit is led a third time. If you can get a discard, the odds are at once reduced to 2 to 1 in your favour, that being the probability that you will escape, even if you have to win two rounds. This is a very large percentage, and should never be lost sight of. If you have a choice between two discards, one being from the K Q J 2 of hearts, and the other from the K Q J of a plain suit, select the plain suit. You can improve your chances little or none in the hearts, while you not only bring the odds to your side in the plain suit, but secure a chance of discarding on the third round of it.

Following the same principle, it is evidently good play to discard from a suit which has been led once or twice, if you have a dangerous card or cards in it. Even if you have a safe tenace in a suit, such as 4 and 2, the 5 and 3 being still out somewhere, it is better to discard from it if there is the slightest danger of your getting the lead. Tenaces are only safe when led up to.

In **Howell's settling**, the object is not so much to load the others as to escape yourself. It is never advisable to attempt to take all thirteen hearts, because there are no Jacks ; but there are many cases in which it is better deliberately to take three or four, in order to avoid the chance of taking six or eight. For an example of these tactics adopted by two playes, see Illustrative Hand, No. 3. On the same principle, there are often cases in which it is advisable to take a trick with one heart in it, in order to get rid of a dangerous card, which might bring you in several hearts later on. The general principles of leading and discarding are the same as in Sweepstake Hearts ; but it is not necessary to take such desperate chances to escape entirely.

THREE-HANDED HEARTS is more difficult to play than any other form of the game, partly because there are so many rounds of each suit, and partly because the moment one player refuses, the exact cards of that suit in the two other players' hands are known to each of them.

There is usually a great deal of cross-fighting in the three-handed game, during which one player escapes by getting numerous discards. When all three have refused, each a different suit, the end game becomes a question of generalship, and the preservation of one or more commanding cards, with which to control and place the lead, is usually the key to the situation. A player who has no high cards for the end game, unless he is quite safe, is almost certain to be loaded in the last few tricks.

TWO-HANDED HEARTS. Before opening the hand, the player should carefully consider what suits are safe and what are dangerous. It is usually best to preserve the safe suits and to lead the dangerous ones, which you should clear your hand of, if possible. It is a great advantage to have a missing suit, and equally disadvantageous to have a number of a suit of which your adversary is probably clear. If a card of a missing suit is drawn, it is usually best to lead it at once, so as to keep the suit clear ; but in so doing, be careful first to place the card among the others in the hand, or your adversary will detect that it is a missing suit.

The lead is a disadvantage if you have safe hearts ; but toward the end of the stock, from which cards are drawn, it is an advantage to have commanding cards, with which you can assume the lead if necessary.

There is some finesse in determining whether or not to change the suit often in the leads. If you have a better memory than your adversary, it may be well to change often ; but if not, it may assist you to keep at one suit until afraid to lead it again.

In Two-Handed Hearts, keeping count of the cards is the most important matter, because the real play comes after the stock is exhausted, and the moment that occurs you should know every card in your adversary's hand. The exact number of each suit should be a certainty, if not the exact rank of the cards. Until you can depend on yourself for this, you are not a good player. The last thirteen tricks are usually a problem in double-dummy ; but the advantage will always be found to be with the player who has carefully prepared himself for the final struggle by preserving certain safe suits, and getting rid of those in which it became evident that his adversary had the small and safe cards.

Some very pretty positions arise in the end game, it being often possible to foresee that four or five tricks must be played in a certain manner in order to ensure the lead being properly placed at the end, so that the odd hearts may be avoided.

AUCTION HEARTS. The cards having been cut and dealt, the player to the left of the dealer, whom we shall call A, examines his hand, and determines which suit he would prefer to play to get clear of. Let us suppose his hand to consist of the ♡ A K 8 ; ♣ J 6 5 4 3 2 ; ◇ K 4 ; and the ♠ 7 3. If the suit remains hearts, he is almost certain to take in a number ; but if it is changed to clubs, he is almost as certain of getting clear. The hand is not absolutely safe, as hearts might be led two or three times before the clubs in the other hands were exhausted by the original leader, whose game would be to lead small clubs. As the pool will contain thirteen counters to a certainty, he can afford to bid in proportion to his chances of winning it for the privilege of making clubs the suit to be avoided, instead of hearts.

It might be assumed, if the odds were 10 to 1 that the player would get clear if the suit were clubs, that therefore he could afford to bid ten times the amount of the pool, or 130, for his chance. Theoretically this is correct, but if he should lose one such pool, he would have to win ten others to get back his bid alone, to say nothing of the amounts he would lose by paying his share in pools won by others. Let us suppose him to win his share, one-fourth of all the pools. While he is winning the ten pools necessary to repair his single loss, he has to stand his share of the losses in the thirty others, which would average about 128 counters. This must show us that even if a player has a 10 to 1 chance in his favour, he must calculate not only on losing that chance once in eleven times, but must make provision for the amounts he will lose in other pools. Experience shows that a bid of 25 would be about the amount a good player would make on such a hand as we are considering, if the pool were not a Jack, and he had first say.

The next player, Y, now examines his hand. Let us suppose that he finds ♡ 6 4 3 ; ♣ A K 10 ; ◇ 8 7 5 3 ; ♠ 6 5 4. If the first bidder is offering on clubs, it is evident that he will lead them, as the successful bidder has the original lead in Auction Hearts ; and it is equally evident that if he does so, a player with A K 10 will have to pay for most of the pool. If any of the other suits is the one bid on, B has as good a chance for the pool as any one, at least to divide it. With two men still to bid, a good player would probably make himself safe by shutting out A's bid, probably offering 26.

Let us suppose B then to examine his hand, finding ♡ J 10 ; ♣ Q 9 8 7 ; ◇ A 10 9 ; ♠ 10 9 8 2. Being unsafe in everything, he passes, and practically submits to his fate, his only hope being that the pool will result in a Jack. Z then examines his hand, finding ♡ Q 9 7 5 2 ; ♣ none ; ◇ Q J 6 2 ; ♠ A K Q J. He sees at once that on spades he would lose everything, and on diamonds he would have a very poor chance. On clubs the result would depend on how often spades were led. In hearts, he has a very good hand, especially as he has a missing suit to discard in. As he is the last bidder he can make sure of the choice for 27, which he bids, and pays into the pool. The result of the play is given in Illustrative Hand No. 4. (As the cards happen to lie, had A been the successful bidder and made it clubs, Z would have won the pool.)

ILLUSTRATIVE HANDS.

No. 1. Sweepstake Hearts. A leads for first trick.				TRICK	*No. 2.* Sweepstake Hearts. A leads for first trick.			
A	Y	B	Z		A	Y	B	Z
10 ♠	Q ♠	8 ♠	K ♠	I	♣ A	♣ K	♣ 10	♣ Q
♣ J	♣ A	♣ 4	♣ K	2	♣ 5	♣ 2	♣ 9	♣ J
6 ◊	A ◊	J ◊	Q ◊	3	10 ◊	J ◊	9 ◊	A ◊
5 ◊	K ◊	10 ◊	9 ◊	4	Q ◊	8 ◊	K ◊	4 ◊
4 ◊	3 ◊	2 ◊	8 ◊	5	2 ♠	J ♠	A ♠	9 ♠
♣ 9	♣ 7	♣ 3	♣ Q	6	Q ♠	10 ♠	K ♠	8 ♠
♣ 6	♣ 5	♣ 2	♣ 10	7	♡ A	7 ◊	3 ◊	♡ Q
3 ♠	6 ♠	4 ♠	J ♠	8	♡ 10	♡ 4	♡ 3	♡ 5
2 ♠	5 ♠	♡ K	9 ♠	9	♣ 4	♡ K	♣ 6	♣ 7
♡ A	♡ Q	♡ 10	♡ 5	10	♡ 9	7 ♠	♡ J	5 ♠
♡ 7	♡ J	♡ 9	7 ♠	11	♡ 7	♡ 2	♣ 8	♡ 8
♡ 6	♡ 8	♡ 4	♣ 8	12	♡ 6	6 ♠	6 ◊	4 ♠
A ♠	♡ 2	♡ 3	7 ◊	13	♣ 3	5 ◊	2 ◊	3 ♠

A 4	Y 6	B 2	Z I		A 4	Y 5	B o	Z 4

Making it a Jack.   B wins the Pool.

No. 1. 2nd Trick. Z sees that with such a hand escape is impossible. As his chief danger is in being loaded with hearts at the end, he clears his hand as rapidly as possible. *9th Trick.* The ♠ A being held up, it looks as if A were safe in that suit with A 5 2. If Z now leads the ♡ 5, and A gets into the lead, returning the spade, Z must take every other trick. *10th Trick.* If Z now leads ♠ 7, he loads A; but if his ♡ 5 should win the next trick he will take all the rest of the hearts, Y and B dividing the pool. If he leads the ♡ 5 first he cannot get more than four hearts, and the other players will inevitably make a Jack of it. *11th Trick.* Y sees that if he underplays the 7 led, B will win the pool, as he has nothing but hearts, A having only one more. He keeps A out of the lead by winning two rounds, so as to be sure of loading B, making it a Jack. The ending is very well played.

No. 2. A has an even chance to escape, and it is better for him to be third or fourth player in hearts than to lead them. *3rd Trick.* B sees from the fall of the clubs that Y has no more, and that A is safe in them and will lead them again; so he holds up ◊ K to keep A out of the lead. *7th Trick.* As A's hand can now be counted to contain either the 7 4 3 of clubs and four dangerous hearts, or the 4 3 of clubs and five hearts, B's game is clearly to lead diamonds, in order to load Y and Z. His only dangerous card, the ♡ J, will go on the next round of spades, which must be led again in the next two or three tricks.

No. 3. Howell's Settling. Z dealt, and A leads for first trick.				TRICK	*No. 4.* Auction Hearts. A, the successful bidder, names Hearts.			
A	Y	B	Z		A	Y	B	Z
10 ◊	J ◊	9 ◊	**K ◊**	I	♡ 5	♡ 8	♡ 6	**♡ J**
7 ◊	6 ◊	8 ◊	**Q ◊**	2	Q ◊	4 ◊	8 ◊	**A ◊**
♣ 4	♣ 9	♣ J	**♣ A**	3	J ◊	**K ◊**	7 ◊	10 ◊
♣ 2	♣ 8	♣ 5	**♣ K**	4	**A ♠**	7 ♠	6 ♠	10 ♠
J ♠	8 ♠	K ♠	**A ♠**	5	♡ 7	**♡ A**	♡ 4	♡ 10
5 ♠	7 ♠	**Q ♠**	10 ♠	6	**K ♠**	3 ♠	5 ♠	9 ♠
4 ♠	**6 ♠**	3 ♠	2 ♠	7	♡ Q	**♡ K**	♡ 3	♣ 9
♡ 5	♡ 3	**♡ 8**	♡ 4	8	♡ 9	♣ J	♣ 10	**♣ Q**
♡ A	♡ J	♡ 7	5 ◊	9	**Q ♠**	♣ 6	4 ♠	8 ♠
♡ 9	♡ 2	**♡ K**	♣ Q	10	**J ♠**	♣ 5	♣ A	2 ♠
A ◊	**♡ 10**	♡ 6	9 ♠	11	6 ◊	♣ 4	5 ◊	**9 ◊**
4 ◊	♣ 3	♡ Q	♣ 10	12	2 ◊	♣ 3	**♣ K**	♣ 8
2 ◊	**♣ 7**	3 ◊	♣ 6	13	♡ 2	♣ 2	**3 ◊**	♣ 7

A 3   Y 2   B 7   Z 1
Z wins 9; Y 5; A 1; B loses 15.

A o   Y 7   B 1   Z 5
A wins the pool.

No. 3. A begins with the intermediate cards of his safe suit. *8th Trick.* Y is afraid to lead away from his club tenace, because it might be at once led back to him. *9th Trick.* Z seizes this opportunity to get rid of the very dangerous ◊ 5. If A does not play the ♡ A now, it is quite possible that he will take every trick, except one in diamonds. *10th Trick.* If A leads the ◊ 2, and hearts are led again, he must take all the remaining hearts. By taking three at once he can escape the rest. B sees that if he passes this trick A will at once lead the ◊ 2, and he will take all the remaining hearts; so he takes these three and throws the lead to Y, who has no chance to injure him. ***11th Trick.*** Z keeps two clubs, hoping that if Y gets in and leads clubs, B may discard a diamond instead of a heart, in which case Z would get clear.

No. 4. A, with his dangerous suit of spades, clears up the hearts at once. ***6th Trick.*** The second round of spades betrays A's dangerous suit to the other players. ***7th Trick.*** A must risk the King and 3 being divided, for if they are in one hand nothing will save him. Z keeps ◊ 9 and ♣ Q in order to be sure of getting a lead, as he is the only player who can load A by putting him in on spades at the end making him take in his own hearts. ***8th Trick.*** B cannot risk playing the high clubs while there is any chance for him to win the pool. He can count A to be safe in diamonds, with two hearts and two spades. ***10th Trick.*** A clears his hand of the very dangerous spade before leading his tenace in diamonds. ***12th Trick.*** A will not give up the heart until he is sure that B has not the ♣ 7.

Text Books. There are at present only two text-books on the game ; *Foster on Hearts,* and *Hearts and Heartsette.*

SLOBBERHANNES.

Cards. Slobberhannes is played with a Euchre pack, thirty-two cards, all below the Seven being deleted. The cards rank : A K Q J 10 9 8 7, the ace being the highest both in cutting and in play. There is no trump suit.

Counters. Each player is provided with ten counters, and points are marked by placing these counters in the pool. The player who first loses his ten counters also loses the game. If stakes are played for, counters of a different colour must be provided, and the player losing the game must pay as many counters to each of the others as they have points still in front of them. One player is usually the banker, and sells and redeems all money counters. The others are re-distributed at the end of each game.

Players. Any number from four to seven may play ; but the two black Sevens must be deleted if there are more than four players. When seven play, the dealer takes no cards. All the preliminaries of seats, cards and deal are settled as at Hearts.

Dealing. The entire pack is distributed, the dealer giving each player in rotation two or three cards in each round. No trump is turned.   All irregularities in the deal are governed by the same laws as at Hearts ; but a misdeal does not lose the deal under any circumstances.   The same dealer must deal again.

Objects of the Game.   The object in Slobberhannes is to avoid taking either the first or the last trick, or any trick containing the Queen of clubs.   The player who wins any of these loses one point, and if he wins all three of them, he loses an extra point, or four altogether.   The penalty for a revoke is also the loss of a point.

Method of Playing.   The eldest hand begins by leading any card he pleases, and the others must follow suit if they can. The highest card played, if of the suit led, wins the trick, and the winner takes it in and leads for the next trick.   The player winning the first trick must pay for it immediately, to avoid disputes. The tricks which are neither the first nor the last have no value, unless they contain the club Queen, which must be paid for as soon as it is taken in.

There is a good deal of play in manœuvring to get rid of cards which might win the last trick, or which would take in the club Queen.   The Ace and King of clubs are of course dangerous cards, and unless the player holding them has small cards enough to make him safe in that suit, he should be on the alert for opportunities to discard.

POLIGNAC.

QUATRE-VALETS, OR FOUR JACKS.

Cards and Players.   When Polignac is played by four persons, a Piquet pack is used, and eight cards are dealt to each player, 3-2-3 at a time.   When five play, the two black Sevens are deleted, and six cards are given to each player.   When six play, each receives five cards.   When seven play, the dealer takes no cards.   In France, the cards usually rank as in Écarté ; K Q J A 10 9 8 7 ; but in England and America it is more usual to preserve the order in Piquet, A K Q J 10 9 8 7.   There is no trump suit. All the preliminaries are settled as at Hearts or Slobberhannes,

Counters.   Each player is provided with ten or twenty counters, as may be agreed upon, and the player first losing his counters loses the game, and pays to each of the others any stake that may have been previously agreed upon, usually a counter for each point they have still to go when he is decavé.

Objects of the Game. The object of the game is to avoid winning any trick containing a Jack, and especially the Jack of spades, which is called **Polignac.** The moment any player wins a trick containing a Jack, he pays one counter into the pool. If he takes in Polignac, he pays two counters. The eldest hand begins by leading any card he pleases, and the others must follow suit if they can. The highest card played, if of the suit led, wins the trick, and the winner leads for the next trick. If a player has none of the suit led he may discard anything he pleases.

The game is sometimes varied by adding a **general,** or **capot.** Any player who thinks he can win all the tricks announces capot before the first card is led. If he is successful he loses nothing; but each of the others must pay five counters into the pool, one for each Jack, and one extra for Polignac. If the capot player fails to win every trick, each player pays for whatever jacks he has taken in.

ENFLÉ,

OR SCHWELLEN.

When Enflé is played by four persons, the Piquet pack of thirty-two cards is used. If there are more than four players, sufficient cards are added to give eight to each person. The rank of the cards and all other preliminaries are the same as at Hearts. There is no trump suit.

The cards are dealt 3-2-3 at a time. The eldest hand leads any card he pleases, and the others must follow suit if they can. If all follow suit, the highest card played wins the trick, which is turned face down, and the cards in it are dead. The winner leads for the next trick, and so on. But if any player is unable to follow suit, he is not allowed to discard, but must immediately gather up the cards already played, and take them into his own hand with the cards originally dealt to him. The players following the one who renounces to the suit led do not play to the trick at all; but wait for him to lead for the next trick. Should any player fail to follow suit on the next trick, or on any subsequent trick, he gathers the cards already played, takes them into his hand and leads for the next trick. The play is continued in this manner until some player gets rid of all his cards, and so wins the game.

Enflé is usually played for a pool, to which each player contributes an equal amount before play begins. The game requires considerable skill and memory to play it well, it being very important to remember the cards taken in hand by certain players, and those which are in the tricks turned down.

THE LAWS OF HEARTS.

1. Formation of table. Those first in the room have the pre-ference. If more than the necessary number assemble, the choice shall be determined by cutting, those cutting the lowest cards having the right to play. Six persons is the largest number that can play at one table. The player cutting the lowest card has the deal.

2. In cutting, the Ace is low. Players cutting cards of equal value, cut again. All must cut from the same pack, and any person exposing more than one card must cut again. Drawing cards from an outspread pack is equivalent to cutting.

3. A complete Heart pack consists of fifty-two cards, which rank in the following order :—A K Q J 10 9 8 7 6 5 4 3 2, the Ace being highest in play. In Three-Handed Hearts, the spade deuce is thrown out. In Five-Handed, both the black deuces are laid aside. In Six-Handed, all four deuces are discarded. In Joker Hearts the heart deuce is replaced by the Joker.

4. When two packs are used, the player next but one on the dealer's left must collect and shuffle the cards for the next deal, placing them on his right. The dealer has the privilege of shuffling last.

5. The dealer must present the pack to his right-hand adversary to be cut. Not less than four cards shall constitute a cut.

6. In case of any confusion or exposure of the cards in cutting, or in reuniting them after cutting, the pack must be shuffled and cut again.

7. If the dealer re-shuffles the cards after they have been properly cut, or looks at the bottom card, he loses his deal.

8. After the cards have been cut, the dealer must distribute them one at a time to each player in rotation, beginning at his left, and continuing until the pack is exhausted ; or in Two-Handed Hearts, until each player has thirteen.

9. The deal passes to the left.

10. There must be a new deal by the same dealer if the pack is proved to be incorrect, either during the deal or during the play of a hand ; or if any card is faced in the pack, or is found to be so marked or mutilated that it can be named. In the last case a new pack must be used.

11. If a card is exposed during the deal, the player to whom it is dealt may demand a new deal, provided he has not touched any of his cards. If the deal stands, the exposed card cannot be called.

12. Any one dealing out of turn may be stopped before the last card is dealt. After that the deal must stand, and the packs, if changed, must so remain.

13. It is a misdeal : If the dealer omits to have the pack cut, and

the error is discovered before the last card is dealt ; or if he deals a card incorrectly, and fails to remedy it before dealing another ; or if he counts the cards on the table, or those remaining in the pack ; or if it is discovered before all have played to the first trick that any player has not his proper number of cards, the pack being perfect.

14. A misdeal loses the deal unless one of the other players has touched his cards, or in any way interrupted the dealer.

15. If, after the first trick is played to, any two players are found to have more or less than their correct number of cards, the pack being perfect, the one having less shall draw from the hand of the one having more, and each shall pay a forfeit of five counters into the pool.

16. If a player omits to play to any trick, and plays to the following one, he shall not be allowed to correct the error ; but shall be compelled to take in the last trick, with whatever hearts it may contain.

17. Should a player be found during or at the end of a hand to be a card short, all the others having the right number, and all having played to the first trick, he shall be compelled to take in the last trick.

18. If a player leads or plays two cards to a trick, he must indicate the one intended, and leave the other face up on the table. Any card exposed, except in the proper course of play, or any card named by the player holding it, must be left face up on the table.

19. A player must lead or play any exposed card when called upon to do so by any other player, provided he can do so without revoking. He cannot be prevented from playing an exposed card, and if he can so get rid of it, no penalty remains.

20. If a player leads out of turn, a suit may be called from him when it is next his proper turn to lead. This penalty can be enforced only by the player on his right. If he has none of the suit called, or if all have played to the false lead, no penalty can be enforced. If all have not played to the false lead, the cards can be taken back, and are not exposed cards.

21. If the third hand plays before the second, the fourth hand may demand that the card be taken back, and may call upon the third hand to play the highest card he has of the suit ; or may call upon him not to discard hearts. If the fourth plays before the third, the second player may demand the penalty.

22. The first player to any trick having led, the others must follow suit if they can. Should a player revoke, and discover the error before the trick in which it occurs has been turned and quitted, he may amend his play, and the card played in error becomes an exposed card. Any who have played after him may withdraw their cards and substitute others, the cards first played not being exposed.

23.   If the revoke is discovered during the play of the hand, the hand must be played out, and at the end the revoking player must pay all losses in that hand.   Should the revoking player win the pool himself, he must pay to the pool thirteen counters and leave them for a Jack.   Should he divide it, he must pay the other winner six counters, and leave up seven for a Jack.

24.   Should two or more players revoke in the same hand, each must pay the entire losses in the hand, as if he were alone in error ; so that if two should revoke, and a·third win the pool, he would receive twenty-six counters, instead of thirteen.   In Auction Hearts the revoking player must pay the amount of the bid in addition.

25.   The claimant of a revoke may search all the tricks at the end of a hand.   The revoke is established if the accused player mixes the cards before the claimants have time to examine them.

26.   A revoke must be claimed before the tricks have been mixed, preparatory to shuffling for the next deal.

27.   If a player is lawfully called upon to lead a certain suit, or to play the highest of it, and unnecessarily fails to comply, he is liable to the penalties for a revoke.

28.   Any trick once turned and quitted must not again be seen until the hand is played.   Any player violating this rule is subject to the same penalties as for a lead out of turn.

29.   In settling at the end of the hand, the player having taken no hearts, [each of the others having taken at least one,] wins the pool.   Two players having taken none, the other two having each at least one, divide it, the odd counter remaining until the next pool.   Three players having taken none, the thirteen counters remain in the pool, forming a Jack, which can be won only by one player taking no hearts, each of the others having taken at least one.   During the time the Jack is played for, and until it is won, each player must add to the pool by paying for the hearts he takes in each hand.

30.   In Auction Hearts, the player to the left of the dealer has the first bid, the dealer the last, and there is no second bid.

THE BÉZIQUE FAMILY.

This family includes three of our most popular games ; Bézique itself, Binocle, and Sixty-Six. These are all comparatively modern games, but are descended from very old stock, the best known of the ancestors being Marriage, Matrimony, and Cinq-Cents. The etymology of the word Bézique is very much disputed. Some claim that it is from the Spanish basa, afterwards basico, a little kiss ; referring to the union of the spade Queen and the diamond Jack, and the various marriages in the game. This was afterwards Basique, transformed by the French to Bésique, and by the English to Bézique. One English writer thinks the word is from bésaigne, the double-headed axe.

Judging from the rank of the cards, which is peculiar to German games, Bézique may have originated in an attempt to play Binocle with a piquet pack, for Binocle seems to have been originally played with a full pack of fifty-two cards. One German writer says the game is of Swiss origin, and that they probably got it from Spain. In one writer's opinion, the name Binocle, is derived from *bis*, until, and *knochle*, the knuckle, which would imply that the original meaning was, until some one knuckled ; *i. e.*, stopped the game by knocking on the table with his knuckles. This interpretation seems far-fetched, but if correct, it would sustain the opinion that Binocle was derived from the old game of Cinq-Cents, in which the player knocked with his knuckles to announce that he had made enough points to win the game. It is much more probable that the word Binocle is from the Latin *binus*, double, and *oculus*, an eye, meaning to see double ; which may have referred in some way to the double combinations which are frequently seen in the game. Stopping the play is a prominent feature in Sixty-Six, another variation of Bézique, and the connecting link between Binocle and Skat. In Sixty-Six, the combination known as bézique, or binocle, is omitted ; so is the sequence in trumps. Sixty-four-card Binocle is simply Bézique, with a slight difference in the counting value of the various combinations. Sometimes twelve cards are given to each player.

Great confusion seems to have existed when the game of Bézique was introduced to England, in the winter of 1868–9, owing to the fact that so many persons rushed into print with their own private opinions of the rules, which were first given by Dr. Pole, in 1861,

No one knew whether "the last trick" was the absolute last, or the last before the stock was exhausted. Whether the highest or lowest cut dealt was also a matter of dispute. "Cavendish" got both these wrong in the first edition of his "Pocket Guide," but corrected himself without explanation or apology in the second edition. It was then the custom of many players to attach no value to the trump suit until the stock was exhausted; so that until the last eight tricks there was no such thing as trumping a trick in order to win it. Disputes also arose as to counting double combinations, many contending that a double marriage should be as valuable as a double bézique. Time and experience have finally settled all these points, and the rules of the game are now practically uniform in all countries.

BÉZIQUE,

OR SIXTY-FOUR-CARD BINOCLE.

There are two forms of Bézique in common use; the ordinary game, which will be first described, and the variation known as Rubicon Bézique, which is to Bézique proper what Railroad Euchre is to Euchre.

CARDS. Bézique is played with two packs of thirty-two cards each, all below the Seven being deleted, and the two packs being then shuffled together and used as one. It is better to have both packs of the same colour and pattern, but it is not absolutely necessary. The cards rank, A 10 K Q J 9 8 7; the Ace being the highest, both in cutting and in play.

COUNTERS. Special markers are made for scoring at Bézique; but the score may easily be kept by means of counters.

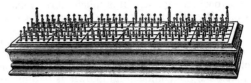

PULL-UP BEZIQUE MARKER.

Each player should be provided with four white, four blue, and one red, together with some special marker, such as a copper cent or a button. The button stands for 500 points, each blue counter for 100, the red for 50, and the white ones for 10 each. At the beginning of the game the counters are placed on the left of the player, and are passed from left to right as the points accrue, exchanging smaller denominations for higher when necessary.

Many persons find it more convenient to peg the game on a pull-up cribbage board, starting at 21, counting each peg as 10 points, and going twice round to the game hole.

STAKES. Bézique is played for so much a game, 1,000 points up; or for so much a point, the score of the loser being deducted from that of the winner.   When a partie of five games is agreed upon, it is usual to have an extra stake upon the odd game, and when three games have been won by the same player, the partie is at an end.   It is usual to count it a double game if the loser has not reached 500 points.

PLAYERS. Bézique is played by two persons, one of whom is known as the *dealer,* and the other as the *pone.* They cut for choice of seats and deal, the player cutting the highest card having the first choice, and electing whether or not to deal himself.   In cutting, the cards rank as in play, and the ace is the highest.   If a player exposes more than one card, he must cut again.

DEALING. The cards are thoroughly shuffled, and presented to the pone to be cut.   At least five cards must be left in each packet.   The cards are then dealt three at a time for the first round, two for the next, and three for the last, each player receiving eight cards.   The seventeenth is then turned up for the trump. If this card is a Seven, the dealer scores 10 points for it at once. The trump card is laid on the table by itself, the remainder of the pack, which is called the **stock** or **talon,** is slightly spread, to facilitate the process of drawing cards from it, and to be sure that none of the cards remaining in the undealt portion are exposed. In sixty-four-card Binocle twelve cards are sometimes dealt to each player.

Misdealing. A misdeal does not lose the deal, but in some cases a new deal is at the option of the adversary.   If the dealer exposes a card belonging to the adversary or to the stock, the pone may demand a new deal ; but if either player exposes any of his own cards, the deal stands good.   If too many cards are given to either player, there must be a new deal.   If too few, the pone may claim a fresh deal, or allow the dealer to supply the missing cards from the top of the stock, without changing the trump card.   If any card but the trump is found faced in the pack, there must be a new deal.   If a card faced in the stock is not discovered until the first trick has been played to, the exposed card must be turned face down, without disturbing its position.   If a pack is found to be imperfect, the deal in which the error is discovered is void, but all previous cuts or scores made with that pack stand good.

METHOD OF PLAYING. The pone begins by leading any card he chooses, to which his adversary may play any card he pleases.   A player is not obliged to follow suit, nor to trump ; but may renounce or trump at pleasure until the stock is exhausted, after which the method of play undergoes a change. If a player follows suit, the higher card wins the trick, and if identical cards are played to the same trick, such as two Jacks of clubs, the leader wins. Trumps win plain suits. The winner of the trick takes in the cards, turning them face down ; but before he leads for the next trick he has the privilege of announcing and scoring any one of certain combinations that he may hold in his hand. After, or in the absence of any such announcement, and before leading for the next trick, he draws a card from the top of the stock and places it in his hand, without showing or naming it. His adversary draws the next card, so that each player restores the number of cards in his hand to eight. This method of drawing from the stock is open to many objections, and in France the pone always draws first, no matter who wins the trick.

All combinations announced and scored must be laid face upward on the table ; but the cards still form part of the player's hand, and may be led or played at any time, although they must not again be taken in hand until the stock is exhausted.

OBJECTS OF THE GAME. The reasons for winning or not winning certain tricks will be better understood in connection with the description of the various combinations that count toward game, and the manner of scoring them.

Brisques. The aces and Tens of each suit are called brisques, and count ten points each towards game. Except for the purpose of getting or keeping the lead, there is no object in winning any trick which does not contain a brisque. Every brisque taken in should be scored at once by the player winning the trick; 10 points for an ace or Ten ; 20 points if there are two such cards in the same trick.

A player holding or drawing the **Seven of trumps** has the privilege of exchanging it for the turn-up trump, and scoring 10 points at the same time ; but he must make the exchange immediately after winning a trick, and before drawing his card from the stock. Should the turn-up card be a Seven, or one exchange have already been made, the exchange can still be made and scored. He cannot score the Seven and make a declaration at the same time.

DECLARATIONS. The combinations which may be announced and scored during the play of the hand are divided into three classes : Marriages and Sequences ; Béziques ; and Fours of a kind. Only one combination can be scored at a time, and it must be announced immediately after the player holding it has won a trick, and before he draws his card from the talon. If he draws without announcing, it is equivalent to saying he has no declaration to make. Having drawn his card, even if he has not looked at it, he cannot score any declaration until he wins another trick.

The combinations and their values are as follows :—

CLASS A

King and Queen of any plain suit, **Marriage** .	20
King and Queen of trumps, **Royal Marriage** .	40
Sequence of five highest trumps, **Sequence** .	250

CLASS B.

Spade Queen and diamond Jack, **Bézique** .	40
Two spade Queens and diamond Jacks, **Double Bézique**	500

CLASS C.

Any **four Aces**	100
Any **four Kings.**	80
Any **four Queens**	60
Any **four Jacks**	40

The four court cards in class C may be all of different suits, or any two of them may be of the same suit.

A great many misunderstandings arise with respect to the manner and order of making declarations, most of which may be avoided by remembering the following rules :

The player making the declaration must have won the previous trick, and must make his announcement before drawing his card from the stock. When the stock is exhausted, so that there is no card to be drawn, no announcement can be made.

Only one declaration can be scored at a time, so that a trick must be won for every announcement made, or the combination cannot be scored. This does not prevent a player from making two or more announcements at the same time, but he can score only one of them.

A player cannot make a lower declaration with cards which form part of a higher one already made in the same class. For instance : Marriages and sequences belong to the same class. If the sequence has been declared, a player cannot take from it the King and Queen and score a marriage ; neither can he add a new Queen to the King already in the sequence, and announce a marriage ; because the higher combination was scored first. But if the marriage is first announced, the A 10 J may be added and the sequence scored, after winning another trick.

Cards once used in combination cannot again be used in combinations of equal value of the same class. For instance : Four Kings have been declared, and one of them afterward used in the course of play. The player cannot add a new King to the three remaining, and announce four Kings again. A marriage in spades has been declared, and the King got rid of in play. A new King of spades will not make another marriage with the old Queen. A bézique has been scored, and the Jack got rid of in play ; a new Jack of diamonds will not make another bézique with the old Queen.

Some judgment is necessary in making announcements, the question of time being often important. Suppose hearts are trumps, and the winner of the trick holds double bézique, sixty Queens, and a royal marriage :—

He cannot lay all these cards down at once, and claim 600 points. Neither can he lay down four Queens and two Jacks, and score 560 ; nor four Queens and a King and score 100. He may announce them if he chooses to expose his hand in that manner, but he can score only one combination, and must win a separate trick to score each of the others. It would be better for him to select some one of the combinations, and declare it, waiting until he won another trick to declare the next one. A beginner would be apt to declare the highest count first, 500 for the double bézique ; but under the rule which prevents a player from making a declaration which forms part of a higher one of the same class already made, he would lose the 40 points for the single bézique. It would be better to declare the single bézique first, scoring 40 points for it, and after winning another trick to show the other bézique, scoring 500 points more for the double combination. A player is not allowed to score 40 for the second bézique, and then 500 for the two combined ; because if new announcements are made in the same class, at least one new card must be added from the player's hand when the announcement is made, even if it is not scored until later.

Double Declarations. It frequently happens that a player is forced to make two declarations at the same time, although he can score only one of them. For instance : A player has announced and shown four Kings, one of them being the King of spades. On winning another trick he shows and scores bézique. One of the bézique cards forms a marriage with the spade King, and as the combinations belong to different classes, both may be scored, although the same card is used in each ; but the player cannot score the second combination until he wins another trick. Under such circumstances it is usual to declare both combinations, scoring the more valuable, and repeating the one left over until an opportunity arises to score it. In this case the player would say : "Forty for bézique, and twenty to score." If he lost the next trick he would continue to repeat at every trick : " Twenty to score," until he won a trick.

A player having a score in abeyance in this manner is not obliged to score it if he has anything else to announce. A player with twenty to score might pick up the sequence in trumps before he won another trick, and he would be very foolish to lose the chance to score 250 for the sake of the 20 already announced. If he had time, he would probably declare : " Royal Marriage, forty, and twenty to score." On winning another trick he would add the A 10 J of trumps, and announce, " Two-fifty in trumps, and twenty to score," still carrying on the small score for a future opportunity.

A player may lay down and score eighty Kings, and afterward sixty Queens, the remaining Kings forming marriages. In such a case he would score the sixty points first, and declare the two or three marriages remaining. In the same manner he may have announced four Kings, and after playing away two of them, leaving two Kings of spades, he may declare double bézique, and claim the two marriages "to score." In all such cases it must be remembered that the cards declared must still be on the table when the time comes to score them. If, in the case just given, one of the cards forming either of the marriages was got rid of in the course of play, that marriage could not afterward be scored, although it had been properly announced. If the stock is exhausted before the player with a score in abeyance can win another trick, the score is lost.

It is often very important for a player to know how much time he has to score. When the talon is spread it is comparatively easy to judge how many more tricks remain to be played. The English laws allow a player to count the stock, the French do not. A trick once turned and quitted cannot again be seen, and the players are not allowed to count the number of tricks they have won.

The last card of the stock is taken by the player winning the trick, and the turn-up trump goes to his adversary.

The Last Eight Tricks. When the stock is exhausted, the players take back into their hands all the cards remaining of the combinations which have been laid on the table. The winner of the previous trick then leads any card he pleases, but his adversary must now not only follow suit, but must win the trick if he can, either with a superior card of the same suit, or with a trump. The same rule applies to all the remaining tricks. Brisques still count for the winner of the trick containing them, and should be scored as soon as made. The winner of the last trick of all scores ten points for it immediately, in addition to any brisques that it may contain.

Irregularities in Play. If a player leads out of turn, and his adversary plays to the lead, whether intentionally or otherwise, the trick stands good. If the adversary calls attention to the error, the card led out of turn may be taken back without penalty.

If a player has too many cards after playing to the first trick, his adversary may either claim a fresh deal or may compel him to play without drawing from the talon, until the number of cards in his hand is reduced to eight; the player with too many cards not being allowed to make any announcements until he has his right number of cards. If a player has too few cards, his adversary may either claim a fresh deal, or may allow him to make good the deficiency by drawing from the stock.

After the stock is exhausted, any player failing to follow suit or to win a trick, when able to do so, may be compelled to take back his cards to the point where the error occurred, and to replay the hand. In France he is penalised by counting nothing from that point on, either for brisques or for the last trick.

Irregularities in Drawing. If a player has forgotten to take a card from the talon, and has played to the next trick, his adversary may elect to call the deal void, or to allow him to draw two cards next time.

If a player has drawn two cards from the stock, instead of one, he must show the second one to his adversary if he has seen it himself. If he has not seen it, he may put it back without penalty. If he draws out of turn, he must restore the card improperly drawn; and if it belongs to his adversary the player in error must show his own card. If both players draw the wrong cards there is no remedy.

If the loser of any trick draws and looks at two cards from the stock, his adversary may look at both cards of the following draw, and may select either for himself. If he chooses the second card, he need not show it.

If, on account of some undetected irregularity, an even number of cards remain in the stock, the last card must not be drawn. The winner of the trick takes the last but one, and the loser takes the trump card.

Irregular Announcements. Should a player announce four of a kind, having only three; as, for instance, laying down three Kings and a Jack, and declaring four Kings, his adversary can compel him not only to take down the score erroneously marked, but to lead or play one of the three Kings. A player may be called upon to lead or play cards from any other erroneous declarations in the same manner; but if the player has the right card or cards in his hand, he is permitted to amend his error, provided he has not drawn a card from the stock in the meantime.

SCORING. It is better to score all points as soon as they are made. The game is usually 1000 points. Some players do not count the brisques until the last trick has been played, but the practice is not to be recommended. Scores erroneously marked must be taken down, and the adversary may add the points to his own score.

Suggestions for Good Play will be found in Binocle.

FOUR-HANDED BÉZIQUE.

In this variation, four persons may play; each for himself or two against two, partners sitting opposite each other. Four packs of thirty-two cards each are shuffled together and used as one. Triple bézique counts 1500. When a player wins a trick, either he or his partner may declare everything in the hand, but only one combination can be scored at a time. The advantage of showing all the combinations in the hand is that they may be built up by either partner. For instance: One partner has declared bézique and royal marriage, scoring the marriage only. His partner wins the next trick and adds A 10 J to the marriage, scoring the sequence; or perhaps shows three Kings or Queens, making fours.

The players usually divide after the stock is exhausted, and for the last eight tricks each takes one of his former adversaries for a partner, but without changing seats. The game is usually 2000 points up.

THREE-HANDED BÉZIQUE.

Three persons play, each for himself. Two packs of thirty-two cards each and one of thirty-one cards are shuffled together. Triple bézique counts 1500, and the game is usually 2000 points.

The deleted card from the third pack should be an Eight.

POLISH BÉZIQUE.

This differs from the ordinary game only in the value of the tricks taken. The winner of each trick, instead of turning it down after counting the brisques, takes from it any court cards it may contain, and the Ten of trumps. He lays these cards face up on the table, but apart from those declared from his own hand, and uses them to form combinations, which may be scored in the usual way. The chief difference is that cards so taken in tricks cannot be led or played to subsequent tricks, nor can they be taken in hand at the end of the stock. Combinations may be completed either by cards in the player's hand, or by cards won in subsequent tricks.

CINQ-CENTS.

This might be described as Bézique with one pack of cards. All the regulations are the same as in the modern form of Bézique, but there is an additional count, 120, for a sequence of the five highest cards in any plain suit. Bézique is called **Binage,** and of course there are no double combinations. Cards which have been used in one combination cannot be used in any other, even of a different class.

Brisques are not scored as they are won; but after the hand is over, and ten points have been counted for the last trick, each player turns over his cards and counts up the value of the points they contain. In this final count, the Ace reckons for 11, the Ten for 10, King for 4, Queen for 3, Jack for 2, no matter what the suit may be, so that there are 120 points to be divided between the players. It is usual for only one to count, the other taking the difference between his total and 120.

From this it might be imagined that no notice was taken of the counting value of the cards taken in during the progress of the play. Early in the game this is true, but toward the end each player must keep very careful mental count of the value of his tricks, although he is not allowed to score them. When either player knows, by adding the mental count of his tricks to his scored declarations, that he has made points enough to win the game, he stops the play by knocking on the table, either with his knuckles or his cards. He then turns over his tricks and counts the points they contain to show his adversary that he has won the game. Even if his adversary has also enough points to go out, the player who knocked wins the game, provided his count is correct. If the player who knocks is mistaken, and cannot count out, he loses, no matter what his adversary may have.

If neither knocks, and at the end of the hand both players are found to have points enough to put them out, neither wins the game, which must be continued for 100 points more; that is, as 500 points is the usual game, it must be made 600 in such a case. Should both reach 600 without knocking, it must be continued to 700. If neither knocks, and only one has enough points to go out he wins the game on its merits.

As the name implies, 500 points is game.

PENCHANT.

Penchant is a complicated form of Cinq-cents and Bézique, played with a single pack of thirty-two cards, which rank as at Piquet; A K Q J 10 9 8 7, the ace being highest both in cutting and in play.

Cutting. The higher cut has the choice of seats, and the lower cut deals the first hand.

Dealing. After the cards have been cut by the pone the dealer gives one card to his adversary, then one to the stock, and then one to himself, all face down. Two more are then given to the stock, one to the pone, two to the stock again, and one to the dealer. This is continued, giving two cards to the stock between the ones given to each player, until the last round, when only one card is dealt to the stock. This will result in each player receiving six cards, and twenty being left in the centre of the table for the talon. No trump is turned. Very few players trouble themselves with this method of dealing, preferring to deal three cards to each player alternately, leaving the remaining twenty for the stock.

Playing. All the regulations for leading, following suit, drawing from the talon, etc., are the same as in Bézique, but the declarations and their values are quite different.

Brisques. There are twelve brisque cards, the Seven of each suit being added to the usual Aces and Tens. The brisques are not scored as taken in, except in the last six tricks. At the end of the hand all the brisques are counted, whether already scored in the last six tricks or not, and the player having more than six counts ten points for each above six. If each has six, neither scores. By this method, a player may make and score several brisques in the last six tricks, all of which he will reckon over again in the total count at the end.

Declarations. The winner of any trick, previous to the exhaustion of the stock, may announce and lay upon the table any one of ten different combinations, which are divided into three classes. These are as follows, with the number of points he is entitled to score for each:

CLASS A. DIFFERENT SUITS.

Any four of a kind, such as four Tens, . .	100
Any three of a kind, such as three Queens, .	30
Any pair, such as two Nines, . . .	20

CLASS B. THE SAME SUIT.

Any sequence of five, containing K Q J, .	250
Any sequence of four, containing K Q J, . .	40
Any sequence of K Q J, . . .	30
King and Queen of any suit, . . .	20
Queen and Jack of any suit, . . .	20
Any flush of five cards, containing K Q J, . .	50

CLASS C. PENCHANTS.

Any Queen and Jack of different suits, .	10

The sequences and flushes in class B must all be of the same suit ; penchant cards must be of different suits.

If the winner of any trick has no declaration to make, he signifies it by drawing the top card from the stock. His adversary, before drawing his card from the stock, may then declare a penchant, if he has one ; but no other combination can be declared by the player who does not win the trick. If the winner of the trick makes any declaration, the loser cannot declare.

The Jack of the first penchant declared makes the ***trump suit*** for that deal, no matter which player announces it. Trumps do not increase the value of any combination, and are only useful to win plain-suit tricks.

All declarations are scored immediately, either on a marker or with counters. It will be observed that with the exception of sequences of five cards, fours, and penchants, the count is ten points for each card in the combination. Only one declaration can be made at a time.

Any card laid upon the table for one declaration can be used again in future declarations, provided the player making the new announcement adds at least one fresh card from his hand. A player having a marriage and a penchant on the table cannot afterward score for the pair of Queens ; but if he adds a Queen from his hand he can score the triplet.

Pairs, triplets and fours are divided into two classes, the major being formed of court cards ; the minor of cards below the Jack. Minor combinations cannot be scored if the adversary has upon the table cards which form a major combination of the same or greater value in the same class ; that is, in class A. For instance : If your adversary has two Queens on the table, you cannot announce any pair below Jacks. His Queens need not have been announced as a pair ; they may be parts of a marriage and a penchant. But if you have on the table a pair as good as his, you can score minor pairs. For instance : He has two Kings on the table, and you have two Aces. Your Aces cancel his Kings, and you can score any minor pair ; but he can not. If you have a minor triplet to declare, such as three Eights, no major pair of his will bar it, because your triplet counts more than his pair. No minor combination on his side will bar you ; it must be one of court cards, and it must be better than any that you have laid on the table yourself.

The Last Six Tricks. After the stock is exhausted, the second player must follow suit if able, and must win the trick if he can. As already explained, brisques won in the last six tricks are scored as they are taken in, and after the last card is played all the brisques are re-counted, the player holding more than six scoring ten points for each above that number. There is no score for winning the last trick.

Four deals is a game. At the end of the fourth deal the lower score is deducted from the higher, and the difference is the value of the game in points. If the lesser score is not at least 400 points, the winner doubles the difference in his favour.

The only text-book on this game introduces a great many technical terms which have no meaning to the ordinary card-player, and which have therefore been omitted from this description.

Suggestions for Good Play will be found in Binocle.

RUBICON BEZIQUE.

Rubicon Bézique bears the same relation to the ordinary game that Railroad Euchre does to Euchre proper. In fact the game might well be called Railroad Bézique, for its chief peculiarity is the rapid accumulation of large scores. The game seems to have originated in France, but is now very popular wherever Bézique is played.

CARDS. Rubicon Bézique is played with four piquet packs of thirty-two cards each ; all below the Sevens being deleted from an ordinary pack. The four packs, which should be of the same pattern and colour, are shuffled together and used as one. The cards rank : A 10 K Q J 9 8 7, the ace being the highest, both in cutting and in play.

MARKERS. The game may be kept on a bézique marker, a pull-up cribbage board, or with counters. Markers must be made to score at least 5000 points. When a cribbage board is used, it is usual to count the outside row of pegs as 10 each, the inner row as 100 each, and the game pegs in the centre as 1000 each. If counters are used, there must be for each player ; four white, to mark 10's ; one red to mark 50 ; nine blue to mark 100's ; and four coppers to mark 1000 each. These counters are moved from left to right of the player as the points accrue. In whatever manner the count is kept, it should be distinctly visible to both persons, as playing to the score is very important.

STAKES. Rubicon Bézique is played for so much a hundred points, and in settling up, all fractions of a hundred are disregarded, unless they are necessary to decide the game. Ten cents a hundred is the usual stake ; sixpence in England. Games are seldom worth less than one or two thousand points.

PLAYERS. Rubicon Bézique is played by two persons, one of whom is known as the *dealer*, and the other as the *pone*. They cut for seats and deal, the player cutting the higher card having first choice, and electing whether or not to deal himself. In cutting, the cards rank as in play, the ace being the highest. If a player exposes more than one card, he must cut again.

DEALING. The cards are thoroughly shuffled, and presented to the pone to be cut. At least five cards must be left in each packet. The dealer then distributes the cards three at a time, first to his adversary and then to himself, for three rounds, so that each player receives nine cards. No trump is turned ; but the first marraige declared and scored is the trump suit for that deal. The undealt portion of the pack, called the *stock* or *talon,* is slightly spread between the two players, and a little to the left of the dealer. If in spreading the stock any card is found to be exposed, there must be a new deal by the same dealer.

Misdealing. A misdeal does not lose the deal, but in some cases a new deal is at the option of the pone. If the dealer exposes a card belonging to his adversary or to the stock, the pone may demand a new deal ; but if either player exposes any of his own cards, the deal stands good. If too many cards are given to either player, and the error is discovered before the dealer plays to the first trick, there must be a new deal. If either player has too few cards, the pone may demand a new deal, or may allow the dealer to supply the deficiency from the top of the stock. If any card is found exposed in the pack, there must be a new deal. If any card faced in the stock is not discovered until the first trick has been played to by the dealer, the exposed card must be turned face down, without disturbing its position. If the pack is found to be imperfect, the deal in which it is discovered is void ; but all previous scores or cuts made with that pack stand good.

METHOD OF PLAYING. The pone takes up and examines his nine cards. If he finds himself without King, Queen or Jack of any suit, he immediately shows his hand to the dealer, and marks fifty points for *carte blanche.* Whether he has carte blanche or not, he begins the play by leading any card he pleases. If the dealer has carte blanche, he must show and score it before playing to the first trick. Players are not obliged to follow suit, nor to trump; but may renounce or trump at pleasure until the stock is exhausted, after which the method of play undergoes a change. Until the first marriage is declared and scored there is no trump suit. If the second player in any trick follows suit, the higher card wins. Trumps win plain suits. If identical cards are played to the same trick, such as two club aces, the leader wins.

The tricks are left face upward on the table until an ace or Ten is played, for tricks not containing either of these cards are of no value. When an ace or Ten is played, the winner of the trick gathers in all the cards that have accumulated, and turns them face down in front of him. These counting cards are called **brisques,** and if a player neglects to gather the brisques he wins, his adversary may do so when next he wins a trick, whether the trick he wins contains a brisque or not; the fact that there is a brisque on the table is sufficient.

Declaring. The winner of any trick, before leading for the next trick, has the privilege of announcing and scoring any one of certain combinations that he may hold in his hand. After, or in the absence of any such announcement, and before leading for the next trick, he draws one card from the top of the stock, and places it in his hand, without showing or naming it. His adversary then draws the next card, so that each restores the number of cards in his hand to nine. This method of playing, announcing, and drawing is continued until the stock is exhausted.

If a player who has already announced carte blanche finds that the first card he draws from the stock is not a King, Queen or Jack, he shows it to his adversary, and scores another fifty points for another carte blanche. This may be continued until he draws one of those cards. Carte blanche cannot be scored at all unless held before a card is played; that is, it must be dealt to the player originally.

All combinations announced and scored must be left face upward on the table, but the cards still form part of the player's hand, and may be led or played at any time, although they must not again be taken in hand until the stock is exhausted.

The first marriage announced and scored, no matter by which player, makes the *trump suit* for that deal; but a player with a marriage on the table is not obliged to announce it if he does not wish to make that suit the trump.

Irregularities in Play. If a player leads out of turn, and his adversary plays to the lead, whether intentionally or otherwise, the trick stands good. If the adversary calls attention to the error, the card led out of turn may be taken back without penalty.

If, after playing to the first trick, one player is found to have more than his right number of cards, the English rules say that the game is to be immediately abandoned, and the adversary of the player in error is to add 1300 points to his score at the time the error is discovered, together with all the points already scored by the player in error ; but the latter amount must not exceed 900.

The same penalties are enforced if one player has too many cards and the other too few ; but in the latter case the hand is played out, the player not in fault scoring all he can.

If both players have more than their right number of cards, the deal is void.   If either has less than his proper number, his adversary having the right number, the deal stands good, and there is no penalty except that the player with the right number of cards wins and scores for the last trick.   If both have less than the right number, the deal stands good, and the actual winner of the last trick scores it.

It will be observed that these rules are quite different from the French rules, which have been given in connection with the ordinary game of Bézique.   In France, it is always the custom to establish the *status quo*, if possible, and to assume that the error was quite unintentional.   In England, all laws are based on the assumption that your adversary is a rogue, and the penalties are absurdly severe, but we have no authority to change them.

Irregularities in Drawing.

If a player has forgotten to take his card from the talon, and has played to the next trick, the English laws compel him to play the remainder of the hand with eight cards ; the French laws give his adversary the option of calling the deal void, or allowing the player in error to draw two cards from the stock next time.

If a player draws two cards from the stock, instead of one, he must show the second one to his adversary if he has seen it himself. If it was his adversary's card, he must show his own card also.   If he has not seen it, he may put it back without penalty.   If he draws out of turn, he must restore the card improperly drawn, and if it belongs to his adversary, the player in error must show his own card.   If both players draw the wrong cards, there is no remedy.

If the loser of any trick draws and looks at two cards from the stock, his adversary may look at both cards of the following draw, and may select either for himself.   If he chooses the second card, he need not show it.

If, on account of some undetected irregularity, an odd number of cards remain in the stock, the last card must not be drawn.

OBJECTS OF THE GAME.

Each game is complete in one deal, and the score of the loser is deducted from that of the winner.   The combinations which may be declared and scored are the same as in Bézique, but owing to the use of four packs of cards double combinations are much more frequent, and triple combinations are not uncommon.

The chief concern of the player must be, first of all, to save himself from a rubicon; that is, either to reach 1000 points, or to score as few points as possible. If he does not reach 1000, his adversary will take whatever he has scored, and add them to his own, besides 1300 in addition for rubicon and brisques. For instance: At the end of the hand A has scored 1200, and B has only 700. B is rubiconed, and his 700 points are added to A's 1200, together with 1300 more for a rubicon game and brisques; giving A a grand total of 3200 points to nothing. Had B reached 1000, he would have saved his rubicon, and A would have scored the difference only, or 200 points, plus 500 for the game; 700 altogether.

Brisques. The aces and Tens of each suit are of no value unless it is necessary to count them to decide a tie, or to save a rubicon. They are never scored during the play of the hand.

Declarations. The combinations which may be announced and scored during the play of the hand are divided into three classes: A, Marriages and Sequences; B, Béziques; and C, Fours. Only one combination can be scored at a time, and it must be announced and laid on the table immediately after the player holding it has won a trick, and before he draws his card from the talon. If he draws without announcing, it is equivalent to saying he has no declaration to make. Having drawn his card, even if he has not looked at it, he cannot score any declaration until he wins another trick. The various combinations and their values are as follows:

CLASS A.

King and Queen in any plain suit, **Marriage** . .	20
King and Queen of trumps, **Royal Marriage** .	40
Five highest cards in a plain suit, **Sequence** . .	150
Five highest cards in trumps, **Royal Sequence** .	250

CLASS B.

Spade Queen and Diamond Jack, **Single Bezique** .	40
Two spade Queens and diamond Jacks, **Double Bezique**	500
Three spade Queens and diamond Jacks, **Triple Bezique**	1500
Four spade Queens and diamond Jacks, **Quadruple Bezique**	4500

CLASS C.

Any four Aces	100
Any four Kings	80
Any four Queens	60
Any four Jacks	40

Besides the foregoing, there is the score of fifty points for carte blanche, which may be announced only before the first trick is played to, and the score of fifty points for the winner of the last trick of all.

In class A, the first marriage declared must of course count 40, as it is the trump suit for that deal. In class C, the four court cards may be of different suits, or any two or more of them may be of the same suit.

The rules governing declarations are as follows :—

The player making the declaration must have won the previous trick, and must make his announcement before drawing his card from the stock. When the stock is exhausted, so that no cards remain to be drawn, no announcements can be made.

Only one declaration can be scored at a time, so that a trick must be won for every announcement made, or the combination cannot be scored. This rule does not prevent a player from making two or more announcements at the same time ; but he can score only one of them.

A player cannot make a lower declaration with cards which form part of a higher combination already shown in the same class. For instance :—Marriages and sequences belong to the same class. If a sequence has been declared, the player cannot take from it the King and Queen, and score for the marriage ; neither can he add a new Queen to the King already used in the sequence, because the higher combination was scored first. The same rule applies to lower and higher béziques. But if the lower combination is first shown and scored—the marriage—the A 10 J may be added afterward, on winning another trick, and the sequence scored. This rule does not apply to cards belonging to combinations in different classes. A Queen used in class A may be used over again in both B and C classes.

Re-forming Combinations. The chief peculiarity in Rubicon Bézique is that combinations which have been laid on the table and scored may be broken up, re-formed, and scored again indefinitely. For instance : A player has declared royal sequence, and scored 250 points for it. He may play away the Ace, breaking up the sequence, and upon winning the trick lay down another Ace, re-forming the sequence, and scoring 250 points again. He might repeat the same process with the Ten, King, Queen and Jack, and in six successive tricks he would score this royal sequence six times, making 1500 points out of it. In actual play it is not necessary to go through the formality of playing away a card from the combination on the table, and then replacing it, for it amounts to the same thing if the new card in the hand is led or played, and the fresh combination claimed.

Marriages, béziques and fours may be broken up and re-formed in the same way. After declaring 100 Aces, the player may lead or play another Ace, and claim another 100 Aces, scoring them when he wins a trick. In this way, eight Aces actually held might score 500 points. In the bézique combinations, a new card simply re-forms the single bézique. In order to score double, triple, or quadruple bézique, all the cards forming the combination must be on the table at one time, but they may be played and scored one after the other, cumulatively. For instance : A player holding quadruple bézique and showing all eight cards at once would score 4500 only; the minor béziques would be lost. If he had time, and could win tricks enough, he might show the single first, scoring 40, then the double, scoring 500, then the triple, scoring 1500, and finally the quadruple, scoring 4500, which would yield him a grand total of 6540 points. He might declare marriage in hearts, and afterward play three more heart Queens, scoring each marriage, and then three heart Kings, scoring three more marriages. These would all be new combinations.

Double Declarations. These are carried forward in the manner already described for the ordinary game. Suppose a player has two spade Kings on the table, and shows double bézique. He of course marks the more valuable score, 500, and simply claims the marriages by saying : " With twenty and twenty to score." On winning another trick he is not compelled to score the previous announcement if he has any other or better to make. He might have two more Queens, and would announce : " Sixty Queens, with twenty and twenty to score." If he scores one of the announcements held over, he still carries on the other.

When announcements are carried forward in this manner, it must be remembered that the cards must still be on the table when the time comes to score them. If one of them has been led or played, or the stock is exhausted before the player wins another trick, the score held over is lost.

Time. On account of the great number of combinations possible at Rubicon Bézique, it is very seldom that a player succeeds in scoring everything he holds. He is allowed to count the cards remaining in the talon, provided he does not disturb their order. This count is often important toward the end of the hand. For instance : You know from the cards you hold, and those played, that your adversary must have in his hand the cards that will make a double bézique on the table into a triple bézique, which would give him 1500 points. If, on counting the stock, you find only six cards remain, and you have three certain winning trumps to lead, you can shut out his 1500 by exhausting the stock before he can win a trick.

Irregular Announcements. If a player announces a combination which he does not show ; such as fours, when he has only three, which he may easily do by mistaking a Jack for a King, his adversary can compel him not only to take down the score erroneously marked, but to lead or play one of the three Kings. A player may be called upon to lead or play cards from other erroneous declarations in the same manner; but if he has the right card or cards in his hand, he is permitted to amend his error, provided he has not drawn a card from the stock in the meantime.

The Last Nine Tricks. When the stock is exhausted, all announcements are at an end, and the players take back into their hands all the cards upon the table which may remain from the combinations declared in the course of play. The winner of the previous trick then leads any card he pleases, but for the last nine tricks the second player in each must not only follow suit, but must win the trick if he can, either with a superior card or with a trump. Any player failing to follow suit or to win a trick, when able to do so, may be compelled to take back his cards to the point where the error occurred, and to replay the hand from that point. In France he is penalised by counting nothing from that point on, either for brisques or for the last trick.

The winner of the *last trick* scores fifty points for it immediately.

SCORING. Each deal is a complete game in itself, and the winner is the player who has scored the most points for carte blanche, combinations, and the last trick. The brisques are not counted, unless they are necessary to decide a tie, or save a rubicon.

The value of the game is determined by deducting the lesser score from the higher, and then adding 500 points to the remainder. In this deduction all fractions of a hundred are disregarded. For instance: A's score is 1830; while B's is 1260. A wins 1800. less the 1200 scored by B, which leaves 600; to this must be added the 500 points for game, making the total value of A's game 1100 points.

If the scores are very nearly equal, being within one or two hundred points of each other, the tricks taken in by each player are turned over, and the brisques are counted, each player adding to his score ten points for every brisque he has won. Suppose that after the last trick had been played and scored, A's total was 1260, and B's 1140. This is close enough to justify B in demanding a count of the brisques. It is found that A has seven only, while B has twenty-five. This shows B to be the winner of the game, with a total score of 1390 to A's 1330.

If the difference between the final scores is less than 100 points, after adding the brisques and throwing off the fractions, the player with the higher score adds 100 points for bonus. In the case just given, B's final score is equal to A's, after dropping the fractions from both; so he would add 100 for bonus to the 500 for game, and win 600 points altogether.

Rubicons. If the lower score is less than 1000, no matter what the higher score may be, the loser is rubiconed, and all the points he has scored are *added* to the score of the winner, instead of being deducted. In addition to this, the winner adds a double game, or 1000 points, for the rubicon, and 300 points for all the brisques, no matter who actually won them. For example: A's score is 920, and B's 440. It is not necessary to count the brisques to see that A wins and B is rubiconed. A adds B's 400 to his own 900, making his score 1300, and to this total he adds 1300 for rubicon and brisques, making the value of his game 2600 points altogether.

The loser is not rubiconed if he can bring his total score to 1000 by adding his brisques. Suppose A has 1740 and B 850. The brisques are counted, and it is found that B has eighteen, making his score 1030, and saving his rubicon. A adds his fourteen brisques, making his total 1880, which makes the value of his game 1800, minus B's 1000, plus 500 for the game, or 1300 altogether.

If B's brisques did not prove sufficient to save the rubicon, A would count them all. Suppose that in the foregoing case B had taken in only eleven brisques, leaving his total 990. As this does not save the rubicon the game is reckoned as if the brisques had not been counted at all, and A wins 1800, plus B's 800, plus 1300 for rubicon and brisques; 3900 altogether.

If the player who is rubiconed has scored less than 100 points, the winner takes 100 for bonus, in addition to the 1300 for rubicon and brisques.

When a series of games is played between the same individuals, it is usual to keep the net results on a sheet of paper, setting down the hundreds only, and to settle at the end of the sitting.

Suggestions for Good Play will be found in Binocle.

CHINESE BEZIQUE is Rubicon Bézique with six packs of cards shuffled together and used as one. The counts run into enormous figures, and 6000 is not an uncommon score for the winner.

In **CHOUETTE BEZIQUE,** one of several players agrees to take all bets, and has the choice of deal and seats without cutting. His adversaries may consult together in playing against him. If the chouette player wins, one of his opponents takes the loser's place ; but if he loses, the same player opposes him for the next game. The adversaries usually cut to decide which of them shall play the first game against the chouette player, the highest card having the privilege. If there are four players, two may play against two, each consulting with his partner and sharing his bets.

BINOCLE.

The word Binocle is spelt in many different ways, all of which are, however, phonetic equivalents of the correct one. The word is evidently from the Latin *binus*, double, and *oculus*, to see, and was probably adopted on account of the importance of the double combinations which are the chief counting elements in the game. In all German works on card games the name is spelt as we give it; but the pronunciation of the initial " b " in the German, is so near that of " p," that " Pinocle " is nearer the correct spelling than any other form. There is no authority for the introduction of the " h," which has led some persons to think the word a compound of " bis " and " knochle," and has given rise to the forms : binochle, pinochle, pinuchle, pinucle, penucle, penuchle, penuckle and pinuckel, all of which may be found in various works on card games.

CARDS. Binocle is played with two packs of twenty-four cards each, all below the Nine being deleted, and the two packs being then shuffled together, and used as one. The cards rank A 10 K Q J 9, the Ace being the highest, both in cutting and in play.

COUNTERS. The game is 1000 points, and is usually scored with counters, each player being provided with four white, worth 10 each ; four blue, worth 100 each ; one red, worth 50, and a copper cent or a button, which represents 500. These counters are placed on the left of the player at the beginning of the game, and are moved over to his right as the points accrue. The game is sometimes kept on a cribbage board, each player starting at 21, and going twice round to the game-hole, reckoning each peg as 10 points.

STAKES. Binocle is played for so much a game of 1000 points, and the moment either player either actually reaches or claims to have reached that number, the game is at an end. If his claim is correct, he wins ; if it is not, his adversary takes the stakes, no matter what the score may be.

PLAYERS. Binocle is played by two persons, one of whom is known as the ***dealer,*** and the other as the ***pone.*** They cut for the choice of seats and deal, and the player cutting the higher card may deal or not, as he pleases. It is usual for the player having the choice to make his adversary deal. A player exposing more than one card must cut again.

DEALING. After the cards are thoroughly shuffled, they are presented to the pone to be cut. At least five cards must be left in each packet. The dealer then distributes the cards four at a time for three rounds, giving to his adversary first, and then to himself. The twenty-fifth card is turned up for the trump. If this card is a Nine, the dealer claims ***dix,*** and counts ten for it immediately. The trump card is laid aside, and the remainder of the pack, which is called the ***stock,*** or ***talon,*** is slightly spread, to facilitate the process of drawing cards from it, and to be sure that none of the cards remaining in the stock are exposed. The trump is usually placed face up under the last card of the stock.

In ***Sixty-four-card Binocle,*** the Sevens and Eights are added to the pack. There are then two ways to play : If eight cards are dealt to each player, the game is simply Bézique, except for some minor details relating to the combinations and their value. These are usually disregarded, and the regular game of Bézique is played. If twelve cards are dealt to each player, the game is the same as the one about to be described, but with eight cards added to the pack, and the Seven taking the place of the Nine for dix.

Misdealing. If the dealer exposes a card belonging to his adversary or to the stock, the pone may demand a new deal ; but if either player exposes any of his own cards the deal stands good. If too many cards are given to either player, and the error is discovered before the dealer plays to the first trick, there must be a new deal. If either player has too few cards, the pone may demand a new deal, or may allow the dealer to supply the deficiency from the top of the stock. If any card is found exposed in the pack, there must be a new deal. If a card faced in the stock is not discovered until the first trick has been played to by the dealer, the exposed card must be turned face down, without disturbing its position. If the pack is found to be imperfect, the deal in which it is discovered is void ; but all previous scores and cuts made with that pack stand good.

METHOD OF PLAYING. After the trump is turned, the pone begins by leading any card he pleases. The second player is not obliged to follow suit, nor to trump ; but may renounce or trump at pleasure until the stock is exhausted, after which the method of play undergoes a change. If the second player follows suit in any trick, the higher card wins. Trumps win plain suits. If identical cards are played to the same trick, such as two club Jacks, the leader wins.

The winner of the trick takes in the cards, turning them face down, but before he leads for the next trick he has the privilege of announcing and scoring any one of certain combinations that he may hold in his hand. After, or in the absence of any such announcement, and before leading for the next trick, he draws a card from the top of the stock, and places it in his hand, without showing or naming it. His adversary then draws the next card, so that each player restores the number of cards in his hand to twelve. This method of playing, announcing, and drawing from the talon is continued until the stock is exhausted. The A 10 K Q J of each suit have certain counting values, which will be described further on.

All combinations announced and scored must be laid face upward on the table ; but the cards still form part of the player's hand, and may be led or played at any time, although they must not again be taken in hand until the stock is exhausted.

Irregularities in Play. If either player leads out of turn, and his adversary plays to the lead, whether intentionally or otherwise, the trick stands good. If the adversary calls attention to the error, the card may be taken back without penalty.

If at any time it is discovered that a player has too many cards, his adversary may either claim a fresh deal, or may compel him to play without drawing from the talon until the number of his cards is reduced to twelve. The player with too many cards is not allowed to make or score any announcements until he has his right number of cards. If a player has too few cards, his adversary may either claim a fresh deal, or allow him to make good the deficiency by drawing from the stock.

Any player looking at any but the last trick turned down, forfeits his entire score for " cards."

Irregularities in Drawing. If a player has forgotten to take a card from the talon, and has played to the next trick, his adversary may elect to call the deal void, or to allow him to draw two cards next time.

If a player has drawn two cards from the stock, instead of one, he must show the second one to his adversary if he has seen it himself. If it was his adversary's card, he must show his own card also. If he has not seen it, he may put it back without penalty. If he draws out of turn, he must restore the card improperly drawn, and if it belongs to his adversary, the player in error must show his own card. If both draw the wrong cards there is no remedy, and each must keep what he gets. If the loser of any trick draws and looks at two cards from the stock, his adversary may look at both cards of the following draw, and may select either for himself. If he chooses the second card, which his adversary has not seen, he need not show it.

If, on account of some undetected irregularity, an even number of cards remain in the stock, the last card must not be drawn. The winner of the trick takes the last but one, and the loser takes the trump card.

OBJECTS OF THE GAME. The aim of each player is to reach 1000 points before his adversary, and the one first reaching that number, and announcing it, wins the game. Points are scored for *dix, melds,* the *last trick,* and for *cards,* which are the counting cards in tricks won.

Melds. The various combinations which are declared during the play of the hand are called melds, from the German word melden, to announce. These melds are divided into three classes : *a*, Marriages and Sequences; *b*, Binocles; and *c*, Fours. Only one combination can be announced at a time, and it must be melded immediately after the player holding it has won a trick, and before he draws his card from the stock. If he draws without announcing, even if he has not seen the card drawn, he cannot meld anything until he wins another trick. The melds and their values are as follows :—

CLASS A.

King and Queen of any plain suit, **Marriage,** . .	20
King and Queen of Trumps, **Royal Marriage,** .	40
The five highest trumps, **Sequence,** . . .	150

CLASS B.

Spade Queen and diamond Jack, **Binocle,** . .	40
Two spade Queens and diamond Jacks, **Double Binocle,**	300
King and Queen of spades, and diamond Jack, **Grand Binocle,**	80

CLASS C.

Four Aces of different suits, . . .	100
Four Kings of different suits, . .	80
Four Queens of different suits, . . .	60
Four Jacks of different suits, . .	40
Eight Aces, ...	1000
Eight Kings, ...	800
Eight Queens, ...	600
Eight Jacks, ...	400

The third meld in class B is not often played in America. The count for it is the same, 80 points, whether the marriage in spades is the trump suit or not. It will be observed that the court cards in class C must be of different suits in Binocle, whereas, in Bézique, any four court cards may be declared. The following rules govern all classes of declarations :—

The player making the declaration must have won the previous trick, and must meld before drawing his card from the stock. When the stock is exhausted, so that no cards remain to be drawn, no further announcements can be made.

Only one meld can be scored at a time, so that a trick must be made for every announcement made, or the combination cannot be scored. This rule does not prevent a player from making two or more announcements, in different classes, at the same time, but he can score only one of them. This is a very important rule, and little understood. Suppose a player lays down four Kings and four Queens. The total count for the various combinations these cards will make is 240; three plain-suit marriages, 20 each; royal marriage, 40; four Kings 80, and four Queens 60. But only one combination can be scored for each trick won, so that it would take six tricks to count these six melds. If all these melds are laid on the table at once, they simply expose the player's hand, without giving him any advantage, and it is much better to meld the most valuable combination first, keeping the others until tricks are won which will entitle the player to score them. After scoring 80 Kings, 60 Queens could be melded, and the marriages, which are in another class, simply announced, to be scored later.

This distinction between classes of melds is often confusing, even to old players. It is frequently claimed that if four Kings have been melded, and the player holds four Queens, the only way to score these eight cards is to marry the Queens to the Kings, one at a time, until the last Queen is to be shown, when the player must either take the 60 for the Queens, and let the last marriage go, or score the marriage and let the 60 Queens go. This is an error, because the marriages and the fours belong to different classes of declarations. The proper way to meld these eight cards is to declare the 80 Kings first; then the 60 Queens; announcing the four marriages, which may be afterward scored, one at a time, as tricks are won. The case is the same as melding bézique, and claiming a marriage with a King already on the table. The marriage is not lost, but may be scored after winning another trick, provided it is claimed when the cards completing it are laid on the table.

A player cannot meld cards which have already been used to form higher combinations in the same class; but he may use cards melded in lower combinations to form more valuable ones in the same class, provided he adds at least one fresh card from his hand. The principle is that cards may be *added* to melds already shown, but they cannot be *taken away* to form other combinations in the same class. For example: Royal marriage has been melded and scored. The player may *add* to this the Ace, Ten, and Jack of trumps to make the sequence, which is a more valuable combination in the same class. But if the first meld is the sequence, he cannot *take away* from the sequence the card or cards to form a marriage. A new Queen added to the King already in the sequence will not make a marriage; because it is not the Queen that is added to the sequence, but the King that is taken away.

The same rule applies to the binocles. If a player has scored double binocle, he can not afterward take away two cards to meld a single binocle; but if the single binocle has been melded and scored first, he may add two more cards, and score the double binocle. He cannot score the second single, and then claim the double, because some new card must be added to form a new meld in the same class.

If four Kings are melded and scored, the other four may be added later; but if the eight Kings are first melded, the score for the four Kings is lost.

Cards may be taken away from one combination to form less valuable combinations in another class. For instance: Four Jacks have been melded; the diamond Jack may be taken away to form a binocle with the spade Queen. If spades are trumps, and the sequence has been melded, the Queen may be taken away to form a binocle, because the binocle is in a different class of melds; but the Queen cannot be used to form a marriage, because the sequence and the marriage are in the same class. As there are three classes, one card may be used three separate times. The spade Queen, for instance, may be used in a marriage, in binocle, and in four Queens, and these melds may be made in any order.

Cards once used in combinations cannot again be used in melds of equal value belonging to the same class; and combinations once broken up cannot be re-formed by the addition of fresh cards. For instance: Four Kings have been melded, and one of them has been used in the course of play. The player cannot add a new King to the three remaining, and meld four Kings again. A marriage in hearts has been melded, and the King played away. A new King will not make another marriage with the old Queen. A binocle has been melded, and the Jack has been played; another Jack will not make a new binocle with the old Queen.

Double Declarations. When a player makes a meld containing certain cards which will form a counting combination with other cards already on the table, it is called a double declaration, that is, a meld in two different classes at the same time. For instance: A player has melded and scored four Kings, and on winning another trick he melds binocle. Two of the cards on the table form a marriage in spades, and as the marriage is in a different class from either of the other melds, it may be claimed, although it cannot be scored until the player wins another trick. If it is not claimed when the cards are laid on the table, it cannot be scored. It is usual to score the more valuable combination at once, and to repeat the one left over, until an opportunity arises to score it. In the foregoing case the player would say: "Forty for binocle, and twenty to score." If he lost the next trick, he would repeat at every trick: "Twenty to score," until he won a trick and scored it.

A player having a meld in abeyance in this manner, is not obliged to score it if he has anything else or better to announce. A player with twenty to score might pick up the sequence in trumps before he won another trick, and he would be very foolish to lose the chance to score 150 for the sake of the 20 already announced. If he had time, or was sure of winning another trick before the stock was exhausted, he might declare : " Royal marriage, forty, and twenty to score." On winning another trick he would add the A 10 J of trumps, and announce : " One-fifty in trumps, and twenty to score ; " still carrying on the small score for a future opportunity.

In all such cases it must be remembered that the cards declared must still be on the table when the time comes to score them. It a player has melded four Kings and four Queens, claiming the marriages, but has to play one of the cards before scoring the marriage of which it forms a part, the score for that marriage is lost, although it was properly announced. If the stock is exhausted before the player with a score in abeyance can win another trick, the held-over score is lost.

Time. On account of the number of combinations possible, and the fact that there are only twelve tricks to be played before the scores for announcements are barred, it frequently happens that a player has not time to score everything he holds. He is allowed to count the cards remaining in the talon, provided he does not disturb their order, and it is often important to do so toward the end of a hand.

Scoring Dix. If a player holds or draws the Nine of trumps, he has the privilege of exchanging it for the turn-up card, and scoring ten points for dix. The exchange must be made immediately after winning a trick, and before drawing his card from the stock. Should the turn-up be a Nine, the exchange may still be made and scored ; and if one player has already exchanged a Nine for the turn-up, the second Nine may still be exchanged for the first, and scored. A player cannot score dix and any other combination at the same time. For this reason a player whose time is short will often forego the dix score altogether unless the trump card is valuable.

Irregular Melds. If a player announces a combination which he does not show, such as fours when he has three only, which he may easily do by mistaking a Jack for a King, his adversary can compel him not only to take down the score erroneously marked, but to lead or play one of the three Kings. A player may be called upon to lead or play cards from other erroneous declarations in the same manner, but if he has the right card or cards in his hand, he may amend his error, provided he has not drawn a card from the stock in the meantime.

The Last Twelve Tricks. When the stock is exhausted all announcements are at an end, and the players take back into their hands all the cards upon the table which may remain from the combinations declared in the course of play. Should a player take up his cards before playing to the last trick, he may be called upon to lay his entire hand on the table.

The winner of the previous trick then leads any card he pleases; but for the last twelve tricks the second player in each must not only follow suit, but must win the trick if he can, either with a superior card or with a trump. Any player failing to follow suit or to win a trick, when able to do so, may be compelled to take back his cards to the point where the error occurred, and to replay the hand from that point on. The penalty for the ***revoke*** varies in different places, but the general rule is for the revoking player to lose his entire count for " cards."

The winner of ***the last trick*** scores ten points for it; and the players then turn over the tricks they have taken, and count their score for " cards."

Cards. The five highest cards in each suit count toward game for the player winning them. The Ace is worth 11 points, the Ten 10, the King 4, the Queen 3, and the Jack 2, no matter what the suit may be, so that there are 240 points for cards to be divided between the players in each deal. It is usual for only one to count, the other checking him, and taking the difference between the total and 240. Cards are not scored as the tricks are taken in, but after the hand is over and the 10 points have been scored for the last trick.

From this it might be imagined that no notice was taken of the counting value of the cards taken in during the play. Early in the game this is true ; but toward the end each player must keep very careful ***mental count*** of the value of his tricks, although he is not allowed to make any note of it, nor to score it. When either player knows, by adding his mental count to his score for melds and dix, that he has made points enough to win the game, he stops the play by knocking on the table. He then turns over his tricks and counts his cards, to show his adversary that he has won the game. Even if both have enough to go out, the player wins who knocks first, provided his count is correct. If the player who knocks is mistaken, and cannot count out, he loses the game, no matter what his adversary's score may be.

If neither knocks, and at the end of the hand both players are found to have points enough to put them out, neither wins the game. If the game is 1000 points, it must be continued to 1250. Should both reach that point without knocking, it must be continued to 1500. If neither knocks, and only one has enough points to put him out, he wins the game on its merits.

SCORING. The game is usually 1000 points. All scores for dix, melds, and the last trick, are counted as soon as made; but the players are not allowed to keep any record of the score for cards, nor to go back over their tricks to refresh their memory. Any player going back further than the last trick turned and quitted, forfeits his entire score for cards. The player first correctly announcing that he has reached 1000 points, wins the game, no matter what his adversary's score may be; but if the announcement is incorrect, he loses the game.

Should a player score more than he is entitled to; as, for instance, scoring 80 for four Queens, his adversary may take down the superfluous score, 20 points in this instance, and may add it to his own score for a penalty.

CHEATING. Apart from the usual weapons of false shuffles, strippers cut to locate or pull out the binocle cards, and the opportunities always offered to the greek when the cards are dealt three or four at a time, the bézique family of games are particularly adapted to the use of marked cards. These will show the philosopher the exact value of both the cards in the next draw, and will enable him to vary his play accordingly. It is for this reason that in France the top card of the stock is always drawn by the same player, no matter which wins the trick. In Rubicon Bézique, a person should be very familiar with the movements peculiar to dealing seconds before he ventures to play in a public café, or he may find his adversary with the most astonishing run of repeated combinations, and will be rubiconed almost every game.

Never play with a man who cuts the pack with both hands, watches the cards closely as he deals, or looks intently at the top of the stock before he plays to the current trick. Players who have a nervous affection which makes them pass over too many counters at once will also bear watching. Colour blindness may lead them to take over a blue instead of a white in a close game.

SUGGESTIONS FOR GOOD PLAY. The general principles of play are much the same in all the Bézique family of games.

It is usually best to give your adversary the deal, because the first lead is often an advantage, especially if the turn-up is valuable, and you have a dix, or if you want to make the trump in Rubicon Bézique.

It is seldom right to make the trump unless you have one or two of the sequence cards with the marriage.

The Lead is a disadvantage unless you have something to declare, or there is a brisque in the trick, or you can get home the Ten of a plain suit. The Tens are of no value in plain suits except as brisques, for they enter into no combination with other cards except in Penchant, Cinq-cents, and Rubicon. If the trick is of no value, or you have nothing important to declare, get rid of your small cards, and lead them when you do not want to retain the lead. The lead is sometimes necessary to prevent your adversary from declaring, especially toward the end of the hand. If you have led a brisque and won the trick, it is better to lead another brisque in the same suit than to change.

Aces are better leads than Kings or Queens, for the court cards can be married, and you may never get 100 Aces. Kings are better leads than Queens, especially if the Queens are spades. Jacks are better than either, but the Jack of diamonds should be kept as long as possible. If you have to decide between two combinations, one of which you must sacrifice, lead that which is of the smallest value, or the least likely to be restored. For instance: If your adversary has shown one or two Kings, but no Ace, and you have three of each, you are more likely to get 100 Aces than 80 Kings.

If you hold duplicate cards, especially in trumps, play the one on the table, not the one in your hand.

Brisques. Beginners often overlook the importance of brisques. Every time you allow your adversary to take in a brisque which you might have won, you make a difference of twenty points in the score. While you are hugging three Aces, waiting for a fourth, your adversary may get home all his Tens, and then turn up with your fourth Ace in his hand.

Discarding. It is usually best to settle upon one of two suits or combinations, and to discard the others, for you cannot play for everything. Having once settled on what to play for, it is generally bad policy to change unless something better turns up.

Your adversary's discards will often be a guide as to the combinations he hopes to make, and will show you that you need not keep certain cards. For instance: If a binocle player discards or plays two heart Kings, it is unlikely that he has either of the Queens, and you may reasonably hope for 60 Queens; but it will be impossible for you to make anything out of your Kings but marriages. In Bézique, where Kings may be of the same suit in fours, you will have a slightly better chance for 80 Kings on account of your adversary's discards, because he certainly has no more, as he would not break up three Kings.

Declaring. It is often a nice point to decide whether or not you can afford to make minor declarations while holding higher ones in your hand. In Rubicon many players will give up the trump marriage if they have the sequence, especially with a good chance of re-forming it several times with duplicate cards. The number of cards in hand will often be the best guide. In Rubicon, if you held trump sequence and double bézique, it would be better to declare the sequence first, and to lead the card you drew. One of the trump sequence on the table would then be free to regain the lead and declare the double bézique ; but if the bézique was declared first, the sequence might have to be broken into to regain the lead. With a plain-suit sequence and four Aces, declare the Aces first. They will then be free to win tricks for the purpose of making other declarations.

It is seldom right to show the bézique cards in other combinations, and four Jacks is a very bad meld, because it shows your adversary that he cannot hope for double bézique. By holding up bézique cards, even if you know they are of no use to you, you may lead your adversary to break up his hand, hoping to draw the card or cards you hold.

Trumps. Small trumps may be used to advantage in winning brisques, but you should keep at least one small trump to get the lead at critical periods of the hand, or to make an important declaration. It is bad policy to trump in to make minor declarations, unless your time is short. It is seldom right to lead the trump Ace, except at the end of the hand, or when you have duplicates, but leading high trumps to prevent an adversary from declaring further is a common stratagem, if you know from the cards in your hand, and those played, that your adversary may get the cards to meld something of importance.

The Last Tricks. Before you play to the last trick, give yourself time to note the cards your adversary has on the table, and compare them with your own, so that you may play the last tricks to advantage. If you wait until after playing to the last trick, he may gather up his cards so quickly that you will be unable to remember them. At Rubicon it is not always advisable to win the last trick. If your adversary is rubiconed in any case, you may add 100 points to your own score by giving him the 50 for the last trick, which may put him across the line into another hundred.

TEXT BOOKS.

Bézique and Cribbage, by " Berkeley."
The Royal Game of Bézique, by Chas. Goodall.
Pocket Guide to Bézique, by " Cavendish."
Bézique, by J. L. Baldwin.
Rubicon Bézique, by " Cavendish."
Bézique, by Reynolds & Son.
Bézique, by English.
Règle du Bésique Japonais.
Articles in *Macmillan*, Dec., 1861 ; *Field*, Jan. 30, 1869 ; *Pall Mall Gazette*, Jan. 23, 27, 1869 ; *Once a Week*, Feb. 13, Mar. 20, 1869 ; *Daily News*, Feb. 10, 1869 ; *Westminster Papers*, Jan., 1869.

THREE-HANDED BINOCLE.

When three persons play, the entire pack is dealt out, giving sixteen cards to each player, four at a time, and turning up the last for the trump. There is no stock. Each plays for himself, and must keep his own score. A triangular cribbage board is very useful for this purpose.

Dix. Each player in turn, beginning on the dealer's left, may show the Nine of trumps if he holds it, and announce that he will score dix, and exchange it for the trump card when he wins a trick. Should two Nines be shown by different players, the one first winning a trick takes the turn-up trump. Even if the dealer has a Nine himself, he is not allowed to keep the turn-up trump unless he wins a trick before the player who holds the other Nine. If the same player holds both Nines he may score twenty on winning a trick. A player with 990 up is not out if he turns up the Nine. He must win a trick.

Melds. All the combinations have the same value as in the ordinary game, but all melds are laid upon the table before a card is played. When he lays down his cards, a player may make as many combinations with them as he can, just as he would in the ordinary game if he had plenty of time. If he has the trump sequence, he may lay down the marriage first, then the A 10 J. If he has double binocle, he may lay down the single first, and then the other, claiming the count for both. Four Kings and four Queens count 240. Eight Kings count 880. The trump sequence and double binocle count 530.

No player is allowed to meld after he has played to the first trick. If he discovers he had more to meld, but has played a card, the unannounced score is lost. An interesting variation is sometimes introduced by allowing the other players to claim any score overlooked by the one who melds.

The total number of points claimed by each player is simply announced, but not scored. The player must win a trick before he can score anything; but the first trick he wins entitles him to score everything he has announced, including dix. It is usual for the two players who do not win the first trick to continue their announcements, " Two-twenty to score," or whatever it may be, until they win a trick.

Playing. The melds are all taken in hand again before play begins. The eldest hand leads for the first trick, any card he pleases, and the others must follow suit if able, and must win the trick if they can, either with a higher card or with a trump. If the third hand cannot win the trick, he is still obliged to follow suit if he can ; but if he has none of the suit led, and the second hand has already put on a better trump than any held by third hand, the latter may discard what he pleases. The winner of one trick leads for the next, as in the ordinary game. The winner of the sixteenth or last trick, counts ten points for it at once.

Scoring. The points for dix, melds, and the last trick are all scored with the counters in the ordinary way, but the score for cards must be kept mentally. The moment any player correctly announces that he has reached 1000 points, he wins the game, no matter what the others may have scored. If his claim is not correct, he retires, and the two remaining players finish alone. If neither wins the game that deal, they play the next deal as in ordinary two-handed Binocle, with a stock, the ultimate winner taking the stakes. If it has been agreed that the lowest score pays when the first player goes out, the game is ended as soon as one retires. If two players reach 1000 points without either having claimed the game, they must both go on to 1250; but if the third player reaches and announces 1000 before either of the others reaches 1250, he wins the game.

FOUR-HANDED BINOCLE.

Four persons may play, each for himself, or two against two as partners, sitting opposite each other. All the cards are dealt, twelve to each player, four at a time, and the last is turned up for the trump.

Melds are not made until the player holding them has played to the first trick. The eldest hand leads and then melds; the second player plays and then melds, and so on. The card played to the first trick may still be reckoned in the melds.

Playing. The general rules of play are the same as in the three-handed game; players being obliged to follow suit and to win the trick if able to do so. The fourth player must win his partner's trick if he can.

Scoring. There are three ways to score: In the first, each player must individually win a trick in order to score his melds. In the second, when either partner wins a trick, the melds in both hands may be scored. In both these the melds are kept separate. In the third, when a player wins a trick he may combine his melds with those of his partner to form fresh combinations, and the scores are made as if the melds of the two partners were in one hand; but cards previously played to the tricks cannot be used in these fresh combinations. The cards must still be on the table, unplayed. For this reason, in this style of game the melds are not taken up until one of the partners wins a trick.

SIXTY-SIX.

Sixty-six is one of the simplest forms of Bézique, and is an extremely good game for two persons with one pack of cards.

Cards. Sixty-six is played with a pack of twenty-four cards, all below the Nine being deleted. The cards rank, A 10 K Q J 9 ; the Ace being the highest, both in cutting and in play.

Markers. The game may be kept with the small cards in the unused portion of the pack, or with a whist marker or counters. Anything that will score up to seven points will do.

Players. The regular game is played by two persons, one of whom is known as the dealer, and the other as the pone. They cut for seats and deal, the highest cut having the choice.

Stakes. Sixty-six is played for so much a game, or for so much a point, the loser's score being deducted from the winner's. If the loser has not scored at all, it is usually counted a double game.

Dealing. The cards having been shuffled and presented to the pone to be cut, the dealer gives six cards to each player, three at a time, dealing first to his adversary. There are several ways of making the trump, one of which should be agreed upon before play begins. One way is for the pone to draw a card from the top, the middle, or the bottom of the talon, after the dealer has given each player his six cards. Another way is for the dealer to turn up the seventh card, after dealing the first round of three to each player. Another, and the one generally adopted in America, is for the dealer to turn up the thirteenth card for the trump, after giving six cards to each player. The trump card is left face upward on the table, and is usually placed under the remainder of the pack, which is slightly spread, face down, for the players to draw from.

The general rules for irregularities in the deal are the same as in Binocle. A misdeal does not lose the deal.

Objects of the Game. The object of the game, as its name implies, is to count sixty-six. If a player can get sixty-six before his adversary, he counts one point toward game. If he gets sixty-six before his opponent gets thirty-three, which is called *schneider,* he counts two. If he gets sixty-six before his adversary wins a trick, which is called *schwartz,* he counts three. The player first making seven points in this manner wins the game.

A player may reach sixty-six by winning tricks containing certain counting cards ; by holding and announcing marriages, which are the King and Queen of any suit ; and by winning the last trick.

The various counts for these are as follows :—

For King and Queen of trumps, ***Royal Marriage,***	40
For King and Queen of any plain suit, ***Marriage,***	20
For the Ace of any suit,	11
For the Ten of any suit,	10
For the King of any suit,	4
For the Queen of any suit,	3
For the Jack of any suit,	2
For the last or twelfth trick,	10

The marriages count for the player holding and announcing them ; all other points for the player actually winning them. The last trick does not count unless it is the twelfth ; that is, not unless every card is played.

Method of Playing. The pone begins by leading any card he pleases. The second player in any trick is not obliged to follow suit, even in trumps ; but may renounce or trump at pleasure until the players cease to draw from the stock. If the second player follows suit, the higher card wins the trick. Trumps win all other suits.

Drawing. The winner of the trick takes in the cards, turning them face down ; but before he leads for the next trick he draws a card from the top of the stock, and places it in his hand without showing or naming it. His adversary then draws the next card, so that each restores the number of cards in his hand to six.

The Trump. If either player holds or draws the Nine of trumps, he may exchange it for the turn-up at any time, provided he has already won a trick. This need not be the trick immediately before exchanging, and he need not wait to get the lead before making the exchange. For instance : A player holding the Nine, and having to play to his adversary's lead, may win the trick with the turn-up card, leaving the Nine in its place, provided he has won some previous trick. There is no count for dix, as in Bézique and Binocle, and the player is not obliged to exchange unless he wishes to do so. If the Nine is the last card in the stock, it is, of course, too late to exchange it, and the player drawing it must keep it.

Marriages. If a player holds both King and Queen of any suit, he may count 20 points towards 66 for the marriage, or 40 for royal marriage, by leading either of the marriage cards. It is not necessary for the King or Queen so led to win the trick ; but the player declaring a marriage must have the lead, and must have won a trick, or he cannot count it. The pone may declare a marriage on his first lead ; but it will not count unless he wins some subsequent trick, and if his adversary gets to 66 before the pone gets a trick, the marriage is lost, and the pone is schwartz.

If the 20 or 40 claimed for the marriage is enough to carry the player's count to 66 or beyond, the marriage need only be shown and claimed, without leading it, and the remaining cards are then abandoned, provided the count is correct. Only one marriage can be shown but not led in this manner.

In the ordinary course of play it is not necessary to show both cards of the marriage unless the adversary asks to see them. The player simply leads the King or Queen, and says : " Twenty," or " Forty," as the case may be. If he leads a King or Queen without claiming any count, it is evident that he has not a marriage. If he has simply forgotten to claim it, he cannot amend the error after his adversary has played to the trick, and the score is lost. To avoid disputes, careful players leave one of the marriage cards face up among their cards, as a reminder that a marriage was claimed in that suit, either by the player with the card turned, or by his adversary.

Counting. A player is not allowed to make any record of his progress toward sixty-six, but must keep his count mentally. It is highly important to keep both your own and your adversary's count, in order that you may always know how many each of you wants to reach 66. A player is not allowed to go back over his tricks to refresh his memory, and if he looks at any trick but the last one turned and quitted, he loses the privilege of " closing."

All *irregularities* in playing and drawing are governed by the same rules as in Binocle.

The Last Six Tricks. After the stock is exhausted, marriages may still be led or shown, and scored ; but the second player in each trick must follow suit if he can, although he is not obliged to win the trick unless he chooses to do so. If all the cards are played, the winner of the last or twelfth trick, counts 10 for it toward his 66.

Announcing Sixty-six. If neither of the players has claimed to have reached 66 until after the last trick is played, both turn over their cards and count their points. If only one has reached 66, he counts one or two points, according to his adversary's count. If neither has reached 66, which is possible if no marriages have been declared ; or if both have 66 or more, and neither has claimed it, neither side scores, but the winner on the next deal adds one to whatever he may make. For instance : A and B are adversaries, and the last trick is played without either announcing that he is sixty-six. On counting, it is found that A has 48 points and a marriage, 68 altogether, while B has 72 points and the last trick, 82 altogether. Neither counts anything. On the next deal let us suppose that A makes 66 before B gets out of schneider, which will give A two points. To these he adds one for the tie on the last deal, and scores three altogether.

Closing. Closing is turning the trump card face down on the remainder of the pack, which signifies that there shall be no more drawing from the stock, and that the second player in each trick must follow suit if he can, although he is not obliged to win the trick.

A player can close only when he has the lead, but having the lead, he may close at any time. The pone may close before leading for the first trick; or after winning the first trick, and before drawing from the stock. The leader may close after one or more tricks have been played, and he may close without drawing from the stock; or he may draw, and then close. If the leader closes without drawing, his adversary must play without drawing.

When the stock is closed, the player holding the Nine of trumps may still exchange it for the trump card, whether he is the closer or not, provided he has previously won a trick. It is usual for the closer, if he does not hold the Nine himself, to take up the trump card and offer it to his adversary. This is an intimation that he is about to turn it down if his adversary does not want it. It is sometimes better not to exchange when the game is closed, as it may give the adversary a good counting card if he can catch all your trumps.

There is no score for the last trick when the game is closed, because the number of tricks played will then be less than twelve.

As closing gives peculiar advantages to the closer, there are certain forfeits if a person closes and fails to reach 66. There are three varieties of closing, which are as follows:—

If, during the play of the hand, either player thinks he has reached 66, he closes, and turns over the tricks he has already won. If he is correct, he scores one, two, or three points, according to the condition of his adversary's count. But if he is not correct, and has not quite reached 66, his adversary scores two points in any case, and if the non-closer had not won a trick up to the time the stock was closed, he scores three; because that is the number the closer would have won if he had been correct in his count.

If a player thinks he would have a better chance to reach 66 first if his adversary was compelled to follow suit, he may close the stock. For instance: A's mental count is 35, and he holds in his hand a marriage, and the Ace of another plain suit; but no trumps. If he closes at once, and leads the Ace, his adversary will have to follow suit, and the 11 points will put the closing player to 46. He can then show his marriage, without leading it, and claim 66. But if the adversary should turn out to have none of the suit led, and should trump the Ace, A might never reach 66, and B would count two points.

A player may close, hoping to make schneider or schwartz. For instance: A knows his score is 13, while B has 32. A has royal marriage and Ace of trumps in his hand, and the Nine is turned up. If A closes, and so compels B to follow suit, he must catch the Jack or Ten of trumps by leading the Ace. If he catches the Jack, that will put him to 26, and showing the royal marriage will put him 66, and make B schneider. If B has no trump, one of the marriage cards can be led without any fear of losing it, and that will put A to 66, even if B plays a Nine to both leads. But if A leads the ace of trumps without closing, B is not compelled to follow suit, and might play the Nine of a plain suit to the Ace of trumps. If A then closed or played on without closing, B might win one of the marriage cards with the Ten, and not only get out of schneider, but reach 66 in plain suits before A could win another trick.

On the same principle, a player may think he can reach 66 before his adversary can win a trick, provided he can compel him to follow suit. With two plain-suit Aces and the royal marriage, the pone would close before playing to the first trick, trusting to catch at least 4 points with his two aces, and then to show the marriage, making his adversary schwartz.

Some judgment is necessary in deciding whether or not to draw before closing. If a player is allowed to draw, he may get a trump, or a guard to one that you suspect he has. Suppose he has exchanged the Nine for the Ten, and you have Ace and royal marriage ; it is very likely that the Ten is unguarded, and if you close without drawing you may catch it, which will make your three trumps alone good for 68. This also shows that the player should not have taken up the Ten until he wanted to use it.

Nothing is gained by closing, except compelling the adversary to follow suit ; because if you close to make him schwartz, and he gets a trick, you count two only ; if you close to make him schneider, and he gets out, you count one only. If you fail in the first case, he counts three, and any failure will give him two points.

THREE-HANDED SIXTY-SIX.

This is exactly the same as the ordinary game, except that the dealer takes no cards, but scores whatever points are won on the hand he deals. If neither of the others score, either through each making 65, or one failing to claim 66, the dealer scores one point, and the others get nothing. The dealer cannot go out on his own deal. He must stop at six, and win out by his own play.

There are two ways to settle : Each may pay a certain amount to the pool, and the first man out take it all; or, after one is out, the two remaining finish the game, and the loser pays both or settles for the refreshments, as the case may be. If the first man goes out when it will be his turn to deal, he must deal the next hand.

FOUR-HANDED SIXTY-SIX.

This game is sometimes called **Kreutz-mariage**, owing to the German fashion of dealing the cards in the form of a cross; but as the cards are not dealt that way, and marriages are not scored in America, the name is not appropriate in this country.

The pack is increased to thirty-two cards by the addition of the Sevens and Eights. After the cards are cut by the pone, the dealer gives three to each player on the first round, then two, and then three again, turning up the last card for the trump. In Germany the dealer first gives two cards to his partner, then two to his left hand adversary, then two to his right hand adversary, and finally two to himself. This is continued for four rounds, so that each player receives eight cards, and the last is turned up for the trump. The turned-up trump belongs to the dealer, and cannot be exchanged.

In this form of the game the players must not only follow suit, but must win the trick if they can, and must trump and overtrump if possible. A player is even obliged to win his partner's trick. Owing to this rule, a player with good plain suit cards will usually attempt to exhaust the trumps as rapidly as possible.

The **counting cards** are the same as in Sixty-six, and the winner of the last trick counts 10. As there is no stock, there is no closing; and as marriages are not counted in America, the 66 points must be made on cards alone.

The scores for **schneider** and **schwartz** are the same as in Sixty-six, and seven points is game. There are 130 points made in every deal, so if one side gets more than 66 and less than 100, their adversaries must be out of schneider, and the winners count one. More than 100, but less than 130 is schneider, and counts two. If the winners take every trick, making 130 points, they score three. Sometimes an extra point is scored for winning the Ten of trumps; but such a count is quite foreign to the game.

NATIONAL GAMES.

There are certain games of cards which do not seem to belong to any particular family, but stand apart from other games, and have been played since their first invention with only trifling variations, giving rise to no offshoots bearing other names. These are usually the most popular games with the middle and lower classes in the countries in which they are found, and may be considered as distinctly national in character. Games that become popular with the masses always last longer than others, and the rules governing them are much better understood, and more firmly established. In the course of a century the English aristocracy have run the gamut of Quadrille, Ombre, Whist, Écarté, Bézique, Piquet, Rubicon, and Bridge ; while the middle classes have stuck steadily to Cribbage for nearly two hundred years.

Six of these popular games are strikingly typical of the national character, both in their construction, and in the manner of playing them. These are : Skat in Germany; Cribbage in England ; Piquet in France ; Conquian in Mexico ; Calabrasella in Italy ; and Cassino in America. All these are excellent games, and have deservedly survived much more pretentious rivals.

With the exception of Skat, little is known of the exact origin of any of these games, although most of them may be traced by their resemblance to more ancient forms. Skat is the most modern, and to-day the most popular, many persons thinking it superior to Whist. The game seems to have originated among the farmers of Thuringia, a province of Saxony, and was probably a variation of the Wendish game of Schapskopf. The first mention of Skat that we can find is in an article in the " Osterländer Blättern," in 1818. Thirty years later Professor Hempel of Altenburg published the rules and principles of the game under the title : "Das Skatspiel, von J. F. L. H." It is said that he learned the game from a friend, who had been taught it by a Wendish coachman in his employ. The game spread rapidly, and soon became popular all over Germany, but with many minor variations in the details of play. To settle these, a Skat congress was finally held in Altenburg in 1886. This was succeeded by others in Leipzic and Dresden, and the result of these meetings has been to weed out all the minor differences in play. and to settle upon a universal code of laws for the game, which is called Reichs-Skat.

In America, Reichs-Skat is no longer played ; the value of some of the games is changed, and all the bidding is by Zahlen-reizen. In all the text-books on Skat which we have examined, this fact has been entirely overlooked.

SKAT.

The etymology of the word Skat, sometimes spelt Scat, is a matter of doubt, but the most plausible explanation is that it is a corruption of one of the terms in the parent game of Taroc ; " scart," from " scarto," what is left ; or " scartare," to discard or reject. " Matadore " is another word from the game of Taroc, still retained in Skat. Others attribute the word to " Skatt," the Old-German or Anglo-Saxon for money ; the modern German, " Schatz," a treasure, referring to the forms of the game in which good counting cards are laid aside in the skat for the count at the end of the hand. This derivation would account for both spellings of the word, with a " k " and with a " c."

The student is advised to make himself familiar with the German terms in the following description, as they are in common use wherever skat is played. Many American players who use the English language in bidding by figures, still adhere to the German names for the suits and positions at the table.

CARDS. Skat is played with a pack of thirty-two cards, all below the Seven being deleted. The rank of the cards differs according to whether the players are attempting to win or to lose tricks. If the object is to win tricks. it is known as a " game ; " if the object is to lose, it is called a " nullo." In nullo the cards rank in their natural order; A K Q J 10 9 8 7, the Ace being the highest. In the various " games," the four Jacks are always the best trumps, and are known as ***Wenzels.*** The other cards follow the usual German rank ; A 10 K Q 9 8 7, the Ace being the highest in plain suits.

The German names for the cards are as follows ;—***Jack :*** Wenzel, Bauern, Bube, Jungen, or Unter. ***Ace :*** As, or Daus. ***Ten,*** Zehn. ***King,*** König. ***Queen :*** Dame, Ober, or Königen. ***Nine,*** Neun. ***Eight,*** Acht. ***Seven,*** Sieben. The most common terms are ; Bube, As, Zehn, König, Dame, etc. The words Unter and Ober for the Queen and Jack, refer to the manner of marking the suits on the German cards. In the Queens, the mark of the suit is always above the figure, which has a single head ;

in the Jacks the suit mark is always under the figure. This distinction is necessary, because in the German cards the Queen is a male figure. The King has two suit marks, one on each side of the head. When the French or American double-head cards are used, with suit-marks in both corners, the words "ober" and "unter" have no meaning; Dame and Bube being used instead.

Rank of the Suits. In addition to the rank of the cards themselves, the suits outrank one another, except in Nullo, clubs being always the best, then spades, hearts and diamonds. The Germans have various names for the suits, that first given in each instance being in common use among modern Germans. ***Clubs:*** Kreuz, Trefle, Eicheln, Eckern, or Braün. ***Spades:*** Pique, Schüppen, Laub, or Grün. ***Hearts:*** Hertzen, Cœur, or Roth. ***Diamonds:*** Carreau, Schellen, Eckstein, Ruthen, or Gelb. In the German notation of card games and problems, the suits are indicated by the French terms: clubs, *tr* for trefle; spades, *p* for pique; hearts, *co* for cœur; diamonds, *car* for carreau. The cards are indicated by the initials; A K D B Z 9 8 7, which stand for As, König, Dame, Bube, Zehn, etc. The winning card in each trick is always printed in full-faced type.

The cards of each suit are divided into two parts, known as counting cards, ***Zahlkarten,*** and those having no counting value; ***Fehlkarten,*** or Ladons. The counting cards and their values are as follows:—Ace 11, Ten 10, King 4, Queen 3, and Jack 2. These are used in reckoning up the value of the tricks won by each side in counting toward 61 in all the "games," but not in Nullo. The Seven, Eight and Nine have no counting value.

The rank of the suits has no influence on their trick-taking powers, nor on the value of the Zahlkarten; but it increases or diminishes the value of the "game" played for. When any suit is made the trump, it takes the precedence of the three others only in so far as trumps will win other suits, and the suits which are not trumps are equal in value so far as trick-taking is concerned. As the four Wenzels are always the highest trumps, there will always be eleven cards in the trump suit, and seven in each of the plain suits; so that if clubs were trumps, the rank of the cards would be :—

In any of the other suits the rank would be :—

Matadores. The club Jack is always the best trump, and every trump card in unbroken sequence with the club Jack is called a Matadore, provided the sequence is in the hand of the same player. This rule holds whether the sequence was in the hand originally dealt to him or part of it is found in the Skat, should he become possessed of the Skat cards. For instance : Clubs are trumps, and a player holds these cards :—

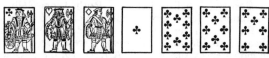

He has only one Matadore; but as the Skat cards will belong to him if he has made the trump, he may find in them the spade Jack, which would complete his sequence, giving him six Matadores, instead of one. As one side or the other must have the club Jack in every deal, there must always be a certain number of Matadores, from one to eleven. If the player who makes the trump has them, he is said to play **with** so many; if his adversaries hold them, he is said to play **without** just as many as they hold. The difficult thing for the beginner at Skat to understand is that whether a player holds the Matadores or not, the number of them has exactly the same influence on the value of his game. If one player held these cards

and wished to make hearts trumps, he would be playing "with two." If another player wished to make the same suit trumps with these cards :—

he would be playing " without two," and the value of each game would be exactly the same, no matter which player actually made the trump. Matadores must be held ; they do not count if won from the adversaries in the course of play.

MARKERS. Counters of any kind are not used in Skat, as the score is kept on a writing pad, which should be ruled into vertical columns for the number of players engaged.

PLAYERS. Skat is played by three persons. If there are four at the table the dealer takes no cards, but shares the fortunes of those who are opposed to the single player, winning and losing on each hand whatever they win and lose. If there are five or six at the table, the dealer gives cards to the two on his left, and the one next him on the right. Those holding no cards share the fortunes of the two who are opposed to the single player.

After the table is formed, no one can join the game without the consent of all those already in, and then only after a **round ;** that is, after each player at the table has had an equal number of deals. Should any player cut into a table during the progress of a game, he must take his seat at the right of the player who dealt the first hand. When six persons offer for play, it is much better to form two tables, but some persons object to playing continuously, and like the rest given to the dealer when more than three play.

There are always three active players in Skat. The one who makes the trump is called **the player,** or Spieler ; the two opposed to him are called the **adversaries,** or Gegners ; while those who hold no cards are called **im Skat,** or Theilnehmer. Of the three active players, the one who leads for the first trick is called **Vorhand ;** the second player is called **Mittelhand,** and the third **Hinterhand.** The person sitting on the dealer's right, to whom the cards are presented to be cut, is called the **pone.**

No person is allowed to withdraw from the game without giving notice in advance, and he can retire only at the end of a round of deals. It is usual to give notice at the beginning of a round, by saying : " This is my last."

CUTTING. Positions at the table are drawn for, the cards ranking as in play, Jacks being the best, and the suits outranking one another in order, so that there can be no ties in cutting. The lowest cut has the first choice of seats, and also deals the first hand. It is usual for the player sitting on the right of the first dealer to keep the score, so that one may always know when a round ends.

STAKES. Skat is played for so much a point, and the single player wins from or loses to each of the others at the table. A cent a point is considered a pretty stiff game, half a cent being more common in good clubs. Many play for a fifth, or even a tenth of a cent a point. At half a cent a point, ten dollars will usually cover a run of pretty bad luck in an evening's play.

DEALING. At the beginning of the game the cards should be counted and thoroughly shuffled, and shuffled at least three times before each deal thereafter. The dealer presents the pack to the pone to be cut, and at least five cards must be left in each packet. The cards are dealt from left to right in rotation, and the deal passes to the left in regular order.

Only three persons at the table receive cards, no matter how many are in the game. If there are are four players, the dealer gives himself no cards. If there are five or six players, the first two on the dealer's left and the pone receive cards. The other persons at the table are said to be " im Skat," because they are laid aside for that deal.

The cards may be distributed in several ways, but whichever manner the first dealer selects must be continued during the game, both by the original dealer, and by the others at the table. Ten cards are given to each player, and two are dealt face downward in the centre of the table for the Skat. No trump is turned. The cards may be dealt five at a time in two rounds ; or three the first round, then four, and then three again ; or three, two, three, two. The two cards laid out for the Skat must not be either the first or the last dealt, and it is usual to lay them out after dealing the first round.

The best clubs have a fixed rule for dealing at Skat. In America the most popular way is to give three cards to each player, then two to the Skat, then four to each player again, and finally three. This is the rule at the Arion Club Skat tournaments in New York.

Irregularities in the Deal. If the pack is found to be imperfect, the deal in which the error is discovered is void ; but any previous scores or cuts made with that pack stand good. If the cards have not been cut, or if a card is found faced in the pack, or if the dealer exposes a card in dealing, any active player who has not looked at his cards may demand a fresh deal by the same dealer. If the dealer gives too many or too few cards to any player, he must shuffle and deal again. If the error is not discovered until the hand is partly played out, the deal is void, and the misdealer deals again. A misdeal does not lose the deal under any circumstances, but it is usual to exact a penalty of ten points for a misdeal.

OBJECTS OF THE GAME. The object of each player is to obtain the privilege of attempting to accomplish a certain task, which is known as his " game," and which he must be able to carry through successfully against the combined efforts of the two other players. The more difficult the task undertaken, the greater the number of points scored for it, and the player who will undertake the game which is of the greatest value of those offered must be allowed the privilege of trying it. In order to determine which player this is, they may all bid for the privilege by naming a certain number of points, usually well within the actual value of the game they intend to play. If a bidder meets with opposition, he gradually approaches the true value of his game, and the player whose game is worth the most will of course be able to bid the greatest number of points, and must be selected as the player, the two others being his adversaries.

Games. These games are divided into two principal classes, those in which the player undertakes to win, and those in which he tries to lose. When he plays to lose, it is to lose every trick, there being no trump suit, and the cards in each suit ranking A K Q J 10 9 8 7. These games are called *Null,* or Nullo, and *Null Ouvert,* the latter being played with the successful bidder's cards exposed face upward on the table, but not liable to be called. The moment he wins a trick in a Nullo, he loses his game. Nullos are quite foreign to Skat, and appear to have been introduced as a consolation for players who always hold bad cards.

When *Ramsch* is played, the object is to take less than either of the other players ; but the cards rank as in the ordinary game, except that the four Jacks are the only trumps.

In all other games the successful bidder undertakes to win ; but his success does not depend on the number of tricks he takes in, but on the total value of the counting cards contained in those tricks. The total value of all the counting cards is 120 points, and to be successful, the single player must win at least 61. If he succeeds in winning 61 or more points, he wins his game, whatever it may be. If he can get 91 points, he wins a double game, which is called *schneider.* If he can take every trick, he wins a treble game, which is called *schwartz.* It is not enough to win 120 points, for if the adversaries win a single trick, even if it contains no counting cards, they save the schwartz.

If the single player fails to reach 61, he loses. If he fails to reach 31, he is schneider ; and if he fails to take a trick he is schwartz. These various results increase the value of the game, as will presently be seen.

There are four varieties of games in which the successful bidder plays to win, the difference being in the manner of using the skat cards, and making the trump. These games are called *Frage, Tourne, Solo,* and *Grand,* and they outrank one another in the order given, Frage being the lowest. The first three : Frage, Tourné and Solo, are each again divided into four parts, according to the suit which is trumps ; a Tourné in clubs being better than one in spades ; a Solo in hearts being better than one in diamonds, and so on. This is in accordance with the rank of the suits already mentioned in the paragraph devoted to that subject.

In a *Fragé,* or Simple Game, the successful bidder takes both the skat cards into his hand, and then declares which suit shall be the trump; discarding two cards face downward for his schatz, or treasure, before play begins. The two cards thus laid aside count for the single player at the end of the hand, provided he takes a trick, and they cannot be won by the adversaries unless they make the single player schwartz.

In a *Tourné,* the successful bidder turns one of the skat cards face upward on the table before looking at the second card. He may turn over whichever card he pleases, but the one he turns fixes the trump suit for that hand, If he looks at one and turns another, or if he sees both before turning either, he must play a Frage. If the card turned over is a Seven, the player may change his game to a Nullo; or if it is a Jack he may change to a Grand; but in either case he must do so before he sees the second card in the Skat.

In a *Solo,* the skat cards are not touched, the successful bidder naming the trump to suit the hand of ten cards originally dealt him. The Skat belongs to him, as in Frage and Tourné, but he must not see its contents until the hand is played out, when any points and Matadores it may contain will count for him.

In a *Grand* there is no trump suit, the four Jacks being the only trumps in play. These four cards preserve their relative suit value, the club Jack being the best, and they are still Matadores. There are three varieties of Grand: A tourné player may make it a Grand if he turns up a Jack, provided he has not seen the other skat card. This is called *Grand Tourné.* A player may make it a Grand without seeing either of the skat cards. This is called a *Grand Solo.* A player may announce a Grand and lay his cards face up on the table; exposed, but not liable to be called. This is called a *Grand Ouvert.* A Frage cannot be played as a Grand under any circumstances, but some players, when they have got the play on a bid low enough to be a Frage game and have a hand almost good enough for a Grand, are in the habit of indulging in a little bit of sharp practice. They will take the skat cards into their hand one at a time, and as they lift them, if they see the first is a Jack, they will turn it over, so as to make it a Tourné, and claim the privilege of playing a Grand. If it is not a Jack, or does not fit their hand well enough to make them a good Tourné, they will put it with their other cards without showing it, and then take up the other card. For this reason it is the law in all good clubs that any player taking up the skat cards one at a time, must play a Tourné; and if he is going to play a Frage, he must lift both of them together.

GAME VALUES. Each of the foregoing games has what is called a unit of value, which is afterward multiplied several times according to the number of Matadores, and whether the game was schneider or schwartz.

These **unit** values are as follows, beginning with the lowest :

	◇	♡	♠	♣	Wenzels trumps.	No trumps.
Frage in	1	2	3	4	Grand Tourné, 12.	Nullo Tourné, 10.
Tourné in	5	6	7	8	Grand Solo, 18.	Null Solo, 23.
Solo in	9	10	11	12	Grand Ouvert, 24.	Null Ouvert. 46.

In some clubs a Nullo is worth 20 or 22 points ; and a Null Ouvert is worth double the amount agreed upon for the Nullo.

Multipliers. The foregoing are simply the standard counting values of these various games. In calculating the actual value of a player's game, in order to see how much he may safely offer in the bidding, and how much he would win if successful in his undertaking, these standard values are multiplied as follows :—

Five classes of games are recognized, beginning with the lowest, in which the player gets the necessary 61 points, but does not make his adversaries schneider. This is simply called "game," and as it must always be either won or lost, it is a constant factor. The value of the game is 1, and each better game is numbered in regular order, the five varieties being as follows :

The Game, 1. Schneider, 2. Schneider announced, 3. Schwartz, 4. Schwartz announced, 5.

These numbers are added to the number of Matadores, and the total thus found is multiplied by the unit value of the game. For instance : A player has obtained the privilege of playing on a bid of thirty. His game is a Solo in hearts, in which he holds the three highest Matadores and announces schneider in advance. His game multiplier is therefore 3, (for the announced schneider,) to which he adds 3 more for the Matadores, 6 altogether. The unit value of a heart Solo being 10, he could have gone on bidding to 60 had it been necessary, and he will win 60 from each of his adversaries if he succeeds in reaching 91 points in the counting cards he takes in in his tricks, together with what he finds in the Skat.

If his adversaries got to 30 with their counting cards, he would have lost 60 to each of them, although he bid only 30, because he announced his game as schneider, and did not make it. Had he not announced the schneider, and reached 91 or more in his counting cards, he would have won a game worth 50, losing the extra multiplier by not announcing the schneider in advance, for a schneider made without announcing it is worth only 2.

If a player announces schneider, and not only fails to make it, but is made schneider himself, his adversaries add one multiplier for the schneider they make.

In reckoning the value of a game it is always safer to bid on playing " with " than " without " Matadores in a Solo or Tourné ; because although you may have a hand " without four," you may find a Wenzel in the Skat, and if it is the club Jack you lose three multipliers at once.

BIDDING. The players must be familiar with the manner of computing the various games in order to bid with judgment, and without hesitation. Suppose you hold the three highest Matadores with an average hand, not strong enough in any one suit to play a Solo, but good enough for a Tourné. Your smallest possible game will be diamonds with three; which will be worth 5 multiplied by 4 ; 1 for the game, and 3 for the Matadores, 20 points. If you can get the game on any bid less than 20 you are absolutely safe, provided you can reach 61 in your tricks. But the opposition of another player may irritate you, [reizen,] and provoke you to bid 24, or even 28, in the hope of turning a heart or a spade. If you go beyond 20, and turn a diamond, you must either find the fourth Matadore in the Skat, or make your adversaries schneider, in order to secure another multiplier. If you fail, you lose 24, or 28, according to your bid.

The great difficulty in Skat is to judge the value of a hand, so as neither to under nor overbid it, and also to get all out of it that it is worth. A person who plays a Frage in hearts when he could easily have made it a Solo, reduces the value of his game just eighty per cent. A player with the four Wenzels, A K Q 9 8 of diamonds, and a losing card, would be foolish to play a diamond Solo with five, schneider announced, worth 72 ; while he had in his hand a sure Grand, with four, schneider announced, worth 126. Of course the schneider is not a certainty. The risk is that the Ten of diamonds will be guarded, and that an Ace and a Ten will make, both of them on your losing card, or one of them on the diamond Ten. A careful player would be satisfied with 108 on such a hand, for if he fails to make the announced schneider, he loses everything.

A player is not obliged to play the game he originally intended to, if he thinks he has anything better ; but he must play a game worth as much as he bid, or the next higher, and having once announced his game, he must play it.

Suppose Vorhand has a spade Solo with two, and on being offered 33 says, " Yes," thinking the bidder will go on to 36, instead of which he passes. It is very probable that the bidder has a spade Solo without two, and will defeat a spade Solo announced by Vorhand. If Vorhand has almost as good a game in hearts, he should change, hoping to make schneider, or to find another Matadore in the Skat. If he loses the game, a heart Solo with two costs 30 points ; but as Vorhand refused 33, and the next best game he could have made with a heart Solo is 40, that is the amount he loses, although he refused only 33.

Method of Bidding. The Vorhand always holds the play, and the Mittelhand always makes the first bid, or passes, the Hinterhand saying nothing until the propositions made by the Mittelhand have been finally refused or passed by the Vorhand. The usual formula is for the Vorhand to say, "How many?" or, "I am Vorhand," whereupon the Mittelhand bids or passes. If Vorhand has as good a game as offered him he says, "Yes," and Mittelhand must bid higher or pass. If Vorhand has not as good a game he may either pass, or bluff the bidder into going higher by saying, "Yes." As soon as one passes, the other turns to the Hinterhand, who must either make a higher bid than the last, or pass. The survivor of the first two must either say, "Yes," to the offers made by Hinterhand, or pass. The final survivor then announces his game. It is usual for the last one to pass to signify that he is done by pushing the skat cards toward the survivor, indicating that they are his, and that he is the player. If a player is offered a game equal to his own he may still say, "Yes;" but if he is offered a better game, and still says, "Yes," he runs the risk of being compelled to play.

The old German way of bidding, adopted at the Skat Congresses in Altenburg, Leipzig and Dresden, was to bid in suits; a bid of club Solo outranking one of spade Solo, no matter what it was worth. This has long been obsolete, the objection to it being that a player might get the play on a game of much inferior value. A player with a spade Solo, six Matadores, and schneider announced could offer only a spade Solo, without mentioning its value, and although his game was worth 99, he could be outbid by an offer of Nullo, which was then worth only 20. This is contrary to the spirit of the game, which requires that the person offering the game of the greatest value shall be the player. The rank of the bids in the old German game was as follows, beginning with the lowest :—

> Frage, in the order of the suits.
> Tourné, in the order of the suits.
> Grand Tourné.
> Solo in diamonds, hearts and spades.
> Nullo, worth 20.
> Solo in clubs.
> Grand Solo, worth 16.
> Null ouvert, worth 40.
> Grand ouvert.

The multipliers were the same as those used in the modern game, but the player had no means of using them in his bids. It will be observed that the modern value of the various games seeks to preserve the old rank by assuming the lowest possible bid on any given game. For instance : The lowest spade Solo would be worth 22; the lowest club Solo, 24. To make the Nullo still come between these bids, it is now worth 23.

THE SKAT CARDS. The successful bidder determined, the skat cards are pushed towards him, and the manner in which he uses them limits the game he is allowed to play. While the player must win or lose a game worth as many as bid, he may attempt to win as many more as he pleases. If he has got the play on a bid of ten, that does not prevent him from playing a club Solo, with schneider announced. But if he has bid or refused eleven, and plays a tourné in diamonds, he must make schneider or play with or without two Matadores in order to bring his multipliers up to three. If both these fail him he loses 15, the next higher game than his bid possible in a diamond tourné.

If the player takes both the skat cards into his hand, his game is limited to a Frage, but may be in any suit, and accompanied by an announcement of schneider or schwartz. His game announced, he lays out any two cards he pleases for his skat, so as to play with ten only.

If the player turns over either of the skat cards his game is limited to a tourné, but he may announce schneider or schwartz if he pleases. If he turns a Seven, he may change to Nullo, but not to Null Ouvert, and if he turns a Jack he may change to Grand, but not to Grand Ouvert. The unit value of a Nullo is 23, a Nullo tourné is 10 only. A Grand tourné is worth 12 only, while a Grand Solo is worth 18. A tourné player must lay out two skat cards to reduce his hand to ten cards.

If the player neither turns over nor takes into his hand either of the skat cards, he may play any of the suit Solos, Grand Solo, Grand Ouvert, Nullo, or Null Ouvert.

Any player looking at the skat cards before the beginning of the play is debarred from bidding that deal, and is penalised ten points in the score. In addition to this penalty, either of the other players may demand a fresh deal. If a player looks at the skat cards during the play of a hand the play is immediately stopped, and if he is the single player he can count only the points taken in up to that time, exclusive of the skat. These points are deducted from 120, and his adversaries claim the difference. The game is then settled, according to this count, exactly as if the hand had been played out. If an adversary of the single player looks at either of the skat cards during the play of a hand, the single player may at once stop the game, and his adversaries can count only the points they have taken in in tricks up to that time. If they have no tricks they are schwartz ; if they have not 30 points they are schneider.

When four or more play, any person holding no cards may be penalised ten points for looking at the skat cards.

METHOD OF PLAYING. The successful bidder having disposed of the skat cards and announced his game, the Vorhand leads any card he pleases for the first trick. Vorhand should be careful not to lead until the player has laid out or discarded for the Skat in a Frage or a Tourné. Players must follow suit if they can, but are not obliged to win the trick. Having none of the suit led they may trump or discard at pleasure. The highest card played, if of the suit led, wins the trick, and trumps win all other suits. The winner of the first trick leads for the next, and so on, until all the cards have been played, or the game is acknowledged as won or lost, and abandoned. In a Grand, if a Jack is led, players must follow suit with the other Jacks, they being trumps.

Abandoned Hands. If the single player finds he has overbid himself, or sees that he cannot make as good a game as bid, he may abandon his hand in a Frage or Tourné, to save himself from being made schneider or schwartz, provided he does so before he plays to the second trick. A Solo cannot be abandoned in this manner, as the rule is made only to allow a player to get off cheaply who has been unlucky in finding nothing in the Skat to suit his hand. For instance : A player has risked a Tourné with a missing suit, and turns up that suit, the other skat card being a different suit. He can abandon his hand at once, losing his bid or the next higher game, but escaping schneider or schwartz.

Irregularities in the Hands. If, during the play of a hand, any person is found to have too many or too few cards, the others having their right number, it is evident that there has been no misdeal if the pack is perfect and there are two cards in the Skat. If the player in error has too few cards, probably from having dropped one on the floor, or having played two cards to the same trick, he loses in any case, but the adversary may demand to have the hand played out in order to try for schneider or schwartz, and the last trick, with the missing card, must be considered as having been won by the side not in fault. If the player in fault is opposed to the single player, his partner suffers with him. If the player discovers his loss, he is not allowed to pick the card from the floor and replace it in his hand if he has in the meantime played to a trick with a wrong number of cards.

Playing Out of Turn. The usual penalty in America for leading or playing out of turn is the loss of the game if the error is made by the adversaries of the single player. If by the player himself, the card played in error must be taken back, and if only one adversary has played to the false lead, he may also take back his card. If both have played, the trick stands good. The single player suffers no penalty, as it is only to his own disadvantage to expose his hand.

The Revoke. If a player revokes, but discovers his error before the trick in which it occurs is turned and quitted, he may amend his play, and the card erroneously played is exposed. If the player in error is one of the adversaries of the single player, his partner may be prevented from leading the suit of the exposed card on the next trick, or when next he gets the lead. If the revoke is not discovered in time to save it, the side in error can count only the points in the tricks taken in up to that time, and the hand is then abandoned. In all cases in which the revoke is not discovered in time to remedy it, the game is lost for the player in error; but he may count the points in his tricks up to the time the revoke occurred, in order to save schneider or schwartz. In Nullos, the game is lost the moment the revoke is discovered.

Seeing Tricks. The tricks must be kept separate as they are taken in, and any player is allowed to look at the last trick turned and quitted. Any player looking at any other trick but the last may be penalised ten points.

Playing Ouverts. The strict rules of the game require Ouverts to be exposed face upward on the table before a card is played; but in some clubs the player's hand is not exposed until after the first trick.

SCORING. The score should always be kept by the player sitting on the right of the first dealer. This will mark the rounds. The score sheet should be ruled in vertical columns, one for each player at the table.

Each player is charged individually with his losses and gains, the amounts being added to or deducted from his score, and a plus or a minus mark placed in front of the last figure, so that the exact state of each player's score will be apparent at a glance.

The score of the single player is the only one put down, and it is charged to him as a loss or a gain at the end of each deal.

If there are four players, a line is drawn under every fourth amount entered in each person's account. If three play, the line is drawn under every third amount. This system of scoring will show at once whose turn it is to deal, if the total number of amounts under which no line is drawn are counted up. For instance : Three persons play ; A dealt the first hand. In the first three columns are shown the amounts won and lost in the three rounds, while the last three columns show the manner in which these losses and gains were entered on the score sheet :—

Points won and lost.			Score Card.		
1st Round.	2nd Round.	3rd Round.	A	B	C
A won 33	A lost 16	C lost 36	+ 33	+ 40	+ 55
C won 55	B won 40	B won 48	+ 17	+ 88	+ 67
C won 12	A lost 24	C lost 12	− 7		+ 31
					+ 19

At the end of the second round a line was drawn under A's account, which then contained three items; and after the first game in the third round a line was drawn under C's account.

If we suppose the game to be stopped at this point, the scores would be balanced as follows:

A is 7 points minus, and he has lost them to both B and C. He has also lost the 88 which B has won, and the 19 which C has won. These amounts are put down one under the other, as shown in the margin. B has won 7 and 88 from A, and 88 from C; but from the total of these amounts he must deduct the 19 won by C. C has won 7 and 19 from A, and 19 from B. From this total he must deduct the 88 points won by B, leaving him minus 43. If the total losses of A and C are now added

A	B	C
− 7	+ 7	+ 7
− 7	+88	+19
−88	+88	+19
−19	+183	+45
	−19	−88
−121	+164	−43

together, it will be found that they exactly balance B's winnings, showing that the account is correct.

If four persons play, each will individually win or lose to each of the three others, the dealer always sharing the fortunes of those opposed to the single player.

A glance at the first score sheet will show that there are three amounts under which no line has been drawn, two in B's column, and one in C's. As three deals make a round, it must be A's deal. If there were only two such open amounts, it would show that only two deals had been made on the round, consequently it would be C's deal.

CHEATING. As in all games in which the cards are dealt in groups, the greek will find many opportunities in Skat. The clumsiest shuffler can usually locate some of the Wenzels at the top or the bottom of the pack, before presenting it to be cut, and if the players do not insist on the cards being dealt always in the same manner, the sharper can secure to himself two or more Wenzels, either in his hand or in the Skat. Any person who deals the cards sometimes three at a time, and again five at a time, should be stopped immediately, and no such excuses as changing his luck should be listened to for a moment. Any person who habitually picks up the cards with their faces towards him, and straightens them by lifting them from their positions in the pack, should be stopped at once, and requested to straighten the cards face down.

Dealing seconds is very difficult when the cards have to be "pinched" in threes and fours. A second dealer holding back a Wenzel on the top may give his adversary two underneath without knowing it. Marked cards are of advantage only when the dealer plays, and are of little use beyond telling him what he can turn up for a trump, or what he will find in the Skat. The rule for having four in the game, if possible, is one of the greatest safeguards, un-less the dealer is in secret partnership with one of the players.

SUGGESTIONS FOR GOOD PLAY. The chief things to master in Skat are the values of the hands, the principles of bidding on them, the best methods of playing them, and the proper methods of combining forces with your partner for the time being, in order to defeat the single player.

Bidding. Some persons attach a great deal of importance to the odds for and against certain cards being in the Skat. If a player without three is forced to risk finding a Matadore in the Skat, it is usually enough for him to know that the odds are about 3 to 1 against it. It is much more important for him to consider what cards may make against him, and what they would count. It is often necessary to estimate very closely the number of points that must fall on a certain number of leads. For instance : You are Vorhand, and hold these cards :—

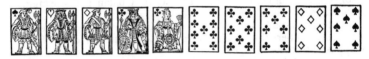

Even if you find the Ace and Ten with the best Wenzel in one hand against you, you have an almost certain club Solo, for if you lead a Wenzel, your adversary must either take it, or give you the Ace or Ten. If he wins it, and his partner gives him a Ten of another suit, and they then proceed to make both the Aces and Tens of your weak suits, that will give them only 56 points, and you will make every other trick. The only thing that could defeat you is for one player on the fourth trick to lead a suit of which his partner had none. This would require one player to have all the spades and the other all the hearts, which is almost impossible.

Another familiar example is the following : You are Vorhand with these cards :—

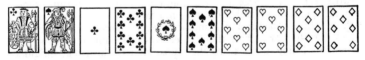

Although you cannot possibly win more than six tricks, and must lose every trick in the red suits, you have an invincible Grand ; because the adversaries have not a sufficient number of Fehlkarten to give you to avoid adding 16 points to the 46 you al-ready have in your hand, which must make you 62 before they get a trick.

It is better to bid on a doubtful Solo than on a risky Tourné ; and if you have a choice of two numerically equal suits, it is better to bid on a suit containing small cards in preference to one containing A 10. In bidding Tournés, you must remember that the more cards you hold of a suit, the less your chance to turn up one.

It is not good play to bid a Solo on four or five trumps unless you have some aces in the other suits. A Grand may be bid even without a trump, if you have the lead, and hold four aces, or three aces and four Tens. A Grand with any two Wenzels is safe if you have two good suits. A Nullo should never be bid unless the player has the Seven of his long suit.

A certain amount of risk must be taken in all bids, and a player who never offers a game that is not perfectly safe is called a *Maurer ;* one who builds on a solid foundation. The player who offers the most games will usually win the most unless he is a very poor player.

Leading. The single player should almost always begin with the trumps, in order to get them out of his way. With a sequence of Wenzels, it is a common artifice to begin with the lowest, hoping the second player may fatten the trick by discarding a Ten or Ace, under the impression that the Hinterhand can win it. This style of underplay is called *Wimmelfinte,* and the Mittelhand should beware of it. With only one Wenzel and the Ace and Ten, it is better to begin with a small trump. If you find all the trumps in one hand against you, or tenace over you, stop leading trumps, and play forcing cards.

If you have no Wenzels it is usually best to lead your smallest trumps. If you have only Ace Ten and small trumps, and know the adversaries have one Wenzel and one trump better than your small one, lead your Ten, so that they cannot make both trumps. In playing for a schneider, it is often advisable to continue the trumps, even after the adversaries are exhausted, so that they shall not know which suit to keep for the last trick.

Laying out the Skat. In a Frage or a Tourné, some judgment is required in discarding for the Skat. It is often necessary to lay aside the Ace and Ten of trumps if there is any danger that the adversaries may catch them. Unguarded Tens should always be laid out, and it is a good general principle to get rid of one suit entirely, so that you can trump it. It is a common practice to put in the Skat the Ace and Ten of a suit of which you hold also the King. When you lead the King, if Mittelhand has none of the suit he is sure to fatten the trick for his partner, thinking he must have Ace or Ten. With the Ten, King, and small cards of a plain suit, lay the Ten and King in the Skat.

The Adversaries should combine against the single player by getting him between them if possible. If you sit on the left of the player, lead your short suits up to him ; but if you sit on his right, lead your longest suit through him. Try to force out his trumps on your plain-suit cards if you can, and avoid giving him discards of his weak suits. With a long trump suit, it is often advantageous to lead it through the player, but seldom right to lead it up to him.

In Solos, the adversaries should lead Aces and winning cards, and change suits frequently. If you are playing against a Grand, and have two trumps, one of them the best, lead it, and then play your long suit ; but if you have the two smallest trumps, lead the long suit first, and force with it every time you get in.

The partners should always scheme to protect each other's Tens by keeping the Aces of plain suits. For this reason it is very bad play to fatten with the Ace of a suit of which you have not the Ten, or to play an Ace third hand when there are only small cards in the trick, and the Ten of the suit has not been played and you do not hold it.

If the player is void of a suit, continue leading it, no matter what you hold in it. This will either weaken his trumps, or, if he is between you, will give your partner discards.

If the player leads a Wenzel, it is usually best to cover it if you can ; but do not play the club Jack on the diamond Jack unless you want the lead very badly.

When the single player does not lead trumps, but plays his Aces and Tens, the Germans call it "auf die Dörfer gehen ;" that is, getting to the villages, or getting home ; equivalent to our expression, "getting out of the woods," or "getting in out of the rain." When the single player runs for home in this way, it is usually best to lead trumps through him at the first opportunity.

In playing against a Nullo, the great point is to give your partner discards. If you find that the player's long suit is yours also, continue it until your partner has discarded an entire suit if possible. If you then have the small card of the discarded suit, you may defeat the Nullo at once.

Fattening. The Germans call this Wimmeln, or "swarming" the points together in one trick. It is always advisable to get rid of Tens in this way, or Aces of suits in which you hold both Ace and Ten ; but it is bad play to fatten with the Ace of a suit of which you have not the Ten, unless the trick wins the game from the player, or saves a very probable schneider.

The following ***Illustrative Hands*** will give the student a very good idea of the manner in which the various forms of the game are played, showing the difference in the play of a Frage, Tourné, Solo, and Grand.

A FRAGE. Mittelhand offered 10 ; Vorhand said, "Yes," and Mittelhand passed. Hinterhand then offered 11 on these cards :—

Vorhand passed, and Hinterhand, afraid of losing a big game if he played a Tourné and found a diamond or a spade, concluded to take both the Skat cards, hoping to make a club Frage without three, which would be worth 16 points. In the Skat he found the ♡ 9 and ♡ 8. Having bid too high to play a heart Frage, he was obliged to stick to his clubs, laying out for the Skat the Tens of hearts and diamonds. The play is given in the margin, C being the single player, and A being Vorhand, with the lead on the first trick. Clubs are trumps.

When leading up to the single player, the rule is to lead the short suit ; but when leading through him, the long suit. B, knowing that A must be very short in spades, leads the suit back through the player. Had A led the heart Seven, B would have put on his best trump and led the spade suit. At trick 5, it makes no difference in the result whether C passes or trumps, for A will discard his diamond if C does not trump.

C is schwartz, not having won a trick, and loses a club Frage, the unit value of which is 4, multiplied by 4 for the schwartz, and 3 for the Matadores ; 7 times 4 equals 28 points.

A FRAGE.

	A	B	C
1	7 ♠	A ♠	8 ♠
2	♣ Q	K ♠	10 ♠
3	♡ 7	♣ A	♡ 8
4	9 ◊	Q ♠	♡ 9
5	♣ 9	9 ♠	♣ 7
6	♣ J	♣ K	♣ 8
7	J ♠	K ◊	J ◊
8	♡ J	Q ◊	♣ 10
9	8 ◊	A ◊	♡ K
10	♡ Q	7 ◊	♡ A

♡ 10 and ◊ 10 in the Skat.

A TOURNÉ. A, Vorhand, has refused ten with the following cards, Hinterhand having passed without a bid :—

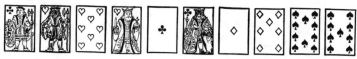

A concludes to play a Tourné, and turns the heart ♡ Q, finding the ◊ King in the Skat. He lays out the ♠ 10 and ♠ 9 in the Skat, and expects to make 12 points ; a heart Tourné, with one Matadore. The play is given in the margin. A is the player, and is also Vorhand, with the lead for the first trick. Hearts are trumps.

A TOURNÉ.

	A	B	C	A wins.
I	♣ J	♡ 7	J ♦	4
2	♡ Q	♡ A	♡ 8	–
3	K ♦	9 ♦	Q ♦	7
4	♡ J	J ♠	A ♠	–
5	♡ 10	♡ 9	7 ♠	10
6	A ♦	♣ 7	8 ♦	11
7	7 ♦	K ♠	10 ♦	–
8	♣ K	♣ 10	♣ 9	–
8	♡ K	Q ♠	8 ♠	7
10	♣ A	♣ Q	♣ 8	14
	♠ 10 and ♠ 9 in the Scat.			10
			A wins 63	

A SOLO.

	A	B	C	A wins.
I	♡ ♠	K ♠	♡ J	–
2	♣ A	♣ K	♣ 7	15
3	9 ♠	Q ♠	10 ♦	–
4	7 ♦	A ♦	Q ♦	–
5	8 ♦	K ♦	♣ Q	–
6	♡ A	♡ K	♡ 8	15
7	♡ 10	♡ 7	♡ 9	10
8	10 ♠	7 ♠	♣ 8	10
9	J ♠	♣ J	♡ Q	–
10	A ♠	J ♦	♣ 9	–
	♦ 9 and ♣ 10 in the Scat.			10
			A wins 60	

The manner in which A exhausts the trumps, and makes both his Ace and King of diamonds, should be carefully studied. At trick 8, if he put on the ace of clubs, B might have the 8, and he would lose both his King and the Queen on the Ten, giving him only 60 points. It must be remembered that A knows every card out against him, because he has seen the skat cards. A wins his 12 points; a heart Tourné with one.

A SOLO. Vorhand has refused a bid of 18, and announces spade Solo with the following cards:—

He has the lead for the first trick, and of course begins with the trumps. The play is given in the margin.

C wins the first trick, and leads his long suit through the player. In the last three tricks A coaxes B to win the Ten of trumps; but if B does so he gives up the advantage of his tenace over the player, which is now the only chance to defeat him. B knows that if he wins the Ten of trumps, B and C can make only 59 points, because A will save his trump Ace.

A, having failed to reach 61, loses a spade Solo without one; twice 11, or 22 points, which was the game he must have won to be as good as the offer of 18 which he refused.

A GRAND. B bids ; both Vorhand and Mittelhand pass, and B announces a Grand, with the following cards :—

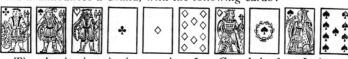

The play is given in the margin. In a Grand the four Jacks are the only trumps.

A has the first, and as he leads through the player, he begins with his long suit, of which he knows that the Ace alone is out, and it may be in the skat. If the player has the Ace, C will probably trump it. If the player has not the Ace, it is just possible that he will not trump the Ten.

C, leading up to the player, opens his short weak suit. At trick 3, C knows that A must have the Ten of hearts, or he would not fatten with the Ace. As this shows that A can stop the heart suit, C guards the spades and lets all his hearts go.

B loses a very strong Grand, which must have been successful if C had had one club,

A GRAND.

	A	B	C	B wins.
I	♣10	♣ A	J ♦	—
2	8 ♠	A ♦	7 ♦	11
3	♡ A	9 ♠	10 ♠	—
4	♣ 7	10 ♦	9 ♦	10
5	♣ 8	♡ J	Q ♦	5
6	♣ 9	J ♠	♡ 9	2
7	♡ 7	K ♦	♡ Q	7
8	♣ Q	♣ J	♡ K	9
9	♣ K	A ♠	7 ♠	15
10	♡ 10	Q ♠	K ♠	—
	◇ 8 and ♡ 8 in the Scat.			—
			B wins 59	

or if A had led anything but the club Ten. A Grand with three Matadores is worth 4 times 18, or 72 points, which is what B loses, although he may have bid only 10 or 12 to get the play.

TEXT BOOKS.

Lehrbuch des Skatspiels, by K. Buhle. 1891.
Deutsche Skatordnung, by K. Buhle. 1888.
Scatspiel. (Anon.)
Von Posert, Quedlinburg. 1879.
Encyclopædia der Spiele, by Fr. Anton. 1889.
Skat. by F. Tschientschy. 1888.
Skat, by L. V. Diehl. 1891.
Skat, by E. E. Lemcke. 1887.
Of the foregoing, only the last two are in English. All of them treat of the old game, in which the bidding was by suits, instead of by figures, but many of them give some fine examples of play. The first on the list is the best for the student, and is a classic in its way.

SKAT LAWS.

The following laws are a liberal translation of the German Skat Laws, approved at the Skat Congresses in Altenburg, Leipzig and Dresden; but the author has modified them to agree with modern practice. The chief changes are in the omission of all laws governing the old-fashioned system of bidding by suits, and in the penalty for adversaries of the single player leading out of turn.

1. Players. Skat may be played by three or more persons; but only three of those at the table are active players in each hand, the others are "im Skat," and share the losses and gains of the adversaries of the single player.

2. Newcomers. After the game has begun, no one can join the table unless those already belonging to it agree, and then only after the first round; that is, after each player has had a deal.

3. Should any person cut into the game after it has begun, he must take the seat to the right of the player who dealt the first hand, unless the others agree to allow him another seat.

4. Stopping the Game. The game cannot be stopped before the time agreed on, unless one of the players gives notice in advance, and then only at the end of a round.

5. Cutting. In drawing for the choice of seats at the table, the lowest cut has the first choice, and the others take their places in order upon his left. The rank of the cards in cutting is the same as in play, and the suits outrank one another in the same order.

6. If the players take their seats without drawing for them, they must cut for the first deal; but if the places have been drawn for, the one who drew the lowest card takes the first deal.

7. Cards. The thirty-two cards in the Skat pack are divided into four suits, which outrank one another in the following order: Clubs, spades, hearts and diamonds. There are eight cards in each suit, of the following rank and counting value, beginning with the highest: Ace 11, Ten 10, King 4, Queen 3, Jack 2. The Nine, Eight, and Seven have no counting value.

8. Shuffling. At the beginning of the game, and after each deal, the cards should be shuffled at least three times, and the shuffling must be done without exposing the face of any card.

9. Cutting. The shuffled pack must be presented by the dealer to his right hand neighbour to be cut. The pone must cut the pack, and at least five cards must be left in each packet. If a card is exposed there must be a new cut.

10. Dealing. The cards must be dealt in such a manner that no player can see the face of any card.

11. Only three persons at the table receive cards, and each of them must be given ten. If there are four players, the dealer gives himself no cards. If there are five or six players, the first two players on the dealer's left, and the one on his right receive cards.

12. The cards must be dealt in two rounds of five each ; or three the first round, then four, and then three again ; or three and then two, and three and then two again. The dealer is allowed to choose any of these methods, but the one first selected must be continued throughout the game, not only by the first dealer, but by each of the other players. A club may make it a rule to deal the cards in a certain manner all the time.

13. The cards must be dealt from left to right, and the deal passes to the left.

14. *Skat Cards.* Ten cards being given to each player, two are left over. These are the skat cards, and they must not be the first nor the last to be dealt. It is usual to lay out the skat cards after the first round has been dealt to each player.

15. No one but the successful bidder is allowed to see the skat cards. Any player who looks at the skat cards before the beginning of the game is debarred from bidding that deal, and loses ten points to each of the other players at the table. In addition to this penalty, the others may demand a fresh deal.

16. Should any one look at the skat cards during the play of a hand, the player in fault can count only the tricks taken up to that time, and the hand is then abandoned.

17. If any player "im Skat" looks at the skat cards, he loses ten points.

18. *Misdealing.* If any card is exposed during the deal, any player who has not touched his cards may demand a fresh deal.

19. If the dealer gives too many or too few cards to any player, the dealer must shuffle and deal again. If the error is not discovered until the hand is partly played out, the deal is void.

20. A player may be penalised ten points for misdealing.

21. *Irregularities in the Hands.* If a player is found to have too few cards, whether from having dropped one on the floor, or playing two or more to one trick, he loses the game ; but the adversaries of the player in fault may demand that the hand be played out, to see if they can make schneider or schwartz ; and the last trick, together with the missing card, must be considered as having been won by the side not in fault. If it is an adversary of the single player who has too few cards, his partner suffers with him.

22. A player who has dropped a card on the floor, or who discovers that he has played two cards to one trick, is not allowed to take the missing card back into his hand if he has played to a trick in the meantime.

23. *Partnerships.* The three active players are divided into two sides. The one who has made the highest bid, for the privilege of playing alone, is called the "player," the others are called the "adversaries."

24. The adversaries share each other's winnings and losses, and all points in the tricks they take in count for them together ; but they are not allowed to make any intimation to each other of the cards they hold.

25. *Payments.* The player, if he wins, receives from each of the opposing partners, and also from the players "im skat," if any, the full value of his game, according to the table of payments. If the player loses he must pay each of the adversaries as much as he would have won had he been successful.

26. *Games.* The winning or losing of the player's game depends on the number of points taken in in tricks.

27. In Skat there are five varieties of games. 1, The simple won or lost game. 2, Schneider. 3, Schneider Announced. 4, Schwartz. 5, Schwartz Announced.

28. The player wins a ***Simple*** game if he gets 61 points in the tricks he takes in, together with the skat cards. The adversaries win if they get 60.

29. The player wins a ***Schneider*** if he gets 91 points. The adversaries win a schneider if the player fails to reach 31, and they add one multiplier to the value of the game.

30. In Solo and Grand, the player wishing to ***announce schneider*** must do so before a card is played. This obliges him to make 91 points, or to lose his game.

31. It either side fails to win a trick, it is ***schwartz.*** A single trick, even if it contains no counting cards, will save the schwartz.

32. In a Solo or Grand, the player wishing to ***announce schwartz,*** must do so before a card is played.

33. A player announcing schneider or schwartz and failing, loses the same amount that he would have won had he been successful. If he is made schneider or schwartz, the adversaries add multipliers to the value of the game.

34. *Trump Suits.* In all games except Grand, Nullo, and Ramsch one of the four suits will become the trump, and the three others will then become equal in value except for the purpose of computing the value of the game.

35. *Wenzels.* In all games except Nullo the four Jacks are the best trumps, and they outrank one another in the order of the suits; clubs, spades, hearts and diamonds, the club Jack being always the best trump. In a Grand or Ramsch the Wenzels are the only trumps.

36. *Trumping.* Any player who is unable to follow suit may play a trump; and the trump so played will win any plain-suit card. A higher trump will win a lower.

37. *Matadores.* Trumps in unbroken sequence with the club Jack form the Matadores. If the single player has the club Jack in his hand or in the skat, he plays *"with"* Matadores; but if either adversary holds the club Jack, the single player is *"without"* Matadores.

38. *Classes of Games.* The variety of game which shall be played is determined by the manner of using the skat cards, and by the announcement made by the successful bidder. Six classes are in general use :—

1. Frage, in any suit.
2. Tourné, in any suit.
3. Grand Tourné.
4. Solo, in any suit.
5. Grand Solo, and Grand Solo Ouvert.
6. Nullo, and Null Ouvert.

39. In the first three the player takes the skat cards into his hand, discarding others in their place. In the last three he must play from his hand, without any knowledge of the skat cards.

40. In a *Frage,* the player takes up both the skat cards at the same time, without showing or naming them, and after discarding others in their place, he must announce the trump suit. In laying out for the skat he may discard either or both the cards originally found there, and the points so laid aside count for him at the end of the hand.

41. In a *Tourné,* the player must select one of the skat cards, and turn it face upward on the table, without seeing the other. The card so turned up determines the trump suit for that hand. Both the skat cards are then taken into the player's hand, without showing or naming the second one, and two cards are then laid out, as in Frage.

42. Should the player see the face of both cards before turning one; or see one and turn the other, he must play a Frage; and if he loses the game he must pay the value of the next higher Frage game above the number of points he bid or refused.

43. Should the turn-up card be a Jack, the player has the option of playing a Tourné in that suit, or announcing a Grand

Tourné. Should the turn-up be a Seven, he may play a Tourné in that suit, or announce a Nullo Tourné. Either announcement must be made before seeing the second card in the skat.

44. The value of a Nullo Tourné must be agreed upon beforehand; or it may be decided not to allow it at all. The usual value of it is ten points.

45. In Solo, Grand Solo, Nullo, or Null Ouvert, the successful bidder must announce his game without seeing either of the skat cards; but whatever points or Matadores are contained therein count for him at the end of the hand.

46. Should the player see either of the skat cards, he cannot play a Solo or Nullo. If he has seen one only, he may play a Tourné; but if he has seen both he must play a Frage.

47. Ouverts. In either of the Ouverts, the player must expose his cards face upward on the table before a card is played. In Grand Ouvert he must win every trick, or he loses his game. The cards so exposed are not liable to be called. In Null Ouvert there are no trumps, and the cards rank in the following order:— A K Q J 10 9 8 7, the Ace being the highest. The Nullo is lost the moment the single player wins a trick.

48. Bidding. The Mittelhand must make the first bid. If Vorhand passes, Hinterhand bids to Mittelhand; but if Mittelhand passes, Hinterhand bids to Vorhand.

49. The person offering the most valuable game is the player, and the skat cards must be pushed toward him, to be used as he sees fit.

50. As between two games of equal value, the elder hand has the preference. That is to say, if the player has a game equal in value to the one offered to him, he may decline the offer, and the bidder must go higher or pass.

51. A bid once offered cannot be withdrawn.

52. A person is not obliged to offer the full value of his game, nor its exact value; but if he is called upon to play, his game must be worth at least as much as he bid or refused.

53. If the Vorhand says: "Go on and bid;" no bid having been made, that does not oblige him to play; and if no offer is made, he may pass also, and the deal goes to the next player on the dealer's left.

54. If the person to whom a bid is offered has as good a game or better, he must say, "Yes," if he wishes to keep his game. If he has not as good a game, and does not wish to run the risk of being called upon to play, he must say, "I pass."

55. All bidding must be done in figures, it being understood that each player making an offer will play a game worth as much as he offers, or more. He is not obliged to state how he proposes to reach the figure named.

56. When the hand is played and the skat cards are examined, if the player's game is not as valuable as his bid, he loses, even if he has reached 61 points ; and the amount he loses is the value of the game that it would have been necessary for him to win to make good his bid. For instance : A player bidding twelve and playing a diamond Tourné, loses fifteen unless he is with or without two, or makes his adversaries schneider.

57. *Abandoned Games.* In a Frage or Tourné, but not in Solo or Nullo, the single player may abandon his game at any time before he plays to the second trick, so that he cannot be made schneider or schwartz. If either adversary of the player abandons his game, his partner is bound to it also, but the single player need not accept the decision. He may claim schneider or schwartz, and if the adversaries will not allow the claim, he may compel them to play the hand out.

58. If the player lays down his cards after he has played to the second trick, he is schneider unless he is already out of schneider.

59. If the player lays down his cards as evidence that his game is a certainty, he must announce his claim before the hand is so exposed, or he cannot count it.

60. *Playing.* After the game has been announced, the Vorhand leads for the first trick. All cards are played from left to right, and the winner of one trick leads for the next.

61. If the single player leads out of turn, the cards must be taken back if the trick is not complete ; but if the error is not discovered before all have played to the trick, it cannot be remedied. Any card played to the false lead can be taken back without penalty.

62. If either adversary of the single player leads out of turn, or if the third hand wins a trick out of turn, or trumps it, the single player can claim his game as won. If it is won already, he can claim schneider ; and if it is already schneider, he can claim schwartz.

63. Players must follow suit if they can ; but having none of the suit led may trump or discard at pleasure. No one is obliged to win any trick.

64. *Revokes.* If a player revokes, the error may be remedied at any time before the trick in which it occurs has been turned and quitted. If the card played in error is of a certain suit the partner of the player in error can be prevented from playing that suit in the next trick, or the next time he has the lead.

65. If the revoke is not discovered in time to correct it, the player in fault can count only the tricks taken up to the time the revoke occurred, and the hand is abandoned, and settled for according to the points won by the side in fault, preceding but exclusive of the trick in which the revoke occurred.

66. In all cases in which a revoke is not discovered in time to correct it, the game is lost by the side in fault. In Nullos it is lost immediately.

67. *The tricks* must be kept separate. Any person may see the last trick turned and quitted, but no other. A person looking at any trick but the last must be penalised ten points.

68. The players "*im Skat*" are not allowed to look over the other hands, nor to advise an adversary of the single player, except with the player's consent.

69. *Ramsch.* If Ramsch is played, each player is for himself, and the four suits are equal, the four Wenzels being the only trumps. The skat cards are not touched, nor are they reckoned in the count. The person winning the most points loses ten. If two players have the same number, but more than the third, both lose. If all three have the same number, the deal is void. If any player takes no trick, the loser must pay him double. If any player takes all the tricks, he must pay three times, or thirty points. Ramsch may be played only when no bid is made, or when the player gets the game on ten.

70. The values of the various games are as follows :—

	◇	♡	♠	♣	Wenzels Trumps.	No Trumps.
Frage in	I	2	3	4	Grand Tourné, 12	Nullo Tourné, 10
Tourné in	5	6	7	8	Grand Solo, 18	Null Solo, 23
Solo in	9	10	11	12	Grand Ouvert, 24	Null Ouvert, 46

71. In calculating the value of the games, the foregoing must be increased by the following multipliers ;—For the game, 1. For schneider, 2. For schneider announced, 3. For schwartz, 4. For schwartz announced, 5 ; and once more for every Matadore, with or without.

72. If the adversaries of the player make him schneider or schwartz, they add to the player's multipliers :—1 if they make him schneider, 3 if they make him schwartz ; but they are not allowed to announce it in advance.

73. There are no multipliers in Ramsch or Nullo.

74. The amount lost by the player, if he fails, is not the amount he has bid or refused ; but the amount he would have won if successful, or that it would have been necessary for him to win in the game he played, in order to make good his bid. This amount must be further increased if the adversaries make him schneider or schwartz.

CRIBBAGE.

Cribbage is not only one of the oldest of the games upon the cards, but enjoys the distinction of being quite unlike any other game, both in the manner of playing it, and in the system of reckoning the points. It is also peculiar from the fact that it is one of the very few really good games which require no effort of the memory ; judgment and finesse being the qualities chiefly requisite for success.

There are two principal varieties of the game ; *Five* and *Six-card* Cribbage ; and these again are divided according to the number of players. The old writers agree in speaking of the five-card game as the more scientific ; but the modern verdict is in favour of the six-card game, which is certainly the more common and popular. The skill in Five-card Cribbage is limited to laying out for the crib and securing the " go " ; but in Six-card Cribbage, while the scientific principles applicable to the crib remain the same as in the five-card game, there is abundant room for the display of skill all through, the hand being as important as the crib, and the play sometimes more important than either. The six-card game will be first described.

CARDS. Cribbage is played with a full pack of fifty-two cards, which have no rank except the order of their sequence ; K Q J 10 9 8 7 6 5 4 3 2 A, the Ace being always the lowest, either in cutting or in play. The cards have also a counting or pip value, the three court cards, K Q J, and the 10 being worth ten points each. All other cards, including the Ace, retain their face value. There are no trumps, and the four suits are therefore equal in value at all times.

MARKERS. The game is 61 points, and is scored or " pegged " on a cribbage board, which has a double row of 30 holes on each side, and a game-hole at each end. The players are each provided with two pegs, and they score the points as they accrue by advancing their pegs from left to right according to the number of points they make. For instance : One player makes 6 for his first count. He places one of his pegs in the sixth hole from the left-hand end of the board. Then he makes 4, and places the second peg four holes in advance of the first, which will show that his total score is ten points. The third time he makes 2, which he scores by lifting out the back peg and putting it two holes in advance of the first one. This system of pegging not only shows the total number of points made by either player, but enables the adversary to check the count, as a glance at the distance between the two pegs will show the number of points pegged last time.

When a player reaches the extreme right of the board, 30 points, he crosses over to the inner row of holes, and goes down from right to left. On reaching the end of the second row he has still one more to go to get into the game-hole, which is in the middle of the board.

When one player reaches his game-hole before the other turns the corner, it is called a *lurch,* and counts two games.

The pegs are so often lost or mislaid that it is much more convenient to use a *pull-up* cribbage board, in which every hole is provided with its own peg, which may be raised to indicate the count. The back pegs can be either left standing or pushed down again.

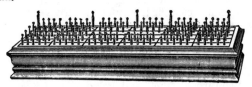

The board is always placed midway between the players.

If three persons play, a triangular board is necessary. This is provided with three sets of holes and three game holes.

When a cribbage board is not at hand, the game may be kept by ruling a sheet of paper into ten divisions, and marking them with the figures 1 to 0 on each side :

0	9	8	7	6	5	4	3	2	1
1	2	3	4	5	6	7	8	9	0

Each player being provided with two coins, one silver and one copper, (or different sizes,) the copper coin can be advanced from point to point to count units, and the silver coin will mark the tens.

PLAYERS. Cribbage is distinctly a game for two players, although three may play, each for himself, or four, two being partners against the other two. When two play, one is known as the *dealer,* and the other as the non-dealer, or the *pone.*

CUTTING. The players cut for the choice of seats, and for the first deal. The lowest cut has the choice, and deals the first hand. The Ace is low. If a player exposes more than one card he must cut again. Ties are also decided by cutting again.

STAKES. Cribbage is played for so much a game, lurches counting double. Players may either settle at the end of each game, or score on a sheet of paper. In the pull-up cribbage boards there are nine extra pegs for counting games won. These are placed in a line with the player's game hole at each end.

DEALING. The cards are shuffled and presented to the pone to be cut, and he must leave at least six cards in each packet. Six cards are dealt to each player, one at a time in rotation, beginning with the player on the dealer's left if there are more than two. No trump is turned, and the remainder of the pack is placed face downward at the end of the cribbage board on the dealer's left.

Irregularities. It is a misdeal if any card is found faced in the pack, or if the pack is found to be imperfect, and there must be a fresh deal by the same dealer. Any previous cuts or scores made with the imperfect pack stand good. A player dealing out of turn may be stopped before the non-dealer lifts his cards from the table. The penalty for dealing out of turn is two points, if the error is detected in time; otherwise the deal stands good.

If the dealer neglects to have the pack cut, exposes a card in dealing, gives too many or too few cards to any player, deals a card incorrectly, and fails to remedy the error before dealing another, or exposes one of his adversary's cards, the non-dealer scores two points by way of penalty. He also has the option of demanding a fresh deal by the same dealer, or of letting the deal stand. If the error is simply an irregularity in the manner of dealing, or an exposed card, the pone must decide without looking at his cards. If either player has too many or too few cards, the pone may look at the hand dealt him before deciding whether or not to have a fresh deal; but if it is the pone himself that has too many or too few cards, he must discover and announce the error before lifting his cards from the table, or he will not be entitled to the option of letting the deal stand. If the pone has too many cards he may return the surplus to the top of the pack, without showing or naming them. If the dealer has too many, the pone may draw from his hand face downward, returning the surplus to the top of the pack; but the pone may not look at the cards so drawn unless the dealer has seen them. If there are too few cards, and the pone elects to have the deal stand, the deficiency must be supplied from the top of the pack.

THE CRIB. The cards dealt, each player takes up his six cards and examines them with a view to laying out two cards, face downward, for the crib; leaving himself four cards with which to play. The four cards which form the crib, two from each hand, always belong to the dealer, and it is usual for each player, in discarding for the crib, to slip his two cards under the end of the cribbage board opposite to that occupied by the remainder of the pack.

Cards once laid out for the crib, and the hand removed from them, cannot be taken up again. A penalty of two points may be scored by the adversary for each card so taken up again, whether it is returned to the player's hand or not. If either player confuses his cards in any manner with those of the crib, his adversary scores two points, and may also claim a fresh deal.

If it is not discovered until he comes to lay out for the crib, that a player has too many cards, the same rules apply that are given for misdealing; but if he has too few cards there is no remedy, as he has lifted his hand. He must lay out two cards for the crib and play with what remain, his adversary scoring two points penalty at the same time.

THE STARTER. Both players having discarded for the crib, the non-dealer cuts the remainder of the pack, and the dealer lifts the top card from the portion left on the table, turning it face up. The two portions being again united, the turned card is placed face up on the pack, and is known as the starter, because it forms the starting-point in the count for every hand and crib. At least four cards must be left in each packet in cutting for the starter.

If the starter is a Jack, the dealer immediately pegs two points ***for his heels.*** If he does not peg these two holes before he plays a card the score is lost. If the Jack of the same suit as the starter is found in the hand or crib of any player, it is called ***his nobs,*** and when the hand is reckoned up after the play is over, one point may be scored for it.

If the dealer exposes more than one card after the pack has been properly cut, his adversary may choose which of the exposed cards shall be the starter.

In order to understand the motives which govern the players in discarding, and the influences which the starter has upon the value of the hands and crib, it will be necessary to describe the objects of the game, before giving the method of play.

OBJECTS OF THE GAME. The chief object in Cribbage is to form and to preserve various counting combinations. As these combinations occur in the course of play, or are shown in the hand or crib after the play is over, their value in points is pegged on the cribbage board, and the player who first pegs a sufficient number of these combinations to reach a total of 61 points, wins the game.

There are five principal varieties of these counting combinations : Pairs, Triplets, Fours, Sequences, and Fifteens ; besides some minor counts which will be spoken of in their proper place.

The various counting combinations in Cribbage may arise in two ways. They may be formed by combining the cards played by one person with those played by his adversary ; or they may be found in the individual hand or crib after the play is over. In the latter case the starter is considered as part of each hand and crib, increasing each of them to five available counting cards.

Pairs. A pair is any two cards of the same denomination, such as two Fives or two Queens, and its counting value is always the same, 2 points. ***Triplets,*** usually called Pairs Royal, Proils, or Prials, are any three cards of the same denomination, such as three Nines. Their value is the number of separate pairs that can be formed with the three cards, which is three, and the combination is therefore always worth 6 points. The different pairs that can be formed with three Nines, for instance, would be as follows :—

Fours, sometimes called Double Pairs Royal, or Deproils, are any four cards of the same denomination, such as four Fours, and their counting value is the number of separate pairs that can be formed with the four cards, which is six. The combination is therefore always worth 12 points. The different combinations of four cards, arranged in pairs, is as follows :—

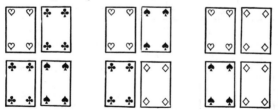

Whether the foregoing combinations are formed during the play of the hand, or found in the hand or crib after the play is over, their counting value is exactly the same.

Sequences. Any three or more cards, following one another in numerical order, will form a sequence. A sequence may also run into the court cards, such as 9 10 J, 10 J Q, or J Q K ; but Q K A is not a sequence in Cribbage. The counting value of a sequence is one point for each card in it. Sequences formed in the course of play must always be single, although the cards forming them need not fall in regular order. Those found in the hand or crib may be double, and those formed with the aid of the starter may be treble or quadruple.

The method of computing the value of double and treble sequences should be thoroughly understood, in order that such combinations may be counted at sight. A few examples will show that each combination belongs to a certain class, to which the same counting value is always attached. These classes are distinguished by the number of duplicates of the sequence cards.

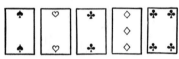

If you hold three cards which form a sequence, and have also a duplicate of any one of them, no matter which, it is evident that by substituting the card of equal value you can form another sequence. Such combinations are therefore always worth 8 points, 6 for the *double run,* as it is called, and 2 for the pair, no matter what the cards are that form the combination.

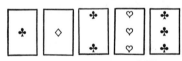

If the five cards in the hand and starter together contain a run of three with two duplicates, it is evident that three separate sequences can be formed by using each of the duplicates alternately. Such combinations are always worth 15 points ; 9 for the triple run of three, and 6 for the pair royal.

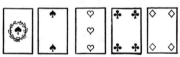

If the duplicates are of two different cards, no matter which, it will be found that four different sequences of three cards each can be formed by changing the Aces and Threes alternately. Such combinations are therefore always worth 16 points ; four runs of three, worth 12, and 4 points for the two separate pairs.

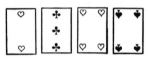

If the five cards contain one sequence of four, and one duplicate, the combination will always be worth 10 points ; 8 for the double run of four, and 2 for the pair.

The foregoing should be thoroughly familiar to every player, so that he may know the exact value of the combination the moment he sees the length of the sequence and the number of duplicates.

Two-card Fifteens. Any combination of two or more cards, the total face value of which is exactly 15, is called *fifteen-*

two, because each fifteen so formed is worth two points in the pegging. There are only three combinations of two cards which will form fifteen; a Five with any court card or Ten; a Nine and a Six; an Eight and a Seven. The manner of counting duplicates is the same as that employed for the pairs and sequences, and the player should be equally familiar with each variety of combination. The fifteens formed by *two cards* only are the simplest, and should be studied first.

 It is obvious that if there is in the hand or the starter a duplicate of either of the cards forming the fifteen, no matter which, another fifteen can be formed, and the combination will therefore always be worth 6 points; 4 for the two fifteens, and 2 for the pair. It must not be forgotten that in the case of *tenth cards,* as they are called, the duplicates may not form pairs, as for instance with K J 5. The fifteen is duplicated, but there is no pair.

 If there are two duplicates of either card, the combination will always be worth 12 points; 6 for the three fifteens, and 6 more, for the pair royal.

If the duplicates are of two different cards, the combination is still worth 12, because four different fifteens can be formed by combining each Nine with each Six separately, and there are two single pairs.

 The same is true of any combinations of two-card fifteens in which all five cards are of value; they are both of the same pegging value, 20 points. If there are three duplicates of one card in the original fifteen, the four separate fifteens will be worth 8, and the double pair royal 12.

If there are two duplicates of one card, and one of the other, six separate fifteens can be formed by combining each Nine with each Six, pegging 12; and the pair royal of one card with the single pair of the other will add 8 more.

Three-card Fifteens may be formed in fifteen different ways, ranging from 10 4 A, to 5 5 5. If you hold any of these combinations, and have a fourth card which is a duplicate of any of the three forming the fifteen, the value of the combination will depend on how many cards you can replace with the duplicate card.

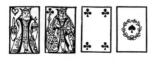

If you have an extra tenth card, you can replace the other tenth card once only, and the total value of the combination is therefore 6 points, which is expressed by the formula; " Fifteen-two, fifteen-four, and a pair."

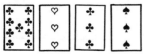

If your combination was 9 3 3, and you had another 9, the same thing would be true ; but if your duplicate is a Three, there are two cards which can be replaced, and the combination is therefore worth 12 ; 6 for the three fifteens, and 6 more for the pair royal.

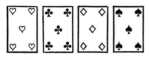

If your combination is one in which all three cards can be replaced with the duplicate, making three extra fifteens, it must be worth 20 altogether ; 8 for the four fifteens, and 12 for the double pair royal.

If you have two duplicates of any one card in the original combination, there are only two extra fifteens, and the combination will be worth 12 ; 6 for the three fifteens, and 6 more for the pair royal.

If you have duplicates of two different cards you can form four fifteens ; because you can replace the Seven first, and then the Six, and then put the first Seven back again with the new Six. This will make the combination of the same value as if you had three duplicates of one card, 12 points ; 8 for the four fifteens, and 4 for the two single pairs.

Combinations. The beginner's greatest difficulty is in counting hands which contain all three varieties of counts ; pairs, sequences, and fifteens. But if he is familiar with the values of the various combinations taken separately, he will have no difficulty in computing them when they are found together. Some regular order should be observed in going over the hands, so that nothing shall be forgotten. The majority of players begin with the fifteens, as they are more liable to be overlooked, and then reckon the value of the runs and pairs together.

Take the following examples :—

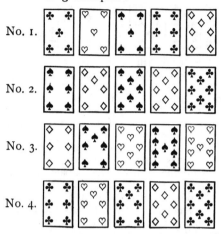

No. 1 contains a fifteen in addition to the three runs of three and the pair royal, and is therefore worth 17 altogether. Nos. 2 and 3 each contain three fifteens; but No. 2 worth 21 points on account of the three runs of three and the pair royal, while No. 3 is worth only 16; a double run of four and a single pair. No. 4 contains four fifteens in addition to the four runs of three and two single pairs, and is therefore worth 24 points.

The best combination that can be held in hand or crib is three Fives and a Jack, with the Five of the same suit as the Jack for a a starter. We have already seen that the four Fives by themselves are worth 20, to which we must add the four extra fifteens made by combining the Jack with each Five separately, and one more point for his nobs, 29 altogether. If the Jack was the starter, the combination would be worth 30 to the dealer, but his heels would have to be counted before a card was played.

Flushes. In addition to the foregoing combinations, if all four cards in the hand are of the same suit the player can peg four points for the flush; if the starter is also the same suit, five points. A flush does not count in the crib unless the starter is the same suit, and then it counts five points. Flushes are never made in play.

Laying Out for the Crib. With this knowledge of the objects of game, and the various counting combinations, it will be seen that each player should keep the cards which count the most for him, or which are most likely to form good combinations with different starters.

Suppose the non-dealer holds these cards :—

If he puts the two Eights in his adversary's crib, he not only gives him two very good cards, which go to form a great many valuable combinations, but he leaves himself absolutely nothing but 2 points for a single fifteen, formed by the 9 and 6. It would be a little better, but still very bad play, for him to discard the 8 and 6, leaving himself a sequence of four cards and a fifteen, 6 points altogether. He might do a little better by discarding the 10 and 8, leaving himself a run of four, and two fifteens, 8 points altogether. If he discards either the 10 and 9, or the 10 and 6, he will leave himself a double run of three, a pair, and two fifteens, 12 altogether. Of these two discards, that of the 10 and 6 is better than the 10 and 9, because the 10 and 9 might help to form a sequence in the adversary's crib, whereas the 10 and 6 are so far apart that they are very unlikely to be of any use.

Cards which are likely to form parts of sequences are called *close cards,* and those which are too widely separated to do so are called *wide cards.*

METHOD OF PLAYING. The crib laid out, and the starter cut, the pone begins by playing any card he pleases. The card he selects he lays face upward on the table on his own side of the cribbage board, and at the same time announces its pip value ; two, five, or ten, whatever it may be. It is then the dealer's turn to play a card from his hand, which is also laid face upward on the table, but on the dealer's side of the cribbage board. Instead of announcing the pip value of this second card, the dealer calls out the total value of the two cards taken together. The pone then lays another card on the table face upward and on the top of the first, which is not turned face down, and at the same time announces the total pip value of the three cards so far played ; the dealer plays again, and so on.

If at any time the total pip value of the cards played is exactly 15 or 31, the one who plays the card that brings it to that number pegs two points for it at once. If any counting combination, such as a pair, pair royal, or sequence, is formed by the cards played, its value is pegged by the person that plays the card which completes the combination ; but neither player is allowed to play a card which will make the total pip value of the cards played pass 31. The method of forming and pegging these various combinations in play will be better understood if they are described separately. A card once played cannot be taken up again, unless it passes 31.

Pairs. If the first card played by the pone should be a 6, and the dealer had a 6 also, the latter would probably play it, announcing : " Twelve, with a pair," and pegging two holes.   If the pone held a third six he would immediately play it, announcing : " Eighteen, with a pair royal," and would peg six holes for the three pairs which can be formed with the three Sixes, although he did not hold all of them.   If the dealer was fortunate enough to hold the fourth Six he might rejoin with : " Twenty-four, with a double-pair-royal."   This would entitle him to peg twelve more holes, although he had already pegged the single pair.

Sequences. Suppose the first card played by the pone was a 4.   The dealer plays a 2, announcing : " Six."   The pone plays a 3, announcing : " Nine, with a run of three," and pegging three holes for the sequence formed in play.   The dealer plays an Ace ; " Ten, with a run of four," and pegs four holes for the sequence of four cards made in play, all of which are face upward on the table, although he held only two of them.

Fifteens. The pone then plays a 5, which, added to the 10 just announced by the dealer, makes 15, with a run of five cards ; seven holes to peg altogether.   (This is quite independent of the sequence previously scored, just as the double pair royal was of the previous single pair.)   The dealer now plays a deuce, and announces seventeen.   This card does not form any sequence with those that have gone immediately before it, because if the order of play is retraced it will be found that another deuce is encountered before we reach the Four.   This illustrates the rule already given, that sequences formed in play must always be single, and cannot be reckoned with substitute cards, like pairs royal.   If they could, the last player in this case might claim a double run of five and a pair.

The pone now plays another 4, which forms the sequence afresh if we go back to the third card played.   He announces : " Twenty-one, with a run of five," and pegs five holes more.   The dealer plays a 3, also claiming a run of five, which he pegs, and as that is the last card to be played in that hand he also pegs one hole for ***last card.***

The total score of the dealer is now 10 points, and that of the pone is 15.   The cards they held, and the order in which they were played is as follows :—

Pone :—

Dealer :—

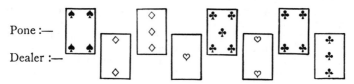

SHOWING. In order to illustrate the manner of counting the hands, which is called showing, let us suppose the starter to be a Queen, and that the pone discarded an Ace and a Ten for the crib, the dealer laying out two Jacks.

The non-dealer always has the first show, as an offset to the advantage of the dealer's crib. The pone therefore shows his hand, which, combined with the starter, is as follows :—

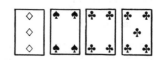

This is worth 10 holes ; the run of three with one duplicate is always worth 8, and the fifteen formed by the starter and the Five counts 2 more. This puts the pone's total score to 25 points.

The dealer then counts, showing his hand first. This, with the starter, is as follows :—

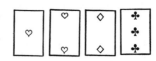

This is worth 14 holes. In addition to the run of three with one duplicate, three fifteens can be formed by combining the starter and a Three with each of the deuces, and then taking the starter and the Ace with both the deuces together. This puts the dealer's total score to 24, with the crib still to count. This is as follows, with the starter :—

This is worth 9 holes ; 8 for the run of three with one duplicate, and 1 for his nobs. There are no fifteens, and the Ace is worthless. This puts the dealer three holes round the corner, and on the homestretch for the game hole.

The deal now passes to the player that was the pone, and the next crib will belong to him.

Beginners often experience difficulty in deciding when a run has been made in play, and when it has not. If there is any dispute about it, the cards should be placed as shown in these diagrams, and if any duplicate is encountered before the run is complete, it cannot be pegged.

Take the following examples :—

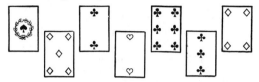

There is no sequence, because we encounter a duplicate deuce before we reach the Five.   If the last player had a Five to play now, it would make a run of five cards, stopping at the deuce of hearts.   Take the following :—

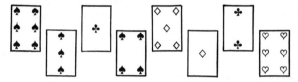

There is no sequence ; but if the pone had played his Five for his second card, the dealer would have pegged two runs ; one of four, and one of six, besides the last card ; the pone making one run of five and a pair, as follows :—

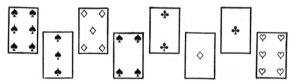

It will be seen that if the dealer had not played his Ace and kept his Six at the last, the pone would have pegged eleven holes on him, instead of seven.

Go, and Thirty-one.   When a person has no card which he can play without making the total pip value of all the cards played more than 31, he must say to his adversary : " Go." That is, " Go on and play, for I cannot." If his adversary has no cards left, the player must say " go " to himself. When a person is told to go, he must play as many cards as he can without passing 31. If he reaches 31 exactly, he scores two points ; if he cannot quite reach it, he scores one point for the go. The principle is that if 31 cannot be made by either player, the one playing the card that brought the count nearest to it shall count one for it, even if he has told himself to go. There is no count for " last card " if it makes 31.

Suppose the first card played is a Jack. The dealer, holding two Nines, an Eight, and a Five, plays the Five, and pegs 2 for the fifteen. The pone plays a Nine, announcing the total as twenty-four. The dealer cannot pair this Nine, because it would run the count past 31, neither can he play the Eight, so he says, " Go." The pone pegs the go without playing, which shows that he is also unable to play, having nothing so small as a Seven.

Both then turn down the cards already played, and the one whose turn it is to play begins all over again with his remaining cards or card, announcing its face value, his adversary playing after him until their cards are exhausted or they reach another 31.

To continue the foregoing example, let us suppose the dealer to play one of his Nines. The pone plays a Jack, and announces " Nineteen." The dealer plays his remaining Nine, and calls " Twenty-eight." The pone tells him to go, and he pegs one. These three cards are turned down. The pone then plays a Ten, and the dealer marks one for the last card. The hands and crib are then shown.

If either player can reach exactly 31, he scores two points for it, whether he has been told to go or not. Suppose the pone begins with a Nine. The dealer plays a Six and pegs 2 for the fifteen. The pone pairs the Six, calls " Twenty-one," and pegs 2 for the pair. The dealer with two Fives and a Four in his hand, plays the Four, and calls " Twenty-five," hoping the pone has no small card, which will allow the dealer to make a run of three with one of his Fives if he is told to go. But the pone plays a Five, calling : " Thirty, with a run of three." The dealer tells him to go, and he plays an Ace, pegging two holes for the 31. The cards are all turned down, and the pone having no cards, the dealer plays his two Fives, and pegs a pair and the last card. The pair counts in this case because the adversary has no cards to interfere with it. A run of three might be played and scored in the same way, because the score for combinations made in play are determined by the order in which the cards are played, irrespective of who plays them.

If a player tells another to go when he can still play himself, he forfeits two points, and his adversary may, if he chooses, take back the cards to the point where the error occurred and have them played over again. The same penalty can be enforced against a player who pegs for a go when he can still play.

Irregularities in Hands. If a player is found to have too many or too few cards, after he has laid out for the crib, his adversary pegs two points, and may also claim a fresh deal. If the deal is allowed to stand, superfluous cards must be drawn at random by the adversary, who may look at the card or cards so drawn before placing them in the pack. If either player is found to have too few cards after having laid out for the crib, he has no remedy. His adversary pegs two points, and the short hand must be played and shown for what it is worth.

Irregular Cribs. If the superfluous card is found in the crib, and the non-dealer had the short hand, the dealer may reckon all the combinations he can make in the six-card crib ; but if it was the dealer who had the short hand, the superfluous crib is void. If the crib contains a superfluous card, both the players having their right number, the non-dealer pegs two holes for the evident misdeal, and the crib is void. If both players have their right number, and the crib is short, it must be shown for what it is worth ; but the non-dealer pegs two holes for the evident misdeal.

Irregular Announcements. There is no penalty if a player announces a wrong number as the total of the cards played, provided he does not peg an erroneous fifteen or thirty-one. If the following player does not correct the announcement, but plays and adds to it, the error cannot be rectified. If any holes are pegged for an erroneous announcement, the adversary may demand that they be taken down again, and may add the number to his own score.

Miscounting. If a player over-counts his hand, crib, or play, and pegs the points erroneously claimed, his adversary may call attention to the error, demand that the superfluous points be taken down again, and may add them to his own score as penalty. Should a player neglect to peg the full value of his hand, crib, or play, his adversary may add the neglected points to his own score, after pointing out the omission. Should a player be mistaken in exacting either of these penalties, he must not only take down what he pegged, but allow his adversary to peg the same number as penalty.

None of these corrections can be claimed until the player in error has pegged and quitted the score ; that is, removed his fingers from the front peg. The claim should always be prefaced by the word ***Muggins.*** If the error is one of omission in play, the adversary must play his own card before claiming muggins. If it is in the hand or crib, the adversary must wait until the points claimed are pegged and quitted. If there are no points claimed, he must wait until the cards are turned face down, thus acknowledging that there is apparently nothing to score. A player is not allowed to tell his adversary whether or not he has counted his hand or crib correctly, until it is pegged.

Nineteen. As it is impossible to hold 19 in hand or crib, it is a common practice for a player, when he has nothing at all to score, to announce, " Nineteen."

Pegging. Neither player is allowed to touch the other's pegs. If the score is erroneous, the player in fault must be called upon to remedy it himself. A player whose pegs are touched by his adversary can score two holes for penalty. If a player removes his adversary's front peg, the latter may immediately claim the game. If a player displaces his own front peg, he must place it behind the other. If both players displace their front pegs, as by accident, they may agree to replace them where they believe them to have stood; but if they cannot agree they must call the game void.

Pegging Out. In pegging during the play, the first man to reach his game hole wins, no matter what either may have in hand or crib. If neither can peg out in play, the non-dealer has the first show. If he cannot show out, the dealer proceeds to count his hand and then his crib. If he cannot show out there must be a new deal.

CHEATING. The greatest advantage at Cribbage is to secure good starters, and for this purpose the greek adopts various methods of trimming and marking the cards so that he may secure a starter exactly suited to his hand. After trimming certain cards a trifle longer or shorter than others, the pack to be cut may be presented to the pone in such a manner that he will unconsciously lift them either by the ends or the sides, according to the wish of the dealer, and so uncover a starter exactly suited to the dealer's hand or crib. When the sharper has the cut, he can of course uncover any card he pleases. With marked edges, the pone can cut down to a card of any desired denomination. Some audacious gamblers make it a rule to get a starter by simply removing the top card and turning up the next one. It is needless to say that the second card has been carefully pre-arranged. Any person who fingers the pack longer than necessary in cutting starters, or who cuts sometimes by the edge and sometimes by the side, will bear watching. Marked cards and second dealing are great weapons in a game where so much depends on a knowledge of the adversary's hand, and on securing good counting cards for yourself.

SUGGESTIONS FOR GOOD PLAY. In the six-card game the hand is more valuable than the crib, because you know what it contains, whereas the crib is largely speculative. In the five-card game, in which there are only three cards in the hand and four in the crib, it is usual to sacrifice the hand very largely for the possibilities of the crib, because of the much larger scores that can be made with five cards, the starter and four in the crib.

Baulking. In both games it is the duty of the pone to baulk the dealer's crib as much as possible, by laying out cards which are very unlikely to be worth anything, either in making fifteens or in filling up sequences. Pairs it is impossible to provide against, and the chance of making a flush is remote, but should be avoided if there is any choice. The best baulk is a King and Nine ; tenth cards and Aces are also very good cards to lay out. Cards which are at least two pips apart, called **wide cards,** are better than **close cards,** as the latter may form sequences. Fives are very bad discards, and so are any cards that form a five or a fifteen.

The Crib. In laying out for his own crib, the dealer should preserve his own hand as much as possible ; but other things being equal, the best cards to lay out are pairs, close cards, and cards that form fives, such as Fours and Aces. If these elements can be combined, so much the better. An Eight and a Seven, for instance, are not only close cards, being only one pip apart, but form a fifteen. The same is true of a trey and deuce.

Keeping. In selecting the hand to keep, much depends on the score. Early in the game you want a counting hand ; near the end, especially if you have only four or five points to go, you want a pegging hand ; that is, one with every card different, so that you can pair several cards, or make fifteens with almost anything that the pone may lead. In keeping a counting hand, much depends on whether it is good in itself, or needs a starter. In reckoning on the possibilities of the starter, it must never be forgotten that there are sixteen tenth cards in the pack, and that they are therefore the most probable starters of all. It is better to keep sequences open at both ends than those open in the middle. With two Sevens and two Eights, either a Six or a Nine will make your hand worth 24 ; but with two Eights and two Sixes, nothing but a Seven will improve your hand more than 4 points. Sequences are the best to keep, especially those of three cards with a duplicate. After them pairs royal are valuable, and next to them cards which will make a number of fives in various combinations, such as two Threes and two deuces.

Leading. There are two systems of playing, known as **playing off,** and **playing on,** and they are selected according to the player's position in the score. Long experience has shown that in six-card Cribbage the average expectation of the non-dealer for his hand and play is 12 points ; and for the dealer, in hand, crib, and play, is 17. This being so, each player having had a deal, their scores should be about 29. If a player is 29 or more, he is said to be **at home ;** and if he is seven or more points ahead of his adversary on even deals, he is said to be **safe at home.** When a player is safe at home, he should play off ; that is, take no chances of scoring himself that might give his adversary a chance to make a still better score. This is usually found in the method of playing sequences. A player who avoids playing cards that might lead up to a run is said to play off. If he invites the run, hoping to make it longer himself, he is said to play on. When a player is behind, it is better for him to play on, and to seize every chance to score, especially with sequences. As it is considered an advantage to be ahead on the first deal, most players prefer a forward game on the opening hand.

Playing Off. In this it is best to play cards on which it is unlikely that your adversary can score. Lead Aces, Twos and Threes, which cannot be made into fifteens. Do not pair his cards unless you have a card which will make you a double pair royal, (without passing 31,) if he should make a pair royal on you. Do not play close cards which he may turn into sequences.

Never play a card which will allow the adversary to make a double score, such as a pair and a fifteen, or a sequence and a fifteen at the same time. Such as the following are all bad plays: 9 on 3; 7 on A; 6 on 3, 4, or 5; 5 on 5; 4 on 7; 3 on 9; A on 7. All these expose you to the immediate rejoinder of a double count. Of course, if you have the card to make a pair royal in return, that is another matter, and is playing on, not playing off.

Do not play a card which brings the pip count to 5 or 21 if you can help it; because any tenth card will enable your adversary to peg two holes. Be a little wary about pairing the first card played, unless you have a third of the same denomination. If you have a choice between a pair and a sequence, your decision will depend on whether you are playing off or on. If you are playing off, make the pair, and take no chances of long runs.

Playing On. In this you play to give your adversary a count, hoping to make a better yourself. It is always advantageous to play one of a pair, and to begin with one end of a sequence. If he pairs your first card, you can reply with a pair royal. If he plays to make a sequence, you can sometimes hold him off until you get the score, and he will be unable to continue the run without passing 31. Play one of two cards that form a five, such as 3 and 2; 4 and A. If he plays a tenth card to it, you can peg fifteen. In playing on, you should make all the sequences possible, taking chances of your adversary's being able to continue the run. If you think he is leading you on, you must be guided by the state of the score as to how much you can risk.

Toward the end, you must reckon pretty closely how many points you can afford to risk your adversary's making without putting him out. If you have enough in your hand to get out on the show, you should not attempt to make a single point in play. Pair nothing, for he might come out with a pair royal; make no runs, for he might extend them. But if you have not enough to show out, you must take every chance to peg the difference, because if you cannot get out in play and first show, the dealer has not only both hand and crib against you, but the first show on the next deal. In six-card Cribbage, the usual pegging for the play is five holes for the dealer, and four or five for the non-dealer. By adding this expectation to your show, you can see how many you can hope to peg yourself, and how many the dealer will probably be on hand, crib and peg altogether. The hands should average 7 points, and the cribs 5.

FIVE-CARD CRIBBAGE.

In this form of the game only five cards are dealt to each player, one at a time. Two of these are laid out for the crib, and the three remaining are used in play, exactly as in the six-card game.

Three for Last. The non-dealer on the first hand of each game is allowed to peg three holes as a compensation for the advantage his adversary derives from having the first deal. Although the rules allow these three to be pegged at any time during the game, they should be put up immediately, in order to avoid disputes.

There is no further play after a go is declared, or either player has reached 31. The score for 31 is two holes; and for the go, one hole. Great importance is attached to the score for the go at five-card Cribbage, because so little is made in play that every point counts.

The Crib. This is the most important thing in the five-card game, and it is much more important to baulk your adversary's crib than to preserve your own hand. The best baulking cards are a King with a 10, 9, 8, 7, 6 or A. Never lay out a Jack, nor two cards which form a five, nor any pair, nor any two close cards. In laying out for your own crib, Fives, Sevens and Eights are the best. Any pair, any two cards that make five or fifteen, and any close cards are also good. Keep pairs royal and runs in your hand, and do not forget that a flush of three counts in the hand; but the starter must agree to make a flush in the crib.

Playing Off and On. The pegging in play is usually small; 2 for the dealer, and an average of 1½ for the non-dealer, hence the importance of the go. The average hand is a little less than 5, and the crib about 5. The player is at home if he has pegged 17 in two deals, his own and his adversary's. He is safe at home if he is 7 ahead, or his adversary is 7 behind.

In Five-card Cribbage, more than any other game, it is true that a game is never won until it is lost. Take the following example, in which the pone is 56 up, and the dealer has pegged only 5 holes altogether. The separated cards show those laid out for the crib, and the odd card is the starter.

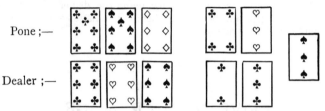

The pone leads a Seven, and afterwards pairs the dealer's Six, pegging to 58. The dealer pegs 6 for the pair royal, and is told to go. This enables the dealer to make a double pair royal and 31, pegging fourteen holes more. (The last card does not count when a go or 31 is pegged). On the show the pone has only a pair, which puts him to 60, within one of the game hole. The dealer shows 12 in hand and 17 in crib, making him 54 up. In the next deal the player who wanted one could not peg, his adversary securing a fifteen and a go, and showing out with a pair and a fifteen, 61 up and game.

THREE-HANDED CRIBBAGE.

Five cards are dealt to each player, and then another, face down, for the foundation of the crib. Each player then lays out one card to make the dealer's crib up to four. The starter is cut by the player on the dealer's left, and the game proceeds as at six-card Cribbage, the eldest hand having the first show, the dealer the last.

FOUR-HANDED CRIBBAGE.

When four play, they cut for partners, choice of seats, and deal; the two lowest pairing against the two highest, and the lowest taking the first deal and crib. The game is usually 121 points up, or twice round the board, and only one player on each side keeps the score.

Five cards are dealt to each player, one at a time, and one of these is discarded from each hand to form the crib, leaving four cards with which to play. The right-hand adversary of the dealer cuts for deal; the left-hand adversary for the starter. The eldest hand plays first, and all pairs, sequences, and fifteens are scored by the side making them. If a player says "go," his left-hand neighbour must play, or pass the go to the next player on his left. In this way it may pass entirely round the table to the last player, who will then peg for it.

At this game there is a great deal more in the play than in either hand or crib. The average hand and crib is the same as at six-card Cribbage, 7 for the hand and 5 for the crib but the play for the partners will run to 8 or 10 holes. Either side should be at home with 48 to 50 on two deals ; four individual hands of 7 each, four plays of five each, and one crib of 5,

---

SEVEN-CARD CRIBBAGE.

This form of the game for two players differs from the others only in the number of cards dealt to each player, which is seven. Two are laid out for the crib, and five kept for playing. There being six cards in each hand, with the starter, the counting combinations sometimes run into high figures, and it is therefore usual to play the game 121 or even 181 points up.

There are no authoritative **LAWS** for Cribbage, but the foregoing descriptions contain all the regulations in force at the best clubs.

TEXT BOOKS.

The Cribbage Player's Handbook, by Walker.
Bézique and Cribbage, by Berkeley.
Pocket Guide to Cribbage, by "Cavendish."
Bohn's Handbook of Games.
Cribbage, by Rawdon Crawley.
Dick's Handbook of Cribbage.

PIQUET.

Piquet is supposed to have been introduced during the reign of Charles VII., and was designed as a motif for a ballet of living cards which was given in the palace of Chinon. Of the etymology of the word piquet, little or nothing is known, but the game itself is one of those perennials that have survived much more pretentious rivals, and, thanks to its intrinsic merits, it has never since its invention ceased to be more or less à la mode.

There are several varieties of Piquet, but the straightforward game for two players, sometimes called *Piquet au Cent,* or 100 points up, is the most common and popular, and will be first described.

CARDS. Piquet is played with a pack of thirty-two cards, all below the Seven being deleted. The cards rank : A K Q J 10 9 8 7, the Ace being the highest both in cutting and in play, There is no trump in Piquet, and all suits are equal in value. Two packs are sometimes used, one by each player in his proper turn to deal.

The cards have a certain pip-counting value, the Ace being reckoned for 11, other court cards for 10 each, and the 7 8 9 10 for their face value.

MARKERS. As the scores are not put down until the end of the hand or play the game is usually kept on a sheet of paper, or it may be marked on a cribbage board.

PLAYERS. Piquet is played by two persons, who sit opposite each other. They are known as the dealer, and the elder hand or pone.

CUTTING. They cut for seats and cards, the lower cut having the choice, and dealing the first hand. If a player exposes more than one card the lowest of those exposed must be taken as his cut. Ties are decided by cutting a second time.

STAKES. Piquet is played for so much a game of 100 points ; but if the loser has not reached 50 points he is lurched, and loses a double game.

DEALING. The cards shuffled, they are presented to the pone to be cut, and at least two cards must be left in each packet. Twelve cards are dealt to each player, either two or three at a time ; but whichever method is first selected must be maintained throughout the game. In England the cards are always dealt by twos. No trump is turned. The remaining eight cards are placed face downward on the table, the five top cards being laid crosswise on the three at the bottom. These eight cards are called the *talon* or stock. Each player deals in turn.

Irregularities in Dealing. If the pack is proved to be imperfect the deal is void, but all previous scores or cuts made with that pack stand good. A misdeal does not lose the deal under any circumstances. If a card is found faced in the pack there must be a fresh deal with the same cards. If a player deals out of turn, and detects the error himself before he sees any of his cards, he may insist on his adversary's dealing, even if the adversary has seen his cards. As the deal is a disadvantage the adversary is not bound to correct the player in error.

If the dealer gives-too many or too few cards to either player a new deal is at the option of the adversary. The error will of course be detected when it is found that there are only seven cards in the talon. If the non-dealer elects to have the deal stand, the error in the player's hand must be remedied in the discard, as will presently be described, and the stock must be divided 4–3 or 5–2, according to which player has too many cards.

Carte Blanche. The cards dealt, each player takes up his twelve cards and sorts them into suits. If the pone finds himself without a K Q or J, he should immediately claim 12 points for carte blanche. If the dealer holds carte blanche, he does not declare it until the pone has discarded.

DISCARDING. The five cards on the top of the talon belong to the pone, and he may discard from his hand any number of cards from one to five, and replace them by an equal number from the top of the stock. He must take at least one card, and he must take from the talon in the natural order of the cards. If he has elected to let a deal stand in which he has been given thirteen cards, he is entitled to four cards only from the talon, and must in all cases leave himself with twelve cards after his discard and draw are completed. If he does not take all five cards, he must announce distinctly how many he leaves, for if he fails to do so the dealer is not liable for having too many cards.

The dealer then discards, first declaring carte blanche if he holds it. In England, he need not draw at all, in France he must draw at least one card. Besides the three cards which belong to him, he is entitled to take as many as he pleases of those left by the pone, and in drawing from the talon he must take the cards in the order in which they come. If two cards are left by the pone, for instance, and the dealer wants three only, he must take the two left by the pone and one of his own three, leaving the two others face down on the table. The number of cards in hand after the discard and draw must be exactly twelve. Only one discard is allowed, and having been made it cannot be changed after the stock has been touched.

If the pone does not take all the cards to which he is entitled, he is allowed to look at those that remain of the first five that were on the talon ; but on no account may he look at any of the dealer's three. If the dealer leaves any cards in the stock, he has a right to look at them, but the pone may not see them until he has led for the first trick, or announced the suit he will lead. If he announces a suit, and after seeing the cards in the stock does not lead that suit, the dealer may call a suit. If the dealer does not look at the remaining cards the pone cannot see them either.

Each player keeps his discards separate from those of his adversary, and is allowed to refer to them at any time during the play of the hand, but on no account can he see his adversary's discards, unless that adversary has mixed with them one or more of the unseen cards that were left in the stock, and afterward picks up and looks at his discard, including the card which the other is entitled to see. For instance : The dealer leaves a card without looking at it. This he afterward mixes with his discard. Now, if he looks at his discard, of course he sees the card left in the stock, and the pone may demand to see not only the card left, but the entire discard. The same rule applies to the pone if he takes into his discards an unseen card of the stock.

Irregular Discards. If a player discards less cards than he intended, it is too late to remedy the error if he has touched the stock. If he discards too many cards, as the dealer frequently will by laying out five instead of three, he may take them back if he has not touched those in the stock, but if he touches any card in the stock, he must play with the short hand if there are not enough cards left in the stock to make his hand up to twelve.

Irregular Drawing. If the pone draws one of the three cards which properly belong to the dealer, he loses the game ; and if the dealer draws any of the first five, before the pone has announced that he leaves them, the dealer loses the game. The dealer has no right to touch any part of the stock until the pone has discarded and drawn ; but if the pone draws without making any announcement about leaving cards, the dealer has a right to assume that five cards have been taken, and that only three remain in the stock. For instance : The pone discards five cards, but draws four only, without saying anything. The dealer proceeds to discard and draw. He has of course taken one of the pone's cards, but it is too late to remedy the error or claim a penalty, and the pone must play with eleven cards. It is evident that the dealer will have too many cards, but as he has been led into the error by his adversary, he must be allowed to discard to reduce his hand to twelve.

If a player takes a card too many from the stock, he may replace it if he has not put it with the other cards in his hand. If he has seen it, he must show it to his adversary. If the superfluous card has been taken into the hand, the player must have too many cards, and can score nothing that deal. This does not prevent the adversary from scoring anything he may have in hand or play, even if it is inferior.

If a player is found to have too few cards after the draw, he may still play and count all he can make, but he cannot win a capot, because he has no card for the last trick, which must be won by his adversary.

The Stock. If a player looks at one of his adversary's cards in the stock before or during the draw, he can count nothing that hand. If he looks at a card left in the talon after the draw, which he is not entitled to see, his adversary may call a suit from him as many times as he has seen cards. If a card of the talon is accidentally exposed, the player to whom it would naturally belong may demand a fresh deal.

OBJECTS OF THE GAME. In order to understand the principles that guide players in discarding, the objects of the game must first be explained. There are three classes of counting combinations at Piquet, and the player that holds the better of each class, scores it. These combinations are : Point ; Sequence ; Fours and Triplets.

The Point is the suit having the greatest pip value, reckoning the Ace as 11, court cards as 10 each, and the 10 9 8 7 at their face value. If one player's best suit contains five cards, worth 48 points, and his adversary has a suit worth 51, the latter would be the only one to count, and it would be called the point for that deal.

The value of the point is the number of cards that go to make it. In England, they count a point containing the 7 8 and 9 as worth one less than the number of cards. This is a modern invention, unknown to the older writers on the game, and not always played.

Sequence. Three or more cards of the same suit, if next in value to one another, form a sequence. The French terms are generally used to designate the number of cards in the sequence : Tierce, Quatrième, Quinte, Sixième, Septième, Huitième. Many English works on cards erroneously spell quinte without the " e," and give " quart " for a sequence of four. If one is going to use the French language at all, it may as well be used correctly.

Sequences outrank one another according to the best card, if they are of equal length ; so that a quinte to a King would be better than a quinte to a Queen ; but a longer sequence always outranks a shorter one, regardless of the high cards. The player holding the best sequence is entitled to score it, together with any inferior sequences he may hold in other suits. Should his adversary hold intermediate sequences, they are of no value. For instance : One player holds a quinte to the Jack in spades, a tierce to the Ten in hearts, and a tierce to the Nine in clubs; while the other holds a quatrième majeure (A K Q J) in hearts, diamonds, and clubs. None of the latter are of any value; but all those in the other hand are good. If the best sequence is a tie, no sequences can be scored by either player.

The value of a sequence is ten more than the number of cards that go to form it, provided that number exceeds four. A tierce counts 3 only, and a quatrième 4 only; but a quinte is worth 15, a sixième 16, and so on.

Fours, and Triplets. Any four cards of the same denomination, higher than a Nine, is called a Quatorze; three of any kind higher than the Nine is called a Trio, or sometimes a Brelan. As a trio is seldom mentioned without naming the denomination, it is usual to say; "Three Kings," or "Three Jacks," as the case may be. The 7 8 and 9 have no value except in point and sequence. The player holding the quatorze of the highest rank may score any inferior ones that he may hold, and also any trios. Should his adversary hold any intermediate ones, they are of no value. In the absence of any quatorze, the best trio decides which player shall count all the trios he may have in his hand, his adversary counting none. For instance: One player holds four Tens and three Jacks, his adversary holding triplets of Aces, Kings, and Queens. None of the latter would be of any value, as the lowest quatorze is better than the highest trio, and the player with the four Tens could count his three Jacks also. Pairs have no value.

The value of any quatorze is 14, as its name implies. Trios are worth 3 only.

In discarding, the object is to secure the best counting combinations, and also to retain cards which will win tricks in play. The combinations take precedence of one another in scoring, the first being always Carte Blanche, then the Point, then Sequence, and lastly the Quatorze or Trio.

DECLARING. Carte blanche must be announced and shown before a discard is made. Each player having discarded and drawn, the elder hand proceeds to announce any counting combinations he holds, which he must declare in regular order, beginning with the point. In announcing the point, the suit is not mentioned, only its value. The sequences are defined by the number of cards and the highest; "sixième to the King," for instance. The fours and trios are defined in the same way; "four Kings," or "three Jacks."

To each of these declarations, as they are made in regular order, the dealer must reply: **"*Good,*" "*Equal,*"** or, **"*Not good.*"** If the point is admitted to be good, the holder scores it; not by putting it down on the score sheet, but simply by beginning his count with the number of points it is worth. If the point is equal, neither player scores it, and secondary points have no value under any circumstances. If the point declared by the elder hand is not good, it is not necessary for the dealer to say how much better his point is; that will come later. To each of the other declarations replies are made in the same manner, except that fours and trios cannot be "equal." As each combination is admitted to be good, the elder hand adds it to his count. For instance: His point is 51, good; his sequence is five to the Ace, good; and his triplet of Aces is good. These are worth 5, 15, and 3 respectively, and his total count is 23, if he has no minor sequences or trios. This is not put down, but simply announced.

The strict rules of the game require the player whose combination is acknowledged to be good, to show it; but among good players this is quite unnecessary, for each usually knows by his own cards what his adversary should and probably does hold.

The elder hand having finished his declarations, and announced their total value in points, leads any card he pleases. If this card is a Ten or better, he claims one point for leading it, even if he does not win the trick, and he adds this point to his score.

An illustration will probably make the foregoing processes clearer. The elder hand, after the draw, holds these cards :—

$$\heartsuit A K Q J : \clubsuit A K Q : \diamondsuit A K Q 7 : \spadesuit A.$$

He announces : "Forty-one." "Not good." "Quatrième to the Ace." "Not good." "Quatorze Aces," which he knows is good; and which admits of his counting his triplets of Kings and Queens. These are worth collectively 20 points, and on leading one of his Aces he announces "Twenty-one."

The dealer, before playing a card, proceeds to claim the count for the combinations which are good in his own hand, which is as follows :—

$$\clubsuit J\ 10\ 9\ 8 : \diamondsuit J\ 10\ 9 : \spadesuit K\ Q\ J\ 10\ 9.$$

The point is worth 5; the quinte 15, the quatrième 4, and the tierce 3; 27 altogether. His trios of Jacks and Tens are shut out by the superior combinations in the elder hand.

Having claimed these 27 points, and their correctness having been admitted by the elder hand, the dealer proceeds to play a card. If either player has forgotten to declare anything before he plays, the count is lost.

Sinking. A player is not obliged to declare any combination unless he wishes to do so, and he may sink a card if he thinks it would be to his advantage to conceal his hand. Sinking is calling only part of a combination, as, for instance, calling 51 for his point when he really has 61; calling a quinte when he has a sixième, or a trio when he has a quatorze. Sinking is usually resorted to only when the player knows from his own hand and discards that what he declares is still better than anything his adversary can hold; but it must be remembered that the part of the declaration which is sunk in this manner is lost.

Irregular Declarations. If either player claims a combination which he does not hold, and does not remedy the error before he plays a card, he cannot count anything that deal, losing any other declarations he may have made which are correct. His adversary then counts everything in his hand, whether his combinations were inferior or not. He also counts for what he wins in the tricks.

If the elder hand's declaration is admitted by the dealer to be good, it is good, even if the dealer afterward proves to have a better point, sequence, quatorze or trio. If any combination named by the elder hand is not actually his best, he cannot amend his declaration after the dealer has replied to it. This is in order to prevent a player from getting information to which he is not entitled. If he holds three Kings and three Tens, for instance, and announces the Tens in order to find out whether or not his adversary has three Queens or Jacks, and the dealer says: "Not good," the three Kings are lost, and the dealer scores his own trios.

It sometimes happens that in order to keep a good point or sequence, a player will discard one card of a quatorze originally dealt him; or one of a trio, of which he afterward draws the fourth. He can score only the trio, of course; but his adversary, having none of that denomination either in his hand or discards, knows that four were possible, and after playing a card he has a right to ask the suit of the card which was discarded.

METHOD OF PLAYING. The elder hand can lead any card he pleases, announcing the suit at the same time. The dealer is bound to follow suit, if able, but he is not obliged to win the trick. As there are no trumps, the higher card, if of the suit led, wins the trick. If the second player does not follow suit, the leader wins. The winner of one trick leads for the next, and so on until all twelve tricks are played.

Every time a card is played which is better than a Nine, the leader counts one for it, adding the number to the total value of his score as already announced. If the second player wins the trick with any card better than a Nine he also counts one; but if the trick is won by the player who led, there is no extra count for winning it. The winner of the ***last trick*** counts one for it, in addition to his count for winning it with a card better than a Nine. If the leader wins it, he gets the one extra.

If each player wins six tricks, there is no further scoring; but if either player wins the ***odd trick*** he adds to his score ten points for **cards,** in addition to all other scores. If either player wins all twelve tricks, which would be the case in the example hand just given as an illustration, he adds to his score forty points for the **capot;** but this forty points includes the scores for the last trick and for the odd trick.

A card once laid on the table cannot be taken back, unless the player has renounced in error. There is no **revoke** in Piquet, and if a player has one of the suit led he must play it. If he fails to do so, when the error is discovered the cards must be taken back and replayed.

REPIC. If either player is able to reach 30 by successive declarations, beginning with the point, all of which are admitted by his adversary to be good, he adds 60 to his score, making it 90 instead of 30, and this is irrespective of what his adversary may have in minor or inferior combinations. The important thing to remember in repic is that declarations always count in regular order, carte blanche taking precedence of everything; then the point, sequences, and quatorze or trio. Suppose elder hand to hold the following cards :—

♡ K Q J 10 9; ♣ A K Q; ◇ A Q 9; ♠ Q.

If the quinte to the King is admitted good for the point, it must be good for the sequence also. That is 20. The four Queens must be good, as the adversary cannot have any quatorze. This makes the total 34, and 60 added for repic, 94 altogether, to which he will add one for leading the first card, if it is above a Nine.

Suppose the elder hand had the following cards :—

♡ A K Q J 8; ♣ A K; ◇ A K; ♠ A K 10.

If his point is good, that and his four Aces and Kings will make him 33 altogether; but his sequence is not good, because the dealer holds five diamonds to the Queen, which comes in order before the score for quatorze, and so saves the repic. Suppose that with the foregoing cards the elder hand was told that even his point was not good. He would count 29 for the 14 Aces, 14 Kings, and the card led. If the dealer had a sixième in diamonds, and a quinte in clubs, for instance, he would claim a repic, 96 points, in spite of the 29 announced by the elder hand ; because point and sequence score before quatorze.

Equalities do not save the repic. Take the following hands :—

Elder :—♡ A J 10 9 8; ♣ 10; ◇ 10; ♠ A J 10 9 8.

Dealer :—♡ K Q; ♣ A K Q; ◇ A K Q J 7; ♠ K Q.

The point is equal. The quatrième to the Jack is not good and the four Tens are not good; so elder hand leads a card, and counts, " One." The dealer then claims repic, 95 points, which is good, although the elder hand had an equal point.

PIC. If either player can reach 30 in hand and play combined, before his adversary scores anything, 30 are added for the pic. Pic can never be made by the dealer unless the elder hand leads a card smaller than a Nine ; he must make repic if anything. To make pic the elder hand must reach 30 in the regular order of scoring. Suppose he holds these cards :—

$$\heartsuit \text{ A } 9; \clubsuit \text{ A K Q J}; \diamondsuit \text{ K Q J 10 } 9; \spadesuit \text{ K.}$$

If the dealer acknowledges the point to be good, everything else in the hand must be good also. This will give the elder hand 27 before playing a card ; 5 for the point, 15 and 4 for the sequences, and 3 for the Kings. By leading out the A K and Q. 3 more points are secured, the dealer having nothing to score, and so the elder hand reaches 30 and makes the pic, counting 60, and still having the lead.

According to the strict rules of the game, a player who is playing for pic is not allowed to count 30 at all, but must jump from his last count, 29, to 60, or he loses the pic ; but this is seldom or never insisted on.

SCORING. The last card played, the total number of points made by each player are put down on the score sheet, or marked on a cribbage board, and if neither player has reached 100 points, the deal passes to the one who was elder hand on the last deal.

The order of scoring should be carefully observed, in order to determine which goes out first, and whether or not a player is lurched. Carte blanche, The Point, Sequence, Quatorze or Trio, Repic, Points for Leading or Winning, Pic, the Odd Trick, Capot.

If one player reaches 100 before his adversary has reached 50, it is a *lurch,* and counts a double game.

Abandoned Hands. If a player throws down his cards, he may still take them up again, unless he or his adversary have mixed their cards with the discards, or with the remainder of the talon.

SUGGESTIONS FOR GOOD PLAY. The chief points for the beginner are good discarding, and taking advantage of tenace positions in the play, so as to secure the count for cards, which is often important.

Elder Hand. In discarding, the pone should consider what there may be against him. If it is unlikely that he will lose a pic or repic, he should try for the *point,* which very often carries with it the sequence. It must be remembered that there are only eight cards in each suit, and by comparing those that you hold with those that your adversary may hold it is comparatively easy, in the majority of hands, to estimate the possible scores against you. Next to the point, the most important thing is the score for **cards.** The point will save pic and repic, but the cards will make the greatest difference in the score in the long run. Sequences are always valuable, especially those that are Ace high in the elder hand, because they enable him to win a succession of tricks in play.

The elder hand should risk a good deal if he has a fair chance to make a pic or repic, which will often settle the game. If there is any choice as to what to keep of two nearly equal chances, always preserve the combination that will be most likely to secure the count for cards.

In **Leading,** it is best to begin with the point, unless you know that you are leading up to tenace, or to high cards that will bring in a long adverse suit. The piquet player soon learns the importance of tenace and fourchette, and can sometimes see how things must be managed for five or six tricks ahead, so as to secure the odd trick. Tenace is the best and third-best of any suit, such as A Q, while a fourchette is any two cards within one of each other, such as K J, or Q 10, and the lead from such combinations should always be avoided. If you have the odd trick in hand, make it at once, before you risk anything else, because the only difference between the odd trick and eleven tricks is the count for each card led in the tricks.

The Dealer. The first thing to guard against is a long run of winning leads from the elder hand, which might make the odd trick, or even capot. As there are no trumps it is very important for the dealer to keep guarded Kings and twice-guarded Queens. The principal thing for the dealer to remember is that if he cannot stop a long suit in the elder hand, he will have to provide in advance for a certain number of discards, and these must be so planned that guards will be preserved in the other suits. He should also get his hand into such condition that when he does get into the lead, he will not have to lead away from tenaces or guarded Kings. Careful attention to his adversary's declarations, and a comparison of his own hand with his discards will usually guide the dealer to a correct conclusion as to what to keep and what to throw away in playing to tricks.

Mathematicians have exhausted their resources on Piquet, but their conclusions are of little use to the average player. The subject of discards has been very fully illustrated by examples from actual play, especially in the *Westminster Papers,* but no one has yet given us any simple rules like the jeux de règle at Écarté.

PIQUET NORMAND,

FOR THREE PLAYERS.

In this form of the game the players cut for seats and deal. The cards are dealt by twos and threes until each has ten, two cards remaining for the talon. The dealer may lay out any two cards in exchange for these, but no other player is allowed to touch them, nor to see the discards.

The elder hand makes the first declarations. He makes repic and counts 90 if he can reach 20 without playing a card ; and he makes pic, 60, if he can reach 20 in hand and play, under the same conditions as in the game for two players. The majority of tricks counts 10 ; if it is a tie, each counts 5. Capot counts 40 if all the tricks are taken by one player ; but if two take them all between them, they count 20 each.

The game may be played for a pool, first man out to take all ; or it may be agreed that after one has retired the others shall decide it between them by playing it out at the ordinary two-handed game.

PIQUET VOLEUR,

FOR FOUR PLAYERS.

The players cut for partners, the two lowest pairing against the two highest, and the lowest cut taking the first deal. Partners sit opposite each other. All the cards are dealt out, two and three at a time, each receiving eight cards.

The elder hand declares first, but instead of announcing one thing at a time, and awaiting the reply of his adversaries, he declares everything, and then plays a card. Suppose the cards are distributed as follows, Z being the dealer :—

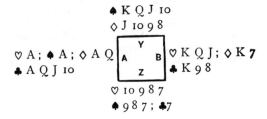

♠ K Q J 10
◇ J 10 9 8

♡ A ; ♠ A ; ◇ A Q   A   Y   B   ♡ K Q J ; ◇ K 7
♣ A Q J 10   Z   ♣ K 9 8

♡ 10 9 8 7
♠ 9 8 7 ; ♣ 7

A announces 41 for his point, sequence of three to the Queen, four Aces, and says, " I play a club," which is his lead for the first trick. If the second player admits all these to be good he says nothing, but plays a card. In this case, Y would announce four to the King, and four to the Jack, and would play a spade, having no club. B would then announce three Kings, which are good on account of his partner's having four Aces ; but both the sequences are shut out by Y's better declarations. The dealer, Z, then declares four to the Ten and three to the Nine, both those sequences being made good by his partner's holding the best sequence at the table.

The first trick played, each person at the table shows what he has claimed, in order that his adversaries may verify the count. A would then gather up the first trick, announcing the total score for his side, which would be 22 ; 4 for the point, 14 Aces, 3 Kings, and 1 for the card led. He would then play another club, announcing 22. This his partner would win but would not count, as he is on the same side that has already counted for the lead. If the play is followed up it will be found that A-B make a capot, The adversaries will then score 15 for their three sequences of four, and one of three.

No point of less than 30 can be announced.

Pic and Repic. If one player, or two partners together, reach 20 in counting, without playing, they count 90 for the repic. If they reach 20 in declarations and play together, they count 60 for the pic. Carte blanche in the hand of one or other partner may count toward pic or repic ; and if two partners each held carte blanche, they would be entitled to 90 points for the repic, no matter what the adversaries held, because carte blanche takes precedence of all other scores.

PIQUET A ÉCRIRE.

This game somewhat resembles Skat in the manner of playing and settling. Any number from three to seven persons sit around the table ; but only two play, and the losses of each individual are charged to him on a score sheet ruled off for the purpose. The players may take turns, each playing two deals, the first with the person on his left, and the second with the one on his right. Or it may be agreed that the loser in each deal shall give way to a new player, the winner of the majority of points in each deal to continue. The game is generally arranged for a certain number of tours or deals, at the end of which the scores are balanced and settled for.

RUBICON PIQUET,

FOR TWO PLAYERS.

The chief difference between this game and the usual form, Piquet au cent, is in the manner of declaring. The usual method in England and America is as follows :—

The Point is scored by the player holding the greatest number of cards in the suit, and the pip value is resorted to only to decide ties. This is done in order to conceal, if possible, the nature of the cards held. When the numerical value is asked, only the last figure is given, " seven," for instance, if the point is 47.

If the point is good, the elder hand immediately names the suit. If it is not good, the suit is not named, and the elder hand proceeds to call his *sequences.* If they are good, the suits must be named ; the same with quatorze and trio.

Undercalling. If a player holds an inferior sequence, quatorze or trio, which he knows is better than any his adversary can possibly hold, he may call it, and afterward score the better combination, provided he is correct in estimating the inferior one that he called as *good against the cards.* But if the adversary can demonstrate that the inferior announcement was not actually good against the cards, and that it was possible for him to hold a better, the score for the higher combination is lost. For instance : A player holds four Kings and three Aces, and on glancing over his hand and discards, sees that his adversary cannot hold any quatorze, so he declares the three Kings, instead of the four Aces. Suppose he mistook a Nine for a Ten, and overlooked the fact that his adversary might have had four Tens, the score for the four Kings would be lost, but the three Aces would be good if his adversary had discarded a Ten, and did not actually hold four. In the ordinary game, the higher combination is lost if it is not called.

In play, every card led, whatever its value, counts one, and winning the trick counts one also. The last trick counts two, and the capot forty. Pic and repic are reckoned as in the ordinary game.

Scoring. Instead of playing 100 points up, six deals is a game, each player dealing three times. The lower score is then deducted from the higher, and 100 points added to the difference to determine the value of the game, which is usually played for so much a point.

If the result of the six deals is a tie, two more deals must be played. If they also result in a tie, the game is void.

Rubicons. If either or both players fail to reach 100 points in the six deals, the one having the most is the winner, and adds to his own score all the points made by the loser, with 100 in addition for game. For instance : A has 113 scored, and B 80. A wins 113 + 80 + 100 = 293 altogether. Again ; A has 88, B has 84. A wins 88 + 84 + 100 = 272 altogether. Again : A has 180, B has 142. A wins the difference in the scores, 38 + 100 = 138 altogether.

TEXT BOOKS.

Jeux de Cartes, by Jean Boussac.
Académie des Jeux, by Van Tenac.
Académie des Jeux, by Richard.
Règles de tous les Jeux, by Dreyfous.
Bohn's Handbook of Games.
Piquet, and Rubicon Piquet, by Berkeley.
Laws of Piquet, by " Cavendish."

Westminster Papers, Vols. II. to IX. inclusive. There are excellent articles on the Laws in Vols. III. and VI., and on discards in Vol. VII.

IMPERIAL,

OR PIQUET WITH A TRUMP.

Impérial differs from Piquet in some minor details, although the leading principle is the same. There are no discards ; sequences of court cards are the only ones that count ; tierces are worthless ; and a trump suit is added.

The **cards** rank K Q J A 10 9 8 7 ; the K Q J A and 7 of trumps are called honours, and in all sequences the four highest cards in the suit are the only ones that count.

Counters. Each player is supplied with six white and four red counters, which are passed from left to right as the points accrue. Each red is worth six white, and when all six white counters have been passed over, they must be returned, and a red one passed over in their place. When all the counters, four red and six white, have been passed over, the game is won.

Dealing. Twelve cards are given to each player, two or three at a time, and the twenty-fifth is turned up for the trump. If this is an honour, the dealer marks one white counter for it. There are no discards.

Impérials. Certain combinations of cards are known as impérials, and the player marks one red counter for each of them.
The best impérial is carte blanche, which is sometimes marked as
a double impérial, and worth two reds. A sequence of K Q J A
in any suit is an impérial. An impérial de retourne may be
formed in the dealer's hand if the turn-up trump completes his
sequence or makes four of a kind. An impérial tombée, or de
rencontre, is made when the player who holds the King and Queen
of trumps catches the Jack and Ace from his adversary. Four
Kings, Queens, Jacks, Aces, or Sevens in one hand is an impérial ;
but the Eights, Nines and Tens have no value.

Declaring. The elder hand announces his point, as in Piquet,
and arrives at its value in the same way, reckoning the Ace for 11,
etc. The dealer replies, " Good," or " Not good," as the case
may be ; but there are no equalities. If the point is a tie, the
elder hand counts it. The point is worth a ***white*** counter. The
impérials are then called, each being worth one ***red*** counter. The
sequences are called first, that in trumps being " good " of course ;
then the fours are called, the best being four Kings, and the
lowest four Aces. In plain-suit sequences there are no " equals,"
the elder hand counting ties as an offset to the advantages of the
deal.

Playing. The elder hand leads a card, and the dealer then
declares and marks any impérials he may have that are good ; after
which he plays a card. No impérials can be claimed or scored
after the holder has played a card. The second player in each
trick must win the trick if he can, either with a higher card or with
a trump. For each honour in trumps in the tricks won the player
marks a white counter at the end of the hand. The winner of the
odd trick scores as many white counters as he has tricks in excess
of his adversary. If either player makes capot, (all twelve tricks,)
he scores two red counters.

Scoring. When one player reaches six white counters and
changes them for a red, his adversary must take down any white
counters he may have scored. For instance : The pone has 2 reds
and 4 whites up ; the dealer has 1 red and 5 whites. The pone
scores two whites, reaching six, and advancing his score to 3 reds,
which are sometimes called impérials. The dealer must take
down his white counters, losing that count altogether, and leaving
himself 1 red. The only exception to this is that at the beginning
of the hand if both have impérials combinations in hand, neither
side takes down its white counters.

In ***Counting out*** the following order of precedence must be observed : The turn-up trump, (if it is an honour). The Point. Impérial in hand, sequences first. Impérial de retourne. Impérial
tombée. Honours in tricks. Odd tricks.

CASSINO.

This is a very old and always popular game, which has lately been much improved by the introduction of the variations known as Royal and Spade Cassino, the latter especially being a very lively game. Like Euchre, Cassino is eminently respectable, and is one of the few games of cards that are unhesitatingly admitted to the domestic circle.

Cards. Cassino is played with a full pack of fifty-two cards, which have no rank in play, their pip or face value being the only element of importance. In cutting for positions at the table, or for partners in the four-handed game, the Ace is the lowest card, the others ranking upward to the King in the order of their sequence.

Markers. When a certain number of points is agreed on as a game, the score may be kept with counters, on a sheet of paper, or on a cribbage board. If each hand is a game in itself, it is settled for immediately, either in counters or in money.

Players. Any number from two to four may play, each for himself, or four may play two against two, partners sitting opposite each other. The players on the dealer's right and left are known as the pone, and the eldest hand respectively.

Cutting. The players draw from an outspread pack for positions at the table, the lowest card having the choice and dealing the first hand. If the first cut does not decide, those tying must cut again. If a player exposes more than one card he must cut again. The ace is low.

Stakes. Cassino may be played for so much a game, or so much a point ; and it may be agreed that the game shall be a certain number of points, or shall be complete in one deal, or that the player making the majority of points on each deal shall score one, and the one first making a certain number in this manner, such as five, shall be the winner. If points are played for, the lower score is usually deducted from the higher, and the difference is the value of the game. It is sometimes agreed that if the winner has twice as many points as his adversary, he shall be paid for a double game.

Dealing. After the cards have been properly shuffled they must be presented to the pone to be cut, and he must leave at least four in each packet. Beginning on his left, the dealer distributes four cards to each player in two rounds of two at a time, giving two to the table just before helping himself in each round. No trump is turned, and the remainder of the pack is left face downward on the dealer's left. The four cards dealt to the table are then turned face up, and the play begins. After the four cards given to each person have all been played, the dealer takes up the remainder of the pack, and without any further shuffling or cutting, deals four more cards to each player, two at a time, but gives none to the table. These four having been played, four more are dealt in the same manner, and so on, until the pack is exhausted, after which the deal passes to the left in regular rotation.

Irregularities in the Deal. If the pack is proved to be imperfect, or if a card is found faced in the pack there must be a fresh deal by the same dealer. If a player deals out of turn, he must be stopped before the cards on the table are turned face upward.

A misdeal loses the deal. It is a misdeal if the pack has not been cut, or if the cards are shuffled after the pack has been properly cut ; or if the dealer deals a card incorrectly, and fails to remedy it before dealing to the next player ; or if he deals too many or too few cards to any player or to the table.

If a card is exposed during the deal, an adversary may claim a fresh deal. If, after the cards on the table have been faced, a card is exposed by the dealer, or is found faced in the pack, the player to whom it would be dealt may reject it, and it must then be placed in the middle of the stock, and he must be given the top card. If a card is exposed in the last round, the dealer must take it, and must allow the player to whom it would have been dealt to draw a card from the dealer's hand, face downward. If he draws the exposed card, he must keep it.

If the dealer gives any player an incorrect number of cards in any round after the first, and does not detect and correct the error before he deals to the next player, the dealer cannot count anything that hand. The number of cards in each hand must be restored to four, either by drawing from them, face down, or adding from the stock. If any player lifts his cards before the dealer has helped all the players, including himself, a misdeal cannot be claimed.

Objects of the Game. The object in Cassino is to secure certain cards and combinations of cards which count toward game. These are as follows :—

	Points.
The majority of *Cards* taken in.	3
The majority of *Spades* taken in.	1
The Ten of diamonds, ***Big Cassino.***	2
The deuce of spades, ***Little Cassino.***	1
The *Ace* of any suit.	1
A *Sweep* of all the cards on the table.	1

The manner in which these points are secured will become apparent from the description of the method of playing the hands.

Method of Playing. Beginning on the dealer's left, each player in turn plays a card from his hand, placing it face upward on the table. Only one card can be played at a time, and each person must play in his proper turn until all four of his cards are exhausted. After receiving fresh cards, the eldest hand again plays first, and so on for every round. Under certain conditions, each player in his proper turn may take up certain cards from the table, together with the one played from his hand, turning them face downward in front of him. He is entitled to count all the points contained in the cards taken in or won in this manner. These conditions are : that he can match or ***pair*** a card or cards on the table ; that he can ***combine*** two or more cards on the table so as to make their total pip value equal to that of the card he plays ; or that he can ***build*** a card in his hand upon one on the table, so as to make their total pip value agree with that of a second card, still in his hand.

Pairing. If the person whose turn it is to play, holds in his hand any card of a similar denomination to any of those on the table, he may play the card from his hand, face upward, and then gather it in again, together with all similar cards, turning them face downward in front of him. For instance : He holds a Eight, and there are one or two Eights on the table. He plays the Eight from his hand, and then gathers in all of them.

Combining. If a player holds any card, not a K Q or J, the pip value of which is equal to that of two or more cards on the table, he may play the card from his hand, and then gather it in again, together with the two or three cards that collectively equal it in pip value. For instance : He holds a 9, and a 4, 3 and 2 are upon the table. He may combine these three cards, calling attention to the fact that their collective value is 9, and then play the 9 from his own hand, gathering in and turning down all four cards. An 8 and Ace, or 6 and 3 might be gathered in the same way ; or two such combinations might be gathered at the same time, 3, 2, 6, 7, for instance, which would make two nines ; all of which might be gathered by a player holding a 9 in his hand.

Pairs and combinations may be taken in together. For instance : Among the cards on the table are a 4, 6, and 10, and the player holds a 10. He can gather in not only the pair of Tens, but the combinations which equal a 10.

Building. A player may have in his hand two cards, the lower of which, if added to a card on the table, would build up its value to that of the higher card still in the player's hand. For instance : A player holds a 9 and 2, and there is a 7 on the table. He may place the 2 on the 7, announcing the total value ; " Nine," which will notify other players that those two cards cannot be separated ; but he cannot take them in until it again comes round to his turn to play, because he is allowed to play only one card at a time, and he has played his card in making the build.

Should any other player following him hold a 9, he would be entitled to take in this build, but he could not separate the two cards forming it. A player holding either a 7 or a 2 could not touch either of the cards in the build, because they are no longer a 7 and 2, but a 9, for all practical purposes.

Increasing Builds. If any player held an Ace and a 10 in his hand, he could increase the 9 build to a 10 build, by putting his Ace on the 7 and 2, and announcing the total value, "Ten." Any following player would then be unable to win the build with anything but a 10, and the player who originally built it a 9 would lose it unless he also held a 10 in his hand. Should the build remain a 9 until it came round again to the player who originally built it, he could then take it in with his 9, or he might himself increase it to 10, if he had an Ace and a 10 in his hand ; but in order to do this the player must have in his hand the cards to win both the original and the increased builds. A player holding in his hand a 10, 3 and 2, but no 8, could not build a 5 on the table to an 8, and afterward advance it to 10. He must have the 2 3 8 and 10 all in his own hand to do this.

Some players imagine that a player cannot increase his own build in this manner, even if he has both the cards for the first and last build ; but there is no reason why a player should be denied a privilege which is freely granted to his adversary. If any player can legitimately make or increase a build, all may do so provided they have the proper cards.

Double Builds. When two cards of the same denomination, or two builds of the same value are put together as one, they cannot be increased. For instance : A player holds 7 and 3, and there are upon the table a 5 2 and 4. He places his 3 on the 4, and gathers the 5 and 2 together, announcing the build as "Two Sevens." This cannot be increased to 8, 9, or 10 under any circumstances, and nothing but a 7 will win it.

Pairs may be doubled in the same manner. If a player has two Nines in his hand, and there is one on the table, he may build on the latter with one of his own, announcing, "Two Nines," which will prevent any player from building either of them to 10, and will entitle the builder to take in both cards with his third Nine when it comes round to his turn. Should any other player at the table hold the fourth Nine, he could of course take in the build.

It is necessary to distinguish between building and combining. In combining cards, those already on the table are gathered together ; in building, or increasing a build, a card must be played from the hand. If one player has made a build of any description, it cannot be interfered with or increased except by other cards from a player's hand, those from the table not being available. For instance : One player has built a 5 by combining two Aces on the table with a 3 from his hand. On the table are also a 2 and 4 and a following player holds a 9 and 7. He cannot use the deuce on the table to increase the build from 5 to 7, nor the 4 to increase it to 9 ; because that would not be building from his hand ; but if he held the 4 and 9 in his hand, he could build on the 5.

The simple rule to be remembered is that no combination of cards once announced, and left on the table, can be changed, except by the addition of a card from the hand of some player.

Taking In. Any player who has made a build is obliged either to win it, when it is next his turn to play, or to win something else, or to make another build. For instance : He has built a 5 into a 9 with a 4, and holds another 4 ; if another 5 appears on the table before it comes to his turn to play, he may build that into a 9 also, with his other 4, announcing, "Two Nines." Or if some player should lay out a 4 he could pair it and take it in, leaving his 9 build until the next round. In the same way a player may increase or win another player's build instead of taking in his own.

In the four-handed game, partners may take in one another's builds, or may make builds which can be won by the card declared in the partner's hand. For instance : One player builds an 8, and his partner holds Little Cassino. If there is a 6 on the table, the Cassino can be built on it, and "two Eights," called, although the player has no 8 in his own hand ; the 8 already built by his partner is sufficient. If a player has built a 9 which has been taken in by an adversary, he still holding the 9 he built for, his partner may build for the declared 9 in the same way.

Sweeping. If at any time a player is able to win everything on the table with one card, it is a sweep, and counts a point. For instance : He holds an 8, and there are upon the table four cards only :— 5 3 6 and 2. By combining the 6 and 2, and the 5 and 3, two Eights will be formed, and the sweep is made. Sweeps are usually marked by leaving the cards with which they are made face upward at the bottom of the tricks taken in by the player. Sweeps made by opposite sides are sometimes turned down to cancel one another.

Trailing. When a player cannot pair, combine, or build anything, he must play a card. This is called trailing, because he is simply following along waiting for opportunities. In trailing it is usually the best policy to play the smaller cards, except Aces and Little Cassino, because as other players will probably trail small cards also, these may be combined and won with the larger cards kept in the player's hand.

Last Cards. In the last round, all the cards remaining on the table are won by the player who takes the last trick, but it does not count as a sweep unless it would have been a sweep under any circumstances. The last trick is usually made by the dealer, who always keeps back a court card if he has one, to pair one already on the table.

Irregularities in Play. If any person plays out of his proper turn, the card so played is laid aside as exposed, until it comes to his turn, when it is simply placed on the table with the others. The player in error is not allowed to build or combine it, nor to win anything with it.

If a player gathers in a card which does not belong to the combination or build, he must not only return the card improperly taken up, but all others taken in with it, together with his own card, the latter, however, being laid out separately from the others. If the combination was his own build, it must be broken up ; if an adversary's, it must be restored, and left as it was.

If a player takes in a build with a wrong card, or takes in a wrong combination, or gathers cards to which he is not entitled, the error must be challenged and proved before the next trick is taken in by another player, because only the last trick gathered can be seen.

If a player makes a build without the proper card in his hand to win it, on discovery of the error, the combination must be broken up, and the adversaries may take back the cards they have played in following the erroneous build, and may amend their play. If, however, another player has won the erroneous build, there is no penalty, nor any remedy.

Showing. After the last card has been played, each player counts his cards face downward, and announces the number. The player having the majority scores the three points for cards. If it is a tie, neither scores. The cards are then turned face up, and the spades counted and claimed ; and then all the points for Cassinos and Aces. It should be remembered that the total number of points to be made in each hand, exclusive of sweeps, is eleven, and the total of the claims made must agree with that number.

Scoring. There are several methods of scoring. The old way was to play 11 points up, deducting the lower score from the higher at the end of each deal. If one side reached 11 before the adversary reached 6, it was a lurch, and counted as a double game. The common method is to count every hand a game, and settle for it in counters.

TWENTY-ONE POINT CASSINO.

This game is usually marked with counters, or pegged on a cribbage board. Nothing is scored until the end of the hand, when each side reckons and claims its points. In order to avoid disputes there should be a previous understanding as to what points go out first in a close game. In the absence of any agreement to the contrary, the points count out in the following order :—Cards first, then Spades, Big Cassino, Little Cassino, Aces, and Sweeps. If the Aces have to decide it, the spade Ace goes out first, then clubs, hearts, and diamonds. If the sweeps have to decide it, only the difference in the number of sweeps counts, and if there is none, or not enough, the game is not ended, and another deal must be played.

It is better to agree to **count out** in twenty-one point Cassino ; each player keeping mental count of the number of cards and spades he has taken in, together with any "natural" points. The moment he reaches 21 he should claim the game, and if his claim is correct he wins, even if his adversary has 21 or more. If he is mistaken, and cannot show out, he loses the game, no matter what his adversary's score may be. If neither claims out, and both are found to be, neither wins, and the game must be continued to 32 points, and so on, eleven points more each time until one player claims to have won the game.

Suggestions for Good Play. The principal thing in Cassino is to remember what has been played, especially in the counting and high cards, such as Aces, Eights, Nines, and Tens. In making pairs and combinations, give preference to those containing spades, and if you have to trail, do not play a spade if you can help it. If three Aces have been taken in, play the fourth, if you hold it, at the first opportunity, because it cannot be paired ; but if there is another Ace to come, keep yours until you can make a good build with it. As between cards which were on the table and those trailed by an adversary, take in those trailed if you have a choice. Take in the adversary's build in preference to your own, if you can, and build on his build at every opportunity. If Big Cassino is still to come, avoid trailing cards that will make a Ten with those on the table. Go for "cards" in preference to everything else, and always make combinations that take in as many cards as possible. If you have a Nine, and the cards on the table are 2 2 5 7, take in the 2 2 5, in preference to the 2 7. It is considered bad policy to take in three court cards, as it stops all sweeps when the fourth appears.

ROYAL CASSINO.

The only difference in this form of the game is that the three court cards, K Q J, have a pip value, and may be used in combining and building, whereas in the ordinary game they can be used only in pairs. The Jack is worth 11, the Queen 12, and the King 13; so that a 9 and 2 can be taken in with a Jack, or a 6 4 and 3 with a King. In the same manner a Queen will win a Jack and Ace, or a King will win a Jack and deuce.

SPADE CASSINO.

In this interesting variation every spade counts one point toward game. The spade Jack counts one in addition to its being a spade, and the extra point so made takes the place of the count for " spades " in the ordinary game, so that 24 points are made in every hand, exclusive of sweeps: Cards 3; Big Cassino 2; Little Cassino 1; the four Aces 4; the spade Jack 1, and 13 spades. It must be remembered that the spade Jack and deuce count 2 points each, the extra point being for the spade.

The game is scored on a cribbage board, every point being pegged immediately; that is, every spade, every Ace, the Cassinos and the sweeps. There is nothing to count at the end of the hand but the cards. Sixty-one points is game, once round the board and into the game hole.

CONQUIAN.

The etymology of this word is very doubtful, and of the origin of the game it stands for, little or nothing is known except that it is a great favourite in Mexico, and in all the American States bordering upon it, especially Texas. It is an excellent game for two players, quite different from any other in its principles, and requiring very close attention and a good memory to play it well. In its finer points, especially in the judgment of what the adversary holds or is playing for, it ranks with our best games, and will probably grow in popularity as it becomes better known.

Cards. Conquian is played with the Spanish pack, forty cards, the 8 9 10 of each suit being deleted. In America, it is much more common to play with a pack of forty cards from which the three court cards, K Q J, have been discarded, leaving each suit an unbroken sequence from the Ace to the Ten. Some persons play with the full pack, but it spoils the game; as it is then possible to win on a sequence of a single suit. There are no trumps, and the cards have no value as to rank, a sequence of 6 7 J being no better than one of 2 3 4. The Ace is not in sequence with the King.

Counters. Each player should be supplied with at least ten counters, which may be used in settling at the end of each deal.

Players. Conquian is played by two persons, one of whom is known as the dealer, and the other as the pone. If there are three at the table, the dealer takes no cards, and has no part in the game for that hand.

Cutting. Seats and deal are cut for, the lowest cut having the choice, and dealing the first hand. The Ace is low, the King high.

Stakes. Each deal is a game in itself, and the loser pays one counter for it. If the game is a tie, called a ***tableau,*** each puts up a counter for a pool, and the winner of the next game takes the pool, in addition to the counter paid by his adversary. If the next game is also a tableau, each player adds another counter to the pool, and so on until it is won.

Dealing. Ten cards are dealt to each player in five rounds of two at a time, and the twenty remaining in the stock are laid upon the table face down, between the players, but a little to the left of the dealer. The stock may be slightly spread, to facilitate the process of drawing cards from it.

Objects of the Game. The object of each player is to form triplets, fours, and sequences, by combining the cards dealt him with others drawn from the stock. These combinations are laid upon the table, face up, and the player wins the game who first succeeds in laying down eleven cards in this manner.

Sequences must be all of the same suit, and cannot be shorter than three cards. The Ace is not in sequence with the King, but the 7 is next below the Jack. A sequence once started can be added to from time to time as the cards are drawn from the stock,

Triplets are any three cards of the same denomination, and they may be increased to ***Fours*** at any time, by adding the other card.

Borrowing. A player with four of a kind on the table may borrow any one of the four to use in a sequence; but he cannot borrow one of three, because no combination may consist of less than three cards. In the same manner a player may borrow the card at either end of a sequence of at least four cards, if he can use it to make a triplet. He cannot borrow an intermediate card, nor one of a sequence of three 'cards only, because three cards must be left to maintain the sequence, but if he had a sequence of at least five cards on the table, he might borrow the top of it to make one triplet, and then the next card to make another triplet.

Method of Playing. The cards dealt, each player sorts his hand into sequences and triplets, and determines what cards he wants to complete his runs, so that he may be on the lookout for them. The pone then draws the top card from the stock and turns it face up on the pack. If this card can be used in combination with any of those in his hand, he draws it over to his side of the table, and takes from his hand the cards completing the combination of three cards, leaving them all face up. Even if he has cards enough in his hand to increase the combination to four or more cards, he should not show them. The cards drawn from the stock must never be taken into the hand.

Let us suppose the pone holds these cards :— ♡ J 7 6 4 ; ♣ 5 3 2 ; ◊ K 7 5 ; and that the ♡ 5 is the first card he draws. He can use this card in three ways : By making a run of three with the ♡ 4 and ♡ 6 ; or a run with the ♡ 6 and ♡ 7 ; or a triplet with the two other 5's. In this case he would probably lay out the 6 and 7, and make the run of three. If he should draw the ♡ Q later on, he could use it by continuing the sequence with his Jack ; or if the ♡ 3 appeared, he could use it with his ♡ 4.

Passing. If he cannot use the card drawn, or does not wish to, he draws it from its position on the top of the stock and places it between himself and the dealer, still face up. The dealer then decides whether or not he wants it, and if he does not he "passes" it by turning it face down, and pushing it to his right. Cards once passed in this manner cannot again be seen by either player. The player who passes the card turns up the next one on the stock. If he does not want it, he places it on the table between himself and his adversary, and if his adversary does not want it either, he turns it down and passes it to the pile of deadwood, turning up the top card of the stock again. In this manner it will be seen that each player has to decide on two cards in succession ; the one drawn but not used by his adversary, and the one he draws himself. This is continued until the stock is exhausted, which ends the game.

Discarding. If a player uses any card drawn from the stock in this manner, it is obvious that he has too many cards, and in order to reduce his hand and show-downs to ten cards, he must discard something, unless he can show down everything remaining in his hand, in which case he would have eleven cards down, and win the game. In discarding, the card thrown out is placed at the disposal of the adversary, as if it were the card drawn from the stock, and if the adversary does not want it, he passes it and draws another. It should be observed that the player drawing the card from the stock always has the first refusal of it. This is sometimes very important, as both players often need the same card.

In the foregoing example, the player's best discard would be his ◊ K, which is too far removed from the others in the suit to make a run possible, and there is no mate to it with which to start a triplet. If the adversary could use this King, he would have to discard in his turn, and the card so thrown out would be at the disposal of the other player, just as if it had been drawn from the stock.

Forcing. A player need not use any card drawn, but if he has upon the table any combination in which it can be used, his adversary may force him with it, even after it has been declined. For instance : A player has eight cards down, two sequences of four small cards each, and in his hand a pair of Kings. Another King will make him game; but if he has to depend on his sequences to put him out, he will have to get three more cards. Suppose he draws a card that will fit one of his sequences ; it is to his advantage to pass it ; but upon laying it on the table his adversary may take it up and force him with it, by placing it at the end of his sequence, at the same time saying : " Discard." In the same manner a player holding one of the cards of his adversary's show-down sequence or triplet may force after using a card, by placing his discard on his adversary's sequence, instead of laying it on the table. If it is laid on the table, the adversary may pass it at once, by turning it down, and it is then too late to compel him to use it. Suppose you think your adversary holds two cards of an unplayed sequence, and has a triplet on the table. If you can use one of those sequence cards in his hand to advantage, and can force him by giving him the fourth card of his triplet, which is of no use to you, you should do so ; but you must remember that you cannot force except after using a card yourself, because you are not allowed to discard under any other circumstances.

If a player looks at any of the cards that have been passed and turned down, his adversary may take up and examine the remainder of the stock, but without disturbing the position of the cards therein, and without showing them. If a player looks at any of the cards in the stock except the one he draws, his adversary may look at all of them. If a player draws out of turn, his adversary simply claims the card.

Showing. After the last card is drawn from the stock and passed, each player shows the remainder of his hand, and as neither can combine his cards so as to get eleven down, it is a tableau, and each puts a counter in the pool for the next hand. The deal passes from one player to the other in rotation as long as they continue to play.

Suggestions for Good Play. Observation of the cards passed will usually show what the adversary is keeping, and what he has no chance for. Toward the end of the stock each player should know what the other holds in his hand by the cards which have not appeared in the drawing. If a player has not a good chance to get eleven down himself, he should play for a tableau, by using nothing that will compel him to discard cards which may put his adversary out. It should be remembered that a player cannot get eleven down in one suit, and careful observation of the cards passed will often show that his runs are blocked, the cards necessary to continue them having been turned down.

One peculiar feature of the game is that a player cannot block his adversary and at the same time win the game, because so long as he holds up the card that his adversary wants he cannot get eleven down himself. His only chance is that he may be able to use the card that his adversary needs. For instance: He holds two 8's, one of which will make his adversary eleven down by completing a sequence. If there is another 8 to come, the player with the pair may use both his 8's, and win; but if there is no other 8 to come, it is impossible for the player with the two 8's to win without first putting his adversary out.

There are no *Text Books* on Conquian, and this is the first complete description of it ever published.

CALABRASELLA.

This is a very popular game with the middle classes and the unoccupied clergy in Italy, and it is one of the very few good games of cards for three players. If the game were better known, the author is sure it would become a great favourite, especially with those who are fond of the whist family, because Calabrasella is an excellent training school for the use of cards of re-entry, long suits, and tenace positions in the end game. In the combination of two players against the third its tactics very closely resemble Skat, and many interesting and difficult positions occur in every game.

Cards. Calabrasella is played with the Spanish pack, forty cards, the 10 9 and 8 of each suit being discarded. The cards rank: 3 2 A K Q J 7 6 5 4, the 3 being the highest, and the 4 the lowest, both in cutting and in play. There are no trumps.

Markers. The game may be scored by paying and taking in counters, each player being provided with about fifty at the beginning of the game, which are purchased from a banker ; but the better way is to keep account of the gains and losses of the single player in each deal, in the manner already described in connection with Skat, balancing the account at the end in the same way.

Players. Calabrasella is played by three persons, two of whom are partners against the third in each hand. If four play, the dealer takes no cards, but shares the fortunes of those who are opposed to the single player, just as in Skat. The players on the right and left of the dealer are known as the pone and the eldest hand respectively.

Cutting. The players cut for seats and deal, the lowest card having the first choice and dealing the first hand. A player exposing more than one card must cut again.

Stakes. The game is played for so much a point. The largest winning or loss for the single player is 140, but such an amount is almost impossible, and the average payments are 10 or 20.

Dealing. The cards are presented to the pone to be cut, and at least four must be left in each packet. The dealer then distributes them to the players four at a time, until each has twelve, four remaining in the stock or talon, which is left upon the table face down. No trump is turned. The deal passes to the left.

There are no misdeals. If the cards are not properly distributed, or four cards are not left in the talon, the same dealer must deal again, without penalty.

Objects of the Game. The chief objects of the game are to win the last trick, and to secure counting cards in the other tricks in the course of play. There are 35 points to be played for in every deal. The six highest cards in each suit, 3 2 A K Q J, have a counting value, the Ace being worth 3, and the others 1 each. The last trick counts 3.

Declaring. The eldest hand examines his cards and determines whether or not he will **stand;** that is, play single handed against the two others. If not, he says **"pass,"** and the next player decides. If all three pass, the deal is void, and passes to the next player on the left. If any player stands, he asks for the 3 of any suit he pleases, and if either adversary holds it, he must give it up. If it is in the stock, the player cannot ask for any other card. If he has all four 3's in his hand he may ask for a 2, but for no lower card. The adversary giving the card asked for must receive a card in exchange from the hand of the single player, but this card must not be shown to the other adversary.

Discarding. Having given a card in exchange for the 3 asked for, the single player must discard at least one more card, face downward on the table, and he may discard as many as four. The four cards remaining in the stock are then turned face up, and the single player may select from them as many cards as he has discarded ; but he is not allowed to amend his discard in any way. The cards he does not take, if any, are turned down again, and are placed with his discards, forming a stock of four cards, which must not be seen or touched until the last card is played, when it becomes the property of the side that wins the last trick, and any counting cards it may contain are reckoned for that side.

Playing. The discards settled, the eldest hand leads any card he pleases, and the others must follow suit if they can, but no one is obliged to win a trick if he has a smaller card of the suit led, and does not want the lead. The two adversaries of the single player do their best to get him between them, and combine their forces to prevent him from winning tricks that contain counting cards, especially Aces. Whatever tricks they win are placed together, and the counting cards contained in them reckon for their joint account. The tricks have no value as such, except the last.

Showing. The winner of the last trick takes the stock, and each side then turns over its cards and counts the total value of the points won. The lower score is deducted from the higher, and the difference is the value of the game. If all 35 points are won by either side, they count double, 70.

Scoring. If the single player loses, he loses to both adversaries, and if he wins he wins from both. His score is the only one put down, and the amount is preceded with a minus or plus sign according to the result. If he secures 23 points, he wins 11 ; if he takes in 16 only, he loses 3. If the amount is less than 18 it must be a loss ; if it is 18 or more it must be a gain. The method of balancing the scores at the end will be found fully explained in connection with Skat.

Irregularities. The penalty for a revoke is the loss of 9 points, which are taken from the score of the side in error at the end of the hand, and added to the score of the side not in fault. If the final score is 24 to 11, for instance, in favour of the single player, and one of the partners has revoked, the score is 33 to 2, and the player wins 31 points. If any player turns over the stock before he has announced to stand and has discarded at least one card, he loses 35 points to each adversary, and the deal is void. If an adversary of the single player turns over the stock before the player has discarded, there is no penalty, and the player may discard as he pleases. If an adversary of the single player leads or plays out of turn, the player may abandon the hand at that point, and claim the stock and last trick, the adversaries being entitled to count only the points they have won up to the time the error occurred.

Suggestions for Good Play. The general tactics of the game are extremely like those employed in Whist and Skat. The player establishes his long suit as rapidly as possible, and preserves his tenaces and cards of re-entry. The adversaries of the player should lead short suits up to him, and long suits through him, and every opportunity should be taken advantage of to discard counting cards on partner's tricks, Aces especially, which are not the best of the suit, but count the most. Both sides scheme to get their hands in shape for winning the last trick, which usually makes a difference of ten or twelve points in the score, owing to the high cards held back, and those found in the stock. Each side should keep mental count of its score, so as to know whether or not it must win the last trick to get to 18. The exposure of the stock, the number of cards discarded by the player, the suits which are led and avoided, will all prove useful guides in determining where the strength or weakness in each suit lies, and proper advantage should be taken of all such inferences.

Some judgment is required in selecting the suit in which the 3 is to be asked for, and the single player must plan in advance for all his discards, one for the exchange, and those for the stock. The player's position at the table makes quite a difference. The leader has an advantage with a good long suit; but with tenaces it is better to be third player, and very bad to be second hand.

Some pretty positions arise in the end game through the refusal of players to win tricks which would put them in the lead, and so lose them the last trick and the stock. After the first few tricks, everything must be arranged with a view to securing that last trick, but the importance of getting home with Aces must never be overlooked. These count 12 points in every hand, and the side that can get in three out of the four has 6 points the best of it.

The only **Text Book** on this game is the Pocket Guide, by "Cavendish"; there are some good articles in Vol. III. of the "*Westminster Papers.*"

ODD GAMES.

There are quite a number of odd games of cards, which come and go as favourites from time to time, and pass round the world from one country to another under many different names. The origin of most of these games is lost in the weedy undergrowth of variations, but the chief family trait in some of them can be traced back to the alpha of cards.

Among the oldest of games was Ombre, immortalised by Pope, the only survivor of which is a variation played by the older Germans, under the name of Solo ; a game which still faintly resists the exterminating influence of Skat. The ancient and honourable games of Comète, Hoc, and Nain Jaune survive to the present day in a large and prosperous family, ranging from Commit to Fan Tan, the latter being to-day quite a favourite among those who like simple and amusing games, free from mental effort. Fan Tan is unfortunately named, as many persons confuse it with the Chinese banking game, and it would be much better under its older name, Play or Pay.

Among the many games of which everyone has heard, and which many thousands have been advised to play, is one which, strange to say, is not to be found described in any work on card games, and that is Old Maid. There was a time when the result of this game was supposed to be final and conclusive, and parties of young men have been known to substitute a Jack or King for the discarded Queen, in order to learn what the future had in store for them. Under such circumstances the game became Old Bachelor, of course.

For those who believe in the verdict of the cards, there are other sources of information. Fortune telling, whether for the purpose of amusement or self-deception, has undoubtedly interested many persons in all stations of life ever since Eittella first explained the art, away back in the sixteenth century. The meanings attached to the cards individually, and the manner of their arrangement, is all that can be given in a work of this kind. The qualifications for success in foretelling the future do not depend so much on the cards as on good judgment of human nature, unlimited assurance, a glib tongue, and a certain amount of ingenuity in making a connected story out of the disjointed sentences formed by the chance arrangement of certain cards, to which an arbitrary or fanciful meaning is attached.

Speculation is considered by some persons an excellent training school for the commercial instincts of the younger members of a family, teaching them to form correct estimates as to the value of certain articles offered for sale in a fluctuating market. Authors is a very good game for the family circle, and does not require special cards, the ordinary pack being easily adapted to the distinctions of the game.

Patience, or Solitaire, has probably claimed the attention of every card-player at some time or other, and one cannot fail to be impressed by the number and ingenuity of the patience games which have been invented. One of the most expensive works on cards ever published is devoted exclusively to Solitaire.

Among all these odd games one should be able to find something to amuse all sorts and conditions of card-players. The only apparatus required in any of them is a pack of cards and a few counters, and for the latter corn or coffee-beans will form an excellent substitute.

SOLO.

Under the name of Solo, the Germans play a great many variations of card games, of which the following is the best known.

Cards. Solo is played with a pack of thirty-two cards, which rank A K Q J 10 9 8 7. One suit is always first preference, or *colour,* and the suit usually selected is clubs. Any suit may be made the trump, but whatever the suit, the club Queen, *Spadilla,* is always the best trump; the Seven of the trump suit, *Manilla,* is always the second-best trump; and the spade Queen, *Basta,* is always the third-best trump.

Players. Solo is played by four persons, who throw round the cards for the deal and choice of seats, the first club turned up deciding it.

Objects. The object of the game is to secure the privilege of naming the trump suit, and of playing, either alone or with a partner, to make five tricks, *solo,* or eight tricks, *tout.* If a partner is required, he is selected by the player asking for a certain ace, but the holder of the ace remains unknown until the ace falls, although from the first he must assist the player who has asked for it. If a player asks for an ace while holding it himself, he of course plays without a partner, unknown to the others however, until he plays the ace asked for.

Bidding. The players bid against one another for the privilege of naming the trump suit, eldest hand having the first say. When no one will bid any higher, the player who has made the best offer names the game he wishes to play, with or without a partner.

Games. The rank of the various games, the amounts bid on them, and the payments made for them, are as follows :—

Simple in suit,. . . . . .2 ; in colour,. . . . . .4.
Forcée or Solo in suit,. . . . . .4 ; in colour,. . . . . .8.
Tout in Suit,. . . . . .16 ; in colour,. . . .32.

Simple Game is to play for five tricks with a partner holding a designated ace. If the trump is clubs, (in colour,) it is worth double, 4 counters.

Solo is five tricks without a partner. With clubs trumps it pays double, 8 counters.

Tout is eight tricks, with or without a partner. If alone, the single player wins or loses all ; if with a partner he must share his gains or losses.

Forcée is when no bid is made, and any player holds both Spadilla and Basta. He must play a Solo, or call for an ace. If he calls, the player holding the ace names the trump suit ; but the suit so named must not be the suit of the called ace. Forcée in clubs is worth double, 8 counters.

Playing. The trump named, the eldest hand leads any card he pleases, and the others must follow suit if they can. The highest card played, if of the suit led, wins the trick, and trumps win all other suits. The hands are abandoned as soon as the bidder takes five tricks, if he is playing anything but a tout. If he goes on he must win all eight tricks, or lose the value of a tout.

Payments. A solo player wins from or loses to each of his adversaries individually the amount of the game in counters. Two partners pay or receive each from one adversary.

HEART SOLO is a game for three players, in which the pack is reduced to twenty-four cards by deleting the Eight of hearts, and all the'diamonds but the Seven. Diamonds are always colour, and there are only three trumps in that suit ; Spadilla, Manilla, and Basta. The only play is for the Solo, and if no one will make a bid, the hands are played in colour, and the winner of the last trick loses the value of a Solo.

AUTHORS.

This game was originally played with cards bearing the names of various authors, and other famous personages, arranged in groups, but the game is much simpler when played with an ordinary pack of fifty-two cards.

Any number of persons can play. The cards are shuffled and spread, and the person drawing the lowest card deals the first hand. The ace is low. Each player then deposits a counter in the pool, and the cards are distributed one at a time until the pack is exhausted. If some players have a card more than others it makes no difference.

The *object* of the game is to secure tricks consisting of four cards of the same denomination ; such as four 6's or four K's, and the player having the most tricks of this kind wins the pool. Ties divide it.

The player on the left of the dealer begins by *asking* for a certain card, which must be of the same denomination as one already in his hand. For instance : He holds the spade Ten. He may ask any one at the table for either of the three other Tens ; but he must designate the suit, and must ask a particular player for the card wanted. If the player asked has the card, he must immediately surrender it, and the player to whom it is given can then ask again—any player for any card, always provided that the asker has one of the same denomination in his own hand.

If the person asked has not the card demanded, the privilege of asking is transferred to him, and he may ask any person at the table for any card of the same denomination as one already in his own hand. If he has just been asked for a Ten, for instance, and has a Ten, but not of the suit asked for, he might turn upon his questioner and get a Ten from him, if he could guess the right suit.

As soon as any player gets together four cards of the same denomination, he lays them face down upon the table in front of him, and they form a trick.

A good memory is necessary to play this game well, as it is very important to recall who has asked for certain cards, and which players were unable to supply them. It is a legitimate artifice in the game to ask for a card you already have in your own hand, although you know it will lose your guess, because it may be the only way to prevent another player from drawing several valuable cards from you. For instance : You hold the Fives of diamonds and spades, and have asked for and received the Five of clubs. If you ask for the heart Five, and miss it, the player with that card may draw all yours ; but if you ask for the spade Five, and he gets into the ask, he will at once betray the fact that he holds the fourth Five by asking you for the club Five ; but he will never think of asking you for the spade Five, because you asked for it yourself. If you can get into the ask again you can immediately make a trick in Fives.

SPECULATION.

Any number of persons less than ten can play, each contributing an agreed number of counters to the pool, the dealer paying double. The full pack of fifty-two cards is used, and the cards rank from the A K Q down to the 2.

In *dealing,* the cards are distributed from left to right, one at a time, until each player has received three. The next card on the top of the pack is turned up, and the suit to which it belongs is the trump, and forms the basis of speculation for that deal. If the turn-up card is an ace, the dealer takes the pool immediately, and the deal passes to the left. If the turn-up is a K Q or J, the dealer offers it for sale, before a card is looked at, and he may accept or refuse the amount offered. Whether the card is sold or not, all the cards that have been dealt out are turned face up, and the highest card of the turn-up suit wins the pool. If the card is not an honour, the dealer proceeds to sell it before any player is allowed to look at any of the cards dealt. If any one buys the dealer's turn-up card, the purchaser places it on his own cards, leaving it face up. Whether it is sold or not, the elder hand proceeds to turn up the top card of his three. If this is not a trump, the next player on his left turns up his top card, and so on until a trump is turned that is better than the one already exposed. The player who possesses the original turn-up, does not expose any more of his cards until a better trump is shown. As soon as a better trump appears it is offered for sale, and after it is sold or refused, the cards are turned up again until a better trump appears, or all the cards have been exposed. The holder of the best trump at the end takes the pool.

OLD MAID.

Strange to say, this oft-quoted and continually derided game is not mentioned in any work on cards, a singular omission which we hasten to supply.

Any number of young ladies may play, and a pack of fifty-one cards is used, the Queen of hearts having been deleted. Any player can deal the cards, which are distributed one at a time until the pack is exhausted ; if every player has not the same number it does not matter. Beginning with the eldest hand, each player sorts her cards into pairs of the same denomination ; such as two Fives, two Jacks, etc., and all pairs so formed are laid upon the table face down, without showing them to the other players. All the cards laid out in this manner are left in front of the player, in order to discover errors, if any. Three of a kind cannot be discarded, but four of a kind may be considered as two pairs.

The discarding of pairs complete, the dealer begins by spreading her remaining cards like a fan, and presenting them, face downward, to her left-hand neighbour, who must draw one card at random. The card so drawn is examined, and if it completes a pair, the two cards are discarded. Whether it forms a pair or not, the player's cards are spread and presented to the next player on the left, to be drawn from in the same manner.

This process of drawing, forming pairs, and discarding is continued until it is found that one player remains with one card. This card is of course the odd Queen, and the unfortunate holder of it is the Old Maid ; but only for that deal.

LIFT SMOKE.

The number of players must be limited to six, each of whom deposits a counter in the pool. A full pack of fifty-two cards is used. The cards rank from the ace down to the deuce, as at Whist. If there are four players, six cards are dealt to each, one at a time ; if five play, five cards to each, and if six play, four cards to each. The last card that falls to the dealer is turned up for the trump, and the remainder of the pack is placed in the centre of the table as a stock to draw from.

The eldest hand leads for the first trick, and the others must follow suit if they can. The highest card played, if of the suit led, wins the trick, and trumps win all other suits. The winner of each trick draws the top card from the talon, and leads again. When any player's cards are exhausted he withdraws from the game, and the others continue. The player who remains to the end, having a card when his adversary has none, wins the pool. If two players remain with a card each, the winner of the trick draws from the stock, and the card so drawn wins the game, his adversary having none.

EARL OF COVENTRY.

This game is sometimes called *Snip Snap Snorem*, by those who are not of a poetical turn of mind. Any number of persons may play, and a full pack of cards is dealt out, one at a time. If some players have a card more than others, it does not matter. The eldest hand lays upon the table any card he pleases, and each player in turn pairs or matches it, if he can, with another of the same denomination, accompanying the action with a rhyme. Suppose the first card played is a King; the person playing it would say: "There's as good as King can be." The first player to lay down another King would say: "There is one as good as he." The player holding the third King would say: "There's the best of all the three," and the holder of the fourth would then triumphantly exclaim: "And there's the Earl of Coventry."

The fortunate holder of the Earl of Coventry in each round has the privilege of leading a card for the next trick, and the first player to get rid of all his cards wins one counter from the others for every card they hold. The words, "Snip, Snap, Snorem," may be substituted for the foregoing rhymes if time is short.

COMMIT.

The etymology of this word has been quite overlooked by those who have described the game. The word is from the French, cométe, a comet; but instead of being an equivalent in English, it is simply a phonetic equivalent; Commit, instead of Comet. Tenac informs us that the game was invented during the appearance of Halley's comet; and the idea of the game is that of a string of cards forming a tail to the one first played, a feature which is common to quite a number of the older games of cards.

Commit is played by any number of persons, with a pack of fifty-one cards, the Eight of diamonds having been deleted. The players draw for positions at the table and for the first deal, and make up a pool. The cards have no value except the order of their sequence in the various suits. The ace is not in sequence with the King, but below the 2. The dealer distributes the cards, one at a time to each player in rotation, as far as they will go, leaving any odd cards on the table face downward, to form what are known as *stops.* As it is desirable to have a number of these stops, it is usual to give only nine cards to each when there are five players.

The eldest hand begins by leading any card he pleases, which he lays face upward in the centre of the table. If he holds any other cards in sequence above it, he must play them, and when he can no longer continue the series, he says aloud: "Without the Jack," or whatever the card may be that he fails on. The player on his left must then continue the sequence in the same suit, if he can; or he must say: "Without the Jack." When the sequence reaches the King, it is stopped, and the player who held the King receives a counter from each player at the table. The same player then begins another sequence with any card he pleases. If a sequence is opened with an ace, a counter may be demanded from each player at the table.

If a sequence is stopped, which it will be if the card necessary to continue it is in the stock, or if the diamonds are run up to the Seven, the person who plays the last card before the stop is entitled to begin another sequence. Should any player who is unable to continue a sequence in his proper turn, hold the Nine of diamonds, he may play that card, and the player following him is then at liberty to continue the original sequence or to play the Ten of diamonds, following up that sequence. When the Nine of diamonds is played, the holder receives two counters from each player at the table; but if it is not got rid of in play, the holder of it must pay two counters to each of the other players.

The first player to get rid of all his cards wins the pool, and the cards remaining in the other hands are then exposed. Any player holding a King must pay a counter for it to each of the other players.

MATRIMONY.

Any number of persons may play, and a full pack of fifty-two cards is used. Each player should be provided with an equal number of counters, to which a trifling value may be attached. A strip of paper is placed in the centre of the table, marked as follows:—

| Matrimony. | Intrigue. | Confederacy. | Pair. | Best. |

Any King and Queen is *Matrimony;* any Queen and Jack is *Intrigue;* any King and Jack is *Confederacy;* any two cards of the same denomination form a *Pair,* and the diamond ace is always *Best.*

The players draw, and the lowest card deals : ace is low. The dealer then takes any number of counters he chooses, and distributes them as he pleases on the various divisions of the layout. Each player then takes a number of counters one less than the dealer's, and distributes them according to his fancy.

The cards are then cut, and the dealer gives one to each player, face down ; and then another, face up. If any of the latter should be the diamond ace, the player to whom it is dealt takes everything on the layout, and the cards are gathered and shuffled again,

the deal passing to the left, the new dealer beginning a fresh pool.
If the diamond ace is not turned up, each player in turn, beginning with the eldest hand, exposes his down card. The first
player to discover Matrimony in his two cards, takes all that has
been staked on that division of the layout. The first to discover
Intrigue or Confederacy, takes all on that, and the first player to
expose a Pair takes that pool. The ace of diamonds is of no value
except as one of a pair, if it is one of the cards that were dealt to
the players face down. The pool for it remains until the card is
dealt to some player face up. Any of the pools which are not won
must remain until the following deal, and may be added to.

POPE JOAN.

This game is a combination of the layout in Matrimony, and the
manner of playing in Commit. There are a great many ways of
dividing the layout, but the following is the simplest. Five cards
are taken from an old pack, and are laid out in the centre of the
table, or their names are written on a sheet of paper.

The cards are thrown round for the deal, and the first Jack
deals. The cards are distributed one at a time, the full pack of
fifty-two cards being used. The following table will show the
number of cards to be given to each player, and that left in the
stock to form stops.

	Players,	15 cards each	7 in the stock.
3	Players,	15 cards each	7 in the stock.
4	"	12 "	4 " "
5	"	9 "	7 " "
6	"	8 "	4 " "
7	"	7 "	3 " "
8	"	6 "	4 " "

Before the deal, the dealer must dress the layout, by putting one counter upon the Ten, two upon the Jack, three upon the Queen, four upon the King, and five on the Pope, which is the Seven (or the Nine) of diamonds.

The eldest hand begins by leading any card he pleases, and if he has those in sequence and suit with it and above it, he continues to play until he fails. He then says " No six," or whatever the card may be that he stops on. The next player on his left then continues the sequence if he can, or if he cannot, he says, " No six," also, and it passes to the next player. If no one can continue, the card must be in the stock, which remains on the table face down and unseen. When one sequence is stopped in this manner, the last player has the right to begin another with any card he pleases.

The object of the game is twofold; to get rid of all the cards before any other player does so, and to get rid of the cards which appear on the layout. If the duplicate of any of those cards can be played, the holder of the card at once takes all the money staked upon it; but if he fails to get rid of it before some player wins the game by getting rid of all his cards, the player who is found with one of the layout cards in his hand at the end must double the amount staked on that card, to which the next dealer will add the usual contribution.

The player who first gets rid of all his cards collects from the other players a counter for every card they hold. These cards must be exposed face up on the table, so that all may see who has to double the various pools. If any of the layout cards are in the stock, the pool simply remains, without doubling.

There are a great many variations of Pope Joan. Sometimes a layout very similar to that in Matrimony is used, Pope taking the place of Pair, and Game that of Best. A trump is turned by the dealer, and Matrimony is King and Queen of trumps, Intrigue Queen and Jack of trumps, Confederacy, King and Jack of trumps. The player holding these cards will of course be able to play both of them if he can play one in a sequence, and will take the pool for the combination. If he holds one card and another player holds the other, they divide the pool. If one of the cards is in the stock, the pool remains. In some places it is the custom to remove the Eight of diamonds, as at Commit, to form an extra and known stop. The player first getting rid of his cards takes the pool on Game, and the holder of Pope takes that pool if he can get rid of the card in the course of play, if not, he must double the pool, just as with the honours in trumps.

NEWMARKET,

OR STOPS.

This game, which is sometimes called Boodle, is Pope Joan without the pope. The four cards forming the layout are the ♥ A, ♣ K, ◇ Q. ♠ J ; but there is no ◇ 7. The dealer names any number of counters that he is willing to stake, which must be at least four, and each player at the table must stake a similar amount. The counters are placed on the layout to suit the players, either all upon one card, or distributed among the four. The cards are dealt as at Pope Joan, and the same number must be left in the talon.

Instead of the player being at liberty to begin a sequence with any card he pleases, he must begin with the lowest card in his hand of the suit which he selects. He is not restricted as to suit, but must play all he has in sequence, and then name the card that he fails on. If a new sequence is opened by any player, he must play the lowest card of the suit in his hand.

If, in the course of play, any of the four cards on the layout can be got rid of, the player holding them takes the pool on that card. If he is left with the card in his hand at the end he is not obliged to double the pool, as at Pope Joan, but simply loses his chance to win it, and it remains until the next deal. The first player to get rid of all his cards receives one counter from the other players for each card they hold.

SPIN is Newmarket, with one variation. The player holding the diamond ace is allowed to play it in order to get the privilege of stopping one suit and opening another. For instance : The sequence in spades has run to the Nine, and one player holds both spade Ten and diamond ace. If this player saw that another was very likely to win the game at any moment, and he had a pool card to play, he might stop the spade sequence by playing both the Ten and the diamond ace together, announcing *Spin.* He can then play a pool card, or begin a new sequence with the lowest of the suit in his hand. He cannot play the diamond ace unless he can play to the sequence first.

SARATOGA. This varies from Newmarket only in the method of making up the pool. Instead of leaving the players to distribute their stakes at pleasure, each is compelled to place an agreed amount on each of the pool cards, as at Pope Joan.

FIVE OR NINE.

This game, which is sometimes called Domino Whist, is simply Pope Joan or Matrimony without the layout. Any number of persons may play, and the full pack of fifty-two cards is used, the cards being dealt in proportion to the number of players, as at Pope Joan.

The eldest hand must begin by laying out the Five or Nine of some suit to start the first sequence. If he has neither of those cards he must pass, and the first player on his left who has a Five or a Nine must begin. The next player on the left must then continue the sequence in the same suit if he can, but he may play either up or down, laying the card on the right or left of the starter. If a Five is led, he may play a Four or a Six. Only one card is played at a time by each person in turn. Any person not being able to continue the sequence may start another if he has another Five, but he cannot start one with a Nine unless the first starter in the game was a Nine. He is also at liberty to start a new sequence with a Five or Nine instead of continuing the old, but he must play if he can, one or the other. If he is unable to play, he must pay one counter into the pool, which is won by the first player who gets rid of all his cards. The winner is also paid a counter for every card held by the other players.

FAN TAN.

This is the simplest form of Stops, and requires no layout. Any number of players can take part, and a full pack of fifty-two cards is used. The players cut for deal and seats, low having the choice. Ace is low. The players are provided with an equal number of counters, and before the cards are dealt, each places an agreed number in the pool. All the cards are dealt out. If some have more than others it does not matter.

The eldest hand begins by playing any card he pleases, and the next player on his left must either play the card next above it, or put one counter in the pool. Only one card is played at a time, and after the sequence has arrived at the King it must be continued with the ace, and go on until the suit is exhausted. The person who plays the thirteenth card of any suit must start another sequence, in any suit and with any card he pleases. The player who first gets rid of all his cards takes the pool.

The great trick in this game is to provide for the last suit to be played, and in order to have the selection of the second suit it is usual for the eldest hand to begin with the higher of two cards next in value to each other, which will make him the last player in that suit. Each suit is turned face down as it is exhausted.

SOLITAIRE.

All games of Solitaire are played with the full pack of fifty-two cards. The games may be roughly divided into two classes; those in which the result is entirely dependent on chance, and cannot be changed by the player after the cards have been shuffled and cut; and those which present opportunities for judgment and skill, the choice of several ways to the same end being offered to the player at various stages of the game. The first class is of course the simplest, but the least satisfactory, as it is nothing more than a game of chance.

Of the many hundreds of patience games, it is possible to give only a few of the best known.

TAKE TEN. Shuffle and cut the cards, and deal out thirteen face upward in two rows of five each, and one row of three. Any two cards, the pip value of which equals 10, may be withdrawn from the tableau, and others dealt from the top of the pack in their places. Only two cards may be used to form a 10. The K Q J 10 of each suit must be lifted together, none of these cards being touched until all four of the same suit are on the table together. When no cards can be lifted, the game is lost.

The object in most patience games is to arrange the cards in sequences. An ascending sequence is one in which the cards run from A 2 3 up to the King; and a descending sequence is one in which they run down to the ace. Sequences may be formed of one suit or of mixed suits, according to the rules of the game.

THE CARPET. Shuffle and cut the pack. Deal out twenty cards in four rows of five cards each, face up. This is the carpet. Any aces found in it are taken out and used to form a fifth row, either at the bottom or at the side. The holes made in the carpet by removing the aces are then filled up from the pack. Cards are then taken from the carpet to build upon the aces in ascending sequence, following suit, and the holes in the carpet are continually filled up with fresh cards from the top of the pack. As other aces appear they are laid aside to start the sequence in the suit to which they belong. When you are stopped, deal the cards remaining in the pack in a pile on the table by themselves, face upward. If any card appears which can be used in the ascending sequences, take it, and if this enables you to make more holes in the carpet, do so. But after having been driven to deal this extra pile, holes in the carpet can no longer be filled from the pack; they must be patched up with the top cards on the extra pile until it is exhausted.

FOUR OF A KIND. Shuffle and cut the pack, then deal out thirteen cards face down in two rows of five each and one row of three. Deal on the top of these until the pack is exhausted, which will give you four cards in each pile, face down. Imagine that these piles represent respectively the A 2 3 4 5 in the first row; the 6 7 8 9 10 in the second, and the J Q K in the third. Take the top card from the ace pile, turn it face upward, and place it, still face upward, under the pile to which it belongs. If it is a Jack, for instance, it will go face up under the first pile in the third row. Then take the top card from the second pile, and so on, keeping the left hand as a marker on the pile last drawn from. When you come to a pile which is complete, all the cards being face up, you can skip it, and go on to the next. If at the end you find that the last card to be turned up lies on its proper pile, and needs turning over only, you win; but if you have to remove it to another pile, you lose.

TRY AGAIN. Shuffle and cut the pack, and deal the cards face upward into four heaps. You are not obliged to deal to each pile in succession, but may place the cards on any of the four piles, according to your judgment or pleasure. In dealing out in this manner it is not good policy to cover one card with a higher, unless you are compelled to do so. Every time you come to an ace, separate it from the others, placing it in a new row, as a foundation for an ascending sequence, which may be continued regardless of the suit of the cards used. The top cards of the four piles are used to build up the sequence. After an ace has appeared, the player may examine the cards in any or all of the piles, but their order must not be disturbed. The object in looking at the cards is to select the pile which is least likely to stop you, or the one having the fewest cards in it.

TAKE FOURTEEN. Shuffle and cut the pack, and deal the cards one at a time, face upward, into twelve piles, and continue dealing on the top of these twelve until the pack is exhausted, This will give you four piles which contain one card more than the others. Then take off any two of the top cards which will make 14, reckoning the Jack as 11, the Queen as 12 and the King as 13, all the others at their face value. Only two cards must be used to make 14. If you succeed in taking off all the cards in this manner, you win. You are at liberty to look at the underneath cards in the various piles, but you must not disturb their positions.

HELP YOUR NEIGHBOUR.   Take from the pack the four aces, and lay them face upward on the table in a row.   These are to be built upon in ascending sequences, following suit.   Shuffle and cut the remaining forty-eight cards, and deal off four starters in a row, below the aces.   These cards are to be built down on, in descending sequence, regardless of suit.   The remainder of the pack is then taken in the left hand, and the cards turned up one by one from the top.   Any card which can be used to build up on the ace row, or down on the second row, is placed on its proper pile at once.   If the card is unavailable for either purpose, it must be placed in a separate and ninth pile, known as the talon, or deadwood.   The ascending sequences may be built up from any of the three sources ; cards from the top of the pack, those on the top of the various descending sequences, or those on the top of the deadwood.

The top card in any descending sequence may be moved from one pile to another, or a card may be taken from an ascending sequence and placed on a descending, always provided that such a card continues the sequence in the pile to which it is removed. If any of the piles occupied by the descending sequences are exhausted, new cards may be placed there at any time the player thinks fit.   Such new piles may be started from the pack, from the deadwood, or from any other pile.

FORTUNE TELLING.

Whatever the arrangement employed for laying out the tableau in fortune telling, the result of the reading will always be dependent on the person's ability to string together in a connected story the meanings which are attached to the various cards.   According to Eittella, the father of all fortune telling, only 32 cards should be used, and it is essential that they should be single heads, because a court card standing firmly on its feet is a very different thing from one standing on its head.   If single-head cards are not at hand, the lower part of the double-head cards must be cancelled in some manner.

The following are the interpretations of the various cards, the initial ***R*** meaning that the card is reversed, or standing on its head.

HEARTS.   Ace.   The house, or home.

King.   A benefactor.   ***R.***   He will not be able to do you much good, although he means well.

Queen.   Everything that is lovely in woman.   ***R.***   You will have to wait awhile for the realization of your hopes.

Jack. A person who may be useful to you. **R.** He will not prove of much account.

Ten. A pleasant surprise.

Nine. Reconciliation.

Eight. Children.

Seven. A good marriage. **R.** Fair to middling.

CLUBS. Ace. Profits from business or gambling.

King. A just man, who has taken a fancy to you. **R.** Something will interfere with his good intentions.

Queen. Your best girl. **R.** She is jealous.

Jack. A probable marriage. **R.** It may have to be postponed.

Ten. Success in business. If followed by ◊ 9, the note will not be paid when it is due; if followed by the ♠ 9 you will lose the entire account.

Nine. Success in love.

Eight. Great anticipations.

Seven. Trifling love affairs. **R.** They will get you into trouble.

DIAMONDS. Ace. A letter, or a written notice.

King. A person to beware of. **R.** Will annoy you in any case.

Queen. A shrew or gossip. **R.** She will make you tired.

Jack. A bearer of bad news. **R.** Worse than you expected.

Ten. An unexpected journey.

Nine. That expected money will not come to hand.

Eight. Some surprising actions on the part of a young man.

Seven. Success in lotteries, gambling or speculation. **R.** The amount will be very small.

SPADES. Ace. Love affairs.

King. Police or sheriffs. **R.** Loss of a lawsuit.

Queen. A gay and deceptive widow. **R.** She's fooling thee.

Jack. Disagreeable young man. **R.** He will do you an injury or injustice of some kind.

Ten. Prison.

Nine. Vexatious delays in business matters.

Eight. Bad news. If followed by the ◊ 7, quarrels.

Seven. Quarrels which will be lasting unless the card is followed by some hearts. **R.** Family rows.

COMBINATIONS. 4 aces, death; 3 aces, dissipation; 2 aces, enmity.

4 Kings, honours; 3 Kings, success in business; 2 Kings, good advice.

4 Queens, scandal; 3 Queens, dissipation; 2 Queens, friendship.

4 Jacks, contagious diseases; 3 Jacks, idleness; 2 Jacks, quarrels.

4 Tens, disagreeable events; 3 Tens, change of residence; 2 Tens, loss.

4 Nines, good actions; 3 Nines, imprudence; 2 Nines, money.

4 Eights, reverses in business or love; 3 Eights, marriage; 2 Eights, trouble.

4 Sevens, intrigues; 3 Sevens, pleasure; 2 Sevens, small affairs and gossip.

THE CONSULTATION. There are several ways of telling fortunes, but one example will suffice. The most important thing is to know what your client wants to be told, and the next is to be sure that she cuts the cards with her left hand.

The cards are shuffled, presented to be cut, and then counted off into sevens, every seventh card being laid face up on the table, the six intermediates being placed on the bottom of the pack each time. When twelve cards have been obtained in this manner, they are laid out in a row, and examined to see if the card representing the questioner is among them. If not, they must be gathered, shuffled, cut, and dealt again. A married man with light hair would be the ◇ K, with dark hair, the ♣ K. If he claims to be single, the ♡ J. If your client is a woman, the ♡ Q will do for blondes, the ♣ Q for brunettes. Do not ask if she is married, and take no notice of rings.

Having obtained the necessary twelve cards, the more you know about the consultant's history, hopes, and prospects, and the better you can judge her character, the less attention you need pay to the cards, and the more satisfactory the result of the consultation will be. It is not necessary to stick too closely to the meanings of the cards, nor to their combinations; the great thing is to tell your client what she wants to hear.

In order to confirm the truth of the pleasing story you have built upon the twelve cards, they must be gathered together, shuffled, presented to be cut with the left hand, and then divided into four packets of three cards each. The first packet is for the Person, the second for the House, the third for the Future, and the fourth for the Surprise. Each packet is successively turned up, and its contents interpreted in connection with the part of the questioner's life which it represents. In case there should be nothing very surprising in the last pack, it is well to have a few generalities on hand, which will be true of a person's future six times out of ten. The expert at fortune telling has a stock of vague suggestions, supposed to be given by the cards, which are so framed as to draw from the client the drift of her hopes and fears. The scent once found, most of the fortune telling is in the nature of confirming the client's own views of the situation. Nevertheless, when well done, by a good talker, fortune telling is very amusing, especially in a small company.

BANKING GAMES.

There are two distinct classes of banking games; those that can be played without any apparatus but a pack of cards and some counters; and those which require a permanent establishment and expensive paraphernalia. Among the first, probably the best known banking games are: Vingt-et-un, Baccara, Blind Hookey, and Fan Tan, the latter requiring only one card, the face of which is never seen. In the second class, which are often called table games, probably the best known are: Faro, Keno, Roulette, Rouge et Noir, and Chuck Luck.

Each of these games has a number of offshoots, and the distinctions between the original and the variation are sometimes so minute as to be hardly worth mentioning. As a matter of reference, and for the convenience of those who hear these variations spoken of, their names and chief characteristics are here given.

Banking games, properly so-called, are those in which one player is continually opposed to all the others. In round games, each player is for himself, but no player is selected for the common enemy. In partnership games, the sides are equally divided, and any advantage in the deal or lead passes alternately from one to the other. In other games, the single player that may be opposed to two or three others usually takes the responsibility upon himself, and for one deal only, so that any advantage he may have is temporary. In banking games, on the contrary, one player is selected as opposed to all others, and the opposition is continual. If there is any advantage in being the banker, it is supposed to be a permanent one, and if the banker has not been at any special expense in securing the advantages of his position he is obliged to surrender it from time to time and give other players a chance. This is the rule in Vingt-et-un, Baccara, and Blind Hookey. If the banker is not changed occasionally, he retains his position on account of the expense he has been put to to provide the apparatus for the play, as in Faro, Keno, Roulette, and Rouge et Noir. To justify this expenditure he must have some permanent advantage, and if no such advantage or "percentage" is inherent in the principles of the game, any person playing against such a banker is probably being cheated.

At Monte Carlo, everything is perfectly fair and straightforward, but no games are played except those in which the percentage in favour of the bank is evident, and is openly acknowledged. In Faro there is no such advantage, and no honest faro bank can live. It is for that reason that the game is not played at Monte Carlo, in spite of the many thousands of Americans who have begged the management to introduce it. The so-called percentage of "splits" at Faro is a mere sham, and any candid dealer will admit that they do not pay for the gas. Roulette, Rouge et Noir, Keno, and Chuck Luck are all percentage games, although the banker in the latter is seldom satisfied with his legitimate gains.

The peculiarity about all percentage banking games is that no system, as a system, will beat them. The mathematical expectation of loss is so nicely adjusted to the probabilities of gain that the player must always get just a little the worst of it if he will only play long enough. Take any system of martingales, and suppose for the sake of illustration that in 1000 coups you will win 180 counters. The mathematical expectation of the game is such that just about once in a thousand coups your martingale will carry you to a point in which you will lose 200 counters, leaving you just 20 behind on every 1000 if you keep on playing. Every system has been carefully investigated, and enormous labour has been expended on the compilation of tables recording for a long series of time every number rolled at Roulette, and every coup raked in at Rouge et Noir, and the result of all systems is found to be the same, the bank succeeds in building up its percentage like a coral island, while the player's money disappears like water in the sand.

VINGT-ET-UN.

Any number of persons may play Vingt-et-un, and a full pack of fifty-two cards is used. The **cards** have no rank, but a counting value is attached to each, the ace being reckoned as 11 or 1, at the option of the holder, all court cards as 10 each, and the others at their face value.

The cards are thrown round for the first deal, and the first ace takes it. The dealer is also the banker. Each player is provided with a certain number of **counters,** usually 25 or 50, and a betting limit is agreed on before play begins. The players on the dealer's right and left are known as the pone and the eldest hand respectively.

The **object** of the game is to get as near 21 as possible in the total pip value of the cards held.

Stakes. Before the cards are dealt, each player except the dealer places before him the amount he bets upon his chances for that deal. This amount may be either at the option of the player, within the betting limit, or it may be a fixed sum, such as one counter. In one variation each player is allowed to look at the first card dealt him before making his bet, and before receiving a second card. When it comes to the dealer's turn, he does not stake anything upon his card, but he has the privilege of calling upon all the others to *double* the amount they have placed on theirs. Any player refusing to double must pass over to the dealer the stake already put up, and stand out of the game for that hand.

Another variation is to allow any player whose second card is of the same denomination as the first to separate them, and to place upon the second card a bet equal in amount to that upon his first card, afterward drawing to each separately, as if they were two different hands.

Dealing. The bets made, the cards are shuffled and presented to the pone to be cut; four must be left in each packet. Two cards are given to each player, including the dealer, one at a time in two rounds. If the dealer gives too many cards to any player, either in the first deal or in the draw, he must correct the error at once. If the player has seen the superfluous card he may keep any two he chooses of those dealt him. If the dealer gives himself too many he must keep them all. The last card in the pack must not be dealt. If there are not enough cards to supply the players, the discards must be gathered up, shuffled together, and cut.

Naturals. The cards all dealt, the dealer first examines his hand. If he has exactly 21, an Ace and a tenth card, which is called a natural, he shows it at once, and the players must pay him twice the amount they have staked in front of them, unless they also have a natural, when it is a stand-off. If the dealer has not a natural, each player in turn, beginning with the eldest hand, examines his two cards to see how nearly their total value approaches 21. If he has a natural, he exposes it immediately, and the dealer must pay him double the amount staked. It is sometimes the rule for the holder of a natural, the dealer having none, to take the stakes of all the other players; but this variation is not in favour.

Drawing. No natural being shown, each player in turn may draw another card, or stand on the two dealt him, which are not shown under any circumstances. If he is content, he says: "I stand." If he wants a card he says: "One," and the dealer gives it to him, face up. If the pips on the card drawn, added to those already in his hand, make his total greater than 21, he is créve, and passes over to the dealer his stake, throwing his cards in the centre of the table, still face down. If the total is not 21, he may draw another card, and so on until he is créve or stands. The first player disposed of in this manner, the dealer goes on to the next one, and so on until he comes to himself. He turns his two cards face upward, and draws or stands to suit himself. If he overdraws, all the other players expose their first two cards to show that they have 21 or less, and he then pays each of them the amount they have staked. If he stands, either before or after drawing, the others expose their cards in the same way, and those that have the same number are tied, and win or lose nothing. Those who have less than the dealer lose their stake; those that have more than the dealer, but still not more than 21, he must pay. When the result is a tie, it is called *paying in cards.*

The Banker. The banker for the next deal may be decided upon in various ways. The old rule was for one player to continue to act as banker and to deal the cards until one of his adversaries held a natural, the dealer having none to offset it. When this occurred, the player who held the natural took the bank and the deal until some one else held a natural. Another way was to agree upon a certain number of rounds for a banker, after which the privilege was drawn for again. Another was for one player to remain the banker until he had lost or won a certain amount, when the privilege was drawn for again. The modern practice is for each player to be the banker in turn, the deal passing in regular rotation to the left. When this is done there must be a penalty for dealing twice in succession, and it is usually fixed at having to pay ties, if the error is not discovered until one player has drawn cards. If before that, it is a misdeal.

Pools. Vingt-et-un is sometimes played with a pool. Each player contributes one counter at the start, and the pool is afterward fed by penalties. Every player who is créve puts in a counter; all ties with the dealer pay one, and the dealer pays one for any irregularity in dealing. The pool may be kept to pay for refreshments, like the kitty in Poker, or it may be won by the first natural shown, as may be agreed.

Probabilities. The only point in the game is for a player to know what hands to stand on, and what to draw to. The dealer is guided by the cards dealt to other players, and by what they ask for. The other players should stand on 17, but draw on 16. In practice it has been found that the odds are about 2 to 1 in favour of drawing at 16; 3 to 1 for drawing at 15. The rules for drawing, etc., are more fully described in connection with the very similar game of Baccara.

MACAO.

In this variety of Vingt-et-un only one card is dealt to each player; court cards and tens count nothing, and the Ace is always worth one. The number to be reached is 9, instead of 21, and if a player has a 9 natural, he receives from the banker three times his stake; if an 8 natural, he receives double, and for a 7 natural, he is paid. If the banker has an equal number of points natural, it is a tie; and if the banker has a 7, 8, or 9 natural he receives from each of the others once, twice, or three times the amount of their stakes. If none of these naturals are shown, the players draw in turn, as at Vingt-et-un, and the dealer receives from those who have less points than he, or who are créve, and pays those who have more, but have not passed 9.

FARMER.

Any number of persons may play. All the 8's and all the 6's but the ♡ 6 are discarded from a pack of fifty-two cards. All court cards count for 10, the ace for 1, and all others at their face value. A pool is then made up by each player contributing one counter. This is the farm, and it is sold to the highest bidder, who must put into it the price he pays for it. He then becomes the farmer, and deals one card to each player, but takes none himself.

The object of the players is to get as near 16 as possible, and each in turn, beginning on the dealer's left must take at least one card. After looking at it he may ask for another, and so on until he is créve or stands. Should a player overdraw himself, he says nothing about it until all are helped, when the hands are exposed. Any player having exactly 16 takes the farm and all its contents. If there is more than one 16, that which is made with the assistance of the ♡ 6 wins, otherwise the one which is made with the fewest cards. If this is a tie the eldest hand wins. If no one has exactly 16, the farm stays with its original owner deal after deal, until exactly 16 is held by some player.

Whether any one wins the farm or not, when the hands are exposed all those who have overdrawn must pay to the one who owned the farm at the beginning of that deal, as many counters as they have points more than 16. These payments do not go into the farm, but are clear profits. Those who have less than 16 pay nothing to the farmer; but the one who is nearest 16 receives a counter from each of the others. Ties are decided by the possession of the ♡ 6, or the fewest cards, or the eldest hand, as already described. If the farm remains in the same hands, the farmer deals again, and collects his profits until he loses his farm. When the farm is won, it is emptied, and re-sold as in the beginning.

QUINZE.

This is a form of Vingt-et-un for two players, but the number to be reached is 15 instead of 21. Court cards are reckoned as 10, and the ace as 1 only. Each player stakes an agreed amount every time, and the dealer then gives one card to his adversary and one to himself. The pone may stand on the first card, or draw; but he does not say anything if he overdraws. The dealer then draws or stands, and both show their cards. The one nearest to 15 wins; but if the result is a tie, or if both have overdrawn, the stakes are doubled, and another hand is dealt, the deal passing from player to player in rotation.

BACCARA.

This very popular variation of Vingt-et-un originated in the south of France, and came into vogue during the latter part of the reign of Louis Philippe. It is neither a recreation nor an intellectual exercise, but simply a means for the rapid exchange of money, well suited to persons of impatient temperament. The word " Baccara " is supposed to mean " nothing," or " zero," and is applied to the hands in which the total pip value of the cards ends with a cypher.

There are two forms of the game in common use; Baccara a deux tableaux, and Baccara chemin de fer. The first will be first described.

Players. Baccara may be played by any number of persons from three to eleven. Those first in the room have the preference, and should immediately inscribe their names. The first eleven form the table, and the privilege of being the banker is sold to the highest bidder; that is, to the one that will put up the most money to be played for. The remaining ten persons draw for choice of seats at the table, the first choice being for the seat immediately on the right of the banker, then for the first seat on his left. Five players are arranged on each side of the banker in this manner, right and left alternately, according to the order of their choice. Sometimes an assistant or croupier is seated opposite the banker, to watch the bets, gather and shuffle the cards, etc. A waste basket is placed in the centre of the table for the reception of cards that have been used in play.

If no one bids for the bank, it must be offered to the first on the list of players; if he declines, the next, and so on. The amount bid for the bank is placed on the table, and none of it can be withdrawn, all winnings being added to it. If no bid is made, the banker may place on the table any amount he thinks proper, and that amount, or what remains of it after each coup, is the betting limit. When the banker loses all he has, the bank is sold to the next highest bidder, or offered to the next player on the list. If the banker wishes at any time to retire, the person taking his place should begin with an amount equal to that then in the bank.

Counters. Each of the players should be provided with a certain number of counters, all of which must be sold and redeemed by the banker or his assistant.

Cards. Three packs of fifty-two cards each are shuffled together and used as one. The players shuffle as much as they please, the banker last, and the banker then presents them to any player he pleases to have them cut. The banker may burn one or two cards if he pleases; that is, turn them face upward on the bottom of the pack.

Object of the Game. The court cards and Tens count nothing, but all others, including the Ace, are reckoned at their face value. The object is to secure cards whose total pip value will most closely approach the number 8 or 9. An 8 made with two cards is better than a 9 made with three.

Stakes. Each player in turn, beginning with the first one on the right of the banker, and after him the first one on the left, and so on, right and left alternately, can bet any amount he pleases until the total amount bet equals the capital then in the bank. When this amount is reached it is useless to place further bets, as they may not be paid. For this reason Baccara is a very slow game when there is not much money in the bank. After all the players have made what bets they wish, outsiders may place bets on the result if they choose to do so.

Either the players or the gallery may bet on either side of the table, which is divided down the middle by a line dividing it into two parts, right and left; hence the name, Baccara a deux tableaux. A person wishing to bet on both sides at once places his money *à cheval;* that is, across the line. If one side wins and the other loses, a bet placed in this manner is a stand-off; if both sides lose, the bet is lost, and if both win the bet is won. A common form of dishonesty at Baccara, and one for which a distinguished Englishman was recently tried, is to place a stake very close to the line, and if it is seen that the side on which it is placed has probably lost; to push the stake onto the line, so that it may be saved if the other side wins. The Englishman in question worked this little game on the Prince of Wales for some time before he was detected.

When the banker loses, he pays the players in their order, right and left alternately, beginning with those who hold cards, until his capital is exhausted. Any further bets are disregarded. If any player bets on the opposite side of the table to that on which he is seated, his bet is not paid until all five of the players on that side have been settled with, because such a bet is regarded as that of an outsider, not belonging to that side of the table. If the player actually holding cards is not the one nearest the banker, he is still the first one to be paid, and then those beyond him in order. For instance : The third player holds cards ; after him the fourth and fifth are paid, and then the first and second, each alternately with a player on the other side of the table.

Banco. Each player in turn, beginning with the one to whom cards will be dealt first, has the right to go banco ; that is, to challenge the banker to play for his entire capital at a single coup. Such a proposition takes precedence of all others. If the bank loses such a coup, it must be put up to the highest bidder again, or offered to the next player on the list. If it wins, the same player, or any other player, may make a similar offer for the next coup, which will now be for double the first amount, of course ; but no player is allowed to offer banco more than twice in succession.

Dealing. The cards cut, the banker takes a convenient number of them in his hand, or better, spreads them face downward on the table, and slips off the top card, giving it to the player next him on the right, face down. The next card he gives to the player on his left, and the next to himself. He gives another card to the right, to the left, and to himself, and then the players take them up and examine them. Ten cards must remain in the stock for the last deal.

Irregularities. After the first card is dealt no bets can be made or changed. The cards must be so held that they shall be at all times in full view of the players. Any card found faced in the pack is thrown in the waste basket. Any card once separated from the pack must be taken. If neither of the players want it, the dealer must take it himself. If the cards are dealt irregularly the error may be rectified if they have not been looked at ; but any player may amend or withdraw his bet before the cards are seen. If the error is not detected in time, the player who holds cards may play the coup or not as he pleases, and all bets on his side of the table are bound by his decision. If a player holds one card too many, he may refuse the coup, or retain whichever two of the three cards he pleases, throwing the third into the waste basket, not showing it. If the banker has too many cards, the players may amend their bets, and the banker's cards are then exposed, and the one taken from him which will leave him with the smallest point, the drawn card being thrown in the waste basket. If the banker gives himself two cards while either player has been given one only, the player must be given another card, and the banker must also take another. If the players have not amended their stake before the error was corrected, the first two cards dealt to the banker are thrown in the waste basket, and the third is his point for that deal. If the banker gives the second card to either player before dealing the first to himself, he must give the second to the other player also, and then take his own. This single card must then be thrown in the waste basket, but the banker may play out the hand as if he had two cards which counted 10 or 20 ; that is, baccara.

Showing. If any of the three persons holding cards finds he has a point of 8 or 9, it must be shown at once, and the two other hands are then exposed. If the banker has 8 or 9, and neither of the others has so many, the bank wins everything on the table. If either player has more than the banker, all the bets on that side of the table must be paid. If either player has as many as the banker, all the bets on that side of the table are a stand-off. If either player has less than the banker, all the bets on that side of the table are lost. If a player wrongly announces 8 or 9, he cannot draw cards unless his point was 10 or 20.

Drawing. If none of the three can show 8 or 9, the banker must offer a card to the player on his right. The card must be slipped off the pack and offered face down. If the player on the right refuses, it is offered to the player on the left, and if he also refuses, the banker must take it himself. If the player on the right takes it, the player on the left may ask for a card also ; but whether he does so or not, the banker is not obliged to draw unless he chooses, after the first card offered has been taken by either player. When the card is taken it is turned face up, and left on the table in front of the person to whom it belongs. Only one card may be drawn by any player, and all the hands are then exposed. Ties are a stand-off. The banker pays all bets on the side that is nearer 9 than himself, and wins all on the side which is not so near 9 as himself. The players on the opposite sides of the table have nothing to do with each other ; each wins or loses with the banker alone.

It should be observed that if a player had 4 originally, and draws a 9, his point is not 13, but 3, because all 10's count for nothing. There is no such thing as being créve, as at Vingt-et-un.

Irregularities. If the banker gives two cards, face up, to the player on his right, the player may retain which he pleases, throwing the other into the waste basket. If two cards are given to the player on the left, he may select which he pleases, and the banker must take the other.

Order of Playing. The coup finished, and all bets paid, the cards which have been used are all thrown into the waste basket, and the stakes are placed for the next coup. The banker deals again, from the top of the stock, without any further shuffling or cutting of the cards. If the player on the right won the first coup, the banker deals to him again ; but if he lost, the banker deals to the next player beyond him ; that is, the second from the banker, on his right. The same with the player on the left. If the player on the right or left wins the second coup, the cards are dealt to him again for the third coup ; if he loses they are dealt to the next player beyond him, and so on, until all five players have held cards and have lost a coup, after which the banker deals to the one nearest him again.

It will thus be seen that there are in each coup only two active players, and that all stakes made upon the game are made upon the result of their hands.

Suggestions for Playing. In justice to those backing him, the player is supposed to draw or not to draw, according to the laws of probabilities, which are exactly the same as in Vingt-et-un. If he has four points, which would be 5 below 9, he should draw ; just as he would if he had 16 at Vingt-et-un, which would be 5 below 21. If he has 5 or more, he should stand ; but if he has 5 exactly it is a matter of judgment, drawing a card being sometimes good play, especially if it is likely to lead the banker to overdraw himself. In some clubs there is a law that a player must draw if his point is less than 5, and must stand if it is more than 5, or he must pay a fine.

As no one is backing the banker, he is at liberty to play as badly as he pleases, and he is really the only one that has an opportunity to exercise any judgment in the matter of drawing. If a player refuses a card, the banker may be able to judge whether or not he has 6 or 7 by his habit of drawing or not drawing at 5. If he is known to be a player who draws at 5, it is useless for the banker to stand at 5, unless he thinks he can beat the player on the other side of the table, and there is more money on that side. If the player demanding a card has been given a 10, the banker should stand, even at 3 or 4. If he has been given an ace, the banker should stand at 4 ; if a 2 or 3, the banker should stand at 5 ; if the player is given a 4, the banker should draw, even if he has 5. If a player has drawn a 5, 6 or 7, the banker should draw, even if he has 5 or 6. If the player draws an 8 or 9, the banker should stand at 4 or 5, sometimes even with 3.

It must be remembered that the banker should have a sharp eye to the relative amounts staked on each side of the table, which will often decide which player he should try to beat. For example : The banker has 5, and the player on his right has drawn a 10, the one on his left a 7. The banker has an excellent chance to win all the bets on the right, and should have a certainty of standing off with them, and unless those on the left very much exceeded them, the banker would be very foolish to risk losing everything by drawing to 5, simply to beat the player on his left.

BACCARA CHEMIN DE FER. In this variation, each player in turn on the left becomes the banker, taking the deal as soon as the first banker loses a coup. The banker gives cards only to the player on his right, and to himself. If this player will not go banco, each of the others in order beyond him may do so. If no one goes banco, each player in turn to the right makes what bets he pleases, within the limit of the bank's capital. If the banker wins the coup, he deals again, and so on until he loses, when the deal passes to the player on his left. The banker, after winning a coup, may pass the deal to the player on his right, if he chooses to do so, provided that player will put up an amount equal to that then in the bank. When this player loses a coup, the bank must go to the player to whom it would have gone in regular order ; that is, the one on the left of the player who transferred his privilege.

Six packs of cards are generally used in Chemin de Fer, and the cards are placed in a wooden box, from which each dealer takes as many as he wants.

CHEATING. Baccara is honeycombed with trickery. Dishonest players, in collusion with the banker, have certain means of informing him of their point, so that he may win all the money staked upon that side of the table by the other players. This may be done in many ways. The player may ask the one sitting next him whether or not he should draw, which shows that he has 5. Or he may make a movement as if to expose his first two cards, and then correct himself. This shows the banker that the player has baccara, and is pretending that he thought he had 9. In addition to this system of communication, which Parisians call tiquer, marked cards, second dealing, and prepared stocks which can be palmed on the true cards, or substituted therefor, are all in common use. If Baccara is honestly played it is one of the fairest of all banking games, but the opportunities for cheating are so many and so easily availed of, and the money to be won and lost is so great, especially at Chemin de Fer, that few who know anything of cheating at cards can resist the temptation to practice it at Baccara.

The Laws of Baccara are very long and complicated. As no official code exists, and as each gambling club makes its own house rules, it is not necessary to give them here, the directions contained in the foregoing description being sufficient for any honest game.

Text Books. The following will be found useful:—
Théorie Mathematique du Baccara, by Dormoy.
Baccara Experimental, by Billard.
Traité Théorique et Pratique Baccara, by Laun.
Westminster Papers, Vols. X. and XI.

BLIND HOOKEY.

This game is sometimes called Dutch Bank. Any number of persons may play, and a full pack of fifty-two cards is used. The cards rank from the A K Q down to the deuce. Any player may shuffle, the dealer last. The pack is then cut, and the re-united parts are placed in the centre of the table. The players then cut it into several packets, none less than four cards, all of which remain on the table face down. Some player then pushes one of the packets toward the dealer, and bets are then made on the others. Any player, except the dealer, can bet what he pleases on any packet.

After all the bets are made all the packets, including the dealer's, are turned face up, exposing the bottom card of each. Any packet disclosing a card lower than the dealer's loses all bets placed upon it. Any packet showing a card better than the dealer's wins from him. The dealer takes all ties. The deal then passes to the next player on the left. Sometimes only three packets are cut, one of which is pushed to the dealer.

This game is a great favourite with card-sharpers, especially on ocean steamers. They use packs in which the cards are trimmed long and short, so that a confederate may cut them by the ends or by the sides for high or low cards, afterward pushing one of the high cuts toward the dealer.

CHINESE FAN TAN.

This is apparently the fairest of all banking games, there being absolutely no percentage in favour of the banker except that the players have to do the guessing.

The one who is willing to put up the largest amount of money to be played for is usually selected as the banker. He is provided with a large bowlful of beans, counters, buttons, small coins, or some objects of which a large number of similar size and shape can be easily obtained. An oblong card is placed in the centre of the table, and the players stake their money upon its corners or upon its edges. These corners are supposed to be numbered in rotation from 1 to 4, the figure 1 being on the right of the banker.

A bet placed on any of the corners takes in the number it is placed upon and the next higher also; so that a bet upon the corner 1 would be upon the numbers 1 and 2; upon 2 it would be upon 2 and 3; and upon 4 it would be upon 4 and 1.

```
 ┌──────────────────┐ X
 │ 3            2   │
 │                  │
 │ 4            1   │
 └──────────────────┘
```

In the illustration, the bet would be upon 2 and 3.

If the bet is placed upon the edge of the card, it takes in the next higher number only.

```
 ┌──────────────────┐
 │ 3            2   │
 │                  │ X
 │ 4            1   │
 └──────────────────┘
```

In the illustration the bet is upon the number 2, and no other.

After all the bets have been placed, the banker takes a large handful of the beans or counters from the bowl, and places them on the table, counting them off rapidly into fours. The number of odd counters remaining decides which number wins; if none remain, 4 wins. If there were 2 or 3 counters over, the banker would pay all bets on the corners 1 and 2, even money. If there were 2 over, he would pay all bets on the edge of the card between 1 and 2 at the rate of three for one, and so on. The counters are then returned to the bowl, and bets are placed for another coup.

Sometimes the banker will draw a handful of beans from the bowl and place them upon the table, covering them with a saucer or with his cap. He then bets any player that there will be 1, 2,

3, or 4 left, the player taking his choice, and being paid three for one if he guesses correctly.

In spite of the fact that this game is apparently perfectly fair for all concerned, the author has never seen an American who could win anything at it while a Chinaman was the banker.

FARO.

This is one of the oldest banking games, and is supposed to be of Italian origin. It belongs to the same family as Lansquenet, Florentini, and Monte Bank. Under the name of Pharaon, it was in great favour during the reign of Louis XIV., and came to America by way of New Orleans. As originally played, the dealer held the cards in his left hand, and any bets once put down could not again be taken up until they were decided. In addition to splits, the dealer took hockelty.

As now played, Faro requires extensive and costly apparatus, the engraved counters used being often worth more than their playing value.

A full pack of fifty-two cards is shuffled and cut by the dealer, and then placed face upward in a dealing box, the top of which is open. The cards are drawn from this box in couples, by pushing them one at a time through a slit in the side. As the cards are withdrawn in this manner a spring pushes the remainder of the pack upward. The first card in sight at the beginning of each deal is called *soda,* and the last card left in the box is *in hoc.*

The first card withdrawn is placed about six inches from the box, and the second is laid close to the box itself.

Every two cards withdrawn in this manner are called a *turn,* and there are twenty-five turns in each deal, Soda and Hoc being dead cards. In making the first turn, the Soda begins the pile farthest from the box, and the next card taken out is called a *loser,* which is placed close to the box. The card left face upward in the box is the *winner* for that turn, so that there must be a winner and a loser for every turn; the loser outside the box, and the winner left in it. On the next and all following turns, the winning card on the previous turn will be placed on the same pile as the Soda, so that it shall be possible at any time to decide which cards have won, and which have lost.

The **Object of the Game** is for the players to guess whether the various cards on which they place their money will win or lose. They are at liberty to select any card they please, from the ace to the King, and to bet any amount within the established limit of the bank.

The Layout. All bets are made with counters of various colors and values, which are sold to the players by the dealer, and may be redeemed at any time. These counters are placed on the layout, which is a complete suit of spades, enamelled on green cloth, sufficient space being left between the cards for the players to place their bets. The ace is on the dealer's left.

There are a great many ways of placing bets at Faro. For instance: A player may make bets covering twenty-one different combinations of cards, all of which would play the Ten to win, as follows :—

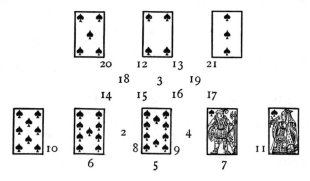

If the first bet is supposed to be flat upon the Ten itself, 2, 3 and 4 would take in the card next the Ten ; 5 the cards on each side with the Ten ; 6 and 7 the three cards behind which the bets are placed, the Ten being one in each instance ; 8 and 9 take in the Ten and the card one remove from it in either direction ; 10 and 11 are the same thing, but placed on the other card ; 12 to 17 inclusive take in the various triangles of which the bet is the middle card ; 18 and 19 take in the four cards surrounding them ; 20 and 21 are *heeled* bets, the bottom counter being flat on the corner of the card, and the remainder being tilted over toward the card diagonally across from the one on which the bet is placed, playing both cards to win. In addition to these twenty-one bets, others might be made by heeling bets that would take certain cards to lose, and the Ten to win. Bets may also be *strung* behind odd or even cards on the side next the dealer. These show that the player bets the next case card that comes will win if it is an even card, and lose if it is odd ; that is, if he places his string behind an even card.

If the player thinks a card will win, he bets it *open*, that is, with nothing but his counters. If he wants to play a card to lose, he *coppers* it, by placing a checker or button on his chips. If a player wishes to reach two cards widely separated, such as the deuce and Seven, and has not money enough to bet on both ; he can ask the dealer for a *marker,* which is a flat oblong piece of ivory. This is placed on the card to be played with the same money, and the dealer may either trust his memory for the bet, or place another marker on it.

After the dealer has waved his hand preparatory to pushing the top card from the box, no bet can be made or changed. After the turn is made, the dealer first picks up all the bets he wins, and then pays all he loses, after which he waits for the players to re-arrange their bets for the next turn. Between each turn a player may make any change he pleases. A lookout sits on the right of the dealer to see that he pays and takes correctly, and to watch that no bets are changed, or coppers slipped off, during the turn.

Splits. If two cards of the same denomination win and lose on the same turn, it is a split, and the dealer takes half the bets on the split card, no matter whether it is bet to win or lose. Splits should come about three times in two deals if the cards are honestly dealt.

Keeping Cases. As the cards are withdrawn from the box they are marked on a case-keeper, which is a suit of thirteen cards, with four buttons running on a steel rod opposite each of them. As the cards come out, these buttons are pushed along, so that the player may know how many of each card are still to come, and what cards are left in for the last turn. In brace games, when the cards are pulled out two at a time to change the run of them, the case-keeper is always a confederate of the dealer, and is sig-nalled what cards have been pulled out under the cards shown, so that he can secretly mark them up. A bet placed or left upon a card of which none are left in the box is called a *sleeper,* and is public property; the first man that can get his hands on it keeps it.

When only one card of any denomination is in the box, it is obvious that such a card cannot be split, and that the bank has no advantage of the player. Such cards are called *cases,* and the betting limit on cases is only half the amount allowed on other cards. It is not considered *comme il faut* for a player to wait for cases, and those who play regularly usually make a number of small bets during the early part of the deal, and then bet high on the cases as they come along. A player who goes upon the prin-ciple that the dealer can cheat those who bet high, and who follows and goes against the big bets with small ones, or who plays one-chip bets all over the board, hoping to strike a good spot to fish on, is called a piker; and when a game runs small this way, the dealers call it a *piking game.*

Keeping Tab. In addition to the case-keeper, score sheets are provided on which the players may keep a record of what cards win and lose on each turn. These tabs are printed in ver-tical columns, about five deals to a sheet. A dot indicates the soda card; a dash, hoc. All winners are marked with a down stroke, and all losers with a cypher. The diagram in the margin will give a very good idea of a faro tab for a com-plete deal. The Queen was soda, the Five split out, and the Eight was in hoc.

A	O O I O
2	O I I I
3	O O I I
4	I O O O
5	O O X
6	I I I I
7	O I I O
8	I I O –
9	O I O I
10	O O O O
J	I I I O
Q	. O I O
K	I O I I

Systems. On the manner in which the cards will go, a great many systems of play are based. There are sixteen different ways for a card to " play," which are simply the permutations of the stroke and the cypher arranged in rows of four at a time. If a player is betting *three on a side,* he will take each card as it becomes a case, and bet that it either wins three times and loses once, or loses once and wins three times. In the fore-going deal he would have bet on the A 3 4 6 9 J to lose on the fourth card out of the box, and would have bet on the case cards of the 2 7 8 10 Q K to win. The Soda, it must be remembered, is really a win-ning card. Of these bets he would have won 5 out of twelve, taking back his money on the 8, as that card was left in hoc. Playing *break even,* these bets would have been exactly reversed, as all the cards would have played either to win and lose an equal number of times, or to *win* or *lose out;* that is, to do the same thing all four times.

Another favourite system is colours. The player takes some definite card, such as the soda, or the first winner or loser, as his starter, and whatever the colour of the third card of each denomination, that is, the card that makes it a case, he plays it to win or lose, according to the system of colours he is playing. Many players reverse on the last turn.

When a player bets one card to lose and another to win, and loses both bets on the same turn, he is *whipsawed.*

The Last Turn. If three different cards are left in for the last turn, the players can *call the turn,* naming the order in which they think the cards will be found. Suppose the three cards left in the box are the 9 8 2, these may come in six different ways :—

$$9\ 8\ 2 \qquad 9\ 2\ 8 \qquad 8\ 9\ 2 \qquad 8\ 2\ 9 \qquad 2\ 9\ 8 \qquad 2\ 8\ 9$$

The odds against any one of these ways are 5 to 1; but the dealer pays 4 for 1 only. In calling the turn, the bet is strung from the selected loser to the selected winner. If the third card intervenes, the bet is strung away from it, to show that it goes round the layout to the other card.

If there are two cards of the same denomination in the last turn, it is called a *cat-hop ;* and as it can come only three ways, the dealer pays 2 for 1. Suppose the cards are 8 8 5, they can come :—

$$8\ 8\ 5 \qquad 8\ 5\ 8 \qquad 5\ 8\ 8$$

If three cards of the same denomination are left, the call is by the colour, and is paid 2 for 1. Suppose two black and one red card are left. These may come :—

$$\text{B B R} \qquad \text{B R B} \qquad \text{R B B}$$

The bets are placed on the dealer's right for red first; on his left for black and red, and in front of him for two blacks.

CHEATING. If Faro were honestly played, it would be one of the prettiest banking games in the world; but unfortunately the money to be made at this game is so great that the richest prizes in the gambling world are offered to the men who can so handle the cards as to " protect the money of the house." All systems are not only worthless, but dangerous to use, when opposed to the skill of the modern faro dealer. A first-class " mechanic " can get from one to two hundred dollars a week, and a percentage of the profits; but it is hardly necessary to say that he is not paid that amount simply for pulling cards out of a box. Before venturing to " buck the tiger " get some one to show you how fifty-three cards are shuffled up, so as to make the last turn come the way that there is most money in it for the house. Watch the movements carefully, so that you will know them the next time you see them in a fashionable house, which you imagine to be " dead square." If you see a dealer with a shuffling board as thick as his dealing box, don't play against that game. If you see a dealer take up the cards already taken from the box, slipping them one under the other, as if to straighten them up, the sooner you cash your chips the better, for you are up against a brace game, no matter where it is dealt.

The proprietors of some fashionable " clubs," especially at watering places, pretend to be above all such things as cheating at faro, and get indignant at the suggestion of the possibility of there being anything crooked in their establishments. The author has but one reply to all such. If it is true that there is nothing unfair in your game, let me put a type-writer girl in the dealer's place to shuffle and pull out the cards, and let your men just see to paying and taking bets.

The boast of all these fashionable gambling houses is that they never won a man's money except in a square game. Strange to say, this is generally true, and the explanation is very simple. If you are losing there is no necessity to cheat you, so you lose your money in a square game. If you are winning, it is the bank's money, and not yours, that they would win if they started to cheat you ; and as the dealer is paid to " protect the money of the house," as they call it, he is perfectly justified in throwing the harpoon into you for a few deals, just to get his own money back ; but he is very careful not to cheat you out of any of your own money. You may lose if you like, but you cannot win ; faro banks are not run that way.

ROUGE ET NOIR,

OR TRENTE-ET-QUARANTE.

The banker and his assistant, called the croupier, sit opposite each other at the sides of a long table, on each end of which are two large diamonds, one red and the other black, separated by a square space and a triangle. Any number of persons can play against the bank, placing their bets on the colour they select, red or black.

Six packs of fifty-two cards each are shuffled together and used as one, the dealer taking a convenient number in his hand for each deal. The players having made their bets, and cut the cards, the dealer turns one card face upward on the table in front of him, at the same time announcing the colour he deals for, which is always for *black first.* The dealer continues to turn up cards one by one, announcing their total pip value each time, until he reaches or passes 31. Court cards and Tens count 10 each, the ace and all others for their face value. Having reached or passed 31 for black, the *red* is dealt for in the same manner, and whichever colour most closely approaches 31, wins. Suppose 35 was dealt for black, and 38 for red; black would win. The number dealt must never exceed 40.

The colour of the first card dealt in each coup is noted, and if the same colour wins the coup, the banker pays all bets placed on the space marked *Couleur.* If the opposite colour wins, he pays all bets in the triangle marked *Inverse.* All bets are paid in even money, there being no odds at this game.

Although black is the first colour dealt for, both it and inverse are ignored in the announcement of the result, red and colour being the only ones mentioned, win or lose.

If the same number is reached for both colours, it is called a *refait,* and is announced by the word, " Apres," which means that all bets are a stand-off for that coup. If the refait happens to be exactly 31, however, the bank wins half the money on the table, no matter how it is placed. The players may either pay this half at once, or may move their entire stake into the first prison, a little square marked out on the table, and belonging to the colour they bet upon. If they win the next coup, their stake is free; if not, they lose it all. Should a second refait of 31 occur, they would have to lose a fourth of this imprisoned stake, and the remainder would be moved into a second prison, to await the result of the next coup, which would either free it or lose it all.

Probabilities. It has been found that of the ten numbers that can be dealt, 31 to 40, the number 31 will come oftener than any other. The proportions are as follow :—

31–13 times,	36–8 times,
32–12 times,	37–7 times,
33–11 times,	38–6 times,
34–10 times,	39–5 times,
35– 9 times,	40–4 times.

The 31 refait also comes oftener than any other. Although the odds against it are supposed to be 63 to 1, the bankers expect it about twice in three deals, and each deal will produce from 28 to 33 coups.

ROULETTE.

It is probable that more money has been lost at the wheel than at any other gambling game in the world. In conjunction with Rouge et Noir, it forms the chief attraction at Monte Carlo, and other public gambling casinos. The rage for these games was so great, and the trickery connected with them so common, that they were banished from France by the law of 18 juillet, 1836, and had to take refuge in Baden and Homburg. Before that time the public revenue from the gaming houses amounted to five or six millions a year, all of which was lost by closing them up. The evil was not exterminated, however, for there are to-day hundreds of gambling hells in Europe, which make up for the brevity of their existence by the rapidity with which they fleece their patrons.

In America, the wheel has always been popular, but Rouge et Noir is practically unknown, the reason being that in the latter game there is no variety, and therefore no chance for the player to exercise any judgment, or to play any "system" in making his bets, as he can in Faro.

The Wheel. The roulette wheel is turned by a small cross-bar rising from its axis. The surface of the wheel slopes from the axis to the outer edge, which is divided into small square pockets, coloured alternately red and black, and each having a number just above it, on the surface of the wheel. These numbers may be in any order, according to the fancy of the maker of the wheel, and they may run from 1 to 27, to 30, to 33, or to 36. In addition to the numbers there are zero marks, which are called *single* and *double 0,* and *Eagle Bird.* All three of these are used in American wheels, and they are green, so that they win for neither colour. In some of the Europeon wheels there are two zeros, the single o being red, and the double o black. The single o also counts as " odd," and as below 19; while the double o is " even," and above 18. Bets on odd or even, above and below, are not paid, however, but must remain on the table until the next roll, when the player either gets back twice his money or loses it all. At Monte Carlo there is only one zero, which is green, and takes everything but bets on itself. The numbers on the wheel are arranged as follows at Monte Carlo, the heavy type being the black :—

0 32 **15** 19 **4** 21 **2** 25 **17** 34 **6** 27 **13** 36 **11** 30 **8** 23 **10** 5 **24** 16 **33** 1 **20** 14 **31** 9 **22** 18 **29** 7 **28** 12 **35** 3 **26.**

The pockets on the edge of the wheel are at the bottom of a sort of circular valley, the centre of which is formed by the revolvng wheel, and the outer slope by a stationary but rising margin or border, at the top of which is an overhanging edge, under which the banker spins a small ivory ball, always in the direction opposite to that in which the wheel is turning. As the ball loses its momentum it strikes some little brass ridges, which cause it to jump onto the wheel, and then to run into one of the pockets. The number, the colour, odd or even, and whether above or below, is immediately announced by the banker, and all bets are taken and paid accordingly.

The Layout.   The wheel is sunk in the middle of a long table, on each end of which is a layout, and on these layouts all bets are placed. The divisions are as follows :—

		o		
	1	2	3	
Passe	4	5	6	Manque
	7	8	9	
	10	11	12	
	13	14	15	
Pair	16	17	18	Impair
	19	20	21	
	22	23	24	
	25	26	27	
Noir	28	29	30	Rouge
	31	32	33	
	34	35	36	
P 12 M 12 D 12				P 12 M 12 D 12

Bets may be made on the following chances :

1.   **En plein.**   Flat upon any number, which pays 35 for 1.

2.   **À cheval,** on the line between two numbers, which pays 17 for 1.

3. *Un carré,* on a cross line, taking in four numbers. This pays 8 for 1.

4. *Transversale,* at the end of any three numbers, and taking in the three horizontal numbers. This pays 11 for 1.

5. *Transversale Six,* placed on the line at the end, taking in the three numbers horizontally above and below. This pays 5 for 1.

6. *Bas.* At the bottom of any of the three vertical columns, taking in the twelve numbers. This pays 2 for 1.

7. *Bas à cheval,* between any two of these columns. This pays ½ for 1.

8. *Premier, Milieu, Dernier.* Bets placed in the spaces marked P 12, M 12, and D 12, are upon the first, middle and last twelve numbers; that is, from 1 to 12, 13 to 24, and 25 to 36 respectively. This pays 2 for 1.

A cheval between any two of the last mentioned, pays ½ for 1.

In addition to the foregoing, all the following chances may be bet upon. They all pay even money.

9. *Impair.* That the number will be odd.

10. *Pair.* That the number will be even.

11. *Manque.* That the number will be from 1 to 18.

12. *Passe.* That the number will be from 19 to 36.

The foregoing are the payments at Monte Carlo; but wheels with less numbers are scaled down accordingly. The players can bet on the zero if they choose, and they will be paid if it comes up, 35 for 1, but all other bets are lost. In wheels with two zeros, red and black, the bank wins on the colour which does not come, and the bets on the right colour are neither paid nor taken, but must remain until the next turn of the wheel, although they may be shifted to another part of the layout.

Systems. As at Faro, gamblers at Roulette are never tired of devising systems to beat the game; but none of them are of any further use than to afford a little passing amusement to their inventors. Persons who are interested in systems will find in the *New York Sun,* July 5, 1896, a very interesting tabulation of every roll of the ball at Monte Carlo for seven successive days, 4,012 in all, of which 120 were zeroes. If they can find a system that will beat the wheel for seven days, and have a return ticket, Monte Carlo will take care of all their spare cash.

One curious fallacy about some systems is to imagine that they will win if the player will quit when he is a certain amount ahead, and not play again until next day. Until some rule can be given by which the exact hour can be fixed to begin play, all such systems must be delusions, as there is no reason why a second man should not begin where the first left off, and therefore no reason why the first should not continue playing all the time.

It is in the interest of the proprietors of all gambling houses to pretend to be afraid of systems. The word is passed round, and the deluded gamesters think they have found the thread which has held the sword of Damocles above the banker's head so long. As a matter of fact, there is no one so welcome at a gambling house as a player with a system. A man may be fortunate enough for a long time to guess right oftener than he will guess wrong, and a lucky man in good guessing form is a very dangerous customer, that no cold deck will beat; but a man with a system surrenders to a double foe; the inevitable percentage of the game, and the skill of the banker, who can beat any system if the player will only promise to stick to it.

KENO, OR LOTTO.

This game is played with a large number of cards, on which are printed various permutations of the numbers 1 to 90, taken five at a time; but each of the five numbers selected for one combination must be in a separate division of tens, such combinations as 2 4 8 16 18 not being allowed on any card, because the 2 4 and 8, for instance, are all in the first ten numbers of the 90. These cards have each a number, printed in large red type across the face of the other figures. The following might be a keno card, No. 325 :—

1		26		45	53		77	
	10	28	3	2	5	62	79	83
4	12		37			67		90

Some cards have more than four rows of figures on them, but none have more than five in one row.

The cards are left on the tables in large numbers, and any number of persons may play. Each selects as many cards as he wishes, or thinks he can watch, and places upon them their price, usually twenty-five cents each. An assistant comes round and calls out the numbers of all the cards to be played, and they are "pegged" on a large board provided for the purpose.

Ninety small ivory balls, with flattened surfaces to carry the numbers, are placed in a keno goose, which looks like a coffee urn with the spout at the bottom. This spout can be screwed out to put in the balls, and is controlled with a spring cut-off like a powder horn, which lets out only one ball at a time. When all the cards have been pegged, the goose is rapidly revolved several times back and forth, and then a number is taken out, and placed in a little tray with ninety depressions in it, numbered in regular order, which hold the balls as they come from the goose. The keno roller calls each number distinctly, and the players who find it on their cards cover it with a button. The first player to get a horizontal row of five numbers covered in this manner, calls out " Keno ! " or bangs the table with a card, and that stops the game. An assistant comes round to the table and calls out the number of the card ; if it has been paid for and pegged, he proceeds to call the numbers forming the keno, and these are checked by the roller from the balls on the tray. If everything is correct, the player is given all the money paid by the other players for their cards, less the ten per cent which goes to the house. If two kenos are made on the same number, they divide the pool equally.

As an illustration of the profitable nature of the game for the house, it may be remarked that if ten men were to play keno for a dollar a card, and each of them made keno ten times, they would all be " dead broke ; " because on each of the hundred kenos at ten dollars each, the bank would have taken out its dollar percentage.

CHUCK-LUCK.

This game is sometimes called *Sweat,* and again, but erroneously, *Hazard.* It is played with three dice, which are usually thrown down a funnel in which several cross-bars are placed. The player is offered five different forms of betting, all of which appear on the *Layout,* and which cover all the combinations possible with three dice.

HIGH.	SINGLE NUMBERS.						LOW.
	1	2	3	4	5	6	

18	17	16	15	14	13	12	11	10	9	8	7	6	5	4	3
180	60	29	18	12	8	6	6	6	6	8	12	18	29	60	180

ODD.	RAFFLES.						EVEN.
	1	2	3	4	5	6	

The Raffles are sometimes indicated by a representation of one face of a die. Bets on single numbers pay even money, if the number bet on comes up on the face of any of the three dice. If it comes up on two of them, such as two deuces, it pays double; but if all three dice are alike it is a *raffle,* and the house takes all bets not placed on raffles. Bets on the numbers from 18 to 3 are upon the total count of the pips on the upper faces of the three dice. The small figures under these numbers show the odds paid; 14, for instance, pays twelve for one. All raffles pay 180 for one; the same as 18 or 3.

Bets on High and Low, Odd or Even, pay even money. High throws are all above 10, and low throws are all below 11. This would be perfectly even betting if the house did not take raffles. Some houses allow a player to bet on raffles generally; that is, to bet that a raffle of some kind will come. Such bets are paid 30 for 1.

The percentage of the house, even in a square game, may be seen from the following table, which gives the odds against the event, and the odds which the house pays:—

The odds against	3 or 18	are	215	to 1;	the house pays	180
"	" 4 " 17 "		71	" 1	" "	60
"	" 5 " 16 "		35	" 1	" "	29
"	" 6 " 15 "		20½	" 1	" "	18
"	" 7 " 14 "		13¼	" 1	" "	12
"	" 8 " 13 "		9¼	" 1	" "	8
"	" 9 " 12 "		7¼	" 1	" "	6
"	" 10 " 11 "		7	" 1	" "	6

Cheating. There are endless ways of swindling at Chuck-luck, the most modern being to turn the dice over after they have reached the table through the funnel. This is done by an apparatus under the cloth, the dealer looking down the funnel to see how the dice lie, and then adjusting them to suit himself. Another method is to hold out one die, throwing only two down the funnel, and slipping the third down the outside, turning it so that when it is combined with the two already in the funnel it will beat the big bets on the layout. Raffles can be forced in this way whenever the two dice in the funnel are paired.

RONDEAU.

This game is played on a pocket billiard table. The banker asks for bets on the *inside* and *outside,* and the amounts staked on each side must balance. So long as they do not balance, the banker must ask for what he wants: " Give me fourteen dollars on the outside to make the game," etc. As soon as the amounts balance, and no more bets are offered, he says: "Roll. The game is made."

A round stick, about a foot long, is placed behind nine small ivory balls. Any person may roll. He takes his stand at one corner of the table and rolls the balls across the table to the pocket diagonally opposite him. At least one ball must go into the pocket and one must be left out, or they must be rolled over again. The number of balls left outside the pocket, odd or even, decides whether the inside or the outside bets win; and after the banker has deducted his ten per cent. the players who have backed the winning side get their money.

UNDER AND OVER SEVEN.

This game is played with a layout, divided and marked as follows :—

U	*7*	*O*
EVEN	3 TO 1	EVEN

The players can bet on any of the three spaces. Two dice are thrown by the banker, and if [the number thrown is *under* seven he pays all bets upon the U, even money, taking all those upon 7 and o. If the throw is *over* seven, he pays all bets upon the o, taking all those upon U and 7. If seven is thrown, he pays all bets upon that number, three for one, and takes all upon U and O.

As there are 36 possible throws with two dice, 15 being under and 15 over seven, the precentage in favour of the banker is always 21 to 15, on U and O. As there are only 6 ways out of 36 to throw seven, the odds against it are 5 to 1; but the banker pays only 3 for 1. In spite of this enormous percentage in his favour, he frequently adds to his revenue by skilful cheating.

TABLE GAMES.

The common form of folding chess-board provides a field for three of our best known games; Chess, Checkers, and Backgammon, which are generally spoken of as " table games," although, strictly speaking, Backgammon is the only game of Tables. These three games were probably played long before history noticed them, and they have survived almost all ancient forms of amusement.

Chess is not only the most important of the three, but the most widely known, and possesses the most extensive literature. According to Chatto, it is probable that all games of cards owe their origin to chess, cards themselves having been derived from an old Indian variation of chess, known as the Four Kings. Chess is also the most fascinating of the table games, its charm being probably due to the fact that, like whist, it is a game that no man ever mastered. Whether or not this is in its favour is an open question. The amount of study and practice required to make a person proficient in chess brings a serious drain upon the time, and the fascinations of the game are such that once a person has become thoroughly interested in it, everything else is laid aside, and it is notorious that no man distinguished as a chess-player has ever been good for anything else.

Mr. Blackburne, the English chess champion, regards the game as a dangerous intellectual vice which is spreading to rather an alarming extent. Discussing the matter, after his game with Mr. Bardeleben, he said : " I know a lot of people who hold the view that chess is an excellent means of training the mind in logic and shrewd calculation, provision and caution. But I don't find these qualities reflected in the lives of chess-players. They are just as fallible and foolish as other folks who don't know a rook from a pawn. But even if it were a form of mental discipline, which I doubt, I should still object to it on the ground of its fatal fascination. Chess is a kind of mental alcohol. It inebriates the man who plays it constantly. He lives in a chess atmosphere, and his dreams are of gambits and the end of games. I have known many an able man ruined by chess. The game has charmed him, and, as a consequence, he has given up everything to the charmer. No, unless a man has supreme self-control, it is better that he should not learn to play chess. I have never allowed my children to learn it, for I have seen too much of its evil results. Draughts is a better game, if you must have a game."

Chess is generally believed to have originated in India, and in its primitive form was called Chaturanga. It is mentioned in the Hindoo Puranas, at least 3000 years B. C. The game seems to have spread eastward long before it came West, going through Burmah to Thibet, Siam, China, Malacca, Java, and Borneo. Owing to the better preservation of historical records in China, many persons have been led to credit that country with the invention of chess, but recent investigations have shown that the Chinese got it from India. At some remote period of the world's history the game was taken from China to Japan, and there are to-day many points in common between the games played in these two countries, especially in the arrangement of the pieces, although the Japanese board has eighty-one squares.

Chess came westward through Constantinople, it having passed through Persia sometime during the sixth century. The Arabs seem to have learned the game, and taken it to Mecca and Medina, afterward passing it along to Syria and the Byzantines, sometime during the seventh century. Disbanded body-guards of the Byzantine emperors carried it to Scandinavia and the North, while it was gradually spreading over Europe by way of the Bosphoros and the Danube.

Draughts, or ***Checkers,*** is sometimes claimed to be an older game than Chess ; but it is much more probable that both are developments of some still older game, all trace of which is lost. In Egypt and Nubia there are illustrations of persons playing at draughts twenty centuries before the Christian era. During recent explorations in Egypt quite a variety of draughtmen have been found, some of which were used during the reign of Rameses III. The usual form seems to have been circular, about an inch in diameter, and surmounted by a round knob, something like a chess pawn, so that the men could be easily picked up. From the manner in which the men are shown mixed upon the board, it is evident that they could not move or take backwards, as in Polish draughts, but whether they advanced diagonally, as at the present day, there is no evidence to show. The Japanese game of draughts has lately been revived in England and America under the name of Go-Bang, but as it requires a special board of 324 squares, it has never been popular.

Backgammon cannot be traced to its origin. Several authorities have fallen into the error of ascribing the game to a certain country because the name is derived from a certain language, forgetting that in ancient times every country invented its own names for games. Chess is called Choke-choo-hong-ki in China, and Shogi in Japan ; but that does not make it either a Chinese or a Japanese game. Either of these names might be used for Backgammon, as they have exactly the same meaning. The Welsh words, bach, and cammen ; or the Saxon bac, and gamen, signify

" a little battle ; " while the Chinese and Japanese names for Chess signify " mimic warfare."

The Welsh and Saxons undoubtedly got Backgammon from the Romans, who played it under the name of Scripta Duodecimo. They seemed to have got it from the Greeks, who are known to have used a table called Abacus, very much like a backgammon board in form, with lines drawn upon it, and the men were moved from one line to another according to the throws of the dice.

There is no trace of Backgammon among the games of the Egyptians or the Hebrews, although the chief factors in the game, the dice, have been known to all nations, and are probably the oldest gaming instruments in the world.

As to the respective merits of these table games, there is little to be said. Curiously enough they are played by entirely different classes of people. Backgammon has always been highly respectable, and seems likely to retain its position as the fashionable game. Draughts is peculiarly the game of the middle classes, popular at the workman's dinner hour, in the sitting-rooms of cheap hotels, in country clubs, and in fire engine stations ; the latter being a favourite training ground for our checker champions. Chess is probably the most universal game of all, and its general character **is** understood by almost every educated person in the world.

CHESS.

Chess is played upon a square board, divided into sixty-four smaller squares of equal size. These small squares are usually of different colours, alternately light and dark, and the board must be so placed that each player shall have a light square at his right, on the side nearer him.

Each player is provided with sixteen men, eight of which are called *pieces,* and eight *pawns.* The men on one side are red or black, and those on the other side are white or yellow, and they are usually of a standard pattern, which is known as the Staunton model.

The eight pieces are :

The King,  The Queen, Two Rooks or Castles,

Two Bishops, and two Knights,

These eight pieces are arranged on the side of the board nearer the player, and immediately in front of them stand the eight Pawns, Diagram No. 1 will show the proper arrangement of the men at the beginning of a game : —

BLACK.

No. 1.

WHITE.

It will be observed that the two Queens are opposite each other, and that each Queen stands upon a square of the same colour as herself. For irregularities in setting up the men, see the Laws of Chess.

The *players* are designated by the colour of the men with which they play, Black or White, and White always has the first move. In a series of games each player alternately takes the white men with the first move. It is usual to draw for the first game, one player concealing in each hand a pawn of a different colour, and offering the choice of hands to his adversary. Whichever colour the chosen hand contains is the one the chooser must take for the first game.

The duplicate pieces of each colour are distinguished by their position with regard to the King or Queen; those on the King's side being called the King's Bishop, the King's Knight, and the King's Rook. Those on the Queen's side are the Queen's Bishop, Queen's Knight, and Queen's Rook. The pawns are designated by the pieces in front of which they stand; King's Pawn; Queen's Knight's Pawn, etc.

The comparative *value of the pieces* changes a little in the course of play, the Rooks especially not being so valuable early in the game. Authorities differ a little as to the exact value of the pieces, but if we take the Pawn as a unit, the fighting value of the others will be about as follows :—

A Knight is worth........ 3½ Pawns.
A Bishop is worth........ 5¼ Pawns.
A Rook is worth........... 9½ Pawns.
A Queen is worth.........15 Pawns.
A King is worth........... 4½ Pawns.

THE MOVES. Each piece has a movement peculiar to itself, and, with the exception of the Pawns, any piece can capture and remove from the board any opposing piece which it finds in its line of movement. The captured piece is not jumped over, but the capturing piece simply occupies the square on which the captured piece stood. The movement of each piece should be studied separately.

The Pawns move straight forward, one square at a time, except on the first move, when they have the privilege of moving either one or two squares, at the option of the player. In capturing, the Pawn does not take the piece directly in its path, but the one diagonally in front of it on either side. Such a capture of course takes the Pawn from the file originally occupied, and it must then continue to advance in a straight line on its new file. In Diagram No. 2, the white Pawns could not capture either of the black Bishops or Rooks, but the Pawn on the left could take either of the black Knights :—

No. 2.

WHITE.

After a Pawn has crossed the middle line of the board into the adversary's territory, it is called a **passed Pawn.** If an adverse Pawn attempts to pass this Pawn by availing itself of the privilege of moving two squares the first time, that would not prevent the passed Pawn from capturing it **en passant.** In the position shown in Diagram No. 3, for instance, if the black Queen's Pawn were to advance two squares, the white Pawn could capture it en passant, lifting it from the board, and taking the position that the black Pawn would have occupied if it had moved only one square the first time ; that is, the first black square in front of the Queen. A Pawn can be taken en passant only by another pawn, never by any other piece.

BLACK.

No. 3.

The **Rook** can be moved any number of squares at a time, forward or backward, but only in vertical or horizontal lines, never diagonally. The Rook's movement is of course limited by pieces obstructing its path, for it cannot jump over anything. At the beginning of the game, for instance, the Rook cannot move at all.

The **Bishop** can be moved any number of squares at a time, forward or backward, but only in diagonal lines, never horizontally or vertically. For this reason the Bishop never leaves the squares of the same colour as that on which it originally stood. A Bishop is often spoken of as a white Bishop or a black Bishop, which does not mean that it is is one of White's Bishops, or one of Black's; but that it stands upon a white or black square. Like the Rook, the Bishop cannot jump over other pieces, and cannot be moved at all until one or other of the two Pawns diagonally in front of it have opened the way.

The **Queen** combines the movements of the Rook and Bishop, and can be moved horizontally, vertically, or diagonally, any number of squares at a time, provided that the path is clear. Like the Rook and Bishop, she cannot move at all until some of the adjoining pieces have made a way for her.

The **King** has the same movement as the Queen, but is limited to one square at a time. The King is not allowed to move to a square which would expose him to capture by adverse pieces, for reasons which will presently be explained.

The **Knight** has a very peculiar movement, which is L shaped, and necessitates his changing the colour of the square he stands on, every time he moves. The simplest way for the beginner to learn the Knight's move is to observe that he must go two squares, neither more nor less, in a vertical or a horizontal direction, and must then change the colour of the square he stands on by going one square either to the right or left, which will complete the L shaped movement. Diagram No. 4 will show that when the Knight is away from the side of the board, he may go to any one of eight different squares; but when he is in a corner he can go to two only. For that reason Knights are much more powerful when placed near the centre of the board.

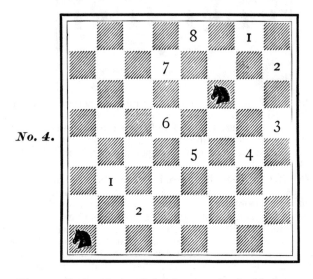

No. 4.

The peculiarity of the Knight's move is that it is not retarded by other pieces, because the Knight can jump over them, a privilege which is not given to any other piece on the board. In Diagram No. 5, for instance, the Knights have been legitimately moved, but no other piece could be moved until the Pawns had made way for it.

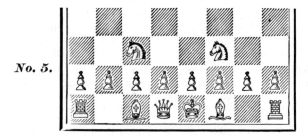

No. 5.

There are one or two peculiar movements which are allowed only under certain conditions. One of these is *Castling*. If there are no pieces between the King and the Rook, and neither piece has been moved, the King may be moved two squares toward the Rook, and at the same time the Rook may be brought round to the other side of the King. The movement must be made with both hands, each manipulating a piece. In the position shown in Diagram No. 6, for instance, the King could castle on either side, with the King's Rook, or with the Queen's Rook:—

No. 6.

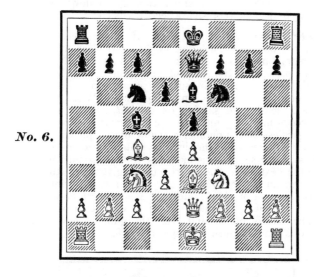

If an adverse piece commands the square that would be passed over by the King in castling, the move is not allowed; because a King must not move into check, nor cross a square that is checked by an adverse piece.

In Diagram No. 7 the position that would result from castling with the Queen's Rook is shown by the black men.

No. 7.

Queening Pawns. If a passed Pawn succeeds in reaching the last or eighth square on any file, the player to whom the Pawn belongs may call it anything he chooses, from a Queen to a Knight. If the piece he chooses has already been captured, it must be replaced on the board, and on the square occupied by the Pawn, which is then removed. If not, some other piece must be put upon the board as a marker; a Rook upside down, or a Pawn with a ring on it, may represent a second Queen.

OBJECT OF THE GAME. If all the pieces could be captured, the object of the game might be to clear the board of the adversary's men, as in Checkers; but the peculiarity of Chess is that one piece, the King, cannot be captured, and the object is to get the adverse King in such a position that he could not escape capture if he were a capturable piece. When that is accomplished the King is said to be ***mated,*** and the player who first succeeds in giving mate to the adversary's King wins the game, regardless of the number or value of the pieces either side may have on the board at the time the mate is accomplished.

When an adverse piece is moved so that it could capture the King on the next move, due notice must be given to the threatened King by announcing " **Check,**" and the player must immediately move his King out of check, interpose a piece or a Pawn, or capture the piece that gives the check. If he cannot do one of these three things he is mated, and loses the game. A very simple example of a mate is given in Diagram No. 8.

No. 8.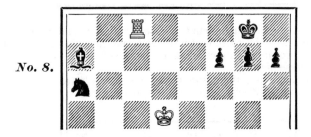

The white Rook has just been moved down to the edge of the board, giving " check." As the black King can move only one square at a time, he cannot get out of check by moving, because the only squares to which he could go would still leave him in check from the Rook. Neither the Knight nor the Bishop can interpose to shut out the Rook's attack; neither of those pieces can capture the Rook; and the Pawns cannot move backward; so the black King is mated, and **White wins the game.**

A mate may take place in the middle of the board, as shown in Diagram No. 9.

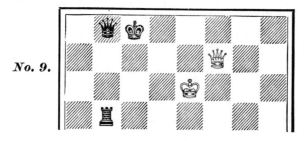

No. 9.

If the black Queen moves diagonally four squares, placing herself in front of the white King, and on the same horizontal file as the black Rook, it will be check-mate, because the white King cannot get out of one check into another by taking the Queen, which is protected by the Rook. For the same reason he cannot move, as the only squares open to him would leave him in check from the Queen, or move him into check from the black King.

Stalemate. If the King is not in check, but cannot move without going into check, and there is no other piece for the player to move, it is called a stalemate, and the game is drawn. In Diagram No. 10, for instance,

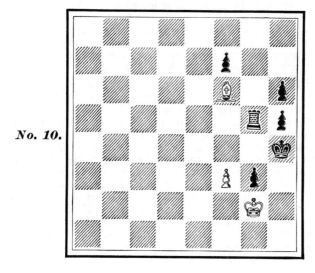

No. 10.

the black King cannot move without going into check from the Pawn or the King ; none of the black Pawns can move, and Black cannot move the Rook without putting his own King in check, (from the Bishop,) which is not allowed.

Perpetual Check. If a piece gives check to the adverse King, and the King moves away, the check may be repeated, and the King must move again, or interpose a piece, or capture the checking piece. If the position is such that no matter how often the King moves or is covered he cannot get out of check, and no matter how much the opposing pieces move they cannot checkmate him, the game is drawn by perpetual check. Diagram No. 11 is an illustration of such a position.

BLACK.

No. 11.

The only way out of the check is to interpose the Queen, whereupon the white Queen will move diagonally to the edge of the board and check again, forcing the black Queen back where she came from, and drawing the game by perpetual check. If the black Queen moves away from the King, she will be captured, and White will give checkmate at the same time.

NOTATION. The various moves which take place in the course of a game are recorded by a system of chess notation, the number of the move being given first, and then the pieces moved and the direction of their movement. The names of the pieces themselves are used to distinguish the various files of squares running vertically from the piece itself to the opposite side of the board, and the seven squares in front of each piece are numbered from 2 to 8. No matter how much the pieces may be moved, the various vertical files still retain the name of the pieces which stood at the bottom of them when the men were first set up. In chess notation, only the initials of the pieces are used, K standing for King, and Kt for Knight. Although the files bear the same names, the numbers count from the side on which the men are placed, so that each square has a double name, depending on the colour of the man placed upon it.

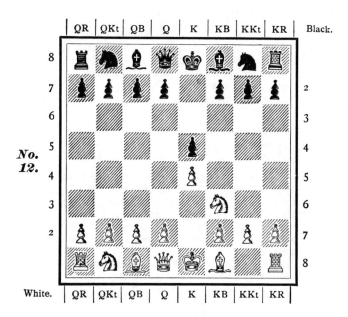

No. 12.

In Diagram No. 12, for instance, both the Pawns that have been moved would be spoken of as on K 4. The Knight that has been moved is on K B 3, because it is a white Knight. If it was a black Knight it would be on K B 6, reckoning from the black side of the board for the black pieces. In order to test your understanding of this system of notation, which is very important in following published games or problems, take the board and men, white side next you, and set up the following position, remembering that when no number is given, the piece stands upon the square originally occupied by the piece which gives its name to the file :—

Black men ;—King on Q R's ; Queen on Q Kt's ; Pawns on Q R 2, and Q Kt, 3 ; Rook on Q R 3.

White men ;—King on Q Kt 5 ; Queen on Q B 6.

Now look at Diagram No 11, and see if you have it right.

In addition to the notation of position, there is that of action. If a dash is placed between the initials of the piece and the definition of the square, it shows first the piece moved, and then the square to which it is moved. In Diagram No 11, for instance, Black's only move to cover the check would be given : Q–Q Kt 2 ; and White's continuation would be given ; Q–K 8.

The first of these might be abbreviated by saying, Q–Kt 2, because there is only one Kt 2 to which the Queen could be moved.

The moves of the white pieces are always given first, either in the left hand of two vertical columns, which are headed " White," and " Black " respectively; or above a line which divides the white move from the black, the latter form being used in text-books, the former in newspapers. The moves in Diagram No. 11 would be as follows, supposing the white Queen to arrive from K8 in the first place :—

White.	*Black.*
1. Q–B 6, ch	Q–Kt 2
2. Q–K 8, ch	Q–Kt's

Or this ; 1. $\dfrac{\text{Q–B 6, ch}}{\text{Q–Kt 2}}$

When the abbreviation " ch," is placed after a move, it means " check." If it is a mate, or a drawn game, or the player resigns, the word follows the move. When the King castles with the King's Rook, which is the shorter move for the Rook, it is indicated by the sign O–O. When the King is castled with the Queen's Rook, which is the longer move for the Rook, the sign O–O–O is used.

A cross, x, placed after the piece moved shows that it captured something, and the letters following the cross do not give the square to which the piece is moved, but show the piece that is captured. K B x Q P, for instance, would mean that the adversary's Queen's Pawn was to be taken from the board, and the King's Bishop was to occupy the square upon which the captured Queen's Pawn had stood.

Beginners usually have some difficulty in following the moves of the Knights, because it frequently happens that the same square can be reached by either of them. The Bishops cannot be confused in this way, because they never change the colour of the square they stand upon. In some sets of chessmen the Knights are distinguished by putting a small crown on the King's Knight, but this is never done in the regulation Staunton model. The beginner will find it very convenient, when following out the play of published games, to screw off the bottom of one white and one black Knight, and to exchange the bases. The white King's Knight will then have a black base, and the black King's Knight will have a white base, and they can be easily identified at any period of the game.

GERMAN NOTATION. Many of our standard chess books, and some of the best edited chess columns, are in German, and the student should be familiar with the German notation, which is much simpler than the English.

The white men are always considered as the side nearer the player ; the vertical columns are designated from left to right by the letters a b c d e f g h ; and the horizontal rows by the numbers 1 2 3 4 5 6 7 8, beginning at the bottom, or white side. The pieces are designated by one capital letter only, as follows :—

K   for König, or King.
D   for Dame, or Queen.
T   for Thurm, or Rook.
L   for Läufer, or Bishop.
S   for Springer, or Knight.

The Pawn is called a Bauer, but when it is moved no initial is given, simply the square it comes from. In Diagram No. 12, for instance, the English notation for the first two moves made by white would be :—P–K 4, and K Kt–B 3, or, Kt–K B 3. The German notation would be :—e 2–e 4 ; and S g 1–f 3. The move of the Knight, it will be observed, gives the initial of the piece and the square upon which it stands, and then the square to which it is moved. A capture is indicated by the letter "n" taking the place of the dash. If the white Knight took the black King's Pawn in Diagram No. 12, for instance, the move would be recorded: S f 3 n e 5, that is, the Springer at f 3 "nimmt" whatever it found at e 5. A check is indicated by a plus sign, +, following the move. In Diagram No. 11, for instance, the last move of the white Queen would be : D e 8–c 6 + ; and Black's reply would be : D b 8–b 7.

THE OPENINGS. Time and experience have shown that it is best for each player to adopt certain conventional openings, in order to develop his pieces. White always has the advantage, usually believed to be equal to 55%, counting drawn games as one half. This is because White can usually take more risks in offering a gambit than Black can in accepting it, and the best judges say that they would rather give a Knight and take the white pieces, than give Pawn-and-move and take the black. *Gambit* is a term used in Italian wrestling, and means that the adversary is given an apparent advantage at the start, in order more successfully to trip him up later on.

There are a great many chess openings, all of which have been analysed as far as the tenth move, including every possible variation on the way. The student who wishes to study them in detail should procure Freeborough's "Chess Openings," or Cook's "Synopsis." In these works, if either side has an advantage before the tenth move, it is indicated by a plus sign ; if the position is equal, it is so marked.

In studying openings, the student should be careful always to play with the winning side next him ; that is, never study how to play a losing game. If the variation ends with a plus sign, showing a win for the white, play it over with the white men next you.

In selecting openings for general use in play, if it is one for the white men, take those openings that have the greatest number of variations ending in favour of white. The Ruy Lopez is a very good opening for beginners, and the Evans' Gambit may be studied later. The French Defence and the Petroff are good openings for Black.

The theory of opening is to mobilise your forces for the attack in the fewest possible moves. Lasker thinks six moves should be enough for this purpose, and he recommends that only the King's and Queen's Pawns should be moved, after which each piece should be placed at once upon the square from which it can operate to the best advantage. He thinks the Knights should be first brought out, and posted at B 3, and then the K's B, somewhere along his own diagonal. The great mistake made by beginners is that they rush off to the attack and try to capture some of the adverse pieces before they have properly prepared themselves for re-inforcement or retreat. It should never be forgotten that the game is not won by capturing the adversary's pieces, but by checkmating his King.

Take the board and pieces, arrange them with the white men next you, and play over the following simple little game. Remember that the figures above the line are for the white men; those below for the black.

| 1 $\dfrac{\text{P–K4}}{\text{P–K4}}$ | 2 $\dfrac{\text{Kt–KB3}}{\text{P–Q3}}$ | 3 $\dfrac{\text{Kt–QB3}}{\text{P–KR3}}$ | 4 $\dfrac{\text{B–B4}}{\text{B–Kt5}}$ |

The third move made by Black accomplishes nothing, and is simply a waste of time. He should have continued by bringing his Knights into play. His fourth move is also a mistake; he should develop the Knights before the Bishops.

| 5 $\dfrac{\text{Kt x P}}{\text{B x Q}}$ | 6 $\dfrac{\text{B x KBPch}}{\text{K–K2}}$ | 7 $\overline{\text{Kt–Q5 mate}}$ |

On his fifth move, Black jumps at the chance to win White's Queen, but this is not of the slightest benefit to him, because the object of the game is not to win the Queen, but to mate the King. At the seventh move the beginner will see that the black King cannot move out of check, neither can he move into check by taking the Bishop. He has no piece that can capture the Knight that gives the check, and nothing can be interposed, so he is mated, and White wins.

Here is another simple little game. Take the black pieces this time, but make the white men move first, of course.

$$1 \; \frac{\text{P–K4}}{\text{P–K4}} \qquad 2 \; \frac{\text{Kt–KB3}}{\text{Kt–KB3}} \qquad 3 \; \frac{\text{Kt x P}}{\text{Kt–QB3}}$$

You don't take the King's Pawn ; it is much more important to develop your pieces rapidly.

$$4 \; \frac{\text{Kt x Kt}}{\text{QP x Kt}} \qquad 5 \; \frac{\text{P–Q3}}{\text{B–QB4}} \qquad 6 \; \frac{\text{B–Kt5}}{\text{Kt x P}}$$

White's sixth move is bad, and you immediately take advantage of it. If he takes your Knight with his Pawn, you will take his K B P with your Bishop, and say " Check." If he takes the Bishop you win his Queen. If he moves his King you check again with your other Bishop, which will force him to take your black Bishop, and lose his Queen.

$$7 \; \frac{\text{B x Q}}{\text{B x Pch}} \qquad 8 \; \frac{\text{K–K2}}{\text{B–Kt5 mate}}$$

If the beginner will examine the position, he will find that there is no way of escape for the King, and Black wins.

Openings are usually divided into five principal classes : Those in which the first piece developed is the ***King's Knight ;*** those in which the ***King's Bishop*** is the first piece brought into play ; those in which a ***Gambit*** is offered on the second move, usually a sacrificed Pawn ; those which are called ***Close*** openings, securing a good defensive game for the black pieces ; and those which are ***Irregular.***

In the following outline of fifty of the openings, only the first four moves are given, and usually only one variation is selected, the object being more to give the student an idea of the development than to exhaust the subject. The arrangement is alphabetical, that being more convenient in a book of reference. For the continuations the student is recommended to study " Freeborough," or the " Handbuch des Schachspiels."

Allgaier Gambit :—

$$1 \; \frac{\text{P–K4}}{\text{P–K4}} \qquad 2 \; \frac{\text{P–KB4}}{\text{P x P}} \qquad 3 \; \frac{\text{Kt–KB3}}{\text{P–KKt4}} \qquad 4 \; \frac{\text{P–KR4}}{\text{P–Kt5}}$$

Boden-Kieseritzky Gambit :—

$$1 \; \frac{\text{P–K4}}{\text{P–K4}} \qquad 2 \; \frac{\text{B–B4}}{\text{Kt–KB3}} \qquad 3 \; \frac{\text{Kt–KB3}}{\text{Kt x P}} \qquad 4 \; \frac{\text{Kt–B3}}{\text{Kt x Kt}}$$

Berlin Defence :—

	1	2	3	4
White	P–K4	B–B4	Q–K2	P–QB3
Black	P–K4	Kt–KB3	Kt–QB3	B–B4

Blackmar Gambit :—

	1	2	3	4
White	P–Q4	P–K4	P–KB3	Kt x P
Black	P–Q4	P x P	P x P	B–B4

Calabrese Counter Gambit :—

	1	2	3	4
White	P–K4	B–B4	P–Q3	P–B4
Black	P–K4	P–KB4	Kt–KB3	P–Q4

Centre Gambit :—

	1	2	3	4
White	P–K4	P–Q4	Q x P	Q–K3
Black	P–K4	P x P	Kt–QB3	B–Kt5 ch

Centre Counter Gambit :—

	1	2	3	4
White	P–K4	P x P	Kt–QB3	P–Q4
Black	P–Q4	Q x P	Q–Q sq	Kt–KB3

Classical Defence, to K. B. opening :—

	1	2	3	4
White	P–K4	B–B4	P–QB3	P–Q4
Black	P–K4	B–B4	Kt–KB3	P x P

Cunningham Gambit :—

	1	2	3	4
White	P–K4	P–KB4	Kt–KB3	B–B4
Black	P–K4	P x P	B–K2	B–R5 ch

Cochrane Gambit :—

	1	2	3	4
White	P–K4	P–KB4	Kt–KB3	B–B4
Black	P–K4	P x P	P–KKt4	P–Kt5

Danish Gambit :—

	1	2	3	4
White	P–K4	P–Q4	P–QB3	B–QB4
Black	P–K4	P x P	P x P	Kt–KB3

English Opening :—

	1	2	3	4
White	P–QB4	P–B4	P–Q3	Kt–QB3
Black	P–QB4	P–B4	Kt–KB3	P–Q3

Evans' Gambit :—

	1	2	3	4
White	P–K4	Kt–KB3	B–B4	P–QKt4
Black	P–K4	Kt–QB3	B–B4	B x KtP

Evans' Gambit Declined :—

1 $\dfrac{\text{P–K4}}{\text{P–K4}}$ 2 $\dfrac{\text{Kt–KB3}}{\text{Kt–QB3}}$ 3 $\dfrac{\text{B–B4}}{\text{B–B4}}$ 4 $\dfrac{\text{P–QKt4}}{\text{B–Kt3}}$

Fianchetto Opening :—

1 $\dfrac{\text{P–K3}}{\text{P–K4}}$ 2 $\dfrac{\text{P–QB4}}{\text{Kt–KB3}}$ 3 $\dfrac{\text{Kt–QB3}}{\text{P–Q4}}$ 4 $\dfrac{\text{P x P}}{\text{Kt x P}}$

Fianchetto Defence :—

1 $\dfrac{\text{P–K4}}{\text{P–QKt3}}$ 2 $\dfrac{\text{P–Q4}}{\text{P–K3}}$ 3 $\dfrac{\text{B–Q3}}{\text{B–Kt2}}$ 4 $\dfrac{\text{Kt–K2}}{\text{Kt–KB3}}$

Four Knights :—

1 $\dfrac{\text{P–K4}}{\text{P–K4}}$ 2 $\dfrac{\text{Kt–KB3}}{\text{Kt–QB3}}$ 3 $\dfrac{\text{Kt–B3}}{\text{Kt–B3}}$ 4 $\dfrac{\text{B–Kt5}}{\text{B–Kt5}}$

French Defence :—

1 $\dfrac{\text{P–K4}}{\text{P–K3}}$ 2 $\dfrac{\text{P–Q4}}{\text{P–Q4}}$ 3 $\dfrac{\text{Kt–QB3}}{\text{Kt–KB3}}$ 4 $\dfrac{\text{B–KKt5}}{\text{B–K2}}$

From Gambit :—

1 $\dfrac{\text{P–KB4}}{\text{P–K4}}$ 2 $\dfrac{\text{P x P}}{\text{P–Q3}}$ 3 $\dfrac{\text{P x P}}{\text{B x P}}$ 4 $\dfrac{\text{Kt–KB3}}{\text{Kt–KB3}}$

Giuoco Piano :—

1 $\dfrac{\text{P–K4}}{\text{P–K4}}$ 2 $\dfrac{\text{Kt–KB3}}{\text{Kt–QB3}}$ 3 $\dfrac{\text{B–B4}}{\text{B–B4}}$ 4 $\dfrac{\text{P–B3}}{\text{Kt–B3}}$

Greco-Counter Gambit :—

1 $\dfrac{\text{P–K4}}{\text{P–K4}}$ 2 $\dfrac{\text{Kt–KB3}}{\text{P–KB4}}$ 3 $\dfrac{\text{Kt x P}}{\text{Q–B3}}$ 4 $\dfrac{\text{P–Q4}}{\text{P–Q3}}$

Hamppe-Allgaier Gambit :—

1 $\dfrac{\text{P–K4}}{\text{P–K4}}$ 2 $\dfrac{\text{Kt–QB3}}{\text{Kt–QB3}}$ 3 $\dfrac{\text{P–B4}}{\text{P x P}}$ 4 $\dfrac{\text{Kt–B3}}{\text{P–KKt4}}$

Hungarian Defence :—

1 $\dfrac{\text{P–K4}}{\text{P–K4}}$ 2 $\dfrac{\text{Kt–KB3}}{\text{Kt–QB3}}$ 3 $\dfrac{\text{B–B4}}{\text{B–K2}}$ 4 $\dfrac{\text{P–Q4}}{\text{P–Q3}}$

Irregular Openings :—

1 $\dfrac{\text{P–K4}}{\text{P–K4}}$ 2 $\dfrac{\text{P–QB3}}{\text{P–Q4}}$ 3 $\dfrac{\text{Kt–B3}}{\text{P x P}}$ 4 $\dfrac{\text{Kt x P}}{\text{B–Q3}}$

Irregular Openings cont'd :—

1 $\dfrac{\text{P–K4}}{\text{P–Q3}}$ 2 $\dfrac{\text{P–Q4}}{\text{Kt–KB3}}$ 3 $\dfrac{\text{B–Q3}}{\text{Kt–QB3}}$ 4 $\dfrac{\text{P–QB3}}{\text{P–K4}}$

1 $\dfrac{\text{P–K4}}{\text{P–QB3}}$ 2 $\dfrac{\text{P–Q4}}{\text{P–Q4}}$ 3 $\dfrac{\text{P x P}}{\text{P x P}}$ 4 $\dfrac{\text{B–Q3}}{\text{Kt–QB3}}$

1 $\dfrac{\text{P--K4}}{\text{Kt–QB3}}$ 2 $\dfrac{\text{P–Q4}}{\text{P–K4}}$ 3 $\dfrac{\text{P x P}}{\text{Kt x P}}$ 4 $\dfrac{\text{P–KB4}}{\text{Kt–Kt3}}$

Jerome Gambit :—

1 $\dfrac{\text{P–K4}}{\text{P–K4}}$ 2 $\dfrac{\text{Kt–KB3}}{\text{Kt–QB3}}$ 3 $\dfrac{\text{B–B4}}{\text{B–B4}}$ 4 $\dfrac{\text{B x P ch}}{\text{K x B}}$

Kieseritzky Gambit :—

1 $\dfrac{\text{P–K4}}{\text{P–K4}}$ 2 $\dfrac{\text{P–KB4}}{\text{P x P}}$ 3 $\dfrac{\text{Kt–KB3}}{\text{P–KKt4}}$ 4 $\dfrac{\text{P–KR4}}{\text{P–Kt5}}$

King's Bishop's Gambit :—

1 $\dfrac{\text{P–K4}}{\text{P–K4}}$ 2 $\dfrac{\text{P--KB4}}{\text{P x P}}$ 3 $\dfrac{\text{B–B4}}{\text{Q–R5 ch}}$ 4 $\dfrac{\text{K–B sq}}{\text{B–B4}}$

King's Bishop's Pawn Game :—

1 $\dfrac{\text{P–KB4}}{\text{P–K3}}$ 2 $\dfrac{\text{Kt–KB3}}{\text{Kt–KB3}}$ 3 $\dfrac{\text{P–K3}}{\text{B–K2}}$ 4 $\dfrac{\text{B–K2}}{\text{P–QKt3}}$

King's Knight Opening.   Irregular Defences :—

1 $\dfrac{\text{P-K4}}{\text{P–K4}}$ 2 $\dfrac{\text{Kt–KB3}}{\text{P–KB3}}$ 3 $\dfrac{\text{Kt x P}}{\text{Q–K2}}$ 4 $\dfrac{\text{Kt–KB3}}{\text{P–Q4}}$

1 $\dfrac{\text{P–K4}}{\text{P–K4}}$ 2 $\dfrac{\text{Kt–KB3}}{\text{Q–B3}}$ 3 $\dfrac{\text{Kt–B3}}{\text{P–B3}}$ 4 $\dfrac{\text{P–Q4}}{\text{P x P}}$

1 $\dfrac{\text{P–K4}}{\text{P–K4}}$ 2 $\dfrac{\text{Kt–KB3}}{\text{B–Q3}}$ 3 $\dfrac{\text{B–B4}}{\text{Kt–KB3}}$ 4 $\dfrac{\text{P–Q4}}{\text{Kt–B3}}$

1 $\dfrac{\text{P–K4}}{\text{P-K4}}$ 2 $\dfrac{\text{Kt–KB3}}{\text{B–B4}}$ 3 $\dfrac{\text{Kt x P}}{\text{Q–K2}}$ 4 $\dfrac{\text{P–Q4}}{\text{B–Kt3}}$

King's Gambit :—

1 $\dfrac{\text{P–K4}}{\text{P–K4}}$ 2 $\dfrac{\text{P–KB4}}{\text{P x P}}$ 3 $\dfrac{\text{P–Q4}}{\text{Q–R5ch}}$ 4 $\dfrac{\text{K–K2}}{\text{P–Q4}}$

1 $\dfrac{\text{P–K4}}{\text{P–K4}}$ 2 $\dfrac{\text{P–KB4}}{\text{P x P}}$ 3 $\dfrac{\text{P–KR4}}{\text{P–Q4}}$ 4 $\dfrac{\text{P x P}}{\text{Q x P}}$

King's Gambit cont'd :—

1 $\dfrac{\text{P–K4}}{\text{P–K4}}$ 2 $\dfrac{\text{P–KB4}}{\text{P x P}}$ 3 $\dfrac{\text{Kt–KB3}}{\text{P–KKt4}}$ 4 $\dfrac{\text{B–B4}}{\text{B–Kt2}}$

1 $\dfrac{\text{P–K4}}{\text{P–K4}}$ 2 $\dfrac{\text{P–KB4}}{\text{P x P}}$ 3 $\dfrac{\text{P–KR4}}{\text{B–K2}}$ 4 $\dfrac{\text{Kt–KB3}}{\text{Kt–KB3}}$

King's Gambit Declined :—

1 $\dfrac{\text{P–K4}}{\text{P–K4}}$ 2 $\dfrac{\text{P–KB4}}{\text{P–Q4}}$ 3 $\dfrac{\text{P x QP}}{\text{Q x P}}$ 4 $\dfrac{\text{Kt–QB3}}{\text{Q–K3}}$

Max Lange's Attack :—

1 $\dfrac{\text{P–K4}}{\text{P–K4}}$ 2 $\dfrac{\text{Kt–KB3}}{\text{Kt–QB3}}$ 3 $\dfrac{\text{B–B4}}{\text{B–B4}}$ 4 $\dfrac{\text{Castles}}{\text{Kt–B3}}$

Muzio Gambit :—

1 $\dfrac{\text{P–K4}}{\text{P–K4}}$ 2 $\dfrac{\text{P–KB4}}{\text{P x P}}$ 3 $\dfrac{\text{Kt–KB3}}{\text{P–KKt4}}$ 4 $\dfrac{\text{B–B4}}{\text{P–Kt5}}$

Petroff's Counter Attack :—

1 $\dfrac{\text{P–K4}}{\text{P–K4}}$ 2 $\dfrac{\text{Kt–KB3}}{\text{Kt–KB3}}$ 3 $\dfrac{\text{Kt x P}}{\text{P–Q3}}$ 4 $\dfrac{\text{K–KB3}}{\text{Kt x P}}$

Philidor's Defence :—

1 $\dfrac{\text{P–K4}}{\text{P–K4}}$ 2 $\dfrac{\text{Kt–KB3}}{\text{P–Q3}}$ 3 $\dfrac{\text{P–Q4}}{\text{P x P}}$ 4 $\dfrac{\text{Kt x P}}{\text{P–Q4}}$

Pierce Gambit :—

1 $\dfrac{\text{P–K4}}{\text{P–K4}}$ 2 $\dfrac{\text{Kt–QB3}}{\text{Kt–QB3}}$ 3 $\dfrac{\text{P–B4}}{\text{P x P}}$ 4 $\dfrac{\text{Kt–B3}}{\text{P–KKt4}}$

Queen's Pawn Counter Gambit :—

1 $\dfrac{\text{P–K4}}{\text{P–K4}}$ 2 $\dfrac{\text{Kt–KB3}}{\text{P–Q4}}$ 3 $\dfrac{\text{P x P}}{\text{B–Q3}}$ 4 $\dfrac{\text{P–Q4}}{\text{P–K5}}$

Queen's Gambit :—

1 $\dfrac{\text{P–Q4}}{\text{P–Q4}}$ 2 $\dfrac{\text{P–QB4}}{\text{P x P}}$ 3 $\dfrac{\text{P–K3}}{\text{P–K4}}$ 4 $\dfrac{\text{B x P}}{\text{P x P}}$

1 $\dfrac{\text{P–Q4}}{\text{P–Q4}}$ 2 $\dfrac{\text{P–QB4}}{\text{P x P}}$ 3 $\dfrac{\text{P–K4}}{\text{P–K4}}$ 4 $\dfrac{\text{P–Q5}}{\text{P–KB4}}$

1 $\dfrac{\text{P–Q4}}{\text{P–Q4}}$ 2 $\dfrac{\text{P–QB4}}{\text{P x P}}$ 3 $\dfrac{\text{Kt–KB3}}{\text{P–K3}}$ 4 $\dfrac{\text{P–K3}}{\text{Kt–KB3}}$

Queen's Pawn Game :—

$1\ \dfrac{\text{P–Q4}}{\text{P–Q4}}$ $2\ \dfrac{\text{P–K3}}{\text{P–K3}}$ $3\ \dfrac{\text{Kt–KB3}}{\text{Kt–KB3}}$ $4\ \dfrac{\text{B–K2}}{\text{B–K2}}$

Ruy Lopez :—

$1\ \dfrac{\text{P–K4}}{\text{P–K4}}$ $2\ \dfrac{\text{Kt–KB3}}{\text{Kt–QB3}}$ $3\ \dfrac{\text{B–Kt5}}{\text{P–QR3}}$ $4\ \dfrac{\text{B–R4}}{\text{Kt–B3}}$

Salvio Gambit :—

$1\ \dfrac{\text{P–K4}}{\text{P–K4}}$ $2\ \dfrac{\text{P–KB4}}{\text{P x P}}$ $3\ \dfrac{\text{Kt–KB3}}{\text{P–KKt4}}$ $4\ \dfrac{\text{B–B4}}{\text{P–Kt5}}$

Scotch Game :—

$1\ \dfrac{\text{P–K4}}{\text{P–K4}}$ $2\ \dfrac{\text{Kt–KB3}}{\text{Kt–QB3}}$ $3\ \dfrac{\text{P–Q4}}{\text{P x P}}$ $4\ \dfrac{\text{Kt x P}}{\text{B–B4}}$

Sicilian Defence :—

$1\ \dfrac{\text{P–K4}}{\text{P–QB4}}$ $2\ \dfrac{\text{Kt–QB3}}{\text{Kt–QB3}}$ $3\ \dfrac{\text{Kt–B3}}{\text{P–K3}}$ $4\ \dfrac{\text{P–Q4}}{\text{P x P}}$

Staunton's Opening :—

$1\ \dfrac{\text{P–K4}}{\text{P–K4}}$ $2\ \dfrac{\text{Kt–KB3}}{\text{Kt–QB3}}$ $3\ \dfrac{\text{P–B3}}{\text{P–B4}}$ $4\ \dfrac{\text{P–Q4}}{\text{P–Q3}}$

Steinitz Gambit :—

$1\ \dfrac{\text{P–K4}}{\text{P–K4}}$ $2\ \dfrac{\text{Kt–QB3}}{\text{Kt–QB3}}$ $3\ \dfrac{\text{P–KB4}}{\text{P x P}}$ $4\ \dfrac{\text{P–Q4}}{\text{Q–R5ch}}$

Three Knights' Game :—

$1\ \dfrac{\text{P–K4}}{\text{P–K4}}$ $2\ \dfrac{\text{Kt–KB3}}{\text{Kt–KB3}}$ $3\ \dfrac{\text{Kt–B3}}{\text{P–Q3}}$ $4\ \dfrac{\text{P–Q4}}{\text{P x P}}$

Two Knights' Defence :—

$1\ \dfrac{\text{P–K4}}{\text{P–K4}}$ $2\ \dfrac{\text{Kt–KB3}}{\text{Kt–QB3}}$ $3\ \dfrac{\text{B–B4}}{\text{Kt–B3}}$ $4\ \dfrac{\text{Kt–Kt5}}{\text{P–Q4}}$

Vienna Opening :—

$1\ \dfrac{\text{P–K4}}{\text{P–K4}}$ $2\ \dfrac{\text{Kt–QB3}}{\text{B–B4}}$ $3\ \dfrac{\text{P–B4}}{\text{P–Q3}}$ $4\ \dfrac{\text{Kt–B3}}{\text{Kt–KB3}}$

Zukertort's Opening :—

$1\ \dfrac{\text{Kt–KB3}}{\text{P–K3}}$ $2\ \dfrac{\text{P–Q4}}{\text{Kt–KB3}}$ $3\ \dfrac{\text{P–K3}}{\text{P–QKt3}}$ $4\ \dfrac{\text{B–K2}}{\text{B–Kt2}}$

GAMES AT ODDS.   Between unequal players it is a common practice for the stronger to give the weaker some advantage. Very few are able to give a Queen, or even a Rook, but a **Knight** is quite common, and one who can concede a Knight to the weakest players in a club is usually spoken of as, "a Knight player." The most common odds between nearly equal players is **Pawn and Move ;** and with a player not strong enough to give a Knight, **Pawn and Two Moves.** The Pawn removed in each instance is Black's K B P, and the Knight is usually the Q Kt. Here are a few examples of the openings in games at odds :—

Pawn and Move :—

1	$\dfrac{\text{P–K4}}{\text{P–K3}}$	2	$\dfrac{\text{P–Q4}}{\text{P–Q4}}$	3	$\dfrac{\text{Q–R5ch}}{\text{P–KKt3}}$	4	$\dfrac{\text{Q–K5}}{\text{Kt–KB3}}$
1	$\dfrac{\text{P–K4}}{\text{P–Q3}}$	2	$\dfrac{\text{P–Q4}}{\text{Kt–KB3}}$	3	$\dfrac{\text{Kt–QB3}}{\text{Kt–B3}}$	4	$\dfrac{\text{P–Q5}}{\text{Kt–K4}}$
1	$\dfrac{\text{P–K4}}{\text{Kt–QB3}}$	2	$\dfrac{\text{P–Q4}}{\text{P–Q4}}$	3	$\dfrac{\text{P–K5}}{\text{B–B4}}$	4	$\dfrac{\text{B–QKt5}}{\text{Q–Q2}}$
1	$\dfrac{\text{P–K4}}{\text{Kt–QB3}}$	2	$\dfrac{\text{P–Q4}}{\text{P–Q4}}$	3	$\dfrac{\text{P x P}}{\text{Kt x P}}$	4	$\dfrac{\text{P–KB4}}{\text{Kt–B2}}$

Pawn and Two Moves :—

1	$\dfrac{\text{P–K4}}{}$	2	$\dfrac{\text{P–Q4}}{\text{P–K3}}$	3	$\dfrac{\text{B–Q3}}{\text{P–B4}}$	4	$\dfrac{\text{P–Q5}}{\text{P–Q3}}$
1	$\dfrac{\text{P–K4}}{}$	2	$\dfrac{\text{P–Q4}}{\text{P–K3}}$	3	$\dfrac{\text{P–QB4}}{\text{P–B4}}$	4	$\dfrac{\text{P–Q5}}{\text{P–Q3}}$
1	$\dfrac{\text{P–K4}}{}$	2	$\dfrac{\text{P–Q4}}{\text{P–Q3}}$	3	$\dfrac{\text{P–KB4}}{\text{P–K3}}$	4	$\dfrac{\text{B–Q3}}{\text{Kt–K2}}$
1	$\dfrac{\text{P–K4}}{}$	2	$\dfrac{\text{P–Q4}}{\text{Kt–QB3}}$	3	$\dfrac{\text{P–Q5}}{\text{Kt–K4}}$	4	$\dfrac{\text{P–KB4}}{\text{Kt–B2}}$

Odds of Queen's Knight :—

1	$\dfrac{\text{P–K4}}{\text{P–K4}}$	2	$\dfrac{\text{Kt–B3}}{\text{P–Q4}}$	3	$\dfrac{\text{P x P}}{\text{P–K5}}$	4	$\dfrac{\text{Kt–K5}}{\text{Q x P}}$
1	$\dfrac{\text{P–K4}}{\text{P–K4}}$	2	$\dfrac{\text{P–KB4}}{\text{P–Q4}}$	3	$\dfrac{\text{P x QP}}{\text{Q x P}}$	4	$\dfrac{\text{Kt–B3}}{\text{P–K5}}$

Odds of King's Knight :—

$$1\ \frac{\text{P–K4}}{\text{P–K4}} \qquad 2\ \frac{\text{B–B4}}{\text{P–QB3}} \qquad 3\ \frac{\text{Kt–B3}}{\text{Kt–B3}} \qquad 4\ \frac{\text{P–Q4}}{\text{P–Q4}}$$

$$1\ \frac{\text{P–K4}}{\text{P–K4}} \qquad 2\ \frac{\text{B–B2}}{\text{Kt–KB3}} \qquad 3\ \frac{\text{P–Q2}}{\text{B–B4}} \qquad 4\ \frac{\text{0–0}}{\text{0–0}}$$

In order to give the student an idea of the value and popularity of the various openings, the following table of the results of 1500 games may be useful. It is from the chess columns of the New York *Sun :*—

OPENINGS.	FIRST PLAYER.			TOTAL PLAYED.	PER CENT. WON BY FIRST PLAYER.	PER CENT. TOTAL GAMES PLAYED.
	WON.	LOST.	DREW.			
Ruy Lopez...........	145	103	58	306	57	20
Queen's Pawn (a).....	97	63	39	199	48	13
French Defence.......	84	48	39	171	60	11
Vienna..............	47	34	15	96	57	6
Sicilian Defence	40	29	10	79	57	5
King's Gambit...... .	36	32	11	79	52	5
Giuoco Piano.........	36	32	10	78	52	5
Evans...............	34	20	12	66	61	4
Irregular............	29	31	14	74	49	5
Scotch..............	22	26	9	57	47	4
Zukertort........	23	17	11	51	56	3
Two Knights Defence.	16	20	10	46	46	3
Staunton's	19	15	5	39	55	3
Fianchetto...........	13	14	2	29	48	2
Petroff Defence......	15	9	3	27	61	2
Centre Gambit (b)	11	11	4	26	50	2
Philidor Defence.....	8	9	3	20	47	1
Miscellaneous........	22	29	6	57	44	4
Total.........	697	542	261	1500	....	....

The first player won 55.2 per cent. of games played, counting drawn games as one-half.

(a). Includes Queen's Gambits and Queen's Gambits declined.

(b). Includes Centre and Counter Centre Gambits.

THE MIDDLE GAME. After a little experience with openings, the player will usually select one or two which he feels that he can handle better than others, and will make a specialty of them. Having mastered a number of variations, and learned the object of them in forming his pieces for attack or defence, he will naturally be led to the study of the middle game. In this there are a few general principles which should be steadily kept in view. For attack, the player should secure command of a wide range of the board ; but for defence he should concentrate his forces as much as possible. He should be careful not to get his pieces in one another's way, and not to leave pieces where they can be attacked and driven back by inferior pieces, because that entails a loss of valuable time. A player should never exchange a man in active service for one that is doing nothing. If several lines of play are open, the one offering the most numerous good continuations should be selected. When a player is not ready for attack, he should develop his pieces, and remember that the more of them he can get to bear on the enemy's King, the better. Supporting pieces should be placed where they are not easily attacked, because good players attack the supports first, so as to isolate the advance guard. Beginners are usually in too great a hurry to give check ; the best players do not check until they are ready to follow it up with a mate, or a winning position, or can gain time in developing their pieces.

END GAMES. There are certain positions in which apparently equal games are not necessarily drawn, and there are others in which a player with a decided advantage cannot win, within the fifty moves which are allowed him, unless he knows exactly how to proceed. If a player is not well up in endings he may lose many a game which could be won if he only knew how to win it. The following games may be abandoned as *drawn :—*

King and Bishop against a King.
King and Knight against a King.
King and two Knights against a King.
King and Queen against two Rooks.
King and Queen against King and two Bishops.
King and Rook against King, Rook and Pawn.
King and Rook against King and Bishop.
King and Rook against King and Knight.
King and Rook against King, Rook and Bishop.

The following games can be *won :—*

King and Queen, or King and Rook, against a King.
King and Queen against King and Rook.
King and Queen against King and Bishop.
King and Queen against King and Knight.
King and Queen against King and Pawn.
King and two Rooks against King and Rook.
King and two Bishops against a King.
King Bishop and Knight against a King.

In order to master all these endings, the student should take up Staunton's Handbook, or the Lehrbuch des Schachspiels, in which they are given very fully. For the beginner only one or two of the most common and important are necessary.

K and Q, or K and R, against K. All that is necessary is to drive the King to the edge of the board, which may be done by holding him below a certain parallel with the Q or R, and then getting your own King in front of him; a check will then drive him one line further back, and when he arrives at the edge of the board, and can no longer go back, he is mated.

K and Q against K and R. Freeborough has devoted an entire volume to this ending, which may be very much prolonged by a skilful player. The object is to drive the King to the edge of the board, and then to get the Rook in such a position that it must be sacrificed to save the mate, or that the mate can be accomplished with the Rook on the board. The player with the Queen must be on his guard against stalemate in this ending.

K and Q against K and B, K and Kt, or K and P. This is easy enough for the Queen if the player is careful to avoid stalemate.

K and two R's against K and R. This can be won easily by forcing an exchange of Rooks.

K and two B's against K. In this position the King must be ruled off into a corner by getting the Bishops together, protected by their King. Start with the men in the following position :—

Black K on his own square. White King on K B 6; white Bishops on K B 4 and K B 5. White to move and win. The mate can be accomplished in six moves, as follows :—

	1	2	3
	B–B7 / K–B sq	B–Q7 / K–Kt sq	K–Kt6 / K–B sq
	4	5	6
	B–Q6 ch / K–Kt sq	B–K6 ch / B–K6 ch	B–K5 mate

K, B and Kt against K. This is one of the most difficult endings for a beginner, but is very instructive, and should be carefully studied. Set up the men as follows :—

Black King on K R sq. White King on K B 6, white Bishop on K B 5, and white Knight on K Kt 5; White to move and win. The object is to drive the King into a corner of the board which is commanded by the Bishop, as he cannot otherwise be mated.

1	2	3	4
Kt–B7 ch / K–Kt sq	B–K4 / K–B sq	B–R7 / K–K sq	Kt–K5 / K–B sq
5	6	7	8
Kt–Q7 ch / K–K sq	K–K6 / K–Q sq	K–Q6 / K–K sq	B–K6 ch / K–Q sq

$$9\ \frac{\text{K--B6}}{\text{K--B sq}} \qquad 10\ \frac{\text{B--B7}}{\text{K--Q sq}} \qquad 11\ \frac{\text{Kt--Kt7 ch}}{\text{K--B sq}} \qquad 12\ \frac{\text{K--B6}}{\text{K--Kt sq}}$$

$$13\ \frac{\text{K--Kt 6}}{\text{K--B sq}} \qquad 14\ \frac{\text{B--K6 ch}}{\text{K--Kt sq}} \qquad 15\ \frac{\text{Kt--B5}}{\text{K--R sq}} \qquad 16\ \frac{\text{B--Q7}}{\text{K--Kt sq}}$$

$$17\ \frac{\text{Kt--R6 ch}}{\text{K--R sq}} \qquad 18\ \frac{\text{B--B6 mate}}{}$$

If, at the fourth move, the black King does not go back to the Bishop's square, but goes on to the Queen's square, hoping to cut across to the other black corner of the board, the continuation will be as follows, beginning at White's fifth move :—

$$5\ \frac{\text{K--K6}}{\text{K--B2}} \qquad 6\ \frac{\text{Kt--Q7}}{\text{K--B3}} \qquad 7\ \frac{\text{B--Q3}}{\text{K--B2}} \qquad 8\ \frac{\text{B--Kt5}}{\text{K--Q's}}$$

$$9\ \frac{\text{Kt--K5}}{\text{K--B2}} \qquad 10\ \frac{\text{Kt--B4}}{\text{K--Q sq}} \qquad 11\ \frac{\text{K--Q6}}{\text{K--B sq}} \qquad 12\ \frac{\text{Kt--R5}}{\text{K--Q sq}}$$

$$13\ \frac{\text{Kt--Kt7 ch}}{\text{K--B sq}} \qquad 14\ \frac{\text{K--B6}}{\text{K--Kt sq}} \qquad 15\ \frac{\text{Kt--Q6}}{\text{K--R2}} \qquad 16\ \frac{\text{K--B7}}{\text{K--R sq}}$$

$$17\ \frac{\text{B--B4}}{\text{K--R2}} \qquad 18\ \frac{\text{Kt--B8 ch}}{\text{K--R sq}} \qquad 19\ \frac{\text{B--Q5 mate}}{}$$

PAWN ENDINGS. There are a great number of these, many being complicated by the addition of Pawns to other pieces. The following example, which is a position that often occurs, should be understood by the beginner :—

Put the black King on K B square ; the white King on K B 6, and a white Pawn on K 6. If it is Black's move, White can win easily ; but if it is White's move it is impossible to win, because whether he checks or not the black King gets in front of the Pawn and either wins it or secures a stalemate.

Put the Pawn behind the King, on K B 5, and White wins, no matter which moves first, for if Black moves he allows the white King to advance to the seventh file, which will queen the Pawn. If White moves first, and the black King keeps opposite him, the Pawn advances. If Black goes in the other direction, the white King goes to the seventh file and wins by queening the Pawn.

If the white King and Pawn are both moved one square further back, the King on K B 5, and the Pawn on K B 4. the win will depend on the move. If it is White's move he can win by advancing the King ; but if it is Black's move he can draw by keeping his King always opposite the white King. If the Pawn advances, he will get in front of it, and if the King is afterward advanced, he will get in front of it; winning the Pawn or securing a stalemate.

THE KNIGHT'S TOUR. Owing to the peculiarity of the Knight's move, many persons have amused themselves in trying to cover the entire chess board with a Knight, touching the same square once only, and returning to the starting-point again. There are several ways of doing this, one of the simplest being the following :—

14	29	34	55	12	27	24	49
35	56	13	28	33	50	11	26
30	15	54	51	58	25	48	23
41	36	57	32	61	52	63	10
16	31	40	53	**64**	59	22	47
37	42	**1**	60	19	62	9	6
2	17	44	39	4	7	46	21
43	38	3	18	45	20	5	8

TEXT BOOKS. Among the very large number of works on Chess there is abundant room for choice, but the following works are considered standard authorities on the game :—

Freeborough's Chess Openings, 1896.
Cook's Synopsis.
Minor Tactics of Chess, by Young and Howell.
Modern Chess Instructor, by W. Steinitz.
Common Sense in Chess, by E. Lasker.
Walker's Treatise on Chess, 1841.
Handbuch des Schachspiels.
Lehrbuch des Schachspiels, by J. Dufresne.
Teoria e Practica del Giuoco degli Schacchi.
British Chess Magazine.
Chess Player's Chronicle.
Chess Monthly.
Westminster Papers, 1868 to 1879.

Of these works, " Minor Tactics " will be found most useful to the beginner, as it simplifies the openings by grouping them, and concentrates the attention on the essential points of chess strategy.

CODE OF CHESS LAWS.

ADOPTED BY THE FIFTH AMERICAN CHESS CONGRESS.

Definitions of Terms Used. Whenever the word "*Umpire*" is used herein, it stands for any Committee having charge of Matches or Tournaments, with power to determine questions of chess-law and rules; or for any duly appointed Referee, or Umpire; for the bystanders, when properly appealed to; or for any person, present or absent, to whom may be referred any disputed questions; or for any other authority whomsoever having power to determine such questions.

When the word "*move*" is used it is understood to mean a legal move or a move to be legally made according to these laws.

When the word "*man*" or "*men*" is used, it is understood that it embraces both Pieces and Pawns.

The Chess-Board and Men. The Chess-board must be placed with a white square at the right-hand corner.

If the Chess-board be wrongly placed, it cannot be changed during the game in progress after a move shall have been made by each player, provided the men were correctly placed upon the board at the beginning, *i. e.*, the Queens upon their own colours.

A deficiency in number, or a misplacement of the men, at the beginning of the game, when discovered, annuls the game.

The field of the Standard Chess-board shall be twenty-two inches square.

The Standard Chess-men shall be of the improved Staunton Club size and pattern.

First Move and Colour. The right of first move must be determined by lot.

The player having the first move must always play with the white men.

The right of move shall alternate, whether the game be won, lost or drawn.

The game is legally begun when each player shall have made his first move.

Whenever a game shall be annulled, the party having the move in that game shall have it in the next game. An annulled game must be considered, in every respect, the same as if it had never been begun.

Concessions. The concession of an indulgence by one player does not give him the right of a similar, or other, indulgence from his opponent.

Errors. If, during the course of the game, it be discovered that any error or illegality has been committed, the moves must be retraced and the necessary correction made, without penalty. If the moves cannot be correctly retraced, the game must be annulled.

If a man be dropped from the board and moves made during its absence, such moves must be retraced and the man restored. If this cannot be done, to the satisfaction of the Umpire, the game must be annulled.

Castling. The King can be Castled only :

When neither the King nor the Castling Rook has been moved, and

When the King is not in check, and

When all the squares between the King and Rook are unoccupied, and

When no hostile man attacks the square on which the King is to be placed, or the square he crosses.

In Castling, the King must be first moved.

The penalty of moving the King prohibits Castling.

En Passant. Taking the Pawn " *en passant*," when the only possible move, is compulsory.

Queening the Pawn. A pawn reaching the eighth square must be at once exchanged for any piece (except the King) that the player of the Pawn may elect.

Check. A player falsely announcing "check," must retract the move upon which the announcment was based and make some other move, or the move made must stand at the option of the opponent.

No penalty can be enforced for any offence committed against these rules in consequence of a false announcement of " check," nor in consequence of the omission of such announcement, when legal " check " be given.

"J'adoube." " J'adoube," " I adjust," or words to that effect, cannot protect a player from any of the penalties imposed by these laws, unless the man or men touched, obviously *need* adjustment, and unless such notification be distinctly uttered *before* the man, or men, be touched, and only the player whose turn it is to move is allowed so to adjust.

The hand having once quitted the man, but for an instant, the move must stand.

Men overturned or displaced accidentally may be replaced by either player, without notice.

A wilful displacement, or overturning of any of the men, forfeits the game.

Penalties. Penalties can be enforced only at the time an offence is committed, and before any move is made thereafter.

A player touching one of his men, when it is his turn to play, must move it. If it cannot be moved he must move his King. If the King cannot move, no penalty can be enforced.

For playing two moves in succession, the adversary may elect which move shall stand.

For touching an adversary's man, when it cannot be captured, the offender must move his King. If the King cannot move, no other penalty can be enforced. But if the man touched can be legally taken, it must be captured.

For playing a man to a square to which it cannot be legally moved, the adversary, at his option, may require him to move the man legally, or to move the King.

For illegally capturing an adversary's man, the offender must move his King, or legally capture the man, as his opponent may elect.

For attempting to Castle illegally, the player doing so must move either the King or Rook, as his adversary may dictate.

For touching more than one of the player's own men, he must move either man that his opponent may name.

For touching more than one of the adversary's men, the offender must capture the one named by his opponent, or if *either* cannot be captured, he may be required to move the King or capture the man which can be taken, at the adversary's option ; or, if *neither* can be captured, then the King must be moved.

A player moving into check may be required, by the opposing player, either to move the King elsewhere, or replace the King and make some other move—but such other move shall not be selected by the player imposing the penalty.

For discovering check on his own King, the player must either legally move the man touched, or move the King at his adversary's option. In case neither move can be made, there shall be no penalty.

While in check, for touching or moving a man which does not cover the check, the player may be required to cover with another piece, or move the King, as the opposing player may elect.

Touching the Squares. While the hand remains upon a man, it may be moved to any square that it commands, except such squares as may have been touched by it during the deliberation on the move ; but if all the squares which it commands have been so touched, then the man must be played to such of the squares as the adversary may elect.

Counting Fifty Moves. If, at any period during a game, either player persist in repeating a particular check, or series of checks, or persist in repeating any particular line of play which does not advance the game; or if " *a game-ending* " be of doubtful character as to its being a win or a draw, or if a win be possible, but the skill to force the game questionable, then either player may demand judgment of the Umpire as to its being a proper game to be determined as drawn at the end of fifty additional moves, on each side ; or the question : " Is, or is not the game a draw ? " may be, by mutual consent of the players, submitted to the Umpire at any time. The decision of the Umpire, in either case, to be final.

And whenever fifty moves are demanded and accorded, the party demanding it may, when the fifty moves have been made, claim the right to go on with the game, and thereupon the other party may claim the fifty move rule, at the end of which, unless mate be effected, the game shall be decided a draw.

Stale-Mate. A stale-mate is a drawn game.

Time Limit. The penalty for exceeding the time limit is the forfeiture of the game.

It shall be the duty of each player, as soon as his move be made, to stop his own register of time and start that of his opponent, whether the time be taken by clocks, sand-glasses, or otherwise. No complaint respecting an adversary's time can be considered, unless this rule be strictly complied with. But nothing herein is intended to affect the penalty for exceeding the time limit as registered.

Abandoning the Game. If either player abandon the game by quitting the table in anger, or in any otherwise offensive manner ; or by momentarily resigning the game ; or refuses to abide by the decision of the Umpire, the game must be scored against him.

If a player absent himself from the table, or manifestly ceases to consider his game, when it is his turn to move, the time so consumed shall, in every case, be registered against him.

Disturbance. Any player wilfully disturbing his adversary shall be admonished ; and if such disturbance be repeated, the game shall be declared lost by the player so offending, provided the player disturbed then appeals to the Umpire.

The Umpire. It is the duty of the Umpire to determine all questions submitted to him according to these laws, when they apply, and according to his best judgment when they do not apply.

No deviation from these laws can be permitted by an Umpire, even by mutual or general consent of the players, after a match or tournament shall have been commenced.

The decision of the Umpire is final, and binds both and all the players.

RULES FOR PLAYING THE GAME AT ODDS.

I.   In games where one player gives the odds of a piece, or " the exchange," or allows his opponent to count drawn games as won, or agrees to check-mate with a particular man, or on a particular square, he has the right to choose the men, and to move first, unless an arrangement to the contrary is agreed to between the combatants.

II.   When the odds of Pawn and one move, or Pawn and more than one move are given, the Pawn given must be the King's Bishop's Pawn when not otherwise previously agreed on.

III.   When a player gives the odds of his King's or Queen's Rook, he must not Castle (or more properly speaking leap his King) on the side from which the Rook is removed, unless before commencing the game or match he stipulates to have the privilege of so doing.

IV.   When a player undertakes to give check-mate with one of his Pawns, or with a particular Pawn, the said Pawn must not be converted into a piece.

V.   When a player accepts the odds of two or more moves, he must not play any man beyond the fourth square, *i. e.*, he must not cross the middle line of the board, before his adversary makes his first move.   Such several moves are to be collectively considered as the first move of the player accepting the odds.

VI.   In the odds of check-mating on a particular square it must be the square occupied by the King mated, not by the man giving the mate.

VII.   The player who undertakes to win in a particular manner, and either draws the game, or wins in some other manner, must be adjudged to be the loser.

In all other respects, the play in games at odds must be governed by the regulations before laid down.

RULES FOR PLAYING CORRESPONDENCE AND CONSULTATION GAMES.

I.   In playing a game by correspondence or in consultation, the two parties shall always agree beforehand in writing or otherwise as to the persons who are to take part in the contest, as to the time and mode of transmitting the moves, as to the penalties to be inflicted for any breach of the contract, and as to the umpire or referee.

II.   In games of this description each party is bound by the move dispatched ; and in this connection the word move refers to what is intelligibly written, or delivered *viva voce*.

In any game the announcement of a move which does not include the actual transfer of a man from one square to another, shall be considered as a move not intelligibly described within the meaning of this section.

III.   Each party must be bound by the move communicated in writing, or by word of mouth, to the adversary whether or not it be made on the adversary's board.   If the move so communicated should prove to be different from that actually made on the party's own board, the latter must be altered to accord with the former.

IV.   If either party be detected in moving the men when it is not their turn to play, or in moving more than one man (except in castling) when it is their turn to play, they shall forfeit the game, unless they can show that the man was moved for the purpose of adjusting or replacing it.

V.   If either party has, accidentally or otherwise, removed a man from the board, which has not been captured in the course of the game, and made certain moves under the impression that such man 'was no longer in play, the moves must stand, but the man may be replaced whenever the error is discovered.

VI.   If either party permit a bystander to take part in the contest, that party shall forfeit the game.

The foregoing laws differ very slightly from those of the British Chess Association, and it is to be hoped that an international code will be agreed upon before a second edition of this work is issued.

CHECKERS,

OR DRAUGHTS.

The Board. Checkers is played upon a board which is not more than sixteen, nor less than fourteen inches square, and is divided into sixty-four smaller squares of equal size. These squares are of different colours, alternately light and dark, and the board must be so placed that each player shall have a light square at his right on the side nearer him.

The Men. Each player is provided with twelve men, which are circular in form, one inch in diameter, and three eighths thick. The men on one side are red or black ; those on the other white or yellow. The men must be placed on the *black* squares.

Diagrams. For convenience in illustrating games and problems the men are always shown as placed on the white squares, type made in that manner being more easily read. The following diagram will show the proper arrangement of the men at the beginning of the game, if the white squares are supposed to be black ones :—

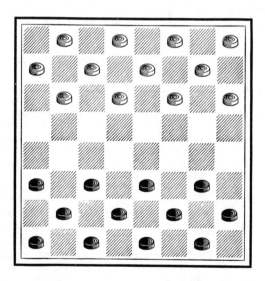

The 'Players are designated by the colour of the men with which they play, White or Black, and Black always has the first move. In a series of games each player in turn takes the black men and the move. It is usual to draw for the first game, one player concealing in each hand a man of different colour, and offering the choice of hands to his adversary. Whichever colour the chosen hand contains the chooser must take for the first game.

The Moves. The men never leave the colour of the squares on which they are originally set up, so that they always move diagonally. At the beginning of the game the men move only one square at a time, and always forward, and can be placed only on squares which are unoccupied. If an adverse piece stands upon a square to which a man might be moved, and there is a vacant

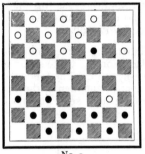

No. 1.

square beyond, the man must jump over the adverse piece to the unoccupied square, at the same time removing from the board the piece so jumped over. In the position shown in Diagram No. 1, for instance, it being White's turn to move, he must jump over the black man, removing it from the board. Black will then have a choice of two jumps, over one man or over two, and will of course select the jump toward the right of the board first, and then over the second man, removing both from the board. A man may jump over and capture several men at one move, provided there are vacant squares between them, and beyond the last man.

Huffing. If a player who can capture a piece neglects to do so, his adversary has the choice of three things :—To compel the player to take back his move and capture the piece ; to huff (remove from the board,) the man that should have captured the piece ; or to let the move stand, and go on with his own move. A huff does not constitute a move ; the piece is simply removed from the board as a penalty, but the penalty must be enforced before the player exacting it makes his own move.

Kings. When a man arrives at any of the four squares on the edge of the board farthest from the side on which he started, he becomes a King, and is **crowned** by putting another man of the same colour on the top of him. In diagrams, kings are distinguished by putting a ring round the single man. ◎ ●. Kings can move either backward or forward, but only one square at a time. If a man arrives at the king-row by capturing an adverse piece, that ends the move, and the newly made king cannnot move again, even to capture another piece, until his adversary has moved. [See notes to Diagram No. 7.]

The Object of the Game is to confine your adversary's pieces so that he cannot move any of them ; or to capture all of them, so that he has none to move. You may succeed in confining the whole twelve of your adversary's men, without capturing any of them, as in Diagram No. 2 ; or such as are left on the board after a certain number have been captured, as in Diagram No. 3.

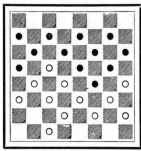

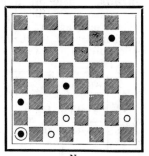

No. 2.   No. 3.

White to Move.   White to Move.

Diagram No. 2 is the ending of our Illustrative Game No. 7.

In No. 3, White gives away a man, bottling up the three black men, and then catches the other black man.   In both these examples it will then be Black's move, and as he cannot move, White wins.

Notation.   The various moves which take place in the course of a game are recorded by giving each square on the board a number, and putting down the number of the square the man is moved from, and the one it is moved to. Only those squares upon which the men stand are numbered, and the black men are always supposed to be originally placed upon the lower numbers, from 1 to 12 ; the white men being placed upon the squares numbered from 21 to 32.   Diagrams Nos. 4 and 5 show the method of numbering the board, and the men placed in position.

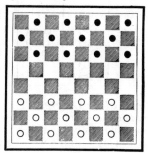

No. 4.   No. 5.

In checker notation the number of the move is never given, as it is in Chess. The moves of the black men are distinguished from those of the white men by being hyphenated, but there are no marks to show when pieces are captured. Letters or figures in the margins are used to refer to possible variations in the play.

Openings. There are a number of standard openings in Checkers which are formed by the preliminary moves on each side. These openings are known by various fanciful names, dear to all checker-players. In the following list they are arranged in alphabetical order for convenience in reference.

ALMA.	AYRSHIRE LASSIE.	BRISTOL.	CENTRE.	CROSS.	DEFIANCE.	DENNY.
11-15	11-15	11-16	11-15	11-15	11-15	10-14
23 19	24 20	24 20	23 19	23 18	23 19	
8-11	8-11	16-19	8-11		9-14	
22 17			22 17		27-23	
3- 8			15-18			

DYKE.	DOUBLE CORNER.	DUNDEE.	EDINBURG.	FIFE.	GLASGOW.	KELSO.
11-15	9-14	12-16	9-13	11-15	11-15	10-15
22 17				23 19	23 19	
15-19				9-14	8-11	
				22 17	22 17	
				5- 9	11-16	

LAIRD AND LADY.	MAID OF THE MILL.	OLD 14TH.	PAISLEY.	SECOND DOUBLE CORNER.	SINGLE CORNER.	SOUTER.
11-15	11-15	11-15	11-16	11-15	11-15	11-15
23 19	22 17	23 19	24 19	24 19	22 18	23 19
8-11	8-11	8-11				9-14
22 17	17 13	22-17				22 17
9-13	15-18	4- 8				6- 9

SWITCHER.	WHILTER.	WILL O' THE WISP.	WHITE DYKE.	IRREGULAR OPENINGS.		
11-15	11-15	11-15	11-15	11-15	11-15	10-15
21 17	23 19	23 19	22 17	22 17	23 19	22 18
	9-14	9-13	8-11	8-11	8-11	15-22
	22 17		17 14	25 22	22 17	25 18
	7-11					

The Middle Game. The best way for the student to learn the manner in which the various openings are followed up, is to play over illustrative games, and in doing so he should be careful always to play with the winning side next him. In selecting openings, take those that show the greatest number of wins for the side you propose to play. In all checker books there are marks at the foot of the column to show which side has an advantage, if any exists, at the end of each variation. The Alma, for instance, shows a great many more winning variations for the black men than for the white, and is consequently one of the best openings for Black.

Any person who plays correctly can always be sure of avoiding defeat; that is, no one can beat him if he makes no slips, and the worst he can get is a draw. It is a common error to suppose that the first move is an advantage. [See Illustrative Game No. 7.]

The strategy of the game consists in so deploying your men that alluring openings are left for your adversary. These openings are always pitfalls of the most dangerous character, and whenever you think a good player has made a mistake and left you a chance, you should examine the position with great care, or you will probably walk into a trap. The first of the example games given in this work is a case in point. White's move, 27 24, is apparently the best possible, yet it immediately and hopelessly loses the game. Sometimes these traps are set very early in the opening, and sometimes after the pieces have been pretty well developed.

There are many cases in which a good player may take advantage of the weakness of an adversary by making moves which are really losing moves, and which would lead to immediate defeat if he were opposed by an expert. But if he feels that his adversary is not skilful enough to take advantage of these losing moves, a winning position may sometimes be rapidly obtained by departing from the regular development of the opening.

The beginner should be satisfied with learning only one or two forms of the openings, committing to memory as many variations as possible. When he meets with a line of play that beats him, he should study out the variation in his text books, and see at what point he made the losing move. To be perfect in any one opening a person must know at least five hundred variations by heart; but if he finds himself caught in a variation which he does not remember, or has never learned, he should trust to good judgment rather than to defective memory.

The End Game usually resolves itself into one of four well-known positions. These four positions are those in which there is a win for one side or the other owing to the peculiar position occupied by the opposing forces, although they may be numerically equal. Every checker player must know these four positions thoroughly, or he may abandon many a game as drawn which he could win, and may lose many a game which he could draw. These four positions are here given as they are usually found in the books, but the player must be able to recognize at once any position which resembles them, or can be made to lead up to them. The student will find many games marked as "won" in which he cannot see any winning position unless he is familiar with the four endings. The expert strives to exchange his men so as to bring about one of these positions, after which he knows he has a won game, although his less skilful adversary may be unconscious of his advantage.

First Position.	*Second Position.*
Black to move and win.	Black to move and win.

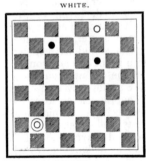

Third Position.	*Fourth Position.*
Either to move ; White to win.	Black to play and win. White to play and draw.

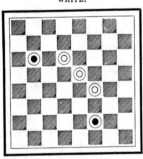
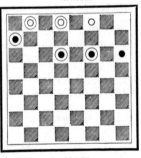

The first position is one of the most common endings on the checker board, and should be very thoroughly understood. The letters in the margin refer to the variations. There are a great many minor variations, for which the student must be referred to Janvier's Anderson, page 265.

First Position	5- 1	10-15	3- 7	10-15	14 10	27-32
	6 9	B 9 5	24 19	24 28	28-32	19 23
27-32	15-18	15-18	7-10	15-19	27 24	5- 1
8 11	17 13	5 9	19 23	28 32	1- 5	6 9
32-27	18-15	1- 5	10-15	19-24	10 6	32-28
11 7	9 14	9 6	23 27	32 28	W wins	23 27
27-23	1- 5	18-15	15-19	11-16	—	W wins
7 10	14 17	21 17	27 32	28 19	*Var B:*	
22-26	15-10	5- 1	19-24	16-23	5- 1	
A 10 6	17 22	6 9	32 28	12 8	6 10	*Fourth*
26-31	10-14	15-18	24-27	23-18	W wins	*Position*
6 9	22 25	9 5	28 32	8 4	—	Black
31-26	5- 1	18-22	27-31	18-14	Black	to play
9 6	25 22	17 14	32 28	4 8	to move	28-24
26-22	1- 6	1- 6	31-27	6- 1	6- 1	32 28
6 10	22 25	5 1	28 32	8 11	18 15	24-20
23-18	6-10	6- 2	27-23	14- 9	C 1- 6	28 32
10 6	25 22	1 5	32 28	13 6	14 10	22-18
18-14	10-15	22-17	23-18	1-10	6- 9	31 27
6 1	22 25	14 9	28 24	11 16	23 19	23-19
22-18	15-18	B wins	18-14	10-15	24-27	27 31
1 6	25 21	—	24 19	16 20	15 18	19-24
18-15	B wins	*Var B.*	6-10	15-19	D 27-32	32 27
6 1	—	9 14	19 23	B wins	19 24	24-28
15-10	*Var A.*	1- 5	10-15	▬▬▬	9- 5	27 32
1 5	30 25	21 17	23 27		10 14	18-22
10- 6	23-18	5- 1	15-19	*Third*	32-28	31 27
5 1	10 6	17 13	27 32	*Position.*	24 27	22-26
14-13	18-14	1- 5	19-24	White	W wins	30 23
1 5	6 1	14 17	32 28	to move	—	28-24
6- 1	26-30	15-10	24-27	18 15	*Var C.*	B wins
5 9	25 21	B wins	28 24	A 6- 1	1- 5	—
1- 5	30-25		27-32	14 9	14 10	White
9 13	1 5	▬▬▬	24 28	24-28	24-28	to play
10-14	25-22	*Second*	32-27	23 19	23 19	31 27
13 9	5 1	*Position.*	28 32	1- 5	28-32	23-19
14-18	22-18	1- 5	27-24	9 6	15 18	27 31
9 6	1 5	8 11	32 28	B 28-32	32-27	19-24
18-15	18-15	5- 9	24-19	19 24	10 6	32 27
30 25	5 1	11 15	28 32	5- 1	27-32	24-20
15-18	15-10	9-14	19-15	24 19	19 23	27 32
6 10	1 5	15 11	32 28	W wins	5- 1	22-18
5- 1	10- 6	14-18	15-10	—	6 9	31 27
25 21	5 1	11 16	28 24	*Var A.*	W wins	28-24
1- 5	14-10	18-15	10- 6	24-28	—	27 31
10 6	1 5	16 20	24 19	23 27	*Var D.*	18-23
18-15	6- 1	15-11	14-10	6- 1	9- 5	31 26
21 17	5 9	20 24	19 24		10 6	Drawn

Traps. The beginner should be on his guard against being caught, "two for one," especially in such positions as those shown in Diagrams Nos. 6 and 7.

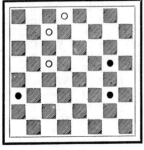
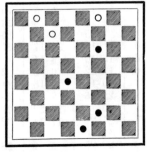

No. 6.   No. 7.

In No. 6, White will play 19 16, forcing you to jump, and will then play 27 23, forcing you to jump again, In No. 7, White will play 30 26, making your man a King. He will then play 32 28, and wait for your newly made King to jump. This will give him three of your men, and he will catch the other before it gets to the king row.

Another common form of trap is to get a player into such a position in the end game, when he has only one or two men, that he cannot get to the king row without being caught; sometimes because he is driven to the side of the board by the man following him, and sometimes because the man meeting him can head him off. The adversary can do this only when he has " the move."

Theory of the Move. When the position is such that you will be able to force your adversary into a situation from which he cannot escape without sacrificing a piece or losing the game, you are said to have the move; and if he does not change it by capturing one of your men he must lose the game. As the move is often of the greatest importance in the end game, every checker-player should understand its theory, so that he may know when it is necessary to make an exchange of men in order to secure the move, and when he should avoid an exchange which would lose it. The move is only important when the number of men on each side is equal.

In order to calculate the move, the board is supposed to be divided into two systems of squares, sixteen in each. The first system is formed by the four vertical rows running from your own side of the board, as shown by the dotted lines in Diagram No. 8. The second system runs from your adversary's side of the board, as shown in Diagram No. 9.

FIRST SYSTEM.   SECOND SYSTEM.

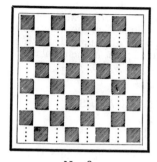

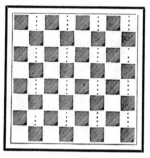

No. 8.   No. 9.

In order to ascertain if you have the move when it is your turn to play, add together all the men, both black and white, in one of the systems, taking no notice of those in the other system, and if the number is ***odd***, you have the move. In Diagram No. 10, for instance, if you have the black men, and it is your turn to play, you will find three men on your own system, and therefore you have the move, and must win by playing 10-15. When White moves, there will again be an odd number of men on your system, and you will still have the move, and he must sacrifice both his men.

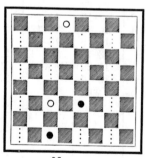

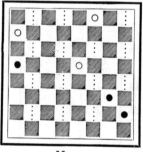

No. 10.   No. 11.

In Diagram No. 11, if you count up the men on either your own or your adversary's system, you will find that the number is even, and as you have not the move you should force an exchange immediately, which will give it to you, and win the game.

Every single exchange of man for man ***changes the move*** when only one of the capturing pieces remains on the board, and the following rule is given for ascertaining how proposed exchanges in complicated positions will affect the move :—The capturing pieces of both black and white in both systems must first be added together, and if the number agrees—in the matter of being odd or even—with that of the number of captured pieces in each system, the move will not be changed ; but if one number so found is odd, and the other is even, the move will be changed.

ILLUSTRATIVE GAMES.

The asterisk shows the losing move.

Play with Black Men.			Play with White Men.			
1	*2*	*3*	*4*	*5*	*6*	*7*
11–15	11–15	10-15	11–15	11–15	11–15	10-15
22 18	23 19	22 18	24 20	22 18	23 19	23 18
15–22	8–11	15–22	8–11	15–22	8–11	12–16
25 18	22 17	25 18	28 24	25 18	26 23	21 17
8–11	3- 8	6–10	4- 8	8–11	4- 8	16–19
29 25	*17 14	29 25	23 19	29 25	30 26	17 14
4- 8	9–18	10-15	*9–13	4- 8	*9–13	9–13
24 20	21 17	*25 22	20 16	24 20	19 16	24 20
10-15	18–22	15–19	11–20	10-15	12–19	8–12
25 22	25 18	23 16	22 17	25 22	23 16	25 21
12–16	15–22	12–19	13–22	*9–13	11–20	12–16
*27 24	26 23	24 15	25 4	20 16	22 17	21 17
15–19	5- 9	9–14	W wins.	12–19	13–22	4- 8
24 15	17 13	18 9		23 16	25 4	29 25
16–19	11–15	11–25		11–20	W wins.	6- 9
23 16	23 18	B wins.		18 4		27 24
9–14	1- 5			W wins.		1- 6
18 9	18 11					32 27
11–25	7–23					6–10
28 24	27 18					27 23
5–14	9–14					8–12
24 19	18 9					25 21
6–10	5–14					2- 6
B wins.	B wins.					31 27
						3- 8
						30 25
						W wins.

LOSING GAME. In this variety of Draughts, the object is to give away all your men before your adversary can give away his, or to block yourself so that you cannot move. The secret of success in Losing Game is to get your men on such squares that they cannot be made to jump to the king row. These squares will be the row next you on your own side of the board, and every second row from that, horizontally. Get your men on those squares as soon as possible, and do not be in too great a hurry to capture your adversary's men.

POLISH DRAUGHTS. Although intended for a special board of 100 squares this game can be played on a common checker board. It differs from ordinary draughts in two particulars:

Although the men can move only forward, they can take backward, and Kings can go any distance at one move.

If in taking a piece, a man arrives at the king row, that does not end the move if he can capture another piece by jumping backward out of the king row again. As this brings him away from the king row before the move is complete, he will not be a king until he can get to the king row at the end of a move.

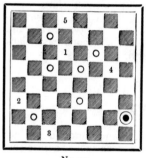

No. 12.

Kings can go any number of squares in a straight line, and can capture any piece which is on the diagonal, not protected by another piece behind it. Kings can also go on for any number of squares beyond the captured piece, and then turn a corner to capture another piece. In Diagram No. 12, for instance, the black King could capture all six of the white men by going over the first one only, and then turning to the left, and continuing to turn to the left after every capture, as shown by the squares with the numbers on them, which indicate his five successive turning-points.

DEVIL AMONG THE TAILORS. This is hardly a variation of the game of Draughts, although it is played on a checker board. Four white men, the tailors, are placed upon 29 30 31 and 32 ; and one black man, the devil, on 1. The men can move only one square at a time, diagonally ; the white men forward only, the black man forward or backward. There is no jumping or capturing, and the object of the tailors is to pin the devil in, so that he cannot move. If the black man can reach the free country behind the white men, he wins the game.

The game is a certainty for the white men if properly played. At the end of four moves they should be lined up on squares 25, 26, 27, 28 and whichever end the devil attacks, the tailors should move in from the other end.

There are two critical positions.

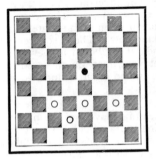
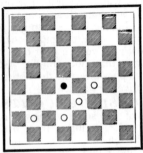

No. 13.   No. 14.

In Diagram No. 13, if White moves 24 19 he loses, because Black goes to 11, and as the tailors advance to head him off, he goes back to 15 and 18, and then gets round by going to 14. White's proper play is 22 18, after which 26 22 will re-form his line.

In Diagram No. 14, if White moves 26 22, or 19 15, he loses immediately. In the first case Black will run to 15 and 11, and either get round or double back to 18. In the second case Black will get round by way of 7, or get through.

CHECKER LAWS.

1. The Standard board must be of light and dark squares, not less than fourteen inches nor more than sixteen inches across said squares.

2. The board shall be so placed that the bottom corner square, on the left hand, shall be black.

3. The Standard men, technically described as White and Black, must be light and dark (say white and red, or yellow and black), turned, and round, not less than one inch, nor more than 1¼ inches in diameter.

4. The men shall be placed on the black squares.

5. The black men shall invariably be placed upon the real or supposed first twelve squares of the board. the white upon the last twelve squares.

6. Each player shall play alternately with the black men, and lots shall be cast for the colour only once, viz., at the beginning of the play—the winner to have his choice of taking black or white.

7. The first play must *invariably* be made by the person having the black men.

8. At the end of five minutes [if the play has not been previously made], "Time" must be called by the person appointed for that purpose, and if the play is not completed in another minute, the game shall be adjudged lost through improper delay.

9. When there is only *one way* of taking *one or more* pieces. Time shall be called at the end of one minute, and if the play is not completed in another minute, the game shall be adjudged lost through improper delay.

10. Either player is entitled, on giving intimation, to arrange his own or his opponent's pieces. After the move has been made, however, if either player touch or arrange any piece without giving intimation to his opponent, he shall be cautioned for the first offence, and shall forfeit the game for any subsequent act of the kind.

11. After the pieces have been arranged, if the person whose turn it is to play *touch* one, he must either play it or forfeit the game. When the piece is not playable, he forfeits according to the preceding law.

12. If *any part* of a playable piece is moved over an angle of the square on which it is stationed, the move must be completed in *that* direction.

13. A capturing play, as well as an ordinary one, is completed whenever the hand has been withdrawn from the piece played, although one or more pieces should have been taken.

14. The Huff or Blow is to remove from the board, before one plays his own piece, any one of the adverse pieces that might or ought to have taken, but the Huff or Blow never constitutes a play.

15. The player has the power to *huff, compel the capture,* or *let the piece remain on the board,* as he thinks proper.

16. When a man first reaches any of the squares on the opposite extreme line of the board, it becomes a King, and can be moved backward or forward. The adversary must crown the new King, by placing a captured man on the top of it, before he makes his own move.

17. A player making a false or improper move forfeits the game to his opponent.

18. When playing, if either player removes one of his own pieces, *he* cannot replace it; but his *opponent* can either play or insist on the man being replaced.

19. A Draw is when neither of the players can force a Win. When one of the sides appears stronger than the other, the stronger is required to complete the Win, or to show a decided advantage over his opponent within forty of his own moves—to be counted from the point at which *notice* was given,—failing which, the game must be abandoned as Drawn.

20.   Anything which may annoy or distract the attention of the player is strictly forbidden ; such as making signs or sounds, pointing or hovering over the board, unnecessarily delaying to move a piece touched, or smoking.   Any *principal* so acting, after having been warned and requested to desist, shall forfeit the game.

21.   While a game is pending, neither player is permitted to leave the room without giving a sufficient reason, or receiving the other's consent or company.

22.   A player committing a breach of any of these laws must submit to the penalty, which his opponent is equally bound to exact.

23.   Any spectator giving warning, either by sign, sound, or remark, on any of the games, whether played or pending, shall be ordered from the room.

24.   Should any dispute occur, not satisfactorily determined by the preceding laws, a *written statement of facts* must be sent to a disinterested arbiter having a knowledge of the game, whose decision shall be final.

TEXT BOOKS.

Spayth's Checkers for Beginners.
Game of Draughts, John Robertson.
Janvier's Anderson.
Bowen's Bristol.
Bowen's Cross.
Bowen's Fife.
E. T. Baker's Alma.
Scattergood's Game of Draughts.
Lyman's Selected Problems.
Backgammon and Draughts, by Berkeley.
Anderson's Checkers.

BACKGAMMON.

OR TRIC-TRAC.

Backgammon is played by two persons, each of whom is provided with fifteen men, two dice, and a dice-box.   The men on each side are of different colours, black and white, and the players are distinguished by the colour of the men with which they play. The board is divided into two tables, *inner* and *outer,* and at the beginning of the game the men may be set up in either of the positions shown in the diagram.

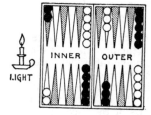

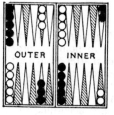

It will be observed that the black men on any point have exactly the same number of white men standing opposite them. In one table there are only two upon one point, and in the other there are only three upon one point. The table with the two men is always the ***inner table*** while the one with three is always the ***outer table.*** This distinction is important, and may be remembered by observing that the number of letters in the words *in* and *out* are two and three respectively.

In setting up the men the inner table is always placed ***toward the light,*** whether it be a window or the gas. Each player must always have the majority of his men, five and three, on the side nearer him : and the minority, five and two, on the side farther from him. The side of the ***inner table*** which is nearer the player will always be his ***home table.*** In all the illustrations in this work you are supposed to be playing with the black side next you, and your inner or home table on your *left* hand.

The raised portion or hinge of the board, which divides the inner from the outer tables, is known as the *bar*, and the points, or flèches, in each player's home table are numbered from 1 to 6, reckoning from the outer edge toward the bar. These six points are spoken of as the Ace, Deuce, Trey, Four, Five and Six points respectively, and they correspond to the six faces on a single die. The points in the outer tables have no numbers, but the one next the bar on each side is called the ***bar point.*** In giving the moves of the men in a game, the names of the six points in the home

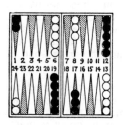

tables are disregarded, and each player, Black and White, numbers the board from 1 to 24, starting from the square on which he has only two men. The notation for the black moves would be as shown in the margin ; that for white being exactly opposite, of course.

The men on each side are always moved in the direction of their notation numbers. In all the following illustrations the black men move round the board from right to left, like the hands of a clock, while the white men go in the opposite direction ; so that the two opposing forces are continually meeting and passing, like the people in the street.

The *Object of the Game* is for each player to move his men from point to point in order to get them all into his home table. It does not matter what part of the home table they reach, so that they get across the bar. The men are moved according to the throws of the dice, each player in turn having a throw and a move. After the men on either side are all home, they are taken off the board according to the throws of the dice, and the player who is the first to get all his men off the board in this manner wins the game.

If each player has taken off some of his men, the player getting all his off first wins a *hit,* which counts as a single game. If one player gets off all his men before his adversary has thrown off a single man, it is a *gammon,* and counts as a double game. If the loser has not only taken off none of his men, but has one or more men left on the side of the board farther from him when his adversary throws off his last man, it is a *backgammon,* and counts as a triple game. In America, gammons and backgammons are seldom played, every game being simply a hit. This spoils some of the fine points of the game, and entirely alters the tactics of the players, as will be seen when we come to the suggestions for good play.

The Dice. Although it is usual for each player to be provided with two dice, some players insist on the same pair being used by each player alternately ; the claim being that luck will then run more evenly. At the beginning of the game each player makes a cast, either with one die or with two, as may be agreed, and the higher throw has the first play. In some clubs the player making the higher throw is allowed the option of playing the first cast, or of throwing again ; but the general practice is to insist that the first cast is simply for the privilege of playing first, and that the dice must be cast again for the first move.

After each throw the dice must fall within the borders of the table on the caster's right, and each die must rest fairly and squarely on one of its faces. If it is *cocked* against a man, the edge of the board, or the other die, or if it jumps over the edge of the table in which it is thrown, both dice must be taken up and cast again. The caster must announce his throw as soon as made.

The Moves. As the men on each side are moved round the board in opposite directions to reach their respective homes, they are of course obliged to meet and pass a number of the adversary's men, and they must pick their way among them by going to points which are unoccupied by the enemy ; for if there are two or more of the enemy in possession of any point, that point is said to be *covered,* and must be jumped over. If only one adverse man occupies a point, it is called a *blot,* and the man may be captured, as will presently be explained.

The numbers that appear on the upper faces of the two dice, when they are thrown, are the number of points that each of any two men, or that any one man may be moved at a time. If a player throws four-deuce, for instance, he may either move one man four points and another two ; or he may move a single man four points and two points, or two points and four points. He cannot lump the throw and call it six points, because if the fourth point from where the man stood was covered by two or more of the enemy, the four could not be played with that man. If the second point from where the man stood was also covered, he could not be moved at all, although the sixth point from where he stood might be unoccupied. If Black's first throw is five-deuce, for instance, he cannot move one of the two men on his adversary's ace point for the five, because the fifth point thence is covered. Neither could he move one of them two and then five, because the seventh point is covered also.

If a player throws *doublets,* that is, the same number on each die, he plays the throw twice over. If a player throws double fours, for instance, he can either move one man four points four times ; or one man four points once, and another man four points three times ; or two men four points twice ; or two men four points each, and then two other men four points, always provided that the points moved to at the end of each four are not covered by the enemy.

If there is only one of the adversary's men on any point which can be reached by a throw of the dice, the blot may be hit, a man being moved to that point, and the adverse man taken from the board and placed upon the bar. In the diagram in the margin, for in-

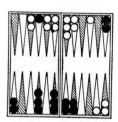

stance, it is White's play, and he has thrown six-four. Black has left a blot on White's four-point, and the single white man in the outer table can reach this with the six throw, taking up the black man, and placing it upon the bar. White now has a blot on his four point, which he should cover by playing in a man four points from the outer table, it being better to leave a blot there than at home.

When a player has a man that has been hit, and placed upon the bar by the adversary, he must re-enter that man before he moves any others. He may choose for the purpose either of the numbers on the next throw of the dice, and must place his man on the point in the adversary's home table which agrees with the number selected. Suppose that in the fore-going example, Black's next throw is five-deuce. He cannot enter the man on the five-point, because it is covered by the enemy: so he must enter upon the deuce point, which is not covered, and must move some other man five points for the throw upon the other die. If both the five and deuce points were covered, Black could not enter on either of them, and as he cannot play until the man on the bar is entered, the throw would be lost, and he would have to wait until his adversary threw and moved in his turn. If two men are upon the bar, both must be entered before any man can be moved. A man may enter and hit a blot at the same time.

If a player could get his men round the board without any of them being hit, seventy-seven points on the dice thrown would bring them all home; but as every man hit has to start all over again from his adversary's home table, it may take a great many throws to get all the men home. For this reason it is obvious that each player should leave as few blots as possible, in order to save his men from being hit; and at the same time he should strive to cover as many points as possible, in order to prevent his adversary from moving round the board freely. It is still more important to cover points in the home table, so that when an adverse man is hit he will have fewer points upon which to enter. It is, of course, unnecessary to say that one can always enter or play on points covered by his own men.

Throwing Off. When either player has succeeded in getting all his men home, he removes them from the board two or four at a time, according to the throws of the dice, provided he has men on the points in his home table corresponding to the numbers thrown. If not, he must move his men up toward the ace point. Doublets may take off four men if there are so many on the point. If there are no men on a number thrown, and the number is so high that the man farthest from the ace point cannot be moved up, that man may be taken off. In the diagram in the margin, for

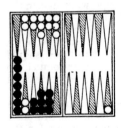

instance, Black has all his men home, and is ready to throw them off. If he threw six-deuce, having no men on either point he would have to move up the deuce; but the farthest man from the ace point cannot be moved up six, so he can throw that man off. This must result in leaving a blot, no matter which man is played up the two Points, and White may hit this blot on his next throw. Should he do so, Black would have to throw an ace to re-enter, as all the other points in White's home table are covered, or "made up." Black could not throw off another man until the one hit had not only been re-entered, but had made the circuit of the board and got home again.

A player is not obliged to throw off a man if he prefers to move, but he must do one or the other. In the foregoing diagram, for instance, if Black threw three-ace, he would be very foolish to take off two men, leaving a blot on his three point. He should move the ace from his four to his three point, and then take off the three, leaving no blots.

SUGGESTIONS FOR GOOD PLAY. Always see that the men are properly set up. It would be a great help to many persons if the manufacturers of backgammon boards would print upon them a small diagram of the correct position of the men.

The first thing for the beginner to learn is the proper manner of playing the opening throws, and this should be practised with a board and men. In some cases there are several ways to play the same throw ; double fours, for instance, it is said cannot be played wrong. All possible throws of the dice, from double six to double ace, and the various ways of playing them, are shown in the diagrams. Black men only are moved, and those with white centres have been brought from the points marked with a small cross x.

The best throws are those which cover the most points, take possession of your own or your adversary's five point, make up your own bar point, or make up points in your home table.

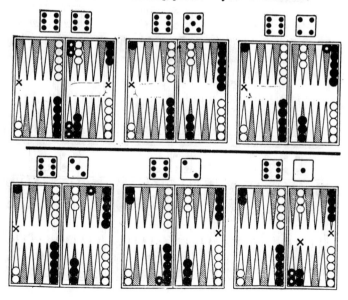

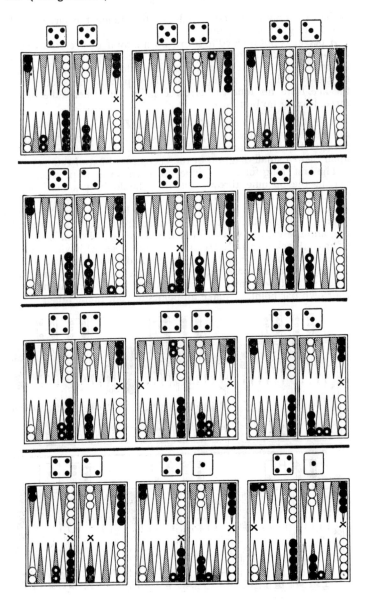

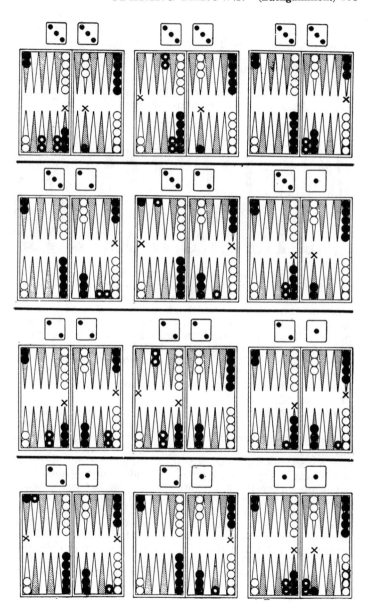

Double aces are the best, because they make up two of the most important points at once. A first-class player will sometimes give an adversary the odds of a first throw of double aces. Double sixes is the next best, and five-ace is considered one of the worst.

Three of these throws require special mention, all of which would be very bad openings in the American game, for reasons which will presently be explained. These throws are five-ace, four-ace, and deuce-ace, when played as follows:—

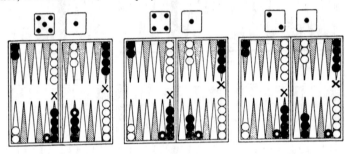

These are all unfortunate opening throws, five-ace being especially bad, and the English players think the best, perhaps because the boldest, way to play them is to leave one or two blots, one of which, however, lays the foundation for possession of your five-point on the next throw, always a great advantage if you can secure it. If neither of the blots are hit, the Englishman pushes forward in the hope of gammoning his adversary, and so winning a double game. In America, where gammons count no more than hits, nothing is to be gained by taking such chances, and the foregoing methods of playing these three throws would therefore be considered very bad.

The English Game. When the players count double and triple games, it is not an uncommon thing to play for the gammon, especially against inferior adversaries, or when one gets a decided advantage at the start. The first thing is to secure your own or your adversary's five point, or both, and if you succeed in that you should play a very forward game, and endeavour to gammon your opponent. After the five-points, secure your bar point, so as to prevent your opponent from " running" with double sixes. Some players think the bar point better than the five point, but it must be remembered that points in the home table are usually better than any outside. If you get the five and bar points made up, try for the four point, and after that you may take some risks to get your men home, and do not take up your opponent's men if you are ahead of him, because they may give you trouble when they re-enter in your home table.

The American Game. When a gammon or backgammon counts you nothing more if you win it, and costs you nothing more if you lose it, the tactics of the game are entirely changed. It is folly to take any risks for the sake of a gammon, and any plays which leave unnecessary blots are very bad; for which reason the three throws shown in the foregoing diagram would be absurd in the American game. On the other hand, you may risk being gammoned, or even backgammoned, if it is the only way to save the game. An Englishman cannot take this risk, for he might lose a triple game in attempting to save a single.

Secure the five point in your own and your adversary's home table as soon as possible, and then the bar and four points. After the first few throws the player should take a general survey of the board, in order to see whether he is ahead or behind, or if he has any advantage of position. He must then decide whether he will play a **backward** or a **forward** game. A glance at the relative positions of the men will usually show if one side is much more advanced than the other, without going into any minute calculations as to how many points nearer home one side may be.

If, at the beginning of the game, one player makes two or three large throws in succession, while his adversary gets small throws only, the latter will have little chance of winning the game simply by running for home, whereas the former's best chance will be to follow up his early advantage and get home as fast as possible. The only hope for the man who is behind is that he can pick up some of his opponent's men, setting them back, and in order to do this he must keep behind his adversary, so as to meet as many of his men as possible.

This enables us to formulate the great principle of the American game, which is that when a player is ahead he should go ahead as fast as he can; and when he is behind, he should stay behind as long as he can. In the first place he is playing a forward, and in the second place a backward game.

The Forward Game. The great point in this game, after having obtained the advantage of several good throws in the opening, is to get home as rapidly as possible without unnecessarily exposing your men by leaving blots. Do not take up your adversary's men if you can help it, because by so doing you place obstacles in your own path, and assist him by allowing him to stay behind, which is just his game. Get past all his men if possible, especially if he has moved his two men out of your home table.

The Backward Game. Exactly the opposite tactics are of course the best for the player who is behind. He should keep two or three men in his adversary's home table, preferably on the ace and deuce points, in the hope of catching some of the enemy, and setting them back. The result of these tactics, if successful, will be to offset the advantage of the adversary's high throws early in the game, because every man captured not only has to start his journey over again, but is liable to be picked up a second or third time. As it is to the advantage of the forward player to avoid picking up men, the one who is behind can leave blots with great freedom, and may even spread his men so that some of them must be taken up. This intense back game is peculiarly American, for in the English game such tactics would usually result in a gammon, and often in a backgammon, and the player dare not risk so much just to save a hit. In the back game it is very important to spread the men freely, so that they may act as **catchers.**

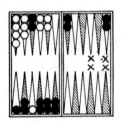

In the position shown in the margin, for instance, White has already thrown off three of his men, but one has been caught and set back. It is impossible for Black to win unless he can catch this man again, or capture one or two of those in White's home table, keeping White from throwing off any more men until Black gets home.

Suppose that in this position Black threw double threes. His play would be to separate all his men in the outer table, so that no matter what White might throw he could hardly escape being caught. The black men might be placed on the points marked with small crosses, and then if the white man cannot be caught and set back long enough for Black to get home, the game cannot be saved. If Black succeeds in picking up this man, he should then complete his home table as rapidly as possible, still keeping his outside men spread, and not disturbing the two men on White's trey point until necessary.

Throwing Off. Always throw off every man possible ; never move up instead of throwing off, unless there are some adverse men in your home table. If you make a throw which will not take off a man, do not move two men, but move up and take off one man if possible.

Chances. Some players profess to attach great importance to the chances of the dice, but such matters are of little practical value except in a general way. It may be interesting to know that the odds were thirty-five to one against a certain throw, but that knowledge does not prevent your adversary from winning the game.

It should always be remembered that it is more difficult for your adversary to hit a man that is very close to him or very far from

Single Die.	Double Dice.
25 to 11 ag'st 1	30 to 6 ag'st 7
24 to 12 ag'st 2	30 to 6 ag'st 8
22 to 14 ag'st 3	31 to 5 ag'st 9
21 to 15 ag'st 4	33 to 3 ag'st 10
21 to 15 ag'st 5	34 to 2 ag'st 11
19 to 17 ag'st 6	35 to 1 ag'st 12

it takes " double dice " to hit him.

him, than one that is about half way. The odds against being hit by a given number, either on one or on both dice, are given in the margin. The throws given in the second column cannot be made without counting both dice, and a player is therefore safer when

---

LAWS.

1. If the men are wrongly set up, the mistake may be remedied if the player in error has moved a man, otherwise they must stand as set up.

2. If a player begins with less than the proper number of men, the error cannot be rectified after the player has made a throw for his move.

3. The players must each cast a single die for the privilege of first move, the higher winning. Ties throw again.

4. By mutual consent it may be agreed to let the higher throw play the points on his own and his adversary's die for the first move; otherwise he must throw again with two dice.

5. Each player must throw the dice into the table on his right hand, and if either die jumps into the other table, or off the board, both dice must be taken up and thrown again.

6. To constitute a fair throw, each die must rest flat upon the board, and if either die is " cocked " against the other, or against the edge of the board or of a man, both dice must be taken up and thrown again.

7. If the caster interferes with the dice in any way, or touches them after they have left the box, and before they come absolutely to rest and the throw is called by the caster, the adversary may place face upward on the die or dice so interfered with, any number he chooses, and the caster must play it as if thrown.

8. Before playing, the throw must be announced by the caster, and if the throw is played as called it stands good, unless an error in the call is discovered before the dice have been touched for the purpose of putting them in the box again.

9. If a player moves a man a wrong number of points, the throw being correctly called, the adversary must demand that the error be rectified before he throws himself, or the erroneous move stands good.

10. If a man wrongly moved can be moved correctly, the player in error is obliged to move that man. If he cannot be moved correctly, the other man that was moved correctly on the same throw must be moved on the number of points on the second die, if possible. If the second man cannot be so moved onward, the player is at liberty to move any man he pleases.

11. Any man touched, except for the purpose of adjusting it, must be moved if the piece is playable. A player about to adjust a man must give due notice by saying, " J'adoube." A man having been properly played to a certain point and quitted, must remain there.

12. The numbers on both dice must be played if possible. If there are two ways to play, one of which will employ the numbers on both dice, the other only one of them, the former must be played. If either, but only one, of the two numbers thrown can be played, the larger of the two must be selected.

13. If a player throws off men before all his men are at home, the men so thrown off must be placed on the bar, and re-entered in the adversary's home table, just as if they had been captured in the course of play. The same penalty attaches to throwing off men while one is on the bar.

RUSSIAN BACKGAMMON.

In this variety of the game, no men are placed upon the board at starting, but each player enters his men by throws of the dice, and both players enter upon the same table, so that all the men on both sides move round the board in the same direction, and both players have the same home table, which is always the one opposite the entering table.

After having entered two men on the first throw, the player is at liberty either to continue entering his men with any subsequent throws, or to play the men already entered. In moving or in entering a player may capture any blots left by his adversary ; but he cannot enter upon a point covered by two or more of the adversary's men. If a player cannot enter a fresh man with the throw made, he must play a man if he can. When a man is captured, he must be re-entered before any other man can be moved.

Except on the first throw of the game, doublets give the player a great advantage. He can not only play the upper faces of the dice twice over, as in the ordinary game, but the faces opposite them also, and can then throw again before his adversary. Should he again throw doublets, he would play both faces of the dice, and throw again, and so on. As the opposite face is always the complement of seven, it is not necessary to turn the dice over to see what it is. A player throwing double four knows that he has four fours and four threes to play and will then get another throw. The upper faces of the dice must be played first, and if all four cannot be played the opposites and the second throw are lost. If the upper faces can be played, but not all the opposites, the second throw is lost.

If the first throw of the game made by either player is a doublet, it is played as in the ordinary game, without playing the opposite faces or getting a second throw.

The chief tactics of the game are in getting your men together in advance of your adversary, and covering as many consecutive points as possible, so that he cannot pass you except singly, and then only at the risk of being hit. After getting home, the men should be piled on the ace and deuce points unless there is very little time to waste in securing position.

TEXT BOOKS.

Backgammon, by Kenny Meadows, 1844.
Backgammon and Draughts, by Berkeley.
Pocket Guide to Backgammon, by " Cavendish."
Bohn's Handbook of Games.

DOMINOES.

Although properly a game for two persons, Dominoes is some-times played by four, two being partners against the other two. There are also some round games in which any number from three to six may play, each for himself.

The Sets. A set of dominoes is a number of pieces of bone, usually about 1½ inches by ¾, and ⅜ths thick. These bones have upon their faces the permutations of the numbers from six to blank, taken two at a time. Some sets begin at double nine, and others at double twelve ; but the standard set is double-six, and is composed of twenty-eight pieces.

The Suits. All the dominoes with the same number upon either end belong to the same suit ; the seven bones with a 4 form-ing the 4 suit ; those with a 6 the 6 suit, and so on. The number of pips in each suit may be easily remembered by observing that the ace suit has the same number of pips as the pieces in the set, 28 ; and that each suit above the ace has seven pips more than the number of pieces in the set, while the blank suit has seven pips less, so that each suit progresses in regular order, seven pips at a time, as shown in the margin.

Blank	21
Ace	28
Deuce	35
Trey	42
Four	49
Five	56
Six	63

Shuffling and Cutting. Dominoes are provided with a small brass pin in the centre of the face, which enables one to spin them round, push them about on the table, and so to shuffle them thoroughly. There are three methods of determining who shall have the first play, or **set,** as it is called : *1.* The player having the higher double ; or, failing any double in either hand, the **heavier** domino, that is, one with a greater number of pips on its face than any held by his adversary. *2.* One player selects any two dominoes, face down, and pushes them toward his adversary, who chooses one. Both are then turned up, and whichever gets the lighter domino has the first set. *3.* Each player draws a domino, face down, and the one getting the lower double sets first. If neither draws a double the lighter domino sets.

The dominoes are then shuffled again by both players, and each draws the number of pieces required by the game they are about to play. The dominoes remaining on the table are left face down, and form the **stock** or **bone-yard.** Each player should sort his dominoes into suits, and either leave them standing on their edges

on the table with their faces toward him, or hold them in his hand. Few persons can hold more than six dominoes in this way, so the seventh is left upon the table, or is the first one set.

Matching. All games of dominoes are based upon the principle of matching, or following suit ; which requires that each domino played shall belong to the same suit as one of the exposed ends of the line of dominoes already played, and exposed upon the table. In playing a domino, it must be so placed that the end of it shall match and adjoin the exposed end of the line ; a six being played to a six, a four to a four, and so on. Each domino, as played, is laid face upward on the table, the ends abutting, and doublets being laid across, or at right angles to the line.

The principal games are divided into two classes ; those in which the object is to **block** a player, so that he cannot follow suit, and those in which the object is to make the ends of the line some multiple of *five* or *three*. The Block Game will be described first.

THE BLOCK GAME. Each player draws seven dominoes, and the one whose turn it is to set lays down any domino he
pleases. If a good player, he will select one of his longest suit, especially if he has three or more, and his object will be to get the
line back to his suit as often as possible. If a player had to set
with the hand of dominoes shown in the foregoing diagram, he
would select the 5–0, because he has four of the 5 suit, and three
of the 0 suit. This would compel his adversary to play some domino having upon it a 5 or a 0. Let us suppose this adversary to
hold the following dominoes :—6–6, 6–3, 6–1, 6–0, 5–1, 5–0. He
would of course play the 6–0, in order to bring the line round to
his long suit of 6's. As this would close the blank end of the line,
the first player, whom we shall call A, would have to play on the 5
end, as he has no 6. In order to get the line back to his second
longest suit, the blanks, he would play the 5–2, hoping to play 2–0
next time. His adversary, B, would play on this end if he could,
but being unable to do so, he gets rid of his heaviest domino, playing the double six. A plays 2–0, and B should now bring in his
suit of aces by playing 6–1, which would win the game ; but for
the sake of illustration we shall suppose that he foolishly plays 6–4.
A plays his double four, and the dominoes on the table present the
following appearance :—

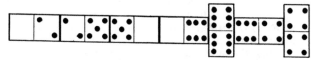

B, having neither 4 nor 0 on any of his remaining dominoes,
says : **" Go,"** which signifies that he is blocked, and cannot play.
A can now play at either end, and with either of two dominoes ;
but it would be bad policy to play the 4–5, because his adversary
might be able to play to the 5 ; but it is a certainty that he cannot play to either 0 or 4. If A plays the 4–5, B gets rid of all his
dominoes before A can play again. If A plays the 4–0 on the
blank end, he will have to play again with his 4–5 ; but if he plays
it on the 4 end he blocks himself.

Whether to block the game or not depends on the probable
comparative value of the dominoes held by A and B. If A blocks
the game by making both ends blank, both players show their remaining dominoes, and the one with the greater number of pips
loses as many points as he has pips in excess of the other player.
In order to judge whether to block or play, it should be remembered that as there are 147 pips in the entire set, the average value
of each domino will be 5¼. If A blocks the game, he will have
17 pips left in his hand, which is above the average value of two
dominoes ; but his adversary will have four dominoes to count,

and it is probable that they will be worth about 21 points. The fact that the seven dominoes already played are 13 pips above the average will reduce the probable value of B's dominoes to about 20. On the other hand, A knows that B has no blanks, which would slightly increase the weight of B's dominoes.

If A blocks the game, as he should do with the odds in his favour, he will win 7 points, the difference between his 17 and B's 24. If he does not block, he must follow the 4–0 with the 5–4. This will bring in B's ace suit, bringing him back to his long suit of 6's. When the 5–1 was played, A would have to say, " go," and B would continue with 1–1, 1–6, 6–3, claiming *domino,* all his pieces being exhausted. Although A can now play, it is too late, for when one player makes domino he counts all the pips remaining in his adversary's hand ; in this case, 8 points for B.

Had B played properly, by putting down 6–1, instead of 6–4, A would have been compelled to play his 4–0, and B would have made both ends 6's, A saying, " go." By then playing his double ace, B would have made certain of domino next time by playing the 6–3, for even if A could play to the 3, he could not shut B out of the ace, and B's 5–1 would make him domino, winning 17 points.

The Block Game is sometimes played 50 or 100 points up, and at the end the winner takes the stakes, if any, or settles at so much a point for the difference between the scores.

In the ***Four-handed Block Game*** the players cut for partners, the two lowest playing against the two highest, and the lowest cut having the first set. Each player draws four bones, and the play goes round from right to left. When any player is blocked, and says " go," the one on his left must play or say " go," also. The game is at an end when one player gets rid of all his dominoes, or all four players are blocked. The pips remaining in the hands of the partners are then reckoned, and the side having the lower number wins the difference.

Another variation is for each to play for himself, but instead of playing only one domino at a time in each round, a player may go on as long as he can follow suit to either end of the line.

DRAW GAME. In this variation of the Block Game, each player has the option of drawing any number of dominoes from the bone-yard except the last two, which must always remain in stock. He may draw while he is still able to play, or not until he is blocked ; but when he is blocked he is compelled to draw until he obtains a domino that can be played, or has drawn all but the last two in the bone-yard.

MATADORE GAME. This is another variety of the Block Game. Each player takes seven bones, and the highest double or the heaviest domino sets. The object is not to follow suit to the ends, but to play a number which will make the end and the number played to it equal *seven.* If the end is a 3, a 4 must be played ; a 2 must be played to a 5, and an ace to a 6. Four dominoes in the set are trumps, or Matadores. These are the double blank, and the three dominoes that have seven on their faces ; 6–1, 5–2, and 4- 3. Any of these trumps may be played at any time on either of the ends, in order to prevent a block ; but the following player, if he does not play a trump also, must play the complement of seven to whichever end of the matadore is left exposed. Doublets are not placed crosswise, and count only for the suit to which they belong ; a double three cannot be played to an ace, because it counts as three only. The trumps are usually placed at right angles to the line. The game is decided and settled for as in the ordinary Block Game.

SEBASTOPOL. In this variety of the Block Game, four persons play. Each takes seven bones, and the double six sets. Nothing but sixes can be played until both sides and both ends of the first set have been played to. When these five dominoes have been set, any of the four ends may be played to. Each player ir turn must play or say, " go." The game is decided and settled for as in the ordinary Block Game.

BERGEN GAME. Two persons play, each of whom draws six bones. The highest double sets, and scores two points for the *double header.* Two points are scored by the player making both ends of the line the same. If there is a doublet at one end, and one of the same suit at the other, it is a triple header, and counts three. Fifteen points is game. In addition to the headers, domino counts one. If both players are blocked, the bones are shown, and the one having the smallest number of pips and no doublet counts one toward game. If he holds a doublet, his adversary scores one ; but if both hold doublets, the lower number of pips wins the point.

DOMINO POOL. Any number from three to six can play, and a pool is made up. They draw for the first set, and after shuffling again, each player takes such an equal number of bones as will leave at least eight in the stock. The leader plays anything he pleases for the first set, and each following player must follow suit if he can, to one end or the other. If a person cannot play, he says " go," and the player on his left plays or passes also. When one makes domino he wins the pool. If all are blocked, the smallest number of pips left in hand wins ; ties divide.

MUGGINS, OR ALL FIVES. This is a game for two, three, or four players. The object is to make the two ends of the line some multiple of five, and for every five so made the player scores five points toward game, which is usually 100 up. If only one point is scored for each five, 20 or 21 may be game. Each player draws seven bones, and the highest double sets, each person afterward playing in turn. If double five is the first set it counts 10. The 5-0 played to this would count 10 for the second player, because one end of the line being 10 and the other 0, the total value of the two ends is still 10. Double blank played to this would count 10 more. If 5–6 is now played on one end, and 0–4 on the other, the count will be 10 again, as shown on the diagram. The figures show the order in which the dominoes were played.

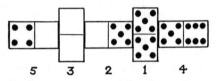

The highest possible score is 20 points, made with the 4–4 and 6–6, at different ends. If either player makes a multiple of five without noticing or claiming it, his adversary says, " *muggins,* " and scores it himself. If a player makes an erroneous score, it must be taken down, and his adversary marks it as penalty.

When a player cannot follow suit, he must draw from the boneyard until he gets a domino that can be played; but the last two in the stock must never be drawn. When one player gets rid of all his bones, he calls *domino,* and scores the nearest multiple of five that is found in the dominoes remaining in his adversary's hand. Remainders of 3 or 4 count as 5; those of 1 or 2 as nothing; so that 12 pips would count as 10; but 13 would count as 15. The players usually settle at the end of the game for the difference between their scores.

Muggins is sometimes varied by playing from both ends of the first doublet set, as well as from the sides. It is not necessary to play on the ends of the first set until one cannot play on the line; but any of the four points may be played to at any time. The end of the first doublet does not count in making multiples of five, but the ends of any dominoes played to it must be counted. If only one end of the first doublet has been played to, there will be three ends to count to make multiples of five; and if both ends of the first doublet have been played to, there will be four ends. Every count must take in all the ends that are in play. The highest count possible is 35; all four lines open, with the 6–6, 4–4, 5–5, and 0–5 at the ends.

ALL THREES. Muggins is sometimes played by making the object to get multiples of three at the ends, instead of multiples of five. Otherwise the game is the same as All Fives.

There are several *card games* with dominoes, but they are little used, and hardly worth description in a work of this kind.

DICE.

Dice are probably the oldest gambling instruments in the world. Chatto thinks that man acquired the passion for gambling as soon as he could distinguish odd from even, or a short straw from a shorter. Simple gambling instruments were probably very early articles of manufacture, and Chatto says that it is not unlikely that after a simple dinner of mutton some enterprising gamester may have taken the small bones from between the shank and the foot, and after burning spots in them to distinguish one from the other, put them into a cow's horn and shaken them up, afterward rolling them upon the ground. From some such beginning Astragali was developed, a game which Dr. Thomas Hyde thinks was known at the time of the Deluge. Later on, other instruments were used in connection with dice, and so the earliest forms of Backgammon were developed.

Dice are still the favourite implements for deciding any matters of pure chance, such as raffling off a horse or a gold watch ; but the rules governing such lotteries are but imperfectly understood by people in general. There are also a number of smaller matters, such as the payment for refreshments or cigars, which are settled by thousands of persons every day, simply by throwing dice. The various methods of throwing, and the rules governing all such games are as follows :—

THE DICE. Although dice may be of any size, the standard pattern are half an inch square, of ivory or bone, with black spots one tenth of an inch in diameter. The opposite sides of the die always equal seven, and if the die is placed upon the table with the ace uppermost and the deuce nearest you, the four will be on the left and the three on the right. The positions of the three and four are sometimes reversed to enable sharpers to distinguish fair dice from those which have been doctored.

At the beginning of any dice game, it is quite unnecessary to examine the dice to be used, because they are always fair. Crooked dice are *rung in* during the game, and the player should make it a point to examine the dice frequently if he has any suspicions. First see that each die has all six figures upon it, for some dice are *dispatchers,* made with double numbers, so as to secure higher throws than the natural average. Double fives are great favourites with backgammon sharps. The next thing is to place the dice together in pairs, to be sure that they are exactly the same height each way. If dice are not square they can be made to roll over and over on the same faces. The faces should then be tested to see that they are not convex, even in the slightest degree. Shaped dice are usually flat on the ace and six faces, especially in crap shooting. Each die should be held between the thumb and forefinger at its longest diameter, to see if it has any tendency to swing on a pivot, for if it does it is loaded. Even if the dice are transparent, it is no guarantee that they are not loaded in the spots. Loaded ivory dice soon get discoloured, and the presence of any darkness in the corners is usually a sign of the presence of mercury. It is a mistake to suppose that loaded dice will always throw high or low; all they will do is to beat averages. Finally, the dice should be tested with a magnet, as they are sometimes made to work in connection with a battery concealed under the table.

DICE BOXES. Although the dice may be perfectly fair, the box may be "crooked." A fair box may be of leather, perfectly smooth inside, or it may be of bone, ivory or wood, with the interior "screwed" or grooved. If the upper edge of the inside presents a sloping flat surface, slightly roughened with sand paper, it will be just as well to refuse to allow such a box to be used, as your adversary is probably an expert at *securing,* which is a method of holding one of the dice securely against this upper edge while the others are shaken and rattled about in the usual manner. A person who is securing dice can be detected by the manner in which he holds the box, keeping his fingers, instead of his palm, over the mouth. When he turns the box face downward on the table, he will still have his fingers under it, and will withdraw them in regular order, the second and third fingers being first separated.

THROWING DICE. There are three methods of throwing dice: The first is to shake them in the box with the palm over the top, and then to shift the hold to the sides, completely exposing the mouth. The box is then turned mouth downward on the table, leaving all the dice completely covered. The box must be lifted by the person who is recording the throws, in a raffle, for instance, after the spectators have had time to assure themselves that all the dice are covered. If the caster has his fingers over the mouth of the box when he turns it over, or lifts the box himself, the throw is foul.

The second method is known as rolling, or the *long gallery,* and is generally used in poker dice and such games. After the box has been shaken, the caster holds it by the side, and gives it a twist and a push, which causes the dice to pour out, and roll along the table.

The third method is called *shooting,* and is always employed in craps. No box is used, the dice being held in the hand and rolled along the table or the ground. The crap shooter is obliged to shake the dice in his hand to show that he is not holding them with certain faces together, which is a common way of preventing or getting certain throws, especially with shaped dice.

Whichever method is employed, each die must lie flat upon one of its own faces after the throw, neither resting upon nor **cocked** against any other die or any obstruction upon the table or the ground. If any of the dice are cocked, all of them must be taken up and thrown again.

RAFFLING.

In a raffle for prizes of any kind, each player has three throws with three dice. The rules already given for throwing dice from a box must be followed, the scorer placing the dice in the box before each throw, and lifting the box after it. The total of the three throws is recorded opposite the name of each player, and the highest throw wins. The odds against throwing a certain number or higher are shown in the margin.

IT IS ABOUT	AGAINST THROWING		
Even		32	or more
9 to	7	33	" "
11 to	6	34	" "
28 to	11	35	" "
3 to	1	36	" "
5 to	1	37	" "
7 to	1	38	" "
10 to	1	39	" "
16 to	1	40	" "
24 to	1	41	" "
39 to	1	42	" "
66 to	1	43	" "
116 to	1	44	" "
215 to	1	45	" "
422 to	1	46	" "
886 to	1	47	" "
2016 to	1	48	" "
5032 to	1	49	" "
14093 to	1	50	" "
45809 to	1	51	" "
183229 to	1	52	" "
1007768 to	1	53	" "
10077695 to	1	54	" "

Suppose the prize in a raffle is a horse which would be worth a hundred dollars to you. The highest throw so far is 42, and there are only twenty more chances to be thrown. It is 2 to 1 that 42 is not beaten or equalled because it is 39 to 1 that 42 is not thrown, and there are only 20 more chances to throw it. If 45 had been thrown, and there were still 21 chances to be thrown, you would be safe in paying liberally for the 45 chance. The great mistake that people make in buying or selling chances on throws already made in raffles is in thinking that because a certain number has not been thrown, that therefore it is likely to be. If there are 116 chances, they argue that 44 or better should be thrown, because that number or higher should come once in 116 times.

This is quite right at the beginning of the raffle, but it is not right to assume that because 100 of the 116 chances have been thrown without reaching 44, that the odds are only 15 to 1 that 44 will not be thrown in the remaining 16 chances. The odds are still 116 to 1 against 44, just as they were before the raffle began.

If you are going back to take into account the previous throws of the dice, you should know the 100 throws that were made with those dice before the raffle began.

CRAP SHOOTING.

This game is a simple form of Hazard, and when played " on the square," is one of the fairest of all games, the percentage in favour of either side being very small. It is rapidly replacing Faro as the gambling game of America.

Any number of persons may play, and any one may be the caster for the first throw. Two dice are used. The players bet a certain amount of money, and the caster covers it, or as much of it as he can. If the caster does not take all the bets offered, players may back him against the other players. The bets made, the caster shoots. If the total of the two dice on the first throw is seven or eleven, it is called a *nick,* or *natural,* and the caster immediately wins the stakes. If the first throw is two, three or twelve, it is a *crap,* and the caster immediately loses. If the caster throws any number, 4, 5, 6, 8, 9, or 10, that number is his *point,* and he must continue throwing until he throws the same number again, in which case he wins ; or throws a seven, in which case he loses.

Two dice may come up in thirty six different ways, each of which will produce one or more of eleven possible throws, running from 2 to 12. The most common throw is seven, because there are six ways that the two dice may come that will make seven ; 6–1, 5–2, 4–3, 3–4, 2–5 and 1–6. The most uncommon are two and twelve, because there is only one way for each of them to come ; double aces or double sixes. The numbers of different ways in which each throw may come are as follows :—

> 7 may come 6 different ways.
> 6 or 8 may come 5 different ways.
> 5 or 9 may come 4 different ways.
> 4 or 10 may come 3 different ways.
> 3 or 11 may come 2 different ways.
> 2 or 12 can come 1 way only.

When the caster makes his first throw, he has 8 chances out of 36 to get 7 or 11, which will win for him ; and 4 chances out of 36 to throw 2, 3 or 12, which will lose for him. It does not follow from this that the odds are 2 to 1 in favour of the caster, because there are only 12 throws out of the 36 possible that will bring any " action " on the bets ; so that the odds are 2 to 1 that the first throw will not settle the bets either way. After the first throw, the caster's chances vary according to his point. If his point was six, he would have 5 chances out of 36 to throw it again, while the players would have 6 chances out of 36 to get a seven. If the player's point is four or ten, the odds will be 6 to 3 against him ; because there are only three ways to get his point, while there are six ways to get a seven.

If the caster wins he shoots again, but when he loses he passes the dice to the next player in turn,

The old game of Hazard was a very complicated affair compared to modern craps, an intimate knowledge of odds and probabilities being requisite for success. The game was generally against the caster, and certain throws were barred when a certain number was the point. Those interested in the subject will find it exhaustively treated in George Lowbut's " Game of Hazard Investigated."

POKER DICE.

If ordinary dice are used, the aces rank above the sixes, the deuces being the lowest. Any number of persons may play, and five dice are used. Each in turn takes the box and has three throws, the first being made with all five dice. After the first throw the caster may lay aside any of the five dice he chooses, putting the others back in the box for a second throw. The same process of selection is allowed for the third throw, any or all five of the dice being available for the last throw. The second and third throws have the same effect as the draw at Poker, except that the dice player may draw twice if he wishes to, and may put back all or any of the dice that he kept on the first or second throws, or he may stand pat on any throw.

The object of the game is to secure pairs, triplets, full hands, and four or five of a kind. Straights do not count in Poker Dice. Suppose the player's first throw to be a pair of sixes. He places them on one side, and picks up the three other dice, throwing them over again. If the second throw produced another six, it would be placed with the first pair, making a triplet, and the two remaining dice would be thrown again. Whatever they produced would be the final value of his hand. The player is not obliged to throw again, if he is satisfied with his first or second throw ; neither is he obliged to leave any pairs or triplets. A player getting two small pairs on the first throw may put either or both of them back in the box again if he chooses.

In throwing for drinks or cigars, it is usual to throw **horse and horse ;** that is, if several persons are in the game the highest man on each round goes out, ties shake it off immediately, one hand each. After it gets down to two men, they shake for the best two out of three hands, and if each wins a hand they are horse and horse, and throw a third to decide it. The last person to throw on each round follows his lead, throwing the first hand on the next round.

TEN PINS WITH DICE.

Any number can play, and the score sheet is ruled off for ten frames, just as in ten pins. Only two dice are used, and they are rolled from a box. Sixes count nothing, and are " off the alley." Each player has three balls or rolls, and he can leave either one or both dice at the end of any throw. If he leaves one he picks up the other and throws it again, but he must abide by the figures appearing on the two dice at the end of his third throw. Suppose he throws double fives on his first throw; that is a *strike,* and is so scored, and the total pips appearing on the two dice at the end of his second throw on the next frame will count on the strike. Suppose he rolls five-deuce the first time. He leaves the five and rolls the other die again, getting another five. That is a *spare,* and the total pips on his first throw on the next frame will count on the spare. If he does not get a spare, it is a *break,* and the total pips on his two dice at the end of his third throw are scored.

It is usual to take up anything but fives on the first throw, on the chance of getting a spare. If a spare is not thrown on the second throw, most players leave anything as good as threes, and always leave fours ; but ace and treys are always thrown again.

BASE BALL WITH DICE.

There are two forms of this game. In the simpler any number of persons may play, and three dice are used. Each player throws in turn, the three dice representing his three strikes. Nothing but aces count, but each of them is a run ; and as long as a player makes runs he goes on throwing. When each player has had nine innings the game is ended, and the highest score wins.

The more complicated form of the game is to have a rough diagram of a base-ball diamond. The players take sides, and each is provided with three markers of different colours, such as red and white poker chips. Only one die is used, and it is thrown from a box. The captains of the teams throw for the first time at the bat, the higher throw winning the choice. Each player in turn of the side at the bat has one throw, and a marker is placed on the base he reaches. Ace, deuce, and trey count for first, second, and third bases respectively ; four is a home run. When a five or six is thrown, the result depends on the number of men on bases, but the striker is always out. If there are no men on bases, or if all the bases are full, the player is out if he throws five or six. If there is only one man on the bases and a five is thrown, the striker is *caught out,* and the man on the base is also caught. If six is thrown, only the striker is caught out, and the man holds his base. If there are two men on bases, they must be in one of three positions : on first and second ; on first and third ; or on second and third. In any position, only the striker is out on six thrown. In the last position, if five is thrown, the striker only is out, as the men cannot run. If there are men on first and second, and five is thrown, the striker is out, and the man on second is caught trying to steal third ; while the man on first holds his base. If five is thrown when there are men on first and third, the striker is out, and the man on third is safe, but the man on first is caught trying to steal second.

When bases are thrown, they are safe hits, and all the men on bases are advanced as many as the man at the bat throws. As soon as three men on each side have struck or been caught out by throwing five or six, the side is out, and all men left on bases count for nothing. As long as three men are not out, the side continues to send its men to the bat in regular order.

GOING TO BOSTON.

This game is known in the colonies as Yankee Grab, or Newmarket. Each player has three throws with three dice, and the highest die in each throw is laid aside. If two are equally high, only one is retained. The others are returned to the box and thrown again. The higher of these two is retained, and the third die is thrown again. The final total of the three dice is the player's score, and the highest wins. In the colonies the ace counts as seven. The game is usually played for a pool.

ACE IN THE POT.

Any number can play, and two dice are used. The game is for a pool, which is won by the final possessor of a single counter. At the beginning each player has two counters, and each in turn throws the two dice. If he throws an ace he pushes one of his counters into the pot ; two aces gets rid of both. If he throws a six on either die, he passes a counter to his left-hand neighbour, who will have the next throw. Two sixes passes both counters if the caster still has so many. The players throw in turn until all the counters but one have been placed in the pot. If a player has no counters, the throw passes him to the next player on his left who has counters in front of him. The last counter of all cannot be put in the pot by throwing an ace ; but it must be passed along to the left when a six is thrown. The player with the last counter in front of him must throw both dice three times in succession, and if he succeeds in avoiding a six, he keeps the counter and wins the pool. If he throws a six, the player who gets the counter must throw three times, and so on, until some one throws three times without getting a six. Instead of a pool, it is sometimes agreed that the final holder of the last counter shall pay for the refreshments.

MULTIPLICATION.

Any number can play, and three dice are used. Each player throws in turn, and the highest die is left on the table; if two are equally high, only one remains. The two other dice are thrown again, and the higher left. The sum of these two is then added together, and the third die is thrown as a multiplier, the result of the multiplication being the player's score.

ROUND THE SPOT.

Any number can play, and three dice are used. Nothing counts but the spots that surround a centre one; so that ace, deuce, four, and six count as blanks. The trey counts as 2, and the five as 4. Each player has three throws with the three dice, and the highest total wins.

VINGT-ET-UN.

Any number of persons can play, making up a pool for the winner. A single die is used, and each player in turn throws as often as he pleases. The object is to get as near twenty-one as possible without passing it, and it is usually considered best to stand at 18, but to throw again at 17. If a player goes beyond 21, he is out of it. The one getting nearest 21 takes the pool; ties divide it.

CENTENNIAL.

Two persons or sides play with three dice. The object of the game is to secure pips on the dice, or multiples of pips, which will make the figures from 1 to 12 in numerical order, and afterward the numbers from 12 to 1 again. The first side to accomplish this wins the game. There must be an ace in the first throw or nothing counts; that obtained, any following numbers may be made singly, or by adding two or more together. Suppose the first throw is 4, 2, 1. The 1 and 2 will make 1, 2 and 3. Then the 4, 1, 2 will make 4, 5, 6 and 7. Each side continues to throw until it fails to score, when the box must be passed to the adversary. If a combination is overlooked by one side, the other may count it if it continues the sequence on their side.

HELP YOUR NEIGHBOUR.

Six persons play, with three dice, and five points is Game. Each player has a number, from 1 to 6, and is provided with five counters, and the first to get rid of them wins. Each player in rotation has one throw, and no matter what he throws, the player whose number appears on the upper face of any die thrown, counts one point toward game. If No. 2 should throw a four and two sixes, for instance, he would count nothing himself, but No. 4 would count 1, and No. 6 would count 2 points toward game.

SHUFFLE BOARD.

Shuffle Board is played on a table 30 feet long and 20 inches wide, with a gutter running all round it. The board is sprinkled with very fine sand. Four weights are used by each side, marked A and B to distinguish them. These weights are of iron or brass, 2¼ inches in diameter, and ½ inch thick. Five inches from each end of the board and parallel with it, is the deuce line.

The object of the game is to push the weights from one end of the board to the other, each side playing one weight alternately until all four weights on each side are played. All pieces over the deuce line count 2, but if a piece hangs over the end of the board it is a **ship,** and counts 3. If there are no ships or deuces, the weight lying nearest to the deuce line counts one point. Only one ship or deuce can be counted in each round, so that only one side can score. The ship that overhangs the most, or the deuce nearest the edge, counts. Twenty-one points is game.

BILLIARDS.

THE TABLE. The standard American billiard table for championship games is ten feet by five ; but that in common use is nine by four and a half. The old tables for the four-ball game had only four pockets, but all modern pool tables have six. The English billiard tables are all twelve feet by six, with six pockets, which are used for both billiards and pool. The head of the table is the end from which the players make their opening shots, and the foot is that on which the red ball is spotted. The baulk is the space at the head of the table behind a line drawn from the second diamonds or "sights" through the white spot. The "D" is the semicircle on the baulk line on English tables.

American tables are made more difficult for championship games by drawing baulk lines 8 or 14 inches from the cushions, barring the rail nurse and the anchor shot. The English game is made difficult by making the cushions higher, the pockets narrower, and barring the spot stroke. The push shot is allowed in the English game, but in America it is permitted only in pool ; never in the carrom game.

The American carrom game cannot be played on an English table on account of the pockets. If the English game is played on an American pool table the red spot should be only nine inches from the bottom rail, and the "D" should be drawn with a radius of eleven inches from the white spot on the baulk line. The D is never marked on an American table, but the opening shot in the three-ball game must be made from within a semicircle of six inch radius from the white spot. In the four-ball game, and in all forms of American Pool, the player may place his ball anywhere within the baulk line.

THE BALLS. The American standard balls are $2\frac{3}{8}$ inches in diameter, while the English are only $2\frac{1}{16}$. Billiard balls should be carefully protected from sudden changes in temperature by being laid away in bran or sawdust in cold weather. It is a mistake to soak the balls in oil ; all they need is to be wiped off with a damp cloth, and polished with chamois skin. The three balls employed in both the English and American games are known as the *red, white,* and *spot white.* In play they are distinguished as the *cue ball,* which is the one struck by the player ; the *object ball,* which is the one that the cue ball first comes into contact with ; and the *carrom ball,* which is the second ball struck by the cue ball in making a carrom.

THE SHOTS. There are three shots common to billiards : The *carrom* or *cannon,* in which a count is made by the cue ball striking both the other balls on the table. The *winning hazard,* in which the object or the carrom ball is driven into a pocket. The *losing hazard,* in which the cue ball goes into a pocket after contact with another ball. There are five ways of making the principal shots at billiards, and they should be thoroughly mastered by every player. These are : The force, the follow, the draw, the massé, and the side stroke.

The first great principle in billiards is that the cue ball will always travel in the *direction* in which the cue is pointed. Hold-

ing the cue upward, downward or sidewise makes no difference ; the line of travel will be a prolongation of the line of the cue. In the three ways of striking the cue ball shown in the diagram in the margin, the ball will go in the direction of the arrow in each instance.

If the cue is held nearly level with the surface of the table the ball will be pushed or rolled along ; but if the cue is held perpendicularly, and the ball is struck directly on the top, the ball will be *pinched* to the table, as in the first figure in the margin, and will not move. If the ball is struck off the centre, as in the second figure, it will travel only a short distance, as a result of the cue's being forced past it toward the cloth, and will then return with a very strong retrograde motion after touching the

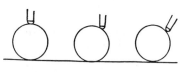

object ball. If the cue strikes too near the top, the pinch will be too strong for the cue ball to reach the object ball, and if the cue is not held perpendicularly, the ball will not return. If the cue points toward the centre of the ball, as in the third figure, the ball will be driven forward, without any tendency to return after striking the object ball. The latter shot is useful in making a "close follow," to avoid making a foul.

The Force Shot. The beginner at billiards should strike his ball always exactly in the centre, until he learns the angles. With moderate strength the effect of the stroke is to cause the ball to roll naturally along the cloth until it reaches the object ball, after which it will be deflected from its original course according to the angle at which the object ball is struck. If the cue ball is struck very hard, however, and very slightly below the centre, it will slide for a certain distance before beginning to roll, and if it reaches the object ball before this sliding motion ceases it will simply come to a stop, or go off at a right angle if the object ball is not struck exactly in the centre. This method of forcing a ball to go off at a right angle is called " screwing " in England.

The Follow Shot. If the cue ball is struck above the centre, the rolling motion is set up at once, no matter how hard the ball is struck, and the effect of contact with the object ball is simply to check the motion for a moment, after which the cue ball rolls forward again, deflected only by the angle at which the object ball was struck. The great art in making follow shots is to let the cue follow the ball, the tip passing at least three inches beyond where

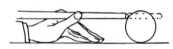

the ball stood, as shown by the dotted lines in the diagram. When the balls are very close together the cue must be lifted, and the ball struck very much on one side, the cue being behind the centre, as shown in the third position in the diagram of pinch shots.

The Draw Shot. This is exactly the reverse of the follow shot, the ball being struck below the centre, and the cue passing at least three inches beyond where the ball stood, as shown in the diagram. This gives the cue ball a retrograde motion, similar to that imparted to a child's hoop by spinning it backward while throwing it forward, so

as to make it return. If the object ball is reached before this retrograde motion is exhausted, the effect will be to stop the forward motion of the cue ball, and to give what is left of the retrograde motion full play, making the cue ball return. The two great mistakes made by beginners in playing draw shots are that they pull the cue back, instead of driving it clear through the ball aimed at, and that they strike so hard that the forward motion of the cue ball is too strong for the retrograde motion to overcome it, or the object ball to stop it. It is never necessary to strike harder **than** sufficient to reach the object ball and get back to the carrom **ball,** unless one is playing for position.

When the balls are so close together that to run the cue through **the** ball would make a foul shot, the draw may still be made by pointing the cue off to the side, and pushing it past the cue ball, instead of through it. This will secure the retrograde motion, but accompanied by a great deal of twist, which must be calculated for if the cue ball is to strike a cushion. A short draw may also be made by using the pinch.

The Massé. Most players imagine this to be a very difficult shot, but it is extremely simple if the principle of the direction of the cue and the effect of the pinch are kept in view. If we place the three balls in a straight line, about four inches apart, we have the simplest form of the massé. To find the exact spot at which the cue ball must be struck, join the centres of the cue and object

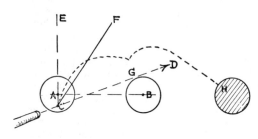

balls by an imaginary line A-B. At right angles to this will be a line A-E, and no matter which side of the ball B you wish to massé upon, your cue must strike the ball A somewhere on the line A-E. Suppose you wish to massé to the left, as shown in the diagram. The pinch must be made on the ball about a quarter from the top, the cue being pointed in the direction in which you want the ball to go, which will be to the extreme edge of B, on the line C-D. The cue must be held at an angle of about 70 degrees. A firm but light blow with a well chalked cue will pinch your ball toward E ; but the direction of the cue will propel it toward D. If the cue has been held at the right angle, and you have not struck too hard, the ball will feel the effect of these two forces equally, which will make it move toward a point half way between D and E, which will be F. The retrograde motion being stronger than the propulsion of the pinch, will gradually overcome it, and the ball will return toward G. Contact with the ball B will cause it to lose all but the forward motion, and it will roll easily toward H, making the carrom.

The Side Stroke. It is a popular delusion that the only way to change the course of a ball is by giving it " twist," " English," or " side." Side has little or no influence on the cue ball until it touches a cushion. Striking above or below the centre is all that is necessary. If it is required to vary the angle at which the object ball is to be struck, the distance below the centre will change the angle of direction in the cue ball without any side stroke. The art of accomplishing this is called *compensation,* an illustration of which is given in the diagram, A being the cue ball, and

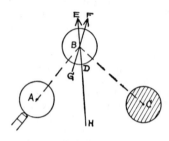

B the object ball. This is a half draw or force shot, the ball being struck about half way between its centre and the cloth. If we draw imaginary lines connecting the centres of A-B and B-C, and bisect the angle, we get the point **D**, which the cue ball must strike to make the carrom. This will drive the object ball in the direction D-E ; but if it is desirable that the object ball should go more in the direction G-F, so as to secure a better position for the next shot, the cue ball will have to strike at G, which will make a draw shot, bringing it back in the direction H, securing the position, but missing the count. In this position the ignorant player puts on side, but all that is necessary to compensate for this deviation in the point of impact is to approach the point of the cue toward the centre of the ball the exact distance that the point G is from the point D. The higher the point of the cue is raised, the further the ball will go from the line D-H. If struck much above the centre, it will follow through the object ball, passing beyond the ball C altogether.

When side is put upon a ball, it spins in that direction. If it is struck on the left, and then goes to a cushion directly in front of it, it will tend to fly off the cushion toward the left, making the angle wider. If a ball spinning to the left goes to a cushion on the left, it will tend to make the angle smaller, and the effect so produced is called *reverse English,* which tends to slow the cue ball.

THE AMERICAN GAME.

In the American game every carrom counts one point, and the number of points that will constitute a game must be agreed upon before play begins. The players string for the lead, the one bringing his ball nearer the head cushion having the choice of balls and of the first shot.

The great art in the American game is to keep the balls in front of you, so as to leave yourself a comparatively easy shot. Every time you get the cue ball between the two others you will find yourself in difficulties ; but whenever both the balls are in front of the cue ball, there will be some chance to score. When there is a choice of several ways of making a shot, the balls being wide apart, it will usually be found that one of them will bring the balls into better position than the others, and for that reason it is

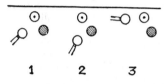

called a *gathering shot.* The expert tries to get the balls on the rail by a series of these gathering shots, and if any of the three positions shown in the diagram can be arrived at, a large run may be made by the *rail nurse.*

When the balls are not left in one of these positions they are said to *break,* but there are several positions in which they may be recovered by a kiss or a massé shot. In No. 4, the player must be careful to come back on the proper side of the carrom ball, so as to get back to position 2, if possible.

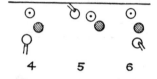

When the player reaches the corner, there are three principal

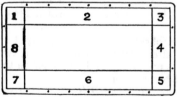

positions for accomplishing the turn. In the first shown, the spot white must be touched very lightly on the left side, the cue ball going to the cushion with a strong English on the right side. In the second position, the red ball is barely touched. The third position is a light force shot · but would be a half follow if the spot white were further out.

BAULK-LINE BILLIARDS.

Professionals became so skilful in rail nursing that the baulk-line was introduced to keep the balls away from the rail. This is a chalk line, eight or fourteen inches from the cushions, according

1	2	3
8		4
7	6	5

to agreement, dividing the table into eight baulk spaces, as shown in the diagram.

It is foul if more than two successive shots are made on balls both of which are within any one of the eight interdicted spaces. Both balls being within the space, the striker can play on them once without sending either out; his next stroke must send at least one out. Should it return, and both balls be again inside, he can play one shot, as before, without sending either out. This process may be repeated *ad libitum*. Should the second stroke fail to send a ball out it does not count, the striker's hand is out, and the next striker plays at the balls as he finds them.

The great art in baulk-line nursing is to get the object and carrom balls astride the line, and then to follow the principle of the rail nurse. The *anchor* shot is now barred in championship games. It consisted in getting two balls frozen to the cushion astride of one end of a line, and then just rubbing their faces with the cue ball. In the baulk-line nurse there are three principal

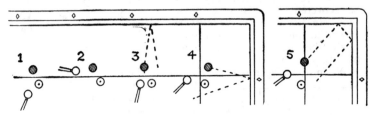

positions, and two turns, as shown in the diagram. In No. 3 the red ball must be driven to the rail and back with great accuracy, leaving the balls in position No. 1 again. The turns are very difficult.

CUSHION CARROMS.

This is a variety of the three-ball game in which a cushion must be touched by the cue ball before the carrom is completed. The cushion may be struck first, and the object ball afterward, or the object ball first, and then the cushion. In the *Three-cushion Carrom Game,* three cushions must be touched by the cue ball before completing the count. In the *Bank-shot Game,* the cue ball must strike at least one cushion before touching the object ball.

The *Four-ball Game* is now obsolete. It was first played on a table with corner pockets, and afterward on a carrom table, two red balls being used, one spotted on the red and the other on the white spot. Two carroms could be made on one shot.

The following are the most important *LAWS* of the carrom game, and are copied by permission from the 1897 edition of the " Laws of Billiards," published by the Brunswick-Balke-Collender Co.

AMERICAN BILLIARD LAWS.

1. The game is begun by stringing for the lead ; the player who brings his ball nearest to the cushion at the head of the table winning the choice of balls and the right to play first or to compel his opponent to play. Should the striker fail to count, his opponent makes the next play, aiming at will at either ball on the table.

2. A carrom consists in hitting both object-balls with the cue-ball in a fair and unobjectionable way ; each carrom will count *one* for the player. A penalty of *one* shall also be counted against the player for every miss occurring during the game.

3. A ball forced off the table is put back on its proper spot. Should the player's ball jump off the table after counting, the count is good, the ball is spotted, and the player plays from the spot.

4. If in playing a shot the cue is not withdrawn from the cue-ball before the cue-ball comes in contact with the object-ball, the shot is foul, the player loses his count, and his hand is out.

5. If the balls are disturbed accidentally through the medium of any agency other than the player himself, they must be replaced and the player allowed to proceed.

6. If in the act of playing the player disturbs any ball other than his own, he cannot make a counting stroke, but he may play for safety. Should he disturb a ball after having played successfully, he loses his count on that shot ; his hand is out, and the ball so disturbed is placed back as nearly as possible in the position which it formerly occupied on the table, the other balls remaining where they stop.

7. Should a player touch his own ball with the cue or otherwise previous to playing, it is foul, the player loses one, and cannot play for safety. It sometimes happens that the player after having touched his ball gives a second stroke, then the balls remain where they stop, or are replaced as nearly as possible in their former position at the option of his opponent.

8. When the cue-ball is very near another, the player shall not play without warning his adversary that they do not touch, and giving him sufficient time to satisfy himself on that point.

9. When the cue-ball is in contact with another, the balls are spotted and the player plays with his ball in hand.

10. Playing with the wrong ball is foul. However, should the player using the wrong ball play more than one shot with it, he shall be entitled to his score just the same as if he had played with his own ; as soon as his hand is out, the white balls must change places, and the game proceed as usual.

ON FOUL STROKES.—It is a foul, and no count can be made :

1. If a stroke is made except with the point of the cue.

2. If the cue is not withdrawn from the cue-ball before the latter comes in contact with an object-ball.

3. If the striker, when in hand, plays from any position not within the six-inch radius.

4. If, in the act of striking, he has not at least one foot *touching* the floor.

5. If he strikes while a ball is in motion, unless it has come to a rest, as provided in Sec. 10 on Foul Strokes.

6. If he plays with the wrong ball, except as provided in foregoing Law 10.

7. If the player touches the cue-ball more than once in any way, or hinders or accelerates it in any other way than by a legitimate stroke of the cue ; or if, during a stroke or after it, he in any way touches, hinders, or accelerates an object-ball, except by the one stroke of the cue-ball to which he is entitled.

8. As touching any ball *in any way* is a stroke, a second touch is a foul.

9. It is a foul against the striker if any ball be disturbed, hastened, or hindered by an opponent or any one but himself, whether the ball or balls are at rest while he is aiming or striking, in motion after he has struck, or at rest again after he has struck, and pending his again taking aim.

10. Should a ball that has once come to a standstill move without apparent cause, while the player is preparing to strike, it shall be replaced. Should it move before he can check his stroke, it, and all other balls set in motion by that stroke, shall be replaced, and the player shall repeat his shot, inasmuch as but for the moving of the ball, he might have counted where he missed, or missed where he counted.

11. It is a foul if the striker plays directly at any ball with which his own is in fixed contact, and the striker must in this instance play from balls spotted, as in the opening stroke of the game.

12. It is a foul to place marks of any kind upon the cloth or cushions as a guide to play ; also foul to practise the banking shot for the lead-off upon the plea of testing the balls.

13. It is a foul against the non-striker, and the striker cannot make a count on the ensuing shot, if a ball in play is lifted from the table, except it be unavoidable in those cases in which it is provided that, because of foul or irregular strokes, the balls shall be transposed or replaced.

14. In order to restrict deliberate playing for safety, it shall be optional with the non-striker, if his opponent makes a miss in each one of three successive innings, to accept the third miss or to reject it and force his antagonist to hit at least one object-ball ; and for this purpose that antagonist's ball shall be replaced by the referee. Should two balls be hit by this stroke, there shall be no count.

FIFTEEN-BALL POOL.

The most successful pool player is not the one who can make difficult winning hazards with the greatest accuracy, but he who thoroughly understands playing for position. If he is familiar with the principles of the force, the follow, the draw, and the side stroke, he should invariably be able to leave himself in a good position for each succeeding shot ; but unless he plans for position in advance, he can never hope to be more than an average player. To attain to proficiency in this there is no better training than playing so many balls or " no count."

There are some shots peculiar to winning hazards which should be understood by every pool player, and they are illustrated in the accompanying diagrams.

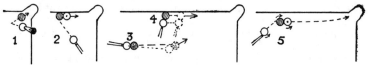

No. 1 is the *stirabout,* and is a combination of the pinch and push shots. It is used when the cue and object balls are both very close to the pocket, but not in such a position as to allow the the player to "cut" the ball in. The cue is held perpendicularly, and as low down on the ball as it will hold without slipping off. The ball is then slowly rolled over with the point of the cue until the cue begins to descend on the other side. The cue ball is then pushed against the object ball, still with the point of the cue. **No. 2** will drive the spot white into the pocket if it is frozen to the red ball. **No. 3** is a very useful push shot when the balls are close together. The cue is kept steadily on the cue ball until the object ball has been pushed to one side. The moment the latter is at the proper angle to run into the pocket the cue is applied sharply, and then withdrawn. **No. 4** is a push shot used when the balls are frozen to the cushion. The cue ball must be kept in contact with the object ball until the latter has acquired sufficient momentum to

reach the pocket. **No. 5** is a shot which was thought impossible until a few years ago. It depends on the communication of side to the object ball. The cue ball is struck very much on the side, almost like a massé, the spin thus given being communicated to the object ball and from that to the second ball, to which it must be frozen. The result will be that the second ball will make a slight curve on its way to the pocket.

False Angles. In playing bank shots it is sometimes necessary to make the object ball come back from the cushion at a smaller angle than the natural one. Some players imagine this can be done by putting side on the cue ball, but such is not the case. It is accomplished by striking so hard that the ball buries itself in the cushion, the result of which is that the angle of reflection is less than that of incidence. It is possible to drive an object ball to the rail at an angle of 60 degrees with such force that after crossing the table twice it will come off at a perfect right angle from the cushion. This is a very useful shot in banking for the side pockets, and also in playing for the 1 or 4 pin at Pin Pool.

The following **LAWS** for Fifteen-Ball Pool are copied, by permission, from the 1897 edition of the rules published by the Brunswick-Balke-Collender Co.

1. The game of Fifteen-Ball Pool is played with fifteen balls numbered from one to fifteen, respectively, and one white ball not numbered. The latter is the cue-ball, and at the opening of the game, the player plays with it from within the string at the head of the table, at any of the numbered balls, and afterward as he finds it on the table, his object being to pocket as many of the numbered balls as he can, the number on each ball he pockets being scored to his credit ; so that not he who pockets the largest number of balls, but he whose score, when added up, yields the largest total, wins the game. Before commencing the game these fifteen balls are placed in the form of a triangle upon the table—a triangular frame being employed for this purpose to insure correctness. The ball numbered fifteen is so placed upon the table as to form the apex of the triangle, pointing upward toward the head of the table, and in forming the triangle the fifteen-ball should rest as nearly as possible upon the spot known as the deep-red spot in the Three-Ball Game. The other balls should have their places in the triangle so that the highest numbers shall be nearest the apex, the lowest numbers forming the base.

2. The player who makes the opening stroke must play from within the string from the head of the table and must strike the pyramid of object-balls with such force as to make at least two of the object-balls strike a cushion, or at least one object-ball go into a pocket. Should he fail to do either he forfeits three points and the next player plays. All balls pocketed on the opening stroke count for the player, and it is not necessary for him to call the numbers of the balls he intends pocketing before making the opening stroke.

3. Before making any other stroke except the opening stroke the player must *distinctly* call the number of the ball he intends to pocket, but he need not designate the particular pocket into which he intends to put it. Unless he calls the ball pocketed it does not count for him, and must be placed on the deep-red spot, or if that be occupied, as nearly below it as possible. The player loses his hand but does not forfeit any points, and the next player plays. Should he call more than one ball he must pocket all the balls he calls, otherwise none of them can be counted for him.

4. After the opening stroke each player must either pocket a ball, make an *object*-ball strike a cushion, or the cue-ball strike a cushion after contact with an object-ball, under penalty of forfeiture of three points. Three forfeitures in succession loses the game for the player making them.

5. Should the player pocket, by the same stroke, more balls than he calls, he is entitled to the balls he pockets, provided he pockets the called ball.

6. A forfeiture of three points is deducted from the player's score for making a miss; pocketing his own ball; forcing his own ball off the table; failing to make the opening stroke, as provided in Rule 2; failing either to make an object-ball strike a cushion or go into a pocket, as provided in Rule 4; striking his own ball twice; playing out of his turn, if detected doing so before he has made more than one counting stroke.

7. A ball whose centre is on the string line must be regarded as within the line.

8. If the player pocket one or more of the object-balls, and his own ball goes into a pocket, or off the table from the stroke, he cannot score for the numbered balls, which must be placed on the spot known as the deep-red spot, or if it be occupied as nearly below it as possible on a line with that spot.

AMERICAN PYRAMID POOL.

The fifteen balls are numbered from one to fifteen respectively, and are usually colored red, but the numbers on the balls are used simply for convenience in calling the number of each ball which the player intends to pocket and do not in any way affect the score of the player, which is determined by the number of balls pocketed. Scratches pay one ball, which must be placed on the deep read spot.

CONTINUOUS POOL.

In Continuous Pool, the scoring of the game is continued until all the balls in each frame have been pocketed, and the game may consist of any number of balls or points up which may be agreed upon. Each ball pocketed scores one point for the striker and the game is usually scored upon the string of buttons over the table, as in regular billiards. Penalties are paid through deducting points from the offending player's score or string of buttons, instead of forfeiting a ball to the table as in regular pyramid pool. The numbers on the balls are simply used for convenience in calling the number of each ball which the player intends to pocket, and do not in any way affect the score of the player.

ENGLISH PYRAMID POOL.

This differs from the American game in several points. There are no "call shots," the player being entitled to every ball he pockets, whether he played for it or not. All balls in hand must be played from a D, 21 to 23 inches in diameter. There is no rule about driving two balls to the cushion on the opening shot. When all the red balls but one are pocketed, the red and white balls are used as cue balls alternately. If there are only two players, and only two balls on the table, the red and white, if either player makes a miss or goes in the pocket himself, that ends the game ; but if there are more than two players another red ball is spotted, as in the American game. The baulk line is no protection, a player in hand being allowed to play on any ball on the table, even if it is behind the D.

SHELL OUT.

This game should not be confounded with Black Pool. It is simply English Pyramids, but instead of making the player with the lowest score at the end pay for the table, each player equally shares the expense, and the balls are pocketed for so much apiece. If the amount of the shell-out was a shilling, and there were six players, any person pocketing a ball would receive a shilling from each of the others, and would play again. A losing hazard or a miss would compel the striker to pay a shilling to each of the others, instead of putting a ball back on the table. The last ball pays double.

HIGH-LOW-JACK-GAME.

This game is played with a set of balls the same as used in Fifteen-Ball Pool.

Any number of persons may play, the order of play being determined by the rolling of the small numbered balls.

The fifteen-ball is High; the one-ball is Low; the nine-ball is Jack; and the highest aggregate is Game. Seven points generally constitute a game.

In cases where players have one and two to go to finish game, the first balls holed count out first, be they High, Low, or Jack.

In setting up the pyramid the three counting balls—High, Low, Jack—are placed in the centre, with High at the head of the three named balls, the other balls as in regular Fifteen-Ball Pool.

When players have each one to go, instead of setting up an entire frame of pyramids, a ball is placed at the foot of the table, in direct line with the spots, and at a distance from the lower cushion equal to the diameter of another of the pool balls. This ball must be pocketed by banking it to one or more cushions. The player who pockets the ball wins the game.

FORTY-ONE POOL.

Forty-One Pool is played with a regular Fifteen-Ball Pool set of balls, the object of play being to pocket a sufficient number of the pool balls which added to the private small ball shall score exactly 41.

CHICAGO POOL.

This game is played with the numbered pool balls from 1 to 15 and a white cue-ball, as in Fifteen-Ball Pool, the object being to play upon and pocket the balls in their numerical order.

The table is laid out for the game by placing the one ball against the end cushion at the first right-hand diamond sight at the foot of the table, the two-ball is placed at the centre diamond sight on same cushion; the remaining thirteen balls are placed in the order of their numbers at the succeeding diamond sights. The three sights on the end rail at head of the table are not occupied by any ball.

The opening stroke *must* be to strike the *one*-ball. If that ball is holed it is placed to the credit of the player, and he continues his hand until he fails to score, but in continuing he must play each time upon the ball bearing the lowest number on the table. After playing upon that ball, however, should any other be pocketed by the same stroke, irrespective of its number, it shall be placed to the player's credit so pocketing it.

If the line of aim at the ball required to be hit is covered by another ball, the player may resort to a bank play or massé, etc., but should he fail to hit the required ball he forfeits three, receiving a scratch.

ENGLISH POOL.

This game is known in England as Colom-Ball, or Following Pool. The balls are placed in a pool bottle, and shaken up by the marker, who then gives one to each candidate for play in rotation. The player who receives the white ball places it on the spot, and the one who gets the red ball plays from within the D at the head of the table. The marker calls the colour of the player whose turn it is, and notifies him which ball will play on him, so that he may play for safety if he can. The following are Brunswick-Balke-Collender Co.'s rules :

The WHITE BALL is spotted.

RED BALL plays upon	. . . .	WHITE.
YELLOW	"	. . . . RED.
GREEN	"	. . . . YELLOW.
BROWN	"	. . . . GREEN.
BLUE	"	. . . . BROWN.
PINK	"	. . . . BLUE.
SPOT-WHITE	"	. . . . PINK.
SPOT-RED	"	. . . . SPOT-WHITE.
SPOT-YELLOW	"	. . . . SPOT-RED.
SPOT-GREEN	"	. . . . SPOT-YELLOW.
SPOT-BROWN	"	. . . . SPOT-GREEN.
SPOT-BLUE	"	. . . . SPOT-BROWN, and
WHITE	"	. . . . SPOT-BLUE.

1. When coloured balls are used, the players must play progressively, as the colours are placed on the pool marking-board, the top colour being No. 1.

2. Each player has *three* lives at starting. No. 1 places his ball on the " winning and losing " spot, No. 2 plays at No. 1, No. 3 at No. 2, and so on—each person playing at the last ball, unless the striker's ball be in hand, when he plays at the nearest ball.

3. When a striker loses a life the next in rotation plays at the ball nearest to his own ; but if this player's ball be in hand, he plays at the ball nearest to the centre of the baulkline, whether it be in or out of baulk.

4. When any doubt arises as to the nearest ball, the marker measures the distance, and the player strikes at the ball declared to be nearest his own.

5. The baulk is no protection.

6. The player loses a life by pocketing his own ball off another, by running a coup, by missing the ball played on, by forcing his ball off the table, by playing *with* the wrong ball, by playing *at* the wrong ball, by playing out of his turn, by striking the wrong ball, or by having his ball pocketed by the next striker.

7. Should the striker pocket the ball he plays at, and by the same stroke pocket his own or force it over the table, *he* loses a life and not the person whose ball he pocketed.

8. Should the player strike the wrong ball, he pays the same forfeit to the person whose ball he should have played at as he would have done if he had pocketed it himself.

9. If the striker miss the ball he ought to play at, and by the same stroke pocket another ball, *he* loses a life, and not the person whose ball he pocketed ; in which case the striker's ball must be taken up, and both balls remain in hand until it be their several turns to play.

10. If the player inquire as to which is his ball, or if it be his turn to play, the marker or the players must give him the information sought.

11. If the striker, while taking aim, inquire which is the ball he ought to play at, and should be misinformed by the marker or by any of the company, he does not lose a life. His ball must in this case be replaced and the stroke played again.

12. When a ball or balls touch the striker's ball, or are in line between it and the ball he has to play at, so that it will prevent him hitting *any part of the object-ball*, such ball or balls must be taken up until the stroke be played, and, after the balls have ceased running, they must be replaced.

13. If a ball or balls are in the way of a striker's cue, so that he cannot play at his ball, he can have them taken up.

14. When the striker *takes* a life, he continues to play on as long as he can pocket a ball, or until the balls are all off the table, in which latter case he places his own ball on the spot as at the commencement.

15. The first player who loses his three lives is entitled to purchase, or **star,** by paying into the pool a sum equal to his original stake, for which he receives lives equal in number to the lowest number of lives on the board.

16. If the player first out refuse to star, the second player out may do so; but if the second refuse, the third may star, and so on, until only two players are left in the pool, when the privilege of starring ceases.

17. Only one star is allowed in a pool.

18. If the striker move his own or any other ball *while in the act of striking*, the stroke is foul; and if, by the same stroke, he pocket a ball or force it off the table, the owner of that ball does not lose a life, and the ball so pocketed must be placed on its original spot. But if by that foul stroke the player pocket his own ball or force it off the table, *he* loses a life.

19. If the striker's ball touch the one he has to play at, he is at liberty either to play at it or at any other ball on the table, and such stroke is not to be considered foul; in such a case, however, the striker loses a life by running his ball into a pocket or forcing it over the table.

20. If, after making a hazard, the striker takes up his ball, or stops it before it has done running, he cannot claim the life for the ball pocketed.

21. If, before a star, two or more balls, each having one life, are pocketed by the same stroke, the owner of the first ball struck can star; but if he refuse, the other player whose ball was pocketed may star.

22. Should the striker's ball stop on the place from which a ball has been taken up, the ball which has been removed must remain in hand until the spot is unoccupied, when it is to be replaced.

23. Should the striker's ball miss the ball played at, no person except the striker is allowed to stop the ball till it has ceased running or struck another ball.

24. Should the striker have his next player's ball removed, and his own ball stop on the spot it occupied, the next player must give a miss from baulk, for which miss he does not lose a life.

25. When a ball has been taken up, and any other than the next player's ball stop on the spot it occupied, the ball so taken up must remain in hand till it can be replaced. But if it be the turn of the ball in hand to play before the one occupying its proper place, the latter must be taken up till there be room to replace it.

26. If the corner of the cushion should prevent the striker from playing in a direct line, he can have any ball removed for the purpose of playing at the object-ball from a cushion.

27. When three players, each with one life, remain in a pool, and the striker make a miss, the other two divide without a stroke.

28. Neither of the last two players can star, but if they are left with an equal number of lives each they may divide the pool; the striker, however, is entitled to his stroke before the division.

29. All disputes are to be decided by the marker; but if he be interested in the game, they shall then be settled by a majority of the players.

BLACK POOL.

This is a variation of English Colour-Ball Pool. A black ball is placed on the centre spot. The colours follow one another just as in English pool, until all the balls have come upon the table. After that, any ball on the table may be played at, and if it is pocketed, the player has the option of playing at the black ball, If he pockets it, each player pays him the amount of a life, so that the player whose ball was first pocketed would have to pay two, one for his own ball and one for the black. If a ball is pocketed before the balls are all on the table, the player may play on the black; but the following players must play on their colours until the first round is complete. No one is ever dead, and the game may be continued indefinitely, although half an hour is the usual limit. The players share the expense of the table, as at Shell-out.

ENGLISH BILLIARDS.

This game is played with three balls, one red and two white. Every winning hazard off the red counts 3; hazards off the white count 2, and all carroms count 2. If a player makes a carrom and a losing hazard on the same stroke, it counts 5 if the red was the object ball; 4 if the white was the object ball. A player may make 10 on one stroke by playing on the red, making a carrom, and pocketing all three balls. A miss counts one for the adversary; but if the player who makes a miss runs into a pocket or jumps off the table, his adversary counts 3.

The secret of success in the English game is not in gathering shots or rail nursing, but in repeated position; that is, playing shots so that the object ball returns to its position, the cue ball falling into a pocket and being played again from an advantageous position in the D. If the red ball is left in a good position for a losing hazard in either of the side pockets, the player should place his own ball in such a position in the D that he can drive the red to the bottom cushion and back again, leaving himself another easy hazard in the side pockets.

If the red is near a bottom pocket, and the player's ball is in hands, the beginner will invariably leave the red ball in baulk, even if he makes the hazard. The reason is that he strikes with just force enough to reach the red and go into the pocket, and this force is just enough to drive the red about the same distance in the opposite direction, leaving it where the cue ball came from—in baulk.

The English do not understand gathering shots, nursing, and cushion carroms so well as the Americans, and play chiefly for the winning and losing hazards. The objective point of the expert is the ***spot stroke,*** which consists in getting exactly behind the red ball when it is on its spot, and then driving it into the corner pocket, returning the cue ball to its position with a light draw shot. If the cue ball fails to come back exactly behind the red the position may be recovered in several ways, some of which are shown in the diagrams.

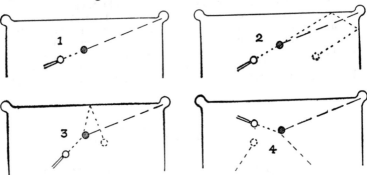

No. 1 is the perfect position for the spot stroke; the dotted lines in the others show the course that must be followed by the cue ball to recover the initial position.

Man-of-war Game is a variety of English billiards in which there are three white balls, each belonging to different players.

The following ***LAWS*** are taken, by permission, from the rules published by the Brunswick-Balke-Collender Co.

ENGLISH BILLIARD LAWS.

1. The choice of balls and order of play shall, unless mutually agreed upon by the two players, be determined by stringing ; and the striker whose ball stops nearest the lower [or bottom] cushion, after being forced from baulk up the table, may take which ball he likes, and play, or direct his opponent to play first, as he may deem expedient.

2. The red ball shall, at the opening of every game, be placed on the top [or red] spot, and replaced after being pocketed or forced off the table, or whenever the balls are broken.

3. Whoever breaks the balls, *i. e.*, opens the game, must play out of baulk, though it is not necessary that he shall strike the red ball.

4. The game shall be adjudged in favour of whoever first scores the number of points agreed on, when the marker shall call "game"; or it shall be given against whoever, after having once commenced, shall neglect or refuse to continue when called upon by his opponent to play.

5. If the striker scores by his stroke he continues until he ceases to make any points, when his opponent follows on.

6. If when moving the cue backward and forward, and prior to a stroke, it touches and moves the ball, the ball must be replaced to the satisfaction of an adversary, otherwise it is a foul stroke ; but if the player strikes, and grazes any part of the ball with any part of the cue, it must be considered a stroke, and the opponent follows on.

7. If a ball rebounds from the table, and is prevented in any way, or by any object except the cushion, from falling to the ground, or if it lodges on a cushion and remains there, it shall be considered off the table, unless it is the red, which must be spotted.

8. A ball on the brink of the pocket need not be "challenged" : if it ceases running and remains stationary, then falls in, it must be replaced, and the score thus made does not count.

9. Any ball or balls behind the baulk-line, or resting exactly upon the line, are not playable if the striker be in hand, and he must play out of baulk before hitting another ball.

10. Misses may be given with the point or butt of the cue, and shall count one for each against the player ; or if the player strike his ball with the cue more than once a penalty shall be enforced, and the non-striker may oblige him to play again, or may call on the marker to place the ball at the point it reached or would have reached when struck first. [The butt may also be used for playing a ball in hand up the table in order to strike a ball in baulk.]

11. Foul strokes do not score to the player, who must allow his opponent to follow on. They are made thus: By striking a ball twice with the cue ; by touching with the hand, ball, or cue an opponent's or the red ball ; by playing with the wrong ball ; by lifting both feet from the floor when playing; by playing at the striker's own ball and displacing it ever so little (except while taking aim, when it shall be replaced, and he shall play again).

12. The penalty for a foul stroke is losing the lead, and, in case of a score, an opponent must have the red ball spotted, and himself break the balls, when the player who made the foul must follow suit, both playing from the D. If the foul is not claimed the player continues to score, if he can.

13. After being pocketed or forced off the table the red ball must be spotted on the top spot, but if that is occupied by another ball the red must be placed on the centre spot between the middle pockets.

14. If in taking aim the player moves his ball and causes it to strike another, even without intending to make a stroke, a foul stroke may be claimed by an adversary. (See Rule Fifteenth.)

15. If a player fail to hit another ball, it counts one to his opponent ; but if by the same stroke the player's ball is forced over the table or into any pocket it counts three to his opponent.

16. Forcing any ball off the table, either before or after the score, causes the striker to gain nothing by the stroke.

17. In the event of either player using his opponent's ball and scoring, the red must be spotted and the balls broken again by the non-striker ; but if no score is made, the next player may take his choice of balls and continue to use the ball he so chooses to the end of the game. No penalty, however, attaches in either case unless the mistake be discovered before the next stroke.

18. No person except an opponent has a right to tell the player that he is using the wrong ball, or to inform the non-striker that his opponent has used the wrong ball ; and if the opponent does not see the striker use the ball, or, seeing him, does not claim the penalty, the marker is bound to score to the striker any points made.

19. Should the striker [whose ball is in hand], in playing up the table on a ball or balls in baulk, either by accident or design, strike one of them [with his own ball] without first going out of baulk, his opponent may have the balls replaced, score a miss, and follow on ; or may cause the striker to play again, or may claim a foul, and have the red spotted and the balls broken again.

20. The striker, when in hand, may not play at a cushion within the baulk (except by going first up the table) so as to hit balls that are within or without the line.

21. If in hand, and in the act of playing, the striker shall move his ball with insufficient strength to take it out of baulk, it shall be counted as a miss to the opponent, who, however, may oblige him to replace his ball and play again. [Failing to play out of baulk, the player may be compelled to play his stroke over again.]

22. If in playing a pushing stroke the striker pushes more than once it is unfair, and any score he may make does not count. His opponent follows by breaking the balls.

23. If in the act of drawing back his cue the striker knocks the ball into a pocket, it counts three to the opponent, and is reckoned a stroke.

24. If a foul stroke be made while giving a miss, the adversary may enforce the penalty or claim the miss, but he cannot do both.

25. If either player take up a ball, unless by consent, the adversary may have it replaced, or may have the balls broken; but if any other person touches or takes up a ball it must be replaced by the marker as nearly as possible.

26. If, after striking, the player or his opponent should by any means obstruct or hasten the speed of any ball, it is at the opponent or player's option to have them replaced, or to break the balls.

27. No player is allowed to receive, nor any by-stander to offer advice on the game; but should any person be appealed to by the marker or either player he has a right to offer an opinion; or if a spectator sees the game wrongly marked he may call out, but he must do so prior to another stroke.

28. The marker shall act as umpire, but any question may be referred by either player to the company, the opinion of the majority of whom shall be acted upon.

PIN POOL.

The game of Pin Pool is played with two white balls and one red, together with five small wooden pins, which are set up in the middle of the table, diamond fashion, each pin having a value to accord with the position it occupies.

4*

3* 5* 2*

I*

The pin nearest the string line is No. 1 ; that to the right of it is No. 2 ; to the left, No. 3 ; the pin farthest from the string line is No. 4 ; and the central or black pin, No. 5. These numbers may be chalked on the cloth in front of each particular pin.

Neither carroms nor hazards count ; for pocketing a ball (when playing on a pocket table), or causing it to jump off the table or lodge on the cushion, or for missing altogether, nothing is forfeited other than the stroke. The only penalty is that the ball so offending shall be spotted upon the white-ball spot at the foot of the table, or if that be occupied then on the nearest spot thereto unoccupied.

When the pins are arranged, the rotation of the players is determined in like manner as in Fifteen-Ball Pool, after which each player receives from the marker a little numbered ball which is placed in the player's cup on the pool board, and the number of which is not known to any of his opponents.

The object of the player is to knock down as many pins as will count exactly thirty-one when the number on the small ball held by him is added to their aggregate ; thus, if the small ball is No. 9, the player will have to gain twenty-two points on the pins before calling game, and whoever first gets exactly thirty-one points in this manner wins the pool.

A white ball is spotted five inches from the lower end of the table, on a line drawn down the centre ; and the red ball placed upon its own spot at the foot of the table.

Player No. 1 must play with the remaining white ball from any point within the string-line at the head of the table at either the red or white ball, or place his own on the string spot. Player No. 2 may play with any ball on the table—red or white. After the first stroke has been played, the players, in their order, may play with or at any ball upon the board.

Unless the player has played on some ball upon the board before knocking down a pin, the stroke under all circumstances goes for nothing, and the pin or pins must be replaced and the player's ball put upon the white-ball spot at the foot of the table or if that be occupied, on the nearest unoccupied spot thereto. But should two balls be in contact the player can play with either of them, direct at the pins, and any count so made is good.

If a player, with one stroke, knocks down the four outside pins and leaves the black one standing on its spot, it is called a Natural, or *Ranche*, and under any and all circumstances it wins the game.

When a player gets more than 31, he is *burst,* and he may either play again immediately with the same ball he has in the pool rack, starting at nothing of course, or he may take a new ball. If he takes a new ball he may either keep it or keep his old one, but he cannot play again until it comes to his turn.

THE LITTLE CORPORAL.

This game is the regular Three-Ball Carrom Game with a small pin added, like those used in Pin Pool, which is set up in the centre of the table. The carroms and forfeits count as in the regular Three-Ball Game, but the knocking down of the pin scores five points for the striker, who plays until he fails to effect a carrom or knock down the pin. A ball must be hit by the cue-ball before the pin can be scored ; playing at the pin direct is not allowed. The pin must be set up where it falls ; but in case it goes off the table or lodges on the top of the cushion it must be placed upon the centre spot. The pin leaning against the cushion must be scored as down, and when the pin lodges in the corner of the table, so that it cannot be hit with the ball, it is to be set up on the centre spot. One hundred points generally constitute a game, but any number of points may be agreed upon.

THE SPANISH GAME OF BILLIARDS.

This game is played in the South, California, and in Mexico and Cuba, and is played with two white and one red ball, and five pins placed similar to those in Pin Pool. The red ball is placed on the red-ball spot, and the first player strikes at it from within the baulk semicircle. The game is scored by winning and losing hazards, carroms, and by knocking over the pins. It is usually played thirty points up.

The player who knocks down a pin after striking a ball gains *two* points, if he knocks down two pins he gains *four* points, and so on, scoring two points for each pin knocked down. If he knock down the middle pin alone he gains *five* points. The player who pockets the red ball gains *three* points and two for each pin knocked down by the same stroke. The player who pockets the white ball gains two points, and two for each pin knocked over with the same stroke. Each carrom counts two. The player who knocks down a pin or pins with his own ball before striking another ball loses two for every pin so knocked down. The player who pockets his own ball without hitting another ball forfeits three points ; for missing altogether he forfeits one point. The striker who forces his own ball off the table without hitting another ball forfeits *three* points, and if he does so after making a carrom or pocket he loses as many points as he would otherwise have gained. The rules of the American Carrom Game, except where they conflict with the foregoing rules, govern this game also.

BOTTLE POOL.

The game of Bottle Pool is played on a pool table with one white ball, the 1 and 2 ball, and pool-bottle. The 1 and 2 balls must be spotted, respectively, at the foot of the table, at the left and right diamond nearest each pocket, and the pool-bottle is placed standing on its neck on the spot in the centre of the table, and when it falls it must be set up, if possible, where it rests.

Carrom on the two object-balls counts 1 point; Pocketing the 1 ball counts 1 point; Pocketing the 2 ball counts 2 points; Carrom from ball and upsetting bottle counts 5 points. The game consists of 31 points. The player having the least number of points at the finish of the game shall be adjudged the loser.

Any number of persons can play, and the rotation of the players is decided as in ordinary pool. Player No. 1 must play with the white ball from any point within the string at the head of the table, at either the 1 or 2 ball at his option. The player who leads must play at and strike one of the object-balls before he can score a carrom on the pool-bottle. If a player carrom on the bottle from either of the object-balls, in such a way as to seat the bottle on its base, he wins the game, without further play.

Should the 1 or 2 ball in any way, during the stroke, touch the bottle and the bottle is in the same play knocked over or stood on its base by the cue-ball, the stroke does not count. If the player forces the bottle off the table or into a pocket, the bottle must be spotted on its proper spot in the centre of the table, the player loses his shot and forfeits one point, and the next player plays.

A player who makes more than 31 points is burst, and must start his string anew; all that he makes in excess of 31 points count on his new string, and the next player plays.

BILLIARD TEXT BOOKS.

American Game :—
Modern Billiards, Brunswick-Balke-Collender Co.
Billiard Laws,   "   "   "   "
Manuel du Biliard, by Vignaux.
Garnier's Practice Shots.

English Game :—
Billiards Simplified, Burroughs and Watts.
Billiards, by W. Cook.
Billiards, by Joseph Bennet.
Billiards, by Maj.-Gen. Drayson.
Practical Billiards, by W. Dufton.
The Spot Stroke, by Joseph Bennet.

CHANCE AND PROBABILITY.

In calculating the probability of any event, the difficulty is not, as many persons imagine, in the process, but in the statement of the proposition, and the great trouble with many of those who dispute on questions of chance is that they are unable to think clearly.

The chance is either for or against the event ; the probability is always for it. The chances are expressed by the fraction of this probability, the denominator being the total number of events possible, and the numerator the number of events favourable. For instance : The probability of throwing an ace with one cast of a single die is expressed by the fraction $\frac{1}{6}$; because six different numbers may be thrown, and they are all equally probable, but only one of them would be an ace. Odds are found by deducting the favourable events from the total, or the numerator from the denominator. In the example, the odds against throwing an ace are therefore 5 to 1. The greater the odds against any event the the more *improbable* it is said to be, and the more *hazardous* it is to risk anything upon it.

When an event happens which is very improbable, the person to whom it happens is considered *lucky,* and the greater the improbability, the greater his luck. If two men play a game, the winner is not considered particularly lucky ; but if one wanted only two points to go out and the other wanted a hundred, the latter would be a very lucky man if he won.

It is a remarkable fact that luck is the only subject in the world on which we have no recognised authority, although it is a topic of the most universal interest. Strictly speaking, to be lucky simply means to be successful, the word being a derivative of *gelingen,* to succeed. There are a few general principles connected with luck which should be understood by every person who is interested in games of chance. In the first place, luck attaches to persons and not to things. It is useless for an unlucky man to change the seats or the cards, for no matter which he chooses the personal equation of good or bad luck adhering to him for the time being cannot be shaken off. In the second place, all men are lucky in some things, and not in others ; and they are lucky or unlucky in those things at certain times and for certain seasons. This element of luck seems to come and go like the swell of the ocean. In the lives of some men the tide of fortune appears to be a long steady flood, without a ripple on the surface. In others it rises and falls in waves of greater or lesser length ; while in others it is irregular in the extreme ; splashing choppy seas to-day ; a storm to-morrow that smashes everything ; and then calm enough to make ducks and drakes with the pebbles on the shore. In the lives of all the tide of fortune is uncertain ; for the man has never lived who could be sure of the weather a week ahead. In the nature of things this must be so, for if there were no ups and downs in life, there would be no such things as chance and luck, and the laws of probability would not exist.

The greatest fallacy in connection with luck is the belief that certain men *are* lucky, whereas the truth is simply that they *have been* lucky up to that time. They have succeeded so far, but that is no guarantee that they will succeed again in any matter of pure chance. This is demonstrated by the laws governing **the probability of successive events.**

Suppose two men sit down to play a game which is one of pure chance ; poker dice, for instance. You are backing Mr. Smith, and want to know the probability of his winning the first game. There are only two possible events, to win or lose, and both are equally probable, so 2 is the denominator of our fraction. The number of favourable events is 1, which is our numerator, and the fraction is therefore $\frac{1}{2}$, which always represents equality.

Now for the successive events. Your man wins the first game, and they proceed to play another. What are the odds on Smith's winning the second game ? It is evident that they are exactly the same as if the first game had never been played, because there are still only two possible events, and one of them will be favourable to him. Suppose he wins that game, and the next, and the next, and so on until he has won nine games in succession, what are the odds against his winning the tenth also ? Still exactly an even thing.

But, says a spectator, Smith's luck must change; because it is very improbable that he will win ten games in succession. The odds against such a thing are 1023 to 1, and the more he wins the more probable it is that he will lose the next game. This is what gamblers call the **maturity of the chances,** and it is one of the greatest fallacies ever entertained by intelligent men. Curiously enough, the men who believe that luck must change in some circumstances, also believe in betting on it to continue in others. When they are **in the vein** they will " follow their luck " in perfect confidence that it will continue. The same men will not bet on another man's luck, even if he is " in the vein," because " the maturity of the chances " tells them that it cannot last !

·If Smith and his adversary had started with an agreement to play ten games, the odds against either of them winning any number in succession would be found by taking the first game as an even chance, expressed by unity, or 1. The odds against the same player winning the second game also would be twice 1 plus 1, or 3 to 1; and the odds against his winning three games in succession would be twice 3 plus 1, or 7 to 1, and so on, according to the figures shown in the margin.

GAMES.	ODDS.
One	1 to 1
Two	3 to 1
Three	7 to 1
Four	15 to 1
Five	31 to 1
Six	63 to 1
Seven	127 to 1
Eight	255 to 1
Nine	511 to 1
Ten	1023 to 1

That this is so may easily be demonstrated by putting down on a sheet of paper the total number of events that may happen if any agreed number of games are played, expressing wins by a stroke, and losses by a cipher. Take the case of two games only. There are four different events which may happen to Smith, as shown in the margin. He may win both games or lose both; or he may win one and lose the other, either first. Only one of these four equally probable events being favourable to his winning both games, and three being unfavourable, the odds are 3 to 1 that he does not win both; but these are the odds *before he begins to play.* Having won the first game, there are only two events possible, those which begin with a win, and he has an equal chance to win again.

GAMES.	
1st	2nd
1	1
1	0
0	1
0	0

If the agreement had been to play three games, there would have been eight possible events, one of which must happen but all of which were equally probable. These are shown in the margin. If Smith wins the first game, there are only four possible events remaining; those in which the first game was won. Of these, there are two in which he may win the second game, and two in which he may lose it, showing that it is still exactly an even thing that he will win the second game. If he wins the second game, there are only two possible events, the first two on the list in the margin, which begin with two wins for Smith. Of these he has one chance to win the third game, and one to lose it.

GAMES.		
1st	2nd	3rd
1	1	1
1	1	0
1	0	1
1	0	0
0	0	0
0	0	1
0	1	0
0	1	1

No matter how far we continue a series of successive events it will always be found that having won a certain number of games, it is still exactly an even thing that he will win the next also. The odds of 1023 to 1 against his winning ten games in succession existed only before he began to play. After he has won the first game, the odds against his winning the remaining nine are only 511 to 1, and so on, until it is an even thing that he wins the tenth, even if he has won the nine preceding it.

In the statistics of 4000 coups at roulette at Monte Carlo it was found that if one colour had come five times in succession, it was an exactly even bet that it would come again ; for in twenty runs of five times there were ten which went on to six. In the author's examination of 500 consecutive deals of faro, there were 815 cards that either won or lost three times in succession, and of these 412 won or lost out. In a gambling house in Little Rock a roulette wheel with three zeros on it did not come up green for 115 rolls, and several gamblers lost all they had betting on the eagle and O's. When the game closed the banker informed them that the green had come up more than twenty times earlier in the evening. They thought the maturity of the chances would compel the green to come ; whereas the chances really were that it would not come, as it had over-run its average so much earlier in the evening. The pendulum swings as far one way as the other, but no method of catching it on the turn has ever yet been discovered.

Compound Events. In order to ascertain the probability of compound or concurrent events, we must find the product of their separate probability. For instance : The odds against your cutting an ace from a pack of 52 cards are 48 to 4, or 12 to 1 ; because there are 52 cards and only 4 of them are aces. The probability fraction is therefore $\frac{1}{13}$. But the probabilities of drawing an ace from two separate packs are $\frac{1}{13} \times \frac{1}{13} = \frac{1}{169}$, or 168 to 1 against it.

Suppose a person bets that you will not cut a court card, K Q or J, from a pack of 52 cards, what are the odds against you ? In this case there are three favourable events, but only one can happen, and as any of them will preclude the others, they are called *conflicting events,* and the probability of one of them is the sum of the probability of all of them. In this case the probability of any one event separately is $\frac{1}{13}$, and the sum of the three is therefore $\frac{1}{13} + \frac{1}{13} + \frac{1}{13} = \frac{3}{13}$; or ten to 3 against it.

In order to prove any calculation of this kind all that is necessary is to ascertain the number of remaining events, and if their sum, added to that already found, equals unity, the calculation must be correct. For instance : The probability of turning a black trump at whist is $\frac{13}{52} + \frac{13}{52} = \frac{26}{52}$; because there are two black suits of 13 cards each. The only other event which can happen is a red trump, the probability of which is also $\frac{26}{52}$, and the sum of these two probabilities is therefore $\frac{26}{52} + \frac{26}{52} = \frac{52}{52}$, or unity.

Another fallacy in connection with the maturity of the chances is shown in betting against two successive events, both improbable, one of which has happened. The odds against drawing two aces in succession from a pack of 52 cards are 220 to 1 ; but after an ace has been drawn the odds against the second card being an ace also are only 16 to 1, although some persons would be mad enough to bet 1000 to 1 against it, on the principle that the first draw was a great piece of luck and the second ace was practically impossible. While the four aces were in the pack the probability of drawing one was $\frac{4}{52}$. One ace having been drawn, 3 remain in 51 cards, so the probability of getting the second is $\frac{3}{51}$, or $\frac{1}{17}$. Before a card was drawn, the probability of getting two aces in succession was the product of these fractions; $\frac{1}{13} \times \frac{1}{17} = \frac{1}{221}$. On the same principle the odds against two players cutting cards that are a tie, such as two Fours, are not 220 to 1, unless it is specified that the first card shall be a Four. The first player having cut, the odds against the second cutting a card of equal value are only 16 to 1.

Dice. In calculating the probabilities of throws with two or more dice, we must multiply together the total number of throws possible with each die separately, and then find the number of throws that will give the result required. Suppose two dice are used. Six different throws may be made with each, therefore. 6 x 6 = 36 different throws are possible with the two dice together. What are the odds against one of these dice being an ace? A person unfamiliar with the science of probabilities would say that as two numbers must come up, and there are only six numbers altogether, the probability is $\frac{2}{6}$, or exactly 2 to 1 against an ace being thrown. But this is not correct, as will be immediately apparent if we write out all the 36 possible throws with two dice; for we shall find that only 11 of the 36 contain an ace, and 25 do not. The proper way to calculate this is to take the chances against the ace on each die separately, and then to multiply them together. There are five other numbers that might come up, and the fraction of their probability is $\frac{5}{6} \times \frac{5}{6} = \frac{25}{36}$, or 25 to 11 in their favour.

Take the case of three dice: As three numbers out of six must come up, it might be supposed that it was an even thing that one would be an ace. But the possible throws with three dice are $6 \times 6 \times 6 = 216$; and those that do not contain an ace are $5 \times 5 \times 5 = 125$; so that the odds against getting an ace in one throw with three dice, or three throws with one die, are $\frac{125}{216}$, or 125 to 91 against it.

To find the probability of getting a given total on the faces of two or three dice we must find the number of ways that the desired number can come. In the 36 possible throws with two dice there are 6 which will show a total of seven pips. The probability of throwing seven is therefore $\frac{6}{36}$, or 5 to 1 against it. A complete list of the combinations with two dice were given in connection with Craps.

Poker. In calculating the probability of certain conflicting events, both of which cannot occur, but either of which would be favourable, we must make the denominator of our fraction equal in both cases, which will, of course, necessitate a proportionate change in our numerator. Suppose a poker player has three of a kind, and intends to draw one card only, the odds against his getting a full hand are $\frac{1}{15}$; against getting four of a kind, $\frac{1}{48}$. To find the total probability of improvement, we must make the first fraction proportionate to the last, which we can do by multiplying it by 3. The result will be $\frac{3}{48} + \frac{1}{48} = \frac{4}{48}$; showing that the total chance of improvement is 1 in 12, or 11 to 1 against it.

Whist. To calculate the probable positions of certain named cards is rather a difficult matter, but the process may be understood from a simple example. Suppose a suit so distributed that you have four to the King, and each of the other players has three cards; what are the probabilities that your partner has both Ace and Queen? The common solution is to put down all the possible positions of the two named cards, and finding only one out of nine to answer, to assume that the odds are 8 to 1 against partner having both cards. This is not correct, because the nine positions are not equally probable. We must first find the number of possible positions for the Ace and Queen separately, afterward multiplying them together, which will give us the denominator; and then the number of positions that are favourable, which will give us the numerator.

As there are nine unknown cards, and the Ace may be any one of them, it is obvious that the Queen may be any one of the remaining eight, which gives us $9 \times 8 = 72$ different ways for the two cards to lie. To find how many of these 72 will give us both cards in partner's hand we must begin with the ace, which may be any one of his three cards. The Queen may be either of the other two, which gives us the numerator, $3 \times 2 = 6$; and the fraction of probability, $\frac{6}{72} = \frac{1}{12}$; or 11 to 1 against both Ace and Queen,

If we wished to find the probability of his having the Ace, but not the Queen, our denominator would remain the same; but the numerator would be the three possible positions of the Ace, multiplied by the six possible positions of the Queen among the six other unknown cards, in the other hands, giving us the fraction $\frac{18}{72}$. The same would be true of the Queen but not the Ace. To prove both these, we must find the probability that he has neither Ace nor Queen. There being six cards apart from his three, the Ace may be any one of them, and the Queen may be any one of the remaining five. This gives us $6 \times 5 = 30$, and the fraction $\frac{30}{72}$. If we now add these four numerators together, we have :—for both cards in partner's hand, 6; for Ace alone, 18; for Queen alone, 18; and for neither, 30; a total of 72, or unity, proving all the calculations correct.

In some of the problems connected with Whist, it is important to know the probability of the suits being distributed in various ways among the four players at the table; or, what is the same thing, the probable distribution of the four suits in any one hand.

DISTRIBU-TIONS.	TIMES IN 1000
8 2 2 1	2
8 3 1 1	1½
8 3 2 0	1
8 4 1 0	½
8 5 0 0	0
7 2 2 2	5
7 3 2 1	19
7 3 3 0	3
7 4 1 1	4
7 4 2 0	3
7 5 1 0	1
7 6 0 0	0
6 3 2 2	57
6 3 3 1	35
6 4 2 1	47
6 4 3 0	13
6 5 1 1	7
6 5 2 0	6
6 6 1 0	1
5 3 3 2	155
5 4 2 2	106
5 4 3 1	130
5 4 4 0	12
5 5 2 1	32
5 5 3 0	9
4 3 3 3	105
4 4 3 2	215
4 4 4 1	30

The author is indebted to Dr. Pole's "Philosophy of Whist" for these calculations. As an example of the use of this table, suppose it was required to find the probability of any other player at the table holding four or more trumps if you had six. Take all the combinations in which the figure 6 appears, and add together the number of times they will probably occur. That will be your denominator, 166. The numerator will be the number of times that the combinations occur which contain a figure larger than 3, in addition to the 6. This will be found to be 74, and the probability will therefore be $\frac{74}{166}$.

MARTINGALES. Many gamblers believe that as the science of probabilities teaches us that events will equalise themselves in time, all that is necessary is to devise some system that will keep a person from guessing, so that he may catch the pendulum as it swings ; and to add to it some system of betting, so that he will have the best of it in the long run. Some content themselves with playing a "system" against banking games, which is merely a guide to the placing of the bets, the simplest example of which would be to bet always on heads if a coin was tossed a thousand times, or to bet on nothing but red at Roulette. Others depend more on martingales, which are guides to the amount of the bets themselves, irrespective of what they are placed on.

The most common form of martingale is called *doubling up*, which proceeds upon the theory that if you lose the first time and bet double the amount the next time, and continue to double until you win, you must eventually win the original amount staked. If there was no end to your capital, and no betting limit to the game, this would be an easy way to make money ; but all banking games have studied these systems, and have so arranged matters that they can extend their heartiest welcome to those who play them.

In the first place, by simply doubling up you are giving the bank the best of it, because you are not getting the proper odds. If you double up five times you are betting 16 to 1 ; but the odds against five successive events are 31 to 1, as we have already seen, and the bank should pay you 31 instead of 16. You should not only double, but add the original amount of the stake each time, betting 1, 3, 7, 15, 31, 63, and so on. If you do this, you will win the amount of your original stake for every bet you make, instead of only for every time you win. This looks well, but as a matter of fact doubling up is only another way of borrowing small sums which will have to be paid back in one large sum when you can probably least afford it.

Suppose the game is Faro, the chips five dollars a stack, and the limit on cases twenty-five dollars. The limit on cases will then be 400 chips. If eight successive events go against your "system," which they will do about once in 255 times, your next bet will be beyond the limit, and the banker will not accept it. At Monte Carlo the smallest bet is a dollar, and the limit is $2,400. They roll about 4,000 coups a week, and if you were to bet on every one of them, doubling up, you would win about $1,865, one dollar at a time, and would lose $4,092 simply through being unable to follow your system beyond the limit of the game during the two or three occasions, in the 4,000 coups, that your system would go against you for eleven or more coups in succession. It is useless to say it would not go against you so often, for probabilities teach us that it would be more wonderful if it did not than if it did.

It must never be forgotten that the most wonderful things that happen are not more wonderful than those that don't happen. If you tossed a coin a thousand times, and did not once toss heads eight times in succession, it would be four times more surprising than if you tossed heads ten times in succession.

Progression. This is a favourite martingale with those who have not the courage or the money to double up. It consists in starting with a certain amount for the first bet, say ten dollars, and adding a dollar every time the bet is lost, or taking off a dollar every time a bet is won. If the player wins as many bets as he loses, and there is no percentage against him, he gets a dollar for every bet he wins, no matter how many bets he makes, or in what order the bets are won and lost, so that the number won equals the number lost. That this is so may be easily demonstrated by setting down on a sheet of paper any imaginary order of bets, such as the ten shown in the margin, five of which are won, and five lost; the net profit on the five bets won being five dollars. No matter how correctly the player may be guessing, and how much the luck runs his way, he wins smaller and smaller amounts, until at last he is "pinched off." But if a long series of events goes against him his bets become larger and

Bets	
Won.	Lost.
10	–
9	–
8	–
–	7
–	8
9	–
–	8
–	9
10	–
–	9
46	41

larger, but he must keep up the progression until he gets even. If ten bets go his way he wins $55; if ten go against him he loses $145.

It is said that Pettibone made a fortune playing progression at Faro, which is very likely, for among the thousands of men who play it the probabilities are that one will win all the time, just as the probabilities are that if a thousand men play ten games of Seven Up, some man will win all ten games. At the same time it is equally probable that some man will lose all ten.

Some players progress, but never pinch, keeping account on a piece of paper how many bets they are behind, and playing the maximum until they have won as many bets as they have lost. Against a perfectly fair game, with no percentage and no limit, and with capital enough to follow the system to the end, playing progression would pay a man about as much as he could make in any good business with the same capital and with half the worry; but as things really are in gambling houses and casinos, all martingales are a delusion and a snare. It is much better, if one must gamble, to trust to luck alone, and it is an old saying that the player without a system is seldom without a dollar. It is the men with systems who have to borrow a stake before they can begin to play.

Such matters as calculating the probability of a certain horse getting a place, the odds against all the horses at the post being given, would be out of place in a work of this kind; but those interested in such chances may find rules for ascertaining their probability in some of the following text books.

TEXT BOOKS.

Calcul de Probabilité, by Bertrand.
Philosophy of Whist, by Dr. Pole.
Winning Whist, by Emory Boardman.
Chance and Luck, by R. A. Proctor.
Complete Poker Player, by John Blackbridge.
Bohn's Handbook of Games.
Betting and Gambling, by Major Churchill.

TEN PINS.

~~~~~~~~

The standard American game of Ten Pins is played upon an *alley* 41 or 42 inches wide, and 60 feet long from the head pin to the foul or scratch line, from behind which the player must deliver his ball. There should be at least 15 feet run back of the foul line, and the gutters on each side of the alley must be deep enough to allow a ball to pass without touching any of the pins standing on the alley.

7 8 9 10   *The Pins* are spotted as shown in the margin, the
 4 5 6   centres 12 inches apart, and those of the back row
  2 3   3 inches from the edge of the pit. The regulation
   1   pins are 15 inches high, 2¼ diam. at the base, 15 inches circumference 4½ from the bottom, and 5¼ at the neck. *The Balls* must not exceed 27 inches in circumference in any direction, but smaller balls may be used.

Frames. Each player rolls ten frames or innings, in each of which he is supposed to have three balls, although as a matter of fact he rolls two only. In match games, two alleys are used, and the players roll one inning on each alternately.

A Strike is made when all ten pins are knocked down with the first ball of the innings, and it is scored on the blackboard with a cross, the number of pins made with the three balls being filled in afterward. *A Spare* is made when all ten pins are knocked down with the two balls of one inning, and it is marked with a diagonal stroke. If the player fails to get either a strike or a spare, it is a *Break,* marked with a horizontal line, under which is written the actual number of pins down. After each ball is rolled any pins that have fallen on the alley are called *deadwood,* and must be removed before the second ball is rolled.

Counting. If a player makes a strike in one inning, all that he makes on the next two balls rolled, whether in one inning or not, counts also on the strike, so as to give him the total score on three balls for the frame. Three successive strikes would give him 30 points on the first frame, with a ball still to roll to complete the second frame, and two balls to roll to complete the third, If he got two strikes in succession, and 5 pins on the first ball of the third frame, 4 on the second ball, the first frame would be worth 25, the second frame 19, and the break on the third frame 9; making his total score 53 for the three frames.

If the player makes a spare in one inning, all the pins knocked down by the first ball of the next inning count also on the spare. Suppose a spare to be followed by a strike, the frame in which the spare was made would be worth 20. If he made 5 pins only, the spare would be worth 15.

Although the player is supposed to have three balls in each inning, and is allowed to count all he makes on three balls if he gets a strike or a spare, he is not allowed to roll three balls on a break. It was formerly the custom to let him roll the third ball on the chance of getting a break of 10. This was afterward changed to giving him 10 pins, without rolling for them, if he got 9 on two balls; but the present rule is to call it a break if he does not get a strike or a spare in two balls, and not to waste time in rolling the third ball.

Scoring. Instead of putting down the amount made in each inning, the total of the frame is added to the total of the previous score, so that the last figure put down shows the total score up to and including that frame. The following illustration shows the total score of a player for ten innings. The top line of figures gives the number of the frame. The second shows the number of pins knocked down by each ball rolled, and the third line shows how the scores would be actually put down on the blackboard, the strike, spare, and break marks being placed above the figures. With the exception of the second line of figures, which is put in for purposes of illustration only, this might be a copy of an actual score.

Frames	1	2	3	4	5	6	7	8	9	10
Pins	8–2	5–5	10	9–0	7–2	8–2	10	8–2	8–1	7–3–9
Score	15	35	54	63	72	92	112	140	149	168

As the player made a spare on the last frame, he had another ball to roll, on what was practically a new frame, with which he made 9 pins.

Averages. If a team is playing a match, and one of the players is unavoidably absent, it is the custom to give him credit for his average, according to the records of his previous games during the tournament or the season. This is considered better than appointing a substitute to play for him.

There are a great many varieties of Ten Pins, but they are of purely local interest. The German clubs, for instance, have a great many games played with Nine pins. Those interested in the subject will find all the variations fully described in the "American League Bowling Guide."

GENERAL LAWS,

FOR ALL CARD GAMES.

Very few games have their own code of laws, and only one or two of these have the stamp of any recognised authority. In minor games, questions are continually arising which could be easily settled if the players were familiar with a few general principles which are common to the laws of all games, and which might be considered as the basis of a general code of card laws. The most important of these principles are as follows :—

Players. It is generally taken for granted that those first in the room have the preference, but if more than the necessary number assemble, the selection must be made by cutting. A second cut will then be required to decide the partnerships, if any, and the positions at the table, the latter being important only in games in which the deal, or some given position at the table, is an advantage or the reverse. The usual method of cutting is to spread the cards face downward on the table, each player drawing one. In some games the cards are thrown round by one of the players.

Shuffling, Cutting and Dealing. In all games in which the cards are shuffled at all, each player has the right to shuffle, the dealer last. In English speaking countries the cards are always cut by the player on the dealer's right, who is called the "pone." In cutting to the dealer in any game there must be as many cards left in each packet as will form a trick ; or, if the game is not one of tricks, as many cards as there will be in any player's hand ; four, for instance, at Whist, and five at Poker. The cards are always distributed to each player in rotation from left to right, and each must receive the same number of cards in the same round. In games in which the cards are dealt by two and threes, for instance, it is illegal to give one player two and another three in the same round.

Misdeals. In all games in which the deal is an advantage, a misdeal loses the deal ; but in all games in which the deal is a disadvantage, or some position is more advantageous than that of the dealer, such as the " age " at Poker, a misdeal does not lose the deal. The only exception to this rule is in Bridge, in which there are no misdeals.

Bidding. In all games in which there is any bidding for the privilege of playing or of making the trump, or any betting on the value of the hands, the privilege must be extended to each player in turn, beginning on the dealer's left. Any bid or any bet once made can neither be taken back nor amended. If any bid is made out of turn in any partnership game, it must be assumed that undue information is conveyed, and the player in error, or his partner, must lose his bid. In round games there is no penalty.

Exposed Cards. No player can exact a penalty for his own error, so that if an adversary of the dealer exposes one of his own cards he cannot claim a misdeal, but the dealer's side may. There should be no penalty for a player's having exposed a card unless he can derive some benefit from the exposure, such as from his partner's having seen it. If there is no partner, there should be no penalty, because the player injures himself only. All exposed cards must be left on the table, and may be called upon by the adversaries to be led or played.

The same principles apply to **Leading out of Turn.** If the player in error has no partner, or his partner is a dummy, and the lead is taken back, no harm is done except to the player himself, and there should be no penalty. If the adversaries fail to observe that the lead was irregular, they are equally at fault with the player, who must be assumed to have erred unintentionally. In games in which a lead out of turn conveys information to a partner, the usual penalty is to call a suit.

If a player is led into error through a previous error on the part of an adversary, he should not suffer any penalty for it, but may take back his card. This is particularly true of following suit to erroneous leads, or playing after a revoke which is afterward amended.

Irregularities in the Hands. In all games in which the player need not follow suit unless he chooses, such as Seven-up, there should be no penalty if the player has not his full complement of cards, because he cannot possibly gain anything by playing with a short hand. But in all such games as Whist, where the absence of a card in plain suits might enable a player to trump, a penalty must be enforced for playing with less than the proper number of cards. In all such games as Poker, it is only to the player's own disadvantage to play with too few cards, provided he is not allowed to call four cards a flush or a straight, and there should be no objection to his playing with a short hand. Many good players "squeeze" their cards, and if they find a good pair in the first two, they put up the ante without looking further. It is manifestly unfair to bar them out of the pool because the dealer has given them only four cards, which gives them no possible advantage, but rather the reverse. This is in accordance with common sense, and is the law in Cribbage and Piquet.

Discrimination. No person should be allowed any advantage over another which is not compensated for in some way. In Seven-up, for instance, the non-dealer counts game if it is a tie ; an advantage which is offset by the dealer's counting Jack if he turns it. In Auction Pitch the dealer has no such advantage, because no trump is turned, and therefore the non-dealer cannot count ties for game. It is a common error among Cassino players to hold that a player cannot build on his own build, but that his adversary may do so. A player holds two deuces, an Eight and a Ten, and builds a Six to an Eight. It is claimed that an adversary may increase this build to ten, but the original builder may not. This is manifestly unfair, because there is no compensating advantage to the player that is denied the privilege to justify its being allowed to his adversary.

Benefiting by Errors. No player should be allowed to win a game by committing a breach of the laws. If a person revokes, for instance, there is a certain penalty, but in addition to the penalty it is always stipulated that the revoking player cannot win the game that hand.

Double Penalties. No person can be subjected to two penalties for one offence. If a player leads out of turn, and a suit is called, the card played in error cannot be also claimed as exposed and liable to be called. If a player revokes, and his adversary wins ten tricks, the revoke penalty adds three tricks to the ten already won ; but these thirteen tricks will not entitle the player to score any points for a slam, because that would be exacting a double penalty ; the tricks for the revoke, and the points for the slam.

Intentional Error. In all games it must be assumed that the player's intentions are honest, and that any errors that arise are committed through inadvertence. Some of our law-makers have attempted so to adjust their codes as to provide against the manœuveres of the blackleg. This is simply impossible. Laws are made for gentlemen, and when it is obvious that a player does not belong to that class the remedy is not to appeal to the laws of the game for protection, but to decline to play with him.

Etiquette. It should be quite unnecessary to legislate against acts which annoy or do injustice to individuals, but there should be some provision in the laws of every game which will secure to each individual equal rights with others in the enjoyment of the game. Some games are especially selfish ; Boston, for instance, in which the four players originally forming the table may monopolise the game for the entire evening, without offering newcomers any chance to cut in. All such games should be limited to a certain number of tournées, at the conclusion of which fresh candidates should be allowed to cut into the table.

Technical Terms.

G. stands for German; F. for French.

*A*bnehmen or Abheben, G., to cut.

Abwerfen, G., to discard.

À cheval, across the line; betting on both sides at once.

Adversary, (G., Feind). In Mort or Bridge, those who play against the Dummy and his partner.

Affranchir, F., to establish a suit.

Age, the eldest hand; sometimes erroneously spelt Edge.

Albany Lead, a lead in Whist, to show four trumps and three of each plain suit.

American Leads, leads that show the number of cards in the suit led, at Whist.

Ames Ace, double aces thrown with dice.

Anchor Shot, getting the object balls against the cushion and astride the line at baulk-line billiards.

Ante, a bet made before playing, but after seeing the hand.

Antepenultimate, the lowest but two of a suit.

Après, the announcement of a refait at Rouge et Noir.

Arroser, F., to be compelled to play a trump which will not win the trick.

Ask for Trumps, playing an unnecessarily high card, when no attempt is made to win the trick.

Auf die Dörfer gehen, to run for home; to make all your aces and kings, instead of leading trumps.

A. Y. B. Z., the letters used to distinguish the positions of the four players at Whist; A–B being partners against Y–Z., and Z. having the deal.

*B*ackgammon. If a player throws off all his men before his adversary has thrown off any, and while one or more of the adversary's men are still on the side of the board next the winning player, it is a backgammon, or triple game.

Bath Coup, holding up Ace Jack on a King led by an adversary.

Battre, F., to shuffle.

Bedienen, G., to follow suit.

Bekommen, G., to win.

Bekennen, G., to follow suit.

Belle, F., the last game of the rubber.

Bidding to the Board, means that the points bid for a certain privilege are not to be credited to any player, but are simply the announcement of the value of an undertaking.

Biseautes (cartes) F., wedges or strippers.

Blätter, G., playing cards.

Blocking a Suit, keeping a high card of it, so that the player with a number of smaller cards cannot win tricks with them.

Blue Peter, the ask for trumps.

Blind, a bet made before seeing the cards.

Blinden, G., a widow, an extra hand dealt at any game.

Board's the Play, a card once played cannot be taken back.

Bobtail, a four-card flush or straight, which is accompanied by a worthless card.

Bone-yard, the stock at dominoes.

Book, the first six tricks taken by either side at Whist which do not count toward game.

Both Ends against the Middle, a system of trimming cards for dealing a brace game of Faro.

Brace Game, a conspiracy between the dealer and the case-keeper at Faro, so that cards improperly taken from the dealing box shall be properly marked by the case-keeper.

Break. In Billiards, a succession of counting shots made by one player, usually called a " run " in America. In Ten Pins, a break is a failure to make either a strike or a spare.

Break Even, a system of playing Faro, betting each card to win or lose an even number of times.

Brelan, F., three cards of the same denomination.

Brelan Carré, F., four cards of the same denomination.

Bringing in a Suit, making tricks in a plain suit after the adverse trumps are exhausted.

Brûler, F., to burn a card.

Bûche, F., cards that count for nothing, such as the tens and court cards in Baccara ; equivalent to the G. Ladons, or Fehlkarten.

Bucking the Tiger, playing against the bank at Faro.

Bumblepuppy, playing Whist in ignorance or defiance of conventionality.

Bumper, a rubber of eight points at English Whist.

Burnt Cards, cards which are turned face upward on the bottom of the pack, usually in banking games.

Calling for Trumps, the ask for trumps.

Cannon, (Am. carrom,) a count made at billiards by causing the cue ball to touch two object balls.

Capot, F., winning all the tricks.

Cards, the number of tricks over six at Whist, such as "two by cards." The majority of cards at Cassino.

Carrer, (se) to straddle the blind. Contre-carrer, to over-straddle.

Carrom, see cannon.

Cartes, F., playing cards.

Carte Blanche, a hand which does not contain K, Q or J.

Carte Roi, F., the best card remaining of a suit.

Cases, when three cards of one denomination have been withdrawn from the box at Faro, the fourth is a case.

Case-keeper, a board for recording the cards as they are withdrawn from the box at Faro. The word is sometimes applied to the person who keeps cases.

Cat-hop, two cards of the same denomination left in for the last turn at Faro.

Cave, F., the amount a player places in front of him at the beginning of play ; table stakes.

Checks, the counters at Poker are checks ; at Faro they are chips.

Chelem, F., a slam.

Chip Along, to bet a single counter and wait for developments.

Chouette, à la, taking all the bets.

Close Cards, those which are not likely to form sequences with others, especially at Cribbage.

Club Stakes, the usual amount bet on any game in the club.

Cogging Dice, turning one over with the finger after they have been fairly thrown.

Cold Deck, a pack of cards which has been pre-arranged, and is surreptitiously exchanged for the one in play.

Colours, a system of playing Faro according to the colour of the first winner or loser in each deal.

Command, the best card of a suit, usually applied to suits which the adversary is trying to establish.

Couper, F., to cut the cards ; also to ruff a suit.

Couleur, F., a suit of cards, such as hearts or clubs.

Coup, a master stroke or brilliant play ; a single roll of the wheel at Roulette, or a deal at Rouge et Noir.

Compass Whist, arranging players according to the points of the compass at Duplicate Whist, and always retaining them in their original positions.

Conventional Play, any method of conveying information, such as the trump signal, which is not based on the principles of the game.

Coppered Bets, bets that have a copper or checker placed upon them at Faro, to show that they play the card to lose.

Court Cards, the K, Q and J ; the ace is not a court card.

Covering, playing a higher card second hand than the one led, but not necessarily the best of the suit.

Créve, F., one who is temporarily out of the game, such as one who has overdrawn his hand at Vingt-et-un ; as distinguished from one who has lost all his money. The latter would be spoken of as décavé.

Crossing the Suit, changing the trump from the suit turned up to one of a different colour, especially in Euchre.

Cross-ruff, two partners alternately trumping a different suit.

Cul levé, (jouer à) playing one after another, by taking the place of the loser. A vulgar expression.

Cutting, dividing the pack when presented by the dealer; or drawing lots for choice of seats and deal.

Cutting In and Out, deciding by cutting which players shall give way to fresh candidates.

Curse of Scotland, the nine of diamonds.

Cut Shots, very fine winning hazards.

*D*ealing Off, the same dealer dealing again.

Deck-head, an Irish name for the turned trump at Spoil Five.

Deadwood, the pins that fall on the alley, in bowling.

Décavé, F., frozen out; the entire amount of the original stake being lost.

Défausser, se, F., to discard.

D'emblée, F., on the first deal; before the draw.

Despatchers, dice which are not properly marked, having two faces alike, such as double fives.

Devil's bed posts, the four of clubs.

Discarding, getting rid of a card in plain suits when unable to follow suit and unwilling to trump.

Donne, (avoir la) to have the deal. Donne, the time occupied in playing the cards distributed during a deal, but "coup" is the term generally used.

Double Pairs Royal, four cards of the same denomination.

Doubleton, two cards only of a suit.

Doubling Up, betting twice the amount of a lost wager.

Doubtful Card, a card led by the player on your right, which your partner may be able to win.

Draw Shot, any shot which makes the ball return toward the cue; in English, a "screw-back."

Duffer, one who is not well up in the principles of the game he is playing.

Dummy, the exposed hand in Dummy Whist, Bridge, or Mort.

Duplicate Whist, a form of Whist in which the same hands are played by both sides, and as nearly as possible under the same conditions.

Dutch It, to cross the suit at Euchre.

*È*carter, F., to discard.

Echoing, showing the number of trumps held when partner leads or calls; in plain suits, showing the number held when a high card is led.

Edge, a corruption of the word "age," the eldest hand.

Eldest Hand, the first player to the left of the dealer in all English games ; to his right in France.

Encaisser, F., to hand the stakes to the banker.

Entamer, F., to lead.

Established Suits, a suit is established when you or your partner can take every trick in it, no matter who leads it.

Étaler, F., to expose a card.

Exposed Cards, cards played in error, or dropped face upward on the table, or held so that the partner can see them.

Face Cards, K, Q and J.

Faire les Cartes, F., to shuffle ; or to make the majority of cards or tricks in a game.

Fall of the Cards, the order in which they are played.

False Cards, cards played to deceive the adversary as to the true holding in the suit.

Fattening, discarding counting cards on partner's tricks.

Feind, G., an adversary ; Gegner is the more common word.

Figure, F., K, Q or J.

Fille, F., see Widow.

Finesse, any attempt to take a trick with a card which is not the best of the suit.

First, Second, or Third Hand, the positions of the players on any individual trick.

Five Fingers, the five of trumps at Spoil Five.

Flèches, the points upon a backgammon board.

Fluke, making a count that was not played for.

Flush, cards of the same suit.

Flux, F., only one suit in the player's hand ; a flush.

Force, to compel a player to trump a trick in order to win it.

Forced Leads, leads which are not desirable, but which are forced upon the player to avoid those which are still less advantageous.

Fordern, G., to lead trumps.

Fourchette, the two cards immediately above and below the one led, such as K J in the second hand on a Q led.

Four Signal, a method of showing four trumps, without asking for them ; usually made by playing three small cards, such as 4 6 2, in that order.

Fourth-best, the fourth card of a suit, counting from the top. The modern substitute for the terms penultimate, and antepenultimate.

Front Stall, one who makes acquaintances for gamblers to fleece.

Frozen, balls touching at billiards.

Frozen Out, a player who has lost his original stake, and cannot continue in the game.

Fuzzing, milking the cards instead of shuffling them.

*G*allery, the spectators who are betting on the game.

Gambling, risking more than one can well afford to lose on any game of chance.

Gambler's Point, the count for " game " at Seven-up.

Gammon. When a player throws off all his men before his adversary throws off any, it is a gammon, or double game.

Gathering Shots, getting the balls together again after driving them round the table. See Nursing.

Geben, G., to deal the cards. Sometimes "Vertheilung der Karten" is used.

Gegner, G., the adversary.

Grand Coup, trumping a trick already won by partner; or playing a small trump on a trick which he has already trumped.

Greek, (grec) a card sharp.

Guarded Cards, cards which cannot be caught by higher cards unless they are led through.

*H*and, the cards dealt to one player; the distribution of the cards in any one deal. A " remarkable hand " might be the play of an entire deal at Whist, for instance.

Heading a Trick, playing a better card than any already played to the trick, but not necessarily the best in the hand.

Heeled Bets, bets at Faro which play one card to win and another to lose, but do not win or lose double the amount if both events come on the same turn.

Hinterhand, G., the last player on the first trick, (Skat).

His Heels, the Jack turned up for a starter at Cribbage.

His Nobs, Jack of the same suit as the starter at Cribbage.

Hoc, or Hockelty, the last card in the box at Faro.

Honours, usually the highest cards in the suit, such as A K Q J, and sometimes the 10. In Calabrasella the 3 and 2 are honours, and in Impérial the lowest card is an honour.

Horse and Horse, each player having one game to his credit when they are playing best two out of three.

Hustling, inveigling persons into skin games.

*I*mpair, the odd numbers at Roulette.

Impasse, F., to finesse.

Imperfect Fourchette, two cards, one immediately above the one led, and the other one remove below it; such as K 10 second hand on a Q led.

Imperfect Pack, one in which there are duplicate cards, missing cards, or cards so marked that they can be identified by the backs,

Indifferent Cards, cards of the same value, so far as trick taking is concerned, such as Q and J.

Inside Straights, sequences which are broken in the middle.

Intricate Shuffles, butting the two parts of the pack together at the ends, and forcing them into each other.

Invite, F., leading a small card of the long suit.

Irregular Leads, leads which are not made in accordance with the usual custom, as distinguished from forced leads.

Jack Strippers, two bowers, trimmed to pull out of the pack.

Jenny, a fine losing hazard, made off an object ball close to the cushion, between the side pocket and the baulk.

Jetons, F., the counters which represent money at any game.

Jeu, F., derived from jocus, a game. The word is variously applied to the game itself; to the player's expectation of success; to his plan of campaign; or to the cards in his hand.

Jeux de Régle, hands which should be played in a certain way on account of their mathematical expectations, (Écarté).

Keeping Tab, keeping a record of the cards that win and lose as they are dealt at Faro.

King Card, the best card remaining unplayed of the suit.

King Row, the four squares on the checker board which are farthest from the player's own side.

Kitty, the percentage taken out of a pool to pay for refreshments, or for the expenses of the table.

Knight Player, one who can give the odds of a Knight to weak players, at Chess.

Last Trick, an expression used to distinguish the last trick when all the cards are played from the last when all the cards are not played, especially in Bézique and Sixty-six.

Last Turn, the three cards left in the box at the end of the deal at Faro, the order of which may be bet upon.

Lead, to play the first card in any trick.

Levée, F., a trick. (Tric, is the odd trick.)

Liées, F., to play rubbers.

Limit, the amount by which one player may increase his bet over that of another.

Long Cards, the dregs of a suit which has been led several times, and exhausted in the hands of the other players.

Long Suits, those containing four or more cards, at Whist.

Lose Out, a card that loses four times in one deal, at Faro.

Losing Cards, those that would lose tricks if they were led.

Losing Hazard, pocketing the cue ball.

Losing Trump, one which is not the best, when only one or two remain.

Love-all, nothing scored on either side.

Main, F., with avoir this expression is indefinite, and may refer to the deal or the lead. With être, to be in the lead. Dans la main, applies to the possibilities of the hand. Placer la main, to place the lead.

Make-up, to get the cards ready for the next deal.

Make the Pass, to put the two parts of the pack back as they were before the cut.

Maldonne, F., misdeal.

Manche, F., one game of the rubber.

Manque, the numbers from 1 to 18 at Roulette.   See Passe.

Marque, F., a score which is kept upon the table by means of counters.

Martingale, any system which controls the amounts wagered on a series of events.   (See chapter on Chance and Probability.)

Massé, a shot made with the cue held nearly perpendicular.

Master Card, the best card remaining of a suit which has been played.

Matsch, G., to win all the tricks, a slam.

Mechanic, a dealer who can make the cards come any way he pleases at Faro.

Melden, G., to announce, claim, or show any counting combination of cards.

Méler, F., to shuffle.

Memory Duplicate, playing over the same hands at the same table ; the players who held the N and S cards getting the E and W for the overplay.

Menage, F., gathering and arranging the cards for the succeeding deal when two packs are used.

Milking, taking a card from the bottom and the top of the pack at the same time with the forefinger and thumb.

Mischen, G., to shuffle.

Misdeal, any failure to distribute the cards properly.

Mise, F., the layout, or the original pool.

Misère Ouverte.   There is no such expression as this in French ; the proper term is Misère sur table.   See Boston.

Mittelhand, G., the second player on the first trick, in Skat.

Mixed Pair, a lady and gentleman playing as partners.

Mort, F., the dummy hand at Whist or Bridge.

Mouth Bets, those made without putting up the money.   One who fails to pay mouth bets is a welcher.

Muggins, to take a score which has been overlooked by an adversary, especially in Cribbage and Dominoes.

Natural, anything which wins the stake immediately ; 7 or 11 at Craps ; 21 at Vingt-et-un ; 8 or 9 at Baccara.

Natural Points, those which must be made every deal, such as big and little cassino, high, low, etc.

Navette, F., a cross ruff.

Neben Farbe, G., plain suits.

Next, the suit of the same colour as the turned trump at Euchre.   Diamonds are " next " to hearts.

Nick, a natural at Craps; 7 or 11 on the first throw.

Nicknames for Cards: The ◊ 9 is the curse of Scotland; the ♣ 4 is the devil's bedposts; the ♣ A is the Puppyfoot; the Jack of trumps at Spoil Five is the Playboy, and the Five of trumps is the Five Fingers.

N. E. S. W., letters used to distinguish the players at Duplicate Whist. N always leads, unless otherwise specified.

Nursing, keeping the balls together at Billiards, as distinguished from gathering, which brings them together.

Odd Trick, the seventh won by the same partners at Whist.

Open Bets, bets at Faro which play cards to win.

Openers, cards which entitle a player to open a jack-pot.

Original Lead, the opening lead of a hand at Whist.

Pair, F., the even numbers at Roulette. See Impair.

Pairs, in Duplicate Whist, the partners sitting N and S, or E and W. Any two cards of the same denomination.

Pairs Royal, any three cards of the same denomination.

Partie, F., a game which requires a number of deals to decide it.

Pass, to decline any undertaking in a game.

Passe, F., the numbers from 19 to 36 at Roulette.

Pat Hands, those which are played without discarding or exchanging any of the cards originally dealt.

Pausirenden, G., one who shares in the fortunes of the game, although not actually playing, as the dealer in four-handed Skat.

Paying in Cards. When the banker and the player's point is equal, the latter is said to "pay in cards."

Penultimate, the lowest but one of a suit at Whist.

Phaser, F., to change the pack.

Philosopher, a card sharp.

Piano Hands, hands which run along smoothly at Whist, and yield no opportunities for loss or gain.

Piking, making small bets all over the layout at Faro.

Playboy, the Jack of trumps at Spoil Five.

Plain Suits, those which are not trumps.

Point, F., the suit containing the greatest number of pips.

Pone, the player on the dealer's right, who cuts the cards.

Ponte, F., one who plays against the banker.

Post Mortems, discussions as to what might have been at Whist, sometimes called, "If you hads."

Pot, strictly speaking, the amount to be played for when a pool has exceeded a certain limit, especially in Spoil Five and Boston.

Premier en Cartes, F., the first to play.

Private Conventions, any system of giving information by the play which could not be understood by a partner unless explained to him.

Probabilities, the odds in favour of any event.

Progression, a martingale which increases a bet a certain amount every time it is lost, and decreases it every time it is won.

Proil, or Prial, Pairs Royal.

Puits, F., only one to go, the whiskey hole.

Punters, those who play against the banker.

Puppy-foot, the ace of clubs.

Quart, the English equivalent of the French word quatrième, a sequence of four cards.

Quart Major, A K Q J of any suit.

Quatorze, F., four cards of the same denomiuation.

Quatriéme, F., a sequence of four cards.

Queue, F., the points added for winning the rubber.

Quinte, F., a sequence of five cards.

Quitted. A trick is quitted when the fingers are removed from it after it is turned down. In Duplicate, a trick is not quitted until all four players have removed their fingers from it. A score is quitted when the fingers are removed from the counters, the peg, or the pencil.

Raffles, the same number appearing on all the dice thrown.

Ranche, leaving the black pin standing alone at Pin Pool.

Re-entry Cards, cards in other suits which bring in long suits at Whist.

Reizen, G., to draw a person on ; to irritate or provoke him to bidding more than he should.

Rejoué, duplicate whist.

Renege, failure to follow suit, having none. See Revoke.

Renounce, same as renege.

Rentrant, F., the player who takes the place of the loser in a previous game.

Renvier, F., to raise the bet, to improve.

Retourne, F., any card turned on the talon, or for a trump.

Revoke, failure to follow suit when able to do so, as distinguished from a renounce or renege.

Ring In, to exchange any unfair for fair gambling implements during the progress of the game. See Cold Deck.

Robbing, exchanging a card in the hand for the turn-up trump, or discarding several for the trumps remaining in the pack. See Cinch and Spoil Five.

Rooking, hustling, inveigling a person into a game for the purpose of cheating him.

Round, a round is complete when each player has had equal advantages with regard to deal, dummy, etc.

Round Games, those which do not admit of partnerships.

Rubber, winning two out of three games. F., Robre.

Rubiconed, lurched, defeated before getting half way.

Ruffing, trumping a suit.

Run, a succession of counting shots at Billiards.

Schnitt, G., a finesse.

Schneiden, G., to finesse.   Schinden is sometimes used.

Scratch, a fluke, a score which was not played for.

Screw Shot, a force shot at Billiards.

Second Dealing, dealing the second card from the top of the pack, keeping back the top card until it can be dealt to yourself or your partner.

See Saw, a cross ruff.

Sequence, three or more cards next in value to one another. The word is sometimes used for two cards only.

Short-card Player, a poker player ; usually a sharper also.

Short Suits, those containing less than four cards.

Short-stop Billiards.   Short-stop players are those who are good enough to play in halls hired for the purpose, but who stop short of the companionship class.

Shuffling, any method of disarranging the cards so that no trace remains of their order during the previous deal or play.

Sights, the diamonds on the rail of an American billiard table.

Signalling for Trumps, playing a higher card before a lower in a plain suit, when no attempt is made to win the trick.

Singleton, one card only of any suit.

Skin Games, those in which a player cannot possibly win.

Skunked, whitewashed, schwartz, beaten without having been able to score a single point.

Slam, winning all the tricks.   Little Slam, winning 12 out of 13 possible.

Sleeper, a bet left or placed on a dead card at Faro.

Sneak, a singleton which is led for the especial purpose of ruffing the second round of the suit.

Snowing the Cards, milking or fuzzing them.

Soda, the first card at Faro, exposed face upward in the box before any bets are made.

Splits, two cards of the same denomination coming on the same turn at Faro.

Spot Stroke, a series of winning hazards with the red ball at English billiards.

Square Game, one in which the cards are perfectly square, and have not been trimmed for wedges, strippers, etc.

Squeezers, cards with indicators on the edges.

Stack of Chips, twenty.   A " stack of whites " is $5.

Starter, the cut card at Cribbage.

Stechen, G., to trump.

Still Pack, the one not in play when two are used.

Stock, cards left after the deal is complete, but which are to be used in the following play.

Stool Pigeon, a hustler.

Straight Whist, playing a hand and immediately shuffling the cards for another deal, as distinguished from Duplicate.

Strength in Trumps, enough to justify a player in passing a doubtful trick ; usually four or five at least.

Strengthening Cards, those which are of no practical trick-taking value to the leader, but which may be useful to the partner ; usually restricted to Q J 10 9.

String Bets, those that take all the odd or all the even cards to play one way, win or lose, at Faro.

Strippers, cards trimmed so that certain ones may be pulled out of the pack at will.

Strohman, G., the dummy at Whist or Bridge.

Strong Suits, those in which a number of tricks can be made after the adverse trumps are out of the way.

Sub Echo, a trump signal in a plain suit, made after partner has led trumps, and the player has not echoed on the trump lead.

Sub-sneak, a two-card suit which is led for the sole purpose of getting a ruff on the third round.

Sweating Out, winning a game without taking any risks, by waiting for the trifling points that fall to your share.

Systems, any guide that keeps a player from guessing in the distribution of his bets ; as distinguished from a martingale, which controls the amount of the wager itself.

*T*able Games, Chess, Checkers, and Backgammon.

Tables, the ancient name for Backgammon.

Taille, F., a number of packs shuffled together, which are not to be re-shuffled or cut until all have been used.

Talon, the same as Stock.

Team Playing, requiring every member of a team to play with every other an equal number of times, at Whist.

Tenace. The major tenace is the best and third best cards remaining, or unplayed, in any suit, such as A Q. The minor tenace is the second and fourth best, such as K J.

Têtes, Kings, Queens and Jacks.

Three-card Monte. A game in which three cards are dexterously thrown on the table by a gambler, and the victim is induced to bet that he can pick out one which has been previously named and shown.

Three-echo, an echo on a trump lead when holding three only.

Three-on-a-side, a system of playing Faro, in which cards are bet to win or lose an odd number of times.

Tournée, F., see Round.

Trailing, playing a card which accomplishes nothing.

Trash, to discard.
Tric, F., the odd trick at Whist or Mort.
Tricon, F., three cards of the same denomination.
Tric-Trac, the European name for Backgammon.
Trump-showing Leads, a system of private conventionalities in leading plain suits at Whist, to show the number of trumps held by the leader.

*U*nblocking, getting out of your partner's way when he has more cards of the suit than you have.
Underplay, leading a card which is not the best of a suit, when the best would naturally be led ; or holding up the best card to let another player win the trick.

*V*ade, F., the pool to be played for.
Vergeben, G., misdeal.
Verleugnen, or Verläugnen, G., to revoke.
Vivant, F., Dummy's partner.
Vole, F., winning all the tricks, a slam.
Vorhand, G., the eldest hand, at Skat.
Vorwerfen, G., to play out of turn.

*W*eak Trumps, not enough to justify a player in passing a doubtful trick.
Wedges, cards trimmed to taper toward one end, so that if certain ones are reversed they can be easily pulled out.
Welcher, one who makes mouth bets, and afterward fails to pay.
Whipsawed, losing two different bets on the same turn.
Whiskey Hole, only one to go.
Whitewashed, defeated without having scored a point.
Wide Balls, those which are near the corner of the table, and are almost sure to be hit by a ball coming from either cushion.
Wide Cards, those which are too far apart to be likely to form sequences.   See Close Cards.
Widow, any extra hand dealt in any game.
Wimmeln, G., to bunch the points together ; to fatten a trick for the partner.
Wimmelfinte, G., leading a card which is calculated to induce the second hand to fatten the trick for his partner.
Winning Hazards, pocketing the object ball.
Winning Out, a card that wins four times in the same deal at Faro.

*Y*arborough, a hand at Whist containing no card higher than a Nine ; the odds against it are 1827 to 1.
Younger Hand, the one not the leader in two-handed games.

*Z*ange, G., a fourchette or tenace.
Zwickmuhle, G., a cross ruff.

FOSTER'S BOOKS ON GAMES.

By R. F. FOSTER, author of FOSTER'S WHIST MANUAL.

FOSTER'S WHIST TACTICS.

In this work the author has followed the same principles which made his manual so successful, first giving the examples with the cards, and then showing the principles underlying their management. The general management of the hand is gone into, and rules are given for the best course when the plain suits and the trumps are in certain proportions.

The examples which the author uses throughout the work consist of 112 hands at Duplicate Whist, played by correspondence between sixteen of the finest players in America. For every card played in this match, each of the players had a week to think over the situation, and the result has been 112 examples of the very best and most carefully studied Whist ever played.

The arrangement and presentation of the subject is quite original, and entirely different from that pursued in any other work on Whist, and the publishers are confident that it will be recognized as the most comprehensive work ever written on the game. The book is very handsomely printed.

Square 12mo, Holliston cloth, stamped with title in gold, and a hand of cards in red ink and silver, gilt edges, $1.25.

HEARTS.

The only work published on this subject by a competent authority. The many admirers of this interesting game will welcome with delight a standard by which all disputes can be settled.

16mo, yellow buckram, stamped with red ink and gold, 50 cts.

FOR SALE BY ALL BOOKSELLERS, OR SENT POST-
PAID. SEND FOR CATALOGUE.

FREDERICK A. STOKES COMPANY

27 & 29, WEST 23D STREET, NEW YORK.

PUBLISHERS' NOTE.

In presenting to the public a new book on games, the publishers desire to call attention to the following points in its favor :—

The book is original from cover to cover. It is the only entirely original book on games that has appeared for 150 years. Instead of being a compilation of various authors, hastily gathered together in book form and published without any regard to completeness or accuracy, and without any of the careful revision needed to bring the various games up to date, this work is that of a single author, who has made the subject of games a life-long study, and every word in the description of each game is written expressly for this book.

The treatment is systematic and uniform. The description of each game begins with the apparatus and the players, and then follows the natural course of play step by step until the end. Each part of the game is described in a separate paragraph, and

Publishers' Note.

every paragraph is preceded by catch words in heavy-faced type, so that the entire work is in the nature of a dictionary, in which any part of any game can be found immediately.

All technical terms are accompanied by a full definition of their meaning, and are printed in full-face type.

All disputed points have been settled in an entirely original manner. Instead of taking any one person as an authority, the history of each game has been traced from its source to its present condition, and its rules have been carefully compared with those of other members of the same family. The times and the reasons for the various changes have been ascertained, and the rules given are not only in strict accord with the true spirit of the game, but are based upon common sense and equity.

The list of technical terms is the most complete ever published.